Y0-CPD-704

WITHDRAWN

The Correspondence of Daniel O'Connell

Volume II

1815–1823

THE CORRESPONDENCE OF DANIEL O'CONNELL

Editor: Maurice R. O'Connell, Ph.D.
Assistant Editor: Gerard J. Lyne, M.A.
Editorial Assistants:
Hugh C. McFadden, M.A. and Elizabeth M. O'Connell

THE
CORRESPONDENCE
OF
DANIEL O'CONNELL

Volume II

1815-1823

Edited by
Maurice R. O'Connell
Professor of History
Fordham University

IRISH UNIVERSITY PRESS
Dublin Ireland
BARNES & NOBLE BOOKS · NEW YORK
(a division of Harper & Row Publishers, Inc.)
for the Irish Manuscripts Commission

ISBN 06–495233–9

941.58092
O18c
v.2

Published in the U.S.A. 1973

by Harper & Row Publishers, Inc.
BARNES & NOBLE IMPORT DIVISION

PRINTED IN THE REPUBLIC OF IRELAND

Contents

The preface, acknowledgments and list of manuscript and published sources for *The Correspondence of Daniel O'Connell* are to be found in Volume I.

Abbreviations

BLG	*Burke's Landed Gentry*
BM	British Museum
Boase	Boase, Frederic. *Modern English Biography* . . .
CMC	*Cork Mercantile Chronicle*
CMP	*Carrick's Morning Post*
DEM	*Dublin Evening Mail*
DEP	*Dublin Evening Post*
DNB	*Dictionary of National Biography*
Ency. Brit.	*Encyclopaedia Britannica*
FJ	*Freeman's Journal*
Gillow	Gillow, Joseph. *A Literary and Biographical History . . . of the English Catholics* . . .
LEP	*Limerick Evening Post*
MC	*Morning Chronicle*
MR	*Morning Register*
NLI	National Library of Ireland, Dublin
PRO	Public Record Office
SNL	*Saunders' News-Letter*
UCD	University College, Dublin

Works Cited

Fagan, William. *The Life and Times of Daniel O'Connell*. 2 vols. Cork 1847–48.

FitzPatrick, William John. *The Life, Times and Correspondence of the Right Rev. Dr. Doyle, Bishop of Kildare and Leighlin*. New ed. 2 vols. Dublin 1880.

Inglis, Brian. *The Freedom of the Press in Ireland, 1784–1841*. London 1954.

Jephson, Maurice Denham. *An Anglo-Irish Miscellany: Some Records of the Jephsons of Mallow*. Dublin 1964.

McDowell, R. B. *Public Opinion and Government Policy in Ireland, 1801–1846*. London 1952.

O'Keeffe, Christopher Manus. *Life and Times of Daniel O'Connell*. 2 vols. Dublin 1864.

Podmore, Frank. *Robert Owen, a Biography*. 2 vols. London 1906.

Strickland, W. G. *A Dictionary of Irish Artists*. 2 vols. Dublin and London 1913.

508
To Father Peter Kenney, S.J.[1]

Merrion Square, 4 January 1815

Dear Sir,

I am anxious to place two sons[2] of mine under your care. The elder will be twelve in June next: the younger was ten in November last. I intend the elder, and indeed both, for the Irish Bar. Of the younger my literary expectations are not as strong as of the elder. My wish would be that he should enter on law studies soon after he commences his eighteenth year; his brother perhaps later in life.

The interval of five years and a half for the elder, and the longer interval for the younger, I should propose to devote to the acquisition of much classical learning, a solid formation in classics, especially in Greek, being in my opinion of great value to real education.

I would wish them also to acquire the French language, and as much knowledge in the simpler branches of mathematics and as great a familiarity with experimental philosophy including, or rather placing at the head, modern chemistry, as may be consistent with your plan of education.

I am thus candid with you as to my wishes, understanding that you desire that parents should be so.

Of course I am most anxious that they should be strongly imbued with the principles of Catholic faith and national feeling. These advantages I should entertain sanguine hopes of, if they were placed under your care.

I therefore beg to know whether you will be pleased to allow me to send them to you and in that case to furnish me with information of all preliminary preparations.

SOURCE : *The Clongowes Record, 1814-1932*, p. 86.

1 Peter James Kenney, S.J. (1779-1841), studied in Palermo; vice-president of St. Patrick's College, Maynooth, 1812-13; revived the Jesuit mission in Ireland; opened Clongowes Wood College, May 1814. First rector of Clongowes, 1814-17, and again from 1821 to 1830. See *DNB*.

2 Maurice and Morgan.

I

509

From Thomas Cloney[1] to Merrion Square

Graig [Co. Kilkenny], 20 January 1815

My dear Sir,

I am proud to see that notwithstanding the very many subjects you have to devote your attention to, you nevertheless do not forget the services of the *Belfast Magazine* to our cause.[2] Well may you complain of apathy and ingratitude in our body when this magazine went down for want of support. At the moment of receiving the *Dublin Evening Post* with your advertisement, I had two acquaintances here with me from the Co. Wexford whose names as subscribers I return you with my own. I have been at your instance a subscriber for the last two years. I shall endeavour to procure more and shall get the subscriptions and forward them as soon as the first number is forwarded as directed. There has been frequently disappointments in receiving publications subscribed for. [I] am therefore delicate on the occasion.

. . . Your Catholic countrymen in this quarter observe with pride and pleasure your unceasing and public-spirited exertions in our common cause. Your inflexible opposition to the schemes and intrigues of the Veto slaves merits their warmest approbation. On this question a change of sentiment in the people need never be dreaded. Let us never enter into a dishonourable compromise with our implacable foes. Their consequence may be considered by superficial observers to have been much enhanced by recent events[3] but this consequence to me, who cannot boast of great penetration, appears ideal and insubstantial. Great as the changes have been for the last twelve months, as great might occur in a short period to come. Why should we then despond or think of surrendering our most sacred rights for anything the wretches in power have to bestow? Let our seceders, if they wish it, go in to *dignified* retirement. Whilst the people have a Scully and an O'Connell, with a few other such Irishmen to direct them, these sham patriots may be spared. Unanimity, however, must be wished for if to be had without a dishonourable compromise.

Subscribers to *B[elfast] Magazine* :
John Quigley, Esq., Donard, Ross
Michael Furlong, Esq., Scobey, Enniscorthy

Thos. Cloney, Graig
Bryan Fitzhenry, Esq., [New] Ross.

SOURCE : O'Connell Papers, NLI 13647

1 Thomas Cloney, known as General Thomas Cloney as a result of
   his part in Co. Wexford in the 1798 Rebellion. Born at Moneyhore,
   near Enniscorthy, and died at Graig, Co. Kilkenny, 20 February
   1850, aged 76. Author of *A Personal Narrative of* 1798 (Dublin 1832).
   He owned a landed estate held under lease from head landlords.
2 O'Connell and Nicholas Mahon were currently advertising for the
   purpose of raising subscriptions for the revival of the *Belfast
   Magazine,* which had recently gone out of circulation. Their
   advertisement claimed that the *Magazine* had rendered invaluable
   services against oppression (*DEP,* 19 Jan. 1815).
3 It appears to have been rumoured at this time that the pope was
   prepared to compromise on the veto (*DEP,* 13, 17 Dec. 1815). In
   the summer of 1813 a secession of some of its members from the
   Catholic Board had occurred, ostensibly because of differences of
   opinion as to the acceptability of a veto. At a meeting with some
   of the seceders in Lord Fingall's house on 17 January 1815,
   O'Connell declared himself prepared to perpetuate the division in
   the Catholic ranks rather than agree to anything less than unqualified Emancipation (*DEP,* 19 Jan. 1815). At a Catholic meeting
   in Dublin on 24 January 1815, he warned the pope and the Irish
   hierarchy that the lower clergy and Catholic masses would revolt
   against any arrangement involving a veto (*DEP,* 26 Jan. 1815).
   Lord Fingall refused to take the chair at this meeting and the other
   seceders did not attend. O'Connell's biographer Fagan claims it
   was at this meeting that O'Connell established his leadership on a
   firm basis, and rendered the cause of unqualified Emancipation
   triumphant (Fagan, *O'Connell,* I, 136).

510

From John N. D'Esterre[1]

11 Bachelor's Walk [Dublin, Thursday], 26 January 1815
Sir,
    Carrick's paper[2] of the 23rd instant (in its report of the
Debates of a meeting of Catholic Gentlemen, on the subject of
a Petition) states that you have applied the appellation of
beggarly to the Corporation of this City, calling it a *beggarly
Corporation*; and therefore, as a member of that body, and
feeling how painful such is, I beg leave to enquire whether you
really used or expressed yourself in any such language? I feel
the more justified in calling on you on this occasion as such

language was not warranted or provoked by anything on the part of the Corporation; neither was it consistent with the subject of your Debate, or the deportment of the other Catholic Gentlemen who were present; and though I view it so inconsistent in every respect, I am in hopes the Editor is under error, and not you. I have further to request your reply in the course of the evening.

SOURCE : FitzPatrick, *Corr.*, I, 27-8

1   John Norcot D'Esterre, 11 Bachelor's Walk, Dublin; provision merchant to Dublin Castle; member of the Trinity Guild of the common council. Captain on half-pay in Royal Marines since 1810.

2   *Carrick's Morning Post*, owned by John Carrick.

510a

To John N. D'Esterre

Merrion Square, 27 January 1815

Sir,

In reply to your letter of yesterday, and without either admitting or disclaiming the expression respecting the Corporation of Dublin in the print to which you allude, I deem it right to inform you that, from the calumnious manner in which the religion and character of the Catholics of Ireland are treated in that body, no terms attributed to me, however reproachful, can exceed the contemptuous feelings I entertain for that body in its corporate capacity; although doubtless it contains many valuable persons, whose conduct as individuals (I lament) must necessarily be confounded in the acts of a general body. I have only to add that *this letter must close our correspondence on this subject.*

SOURCE : FitzPatrick, *Corr.*, I, 28.

511

To Nicholas Purcell O'Gorman, Saturday, 28 January 1815

Desires to see him urgently.[1]

SOURCE : FitzPatrick, *Corr.*, I, 29

1   O'Gorman was one of O'Connell's friends in the affair with D'Esterre.

512

From George Lidwill to Merrion Square

Kearn's Hotel, Kildare St. [Dublin], 30 January 1815

My Dear O'Connell,

I have remained in town on this business longer indeed than was necessary for you or than I ought, circumstanced as some of my family are at present. This is now the fourth day since this person intimated his intention (most wantonly) of taking personal notice of your conduct in case you did not deny having used an epithet respecting the Corporation of Dublin which was attributed you in some of the papers. You refused not only to disclaim it but avowed that no term however reproachful could exceed the contemptuous feelings you entertained for that body in its corporate capacity, and you desired your letter should terminate the correspondence. You have been prepared now more than three days to meet the only notice he should have taken of your letter, had his intentions been such as he professed.

In the interim (during that absence from your house which I recommended), your brother[1] returned (unread) a second letter from this man declaring in a note, in which he enclosed it, that you would receive no letter but expected he would have adopted a different course. It has also happened that Mr. Nugent,[2] the Sheriff's peer (with whom I have had very long dealings), mentioned to me last Saturday morning all the circumstances of this transaction on the side of this man (I forget his name) and that he was prevented from sending you a message lest you should have recourse to legal proceedings. On your part I assured him that you would not, that you had been prepared since your answer to his letter to have gone out with him instanter if called on, that you would enter into no explanation but that you were ready to meet him without a moment's delay. Under all these circumstances your having heard no further on the subject convinces me that this aggression, originating in folly and perhaps urged on by party, has been abandoned altogether and that you may dismiss it entirely from your mind.

SOURCE : O'Connell MSS, UCD

1 James.

2 Edmond Nugent, College Green; sheriff's peer; lord mayor of Dublin, 1828.

513

To Richard Newton Bennett

Tuesday, 31 January 1815

My dear Bennett,

Your general notion is exact, the detail perhaps long. The ruffian[1] appeared in the Hall[2] for a moment with a whip. The instant I heard of it I left the King's Bench and he disappeared. He paraded the quay with his whip. R[ichard] O'Gorman[3] met him, asked him did he want me, for that I told him I would fight him (D'Esterre) in three minutes whenever he chose; that he had but to send me a message and that he should instantly be met. He (D'Esterre) said the message ought to come *from me,* at which O'Gorman laughed. The fellow then took post at Briscoe and Dicksons in College Green. I came there with my friend, Major MacNamara,[4] but the delinquent had fled. His companions there, before I came up, were young Saurin,[5] Sir Richard Musgrave[6] and Abraham Bradley King,[7] the alderman.

The crowd accumulated so fast that I took refuge in Exchequer Street, where Judge Day followed me and bound me to keep the peace on *my honour.* Was there ever such a scene?

SOURCE : NLI, MSS 837

1 D'Esterre.

2 The hall of the Four Courts.

3 Richard O'Gorman (died 1867), third son of James O'Gorman, Ennis, and Susanna, sister of Nicholas Mahon, Dublin. He was a brother of both James O'Gorman, Ennis, and Nicholas Purcell O'Gorman and was a junior partner in the woollen business of his uncle Nicholas Mahon.

4 William Nugent MacNamara (1775-1856), Doolin, Co. Clare; M.P. for Co. Clare, 1830-52.

5 A son of the attorney-general.

6 Sir Richard Musgrave (1757?-1818), created baronet, 1782; author of many anti-Catholic pamphlets. See *DNB.*

7 Abraham Bradley King (1773-1838), alderman and king's stationer. Lord mayor of Dublin, 1813 and 1821; former deputy grand master of the Orange Order; created baronet, 1821.

514

To his wife[1]

Friday [probably 3 February 1815]

My darling Love,

Send any *commands* for me by Scully.[2] If any suspicious person should come do not send *here* at all. Send to McCann's [? Mr. Cairn's][3] in some considerable time after. I need not, dearest, say a word to you in the way of consolation for this momentary absence. The cause of it, however to be regretted, will purchase years of safety.

I cannot describe to you how kindly in every sense of the word I am treated here. My brother James could not behave better to me than Scully and his family. Tell my sweet babes and my boys that I doat of them.

[P.S.] Take care of *this* note.

SOURCE : Fitz-Simon Papers
1 This letter appears to have been written shortly after O'Connell's duel with D'Esterre.
2 Denys Scully.
3 Unidentified.

515

From his brother-in-law Rickard O'Connell to Merrion Square

Tralee, 4 February 1815

Copy

My dear Dan,

An event of all others I most wished for has taken place. To express to you my feelings this morning, on reading the *Freeman's Journal* giving a full and accurate account of the duel between you and Mr. D'Esterre, is beyond my powers of description particularly as the unfavourable impression that remained fixed on my mind and which I could not divest myself of, relative to the manner in which your affair with Mr. Magrath was patched up by that miserable meddler in Catholic affairs,[1] gave me the most serious uneasiness. On this subject I never spoke to you. Though you mentioned it to me in Cork shortly after it occurred, I did not give any opinion about it. But I was decidedly aware, whenever it came to the point and when you were fairly committed and left to your own judgement and with such a friend as Mr. McNamara, that you would have conducted yourself with that steadiness, carriage and coolness which are the true and leading character-istics of an O'Connell. . . . You have laid low the champion of intolerance and the beggarly Corporation of Dublin, to use your own words, who selected the unfortunate D'Esterre as the man, the only man, they could prevail upon of that highly respectable body to put down the troublesome Counsellor O'Connell.

Is it true that James[2] is committed with young Saurin[3] and that they are to fight? If they are, I trust the result will be such as we all wish it to be. John[4] came over here today: we met with a cordial shake of the hand and congratulated each other on the glorious result of the duel. He talks of going up to Dublin if he does not receive a satisfactory answer about James' affair on Monday. . . .

Make allowances for my manner of writing. You know my education was rather limited. . . .

SOURCE : O'Connell Papers, NLI 13647
1 Nicholas Philpot Leader. See letter 437.
2 O'Connell's brother.
3 A son of the attorney-general. He had been one of D'Esterre's companions in the affair with O'Connell.
4 O'Connell's brother.

516
From Sir Edward Stanley[1]

Royal Barracks [Dublin], 4 February 1815
Sir,
    Lest your professional avocations should be interrupted by an apprehension of any proceeding being in contemplation in consequence of the late melancholy event, I have the honour to inform you that there is not the most distant intention of any prosecution whatever on the part of the family or friends of the late Mr. D'Esterre.

SOURCE : FitzPatrick, Corr., I, 33
1 Sir Edward Stanley, Kt. (died c. 1852), deputy barrack master to the city of Dublin, sheriff's peer; wine provision supplier to Dublin Castle.

517
To Sir Edward Stanley

Merrion Square, 5 February 1815

Sir,

. . . It is to me a mournful consolation to meet such generous sentiments from those who must be afflicted at the late
unhappy event. But, believe me, my regret at that event is most
sincere and unaffected, and if I know my own heart, I can
with the strictest truth assert that no person can feel for the
loss society has sustained in the death of Mr. D'Esterre with
more deep and lasting sorrow than I do. Allow me again to
thank you, sir, for the courtesy of your letter—a courtesy quite
consistent with the gentlemanly demeanour of your entire
conduct in this melancholy transaction.

SOURCE : FitzPatrick, *Corr.*, I, 33-4

518
To George Bryan, Jenkinstown, Kilkenny

Merrion Square, 6 February 1815

My dear Bryan,

I thank you sincerely and feelingly for your very kind
letter. I am proud of your kindness and friendship.

It has been a melancholy occurrence[1] but all parties here
admit that I was in nothing to blame. The affair was forced
on with a strange perverseness by the unhappy man. From my
soul I am sorry for him but I could not have acted otherwise
and I am therefore free from self-reproach.

It has been *officially* announced to me that there would be
no prosecution. The letters which have passed on the subject
are published. You will see them in the papers. This therefore
prevents me from availing myself of your affectionate offer. I
can only say I would have embraced it with precisely the same
cordiality with which it was made.

Those are, my dear friend, the consequences of labouring
for the country. To you I deplore its fickleness and ingratitude.
For myself I have got more than I deserved of gratitude and
kindliness, and right happy would I be could I induce you to
forgive the ingratitude and folly of your countrymen and
return to that cause of which you were a pillar and an orna-

ment. I say it unaffectedly, I would give now the right arm to have you with us again hand as well as heart.[2]

SOURCE : Papers of the Hon. Bryan Bellew

1 The duel with D'Esterre.
2 Bryan had apparently become estranged from the Catholic cause due to the recriminations levelled at him a year earlier in connection with the trial of John Magee (see letter 457, note 3).

519

From Christopher Hely Hutchinson to Merrion Square

2 Bulstrode Street, Manchester Square [London],
Monday, 6 February 1815

My dear O'Connell,

I have this moment heard that you have had a duel with a Mr. D'Esterre, and that he is badly wounded. Pray let me have one line from yourself to say how things are, for be assured that in anything in which your life is risked or the peace of your family in any way concerned, I have long felt and shall ever feel a deep and sincere interest.

SOURCE : Fitz-Simon Papers

520

To his wife, Merrion Square

Monasterevan [Co. Kildare], 3 March 1815

My darling Love,

. . . Order the *Impartial Enquirer*[1]. . . . Get one for yourself, also, as my letter to Curran[2] will be continued in my absence from town. . . .

Say everything *imaginable* to our dearest boys and darling, darling girls. Kate's breath this morning smelt most terribly of worms. Darling, see what can be done for her. Hug the doats for me.

SOURCE : Fitz-Simon Papers

1 Not extant.
2 Unidentified.

521

To his wife, Merrion Square

Ennis, 6 March 1815

My darling Love,

I found your letter here before me yesterday evening and I have grieved a good deal at your attributing any want of the warmth of affection in my parting with you. Do believe me for I say it with the greatest truth that, if there was any appearance of that kind, it was only an appearance for the truth is, my own sweetest love, no man ever loved with more constant and unremitting tenderness than I love you. . . . You wrong me if you imagined my manner cold or less affectionate than usual. If it were so, I would instantly return to Dublin and not leave my own darling till I convinced her that my affection for her is as ardent as ever. . . .

I got Cox's *Magazine*.[1] I am sorry the scoundrel has made such an exhibition of me. . . .

SOURCE : Fitz-Simon Papers

1 Walter ('Watty') Cox was editor of a monthly periodical entitled the *Irish Magazine*. In it he published an account of O'Connell's duel with D'Esterre, together with a large-scale engraving of the scene after the encounter. The *Magazine* rejoiced at the death of D'Esterre as an act of public justice upon the Orange faction, which, it claimed, was responsible for the shootings of a number of Catholics at Shercock, Co. Cavan (*Irish Magazine,* Mar. 1815, pp. 97-103).

522

From his wife, to Ennis

[Dublin] 7 March 1815

My dearest Love,

. . . Another thing I wish to remind you of is the balance of Mr. Kearney's[1] bill furnished to us two years since and which I believe you directed Mr. James Sugrue to pay. £50 remains yet due and I have reason to know Kearney wants the money. You are aware that his bill was going on for nine years. I feel most anxious to have this balance paid for many reasons and if you possibly can, send it to me from circuit. James[2] is this moment come in and was told by FitzPatrick that the Pope had positively consented to the Veto and that

it will appear in this night's [*Dublin*] *Evening Post*.[3] God
grant it may not be the case. At all events, darling, won't the
honest Catholics remain as they are, sooner than accept of
Emancipation on such terms? Con Lyne[4] was here when James
mentioned the news. He seemed greatly pleased and said he
would take you the [*Dublin*] *Evening Post*. . . .

SOURCE : O'Connell Papers, NLI 13651
1 Probably J. F. Kearney, M.D.
2 O'Connell's brother.
3 Edward Jerningham, secretary of the English Catholic Board,
   announced on 28 February 1815 that he had received from the pope
   a letter addressed to the Catholic inhabitants of Great Britain,
   stating His Holiness' determination on the veto (*DEP*, 7 Mar. 1815).
   The *Dublin Evening Post* expressed its belief that the pope had in
   his letter agreed to accept the veto (*DEP*, 9 Mar. 1815).
4 Cornelius (Con) Lyne, born in Cork, 1775; son of Timothy Lyne,
   merchant. Called to the bar, 1801. Known as 'Con of the 100
   Bottles' because of his conviviality though he did not drink to
   excess. Died 1841.

523

To his wife, Merrion Square

Ennis, 9 March 1815

My darling Heart,

I wrote to you a hasty line late yesterday after coming out
of court. I am of course quite satisfied with any agreement you
make with Fogarty[1] and indeed altogether agree with you in
thinking that the roof of the house should be put in immediate
repair. . . . It will be best to get Fogarty to enter into a contract for the work and also to keep *all* the roofs in repair by
the year. Have you heard anything more of the fellow Moore[2]
was to get to cure the chimneys of the back buildings? I certainly approve of the plan of double doors to each room. . . .

I will send you the money for Mr. Kearney. I assure you,
heart, I was quite convinced he was paid, and my recollection
distinctly is that James Sugrue charged me in account with the
amount. However, there is now no use in taxing him with the
fact. Beg of James[3] to exert himself with Sugrue and his
partner and to get me any money he possibly can or to ascertain that there is no money to be got. I believe the fellow is
only humbugging me.

The business is just over here. I was concerned in every cause and certainly had more business than any other counsel. Yet I think that little more than seventy pounds will cover the entire of my receipts in this town. The times are bad for all trades.

SOURCE : Fitz-Simon Papers
1 Probably John Fogarty, bricklayer, 6 York Street, Dublin.
2 Probably Daniel of 45 Stafford Street, Dublin.
3 His brother.

524

From his daughter Ellen

Friday, 10 March 1815

My darling Father,

I am delighted to have an opportunity of writing to you. I have been longing to write to you ever since I got my new name[1] that I might have the pleasure of signing it. I am sure I ought to be very fond of it and to have great devotion to Saint Bridget all the days of my life, and so I hope I shall. . . .

SOURCE : O'Connell Papers, NLI 13645
1 Obviously the name taken at the religious ceremony of confirmation.

525

To his wife, Merrion Square

Limerick, 12 March 1815

My darling Heart,

. . . Do not believe a word about the Veto.[1] The letter from the Pope to the English Catholics is nothing more than one of mere civility, in which he praises the English government, but not a word of the Veto. I have *this* from the best authority. Send James[2] to Fitzpatrick's[3] to say so.

. . . There is not much civil business here but an immense deal of criminal. As yet I have had no conviction but I do not expect to escape so well the rest of the assizes.

SOURCE : Fitz-Simon Papers
1 See letter 522, note 3.
2 His brother.
3 Hugh FitzPatrick's establishment at 4 Capel Street, Dublin, where the Catholics held their meetings.

526

To his wife, Merrion Square

Limerick, 13 March 1815

My darling, darling Mary,

I can write but a few words to you today. Indeed I cannot write more. I never in my life was so exquisitely miserable as your last letter made me. I wept over it for two hours this morning in bed and I am ready to weep over it again. When once suspicion enters the human mind, there is an end of all comfort and security. It is, I see, in vain to make any protestations to you. You are, I see, irrecoverably unhappy. I blame, indeed I do, my brother James for instilling this poison into your mind. I know he did it for the best but it was a cruel experiment to render the sweetest, the dearest, the tenderest, the best, the most beloved of wives and mothers unhappy on a loose and idle suspicion. Indeed, indeed, indeed, you have no cause of uneasiness, but my heart is too full and I cannot write more.

Tell my Nell, my angel Nell, that I will write to her as soon as I can.

Darling believe me, do believe me, you have no cause for your misery. Did I ever deceive you?

Ever sweetest Mary,

Your most tenderly and faithfully doating

Daniel O'Connell

SOURCE : Fitz-Simon Papers

527

From his wife to Limerick

[Dublin] 13 March 1815

My darling Love,

. . . The remedy I have given Kate for the worms has served her materially and as I am promised tansy this week, I shall continue to give it to her the remainder of the spring. . . . Maurice and Morgan are quite stout and merry. The former got an *optime* in everything last Saturday and the latter got four. . . .

I am quite pleased at what you tell me of the Pope. It is, I think, very probable that if he had consented to the Veto, government would not still keep it secret. What do you think of the English mob? James[1] is highly delighted with their proceedings. . . .

My finances are exhausted. This day I gave the last £15 to Mrs. Shiel. I do not like calling on Hickson until you bid me. I have this day sent *him* a docket which was left of £96.11.0, an acceptance of yours for O'Leary[2] due in Aungier Street [about one word illegible] money from him yet. . . . I shall not forgive myself until I hear from you in reply to my letter last Saturday. I am sorry for writing to you as I did but, love, I could not help it. My mind was in such a wretched state from trying to suppress my feelings.

[P.S.] Just as I concluded my letter another acceptance came in for O'Leary to the amount of £364. *This,* I also sent to the Hicksons. Have I done right? . . . Maurice has got an *optime* in everything this day. Morgan has got five *optimes,* two V.B. and one B.

SOURCE : O'Connell Papers, NLI 13651
1   O'Connell's brother.
2   James O'Leary.

528

To his wife, Merrion Square

Limerick, 14 March 1815

My darling Love,

I was so agitated and frightened when I wrote to you yesterday that I could scarcely express myself intelligibly. But now, my tenderest heart, let me conjure you to calm your mind and to quiet your fears. If it be true, as I think it is, that I never once deceived you, do believe me now, my own sweetest love. I do not, Mary, deceive you when I tell you that there is not the slightest cause for your apprehensions. Indeed, indeed, my love, there is not. I wish to God my brother James would calculate upon the extreme mischief which he may occasion, by circulating such reports as those about the executions against O'Leary and, what is infinitely more interesting to me, the evils which may follow from his exciting uneasiness in your mind. The fact is, darling, that I am not as yet cool enough to write to James and indeed I do not know when my mind will descend from its present high tone of irritation. I cannot, my heart, conceal from myself that all confidence between us is torn up by the roots. Every line of your very strange letter convinces me of that, and indeed, my ever loved and adored Mary, this letter most amply accounts to me for your letter to Ennis. I do not know what to say to you but I would wish to say anything that could sooth and tranquillize your mind and convince [you] how idle those fears are, which have been suggested to you so industriously. But what is the use of protestation when a suspicious disposition has been excited. Indeed, indeed, two things are equally true—that no wife was ever so ardently loved as you are, and that no man was ever so exquisitely miserable as I am. Every faculty of my mind is literally *astounded* by your letter. I believe I will burn it but I have read it so often that I have it by heart.

Will you send to Mr. Bric,[1] my clerk, and get him to transmit to me by tomorrow's post copies of the accounts of Mr. Boyse, Mr. Hartnett and Mr. Scott . . .

SOURCE : Fitz-Simon Papers

1 John Bric (1793-1826), third son of Laurence Bric (died 1816), Tralee. Clerk to O'Connell in 1815; admitted to King's Inns, 1816, and Middle Temple, London, 1819. Called to the bar, Dublin, 1824. Killed in a duel in Dublin in December 1826.

529

From his wife to Limerick

[Dublin] 14 March 1815

My Dearest Life,

Believe me when I assure you that two or three days previous to your leaving home I had a suspicion of your having accepted a bill for O'Leary. I met a man coming from the study with a paper in his hand. The writing was certainly O'Leary's but further I could not judge. James certainly confirmed this suspicion but he did it from the best motive and unaware that you had made me any positive promise. I am perfectly satisfied with your declaration to me in your letter this morning. I know it is not in your nature to deceive me, and I declare most solemnly that any unhappiness I did feel on the subject is now completely done away. Let me then, darling, entreat of you to forget what is past, and do not for one moment think me capable of having no confidence in your protestations. It grieves me to have caused you to weep, but if you knew how much I struggled to suppress my feelings you would forgive me. I thought to have spoken to you on this odious business the night we were together in the parlour, that they all went to the play, but I could not bring myself to talk on what I knew must make you low spirited and unhappy on the eve of parting with your family. Let me now, love, request you will not write or speak in anger to your brother James. To be the cause of any jealousy between you would indeed render me truly miserable. I have this day answered a gentleman who called with an order on you for acceptance in Mr. O'Leary's handwriting, dated Killarney, to the amount of £96.11.6. I told the gentleman you were not in town nor would you be for six weeks more, and his exclamation was ' My God, what shall I do?' It is a shame for O'Leary to be putting his creditors to stress in this way. I had a higher opinion of his honour. The bill of £15.15.6 endorsed by James Connell and Peter Connell which you sent Hastings,[1] the butcher, is this moment returned protested. What am I to do with it? Hastings has paid it and I must pay him. . . . Maurice got an *optime* in everything again today. Indeed, he seems determined to deserve one every day. He is a very excellent boy and, I trust, will one of these days be a pride and a comfort to us. Morgan got five *optimes*. He is also a very good boy, only a little careless of his improvement.

SOURCE : O'Connell Papers, NLI 13651

1 Stewart's (Dublin) *Almanack* for 1817 lists a Richard Hastings, victualler, 53 William Street, Dublin.

530

From his daughter Kate

15 March 1815

My Darling Father,

I had a great wish to write to you last week but was obliged to give the way to *Miss O'Connell*.[1] I hope you will be as glad to get it now. Saturday will be my birthday. I am so sorry you will not be here but I hope you will think of me and don't forget to drink my health. I shall not forget to drink your's on Patrick's Day.

SOURCE : O'Connell Papers, NLI 13645

1 Her eldest sister, Ellen.

531

From his wife to Limerick

[Dublin] 16 March 1815

My dearest Life,

Though I wrote yesterday I write again today to try and make up for the unhappiness I have given you. Believe me, darling, you cannot possibly feel it more than I do and shall continue to do so until you tell me you have got rid of the impressions which you say my unfortunate epistle has caused you. I trust in God tomorrow's post will bring me a different letter from those I have lately received from you. Do, darling, forgive me what is past and rest assured I will never again cause you or allow myself to feel any unhappiness upon pecuniary matters.

Bric cannot be found. He is somewhere in the country and Mr. Sugrue has not kept to his word relative to the money he was to have given James[1] this day. . . . I have got no money from the Hicksons. James lent me twenty pounds, which will answer until I hear from you, fifteen of which I have been obliged to send Hastings beside the costs of the protest on Connell's acceptance. James had a letter today from Myles McSwiney saying it was almost impossible to get the rents from the tenants. He mentions that Maurice Geoffrey[2] is immediately to set out for Vienna. His uncle[3] has sent for him. . . . The report of this day is that Castlereagh has been assassinated and that B[onaparte] is advancing fast into France. I have just got the [*Dublin*] *Evening Post*. It says he has got sixty thousand men to join him. . . .

SOURCE : O'Connell Papers, NLI 13651

1   O'Connell's brother.
2   Maurice Geoffrey O'Connell, a cousin of O'Connell.
3   Moritz O'Connell (1738-1830), *recte* Muircheartagh or Mortimor, baron of the Holy Roman Empire, son of Maurice O'Connell, Tarmons, Waterville, Co. Kerry, and Mary née O'Sullivan Beare. Chamberlain to Emperors Joseph II, Leopold II and Francis I. Originally of the French service, he transferred to the Austrian army.

532

To his wife, Merrion Square

Limerick, 17 March 1815

My darling Mary,

I am greatly afflicted now at having given you and myself so much uneasiness, and I now am anxious to find words in which to convey any idea to you of the tenderness and fervour of my love for you. Your letter of yesterday was the exact picture of your mind, my own sweetest darling. How my heart pours itself out in doating affection for you. There never, *never, never* was a man so blessed in a wife. You are everything my most anxious heart could desire or even imagine. My sweet Mary, let us forget this momentary uneasiness or think of it only as a proof of the lively sentiment of pure love which we reciprocally entertain for each other. Believe me, sweetest, you have nothing to apprehend, and forgive me, heart treasure, for making you uneasy.

I have a thousand reasons to be in good spirits. My little Kate's letter was a great comfort to me. I cannot describe to you how I adore that child. She is a most charming creature. I have also been eminently successful this assizes. There was a man called Quan[1] tried last assizes for murder. The jury disagreed and after remaining in four days were discharged at the end of the assizes. The crown prosecuted but the prosecutors retained me in Dublin and gave me a brief here. The man had counsel but his cause was not well managed. This assizes the prosecutors *turned me off.* They were sure they could do without me and the prisoner employed me and by my exertions *alone* I got him *easily* acquitted. Darling, an incident of this kind serves much to cheer my restless mind and then, love, the public news—the public news! ! I can scarce draw my breath. Good God, how I die with impatience for the next packet. The fate of the Bourbon is decided before now for good or for ill. Poor Ireland—but I cannot write on the subject. . . .

SOURCE : Fitz-Simon Papers
1 Unidentified.

533

To his wife, Merrion Square

Limerick, 19 March 1815

My darling Love,

. . . I have been detained here by an accumulation of business so that this day I have given no less than nine opinions. I have lodged at Kennedys Bank[1] here £280: for which a bill will be transmitted to the Hicksons[2] by Tuesday's post. . . . Take as much of this money as you choose. I know you will not take more than is essentially necessary, and you know I would not wish you to take one penny less than what pleases and satisfies you. Darling, I hope and trust you have forgiven me my pettishness on the subject of your *long* letter. But the truth is, sweetest, that I love you too much to be able to bear the smallest displeasure or uneasiness of yours. I will not write more to you on this subject and we will forget that letter but, my own dearest darling, be assured your wishes are to me sacred and solemn commands.

Tell James[3] I will write to him certainly from Tralee. I will, my heart, write to him precisely as you desire. Tell my sweet Kate too that I will write to her. . . .

SOURCE : Fitz-Simon Papers

1 Known as the ' Bank of Limerick ', it operated from 1789 until its failure in 1820. In 1815 John Kennedy was one of its partners.
2 John and Robert Hickson, College Green, Dublin.
3 His brother. See letter 529.

534

To Nicholas Mahon[1]

Limerick, 19 March 1815

My dear Friend,

You have at the other side a letter to Lord Hutchinson, the best I can compose. Alter it as you please and put my name to it. I have not as yet heard from Ponsonby,[2] but I expect to be able to give you satisfactory information from him before the close of the week. The truth is that the late news[3] has, I believe, postponed all communications.

SOURCE : FitzPatrick, *Corr.,* I, 39

1 Nicholas Mahon (c. 1746 5 May 1841), 26 Merchants' Quay, Dublin, wealthy woollen merchant, in business in Dublin for over seventy years. Married 1791 his first cousin, Margaret, daughter of Nicholas Mahon, merchant, Limerick. A delegate to the Catholic Convention of 1792.

2 George Ponsonby.

3 ' The late news . . .' may refer either to Napoleon's return to France from Elba, or to a current report that the rescript of Quarantotti had been set aside by the pope (*DEP,* 16 Mar. 1815).

535

To Lord Hutchinson

[19] March 1815

My Lord,

We are quite convinced that your Lordship will at least excuse the liberty we take in addressing you on a subject mightily interesting to us, as you cannot mistake the motives which induce us to address you; they are easily to be found in the entire and unlimited confidence which we, in common with all the other Catholics of Ireland, place in your hereditary attachment to religious liberty, and in that high and ever un-tarnished honour which has distinguished every member of your noble house.

We have been appointed by the Catholic Association[1] to procure our Petition to the Commons to be presented by a member of that House who concurs with the Earl of Donough-more, and with us in the propriety of a discussion, on our claims, during the present session. We feel the great importance to our cause of entrusting our Petition to the member between whom and the Earl of Donoughmore a cordial communion of sentiments and co-operation of arrangements may be expected. We, however, feel a delicacy in applying to that noble Lord on this subject, but the causes of that delicacy not applying to your Lordship, we take the liberty of requesting your advice and assistance upon this occasion.[2] We entreat the honour of a reply addressed under cover to Nicholas Mahon, Merchants' Quay, Dublin. That reply, as well as the contents of this letter, shall ever remain under the seal of confidential and inviolable secrecy.

Daniel O'Connell

SOURCE : FitzPatrick, *Corr.*, I, 39-40

1 This body must not be confused with the organization of the same
name founded in 1823. It arose out of a meeting of Catholic
gentlemen in Clarendon Street chapel on 24 January 1815. It was
there resolved that the former members of the Catholic Board
should ' form themselves into a voluntary association, as individuals
. . .' for the purpose of petitioning parliament (*DEP*, 2 Feb. 1815).
The first reported meeting of the Catholic Association was held on
4 February 1815 (*DEP*, 7 Mar. 1815).

2 At a Catholic meeting on 24 January 1815 it was resolved to request
Donoughmore and Grattan to present petitions to parliament for
unqualified Emancipation (*DEP*, 2 Feb. 1815). Donoughmore agreed
to this but Grattan returned an indecisive answer (*DEP*, 16 Feb.
1815). On 21 February 1815 O'Connell in the Catholic Association
moved that some alternative member be selected to present the
petition in the Commons (*DEP*, 28 Feb. 1815).

536

From his wife to Tralee

[Dublin] 21 March 1815

My Darling Dan,

When I wrote to you on Saturday last I said I would give
you my reason for cautioning you respecting my letters. When
you were last at Derrynane your sister[1] took from your pocket
two letters of mine, the contents of which she not only published in her kitchen but to every individual who came across
her, amongst others James Butler, Charles Sugrue and Dick
Mahony. Had she even adhered to truth in her statement it
would have lessened the baseness of the act. One of those letters
was relative to your mother's coming to Dublin, written indeed
very differently from what was represented to your mother by
Mrs. O'Connell and which representation was the cause why
your mother did not come up last October. This information
I have from an authority I cannot doubt as it was sanctioned
by your mother in case I asked if she purposed coming up next
month with you. To the best of my recollection I never wrote
to you on the subject in any way that I would wish to conceal
from her. I certainly more than once expressed my wish she
may not come until our new building was fit to inhabit when
we could accommodate her with more comfort and more convenience to ourselves. In *this* letter, which Mrs. O'C *stole*, . . .

the whole of the letter has been grossly misrepresented, and your mother has given credit to it which surprises me not a little as she ought to be quite aware of the facility with which Mrs. O'Connell always told lies. God forgive her. She often tried to set me at variance with every individual of your family by telling me what they said and did not say of me, but I never relied much on her veracity. I think I shall write to your mother this week but, in case I should not, I beg you will speak to her on this subject and exactly tell her what I did write to you concerning her. Should she be induced to accompany you now, I do not think your uncle, the General, will interfere with her accommodation. What has occurred in France must, I should suppose, prevent his leaving that country. . . .

At length James[2] has got cash to the amount of £130 from James Sugrue and a bill at four months date for £170. He promised another £100 this week. Shall I give Hickson the bill? The £130 I shall keep so that I need not apply to the Hicksons for any money while you are away. I need not, I am sure, tell you that of this money I shall be as economical as I possibly can. There are some articles of furniture absolutely necessary which I must buy, and from James I was last month obliged to borrow £30 which I paid him today. . . .

. . . Of the public news I shall say nothing as the papers will arrive as soon as any information I can give you. I hope I shall read your speech at the Limerick meeting this week.[3] It is promised in the next paper. Some gentleman from Limerick told James you made a most brilliant one and paid many handsome compliments to the Limerick *ladies*.

[P.S.] God bless you, love, burn every letter that you get from me. It is the only way to *secure* them. . . .

SOURCE : O'Connell Papers, NLI 13651

1   Ellen O'Connell.
2   O'Connell's brother.
3   An aggregate meeting of Limerick Catholics held on St. Patrick's Day (*LEP*, 22 Mar. 1815; *DEP*, 1 April 1815). There is no mention of O'Connell's speech in the reports.

537

From his wife to Cork

25 March 1815

My darling Dan,

Nothing could exceed the delight of our sweet Kate on getting your letter this morning. Before she would allow me to open it, she repeatedly kissed it. She was much amused and seemingly gratified at your saying she would be an inestimable present to her future husband. She is a sweet child, affectionate and well disposed as indeed *they* all are. . . .

I heard of Ally[1] yesterday through a Mr. O'Callaghan who saw a gentleman just returned from Tours. As soon as William[2] heard of B[onaparte]'s movements he set out with his family to Paris on their way to the cantons of Switzerland. . . . Sugrue is *certainly* to give James[3] another £100 tomorrow. I am told he is in great spirits since the *good* news came.[4] . . .

SOURCE : O'Connell Papers, NLI 13651
1   O'Connell's sister Ally Finn.
2   William F. Finn.
3   O'Connell's brother.
4   'The *good* news' probably refers to the recent return of Napoleon to France from Elba.

538

From his wife to Cork

[Dublin] 28 March 1815

My Darling Love,

. . . The account you give of Maurice's[1] situation has impressed on my mind a strong conviction that he is coming to die with me. In my present situation, expecting in the course of six weeks to be confined, this impression must necessarily damp my spirits very much, particularly when I reflect on the severe loss I have so lately sustained[2] but, circumstanced as you were respecting Maurice, I cannot blame you. . . . Then tell me, love, how I am to accommodate every person. I must first tell you I am positively forbid by Kearney[3] to allow the children to sleep in the new building until the first of May. His advice I am determined to follow. Should your uncle[4] come I must put your mother off until October.

. . . I much fear your uncle will not be allowed to come to England. Should he come I will write to your mother and tell her exactly how I am situated, and as she is a woman of sense and reason I am convinced she will give me every credit for the wish I feel in not having her come to us until I can settle her and her servant comfortably, which would be in October. She could then stay until the next summer. . . . My illness was merely an affection in my stomach attended with a weakness and a very great depression of spirits, but I am this moment after taking a bowl of broth and toast and I feel quite stout. I got an acceptance of Kit Moriarty's at sixty-one days sight from James Sugrue for £60.19.10. Tomorrow he promises to make it a £100 by giving the balance in cash. Hickson got £50 this day from O'Leary.⁵ . . .

SOURCE : O'Connell Papers, NLI 13651
1 Mary O'Connell's brother.
2 Mary O'Connell's sister Betsey, wife of James Connor, solicitor, Tralee, died in January 1815.
3 Dr. J. F. Kearney.
4 Count O'Connell.
5 James O'Leary.

539

From his wife to Cork

Dublin, 30 March 1815,
half past four o'clock

My darling Dan,

I am this moment returned from the mail-coach office with Maurice¹ who looks to me uncommonly well. After the description you gave me of his appearance and state of health, it is the greatest relief to my spirits not to see him the object I expected. . . . He tells me you are in perfect health and spirits and greatly elated at the good news.² I wish, heart, you may have cause to be so but I much fear there is little to be expected particularly as the report of this day is that the Allies have declared against Bonaparte. . . .

I did not get the remainder of the £100 from Sugrue yet. He went down to Clongowes Wood [College] with James³ this morning. *He* says he will be very fond of him while he is giving him the money. He has an expectation of getting a settlement in the course of the next week for £600 more. I

hope he may not be disappointed, but I confess I am not very
sanguine where that gentleman is in question. . . .

SOURCE : O'Connell Papers, NLI 13651
1 Mary O'Connell's brother.
2 Napoleon's triumphal return to Paris from Elba.
3 O'Connell's brother.

540

To his wife, Merrion Square

Cork, 2 April 1815

My darling Love,
    . . . I am happy that you have so fully as well as so freely
forgiven me. It was like you, sweetest dearest Mary, best of
wives, tenderest of mothers. Where is the language that could
express my *admiration* of my own darling heart. You will
smile at the *admiration* but it is true though, love.

Do not be uneasy about the Allies. They will only tend to
consolidate the great man's power if they attempt to attack
him. His popularity with the French people is the most glorious and extraordinary of his achievements.

    . . . Though this *is* Sunday, heart, I am surrounded by
business.

SOURCE : Fitz-Simon Papers

541

To his wife, Merrion Square

Cork, 3 April 1815

My darling Love,
    . . . Do what you please with respect to a governess,
darling, and with respect to any other matter, just the same.

There are still two heavy records untried in both of which
I am counsel, and I have eight or ten criminal briefs undisposed of in the County, and the City criminal business will take
an entire day. This is what makes me dread that I shall not
get out of this before Saturday. . . .

SOURCE : Fitz-Simon Papers

541a

From his brother James to Merrion Square

Cork, 16 April 1815[1]

My dearest Dan,

I yesterday received your very affectionate letter covering one for my Uncle Maurice which I think will induce him to consent to your going to London. At all events he can have no blame to you as your going entirely depends on his wish. . . .

The enclosed letter Edward O'Mullane received this morning from Mr. Hart, the attorney, by which you perceive White Church[2] is lost for ever to this worthy family if the sum of one hundred pounds is not paid into court on [or] before Tuesday next. Now though I am at present in advance what to me is a large sum for Edward, I have procured him a hundred pounds and you will therefore on receipt of this letter pay this money (when it ought to be paid) and I will tomorrow morning remit you a Banker's Bill at 31 days for £100.10.0 to cover the discount.

SOURCE : O'Connell MSS, UCD
1 This letter was erroneously dated 16 *September* 1815 by the writer.
2 Near Mallow, Co. Cork, property of O'Connell's mother's family, the O'Mullanes.

542

From his brother James to Merrion Square

Cork, 19 April 1815

My dear Dan,

. . . Edward O'Mullane has agreed to sell Charles Sugrue a life annuity of £100 a year on the lands of Brittas for O'Mullane's own life for six hundred pounds with a clause of redemption to Edward. . . . Hart,[1] the attorney, has a copy of my uncle O'Mullane's[2] will where you will see how this property is circumstanced as to title etc. The present profit rent is £470 and O'Mullane is only subject to £17 a year head rent, and the tenants on the lands with the exception of one man, have very great bargains. . . . Now, my dear Dan, as there is £160 due to you and a much larger sum to me, let me entreat of you to give this business as little delay as possible. . . .

[Charles Sugrue] has become a butter buyer and will after some time have extensive dealings with the country.

I had a letter from Myles McSwiney this morning. He has not been able to get five pounds of the arrears due on your November rents and I have been equally unfortunate on my small property. There is over £130 due to me. How is my mother to be paid? I am convinced she would be glad to take part of her gale. For God's sake, try and send her at least fifty guineas. . . .

SOURCE : O'Connell MSS, UCD

1 William Sterne Hart (died c. 1842), 15 Fownes Street and 17 Fitz-william Square, Dublin. A major in the insurgent forces in 1798.
2 John O'Mullane.

543

From the Knight of Kerry[1]

Ballinruddery, Thursday, 20 April 1815

My dear O'Connell,

I send under another cover the answer[2] which is extorted from me by the irresistible decision of my judgement against every motive of vanity and self-gratification. I need not state the pain which accompanies that decision. Unquestionably to be at all thought of, even as one amongst several, to whom a trust so important might be confided is subject of just pride. If I were less zealous in your cause I should probably have yielded to it. This is no commonplace apology, still less is it anything evasive. I trust that I stand above any necessity of protestations to the Catholic body.

I am conscious that in *secret*, as in open day, in the recesses of Office as in Parliament I have uniformly, incessantly and honestly endeavoured to promote their cause. I should have done exactly the same had I been a Member for a close Borough instead of a very Catholic county. I will say then, I think it has been in my power to serve their cause in ways which never *can* come to their knowledge. Under the same motives I would now obey the wish you convey, were I not certain that it would injure that cause. As I feel sincerely I write to you with the utmost frankness. Had you made the suggestion at the assizes I think I could have convinced you by reasons which it is

impossible to include in the space of a letter. You must therefore allow for haste as well as surprise.

I am not competent to advocating, in chief, your great
question in the character of a competitor of Mr. Grattan. Even
were I capable of introducing it originally, the responsibility
as well as difficulty are now immeasurably enhanced. It
would require not only a station and importance in the House
of Commons which I do not possess but discretion and prudence which belong to no one less than to me. It is not that I
shrink from personal difficulty, misconstruction or envy as
they would affect myself but as they would prejudice your
cause through your advocate. I even exclude from consideration the feelings of friendship and connection which exist
between Mr. Grattan and me, and solemnly affirm on public
grounds my persuasion not only that the loss of him would be
fatal, but the substitution of *me* would be mischievous. I have
upon more than one question besides yours taken a part so
ardent as to subject me to imputations of violence from a
majority of the House, and although I shall never shrink from
my opinions I should be criminal if I were to implicate them
with the management of a question so delicate and difficult.
Many individuals would be detached by the loss of Mr. Grattan
and many by the substitution of me. Many of the more
temperate English would be revolted and all the most violent
of our countrymen further exasperated. Mr. Grattan has done
more by his management and manner even than by his great
abilities. That body who stand clear of the Ministers and the
Opposition have been conciliated by him and would be
alienated by the choice of a person whose misfortune it has
been to shock some of their strongest prejudices.

But above all with the opinions I entertain as to the
principle on which your measure should proceed I must either
suppress them on introducing it or, by their avowal, detach
almost all those on whose support you can reckon for any
advantage. Now, although your Committee may choose to risk
in their own cause such an issue, to be the instrument of
committing the House to such a decision with my view of
its consequences, is too awful a responsibility for me to contemplate for a single moment.

Would to Heaven that I could be instrumental to your
replacing the petition in the hands of your oldest and best
advocate in a manner humiliating to neither party. Mutual
misunderstandings and want of candid intercourse may have

carried each party too far but, when your country is at stake, all should be forgotten but the means to save it. I am convinced Mr. Grattan always intended to move the discussion in this session. I may say it is my earnest *prayer* that you would devise some means to bring about an honourable reconciliation.

How can we go confidently to battle with dissension in our ranks?

Could I with any sense of honesty to your cause undertake the honour which was intended me, I need hardly say that your personal concurrence in conveying it would have enhanced my gratification. I shall not mention the communication to any human being.

SOURCE : O'Connell MSS, UCD

1 O'Connell was a member of the committee appointed by the Catholic Association to select an M.P. to present the Catholic petition to the Commons. On 15 April 1815 the committee was criticized for being inactive (*FJ*, 17 April 1815). O'Connell sought and obtained extra time for the committee to present its report (*FJ*, 17, 19 April 1815). On 23 April 1815 O'Connell and the committee obtained Sir Henry Parnell's agreement to present the petition (*FJ*, 26 April 1815).

2 Probably a letter formally declining to present the Catholic petition to the Commons.

544

To Owen O'Conor, Belanagare

Merrion Square, 29 April 1815

My dear friend,

I have discovered the names of the two principal distributors of the Ribbon System in your county—Pat Byrne, otherwise call[ed] Pat Fatcheen or Faddeen, and a great rioter of the name of Fitzmaurice. The former is supposed to be instigated under hand, the latter probably only by his own inclinations. I am sure you will use every exertion to prevent the poor people from being duped by those or any other combinators. It would be the destruction of our cause and their own ruin. The plan of getting those scoundrels arrested and then enforcing evidence from others would be the very best. The Catholic clergy would, I am sure, assist you to stop the progress of this mischief, and I should not be sorry that you prosecuted one or two of the most guilty at the assizes to convince the people how decided our opposition to those plans is and will continue.

SOURCE : Clonalis Papers

545

To his son Maurice, care of the Rev. Mr. Kenney,
Clongowes Wood College

Merrion Square, 5 May 1815

My dearest Maurice,

I have deferred writing to you for some days that time might reconcile you to your separation from your mother and me. That separation from you and your brother is very painful to us both but we submit cheerfully to the loss of your dear society and Morgan's because we are convinced that it is for the benefit of both of you. Indeed, with respect to you, that separation was become necessary principally because without it you never would have submitted your mind to that regular and systematic course of study which is essentially necessary for you, perhaps more necessary for you than for any other child I have ever met. Your father's partiality makes him imagine that nature has not been deficient to you, but it does not prevent him from seeing that there is a loose and rambling turn in your mind which naturally distracts and takes you off from the regular plan of acquiring knowledge which alone can enable you to contend with superior men or become a source of satisfaction to your family and perhaps of utility to your country.

Your mother, your brother and your sisters are perfectly well and each of them desires to be particularly remembered to you and to Morgan. John asks constantly for you, and your sweet little Betsey in her most musical notes inquires when she shall have the happiness of seeing you both. I intend going down to see you as soon as I possibly can. I thought I should have been able to do so on Tuesday next but the Equity Courts sit that day and I cannot leave town till the ensuing week. I will then go to you, and I think you and Morgan would take pains to enable Mr. Kenney to give me a good account of you if you knew how delightful to my heart that account would be. Tell Morgan this letter is for you both.

SOURCE : Fitz-Simon Papers

546

From Eneas MacDonnell to Merrion Square

Cork, 12 May 1815

My Dear O'Connell,

I received yours late yesterday. . . .

I had two letters from Magee[1] within these ten days. They
were both in most friendly style but stating the impossibility
of his meeting my wishes under the present heavy state of
expenditures of his office owing to legal contests and the large
sums required for procuring foreign news, private correspondence, etc. In the first he told me of your interview with him
for which I owe you many obligations, and in the second he
informed me of O'Gorman's following up his threatened
action[2] and your having subscribed the declaration and supported it as counsel for O'G[orman], the whole of which gave
me much pain, particularly the latter circumstances as I would
much rather have seen you filling the station of mediator.
And I know you will not complain of my candour when I
tell you that I do not like even the sound of the words ' Counsellor O'Connell, Counsel against John Magee '[3] for, after
all, we must all know that it is his property must pay the
piper. His services and still more his sufferings entitle him to
our regard and, though his editor may have done, as he certainly has done, many acts which I sincerely disapprove, still
I would recommend an Irish Catholic to hesitate before he
determines on putting John Magee in jeopardy. I have com-
plained in unreserved terms to Magee himself of the acts to
which I refer, and he certainly met my complaint in most
friendly humour, even in a letter which I wrote to him on last
Tuesday. . . . I renewed my complaints, adding at the same
time my surprise that O'G[orman] should have proceeded to
extremities as I did not recollect that any attack had been
made on him since the commencement of legal proceedings
by him. . . . I suggest a submission of all matters in dispute
to such an Irishman as George Lidwill. . . . Would it not
be a source of most gratifying reflection . . . to communicate
to the world and particularly to our enemies that all those
differences between the Press and the People had been adjusted
in a manner satisfactory and honourable? The [*Dublin*]
Evening Post has a name and character with the public which
would make it a most useful and indeed almost commanding

instrument in the propagation of good principles if properly
directed. . . . The [Dublin] Evening Post took the wrong
course. . . . This was the natural consequence of unregulated
spleen and therefore should not in my mind be visited on the
unfortunate man who was merely the dupe and victim of the
sophistry and frenzy of another. The writer may have felt
himself justified and, indeed, when I recollect some angry
ebullitions of my own I am the less inclined to attach inten-
tional premeditated guilt of acrimony to another. . . .

The Freeman is false in stating that he knew you wrote
the speech.[4] . . .

SOURCE : O'Connell MSS, UCD

1   James Magee.
2   This was an action of complex connections. In January 1814
    Nicholas Purcell O'Gorman was sent by the Catholic Board to
    Londonderry to defend a local priest who was indicted for riot and
    assault (DEP, 13 April 1816). For details of this case see letter 627,
    note 1. An account of the case was published in the Dublin Evening
    Post, which contained an alleged libel on the counsel for the pro-
    secution, Richard O'Doherty. (DEP, 13 April 1816. The alleged
    libel was contained in a comment upon O'Doherty's character
    within parentheses and apart from the verbatim account of the
    proceedings.) O'Doherty took an action against James Magee,
    current proprietor of the Dublin Evening Post, and was awarded
    damages of £500 (DEP, 13 April 1816). Magee claimed the entire
    publication, including the allegedly libellous comment, had been
    taken from a manuscript given him by O'Gorman as a true account
    of the proceedings. He claimed compensation from O'Gorman and
    on the latter's failing to compensate him, took an action against
    him. The case was due to come to trial in July 1815, but was
    suspended when O'Gorman's counsel, influenced perhaps by the
    letter above, moved its postponement pending arbitration by George
    Lidwill (DEP, 13 April 1816). Lidwill's intervention was unsuccess-
    ful. In December 1815 Magee was awarded nearly £1,000 damages
    against O'Gorman, O'Connell acting in this case as counsel for
    O'Gorman. (For an account of this trial see DEP, 16, 19, 21, 23, 26,
    30 Dec. 1815; 4, 9, 11, 18 Jan. 1816.) Meanwhile, O'Gorman
    had commenced an action against the Dublin Evening Post for hav-
    ing published an alleged libel on himself in November 1814. In
    April 1816 O'Gorman sought damages in this case of £1,000 from
    James Magee, but was awarded only £150 (DEP, 4, 11, 13 April
    1816). The reference in the above letter alludes to the latter action
    (April 1816) in which O'Connell did not subsequently take part.
3   This is a mistake. O'Gorman's action was brought not against John
    Magee but his younger brother, James, who from 29 November 1813

had taken over legal proprietorship of the *Dublin Evening Post* and
agreed to accept all liability for prosecutions (*DEP*, 11, 13 April 1816).

4 ' The *Freeman* is false . . .' In his charge to the Westmeath grand
jury in March 1815, Judge Day accused the Catholic Association of
fomenting disturbances in that county and declared it an illegal
body (*DEP*, 25 Mar. 1815). At a Cork Catholic meeting in April
1815, O'Connell severely criticized Day for having made such an
attack (*FJ*, 18 April 1815). The *Freeman's Journal* published
O'Connell's speech and was in consequence prosecuted for libel
(*FJ*, 8 May 1815). In such cases it was usual for the person who
had originally uttered the libel to evade prosecution through plead-
ing possible inaccuracies in reporting. In the case in question the
Freeman's Journal tried to make O'Connell accept responsibility by
claiming to know he had written the speech as published (*FJ*, 10
May 1815).

547

To his son Maurice, Clongowes Wood College

Merrion Square, 15 May 1815

My dearest Maurice,

I am very much obliged to you for both your letters. They
have given me very sincere pleasure because they showed that
you and Morgan had the good sense and good feeling to be
contented with your present situation, and cheerful in the
prospect of improvement that lies before you. . . .

I expect to be able to see you both during the week or at
the latest on Sunday next. I have purposely remained away
from you that you may be the more reconciled to part with
me after a short visit. Your mother cannot go down to see you
till after her confinement but, as soon as she is quite well, I
will take her and the girls to pay you a visit. They are very
happy to find that you both are so well satisfied with College.
. . . Your Aunt Finn is arrived in London as is my Uncle,
the General. They are all coming to Ireland shortly, and I
shall take them to visit you especially if I find that Mr. Kenny
is able to give a satisfactory account of you. Let me know
what books you read, and how many boys are in your class,
and if your place in the class admits of being told, let me
know it. I mean those directions for Morgan as well as for
you and, indeed I am very well pleased at the account you
give of Morgan and hope he will have the same account to
give of you.

SOURCE : Fitz-Simon Papers

548

To the Knight of Kerry

Merrion Square, 15 May 1815

My dear Sir,

Will you allow me to entreat your kind attention to the support of Sir Henry Parnell[1] at the present most interesting period? It is easy to see that, except from *you* and some few others who are attached to the principle of Religious Freedom, we can expect no cordiality of co-operation. The hackneyed part of the opposition, led by Mr. Tierney,[2] seem disposed to take him in flank, whilst he is met by Abbot[3] and Banks[4] in front and harassed in the rear by the most ridiculous of all possible casuists, Cox Hippisley.[5] Add to these the confident assertion of Mr. Plunket[6] that the Petition does not speak the sense of the Catholics of Ireland. I am greatly astonished at Mr. Plunket. He cannot but know that the fact is otherwise, and little as I am disposed to respect the entire of his political life, I did not imagine he was so destitute of that feeling which should place him so far beyond any deviation from truth as to allow him thus to assert. With respect to Kerry, you cannot, with your decisive evidence to contradict that gentleman. You will find to the Petition the name of every Catholic of property in the county—the Galweys[7] and D. Mahony,[8] who hold places, and Hussey,[9] who wishes for at least one, only excepted.

It is, perhaps, a most imperative duty to contradict Mr. Plunket upon this point. As Emancipation of some sort is probably not very distant—with restrictions, besides being wrong in principle—it would tend to make Ireland what Scotland is—as Ireland is what Scotland was—an impoverished and discontented people. If they enact restrictions, the effect will be worse than the present state of affairs. The *Crown Priests* will be despised and deserted by the people, who will be amply supplied with enthusiastic anti-anglican friars from the Continent. There is a tendency *already* to substitute friars for any priests who are supposed to favour the Veto. It is very marked in Dublin already, and they know little of Ireland who suppose that they could *abolish friars* by law. There really is but one resource—to bestow a *generous* Emancipation that would at once take the people out of the hands of us agitators and of every species of enthusiasts, and by destroying the cause of excitement terminate the fever in the public mind. Dr.

Addington[10] and his medical school may recommend bleeding and boiling water, but the patient is already too strong for these remedies.

I have written an inexcuseably long letter to Sir H. Parnell, and am half disposed to bestow my tediousness equally on *you*. Will you pardon me for doing so, and for again—I am sure unnecessarily—hoping your attention to assist Sir Henry, and to protect him and us from our friend Mr. Plunket? It would amuse me very much to have an opportunity of reasoning with that acute and very sagacious personage.

SOURCE : FitzPatrick, *Corr.*, I, 35-7

1   Sir Henry Parnell opened the parliamentary debate on the Catholic question on 11 May 1815 (*FJ*, 16 May 1815). He was due to introduce resolutions for a Catholic relief bill on 30 May 1815 (*FJ*, 24 May 1815, quoting *Dublin Evening Post*).
2   George Tierney, M.P.
3   Charles Abbot (1757-1829), chief secretary for Ireland 1801-02; speaker of the House of Commons, 1802-17; created Baron Colchester, 1817. See *DNB*.
4   Henry Bankes (1757-1834), M.P. for Corfe Castle, 1780-1826. See *DNB*.
5   Sir John Coxe Hippisley, first baronet (1748-1825), M.P. for Sudbury, 1790-96, 1802-19. See *DNB*.
6   William Conyngham Plunket (1764-1854), M.P. for Midhurst, 1807; for Dublin University, 1812-27; attorney-general, 1805-07, 1822-27; chief justice of the common pleas, 1827-30; created Baron Plunket, 1 May 1827; lord chancellor of Ireland, 1830-34, 1835-41. See *DNB*.
7   Of Killarney, land agents to the earls of Kenmare c. 1750-1861. Stephen Gallwey was seneschal to the Manors of Ross and Molahiff and a cess collector.
8   Daniel Mahony (died 1832), Dunloe Castle, Killarney, Co. Kerry. Landowner and kinsman of O'Connell.
9   Unidentified.
10 Anthony Addington, M.D. (1713-90), physician to George III; father of the first viscount Sidmouth. See *DNB*.

549

From his brother James to Merrion Square

Killarney, 15 May 1815

My Dearest Dan,

On my arrival here I found my mother in the most unhappy state of mind in consequence of not being paid her last March gale. She said she had not one guinea and that she wanted to go to the Tralee Spa. I gave her thirty guineas of my own to relieve her *present wants* and assured her, if I was obliged to borrow the seventy guineas more in ten penny pieces, I would pay it to her before a fortnight. This seemed to satisfy her. Now, my dear Dan, for God's sake send this money either to John or me as I really believe she wants it, having lent any money she had last April to Humphrey Moynihan for which he passed his bond payable with interest.

Myles McSwiney cannot get a shilling of the November rent due of your tenants before the middle of August next, and on my small property I am even worse off than you.

SOURCE : O'Connell MSS, UCD

550

To his son Morgan at Clongowes

Merrion Square, 19 May 1815

My dear Morgan,

Your mother and I are greatly pleased at the regularity with which Maurice and you write to us, and we have a notion that it is a greater compliment from you than from Maurice, because he has at least the appearance of being more attentive. I am quite sure that you, my dear child, are as affectionate as he is, and you cannot possibly take any better method of proving that you are so than by attending to your improvement.

John and the girls are in great spirits at finding that you and Maurice consider yourselves so happy and comfortable at College. I, too, am myself very much pleased at that circumstance. I will contrive to see you both in a very few days; sooner I could not do it, as the Courts have continued to sit all the latter part of this week.

SOURCE : FitzPatrick, *Corr.*, I, 46-7

551

From Sir Henry Parnell

23 Bury Street, [London], 22 May 1815

My dear Sir,

You very much overrate my services and form, I fear, much too sanguine an expectation of the good that will result from them.[1] I trust, however, the making your body better acquainted with the House of Commons and the House better acquainted with you will contribute to produce that conciliation which, you may justly say, is the great object of all our exertions.

I have been applied to to present a petition of the Catholics of Lancashire and having undertaken to do it, I shall have an opportunity of bringing before the House the information you have given me on the assertion that your petition did certificate the sentiments of the Catholic body.

Letters have been received here from Italy which say that arrangements are certainly under the consideration of the Pope relative to the future nomination of your bishops, at the instance of Government. I rather think they must relate to the English Catholics and not to you but, at all events, it is certain that Government have the final settlement of the question in their contemplation.

The idea of the necessity of some ecclesiastical arrangements has so fixed itself generally in this country that there is no rational prospect of the measure ever being carried without them.

I shall oppose them in every way, not with any hope of succeeding in getting rid of them, but of showing that they ought to be free from all imputation of an intention to affect the Catholic religion or our civil liberty.

I really believe that those public men who have hitherto been forward in pressing them have fair objects in view and that, if the Irish Catholics could see the subject divested of all remembrance of the existence of an Irish government, their feelings would not be so adverse as they now are.

It would be a great matter gained if your body could bring themselves to place less importance than they do on what the Irish government and its press say or do for they really are no parties to your question. I believe no minister or no Member ever pays the smallest attention to one or the other.

Not a single adverse comment to your cause has as yet appeared in any public paper in this city.

This circumstance proves a great alteration in the opinion of the English since 1813 and may be considered as the sure forerunner of success. If you could in any way exhibit a disposition to meet this favourable indication of a willingness to comply with your wishes, without any inconsistency with

your declared sentiments on the subject of arrangements, it
would produce a very salutary effect.

As I consider the legitimate object of discussion this session
to be the advancement of the measure, I hope the failure of
my motion will not be set down in Ireland as any proof of a
secession of friends in Parliament, but that it will be received
as it really ought to be as the sense of the country on the
distinct claim of unqualified Emancipation.

SOURCE : FitzSimon Papers

1 On 11 May Parnell presented a petition from the Roman Catholics
   of Ireland in favour of full emancipation and gave notice of his
   intention to move on that day fortnight that the House should
   consider ' the laws affecting Roman Catholics ' (*Hansard*, N.S., 1815,
   XXXI, 246-7; *Commons Journal*, LXX, 293). On 18 May Parnell
   read certain resolutions embodying the Catholic claims and moved
   one of them, but finding the House not disposed to receive his
   motion he withdrew it, remarking that ' the only object he had
   in view was accomplished, namely, that of explaining to the House
   the objects necessary to satisfy the wishes of the Catholics of Ireland '
   (*Hansard*, N.S., 1815, XXXI, 257-65). On 30 May Parnell's motion
   that the House go into committee on the Catholic claims was
   defeated 228 to 147.

551a

To Sir Henry Parnell, 23 Bury Street, St. James, London

[postmarked 31 May 1815]

[first part of letter not extant]

of Catholic bishops in Ireland or rather to prevent the office
being filled by any person but a man of whose fidelity to the
state the King should be satisfied. Let *our bill* pass now, and
his bill be announced for the next Sessions. The Minister[1]
would be certain—it appears for a thousand and one reasons—
of carrying his bill next Sessions. *Then* you could with perfect
consistency support it. *Then* it would meet with no opposition
from agitators or aggregate meetings. In the interval that tie
of common feeling and common suffering which at present
keeps the Catholic body in a state of irregular combination
would be worn away and broken. Confidence in the government would be created and a *communion* between the Irish

people and the English government for the first time in history be promoted.

This plan is perhaps with the materials we have to work upon in the house impracticable and is perhaps the less likely to succeed from its obvious efficacy for every useful purpose. *The Irish people are those in the world most likely to be led away by first impulses, and if they were treated to a free emancipation bill in this Sessions they would cheerfully and as a matter of little moment leave the Government and the bishops to make any arrangement they pleased.* Indeed in that case it would not be difficult to make the bishops *listen to reason.* But it is quite impossible, impossible to the last degree, to induce the people or the priests at present and without some such bill as ours being previously and unconditionally passed, to consent to any arrangements or securities. The person who attempts as a Catholic to prevail on the people to [one or two words illegible] would be treated as corrupt and treacherous. In short unless Emancipation come in the *first instance* without securities the people will not consent to any bill, and a bill without this consent destroys its only useful object. *You seem to me to treat the Government of Ireland and its hired press too lightly. They are the first and most serious obstacles in the way of any assent to securities.* That press is vulgar and vile to be sure *but then it is virulent, disgusting and inflammatory, and it bears a kind of official stamp which conveys back to the government of all the effects of its faults and follies.* The Irish Secretary[2] *too is the champion of the Orange Lodges.* The Irish *Attorney-General[3] without manliness to resent* his private quarrel revenges himself on the population at large. *The chancellor[4] a mere unresisting instrument* in the hands of both. *Can you conceive it possible for the people of Ireland, warm as they are with permanent hostility and recent persecution, to consent to give those men any control over their religion.* No. It is only by changing the scene, with a little alteration in the actors that the temper and disposition to allow *Securities,* and to see and estimate them at their just value can be cultivated or expected. Let Emancipation come first, generously and unconditionally, and if experience shall show *securities* to be necessary let the next Sessions impose them.

But whatever shall be the result there is and there can be but one opinion as to the mode in which you have conducted the cause. It is an opinion which I will not *here* and could not anywhere sufficiently express. If we succeed we shall owe it first and principally to you. If we fail we owe it to our own preference of our present degradation to a Vetoistical emancipation. In either case our gratitude to you ought to be equal, and I trust will be permanent and ever lively.[5]

SOURCE : Congleton Papers
1 The prime minister or home secretary. O'Connell was obviously referring to the office rather than the particular incumbent.
2 Robert Peel.
3 William Saurin.
4 The lord chancellor, Lord Manners.
5 The excessive amount of underlining in this letter, and the thinness of the line, suggest that it was not underlined by O'Connell.

552

From the Knight of Kerry to Merrion Square

London, Thursday [1 June 1815]

My dear O'Connell,

The division[1] was better than we[2] could have expected and shows that against the principle of concession they can rally no great force under any circumstances. At the same time, were we to go to a vote on unqualified relief, we should not divide with fifteen.

Parnell managed with considerable prudence. Castlereagh says the measure is thrown back considerably, that in the counties there is a strong prejudice rather increasing. I had wished to speak late in the debate but Parnell thought it advisable that I should get up after Yorke[3] and Knox.[4] The only paper that has not misrepresented me is the *British Press*. I fancy I am no favourite with the reporters.

I think Parnell will introduce a Bill on some of the subordinate points to catch Yorke, etc., and get another discussion.

SOURCE : O'Connell MSS, UCD
1 See letter 551, note 1.
2 The Knight of Kerry had supported the Catholic claims in parliament (*DEP*, 6 June 1815).
3 Charles Philip Yorke (1764-1834), M.P.; half-brother of third earl of Hardwicke; home secretary, 1803-04; first lord of the admiralty, 1810-11. See *DNB*.
4 Hon. Thomas Knox (1786-1858), M.P. for Co. Tyrone 1812-18; for Dungannon, 1813-30 and 1837-38. Styled Viscount Northland 1831-40 when he succeeded as second earl of Ranfurly.

553

To his son Maurice, Clongowes Wood College

Merrion Square, 2 June 1815

My dearest Maurice,

. . . I cannot go down to see you until Sunday week. Your Uncle Maurice[1] is out for a fishing-rod and flies for you as I am most happy to give you and your brother any indulgence which your superiors in the college think you may deserve or be permitted to have. I am also very well pleased that you had nothing to do with the shameful plot to turn the professors into ridicule. I hope Morgan kept himself quite free of it also. . . .

SOURCE : O'Connell Papers, NLI 13645
1   Maurice O'Connell, brother of Mary.

554

From Eneas MacDonnell

39 Lower Ormond Quay
[Dublin], 8 June 1815

Dear O'Connell,

In answer to your inquiries . . . I was and still am convinced that a sum of not less than eight hundred pounds would be necessary to put a three day paper[1] in motion. You know my objection to being the responsible proprietor is founded on an apprehension that some malicious enemy might manage by the agency of a corrupt clerk or printer to insert a libel and thereby place me at the mercy of some bigoted prosecutor. I would however feel as much interest and take as much trouble in the general management of the concern, as well financial as editorial, as if I were the registered proprietor. . . . [He suggests that the interest should be vested in trustees until the money advanced was repaid, after providing for all necessary expenses.] I have had several interviews with Nolan the printer[2] in Church Lane . . . he could publish the first number in the latter end of next week. As to setting up a regular printing office, it could not be *possibly* done in less than two or three months and then with an additional expense of at least four or five hundred pounds.

SOURCE : O'Connell MSS, UCD

1   See letter 559, note 1.
2   James Joseph Nolan, 4 Church Lane, Dublin.

555

From Michael Staunton[1]

17 St. Andrew's Street [Dublin], 8 June 1815

Sir,

Pending the filing of the *ex officio* information against the *Freeman's Journal* for the insertion of your speech at Cork,[2] you had frequently hinted at some step which it seemed to be your intention to take with regard to that proceeding, and on one occasion you went so far as to agree upon meeting me at a specified hour at your own house for the purpose of having it explained to me. I am yet ignorant of the measure you contemplated. It is true I had a conversation with you in the Hall of the Courts, in which, reminding you of the knowledge you had of my intentions relative to this document before it was given for publication, the declarations of readiness to hold yourself personally responsible for all your words and actions which you had so often made,[3] and the reliance I had been ever taught to place on your honour and, I may say, magnaminity, I called upon you to extricate Mr. Harvey[4] from the dilemma in which, without his knowledge[5] and with not one atom of advantage to him or his establishment, you had been the cause of involving him. But you had not thought proper to give me a more definite answer than that you had ' come to no determination and would neither avow nor disavow anything '. This was not compatible with your previous professions, or at least it went but a short way in elucidating the nature of those arrangements upon which you had meditated for a whole week and which you had appointed a time and place for the purpose of developing. I am therefore constrained, now that notice of trial for the 19th inst.[6] has been served, to request you to be more explicit. You have told me you felt yourself under a heavy obligation on the score of the publication of this speech, if not to Mr. Harvey, to whom I should much rather you had conceived it due, at least to myself. The object of this letter is to request you to state your sentiments as to its amount and how it should be discharged, and this I am persuaded you will do as speedily as leisure will admit.

SOURCE : O'Connell MSS, UCD

1   Michael Staunton (1788-1870), editor of *Freeman's Journal*, 1813-24; proprietor of the *Dublin Evening Herald*, 1821-23; editor and proprietor of the *Morning Register*, 1824-43; lord mayor of Dublin, 1847.
2   See letter 546, note 4.
3   A reference to O'Connell's reported statement at the time of the trial of John Magee, in which he is said to have declared: ' I shall *ever* hold myself personally responsible for all my actions and words; I shall *ever* be ready to answer here [i.e., in the courts of law] and everywhere else.' (*FJ*, 10 May 1815, quoting *FJ*, 25 May 1814).
4   Philip Whitfield Harvey (died 1826), was proprietor of the *Freeman's Journal*, c. 1802-26; proprietor of the *Evening Packet*, 1807-10. His only child married Henry Grattan the Younger, M.P., in 1826 so that Grattan became thus the owner of the *Freeman's Journal*.
5   Harvey claimed that Staunton had published O'Connell's allegedly libellous speech without his (Harvey's) knowledge (*FJ*, 9 May 1815).
6   On 19 June Harvey appeared before the court of King's Bench charged with having published O'Connell's speech at the Cork meeting (see letter 556). He then ' in order to save the Crown all trouble in this case ' substituted a plea of guilty for not guilty. He declared, however, that he was morally innocent as ' the publication was procured in his absence, without his knowledge, and contrary to the express direction he had given for the conduct of his paper.' Consequently, the attorney-general allowed him to remain at large but directed him to appear for trial on the first day of the following term (*FJ*, 20 June 1815). It is not known if the proceedings against Harvey were further pursued.

556

To Michael Staunton

Merrion Square, 9 June 1815

Draft

Sir,

I have little leisure for letter-writing at this period of the term, but my answer to your letter shall be explicit. I am wholly unconscious of any claims Mr. Harvey, the proprietor of the *Freeman's Journal*, can have on me. It seems he has published from the *Cork Chronicle* a report of a speech attributed to me, and this without any interference or encouragement on my part, without any connection subsisting between us or other inducement save those which I presume usually regulate the proprietor of a newspaper. It would be strange indeed if such a proprietor, governed solely by views of emolument—as far as I can perceive—should be deemed entitled to turn around upon the individual without any previous intercourse, and to exact from him an indemnity against what is called the law of libel as administered by the Law officers in Ireland.

But this claim must appear the more strange and its object *mysterious,* after the proprietor has deliberately proclaimed in his paper that the article in question is a heinous libel, and after he has thus not only bespoke a conviction for himself, but gratuitously criminated other persons.[1]

Indeed, what can be the serious objects of a trial under those circumstances? To talk of a trial after so complaisant a plea of ' guilty ' would be but a mockery. He has thrown himself on the mercy of an Attorney-General, and as far as in him lay implicated and prejudged the remaining objects of vengeance.

There may possibly be ulterior objects of a trial, but surely Mr. Harvey's defence ceases to be one.

Of the conversation you allude to my recollection is wholly different from the statement in your letter, so is that of Mr. Phillips[2] who was present. I did more than once express my regret for the apprehension you felt for the probable loss of your situation under Mr. Harvey. And certainly I was perfectly willing to do my utmost towards compensating you personally for any pecuniary inconvenience arising from the publication of a speech which you conceived to be mine. This was a leading object in my mind at the time. I apprehend that the error into which you have fallen proceeds from your mistaking this sentiment towards you for a sense of obligation towards the proprietor. But I have never felt or avowed any such obligation. There was no room for it between Mr. Harvey and me.

If *he* seriously conceives himself to have any well-founded claim on me, let him bring it forward distinctly and in person, and if in the judgement of any impartial Gentleman of honour acquainted with the facts it shall be deemed a well-founded claim in *honour* or *justice*, it shall be yielded to. I make this offer as my final answer, and you will allow me, in conclusion, to express my hope and wish that any future communication *on this* subject may proceed from him alone.

SOURCE : O'Connell Papers, NLI 13645

1 On 11 May 1815 the *Freeman's Journal* described O'Connell's speech, which it had published, as a gross libel.
2 Probably Charles Phillips.

557

From Eneas MacDonnell to Merrion Square

Saturday morning, 10 June 1815

Dear O'Connell,

. . . I propose to commence and establish without delay an independent three-day newspaper[1] to be conducted and directed by myself alone, in my own name, for my own account and upon my own sole responsibility. . . .

To enable me to establish this paper I will have occasion for a sum of eight hundred pounds. . . .

SOURCE : O'Connell MSS, UCD

1 The *Dublin Chronicle*. See letter 559, note 1.

558

To Michael Staunton, 17 St. Andrew's St., Dublin

Merrion Square, 13 June 1815

[*Draft or copy*]

Sir,

I am favoured with your letter dated yesterday.

Your statement of facts is so very wide of my conception of them that as I have neither leisure nor inclination for polemics I must assert my right to close the correspondence with this letter.

I refer you to my last letter for my definitive answer with respect to the trial of Mr. Harvey.

SOURCE : O'Connell Papers, NLI 13645

558a

To Sir Henry Parnell

Merrion Square, 13 June 1815

My dear Sir,

I must beg leave to repeat my conviction that *you* will procure for us emancipation. The course you pursue is in my humble judgement the only wise one. You have disengaged our question altogether from party and disembarrassed it from the intricacies of opposition politics.

There is but one danger of failure—and that is your involving it in any connection with *securities*—as they are called. As accompanying relief, as making part of a relief bill they will never, never be accepted. They would destroy the only useful object of emancipation—the conciliation of the population of Ireland. *Nay, so strongly is the notion impressed on the popular mind that securities mean the control over and consequent destruction of their religion that I am convinced that Emancipation accompanied with ecclesiastical arrangements would aggravate every existing evil* and so help me God but I apprehend that instead of conciliating, it would promote a religious war in Ireland of the most furious and ferocious nature. Believe me that there are abundant materials for a sect of popish ' *Cameronians* '[1] who in that event would certainly aid any foreign Standard and probably raise one of their own even without foreign aid. . . . The very anxiety of the enemies of the Catholics to obtain them [the securities] renders them doubly suspicious to the people, and at this moment *a Priest suspected of Vetoism loses all his respect.* It *follows that they exaggerate their hatred* of it to preclude the suspicion but their exaggerations are not unproductive when flung on the hotbed of Irish *excitability.*

. . . *Leaving the people as they are is dangerous—much more dangerous than the administration either here or in England imagine* but, believe me, the danger would only be increased by the proposed remedy. *There is one plain course which* the minister[2] could pursue, and one only, by which he could attain the two objects—*first*—the reconciling the people of Ireland so to England that he may have in Ireland as well as in England local militia and perfect unanimity *and secondly*—any *Securities* that may be wanted or wished for. The plan which I suggest is perhaps not practicable. There are perhaps a thousand secret reasons of State management to prevent it but it would be efficacious. It would be this.

Let Emancipation—*unqualified* at any rate, *full* if possible —be announced. Let the minister announce his patronage to a bill for relief, *unmixed* relief, *and let him declare his intention to postpone ' the Securities'* until the relief bill had passed into a law and gone into operation in fact. *He may pledge himself as strongly as possible that ' the securities' were not given up but merely postponed.* The relief being thus certain, the *Securities deferred, every obstacle to reconciliation, every reason for and topic* of irritation *would be at an end.* The species of *corporate* feeling by which the Catholics are kept in a state of combination would cease and the *influence of Agitators would necessarily die a natural death.* In *the very tumult of joy* and gratitude for kindness bestowed—and there is not in the universe a people so sensitive to kindness—every suspicion would be hushed and every effort to keep alive discontent would be easily defeated. *Afterwards the Minister might deliberately investigate and calmly arrange any ' Securities'* or patronage he may desire, and his objects in that respect would be greatly promoted by a little attention to what the Doctors call *' the predisposing causes'.*

For the purpose of creating a *predisposition to perfect conciliation* and also to *Securities* it would be necessary to change the stations *of three* or four individuals, and to alter the *tone of the Government press.* Insulting language is very silly on the *part and behalf* of any government. It never convinces anybody. It excites insolence in the ruling party, hatred in the governed and *then* the reaction of those passions upon each other. But indeed for every reason this should be taken away altogether. At the popular side there has latterly been no press, and *I promise you* that we would zealously second any efforts made to tranquillize.

The individuals I allude to may be got rid of in this way. The Chancellor[3] should be promoted or at least removed to England. He is *committed* with the country and is besides under the entire control of Saurin. If you had the chancellor out of the way, the Master of the Rolls *should* fill his place for two reasons. First, McMahon is an admirable judge, the best equity judge, Redesdale excepted, that this country ever saw, and he is a man of great conduct, temper, management and manner. All parties like him. He is singularly fortunate in his conduct. Secondly, his promotion would leave a place vacant for Saurin who would, I suppose, be easily induced to take it. Thus he would be removed from politics without the administration giving him up or behaving ill to him which however *we* dislike him, they ought not perhaps to do. Let any other person be attorney-general and the *very temper* of the times will change. There is a stiff and bitter bigotry about the present Atty-General which is not the less hateful and irritative for being conscientious—if it be so—on his part.

There would then be two minor posts to be disposed of. Peele[4] [*sic*] could I suppose be without difficulty disposed of in the diplomatic line or as Under-Secretary in England. In short there is so much promotion before him that he might be promoted off speedily. Gregory[5] *must* follow. He is in the constant habit of using foul language of the Catholics and upon a system of conciliation he could not remain here with propriety.

Thus you see with a smile how we agitators would commence the plan of a useful and efficient Emancipation. . . . Believe me, this country is in a terrific State. The fall of prices has beggared the peasantry and ruined the farmers. The restoration of Buonaparte has given a new direction to their hopes and wishes. England is doing nothing for them. She gives them insults and taxes. Are you surprised that there should exist a frightful propensity to illegal combinations. There are facts on this subject within my knowledge that would appal you. However the lucky circumstance of one or two *sham* plots having been attempted enables us and the Clergy to discountenance and to retard if not to stop real conspiracies. I shall when you come to this country mention to you one instance or two in which success has been certainly great, probably quite complete, in opposing the progress of combination. But if the war continues, if Napoleon be not put down this campaign, if he be in any degree successful and that another doubtful year of war be in prospect, the man has stronger nerves than I have who could know the real state of Ireland and rest quiet without apprehension. My God, how foolishly mistaken the men are who imagine that the agitators and leaders guide and direct the popular sentiment. They may echo that sentiment or give it voice but it pre-exists and operates only the stronger during its periods of silence. I am so deeply convinced of the necessity of emancipation for the safety of the present order of things and of the connection with England that I feel disposed personally to go nearer to

' Securities ' than my principles could justify at any [? other] period. But again and again I disclaim any relief *joined* with ' Securities '. Bad as things are they are better than a relief bill connected immediately with Securities. That bill we would one and all oppose. Be no party to it if you value the gratitude and esteem of the Irish Catholics. But if the bill be *first* carried there will certainly be no popular opposition to the discussion and arrangement of the second.[6]

SOURCE : Congleton Papers

1   The most uncompromising Presbyterian communion in Scotland, dating from the seventeenth century. Until the middle of the nineteenth century they refused to recognize the British constitution or to take part in civil government (*New Catholic Encyc.*).
2   The prime minister or home secretary. O'Connell was obviously referring to the office rather than the particular incumbent.
3   The lord chancellor, Lord Manners.
4   Robert Peel, the chief secretary.
5   William Gregory, the under-secretary.
6   The excessive amount of underlining in this letter, and the thinness of the line drawn, suggest that it was not underlined by O'Connell.

559

From Thomas Cloney to Merrion Square

Graig [Co. Kilkenny], 21 June 1815

My dear Sir,

I received this moment your favour with the prospectus of the *Dublin Chronicle*.[1] I hasten to assure you that any publication coming with your recommendation must cheerfully command my humble support. Several years' unrelenting persecution have pressed so hard on my little property that it often vexes me not to be able to give that pecuniary aid I could wish on many public occasions to forward our cause but what I give comes not with reluctance. . . . I hail the appearance of a newspaper recommended as the *Dublin Chronicle* is and strongly felt the necessity for it. We must soon fall in to complete insignificance and contempt if our consequence and characters depend solely on the *fiat* of any dictatorial editor of any one newspaper. There could not be a warmer supporter (as far as my humble means and influence extended) of a portion of the Dublin press than I have been, but to imperious and unwarrantable dictatorship coming from any source I will never submit. The Catholic Board as a body has been vilely abused by pretended friends; this kind reprehension is bestowed in a parental way on the Association. The Vetoists got it in their turn with a vengeance but lo, it is now discovered that the pusillanimous Seceders are the bravest and most virtuous of all. If this be consistency I never knew what it meant before.[2] The French people have been called on to give up their chief. The Irish Catholics have been also called on to abandon their most intrepid champions but neither, I think, will be found pliable. If we could only keep within the strict letter of the law and not to give advantages to our enemies, things would be better but God knows it is hard to be prudent under such degradation, such insulting and base ingratitude and injustice.

SOURCE : O'Connell Papers, NLI 13647

1   The *Dublin Chronicle* was owned and edited by Eneas MacDonnell. According to Peel, it was established by O'Connell ' when he and his colleagues had brought the editors of all other papers into Newgate. . . . ' It was the only Dublin newspaper which received no government subsidy. In May 1816 MacDonnell was prosecuted by the government for libel. He was imprisoned and fined £100. The *Chronicle* went out of circulation in 1817 (Inglis, *Freedom of the Press*, pp. 142, 146, 239). In its first edition it supported O'Connell and the advocates of unqualified Emancipation (*Dublin Chronicle*, 26 June 1815).
2   The failure of the Catholic cause in parliament at this time was blamed by a section of the press on what it considered the intemperate actions of the Catholic leaders (*FJ*, 13 June 1815; *DEP*, 3, 6 June 1815).

560

From Bryan Fitzhenry[1] to 4 Capel St., Dublin

Gobbinstown [New Ross, Co. Wexford],
30 June 1815

Dear Sir,

Your esteemed circular of the date 30th May only came to hand this day; the delay must have been in Dublin. Any recommendation coming from you I shall be always happy in paying attention to but as to the subscription of 1811, I can say nothing more of than that I sent up *five guineas* to Mr. Hay, as was in or about that time required, and I have regularly paid my part of expenses attendant on our county meetings, and at our last meeting in Wexford we appointed Mr. Thomas Cloney, our treasurer, and to receive all subscriptions, which according as they will be paid him, he will faithfully and honourably account for. I shall exert myself in getting subscriptions, and if I succeed will remit them to Nicholas Mahon, Esq. as you desire. Such sanguine friends of us as have proved true to the cause are almost crestfallen by the division of aristocrats and seceders in this county but we have done our duty and will continue it in opposition to such *time serving vain animals*.

SOURCE : Dublin Diocesan Archives
1 Bryan Fitzhenry, died 12 June 1833.

561

To his wife, Merrion Square

Ennis, 10 July 1815

My darling Love,

I have felt uneasy since I parted you least you should have taken cold the day we were at Clongowes. I perceived the grass wet some minutes sooner than you turned back and I have been blaming myself every hour since I left you for not getting you to go back at once. Indeed if you take cold I shall blame myself bitterly. Tell me, darling, precisely how you are. . . .

Darling, were you not delighted to see your boys? What a fellow my Maurice is! Write, heart, to Morgan about his idleness. I will do so too. . . .

The business [in Ennis] at the civil side but small, a good deal at the criminal side. . . . The business will be quite over here on Thursday. We will then have a Catholic meeting[1] and I will afterwards go to Limerick. . . .

Write to me much about my little girls and watch their new governess. If she does not take a decisive tone of command with them at once, if she does not preserve their respect without relaxation, it will be in vain to attempt to regain it. Darling, it will require your interference to impress this on her mind.

SOURCE : Fitz-Simon Papers
1 The Catholic meeting at Ennis on 13 July 1815 in which O'Connell participated. The meeting is noteworthy in view of a report that

Sir Edward O'Brien (father of William Smith O'Brien, the Young Irelander) had declared in favour of ' Unqualified Emancipation, without Veto or Securities ' (*DEP*, 25 July 1815).

562

To his wife, Merrion Square

Ennis, 12 July 1815

My darling Love,

I am horribly out of spirits. There is all the bad news confirmed even beyond all our fears and liberty for ever crushed in France.[1] And here we have had the bloodiest assizes ever known. No less than five persons capitally convicted, four of them were clients of mine, one *certainly* innocent but he will be hanged. God, God, how cruel, how wretchedly cruel! Darling, do you know *how* I comfort myself?—literally thus, I read your letter over and over again and cheer myself with thinking of you and my own darlings. . . .

And in addition, heart, there is the death of Whitbread!!![2] Just at the moment a great and good man could be least spared. Well, well, Fate seems strangely perverse. The scoundrels of society have now every triumph. The defeats and disasters are reserved for the friends of liberty. Darling, I am indeed melancholy. But it is a folly to grieve and *now* I will try to rouse my spirits. . . .

SOURCE : Fitz-Simon Papers
1   The fall of Napoleon.
2   Samuel Whitbread.

563

To his wife, Merrion Square

Limerick, 16 July 1815

My darling Love,

Your letter of Friday delighted me. How grateful ought I not to be to you for your tenderness. I never read such a letter. It was an exquisite delight to my heart and it would have been a complete cordial to my spirits had I need of one. But, sweetest, you know the elasticity of my mind. I shook off my **gloom** on my way from Ennis. On Friday I was successful in my records and yesterday I saved a number of poor fellows in spite of the scoundrel Chief Baron.[1] . . .

Tell her [Ellen] from me how tenderly I love her, but say that I often felt hurt to the heart at hearing her say silly things and things which she herself knew as well as anybody living to be silly. She seemed to imagine that it was pretty but she, poor child, was greatly mistaken. It was very disgusting. . . . Will you give my respects to Miss Gaghran[2] and tell her I am *half in love* with her on your description. . . .

SOURCE : Fitz-Simon Papers

1   Standish O'Grady.

2   The new governess, Mary Jane Gaghran (c. 1787-1854), sister of John Gaghran, physician, 63 Great Britain Street, Dublin. Married William Ford, town clerk of Dublin city.

564

From his wife to Limerick

Dublin, 17 July 1815

My darling Heart,

. . . *That* part of your letter relative to Ellen I read in the presence of Miss Gaghran. The former promised to exert herself to get rid of *all* her bad habits and Miss G. begged I would say to you that she expected you would see an improvement in Ellen as she had made up her mind to act with a determined manner by her. . . .

You say nothing, heart, of *how* or where I am to get money. I sent the bill for acceptance to Fitzgerald[1] and he has acknowledged the receipt. I also accepted a bill for £1,030 which he drew on you. . . .

SOURCE : O'Connell Papers, NLI 13651

1   Thomas Fitzgerald (died 1834), Fane Valley, near Dundalk, Co. Louth, and 42 Dame Street, Dublin. Born in Ireland; early in life he settled in Demerara, West Indies, where he acquired considerable property; returned to Ireland and purchased property in Co. Louth. M.P. for Co. Louth, 1832-34.

565

To his wife, Merrion Square

Limérick, 18 July 1815

My darling Love,

. . . There is not I am told a single record in Kerry.
Scarcely any of the Bar will go there. I wish I could go up to
you instead of proceeding on to Tralee but it is vain to wish it.
The criminal business here is very heavy and the civil business is also considerable. On the whole it is a good assizes. I
am in the fullest business and am now, sweetest, in the best
possible spirits. I have completely rallied and I again *hope* for
the best. No country was ever put down that was true to itself
and France will rise again in spite of them all.[1] Indeed it
will. . . .

SOURCE : Fitz-Simon Papers

1   See letter 562.

566

To his wife, Merrion Square

Limerick, 20 July 1815

My darling Heart,

You will easily believe that I am in good spirits this day.
I heard from you and both of my boys yesterday. I also was
counsel for more than thirty persons all of whom were
acquitted. There were some of them in very considerable
danger, indeed in imminent peril, but I got them all off. This
is some comfort after the poor wretches the scoundrel Chief
Baron[1] hung *on me* in Ennis.

I thought, heart, I told you to call on John Hickson[2] for
any money you may want. I this day enclose him a bill. He will
supply you. . . .

I thought to have written to the general[3] but have mislaid
his address. Should he arrive in Dublin before I return, *take
no excuse* from him and his stepdaughter for not living with
you. I should be intensely mortified if they were an hour out
of the house. I need not, I am sure, recommend them to your
attention.

The business will not be over here till tomorrow as the

Chief Baron left us an entire day in the middle of the assizes. He is the greatest and vilest rascal that lives. . . .

SOURCE : Fitz-Simon Papers
1   Standish O'Grady.
2   John C. Hickson, 26 College Green, Dublin, wealthy woollen merchant in partnership with his brother Robert.
3   His uncle, Count O'Connell.

567

To his wife, Merrion Square, 22 July 1815, from Limerick

Leaving for Tralee. No civil business there so that only one judge goes.

SOURCE : Fitz-Simon Papers

568

To his wife, Merrion Square

[postmarked Cork] Saturday, 5 August 1815

My darling Heart,

. . . Darling, I am now in the most interesting record that I was ever concerned in. It is a question of legitimacy. It will not be over this day, I may say this night. Then there will remain but one record to be tried, but that is Lord Cork's[1] great case[2] and will take at least a day and a half. I never, darling, was better in my life but I cannot disguise the painful sensation I experience when I think of your having any attack on your lungs. . . .

I must now return to court. I go down with a large party in the steamboat tomorrow to Cove but will be up early enough to write to you.

SOURCE : Fitz-Simon Papers
1   Edmund (Boyle), eighth earl of Cork (1767-1856).
2   Not identified.

569

From his wife to Parade, Cork

11 August 1815

My dearest Love,

. . . What an escape you had, love, from being *exhibited* through Cork.[1] Are you not very proud of having your health drunk at Glasgow? I know I am. Some person sent you the *Glasgow Chronicle*. I suppose *they* feared you would not read the honour you were paid in any of the English papers. I hope your speech was not an *impertinent* one. What induced Doctor Baldwin to consent to being chairman? I thought he was quite of a different opinion but probably he has seen his *error*, and now joins the right *party*. . . .

SOURCE : O'Connell Papers, NLI 13651
1 A Catholic meeting was held in Cork on 9 August 1815, under the chairmanship of Dr. Herbert Baldwin, O'Connell's cousin. O'Connell was acclaimed at the meeting as 'The Man of the People' (*CMC*, 11 Aug. 1815). He was obliged at the end of the meeting to escape by means of a ladder into an adjoining yard from a crowd who wished to chair him through the streets (*CMC*, 16 Aug. 1815).

570

From John Hancock

Lisburn [Co. Antrim], 13 August 1815

[No salutation]

Agreeably to thy request I made out a sketch of the state of parliamentary representation in the counties of Antrim, Down and Armagh, supported by some facts which [one or two words illegible] within my knowledge and sent it to the editor of the [?*Dublin*] *Chronicle* in which it has since appeared. I am insufficiently acquainted with the county of Derry to venture [about one word illegible] similar detail. If thou art not supplied with it by some other quarter, I think I could furnish [?it].

I have had a letter from Major Cartwright,[1] dated the 26th ult., where I find he has been busily engaged in promoting petitions for parliamentary reform. He intimates that my letter to him in which I sent some copious extracts from thy letter to me has been of much use to him in opening the Scottish mind to the real state of Ireland. On the subject of his presumed want of liberality in the article of religion he writes, ' You was [sic] perfectly right in answering for me to Mr. O'Connell, and I thank you for it. To interfere with another man touching his religion is in my judgment a direct offence to the deity. I speak of a coercive interference.' I presume thou has seen the list of toasts at the Glasgow meeting. I was pleased to see thy name coupled with a favourite sentiment of mine that Catholic Emancipation is only likely to be obtained substantially, unreservedly and honourably through parliamentary reform.

I send on the other side some additional extracts from the Major's letter[2] to give thee a view of the prospects of reform in Scotland. This communication is [?confidential] and though I have no objection to the information being [about one word illegible] to the Irish public, yet if it is done, I think the circumstance of its being communicated directly by the [about one word illegible] ought to be suppressed. I have written to [one or two words illegible] him to extend his visit to Ireland to see our [about two words illegible] with his own eyes but I could not hold out [about two words illegible] of active co-operation. . . .

The Duke of Sussex has not treated the Anti-Orange petitioners handsomely. He declined to answer my letter or to give a positive answer to Sir H. Parnell.[3] In consequence, he neither presented the petition to the House of Lords [three or four words illegible] us an opportunity of applying to the Earl of Donoughmore who I expect would have willingly presented them.

SOURCE : O'Connell Papers, NLI 13647

1   John Cartwright (1740-1824), English radical. From 1775 he was the advocate of universal suffrage, annual parliaments and the ballot. Known as the ' Father of Reform '. See *DNB*.

2   The extracts stress Cartwright's view that support for reform is strong in Scotland.

3   On 4 July 1815 Sir Henry Parnell moved in the Commons an address to the Prince Regent ' requesting his Royal Highness would appoint a commission to inquire into the proceedings of the Orange Societies in the North of Ireland '. His motion was defeated by 90 to 20.

571

To Owen O'Conor, Castle [or Park] Street

Merrion Square, 29 August [1815], Tuesday

My dear Friend,

Esmonde *ambitions* the chair.[1] If giving it to him for his *title* be anywhere construed into a slight upon you, we would all die ten thousand deaths sooner than permit it. . . .

Could I then ask for the smallest hint to govern my conduct? I need not, I am sure, say how confidentially I will receive it.

If I am *quite* wrong in supposing *such* a feeling, will you allow me to beg of you in the name of the Association to move the four first resolutions[2] and the two last. That relative to the deputation[3] I will move myself.

SOURCE : Clonalis Papers

1 A Catholic' meeting was held in Clarendon Street chapel on 29 August 1815 under the chairmanship of Sir Thomas Esmonde (*DEP,* 31 Aug. 1815).

2 At the Catholic meeting on 29 August 1815 O'Conor proposed four resolutions expressive of gratitude to the Catholic hierarchy and clergy and in denunciation of the veto (*DEP,* 31 Aug. 1815).

3 A deputation composed of Sir Thomas Esmonde and Owen O'Conor, with the Rev. Richard Hayes, O.F.M., as their secretary, was appointed by the Catholic Association on 29 August 1815 to present to the pope a remonstrance from the Catholic laity of Ireland, praying him not to countenance state interference in the appointment of bishops in Ireland (*DEP,* 31 Aug. 1815). According to his own report, Hayes ultimately set out for Rome unaccompanied. He arrived there on 25 October 1815 and during the following twelve months had five audiences with the pope. He failed, however, to secure a papal pronouncement against the veto, and ill and in debt was forcibly deported from the Papal States on 16 July 1817. (See 'Report of the Rev. Richard Hayes', 13 December 1817, in John O'Connell, *Life and Speeches of Daniel O'Connell,* 2 vols. [Dublin 1846], II, 519-24. Also O'Keeffe, *O'Connell,* II, 236-7, and Fagan, *O'Connell,* I, 236-7.)

572

From Owen O'Conor

[September 1815]

My dear O'Connell,

Before I write to you on business, permit me in the most fervent manner in concert with millions of my countrymen to send up my prayers to Heaven that you may triumph over the malignity of your enemies and the intolerance of a faction.

Finding from the most mature deliberation I could give the subject of my mission to Rome,[1] that it would be impossible for me to render any service to my countrymen, that I should put myself to much expense, risk and inconvenience, I have on my arrival in town sent my resignation to Mr. Hay. I do not know any act of my life which gave me more pain. I have, as well as I could do it, explained my reasons to Mr. Sugrue[2] who called on me here this day. Those reasons, though perfectly consistent with my honour and integrity, I could not venture to state in a letter exposed to public [view], lest they should find their way into the public prints which could do no service whatever.

As I should feel no reluctance, however, to disclose to you every circumstance which operated on my mind and induced me to decline their honourable trust, therefore, in addition to the reasons I have already assigned to you, I shall now transmit extracts from three different letters I received from a particular friend of mine with whom I corresponded on the subject. You will thence be enabled to form some estimate of the length of time I took to form my determination and consequently my unwillingness to decline the honour proposed to me. These extracts which I read for Mr. Sugrue are from Doctor McDermott,[3] my near relative and still nearer friend. Of him I suppose it is unnecessary to speak. His abilities, his soundness of understanding are too generally known to require any comment. The following are his sentiments. His first letter: ' Either the matter in dispute (the Veto) is a *religious* or it is a *political* question. If you Catholics oppose it on the *latter ground* as giving the Crown too much influence, what right will the Pope have to interfere in the politics of another country, or receive a deputation from subjects against the long established government? If you oppose it as a mere *religious question* as endangering the Catholic religion, what right have laymen to interfere in a question out of their competence?

Should they not leave that matter to their priests and their prelates? When the Council of Trent met, had the Catholic laity of Europe sent them a deputation stating these opinions as to matters of faith and discipline, how do you think would they be received? Why, they would be laughed at. The " *ne sutor ultra crepidam* "⁴ would be flung in their faces. There is nothing Popes and prelates are in general more jealous of than lay interference; and justly. It is an encroachment on their exclusive privilege—that of deciding in all ecclesiastical matters. Your Deputation will be thought little of in Rome, in Ireland it will be considered as the 2nd edition of *the Spanish Cortes business*.⁵ Your name and your object will reach Rome before you, where you will be represented as the organs of a Party disaffected to that very Government which has contributed more than any other to restore the Pope to the throne of St. Peter.'

Speaking of the honour of being admitted to the Pope's presence he says: ' But will you be admitted to that honour? I doubt it. I should not be surprised if Lord Castlereagh found means to shut the door of the Vatican against you or at least render your mission inefficient.' [Remainder of letter missing.]

SOURCE : Fitz-Simon Papers
1   See letter 571, note 3.
2   James Sugrue.
3   Hugh MacDermot, MD., Coolavin, Co. Sligo, The MacDermot; delegate for Co. Sligo to the 1792 Catholic Convention; married 1793 Elizabeth Frances O'Conor, sister of Owen O'Conor.
4   A shortened version of the Latin for ' Let the cobbler stick to his last.'
5   Unidentified.

573

From George Lidwill

Friday [1 September 1815]

My dear O'Connell,

Sir Charles Saxton¹ called on me twice while I was absent from this. The last time he left a note to say, when he would hear I was at home, he would again call on me. I expect him every moment; and therefore write this to you to have horses ready as I will appoint the first field adjoining Celbridge, in the county Kildare, and an immediate hour for meeting, which I must naturally think he is now coming to require.²

SOURCE : John O'Rourke, *The Centenary Life of O'Connell*, 92

1 Sir Charles Saxton, second baronet (1773-1838), under-secretary for
   Ireland, 1808-12; M.P. for Cashel, 1812-18.

2 At a Catholic meeting in Dublin on 29 August 1815, O'Connell
   spoke offensively of Robert Peel, who had recently criticized him
   (*DEP*, 31 Aug. 1815). In September 1815 several unsuccessful attempts
   were made to arrange a duel between them. (For a detailed account
   of this episode see Fagan, *O'Connell*, I, 163-210.)

574

To George Lidwill

Harcourt St. [Dublin],
Friday [1 September 1815]

My dear Friend,

Do just as you please. I only think the county of Kildare
ought to be the place. I care not where there. Everything will
be ready expeditiously. My family would be less alarmed if we
postpone it till morning; but do just as you please. I will
remain here.

SOURCE : FitzPatrick, *Corr.*, I, 42

575

From George Lidwill to Merrion Square

Kearn's Hotel, Kildare St. [Dublin],
Saturday, 2 September 1815

My dear O'Connell,

The statement relative to your affair with Mr. Peel[1] made
by Sir Charles Saxton in the *Correspondent* of this night in
which he says so little and suppresses so much of what passed
between himself and me on that subject, renders it necessary
that I should communicate to you in regular order the whole
of what occurred between us on both the days he waited on
me here. . . . [Lidwill gives a very long and detailed account
of the matter which scarcely merits publication because of its
length.]

SOURCE : Huish, *O'Connell*, p. 172

1 Robert Peel (1788-1850), later (1830) second baronet. Chief secretary
   for Ireland, 1812-18; home secretary, 1822-27, 1828-30; prime minister,
   1834-35, 1841-46. See *DNB*.

576

From Robert Peel

Dublin Castle, six o'clock, 4 September 1815
[No salutation]
Having seen in a newspaper of this evening a letter bearing
your signature, connected with a communication which I have
recently made to you, imputing to me ' a paltry trick ', and
concluding with the expression of your regret that I had ' ultimately preferred a paper war ', I have to request that you will
appoint a friend who may make with Colonel Brown,[1] the
bearer of this letter, such arrangements as the case requires.

SOURCE : FitzPatrick, *Corr.*, I, 41
1 Samuel Browne, 20 North St. Stephen's Green, Dublin; colonel of
   York Light Infantry and deputy quarter-master general, c. 1814.

577

To Richard Newton Bennett near Castle Carbury [Co. Kildare]

9 o'clock, Monday night [4 September 1815]
[No salutation]
Peel has sent me *a challenge.* Lidwill is himself engaged
with Sir Charles Saxton. I entreat of you to come to me
instanter. The Knight of Kerry or McNamara[1] or anybody
would answer my purpose if you were by.

SOURCE : NLI MSS 837
1 Major William N. McNamara.

578

To the Knight of Kerry

Merrion Square, Monday evening
[4 September 1815]
(Private)
My dear Sir,
I want a friend most sadly and venture to think of you.
Mr. Lidwill cannot assist me, for he is himself involved with
Sir Charles Saxton. My affair is, as you may imagine, with

Mr. Peel. He has just sent me a well-written challenge from the Castle, and if you would allow me to trespass upon you, I would wait on you as early as you pleased in the morning and explain to you how the matter stands. A Colonel Brown is the person who has called on me from him. His address is Stephen's Green North.

Should you have any difficulty or delicacy in granting me this favour—and there are a thousand reasons which may most properly prevent you—let me have a line by the bearer to say so. If the contrary, let me know at what hour in the morning I could see you. The sooner this affair is over the better.

SOURCE : FitzPatrick, *Corr.*, I, 42

579

To the Knight of Kerry

Tuesday [5 September 1815]

[No salutation]

I wish to see you to express my sincere gratitude for your kindness, and to take your friend's advice on my present most unfortunate predicament. The triumph of those who will *now* traduce me ought to be but shortlived. However, I must say that I am very awkwardly circumstanced, and require more than ever your friendly aid. I wish it may be possible for me to express to you how truly grateful I am for your kindness.

SOURCE : FitzPatrick, *Corr.*, I, 43

580

To the Knight of Kerry

Merrion Square, 5 September 1815

My dear Sir,

I *cannot* go out in the morning—at least before twelve o'clock, and yet I wish very much to see you. The very kind and active interest which you took in my affair this day will be ever remembered by me, and induces me to ask you to favour me, if possible, with a call in the morning, or to be at home for me at three in the afternoon. I want not a little to speak to you.

SOURCE : FitzPatrick, *Corr.*, I, 43

581

From Colonel Brown

Dublin, 5 September [1815], 7 o'clock

Copy

Col. Brown presents his compliments to Mr. O'Connell. From the communication made to him by Mr. Baldwin[1] at eight o'clock last evening, he has been in waiting since four o'clock this morning in expectation of the visit he was to receive from Mr. Lidwill.

At this hour Col. Brown feels himself under the painful necessity of reminding Mr. O'Connell of the letter which he delivered yesterday from Mr. Peel and of the impropriety of any delay in a case of so much delicacy.

SOURCE : Liverpool Papers, BM Add. MSS 38,262, f. 31

1 Probably O'Connell's first cousin, either Walter, Connell or Herbert Baldwin.

582

To Colonel Brown

Merrion Square, 8 o'clock, 5 September [1815]

[No salutation]

Mr. O'Connell presents his compliments to Colonel Brown, and with the utmost concern begs to inform him that the delay to which his letter alludes has been caused by a circumstance of the most painful nature—his having been put under arrest by the Sheriff—which is still aggravated, in his feelings, from having been done at the instance of Mrs. O'Connell, who, agitated by the publications in the newspapers, sent privately, after he had gone to bed, to the Sheriff for that purpose. Mr. O'Connell will, the first possible moment, send a friend to Colonel Brown, to make such arrangements as the present state of things renders necessary.

SOURCE : O'Connell Papers, NLI 13645

583

To Owen O'Conor, Belanagare

Merrion Square, 6 September 1815

My dear friend,

The Committee of the Association met this day. I read your letter to them but I could not make any excuse for you, because I myself feel that you *must* go.[1] It really is inevitable. You cannot refuse, believe me. Everything will be arranged very *expeditiously,* so be ready.

I leave town early in the morning.[2] Many many thanks for your kind wishes. Believe me, I am gratified beyond what I can express by your kindness.

SOURCE : Clonalis Papers

1 O'Conor was apparently reluctant to accompany the delegation to Rome (see letters 571, note 3, and 572).
2 O'Connell was setting out for Ostend where he intended to fight a duel with Peel.

584

To Denys Scully, Merrion Square

Waterford, Wednesday, 13 September 1815

My dear Scully,

I was surprised and not a little disappointed at not meeting Bennett[1] here. I much fear my letter to MacDonnell . . . was retarded or lost. . . . It contained a letter for Sugrue and also one for Bennett. Bennett's letter was enclosed in Sugrue's. I specified to him my plan of leaving my wife in Killarney, remaining there on Sunday to procure an express to follow me on professional business and of coming off for Cork as if *on that business* on Monday and being here on Tuesday.

My plan has completely succeeded. I have left my wife tranquil and unsuspicious and here I am since last evening. I beg of you the moment you receive this letter to go to MacDonnell and Sugrue and inquire after my letter. Let them, particularly Sugrue, find out Bennett. If he be still at New-bury, let a *horse express,* not a carriage, be sent for him. . . . Let him [Sugrue] inform Bennett that my brother James will leave his address at the bar of the Spring Garden Coffee-House. My brother's address is better to be left there than mine as it may excite less attention. Urge Bennett to be with us as expeditiously as possible. We sail in this evening's packet and, as the wind is fair, hope to reach Milford before the coaches start in the morning. If we do not, we will proceed by post carriages. We mean, I believe, to go by Gloucester.[2]

We have debated the point as to travelling under feigned names but have determined not, for many reasons but especially because there does not appear to be the least danger of being *retarded*. . . .

SOURCE : Scully Papers
1 Richard Newton Bennett.
2 En route to Ostend for the duel with Peel.

585

To Denys Scully

Cheltenham [Glocs., England],
Saturday, 16 September 1815

My dear Scully,

. . . On our arrival at Milford *our names* were carefully inquired after and carefully taken down. What was this done for? No matter.

We got to Milford on Thursday. Bennett reached us before we left Waterford. We could not travel beyond two stages on Thursday, and Friday and this day have been consumed in the most vexatious posting through South Wales. . . . Bennett and I will reach London tomorrow.

I presume Monday will be consumed in procuring passports. On Tuesday we reach Dover; Wednesday, Calais, and on Thursday our affair[1] will be over. It is perhaps absurd but I cannot bring myself even to doubt success. However the event is of no importance to the country, as the real value to poor Ireland is the very contest itself. There never was such a battle. Waterloo was nothing to it.

Be assured, so Bennett bids me say, that the enemy has not the least advantage in the time we have consumed.

SOURCE : Scully Papers
1 The duel with Peel.

586

This letter is now numbered 541a

587

To James Connor, Attorney, Tralee

Holilands, Strand, London, 19 September 1815

My dear James,

You will find with this a letter for Mary, and the newspapers will tell you of the ludicrous termination of our once
serious affair. Prepare Mary for my letter before you hand it
to her. Lidwill was arrested the moment of his arrival here,
and I escaped until I was putting my foot into the chaise for
Dover this morning. After all, I do not think our enemies have
the smallest triumph, nor is there any reason for regret, as we
did all in our power to give the gentlemen a meeting, and that
it has been prevented is altogether occasioned by the Government of which they are the representatives in Ireland. They,
too, were the challengers, so that any injury they have to complain of remains unredressed.

I will stay in London this night to refresh myself, and then
be back to my family and trade as speedily as possible. A
thousand and a thousand loves to all with you.

SOURCE : FitzPatrick, *Corr.,* I, 44

588

To Denys Scully, Merrion Square

20 September 1815

My dear Scully,

. . . *They* have got their wicked will of us. Our hands
are tied behind our backs and they have full liberty to abuse
us. What a glorious opportunity have they not deprived me
of—living or dying—but regret is vain and would console our
enemies.[1]

The information on which Lord Ellenborough[2] issued his
warrant was sworn—for I called for the reading of it—by a
Mr. James Becket[3] who is either the Under-Secretary of State
or his brother. And Sir Nathaniel Conant[4] very distinctly
intimated to me that any fatal consequences of a duel would

now be followed up by a rigorous prosecution in England and a certain execution in case of a conviction. There were no less than one hundred constables on the coast waiting *our* arrival. A number of them were sent on at least to Calais where they actually broke into a gentleman's room in search of me. At least so Vesey,[5] brother to Lord De Vesci, told Ridgeway[6] this day. Lieut. Col. Arthur[7] from the Co. Clare was shown eight Bow Street officers at Ramsgate so, you see, it was impossible to escape. A police spy actually travelled on the carriage that brought up Lidwill and Pritty.[8]

And after all this vigilance, our adversaries advertised themselves at every stage and were allowed to go on unimpeded. This is called ' *activity* '.

My heart is still very sore. The scoundrels can now so easily and so safely calumniate us.

SOURCE : Scully Papers

1 O'Connell was taken into custody in England in order to prevent his threatened duel with Peel. See letter 708.
2 Edward (Law), first Baron Ellenborough (1750-1818), lord chief justice, 1802-18. See *DNB*.
3 James Becket, brother of John Becket, under-secretary of state, home dept.
4 Sir Nathaniel Conant, Kt. (1745-1822), chief magistrate, Bow Street, London, 1810-20.
5 Hon. Charles Vesey (1784-1826), son of first Viscount de Vesci.
6 William Ridgeway, B.L., 40 Harcourt Street, Dublin, and Ballay, near Dundrum, Co. Dublin, a surrogate of the High Court of Admiralty, Ireland.
7 Probably George Arthur, lieutenant-colonel, 5th West India Regiment; appointed lieutenant-colonel, 1815; major, 7th West India Regiment, 5 November 1812.
8 Probably Hon. Francis Aldborough Prittie, (1779-1853), younger brother of second Baron Dunalley, Corville, near Roscrea, Co. Tipperary. M.P. for Carlow borough, 1801; Co. Tipperary, 1806-18, 1819-31.

589

From George Lidwill to Merrion Square

Monday, one o'clock [25 September 1815]

My Dear O'Connell,

Now that there cannot be a possibility of your fighting Peel, you may stay quietly at home as it will not signify if any

of *his* friends should get you bound over. Now that all is over
your best way would be to tell Mrs. O'Connell everything. It
was very lucky she never suspected anything as, besides her
uneasiness, she might have attempted to have you bound over
which, coming from any of *your* friends, would destroy for
ever and encourage the enemy to do that which he otherwise
would not, to send you a message.

SOURCE : O'Connell MSS, UCD

590

To his wife, Killarney

Merrion Square, 30 September 1815

My darling Heart,

. . . I left London on Monday and posted to Shrewsbury,
and travelled thence in the day-coach to Holyhead. We reached
the Head on Thursday at one o'clock, and sailed at three. The
night came to blow tremendously and the packet was crowded
to excess. Not a berth could be had for love or money. I lay
on the cabin floor as sick as a dog, with three gentlemen's legs
on my breast and stomach, and the sea water dripping in on
my knees and feet. I was never so completely punished, and
of all the wretched nights that we ever spent it really was the
most miserable. We, however, got in rather early yesterday.
I tumbled into bed as soon as I breakfasted, and am as well
this day as ever I was in the whole course of my life—so much
so that, but for Bess'[1] letter, I should have set off to-day for
Kerry. Bess says you will be here on Tuesday. Darling, I shall
remain till Monday, and unless I hear by that day's post of you,
I will be off for Tralee by the way of Limerick. Kiss my darling
Kate for me, and believe me beyond the power of words.

SOURCE : FitzPatrick, *Corr.,* I, 44-5
1 Bess O'Connell, John's wife.

591

From Jane Swiney[1] to Merrion Square

1 October 1815

My dear Sir,

Will you have the goodness to give Mr. McCarthy my

marriage settlement in order to have it registered? He is a witness to it and I may not have so good an opportunity for a long time. Excuse all this trouble. I have with great pleasure read just now of your return to Dublin. You have made all your friends here very uneasy but, thank God, all our fears are over. Your life is too precious to be put in any danger[2] and, I trust sincerely, it never will again. I am making very free but indeed I could not hold offering my sincere congratulations at your safe return. Mr. Swiney joins me.

SOURCE : O'Connell Papers, NLI 13647
1 Unidentified.
2 A reference to O'Connell's recently attempted duel with Peel.

592

To his wife, Merrion Square

Waterville, 15 October 1815

My darling Love,

. . . I have almost consumed my time in Iveragh. The General[1] comes up to Dublin with me and of course *Mademoiselle*.[2] He says he will remain with us but eight or ten days at the longest. He talks of making a will and leaving his money equally between John, James[3] and me. It amounts he says to £12,000 in the 3 per cents worth, therefore, not above seven thousand pounds. My share would be only about £2,300. Darling, it is well we do not want this legacy as thank God he is likely to live *many*, many years to enjoy his little property. Of course I need not tell you that this is *all a secret*.

Keep all the letters you receive for me till I return. Do not forget the letter about the County of Tipperary as I am anxious to know by whom it was written. It would be worth my while to cultivate any of the *great* London papers, and I assure you solemnly that I could do it with the greatest *safety*. . . .

SOURCE : Fitz-Simon Papers
1 His uncle, Count O'Connell.
2 The count's stepdaughter, Aimée de Bellevue.
3 His two brothers.

593

To his wife, Merrion Square

Carhen, 19 October 1815

My darling Love,

Here I am without being able to leave Iveragh till Monday. Be assured that the fault is not mine. The truth being that the General[1] keeps me to insure leaving the country along with me, and the old gentleman[2] would not allow him to depart until the close of this week. This annoys me for a thousand reasons, one of which is that I owe you a pulling by the *cock nose* for your *saucy* letter. Dearest love, the fact is that I ought rather to make my peace with you than to *threaten* you, but I believe you are not much afraid of the threatenings.

. . . We have made a new pattern in honour of my coming. It will take place tomorrow, Friday, and Saturday we spend at Derrynane and then, heart, I proceed by Tralee, the General and Aimee[3] by Killarney.

. . . The rents coming in very slowly. No person but me paid by anybody.

SOURCE : Fitz-Simon Papers
1 Count O'Connell.
2 Hunting-Cap.
3 Aimée de Bellevue, stepdaughter of Count O'Connell and later wife of Baron Benjamin D'Etchegoyen.

594

To his wife, Merrion Square

Tralee, 26 October 1815

My darling Love,

I have time only to tell you that I could not *escape* from Iveragh till yesterday. I got a great rating from the old man[1] but we parted as good friends as ever. I promised to be a good boy in future. . . .

SOURCE : Fitz-Simon Papers
1 Hunting-Cap.

595

From Rev. Peter Kenney, S.J., to Merrion Square

Clongowes Wood, 5 November 1815

Dear Sir,

I am happy to inform you that your sons are very well and continue to do well. Maurice is now more attentive than he was at the commencement of the present academic year. He continues to give proofs of talent and at the end of his course will certainly be a good classical scholar. Of Morgan, I cannot promise so fairly. He is rather giddy and has been inattentive to school duties. At present he is more diligent. They are both good children, well behaved when kept in training and consequently easily governed.

[On the other side of the sheet the following is written:]

Sir,

I beg leave to furnish you in due course with the Master O'Connells' account which is as follows:

Master Maurice:

To half year's pension payable in advance on 30th ulto.	£28.	8.	9
To postage, hairdresser, amusement etc.		6.	6
To clothes for vacation	4.	19.	2

Master Morgan:

To half year pension payable etc.	25.	0.	0
To postage etc. etc.		4.	5
To clothes for vacation	4.	19.	2
	£63.	18.	0

The amount will on receipt be duly acknowledged and placed to their credit.

SOURCE : O'Connell MSS, UCD

596

To his son Maurice, Clongowes Wood College

Merrion Square, 16 November 1815

My dear child,

. . . I will write to you more frequently in future, but I cannot go to see you until after term. . . . I am pleased to hear that you are now become more attentive. It would be a disgraceful thing after having been in the first class to make but a bad figure in the second. And yet I am told that after your return from vacation you were for some time neglectful. I am sure, my child, that if you were to recollect how much it would delight me to have you obtain first place in your class, you would make an effort to procure that station. . . . Tell him [Morgan] to write to me and do you write to me as often as you are allowed. Tell me candidly what your own expectations are of getting a good place in your class but remember I expect from you to get the first place.

The General and his stepdaughter[1] spent a week here. They are gone off to England on their way to France. I expect your Uncle James hourly. I will take him with me to see you and Morgan, and we will spend the greater part of a day with you. Your foster father and nurse are very well. Your mother gave the latter a suit of clothes and I treated the former to one in honour of you.

SOURCE : Fitz-Simon Papers

1 Count O'Connell and Aimée de Bellevue (see letter 593, note 3).

597

To Nicholas Purcell O'Gorman

[probably c. 1 December 1815]

(Private and confidential)

My dear Purcell,

I wish to God I could settle this business of Magee's.[1] I am anxious for it on your account and on account of *the cause*. I could get the thing closed for £700, payable annually. And as you being under any tie to pay it, arises from your being a public man. I think your friends ought to contribute. If your uncle[2] would pay the first £100, allow me to say that I would cheerfully pay the second, your brother[3] may perhaps pay the third, and then you should be prepared with the remainder. I repeat, however, that as a private gentleman, I do not think you bound to pay anything. But I reckon on it *that the cause* requires of you to make this payment.

Excuse me if I take a liberty with you in making *this offer,* but you will easily appreciate my motives, and those motives will probably serve to show you that I always am

Yours most sincerely,

Daniel O'Connell

SOURCE : FitzPatrick, *Corr.*, I, 23

1 A reference to the action taken by James Magee against Nicholas Purcell O'Gorman which came to trial in December 1815 and in which O'Connell acted as counsel for O'Gorman (see letter 546, note 2).
2 Nicholas Mahon.
3 Richard O'Gorman.

598

From his brother James to Merrion Square

Holylands Coffee House [London],
5 December 1815

My dearest brother,

I arrived here yesterday evening and in a few hours after delivered your letter to the General,[1] and am truly sorry to say that he positively refused complying with your request though I did everything in my power to show him he ran no risk but all in vain. He said that Government brought him in debt for a large sum at the War Office, and that a great proportion of his pay was to be stopped until the balance was discharged so that his principal means of support was to be derived from the *small* sum of money he had in the funds, and he added the present was a very unfavourable moment for selling out, as the three per cents, where his money is, have fallen to £60 per cent, but why do I trouble you by repeating what he said? From the moment I mentioned my business to London (just having given him your letter) I saw he was determined not to comply with our request. I offered to join you in a bond for the £4,000 which he could also hold over as an additional security but alas, alas, he was obdurate.

Now, my dearest Dan, I have to entreat you will bear up against this disappointment with the fortitude of a man and a Christian. When I reach Dublin I trust I may be able to suggest some plan for raising the sum you require. I will leave London in two or three days at farthest. . . .

SOURCE : Fitz-Simon Papers
1 Their uncle Count O'Connell.

599

To Messrs Pim's,[1] *Merchants, William St., Dublin*

Merrion Square, 23 December 1815

Gentlemen,

My friend Mr. Sugrue[2] has communicated to me your desire to be secured in the large sum for which Mr. James O'Leary has involved me with your house. That desire is extremely reasonable and just, and I am disposed and indeed anxious to comply with it. If you will send me your law agent, I will satisfy him and you in the payment of the entire sum now due of O'Leary by mortgage and bonds so as to leave *no possible* contingency either as to the certainty or punctuality of payments. It would be even pleasant to myself to put the business on this footing as speedily as you choose. I propose to secure the entire sum thus, by four instalments each payable with interest in six, twelve, eighteen and twenty-four months. My proposal includes giving such satisfaction as your legal advisers shall deem requisite as to the certainty and punctuality of the payments.

In the meantime I beg of you to take up the bill of this day. Waiting your reply at your leisure.

SOURCE : Library of Religious Society of Friends
1   Thomas, Jonathan and Joseph Pim.
2   James Sugrue.

600

*From his brother James to Merrion Square, redirected
to Limerick*

Killarney, 4 January 1816

My Dear Brother,

Both your letters I duly received here and am glad to find by the style of the last that your spirits have been cheered by the prospect you have of being relieved at least for the present from the very heavy demands on you by the creditors of that villain O'Leary.[1] The bargain you have made with Mr. John Hickson is indeed for *that gentleman* a most advantageous one and such as no person who was not circumstanced in the unfortunate way you are would think of entering into. I will not now take up your time by showing the *advantage* your *friend,* Mr. Hickson, took of you, as he was well aware you *should* submit to his very *unfair and usurious* terms. Let me however entreat of you to take care to have no doubt left as to your being at liberty to redeem this annuity within the three years. For God's sake, take care of this surety. Surely you ought now place no reliance on the *disinterestedness* of any person save a very *few* individuals of your own family. The *other* hopes you say you have beginning to open on you really astonish me. Alas, I fear your too sanguine disposition makes you calculate on some ideal *good* that may never occur but do not, I beseech you, enter into any other *bargain* without consulting either James Connor or me who are your real *friends.* I know you were obliged to submit to any *terms* Mr. Hickson pleased to suggest but this can and *must* be got over within twelve months by paying that *candid* gentleman his prin[cipal] and interest.

You have nothing to fear with respect to my Uncle Maurice. I think it is now almost impossible he can hear it. I will also attend to your instructions about *Crook*[2] and think the suggestion a good one. The family of O'Leary are selling off the stock for anything they can get. . . .

SOURCE : O'Connell MSS, UCD

1   James O'Leary, who was declared a bankrupt in the *Dublin Gazette* of 9 January 1816.
2   Unidentified.

601

From Sir Henry Parnell to Merrion Square, readdressed to Limerick

Emo Park [Queen's Co.], 7 January 1816

Private and Confidential

My dear Sir,

I send you back the draft of the address[1] by this night's post. I have made no alterations except where I thought it required to be made more clear and strong, and where the expressions might possibly give offence. The part relating to the securities would certainly be considered as absolutely declaring a new war with all the advocates of them, but by modifying some expressions and confining the matter to a mere argument against them, all the spirits and use of the proposed remarks and conclusions may be fully preserved. I have always wished things should be reasoned against, but not resolved against. The former course would obtain converts but the latter never will, though it will certainly give new life to your enemies.

I think the address a very excellent one, and just what an address ought to be in respect to its contents and the manner of expressing the sufferings and claims of the party addressing. It is particularly well adapted to English feelings and will, I trust, produce a very good effect in settling the doubts of a vast number of very well meaning people.

As the responsibility of giving advice in so very important a measure is a very heavy one, I hope I shall be excused in suggesting the propriety of showing the amended copy to Judge Fletcher[2] before it is acted upon.

I beg you will consider my alterations rather as hints than as fixed opinions upon the necessity of making them.

SOURCE : Fitz-Simon Papers

1 Perhaps a draft of the address to the Prince Regent which the Catholic Association later resolved (16 March 1816) to entrust to Sir Henry Parnell (*DEP*, 19 Mar. 1816).

2 William Fletcher (1750-1823), son of George Fletcher, M.D., of Dublin; justice of the common pleas, 1806-23.

602

To his wife, Merrion Square

Limerick, 10 January 1816

Darling heart,

You did just right about Sir Henry Parnell's letter.[1] You always do right, sweetest, indeed you do, and your fond husband's heart is truly grateful to you who are the greatest blessing that ever man had. . . . I never before travelled at this time of the year without getting some little cold but I have not a particle of it at present. . . .

Do not be uneasy about the Hicksons or their reports. The best way of putting an end *to talk* on that subject is not to affect any secrecy. James's[2] letter to me was very consolatory —he is a darling fellow. . . .

SOURCE : Fitz-Simon Papers
1 Probably a reference to the fact that Mary had redirected Parnell's letter of 7 January 1816 to him at Limerick where he spent some time before proceeding to Tralee.
2 His brother.

603

To his wife, Merrion Square

Tralee, 13 January 1816

My dearest darling,

. . . I left Limerick early on Thursday in a perfect storm and spent the entire day in a miserable journey to Tarbert where I slept and came on here the next day by the Cashin ferry as the *pass* at Listowel is now unpracticable. . . .

I have found the prospect of things rather better here than I had any kind of idea of. It seems to be that O'Leary's stock-in-trade will sell for much more than I could have conceived. We will, with the blessing of God, get over this *tolerably*, nay much better, sweetest, and be ourselves a great deal the better for it. Tell Mr. L'Estrange,[1] darling, that I long to be back with him. I promise you, love, I feel myself beyond any comparison happier in *this* change[2] which, with the grace of God, I hope will prove complete. Pray for me, darling, fervently and often. . . .

SOURCE : Fitz-Simon Papers
1 Rev. William L'Estrange, O.D.C. (Francis Joseph in religion), St. Teresa's, Clarendon Street, Dublin. Born in Dublin; educated and ordained on the continent; provincial of the Irish Carmelites; a spiritual director to O'Connell; died 6 September 1833.
2 This reference is somewhat obscure. See letter 624.

604

From his son Maurice to Merrion Square

[Clongowes Wood College] 13 January 1816

Dear Father,

I hope you will excuse me for not writing to you for this fortnight back, or rather for this three weeks. I have studied harder since you saw me last than I ever did before and hope to continue to do so. I shall endeavour to fulfill my promise to you and, please God, shall perform it. Tell Mamma that I am very angry with her for not answering my last letter and that I hope she will do so soon. Morgan, I hear, is mending rapidly but, however, I think a lecture from Mr. L'Estrange would do him a great deal of good. . . . When does Uncle Connor[1] intend to send Edward and Dan here? He had better do it soon.

SOURCE : O'Connell MSS, UCD
1 James Connor.

605

To his wife, Merrion Square

[Tralee, postmarked Cork] 16 January 1816
[No salutation]
I am detained here for this day also but shall certainly go off for Cork tomorrow and leave it the next day, Thursday. . . . Things are assuming a much more *pleasant* appearance here than I had any idea of. I do not think I shall lose near as much as I supposed. Certainly I shall work [? for] funds enough to keep myself above water. . . .

SOURCE : Fitz-Simon Papers

606

From his brother James to Merrion Square

Tralee, 22 January 1816
My Dearest Dan,
I have this moment *signed the Deed* and will forward it by the Macroom coach to our friend, Charles Sugrue.
. . . You will have this *precious deed* by Thursday morning and I sincerely hope it will be the means of saving you from *destruction*, whatever my fate may be, but now *that the die is cast* I can with truth say that I am, by being made a party to this business, exquisitely miserable as I am no longer master of my own time or of the very limited property I inherited in right of my father. We both are at the mercy of the men in the world I detest most, and should this affair come to the knowledge of my Uncle Maurice I am convinced he never will give me a guinea. However, be assured, I will never

mention this subject to you again as I was well aware when I affixed my name to this accursed deed that in all human probability my prospects in life were for ever blasted. I again repeat, whatever my sufferings may be, I will never be guilty of the folly of blaming any person as, alas, alas, I am too well aware of the consequences, though by the contents of your letters you seem to think that I have the egregious folly to suppose I am only doing a mere act of courtesy. I now conclude this, to me, most disagreeable subject by saying you have involved me in the ruin you have been so long preparing for your amiable wife and interesting family.

SOURCE : O'Connell MSS, UCD

607

To Richard Newton Bennett

Sunday, 4 February 1816

My dear Friend,

Excuse me for teasing you at this hurried time of term but I would wish to *do* this thing and think no more of it. I think Brewster[1] would be the less complicated. I would take £2,000 giving bond for £2,200 payable within two months after my uncle's[2] death or in four years, whichever shall first happen, insuring my life and with liberty to issue [? executions] unless the interest be regularly paid one half year before the other. This would place me beyond any further trouble whatsoever. Do, my worthy friend, see whether we could not do it at once and leave my mind at rest.

SOURCE : Connolly Autograph Collection
1 Unidentified.
2 Hunting-Cap.

608

To Unknown

O'Leary[1] a Bankrupt

Merrion Square, 8 February 1816

Sir,

If you refer the persons who apply to you for information to me at any reasonable hour they shall—if creditors or other-

wise interested in the estate—have every information they may
desire, or if you bring me the letter or other authority of any
creditor or other person interested in his estate, you shall have
that information yourself. The next gazette[2] will contain a
summons for a meeting of the creditors. You will in the meantime act as you please.

I am

Your obedient servant,

Daniel O'Connell

SOURCE : Fitz-Simon Papers
1 James O'Leary.
2 The *Dublin Gazette* of 13 February 1816 carried this notice, the
meeting being called for 26 February.

609

From his son Maurice to Merrion Square

Clongowes, 13 February 1816

Dear Father,

I am surprised at not receiving an answer to the last letter
I wrote to my Mama. She was very punctual but has now been
a week in my debt. . . . The compositions begin on the
seventh of March. This is the shortest term of the year. I will
endeavour to satisfy you this term. The vacation is at hand.
Iveragh! I shall see it once more, please God! . . . Morgan
unites in love to you.

[P.S.]   How does Charles Phillips go on? Remember me to
Miss Gaghran. How is Eneas MacDonnell?

SOURCE : O'Connell MSS, UCD

610

From Myles McSwiney, Carhen, 16 February 1816 to Merrion Square

States that Hunting-Cap has no suspicion that O'Connell is
involved in James O'Leary's bankruptcy.

SOURCE : O'Connell Papers, NLI 13646

611

From his brother James to Merrion Square

Derrynane, 17 February 1816

My Dear Dan,

I have no doubt you will be impatient to hear what excuse I gave my uncle for my long delay both in Tralee and Killarney. I only arrived here on Tuesday last and found him in good health and spirits. I told my uncle I was detained by bad health as I had a slight return of the bilious complaint. He had heard last week of O'Leary's failure. He repeatedly asked me if you were engaged for him for any sum. I assured him you were not. Indeed, he was at first so earnest and particular in his inquiries that I feared some person had made him acquainted with the facts, but on my *solemnly* assuring him you would not lose a guinea by the fellow as you never became security for him to any amount, he seemed quite satisfied and says that you possibly may loan something to this blackguard but that he himself told you last year O'Leary would unquestionably *snap* from the expensive manner in which he lived. I, of course, allow him to take what merit he pleases for his friendly caution.

You have a right to feel much obliged to Ellen[1] for her exertions in preventing my uncle from hearing this unfortunate business. She had two confidential men stationed, one at the upper gate and the other at the strand, to caution every person who was coming to Derrynane not to mention this business. This, I assure you, was a very necessary caution as every individual in this country knows every circumstance connected with O'Leary's failure. I now hope we have little to fear but we must still keep a sharp look out.

I hope you will take care to bring me my acceptance for £300 which remained in *your friend* Mr. Hickson's[2] hands to the assizes. I assure you there is no man in existence who [*sic*] I wish to have less pecuniary dealings with than that gentleman. I must again and again repeat that I will expect either to have you [? enclose] me this bill on receipt of this letter or at all events to get it at the assizes. I could neither *eat, drink* [*n*]*or sleep* if I was in the power of this gentleman, and it is impossible to describe the wretched state of this country with respect to money. I do not think with all my exertions I will be able to carry to the assizes the head rents you pay Sir R[owland] Blennerhassett, Charles O'Connell[3] etc. What is to become of us if the times do not improve! I have had recourse to the harshest methods to try and extort some payments from your tenants for the last week, all the pounds of the country filled with their cows but all to no purpose. My Uncle Maurice has over £1,500 of his last May rents due to him.

SOURCE : O'Connell MSS, UCD

1   Their sister Ellen.
2   John C. Hickson.
3   Charles O'Connell (1805-77), son of Daniel O'Connell (died 1811), Ballinabloun, the Glen, and Portmagee, both Co. Kerry, and Theresa Lombard. Cousin of O'Connell. He married Kate, second daughter of O'Connell. M.P. for Co. Kerry, 1832-34; appointed resident magistrate, April 1847; lived for some years at Bahoss, Cahirciveen.

612

To his wife, Merrion Square

Ennis, 11 March 1816

My darling love,

I arrived here last night too late and too fatigued to write to you. I got on Saturday to Nenagh and slept there in a wretched cold room but instead of finding myself the worse for it I am considerably better, indeed quite rid of the cold in my head of which every symptom has vanished.

The business here is better than I could reasonably have expected. . . . Darling, I am become one of the most attentive fellows living, taking most excellent care of my money and of myself. . . .

SOURCE : Fitz-Simon Papers

613

From his wife to Ennis

Dublin, 11 March 1816

My dearest Love,

I am indeed most anxious to hear how your *fasting* journey agreed with you. . . . I fear you are observing this Lent too strictly. At all events, while on circuit, I think you ought to relax in some degree. Wednesday, Friday and Saturday would be quite sufficient for you to fast from breakfast. To be from nine o'clock in the morning to perhaps ten at night without eating a morsel in a cold court-house is more than any constitution (however good) will be able to bear. I am sure you are too good a Christian to persevere in anything that would be injurious to your constitution, and I therefore hope you will promise me to give up fasting should you in the slightest degree find it disagrees with you. . . .

James Connor came to tell me the result of the meeting at the Exchange on Saturday last. He desired I should tell you the Commissioners Leyne[1] and Ryan[2] behaved with the strictest justice. They were very near committing Mr. O'Leary[3] for refusing to show some accounts and they were only prevented by his promising to produce them this day when another meeting is to take place. *They* were very harsh to Mr. [? Tinkler][4] and would not allow him to answer for Mr. O'Leary. The latter swore positively that he, nor no person for him, received any money for some time before the messenger went to Kerry to the present moment. He swore he had lost to his tan-yard £1,500 and to the cotton business about £50. This day's meeting is to be the last for some time. His protection will be taken from him and Mr. Henchy[5] has advised the final examination to take place as soon after James Connor can ascertain how Mr. O'Leary is situated respecting his accounts in Kerry. James will go to Killarney immediately after the assizes to ascertain everything necessary previous to the final examination. Mr. Henchy is most indefatigable. He and Mr. Huband[6] were rather smart on each other last Saturday and the Commissioners were very strict upon Huband and *his party*. They seemed greatly disgusted with O'Leary's conduct. *That gentleman* appeared somewhat humbled since you proved your [? debt]. He does not dare talk of you as he did before but his bosom friend, Mr. Hty,[7] says you did not prove the debt, you only claimed it. From the reports that he and Mr. O'L. circulated, it was generally believed you could not prove £500 against him but the public are now of a different opinion. I shall by tomorrow's post let you know the result of this day's meeting.

[P.S.] . . .

SOURCE : O'Connell Papers, NLI 13651

1 James Lyne, B.L. (born 1770), 2 Lower Mount Street, Dublin; commissioner of bankrupts and assistant barrister for Co. Westmeath.

2 John Burke Ryan, B.L. (born 1761), 27 Baggot Street, Dublin; commissioner of bankrupts.

3 James O'Leary.

4 Unidentified.

5 Peter Fitzgibbon Henchy, K.C. (born c. 1773), Merrion Square, Dublin. Commissioner of bankrupts.

6 Wilcocks Huband, B.L. (born 2 July 1776) (son of Joseph Huband, B.L., commissioner of bankrupts) 21 Baggot Street, Dublin. Commissioner of bankrupts.

7 Unidentified.

614

To his wife, Merrion Square

Ennis, Wednesday, 13 March 1816

My darling Love,

You promised to write me a *second* letter, darling, on Tuesday about that scoundrel O'Leary and I felt a sensation of more than regret at not hearing from you this day, but I suppose you did it out of *revenge* for not having heard from me on yesterday morning. I suppose this because I know you are *so spiteful*. Dearest love, I would really have written to you on Sunday night but that I was so excessively tired. . . . My business is far beyond that of any other barrister. In fact, darling, I am quite and without any rival at the head of this circuit. I am not drawing upon my vanity in telling you so. I am saying just what is the simple truth.

. . . We have hourly the most ludicrous scenes with Judge Mayne.[1] He is *an animal,* easily managed, and he and I agree perfectly and I have the pleasure of laughing at him by the hour.

SOURCE : Fitz-Simon Papers

1 Edward Mayne (c. 1756-1829), justice of the Common Pleas, 1806-17; justice of the King's Bench, 1817; resigned in 1820.

615

From his wife to Limerick

[Dublin] 16 March 1816

My dearest Love,

I am not altogether so *very* spiteful as you say for I wrote to you on Tuesday last as I promised but you could not possibly get the letter sooner than Thursday morning. . . . Since James Connor left this I heard nothing of Mr. O'Leary. Mr. Hussey[1] was here this morning and told me he was quite delighted that you had proved your debt. *It* has made a very great change in the opinion of the public and silenced Mr. O'Leary's boasting. I got £15.16.10 from Hickson. This sum is the full amount of *all* I got since you left this. I hope you will send me a remittance by Monday's post. You know Mrs. Shiel is not yet paid. Mr. Bric called on me yesterday to know if you said anything of him in your letter to me on Wednesday last. An acceptance of yours in his favour was brought here to be paid and I sent it off to Hickson's. The amount was £70. This bill, I believe, is the only one Mr. Hickson paid this week. At least no other notice came here. . . .

Let me know particularly how you are. I cannot divest myself of a dread that fasting will injure you. Consider, darling, how dear in every sense of the word is your health to me and your little family.

SOURCE : O'Connell Papers, NLI 13651

1   Rice Hussey (born c. 1790), attorney, 2 Upper Fitzwilliam Street, Dublin; second son of Thomas Hussey, Dingle, and Bridget who later married Stephen H. Rice. Educated at Stonyhurst. Married 1821 Catherine Eliza, daughter of John Grace, Mantua, Co. Roscommon.

616

To his wife, Merrion Square

Limerick, 18 March 1816

My darling Love,

. . . I will send tomorrow a remittance to the Hicksons with directions to give you money out of which you are to give Mrs. Shiel ten guineas. Darling, I am become really an economist, and if the times had continued as they were—but

no matter, sweetest. Let not Rice Hussey's silly chat or anything that is *so* said annoy you in the least. Let it not, my
darling. We shall be, I hope we are, the happiest and the
better for *this* event. As to the happier, that alone relates to
you for better, sweetest, you could not be.

SOURCE : Fitz-Simon Papers

617

To his wife, Merrion Square

Limerick, Wednesday, 20 March 1816

My darling Love,

I write to you today only because I did not write yesterday.
So, darling, I have only time to tell you that I was too much
pressed in point of time to get a bill to send to John Hickson
yesterday but I will get it today and send it tomorrow.
Sweetest Love, I am as well, notwithstanding my fasting, as
any man in Ireland. It fatigues me sometimes a little but it
agrees perfectly with me and I eat on abstinence days an
enormous dinner of fish. . . .

SOURCE : Fitz-Simon Papers

618

To his wife, Merrion Square

Limerick, 21 March 1816

My darling Love,

. . . I send by this post money to John Hickson. He will
give you twenty-one pounds out of it and I will, before I leave
this, remit you at least ten guineas for Mrs. Shiel. You have
not said whether you got from Hickson the £15 he promised
but I presume you must. Otherwise you could not have *sub-
sisted* so long.

Bad as the circuit has been, I have already received or
earned upwards of 200 guineas so that, darling, with health,
spirits and the assistance of God we will work over the difficulties into which my most absurd credulity involved me.
Dearest sweetest, how I *ought* to love you for the manner in
which you have met those difficulties. . . .

Darling, I was concerned in all the records in the County and City except one, and in all that were tried in Ennis. And I flatter myself that the public will not be *less* inclined to employ me again because of the *exhibitions* I have made on those occasions. We have been unfortunately foiled for the present in our Corporation cases. They have fairly *tricked* us out of a trial.[1]

SOURCE : Fitz-Simon Papers

1 One of the cases referred to was that brought by John Tuthill, a freeman of Limerick, against Edward Parker, town clerk, concerning the withholding by the latter of a copy of the list of freemen of Limerick from Tuthill's inspection (*LEP*, 23 Mar. 1816). In this case some of the jury claimed illness, and in consequence the entire jury was discharged, with the result that the case had to be commenced *de novo*. Several other cases affecting Limerick corporation were, due to alleged irregularity in the proceedings, held over to the next assizes (*LEP*, 23 Mar. 1816). According to the *Limerick Evening Post*, several thousand pounds had recently been collected for the purpose of procuring for the citizens of Limerick their corporate rights (*LEP*, 23 Mar. 1816). See also letter 462.

619

To his wife, Merrion Square

Tralee [Tuesday], 26 March 1816

My darling Love,

I came yesterday all the way from Limerick. I left it at five in the morning and did not get here till near nine, very much fatigued, having *worked* at my trade till past twelve on Sunday night, and of course, darling, slept very little. However, it is not possible to be better than I am today or indeed half so well but for the miserable state of business. Only *two* records . . . so that for the first time since I was called to the Bar I have had [? but one] record brief, but there is a good deal of criminal business. So much, heart, for trade.

I sent John Hickson £62 more from Limerick with a request to let you have ten guineas for Mrs. Shiel. I did not say *that* to him. . . .

I got my sweet Nell's French letter yesterday. It was so perfectly well written that *of course* Miss Gaghran assisted in

the language. It is impossible Ellen could have written it
without aid and in fact is an excellent specimen of Miss
Gaghran's own knowledge of the true genius of the language.
Darling, thank my Nell for me. . . .

SOURCE : Fitz-Simon Papers

620

From his wife to James Connor's Esquire, Tralee

Dublin, 26 March 1816
[No salutation]

You have indeed, my darling, a great deal of merit for
your attention at present to your religious duties, and it is a
delightful reflection to me that amidst all your bustle and
business you continue a pattern of piety to all of us. I had
yesterday the happiness of being at Communion and as my
health will now permit me to be more regular than I have
been this time back, I shall with the assistance of God try to
follow your example. God be thanked, darling, the times are
changed. You are now the better *Christian*. My girls are to pay
Mr. Walsh¹ a visit this week and, as for our darling boys, I
need have no fears that their religion will be neglected. . . .
Ellen is equally as anxious for a reply to her letter written on
Saturday. How do you like her first attempt in French? I
should like to know from you if she understands the language
and how you approve of Miss G's instruction in English and
writing. . . . I called to see Mrs. O'Sullivan² and, in the
course of our conversation, she told me her niece, Mary
Coppinger,³ had at present a £1,000 to put at interest. *It*
immediately occurred to me that you may wish to get it, and
Mrs. O'S joined me in opinion that Mrs. Coppinger would give
it. What would you think of writing to her on the subject
without mentioning her aunt's name but, except you want the
money very much, darling, I should prefer your not taking it.
Interest money to you must be so heavy just now. I have this
moment sent Hickson a notice to pay £90 to some house in
Pill Lane. O'Leary is yet in town. . . . Has your uncle⁴ gone
through the operation for which he went to Cork? . . . With
the strictest economy our book has been ten pounds last week
and the week before. . . .

source : O'Connell Papers, NLI 13650
1 Probably the Rev. Pierse Walsh, Townsend Street chapel, Dublin.
2 Unidentified.
3 Unidentified.
4 Hunting-Cap.

621

To his wife, Merrion Square, 28 March 1816, from Tralee

Fasting ' agrees perfectly well with me in every respect '.

source : Fitz-Simon Papers

622

From his wife to Cork

Friday night, 29 [and 30] March 1816

[No salutation]

[Long account of Morgan's indisposition as described in a letter from the Rector of Clongowes Wood College.]

All our darlings here are quite well, Ellen in great spirits at your approbation of her French letter. Miss G[aghran] declares Ellen deserves all the merit. *She* only assisted her in two words. I *want* money, love. Miss G. has asked me for ten guineas and I have got the Insurance Office to pay £5 to. I hope Cork will have good business. In truth I believe the people have not money *even* for law.

Saturday evening, half past five o'clock [30 March 1816]

My darling, I am but this moment returned from Clongowes after spending three hours with our darling boys and have the happiness to tell you our dear Morgan is considerably better. . . . He is taken as much care of as if I had him at home. . . .

source : O'Connell Papers, NLI 13651

623

To his daughter Ellen, Merrion Square

Tralee, 1 April 1816

My darling Ellen,

I had not time to write to you since I got your French letter on Thursday last though I was determined to do so for many reasons but especially because I was greatly pleased with your letter. Indeed I was greatly surprised at its being so extremely well written. I am sure Miss Gaghran must have assisted you in the composition as the style and the construction of the sentences was certainly greatly superior to anything you could be expected to write. I repeat, my sweet child, that it gave me the most sincere pleasure.

Will you give my tenderest love to your darling mother and tell her to do just as she pleases about buying the new piano. . . .

I am myself as well as ever I was in my life but a little out of spirits as this was a very bloody assizes. There were no less than seven men capitally convicted and I really believe they will all be executed. . . .

SOURCE : Fitz-Simon Papers

624

From his wife to Parade, Cork

[Dublin], 1 April 1816

[No salutation]

. . . Both he [Maurice] and Morgan told me it was quite impossible for them to be happier or more contented than they were at Clongowes. They had not the slightest fault to find with anything. Indeed Mr. Kenny[1] seems to be more like a kind parent than anything else to them. Nothing can exceed his attention to Morgan since his illness. . . . He was the only boy ill out of a hundred and thirty-one. The new building is completed and looks very handsome. *They* are to inhabit it during the summer. In short, love, I came home quite delighted with everything I saw and heard of the establishment and as happy as possible on leaving our dear boys so happily situated. Maurice is grown but his appearance of health is beyond anything I can say. He had many questions to ask about you, thanked God with his hands clasped for your *conversion.*[2] . . .

For goodness sake, write to Kate. She is all impatience for a reply to her letter. . . .

SOURCE : O'Connell Papers, NLI 13651

1 Rev. Peter Kenney, S.J.

2 The *conversion* can scarcely have been his return to the belief and practice of the Catholic religion since that must have occurred sometime before 1809 (see letter 237). Probably it was a determination not to lend money or go security for others. See letters 501 and 603.

625

From his wife to Parade, Cork

[Dublin] 2 April 1816

My darling Dan,

. . . I have no society but theirs [her children] with the exception of a visit now and again from Mr. L'Estrange and Miss Conry, and I feel as happy as it is possible for me to feel in your absence.

Mr. L'Estrange paid me a long visit this morning. He was very anxious to know if you had a meeting in Kerry. On this subject, I could give him no information. The only news he told me was that Lord Trimleston[1] dined a second time with the Lord Lieutenant and on Saturday last with the Attorney-General. *This* I think *looks well.* In Cork I suppose the seceders will make a great noise about getting signatures to the Vetoistical petition[2] and I much fear they will succeed. What a shocking scene has taken place in Skibbereen Chapel.[3] I think Mr. Sandy Tim[4] has no great cause to be proud of himself. I could forgive him anything but attacking the clergyman in the house of God. I fear the Veto will do more mischief but I trust in Providence *it* will never pass. *I feel* almost confident it never will. . . .

Ellen is impatiently expecting your answer about the piano, and Kate an answer to her letter. They are both very deserving children and I am satisfied you will indulge *them* if in your power. . . .

SOURCE : O'Connell Papers, NLI 13651

1   One of the seceders from the former Catholic Board who were
    prepared to compromise on the veto.

2   The petition to parliament adopted at a meeting of Catholics in
    Lord Trimleston's house on 13 February 1816. It declared the
    Catholics of Ireland ready to accept a qualified Emancipation (*DEP*,
    17 Feb. 1816). This petition was circulated throughout Ireland for
    signature, one copy being forwarded to Cork (*CMC*, 13 Mar. 1816).
    The Catholic Association was at the same time circulating a rival
    petition for unqualified Emancipation (*DEP*, 13 Mar. 1816) though
    ' a great part ' of the expenses of the Catholic petitions since 1811,
    for which the Association apparently held itself liable, were still
    unpaid (see circular letter of Edward Hay, dated 8 Mar. 1816, to
    the Catholics of Ireland, *DEP*, 16 Mar. 1816).

3   On 17 and 22 March 1816 some noisy altercations had taken place
    in the chapel of Skibbereen between vetoists and anti-vetoists over
    the rival Catholic petitions to parliament. The Rev. Michael Collins,
    parish priest of Skibbereen, apparently opposed the signing of the
    vetoist petition (*CMC*, 25 Mar. 1816).

4   Alexander O'Driscoll of Clover Hill, Skibbereen, Co. Cork. He had
    been a member of the Cork Catholic Board, and was among those
    satirized in the ' Blarney Lane ' letter (see letter 469, note 1; also
    DEP, 7 April 1814). He had apparently been canvassing in Skib-
    bereen for signatures to the vetoist petition and was one of those
    who clashed in consequence with the local parish priest (*CMC*, 25
    Mar. 1816; see also letter of the Rev. Michael Collins to the editor
    of the *Cork Mercantile Chronicle*, 5 April 1816).

626

To his son Maurice, Clongowes Wood College

Cork, 3 April 1816

My dear child,

As soon as you get this letter, ask permission of Mr. Kenny
to write to me daily whilst your brother is ill. Direct to me,
' Cork '. Be quite candid and explicit with me as to his state
and whether the physician apprehends any danger.

Tell him from me, I mean, tell your brother from me that
I doat with the tenderest affection on him and entreat of him
if he loves me to take his medicines and to keep himself as
quiet as he possibly can. I will write to him by the post of
tomorrow, and you will in the meantime say to him from me
the kindest and most affectionate things you can imagine.

. . . He has every promise of being a delightful fellow. . . .
I intend to be more punctual in writing to you and your
brother than I have been. Tell my Morgan so.

I hope, my child, your reply will be cheering to my heart.
I have heard a most excellent account of you. I mean to call to
see you and my darling Morgan on my way up.

SOURCE : Property of John V. Kelleher

627

From his wife

Dublin, 4 April 1816

My darling love,

. . . Our dear Ellen got your letter of Monday this day. It
was indeed a most unexpected pleasure to her, and you could
see delight pictured in her countenance while reading the
letter. I shall wait to hear from you before I do anything
decisive respecting the piano. I would rather, darling, you
would at once say to me buy or don't buy it, for I feel delicate
in putting you to any expense at present, though, as I before
told you, I think we ought to trespass a little for the advantage
of our children. . . .

Poor Mr. O'Mullane, how sorry I am to hear of his bad
luck.[1] What extraordinary conduct in Mr. Magee. O'Gorman,
I fear, will fare as badly.[2] We are all anxiously expecting to
hear some account this evening. . . .

For your sake I wish next week was over. I really fear you
will starve yourself. The Lent is observed so much more
strictly in Cork than here, but recollect, Darling, you ought
to take care of yourself.

SOURCE : O'Connell Papers, NLI 13651

1 Cornelius O'Mullane, parish priest of Templemore, Co. Londonderry
   (*DEP*, 29 Jan. 1814) was indicted for riot and assault in January
   1814. According to a hostile source, the alleged offences arose out
   of the latter's attendance at a banquet in October 1812 to celebrate
   the return of Sir George Hill as M.P. for Londonderry city.
   O'Mullane, in an account of the banquet which he is said to have
   sent the *Dublin Evening Post,* claimed Hill had promised to support the Catholic petition to parliament. Hill denied this, and in a
   subsequent newspaper controversy with O'Mullane was supported

by Richard O'Doherty in whom the Catholics of Londonderry had
recently expressed their confidence. O'Doherty thereby fell foul of
O'Mullane's supporters, and claimed O'Mullane had him forcibly
ejected from a meeting in his chapel (*DEP*, 16 Dec. 1815). The
bishop of Derry had O'Mullane suspended from his clerical
functions and was said in consequence to have been assaulted by
O'Mullane's supporters (*DEP*, 29 Jan. 1814). For these and other
alleged offences of a similar nature, O'Mullane was sentenced to
one month's imprisonment. (*DEP*, 11 Jan. 1814. According to the
Dublin Evening Post of 27 January 1814, two of the judges at
O'Mullane's trial declared this verdict was 'contrary to justice, law
and evidence'. For O'Mullane's trial see *DEP*, 29 Jan.; 5, 19,
22 Feb. 1814). In April 1816 O'Mullane brought an action at Galway
assizes against the proprietor of the *Londonderry Journal* for having
published an alleged libel on him in connection with this case.
O'Mullane sought damages of £5,000. The judge, however, declared
that in view of his political turbulence and insubordination to his
bishop, O'Mullane did not deserve compensation. He was awarded
6d damages and 6d costs (*DEP*, 4 April 1816).
2   See letter 546, note 2.

628

To his wife, Merrion Square

Cork, 7 April 1816

My darling Mary,

   I can *this* night only tell you that I never was better in
health or spirits or half so busy. Surely, darling, you *have* paid
the insurance. I did not think it necessary to write to you about
it. I have found a letter from Mr. Kenny[1] on my table. He
gives a most delightful account of both my boys. Maurice rates
very high with him. Dearest, it is just ten.

SOURCE : Fitz-Simon Papers
1   Rev. Peter Kenney, S.J.

629

From his wife to Cork

Dublin, 8 April 1816

My dearest love,

   From your letter to Kate (which she got this morning) I
am happy to perceive you are at length satisfied. *We* are not

deceiving you respecting Morgan's state of health. The enclosed will convince you he is no longer an invalid. . . . What a scolding, darling, I *will* give you when we *meet* for giving yourself such a world of misery without the slightest cause. Anything to equal your Kate's joy on receiving your letter! ! I happened to be in my room and she came up quite breathless with the letter in her hand. You have made Ellen and *her* quite happy by *commanding* me to buy the piano. Tomorrow we purpose after prayers going to several music shops where we are told there are second hand pianos to be sold cheap. If we succeed in getting as good a one for less money than the one we are in treaty for, we shan't come home without making a purchase.

I paid the insurance money this morning and for this week I have but £5. I have this moment sent Hickson a docket to pay fifty pounds this evening. It is the only one that has been sent here this fortnight or more. Mr. Hickson wanted to get the half notes for thirty pounds from me instead of my getting *them* from him. From your letter he understood the money was for him, but surely, darling, you very plainly told me to send to Hickson for the remaining halves of *these* you sent me. . . . You did not yet tell me anything of your uncle, your mother, or any of your friends. The former, I hear, was in Cork. Had he the operation performed and has he received any benefit from it? How happy I am to hear from Ellen Connor that your spirits were so good in Tralee. I am sure, darling, your fasting and abstinence ought to have kept them down for by what I can learn you have observed *both* most strictly. I will venture to say there were few priests did more. . . .

SOURCE : O'Connell Papers, NLI 13651

630

To his wife, Merrion Square

Cork, Tuesday, 9 April 1816

My dearest Heart,

Forgive me, love, for being so uneasy about *your* Morgan but the fact is that I felt as if I had treated the poor fellow badly and my grief was embittered by a very painful sensation like remorse. . . . I heard from Mr. Kenny yesterday and from Maurice today. The latter is head of his class and Mr. Kenny speaks of him in the highest possible terms.

The hurry here is extremely great but the quantity of business done is sufficiently small. Both judges[1] are miserably slow and I do not expect to have the assizes over before next Saturday week. I have, darling, been concerned in every cause criminal and civil or at least in so many that there is scarcely any exaggeration in calling it *all*. . . .

I hope my Kate was pleased with my letter to her. . . .

SOURCE : Fitz-Simon Papers
1   Robert Day and Edward Mayne.

631

From his wife to Cork

Dublin, 10 April [1816]

My dearest love,

. . . I learn from the Cork paper you are well and not unemployed and I hope tomorrow's post will bring me a letter. . . . I have not bought the piano. First I had not money and secondly I wish to look elsewhere in hopes of getting a better bargain. Yesterday we were not successful. . . . I see by the Cork paper that an aggregate meeting is to take place on Tuesday next. I may therefore, love, take for granted you will remain to attend it.[1] . . . God only knows how well you are earning Emancipation at whatever time it is given. Does not the present disposition of some of the Ministers give some hope that Emancipation will be acceded [*sic*] and without requiring the Veto. If so, what a victory over the *Lords* and *Pensioners*! Your speech at Limerick[2] we were promised in the *Dublin Chronicle* but as yet it has not appeared, and it is too provoking that, until everything interesting was over in Limerick, *they* did not condescend to send us *here* the *Limerick Evening Post*. I should be greatly gratified if you stopped that paper. Indeed it is no acquisition. The Cork paper is something like *our Chronicle* and tells us all the provincial news. The last *Dublin Chronicle* was most entertaining. Some of *us* suspect you for writing the attack upon the Vetoists[3] but I think it is more like Scully.[4] I do not think it likely you would *talk* of yourself.

I got wine from James Sugrue yesterday. I desired he should

send me two dozen of port and two of white wine but he had only six bottles of port to send. Let me know where I am to get port as it will be necessary, love [? to have] it in before you return. . . .

SOURCE : O'Connell Papers, NLI 13650

1 A Cork Catholic meeting held on 19 April 1816 and attended by O'Connell which passed resolutions in condemnation of the veto and of the pro-veto petition. It was described as 'one of the most numerous and respectable of its kind' (*CMC*, 19 April 1816).
2 O'Connell spoke at a Catholic meeting in Limerick on 23 March 1816, which the *Limerick Evening Post* claimed to have been attended by 200,000 persons (*LEP*, 27 Mar. 1816). Because of 'the variety and range it embraced', publication of O'Connell's speech was postponed (*LEP*, 27 Mar. 1816), and it was not subsequently published. The meeting passed resolutions in favour of unqualified Emancipation and in condemnation of the pro-veto petition (*LEP*, 30 Mar. 1816).
3 A letter apparently published in the *Dublin Chronicle*, 8 March 1816, implying that the signatures of Lords Fingall, Killeen, Kenmare, Gormanston and Southwell had been affixed to the pro-veto Catholic petition without their consent (see letter of Le Chevalier de MacCarthy to the editor of the *Dublin Evening Post*, dated 9 April 1816, claiming the signatures to have been genuine, *DEP*, 9 April 1816).
4 Denys Scully.

632

From his wife to Parade, Cork

Dublin, 12 April 1816

My darling Love,

. . . Surely, darling, you must certainly have made a mistake when you say the business of Cork will not be over until tomorrow week. I never knew the assizes *business* to hold longer than a fortnight and you were scarcely ever delayed beyond three or four days after. . . . I should be sorry you lost any business by quitting Cork, nor would I say a word on the subject if I was not quite convinced the business you would get here would amply compensate you for any you may lose in Cork beside the happiness to your family of having you at home with them. . . .

Was it you, darling, that examined Mr. Galwey about the Skibbereen business?[1] He *cut* a most ridiculous figure. I hope

Mr. Sandy Tim[2] will be made quite as ridiculous. Doctor
Murray preached this morning in Townsend Street. He spoke,
I am told, much against the Veto[3] which I hope will have a
good effect on many who were listening to him. Nurse was
there and when she came home she says, ' Oh, Madam, I
wish my master was hearing Doctor Murray this morning
speaking against the Veto. How happy it would make him.'
I am delighted to see [? in the] *Chronicle* that both Doctor
Troy and Dr. Murray have intimated their intention of [one
word illegible] *our* petition.[4] . . .

SOURCE : O'Connell Papers, NLI 13651

1 O'Connell was counsel for some Skibbereen Catholics who summoned a local magistrate before the courts for having brought a
military force to their chapel during Mass on Sunday 22 March
1816, ostensibly for the purpose of keeping the peace between vetoists
and anti-vetoists (*CMC*, 8 April 1816; see also letter 625). Henry
Galwey of Oldcourt, Skibbereen, a brewer (see letter of Michael
Collins to the editor of the *Cork Mercantile Chronicle*, dated 28
March 1816, *CMC*, 1 April 1816), had been involved on the side of
the vetoists in the recent altercation in Skibbereen chapel. He signed
an affidavit exonerating Alexander O'Driscoll from charges of having acted offensively on that occasion (*CMC*, 10 April 1816). He was
summoned as a witness in the case described above, and was cross-
examined in such a manner as to question his social status (*CMC*,
10, 12 April 1816). The name of his questioner was not published.
2 See letter 625, note 4.
3 In his sermon Murray, according to himself, censured ' those mis-
guided Catholics, who seem willing to impose new and disgraceful
bonds . . . on the church (Daniel Murray to the *Dublin Chronicle*,
15 April 1816, *DEP*, 16 April 1816).
4 In answer to Murray's letter the vetoists promptly secured in a letter
from Archbishop Troy an assurance that Catholics might sign the
pro-veto petition without breaking the law of the church, or incur-
ring Troy's personal displeasure (*DEP*, 23 April 1816).

633

From his wife to Parade, Cork

Dublin, 13 April [1816]

My dearest love,

No letter from you this day, which is indeed a very great
disappointment as I have not one farthing of money and
Saturday with me is always *pay* day. I have kept a regular

account of every shilling I received and of every penny I laid
out since you left home with the strictest economy. I have
already expended £81.14.4 but then, heart, you are exactly
five weeks away this day and I have paid some large sums out
of the above money. At all events, I can with truth assure you,
not a penny was laid out that could in any way be avoided.

. . . Most truly, darling, do I congratulate you on the
conclusion of Lent. Very few, I believe, have observed the fast
and abstinence so strictly. God grant you have not suffered by
doing so. If I see you looking thin and pale when you return
home I will indeed be seriously displeased with you. . . .

SOURCE : O'Connell Papers, NLI 13650

634

To his wife, Merrion Square

Cork, 14 April 1816

My darling Heart,

. . . Darling, there never was so weighty or so tedious an
assizes. I have still 15 briefs in criminal cases undisposed of
and we begin tomorrow the third week of the assizes. . . . I
fancy I must return by Limerick but one day *shall* finish my
business there. . . .

Darling, Dr. Murray's sermon[1] delights *us all* here. He has
marked the name of Judas on the Vetoists. Our aggregate is
postponed till *Friday* next.[2] What think of that, sweetest? You
may well imagine that I do not deceive you with regard to the
state of the business.

. . . Darling, I hardly knew the taste of meat this morning
but I never in my life was half so well.

SOURCE : Fitz-Simon Papers
1   See letter 632, note 3.
2   See letter 631, note 1.

635

From his wife to Cork

Dublin, 16 April 1816

My dearest Love,

. . . Thank God, you are so well after all your fasting and
abstinence. I assure you, heart, I was more delighted for your

sake to have Lent over than for any other reason for I all along had my fears that your health would suffer from this strictness with which you observed the fasting. You will be quite pleased with Doctor Murray's letter[1] in the *Chronicle*. In substance it is precisely the same as what appeared in Friday night's paper. It is a great blow to all the Vetoists and perhaps it may prevent many more from joining them. . . .

James Sugrue was here this morning. He told me that Finlay and Phillips had a falling out with John Magee. Magee considered the evidence which Finlay gave in the trial between him and O'Gorman[2] too favourable to the latter party. This is the report of the day but Mr. *Bric* told Roger[3] this morning there is certainly a cool[ness] between the *parties* which he fears will be the means of Finlay's quitting Magee. Should this be the case, heart, surely you will not continue a subscriber to the [*Dublin*] *Evening Post*. In my opinion no Catholic but a *Vetoist* should subscribe to it. *You don't* tell me a word of news for *all* I tell you. . . .

I hope, darling, you will not *attack* any person in your speech at the Aggregate next Friday. Is it not better be silent respecting the Vetoists? Doctor Murray's letter is quite sufficient. . . .

SOURCE : O'Connell Papers, NLI 13651

1   See letter 632, note 3.
2   See letter 546, note 2.
3   Roger O'Sullivan (born c. 1797), eldest son of Daniel O'Sullivan, Reendonegan, Bantry, Co. Cork, and O'Connell's sister Honora. Clerk to O'Connell and later an attorney. Admitted King's Inns, 1814.

636

To his wife, Merrion Square

Cork, 17 April 1816

My darling Love,

I ought indeed to have been more punctual in writing to you last week. I acknowledge that I ought, but, sweetest, the business was so excessively pressing. Judge Mayne sat so early and Judge Day so late that there was not a moment left for me to breathe in. Indeed, best of darlings, this was and could be the sole cause of my not writing to you every day. Writing to you is one of the most pure pleasures which this world affords me. . . .

I have at length got rid of all my briefs and wait now in Cork only for the aggregate and to do my *chamber business* in the meantime. I have enough to keep me a fortnight but I will certainly leave this on Saturday. . . .

SOURCE : Fitz-Simon Papers

637

To his wife, Merrion Square

Cork, 18 April 1816

My hearts darling,

I will talk to you about *all* your *questions* when we meet. Now, darling, I must go to bed for I have laboured more this day at my trade than if my court business was still going on. . . .

SOURCE : Fitz-Simon Papers

638

From Myles McSwiney to Merrion Square

Carhen, 31 May 1816

My Dear Dan,

. . . I kept back the *Chronicle,* with the account [of] your business with the Attorney-General,[1] from your uncle. We are getting in no money and fear it will be impossible to remit the sum you mention. I am still annoyed by the Mahonys[2] to know where the old woman is to call for her jointure, as they expected to hear from you on that subject. . . .

SOURCE : O'Connell Papers, NLI 13646

1 On 18 May 1816 O'Connell was counsel for the defence of Harding Tracy, printer of the *Cork Mercantile Chronicle,* in an action for libel brought against Tracy by the government. The *Cork Mercantile Chronicle* had published O'Connell's speech at a Catholic meeting in Cork on 15 April 1815 in which he criticized the administration of justice in Ireland. In court the attorney-general accused O'Connell of having used language calculated to incite rebellion. O'Connell replied by disparaging the attorney-general (*DEP,* 21 May

1816). Despite a plea from O'Connell for clemency to his client in view of the latter's poor health and the straitened circumstances of his family, Harding was sentenced to two years' imprisonment in Newgate and fined £300 (*DEP*, 21 May 1816).
2 Unidentified.

639

To his wife, Merrion Square, 30 July 1816, from Ennis

Very pleased that he was engaged in all the records at the assizes.

SOURCE : Fitz-Simon Papers

640

To his wife, Merrion Square

Limerick, 4 August 1816

My darling Love,

. . . I walked into town yesterday morning no less than fifteen miles from Dr. O'Shaughnessy's[1] where I had slept. I was in before breakfast and felt not one bit tired though my feet blistered from *road walking*. . . .

The favour, love, which I had to beg of you is this, that you would ask young Mahon[2] to spend the vacation with your boys. I am under very great obligations to his father[3] and I would be most happy to return him any compliment. Ask him then, sweetest, and write to Mr. Kenny to send him up. I got his father's leave, so you see I am committed. Do, darling, gratify me in this—do, sweetest.

The great cause of *Grady* v. *Bruce*[4] is fixed for Thursday. Burton[5] comes down but Curran[6] does not. What a wavering inconsistent fellow!

SOURCE : Fitz-Simon Papers
1 Bishop of Killaloe.
2 James Patrick O'Gorman Mahon (1800/1803-16 June 1891), known later as The O'Gorman Mahon. Educated Clongowes, 1815-19: T.C.D., 1819-22. Son of Patrick Mahon and grandson of James O'Gorman, Ennis; nephew of Nicholas Purcell O'Gorman. Married 1830 Christine O'Brien, Fitzwilliam Square, Dublin. M.P. for Co. Clare, 1830-31, 1879-85; Ennis, 1847-52; Co. Carlow, 1887-91.

3   Patrick Mahon (died 1821), Newpark, Ennis. Married a daughter of
    James O'Gorman.

4   A celebrated libel action. George Evans Bruce, a Limerick banker,
    claimed damages of £20,000 from Thomas Grady, a barrister, in
    consequence of the latter's having published a poem concerning
    him entitled ' The Nosegay '. Bruce and Grady had originally been
    friends. They appear to have quarrelled in consequence of a loan
    which Grady had obtained from Bruce, for which he claimed he
    was charged a usurious rate of interest. The jury awarded Bruce
    damages of £500, and it was joked that their doing so was occa-
    sioned by the fact that the defendant had failed to prove one (one
    fortieth) of the forty charges brought by him against Bruce in the
    poem. As a counsel for Grady, O'Connell delivered a speech of two
    hours duration. See *An Authentic Report of the Interesting Trial for
    Libel Contained in the Celebrated Poem called ' The Nosegay '*
    (Limerick 1816?).

5   Charles Burton was a counsel for Grady in this case.

6   The retired John Philpot Curran had been expected to act as a
    counsel (*DEP*, 8 Aug. 1817).

641

To his son Maurice

Limerick, 5 August 1816

My darling Maurice,

I had great pleasure in receiving your letter . . . but I
must own I felt a passing shade of disappointment that you
are not higher in your class. I am very willing to believe that
it was not your fault, and do not blame you; and yet, my
child, I consider *you could* have worked out a better place.
However, be assured I say this without one particle of anything like anger. Will you make an effort to gratify me next
time? . . .

Join with me in soliciting your mother to allow you to
invite young Mahon[1] to spend part of the vacation with
you. . . .

SOURCE : *Irish Monthly*, XV (1887), 598-9

1   James Patrick O'Gorman Mahon.

642

To his son Morgan

Limerick, 6 August 1816

My darling Morgan,

I was greatly pleased with your letter. It delighted me to find that you were advanced in your class. The truth is that if you took it into your red head you could easily be head of the class. I am quite sure you could, but a little laziness and a little carelessness combine to keep you down. At all events it is pleasing to see that you are rising in the class, and makes me hope you will soon determine to be first of it. Do, my sweet Morgan, take the trouble for one examination, and I promise you that you never will think it a trouble again. . . .

Give my tenderest love, my love beyond expression in softness and constancy, to your sweet mother, the best darling that ever blessed man with delightful children. . . .

SOURCE : FitzPatrick, *Corr*, I, 47-8

643

From his wife to Limerick

Dublin, 6 August 1816

[No salutation]

. . . I yesterday wrote to Mr. Kenny[1] agreeable to your wish, and have prepared James, the servant's, room for Master Mahon. . . . The boys are most anxious for his arrival. He seems to be one of their favourites, but in what way, darling, are you under any obligations to Mr. Mahon?[2] I never heard you speak on the subject. Is it any accommodation he has given in money matters? . . . My boys and girls, when I am confined, will write to you in turn. . . . I hope I shall read the *trial*[3] in the *Chronicle*. Let me know what you get for stating the case. I hope, darling, to hear you will come off with *éclat*. At all events I flatter myself you are a better orator than Mr. Burton. *This* is your birthday, my heart. I shall drink your health and may *we* and *our* little ones live to see many, many happy returns of this day. . . .

SOURCE : O'Connell Papers, NLI 13651
1 Rev. Peter Kenney, S.J.
2 Patrick Mahon.
3 *Bruce* v. *Grady*.

644

To his wife, Merrion Square

Limerick, 8 August 1816

My darling Love,

. . . I was unable to write yesterday because of our preparations for Bruce's trial. It came on about ten o'clock. Goold[1]
stated the case in a speech of three hours and three quarters,
an excellent speech it was but very tedious. There were but few
witnesses for the P[lain]tiff. At four o'clock I rose and spoke
for just an hour and a half. It was *my* best speech I think and
the entire Bar think so too. This day will be consumed by the
evidence and other speeches but *my part* is done and I am
satisfied with it.

The business is *besides* this mainly over. There is one
tremendous murder case[2] in which I am concerned and in
which eleven of the finest looking young fellows I ever saw
are in great jeopardy. They will be tried tomorrow.

SOURCE : Fitz-Simon Papers
1 Thomas Goold, K.C., counsel for Bruce. See letter 640, note 4.
2 Apparently that which concerned the murder of Thomas Dillon
   and Margaret, his wife, on the night of 4 September 1815 near
   Pallaskenry, Co. Limerick. The Dillon house was allegedly attacked
   by a large number of men who shot and stabbed Dillon and his wife
   to death, while the latter held an infant in her arms, and their
   daughter watched from a loft in which her mother had placed her
   for safety. Thomas Bourke, Michael Hehir and John Evans were
   convicted of the crime and hanged at Pallaskenry on 10 August
   1816. An unspecified number of other defendants were remanded
   in custody in connection with the case (*LEP*, 12 Aug. 1816).

645

To his wife, Merrion Square

Limerick, 9 August 1816

My darling Love,

. . . Bruce's trial is over. He got a verdict for £500—
shabby enough after being accused of the foulest crime that
ever disgraced human nature.[1] The verdict was given rather
to punish the defendant than remunerate the plaintiff. For my
part I am perfectly satisfied with the entire.

The business will be over tomorrow but I will not leave this for Tralee till Monday late as I have one thousand things to do here. . . .

SOURCE : Fitz-Simon Papers

1 A reference to Bruce's being accused in ' The Nosegay ' of incestuous relations with his sister. See letter 640, note 4.

646

From his wife to Limerick

Dublin, 9 August [1816]

My dearest Love,

. . . Dumas[1] told me there was not a greater buck in Bond Street than Mr. James O'Leary, dashing away at his usual rate and most elegantly dressed, at the opera and theatres every night, and living at one of the most expensive taverns in London. This is the way, darling, he is spending your eight thousand pounds. My God, what a horrid perjured fellow he is. Surely, heart, you will never think of signing his certificate.[2] Believe me, you owe to your own character not to do so and I ask you as a favour not to sign it. You do not want further proofs of his base disposition than his present conduct. Dumas also met James Sugrue on 'change. He is but just returned from Genoa and is now engaged on some chemical speculation. He has no notion of returning to Dublin. Mrs. Dumas seems to me quite an altered being which I am sincerely rejoiced at for her husband's sake who appears to me to be a very sincere friend of yours. Shall we read your speech on the trial? I shall be much disappointed if it is not well reported. How did Mr. Grady get off?[3] . . .

SOURCE : O'Connell Papers, NLI 13650

1 Thomas Collins Dumas, attorney, Hen Street, Killarney, Co. Kerry.
2 Presumably some procedure whereby a bankrupt is released from some of the penalties of bankruptcy.
3 Thomas Grady, defendant in the case *Bruce* v. *Grady*. See letter 640, note 4.

647

From his wife to Limerick

Dublin, 10 August 1816

My dearest Love,

. . . Mr. Bruce had no great triumph in my opinion. It would have been more wise of him not to bring *such* scurrilous business before the public. The *Limerick [Evening] Post* pays you a handsome compliment.[1] *We* shall all *here* be much disappointed if your speech does not appear in the next *Chronicle*.[2]

. . . Don't forget, love, to send me a remittance this day. Nurse has called upon me for three guineas which will be due to her the thirtieth of this month and as I yesterday told you I want provision for the next week. . . . Morgan as you may well suppose was greatly pleased with your letter. . . .

SOURCE : O'Connell Papers, NLI 13651

1 The *Limerick Evening Post* declared of O'Connell in the 'Nosegay' trial that 'his humour, wit and nervous eloquence were equal to anything we ever heard from the distinguished orator' (*LEP*, 8 Aug. 1816).
2 The *Dublin Chronicle*.

648

To his wife, Merrion Square

Limerick, 11 August 1816

My darling Love,

. . . These assizes are nearly closed. The trial of a most shocking murder[1] occupied the last two days and there remain seven or eight others to be tried for it, but I shall be off for Kerry tomorrow evening. . . .

Write to me, darling, *every day* whilst I am in Kerry. Do not, dearest, omit any one day. . . . And get my boys and my girls to write to me. Beg of Miss Gaghran to allow the girls to *compose* altogether their own letters and to write to me in English, for the sake of having their genuine expressions.

I have just had a letter from Myles McSwiney. My poor mother is ill, very ill—poor woman. She was to me in my infancy the most tender of mothers. May the good God pour his choicest blessings on her head. . . .

I promise you, darling, not to sign O'Leary's certificate.[2]
I only despise myself heartily for allowing so contemptible a
scoundrel to impose on me.

SOURCE : Fitz-Simon Papers
1   See letter 644, note 2.
2   See letter 646.

649

To his wife, Merrion Square

Limerick, 12 August 1816

My darling Love,
    . . . If you are pressed [for money] call to Hickson but
avoid *that* if you can. . . .
    Tell Maurice to call at Fitzpatrick's and bid him send me
' Moore's Index ' when bound. . . . Tell Maurice, also, that it
certainly is the 52nd number of the *Edinburgh Review* which
I want. . . . Get Maurice to call on MacDonnell[1] and beg of
him not to print any report of Bruce's trial[2] in any detail until
he hears from me, as certainly any report from Bruce's side
will be imperfect. . . .

SOURCE : Fitz-Simon Papers
1   Eneas MacDonnell, editor and proprietor of the *Dublin Chronicle*.
2   *Bruce* v. *Grady*. See letter 640, note 4.

650

From his wife to Tralee

Dublin, 13 August 1816

My dearest Love,
    . . . In all probability you may hear by the post of Monday
next of the birth of another *red haired* daughter. Should it
happen to be a son perhaps we had better call it, as we first
intended, after James.[1] He certainly deserves any compliment
we can pay him for he is everything that is kind and
affectionate to us and to our children. . . .
    The boys, as you may well suppose [are] enjoying their
vacation but greatly afraid they will be gone before your
return. They tell me if you write to Mr. Kenny[2] for permission
for them to remain until the middle of next month, he will

give it provided you give him some very good *reason* which,
darling, you *must* do. It would be such a disappointment to
my poor fellows not to have some days with you. . . .

SOURCE : O'Connell Papers, NLI 13651
1   O'Connell's brother.
2   Rev. Peter Kenney, S.J.

651

To his wife, Merrion Square, 14 August 1816, from Tralee

Very poor assizes: 'Except me, not a lawyer will get one
guinea.'

SOURCE : Fitz-Simon Papers

652

From his wife to Tralee

Dublin, 15 August 1816

My dearest love,
    . . . The claret is arrived, a hogshead, the duty and freight
of which amounts to something more than forty pounds. This
sum I must call upon Hickson to pay. Otherwise the claret
will be kept in the stores of the Custom House and perhaps
adulterated. I wish the old gentleman[1] had paid the freight and
duty as well as the insurance. However it is well to get such
wine for merely paying the duty. I thought I was *going* to be
ill last night but *it* was a *false* alarm for I was well enough
this morning to go to my duty and hear three Masses. Would
to God I was once well, but I must have *patience* and trust in
the goodness of God for a happy time. . . .

SOURCE : O'Connell Papers, NLI 13651
1   O'Connell's uncle Count O'Connell.

653

To his wife, Merrion Square, 16 August 1816, from Tralee

'Darling, there have been two convictions but I was *not* concerned for either of the men. All my men have been hitherto
acquitted.'

SOURCE : Fitz-Simon Papers

654

To his wife, Merrion Square, 17 August 1816, from Tralee

' Think what a Tralee assizes when I received but thirty-four guineas.'

SOURCE : Fitz-Simon Papers

655

To his wife, Merrion Square

Tralee, 18 August 1816

My own darling Mary,

I am going out to dine at the worthy Sir Rowland's[1] to Blennerville. . . .

I am sorry the old gentleman in Paris[2] did not keep his claret to himself. He could not make us a present less wanting at this time. There never was such distress and want of money known in any former times. Half the gentry of the country are ruined. Iveragh holds out better than other places but still bad enough even there. We must not, however, let our spirits fail us even in these times. . . .

SOURCE : Fitz-Simon Papers
1 Sir Rowland Blennerhassett.
2 His uncle Count O'Connell.

656

From Judge Mayne

Killarney, Tuesday night,
20 August 1816

Judge Mayne would not lose a moment in acknowledging the receipt of Mr. O'Connell's note and the affidavit which accompanied it. He received them in such time only this evening on leaving court as to send them in the carriage, has enclosed them in a letter to Mr. Peel, and writes this as the earliest mode to apprize Mr. O'Connell, that any circumstances important to the prisoner in question, John Thomas,[1] must now be communicated, if at all, directly to the Lord Lieutenant and not through Judge Mayne, the day for the execution appointed being the 24th instant. Leaves this note to meet Mr. O'Connell at the Inn.

SOURCE : O'Connell Papers, NLI 13647
1   Unidentified.

657

From his wife to Parade, Cork

Dublin, 21 August 1816

My dearest Love,

Would it not be a prudent thing for you to dispose of the claret? Really, heart, I see no use you have for it. You do not drink claret at present nor do you give it to drink. . . . I got a few lines from the General[1] by this post enclosing me the invoice of the wine. The freight alone is three pounds. Had *he* paid the entire expense the wine would indeed be a handsome present. Your account of the distress of the country is truly melancholy and, what is worse, there is very little prospect of any change in the times for the better. Provisions of every kind, bread and butter excepted, are becoming cheap here. I now get the best meat of every kind for sixpence halfpenny a pound and it is expected to fall a penny more. . . .

I hope, my heart, you will be more fortunate in Cork than you have been in Tralee. You did not tell me what you made at Ennis and Limerick. I don't suppose (excepting your first assizes in Tralee) you ever got so trifling a sum as you did this time but if the business was there you would get it. I believe there is no barrister has less cause to complain than you have. The public say so and it is a great satisfaction to me to hear it said. . . .

SOURCE : O'Connell Papers, NLI 13651
1   O'Connell's uncle Count O'Connell.

658

To his wife, Merrion Square

Cork, 22 August 1816

My darling Love,

. . . Tell my sweet Nell that she shall have the piano as

speedily as I possibly can get it for her but, love, the fact is
that I have still near £1,700 of guarantees or bills of that
scoundrel O'Leary outstanding and I want every shilling
which I can put together to avoid being obliged to have my
bills protested, and myself sued. Another year, darling, will
with the help of God, hard labour and economy get us over
all, but it requires *all* these to work through the storm which
I have raised around me. Nobody can be more prudent than
you are, *that* is quite certain and, darling, I owe you my
deepest debt of gratitude for the manner in which you have
borne the privations which my absurd credulity has compelled you to endure. . . .

Darling, when do you mean to give me this other
daughter? This is almost the first time that you were *after*
your calculation. I am indeed impatient. . . .

There is very little business in the city and not much in
the county. . . .

SOURCE : Fitz-Simon Papers

659

To his wife, Merrion Square

Cork, Saturday [24 August 1816]

Darling heart's treasure,

May God bless and protect you, love, sweetest love. Hug
to your heart your little Dan[1] and tell him, whisper him of
his father. Just say to him what you think of his father, but,
darling, tell him it would not be possible to describe what I
think and feel of his beloved mother.

I am, dearest, in the gayest spirits. I will suffocate my
Nell for her darling letter. I am just out of court after a *great*
acquittal[2] and as soon as I dine I will go to the play.

Darling, *sell* the claret.

SOURCE : Fitz-Simon Papers

1 Daniel O'Connell (22 Aug. 1816-1897), youngest son of O'Connell.
   M.P. for Dundalk, 1846-47; Waterford city, 1847-48; Tralee, 1853-63;
   appointed commissioner of income tax, 1863. Married 1866 Ellen
   Mary, daughter of Ebenezer Foster, The Elms, Cambridge.
2 Unidentified.

660

From Rev. John T. O'Flaherty[1]

George's Quay, Cork, 26 August 1816

Dear Sir,

The annexed inquiries into the family of O'Connell are extracted from the notes to the topographical tables in my *History of the County and City of Limerick*. . . . [The writer goes on to discuss the scope of his historical work.]

When I had the pleasure to see you in Glin last year, you expressed a wish to have a view of so much of my manuscript as regarded your family, previously to its committal to the press. It is at the foot of this letter. . . .

The printing will be done in Cork, and those who mean to subscribe ought to send their names as early as possible. . . . I hope to have, through you, 200 subscribers at least. I know you could get me many here in Cork. . . . Of one thing, however, I am quite sure. It is that no county historian of Ireland has taken the twentieth part of my labour in the vindication of our ancient history, our origin, language, laws, institutions and manners.

[There follows a very brief statement on the origins of the O'Connell family.]

SOURCE : O'Connell Papers, NLI 13647

1 Author of *A Sketch of the History and Antiquities of the Southern Islands of Arran . . . with Observations on the Religion of the Celtic Nations, . . . Druidic Rites etc.* (Dublin 1824), *A Glance at Ancient Ireland* (Cork 1842), *Thoughts on the Origins and Language of the Ancient Scots.*

661

To his wife, Merrion Square

Cork, 27 August 1816

My darling Love,

I was in such spirits that I went down to Cove on Sunday in a row-boat and came up in the steamboat too late to write, and yesterday I was kept in court until it was impossible for me to put pen to paper. . . .

You frightened me with your alarms and my heart feels at ease now that you and your stout *rascal* are well. How much obliged I feel to my children for writing to me. Tell each of them so. I cannot indeed express my love for them. I hope good Mr. Maurice will condescend to write to me *also.* . . .

SOURCE : Fitz-Simon Papers

662

To his wife, Merrion Square

Cork, 30 August 1816

My darling Heart,

I never was so hurried as I have been this week between the two courts, criminal and civil. There is a dreadful load of criminal business. So much indeed that I doubt if Judge Mayne will have finished before this day week. I have had an immense number of cases and as yet but one conviction. I fear, however, that I shall not continue to be so fortunate. . . .

Darling, call the boy[1] what you please. A thousand loves to boys and girls. I must run off to court.

SOURCE : Fitz-Simon Papers
1 His youngest son, Daniel.

663

To his wife, Merrion Square

[Postmarked Cork] 31 August 1816

My own Love,

I was cheered with your letter. I am not, I could not be angry with my beloved Maurice.

I will write to Mr. Kenney tomorrow. In the meantime, the boys *must* stay at home.

Darling, I *must* run back to court in a shocking murder case.[1] I go to court every day before nine and leave it after seven, but I never was better or in *half* such spirits.

SOURCE : Fitz-Simon Papers
1 Unidentified.

664

To his wife, Merrion Square

Cork, 1 September 1816

My darling Heart,

. . . On Friday we shall have an *aggregate,* and on Saturday I expect to be quite able to leave this. . . . *All this* is a secret for I promised my poor mother and James Butler not to go up to Dublin till I saw the one and made the other *happy.* I regret to disappoint my mother but, as she is in no immediate danger, I can afford to run to see you; and as to Butler, he will excuse me for a few days but, darling, it can be only for a few days because I must for one thousand reasons be back in Kerry without delay. . . .

Tell my dearest Maurice and Morgan that I write by this post to Mr. Kenney so that they may remain until I have an opportunity of personally expressing my affection for them. . . .

The times are very distressing to the country and there is no prospect of alleviation. But my trade is excellent. I will send you more money on Tuesday and take you *more* myself. . . .

There still remain seven records untried; I am in *all* of them, and about a dozen criminal cases. The judges are indeed cruelly slow but they do the business tolerably well. . . .

SOURCE : Fitz-Simon Papers

665

From his wife to Cork

3 September 1816

Dearest love,

. . . Had you gone to Kerry without coming to see me and my boys, I should be most highly *offended* with you. Your mother is not in that dangerous state that you should hurry off to her, and James Butler having lived so long a bachelor, the delay of a week cannot add much to his *age.* I am sincerely glad he is to be married for many reasons. As to your being back from Iveragh until November I have not a hope nor do I expect it. I must own I would rather you did not spend much of your time in *that* country. A fortnight to amuse you is all I should *allow* and a week to spend entirely with your uncle. . . .

SOURCE : O'Connell Papers, NLI 13645

666

From Rev. John T. O'Flaherty, 3 September 1816
from Cork.

A long (unscientific) account of the ancient history of the O'Connells.

SOURCE : O'Connell MSS, UCD

667

To his wife, Merrion Square

Killarney, 20 September 1816

My darling Love,

I came here yesterday by the coach very pleasantly with Mrs. Chute and her sister, the beautiful Miss Yielding.[1] I have not as yet drawn the articles for Butler but he is *waiting* for me and so is the lady.[2] I shall go off tomorrow at all events for Iveragh and let them send after me. I have spent the entire of this day here working as hard as if I was in my own shop in Dublin. I drew marriage articles for a Miss Lynch of this town today and two other [nearly half a line illegible].

Sweetest love, I saw John [surname illegible] today. He bid me tell you that his daughter was quite well and had quite succeeded in making papists of the young *Bantrys*. We laughed a good deal at the vexation *they* experience at this trick she has played on the bigots. . . . I will write to you on Sunday from Iveragh. My poor mother is not well. . . .

SOURCE : Fitz-Simon Papers

1 Elizabeth (died 1851), wife of Capt. Caleb Chute, 69th Foot, and her sister, daughters of Theophilus Yielding, Caheraan, Killarney, Co. Kerry.
2 James Butler, Waterville, and Agnes Day, daughter of John Day, mayor of Cork, 1806, were married in 1817.

668

From his wife, 20 September 1816, to Derrynane

'Take care, love, of my letters. What your sister [Ellen] did once, she may do again, and you are too apt to leave letters behind you in your coat pockets.'

source : O'Connell MSS, UCD

669

To his wife, Merrion Square

Derrynane, 25 September 1816

My darling Love,

I came here on Monday and found my uncle poorly. He looks very much broken and shook but he is at present afflicted with a very severe cold. He is however much better than he was and received me with great affection.

I will certainly send you money in my next letter. In the meantime John Hickson will give Mrs. Shiel ten or twenty pounds on my account. I am much pleased you sent the carriage to poor Robert Hickson's funeral. Do you know that he was really disposed to act a very friendly part by me. . . . I do not wish, sweetest, to have O'Riordan[1] go to Clongowes. Depend on it, if anything serious should ail Maurice, Mr. Kenney would not conceal it a moment. I was myself very subject to those headaches, and bleeding was never resorted to —besides bleeding always leaves a permanent injury though it may give a temporary relief. . . .

source : Fitz-Simon Papers
1   Dr. John O'Reardon.

670

To his wife, Merrion Square

Derrynane, 26 September 1816

My darling Love,

. . . I did not like to leave my uncle who is really unwell with a very severe cold and a good deal oppressed. He would not listen to sending for a physician nor indeed is there any occasion but still I did not like to leave him in his present situation. He certainly looks much broken.

Darling, I will be at Carhen on Saturday and we are to have great racing at the pattern. All my schoolboy feelings are alive again and I am as merry as ever I was. . . .

Darling, we are under great obligations to Ellen[1] and it is not *my habit* to forget kindness.

SOURCE : Fitz-Simon Papers
1   His sister.

671

From his wife to Carhen c/o Myles McSwiney

[Dublin] Saturday, 28 September 1816

[No salutation]

. . . From your Limerick *correspondent* I had yesterday another letter, the style similar to the two *last*. The writer certainly seems to be insane. . . . You will be sorry to hear poor Dora[1] is very near her end, poor creature wishes to remove to her daughters and this day she goes there. I of course continue my kindness to her the same as if she was in the house. . . .

Thank God, I am perfectly well. I have been three times and tomorrow I shall for the fourth time go to Chapel. What a dreary disappointment to you country folks if tomorrow be unfavourable for the Patron. . . . We do not see a creature here but Miss Conry and Mr. L'Estrange and know as little of what is going forward in town as you do at Derrynane.

SOURCE : O'Connell Papers, NLI 13651
1   Maidservant.

672

To his wife, Merrion Square

Carhen, 29 September 1816

My darling Love,

I am just come here from Derrynane and just going to the *Patron* with a miserably bad day. My Uncle is much better and will not require any further medical assistance. I will send

tomorrow twenty pounds to James Connor to remit to you.
The rents are coming very slowly, and between the fall of
prices and the dreadful weather there is nothing but rain and
wretchedness.

I think I have discovered my Limerick correspondent. The
handwriting struck me as being quite familiar to me though I
am not quite sure that I have made it out. It is more closely
written I think than Tom Codd's[1] yet it cannot well be any
other. He has for years teased me with letters for money,
insisting that it was he brought me forward in the world, lent
me money, etc. The last time my uncle was in Cork, he made
a bitter complaint of my ingratitude. I have for a length of
time left his letters unread or returned them upon him. He is
full of schemes though quite mad, and indeed I should have
no doubt the letters were his but that the one you sent me is
written in a closer and I think a much better hand than his.
It vexes me not to be certain but if you get any more of them,
send them to me and I will endeavour to trace out the writer.
Or keep them till I go up and I will then send them in a
packet to his brother-in-law, poor Jerry Mahony of Cork. . . .

SOURCE : Fitz-Simon Papers
1 Unidentified. See letters 673 and 674.

673

To his wife, Merrion Square

Portmagee [Co. Kerry], 2 October 1816

My darling Love,
    . . . We have not had one single dry day since I came to
this country. The wet weather spoiled the pattern races etc. but
what is worse, it is ruining the peasantry *out* and *out*. . . .

I have written to Jerry Mahony about *your* Limerick correspondent. I have no doubt from the last letter that I am
right in my conjecture.

The account you give me of John[1] pleases me extremely.
He is a darling infant and will make a most excellent
priest. . . .

SOURCE : Fitz-Simon Papers
1 His six-year-old son.

674

From his wife to Tralee c/o J. Connor

Dublin, 16 October 1816

My dearest Love,

From your unknown correspondent[1] I got a letter this morning exactly similar to those I tendered to you. I am quite of your opinion respecting the intention of the writer. I also suspect that the writer of *those* letters is the same person whom you might recollect four years ago wrote to you from *Bristol* and took special care the letters should arrive in your absence. The handwriting, I think, to the best of my recollection is the same. I hope you kept the English letters that we might compare them with the Limerick ones. I am quite displeased that you should for a moment suffer the slightest uneasiness on *this* subject. Believe me, my *own* Dan, when I assure you that the machinations of *our anonymous friend* has not lessened my confidence in you. I should indeed be most ungrateful for your tenderness and affection if I allowed myself to fret or felt less happy than I did before the receipt of those contemptible scrolls. When I got the first letter (which I still have) I really thought it might have come from one of your female *acquaintances before I knew* you, and recollecting you had contributed to the support of Mrs. Y, I considered you might think it incumbent upon you to contribute to the support of *this person,* and the style of the first letter was calculated to make me think so and, on your return, I was determined to represent to you that in our present circumstances you could not in justice to your family contribute to *her* support, particularly if *she* was able to earn her bread which I know she must be when she wished to get an engagement from Talbot.[2] On this subject I will say no more until we meet and then I will scold you well. . . .

SOURCE : O'Connell Papers, NLI 13651

1   See letters 672 and 673.
2   Unidentified.

675

From his wife to Tralee c/o J. Connor's

Dublin, 17 October 1816

My dearest Love,

From the style of your letter written from Carhen last Sunday you must have been seriously displeased with me but let me ask you, how was I to act? For nearly a week I got no letter from you. Consequently, I could not be certain where to address you, not knowing the cause of your delay and expecting you to leave the country every day. . . . *This nasty* letter from Carhen has dispirited me. It is the first *serious* letter I ever got from you and I exactly feel like a *spoiled child.* . . .

I heard today from our boys, a letter from Maurice to you. He complains as Morgan *does* of your not writing to him since you went to the country. Scarcely a day passes without gentlemen calling to know if you are come here and regretting you are not. John Hickson is particularly anxious for your return. . . .

SOURCE : O'Connell Papers, NLI 13651

676

To his son Morgan, Clongowes Wood College

24 November 1816

My dearest Morgan,

I intended to have gone down to you on Thursday, but, finding that it will not be in my power to see you till next week, I write lest you should be disappointed. . . . I promise to go down next week and to take Mr. Phillips[1] to see you. Tell my darling Maurice that I shall bring down the books he wishes for. . . .

Professional hurry makes me forget those things, but your mother does not love you better or more tenderly than I do. . . .

SOURCE : FitzPatrick, *Corr.,* I, 48-9

1 Charles Phillips.

677

From John Hancock to Merrion Square

Lisburn, 1 December 1816

My dear friend,

I am glad to find that an aggregate meeting of Catholics is to be held.[1] I was peculiarly gratified to find thy name connected with the address to the inhabitants of Britain[2] as affording a security that the cause of parliamentary reform will be ably supported as I had previously remarked with great satisfaction in the proceedings at Cork.[3]

I have frequently expressed my decided opinion to thee that the parliamentary reformers, as the real friends of civil and religious liberty, are the only consistent advocates on principle of Catholic Emancipation. Ministers may be willing to barter privilege for patronage, but the concession of equal rights without regard to opinions will proceed only from men themselves resolved to be free and who only are capable of appreciating the value of freedom to others.

I hope the Catholic meeting[4] will be distinguished by firmness and decision. I always deprecate compromises on such occasions. A friend of mine used to call this line of acting by the appropriate name of "*unrighteous condescension*". Some, however, attempt to dignify it by asserting the sound policy of getting all to draw together, and the right is thus sacrificed to the supposed expedient. Hence Dr. [Benjamin] Franklin called a large assembly the greatest fool in the world. I will candidly tell thee that my fears were lately excited on this head by an article in the *Dublin Chronicle* about 10 days ago under the head of Catholic Cause. In my view it appeared to hold out some indirect hints to ministers of joining them against the political reformers in England provided Emancipation were granted and censure was attempted to be thrown on the public meetings in England as being more violent than the former proceedings of the Catholics in Ireland. Comparison was made between the agitators in both countries. Why should friends fall out? For my part I consider the *agitators* on both sides of the Channel as the best friends of liberty. I do not know how the paragraph to which I allude found its way into the *Chronicle* as it is contrary to the general line of politics adopted in that paper. I most sincerely wish to see Catholics emancipated without any compromise of their civil and religious liberties, without veto, without sale to the government, without any illiberal conditions on the broad and comprehensive principle of equal rights to all. And above all the rest, I ardently desire to see the downfall of the Orange system as, if it be suffered to remain, emancipation will be incomplete and an envenomed wound left rankling in the bosom of our country.

Sometime ago I meditated to have published a letter to Major Cartwright on the subject and thus to have appealed to the British public on this mighty grievance and at least to have attempted to impress reformers with the horrors of the Orange system daily producing such dismal effects in Ireland both directly and indirectly. But somehow I got discouraged and the project dropped for that time. There was little in the state of Ireland then to encourage exertion. The north and the south exhibited ' one sterile swamp of soul '. Catholics divided and paralysed. Such portion of the Protestants as formerly showed spirit were either apostatized and gone over to the enemies' ranks or under the influence of such culpable timidity that ' virtue had no tongue ' to proclaim the infamy of vice. Such with a few exceptions is the state of Ireland. Let us contrast our enfeebled, languid state with the present state of Britain, as described in a letter I received yesterday from Major Cartwright. I subjoin some extracts from his letter.

' Reform is at length coming upon us almost faster than we can be prepared for it. Apostles are springing up and preaching the doctrine to auditors who come 5, 10 or 15 miles to hear them. Lancashire and the West Riding of Yorkshire are in activity almost to a man, the grandees, the clergy and the magistracy excepted, but converts among them are daily coming over. Scotland is growing warmer. With regard to the people of Ireland we know that parliamentary reform must have their hearts and I trust that the breaking of the ice on that subject at the aggregate meeting at Cork augurs well, but they must in their present condition, with the bayonet at their throats, have time allowed for giving expression to their wishes. It being now probable that circumstances will accelerate our movement in England, I am the more anxious that Ireland should participate in the glory of our proceedings by sending us a cargo of petitions. We see strong symptoms of apprehension at the helm, and if we can but preserve peace at our public meetings, we trust we shall have a tranquil victory but, as of course the stronger we become in public opinion, the more sure we shall be of a peaceful victory, a cargo of petitions coming in time will be of infinite use.'[5]

So writes the honest Major, full of hope and confidence. I have more doubts. The present struggles in England and Scotland appear to me to be less the result of an enlightened philosophy and a full comprehension of the principles of liberty than of the temporary pressure of taxation and of a dread of scarcity which now appears inevitable. . . .

Lord Castlereagh threatens to take the *pension*,[6] as he expressly calls it, from the Presbyterian ministers if they support the Belfast Academical Institution[7] contrary to the wishes of government. They at present talk big and make a show of resistance. I hope their spirit may not evaporate but keep in full strength to the time of need. Catholics be warned by example! Beware of the wily statesman using soft words till he bind the ignominious fetters on the generous horse.

Timeo Danaos et dona ferentes.

It was often argued that the Regium Donum was a harmless gift without any pledge. If any seriously believed so, the fallacy must now be apparent to all.

SOURCE : O'Connell Papers, NLI 13647

1 The holding of an aggregate meeting was arranged for 17 December 1816 at a meeting of Catholic gentlemen in D'Arcy's Globe Tavern, Essex Street, Dublin, on 29 November 1816 (*DEP,* 30 Nov. 1816).

2 On O'Connell's proposal the meeting of 29 November resolved to prepare an address to the people of England (*DEP,* 30 Nov. 1816).

3 At a Catholic meeting in Carey's Lane chapel, Cork, on 6 September 1816, a resolution was passed declaring the defective state of the current system of parliamentary representation to be responsible for the rejection of the Catholic petitions for unqualified Emancipation, and urging ' our fellow subjects of every religious persuasion, to leave no constitutional means untried, in order to procure a full, free and frequent election of *Real Representatives* of the people of these Nations in the Commons House of Parliament ' (*CMC,* 9, 11, 13, 16 Sept. 1816).

4 The meeting took place in Clarendon Street chapel on 17 December 1816 under the chairmanship of Sir Thomas Esmonde. It was agreed that the Catholic petition of 1812, which had been signed by Fingall and the seceders, should be readopted for presentation to parliament. A resolution was also passed strongly favouring introducing to Ireland domestic nomination of bishops by dean and chapter (*DEP,* 18, 19 Dec. 1816).

5 At the above meeting (see note 4) O'Connell said he had intended

moving a resolution on parliamentary reform but had sacrificed his judgment for the sake of unanimity (*DEP*, 19 Dec. 1816).

6 The *regium donum*, the state grant to the Presbyterian church. In 1802 it was increased to such an extent that radicals feared it would undermine the independence of their church (McDowell, *Public Opinion*, pp. 84-5).

7 Founded in 1807, the Belfast Academical Institution was designed to provide both elementary and advanced instruction in a wide range of subjects, including the Irish language (*An Account of the System of Education in the Belfast Academical Institution*, Belfast, 1818, pp. 4-6, 31). In theory non-sectarian, it was in fact ' meant to be the germ of a northern university catering mainly to presbyterians ' (McDowell, *Public Opinion*, p. 53).

678

From John Cartwright to Merrion Square

James Street, Westminster, 24 December 1816

Sir,

It has been with the most lively satisfaction that, in the *Dublin Chronicle,* for which I have been indebted to an unknown friend, I have seen a full proof that the question of a reform in our representation has struck a vigorous root in the mind of Ireland.

It would be difficult, Sir, to draw a faithful picture of the present state of that cause in this island, as every day teems with evidence of its increasing strength, as well as of the sound knowledge in which it has its foundation.

As in the day of the great moral reformer, so in this with us, the truth has made infinitely more progress among those in low stations than among those of the higher classes; but I trust it is working its way upwards.

To this end a requisition is now in circulation in the city of London expressing a hope that the Lord Mayor[1] will invite ' those noblemen, country gentlemen, Magistrates of Counties, cities and towns, and those merchants, bankers and common councilmen of London, who interest themselves in the Liberties of their country, to meet at the Mansion House early in Feby. to consider how far a constitutional reform in the representation of the people in the Commons House of Parliament would be calculated to arrest the present dreadful career of public calamity, to remove its existence, and to prevent its return:—and likewise to consider what other measures ought, with all possible promptitude and decision, to be adopted for relieving, to the extent of practicability, that distress which it now almost universally experienced, and, by a large proportion of the community, most acutely felt'.

If the aristocracy be in their senses, they will appear at that meeting, and conduct themselves as justice and public feeling dictate; for it seems to be the general sentiment of reflecting men that we are on the eve—either of a radical reform, restoring our rights and liberties, or of a hurricane, the result of which no one can calculate. . . .

May the *Petitions* of Ireland, therefore, be, if it were possible, as numerous as her *wrongs*! This, after all, is the artillery with which the fortress of corruption must be battered down.

By favour of my friend, Mr. Thomas,[2] son of Dr. Thomas, I take the liberty of sending you a few essays and papers, of which I have to request your acceptance and distribution for promoting the cause of Reform.

Compelled to write in great haste, I can only offer it as an opinion that we are likely to be in a condition to carry *annual* election and suffrage to the extent of all *householders,* whether taxed directly or indirectly; but, should Ireland pour in her hundreds of petitions—and why shall she not?—I should reckon on the thing as certain.

Trifles, Sir, have influence on men's imaginations. I therefore believe we derive great advantage in using *sheet* petitions in preference to *rolls.* . . .

The Liberty and Happiness of both our countries probably hinging on the success or failure of our approaching effort, I am indeed most anxious to hear that Ireland has *begun the work of petitioning,* and that it will be prosecuted with her characteristic ardour! We hope to have a *notice* given on the very first day of the session that, on a certain day then to be announced, a *Motion* will be made for leave to bring in our Bill. On that motion we, many of us, think the fate of our country will depend. That the evil genius of procrastinators may not lull Ireland into a fatal repose until it be too late is the devout prayer of

Sir your most obed. Svt.
J. Cartwright

P.S. A strong committee of the Hampden Club[3] (of which the

Lord Mayor is a member) join in the application for the meeting at the Mansion House.

SOURCE : Fitz-Simon Papers

1   Matthew Wood (1768-1843), lord mayor of London, 1816 and 1817; M.P. for London city, 1817-43; created baronet, 1838. Grandfather of Katharine Wood, wife of Capt. W. H. O'Shea, M.P., and later of Charles Stewart Parnell, M.P. See *DNB*.
2   Unidentified.
3   A political society in London whose aim was parliamentary reform. During the winter of 1816-17 many local Hampden clubs were organized throughout the country.

679

From Myles McSwiney to Merrion Square

Carhen, 25 December 1816

My Dear Dan,

Your poor mother still holds out, in fact she is somewhat relieved for the last two days though she was very ill since I wrote to you. She cannot lie down on the bed but is supported sitting in the bed day and night and takes very little drink. It is impossible to say how long she may linger in this state, but I regret to say any hopes of recovery must be given up. She is quite collected and resigned to her situation, and *very, very* often since her illness has she in the most solemn manner left her blessing to you and all your family. I enclose you a receipt sent here some time back by your uncle[1] to be forwarded to you relative to the statutes[2] to be had from Grierson[3] etc. . . .

SOURCE : O'Connell Papers, NLI 13646

1   Hunting-Cap.
2   Parliamentary statutes.
3   George Grierson, 28 Parliament Street, Dublin, king's printer. His former country house, an exceedingly fine Georgian mansion, is now part of Loreto Abbey, Rathfarnham, Co. Dublin, a convent boarding school.

680

From John Cartwright to Merrion Square

[postmarked 4 January 1817]

Sir,

Being enabled to report that the most energetic exertions are making in the populous parts of both England and

Scotland in the cause of a radical parliamentary reform, as well as a rapid increase of activity in the other parts of this island in that great work of national salvation, leaving not a doubt of complete success at *one* effort provided Ireland from her 1446 parishes shall timely pour in her petitions by hundreds. Allow me to express a hope that your exertions to that end will not be wanting. By native gentlemen I am taught to understand that if this work be taken up by the clergy of the Roman Catholic persuasion in particular, it may be effected with great dispatch.

P.S. In the Bill[1] that is preparing it is proposed that England shall lose 45 representatives and Ireland gain 27.

SOURCE : O'Connell MSS, UCD

1 The bill which Sir Francis Burdett had been requested to draft by delegates of the Hampden clubs meeting in London in January 1817, a few days before the opening of parliament (Melville W. Patterson, *Sir Francis Burdett and His Times* (1770-1844), 2 vols. [London 1931], II, 417; *DEP*, 25 Jan. 1817). On 20 May 1817 Burdett's motion that a select committee be appointed to consider the state of the English representation was defeated 265 to 277.

681

From John Hancock to Merrion Square

Lisburn, 5 February 1817

My dear Friend,

My silence is not so long as thou seems to suppose. I wrote to thee about two months ago to object to a paragraph which appeared to have crept inadvertently into the columns of the *Dublin Chronicle*.

I would have replied sooner to thy letter of 24th ult. if I had not waited in hopes of giving some better account of the cause of reform in Belfast. I almost despaired but still I endeavoured to hope, but now I fear my despair will be confirmed. As usual there was much talk and that inert consultation which has so direct a tendency to perplex counsel by timidity and indecision. The timid increase their fears and infect others with the debasing contagion. A requisition was presented to the Sovereign of the town. This was a useless formality. He refused, and here I find the matter rests. I was ready to attend if the call was worded so as not to exclude non-residents. Few or none of the commercial aristocracy would have attended: probably few even of the middling classes, so broken down by the influence of the petty tyrants, the bankers and the pressure of the times is the state of public spirit. But I expect thousands of the working classes would have attended and to them the business ought to have been trusted in the default of others. I am a decided democrat.

A sketch of a petition and resolution had been prepared by Dr. Drennan.[1] To these I agreed with one or two alterations which I pointed out; I also drew up 3 additional resolutions which I designed to propose. The first entered into the causes of the distress affecting all classes of the community both rich and poor in one common calamity from enormous taxation and an expensive government, and pointing out the tendency of revenue and stamp laws to lead to despotism by their vexatious operations. My second went to give a pledge on the part of reformers in favour of unconditional Catholic Emancipation on principle, contrasted with Lord Castlereagh's bargain for the barter of privilege for additional subjugation of the Catholic mind; and 3dly a vote of thanks to Major Cartwright. I did not hear of any objections to my resolutions but the matter appears likely to fall more from apathy than any other cause. We have neither wind nor tide to advance reform. I hear some now say it is useless to apply to Parliament in its present temper. Thus fears increase and produce evasions.

From the foregoing observations thou may perceive there is no probability even *now* of procuring a reform club in Belfast. How goes on the one in Dublin? I wish to know the terms of becoming a member and if you admit from other parts of Ireland besides Dublin.[2]

Ministry are thoroughly alarmed and both they and their adherents and the Whigs appear inclined to make a common cause against thorough reformers. They hold a high language in Parliament approaching to treason against their sovereign lords, the people. The most will be attempted to be made of the stones thrown at the coach of the Regent. I think no bullets were used and it will be difficult to get up a second act of Le Maitre's pop-gun plot.[3] If the people know their duties and coolly but determinedly assert their rights, the idols of power, which a political superstition has set up, must fall before the authority of reason. . . .

[P.S.] In this town the influence of the landlord, the Marquis of Hertford,[4] with the trained bands of Orangemen prevents all idea of a public meeting. In Belfast a large majority of the working classes are on the right side. Since I wrote the foregoing letter I find by an advertisement in today's *Belfast Chronicle* a call for a public meeting in that town on the 13th.[5] So far as a call goes, I own myself mistaken in my foregoing forebodings. Whether public spirit will really and effectually arise from the dead on this occasion remains to be seen. I still anticipate and fear half measures.

SOURCE : O'Connell Papers, NLI 13647

1 William Drennan (1754-1820), Belfast physician, United Irishman; tried for sedition and acquitted, 1794; poet; founded the *Belfast Magazine*, 1808. See *DNB*.

2 Some agitation in favour of parliamentary reform was at this time being carried on in Cork and Dublin (*DEP*, 9, 14 Jan.; 6, 13 Feb. 1817). The ' Friends of Reform ' were founded on 13 January 1817 at a meeting in Dublin (*DEP*, 14 Jan. 1817). This organization was designed to prepare petitions and disseminate information on parliamentary reform (*DEP*, 1 Feb. 1817). Members paid five shillings per annum plus tenpence per week (*DEP*, 14 Jan. 1817). O'Connell attended its meetings which were ' select rather than numerous ' (*DEP*, 28 Jan. 1817), about forty persons attending its second dinner (*DEP*, 1 Feb. 1817).

3 A reference to the alleged attempt on the life of the Prince Regent on 29 January 1817, when two shots from an air-gun are said to have been fired through the window of his carriage (*Annual Register*, 1817, p. 3).

4 Francis (Seymour-Conway), second marquis of Hertford (1742/3-1822); lord chamberlain, 1812-21.

5 This meeting was held at the Brown Linen Hall, Belfast, on 13 February 1817 under the chairmanship of Dr. Tennent (*DEP*, 15, 20 Feb. 1817). Resolutions were passed in favour of parliamentary reform and petitions to the House of Commons and Prince Regent prepared for ' a pure and uncorrupted House of Commons, fairly, freely and frequently chosen ' (*DEP*, 22 Feb. 1817).

682

From his brother James to Merrion Square

Cork, 8 February 1817

My dear Dan,

I yesterday received a letter from John Hickson, in which he has the kindness to say that he will, at any time he is paid his principal sum of £3,600 and the proportion of the gale then due, without *further notice,* give up the annuity. By my letter to you of the 2d inst. you are aware that John[1] and I *as trustees* for the General[2] must get a regular assignment of that annuity before we can pay the money, so that the sooner this is done the better as exchange is now up to 11½ per cent and the money unproductive in the Bankers' hands in London. I have this day written to John either to come to Cork himself or to send me bills on Coutts and Co. for £3,600 in order that I may get money for them here to pay John Hickson, the General's money being lodged in Coutts Bank to *John's credit* and, letters having passed between him and *that House,* he is of course the only person they know in the transaction. I therefore think you ought on receipt of this write to John to Grenagh and say how this annuity is to be conveyed over to *him* and *me* as *trustees* for the General. John will, I presume, feel himself bound to lay the deed before Stephen Rice as counsel for *our uncle.* In your letter to me be also very particular in saying how this business is to be arranged as it is probable John may come to Cork tomorrow or the day after. . . .

SOURCE : Fitz-Simon Papers
1   His brother John.
2   His uncle Count O'Connell.

682a

To Rev. William O'Brien,[1] P.P., Doneraile

Merrion Square, 13 February 1817

My dear friend,

The day after I got your letter the melancholy account of the death of my beloved mother reached me. This will I am sure excuse me to you for not sooner replying.

I solemnly assure you that I did not receive the former letter to which you allude. If I had it should certainly have been answered.

I write this day to Morty O'Sullivan[2] about your annuity and I promise you that if he does not pay you at the Cork assizes *that I will.* Write me a line there by the third day of *the county* assizes saying where your receipt will be and it shall be taken up.

I am surprised you should think that any account respecting your health would be uninteresting to me. This is not kind towards one who has always respected and regarded you as one of his oldest and most esteemed friends. Believe me that it gives me sincere pleasure to hear that Morty O'Sullivan will have a prospect of paying your annuity for many, many long years. I trust in God I shall yet obtain receipts for that annuity under an episcopal seal; and I congratulate you personally on the prospect we now have of dispersing the Vetoists for ever. They are become an object of ridicule and contempt, and if the blow be followed up by clergy and laity we shall be rid of all similar attempts for ever.

SOURCE : NLI, MSS 17070

1 Rev. Dr. William O'Brien, parish priest of Doneraile, 1815-34.
2 Morty O'Sullivan (died 1 June 1825), a cousin of O'Connell; son of John O'Sullivan (died c. 1796), Coulagh, Eyries, Berehaven, Co. Cork. Married first Mary (died 1822), daughter of Roger O'Sullivan of Garnish; second, Ellen O'Sullivan on 11 April 1823. A popular magistrate and noted smuggler.

683

From his brother James to Merrion Square

Carhen, 1 March 1817

My Dear Dan,

It was only yesterday I received your letter of the 13th ult. and candidly confess that the statement of the bills of yours still undischarged on account of O'Leary's business has astonished me, for I flattered myself that the large sums you got in December 1815 and in February 1816 together with your dividend of this *fiend's estates* had ere now rid you of all demands on O'Leary's account. . . . I am well aware that if you cannot procure at least £1,500, it is impossible for you to wade through all those bills that must be *paid to the hour*. John and I have promised to lend Lord Ventry[1] £6,400, the balance of the General's[2] money after redeeming Hickson's[3] annuity. In fact I believe John has before now given Lord Ventry this money but in any event nothing can be done until the Tralee assizes and then when *we all* meet, we can see what is to be done. You know John and I are but trustees for the General and we cannot think of disposing of one guinea of his property without his consent. But in the event of our advancing the £1,800, how in the name of wonder could you secure the principal sum to the representatives of the General? Surely you are strict tenant for life and even if you were not, all the property you got in right of your father would not now, if sold out, do more than pay the enormous debt you owe. As to professional resources, if you are by the receipts of your profession able to support your family, it will be doing wonders. It is quite impossible you can do so if you do not put some restraint on your *own personal expenses,* which I know from what occurred when last you were in Iveragh, are to a man circumstanced as you are, ruinously heavy. You have in this letter a statement of *debts I know you owe* and of course there are many more I can know nothing about but the bare interest of those I made will absorb the entire of your landed property and scarce leave a guinea to the paying of the principal. My dearest fellow, what do you mean by saying that in two years the far greater part of your debts will be discharged? Surely, when you speak in this way, you are not aware of the magnitude of them. . . .

Debts due of D. O'Connell Esq

To the General [Count O'Connell]	3,600
To Counsellor Scully lent you in December 1815	2,274
A balance due of you to the representatives of Mrs White[4] of Limerick	1,200
Due of you of O'Leary's Bills out	1,945
Due of you in Iveragh to common men in *all at least*	3,000
Due to Charles Sugrue	950
Due to Counsellor Finn at least	800
Due to John Primrose	600
Due to Collins Dumas	500
Due to Widow Connor,[5] Killarney	500
To Peter Hussey[6]	500
To George Hickson,[7] Fermoy [le]	500
To the representatives of Mrs. Tuohy[8]	500
To your sister Ellen	300
To Humphrey Moynihan's family	200
To Dan O'Sullivan, Reendonegan	200
To money due of you to Maurice, my uncle's clerk[9]	130

£17,699

To Jerry Mahony 16th Foot   300
Due to my mother, now to Honora Sullivan
    [wife of Dan O'Sullivan of Reendonegan]   100
Due to Terry O'Brien, Attorney, Limerick   200
Colonel Crosbie's[10] bond given you by Rick O'Connell   400
                            ————
                         £18,699

In addition to the above enormous debt of eighteen thousand, six hundred and ninety-nine pounds I [? know] you borrowed from Mr. Hartnet of Maunsel and Kennedy's Bank[11] in Limerick in November 1815 five hundred pounds and which I presume is not yet paid . . . so that rating the entire of your debts at twenty thousand pounds I fear a very low estimate. . . .

SOURCE : O'Connell MSS, UCD
1 Thomas (Mullins), first Baron Ventry (1736-1824), Burnham, Dingle, Co. Kerry.
2 His uncle Count O'Connell.
3 John Hickson, College Green, Dublin.
4 Unidentified.
5 Unidentified.
6 Peter Bodkin Hussey.
7 George Hickson, Fermoyle, Co. Kerry.
8 Unidentified.
9 Unidentified.
10 Col. James Crosbie.
11 This bank was opened in 1789 but failed in 1820. In that period there were several alterations in partnership. It began with the partnership of Thomas Maunsell, Robert Maunsell, Sir Matthew Blakiston, Bart., Thomas Brooke and Richard Maunsell; and ended with the partnership of George Maunsell, John Kennedy and Robert Maunsell.

684

To Mathias Joseph O'Kelly,[1] 147 James' St., Dublin

Merrion Square, 5 March 1817

My dear O'Kelly,

I hereby undertake in consideration of your having become security for the *Dublin Chronicle*[2] at the Stamp Office at my

request to indemnify and save you harmless from any loss
whatsoever on account of such security.[3]

SOURCE : Fitz-Simon Papers

1 Mathias Joseph O'Kelly (1786-1868), son of Joseph O'Kelly, Co.
   Kildare. Later secretary to the Dublin cemetries committee.
2 Eneas MacDonnell's pro-Emancipation newspaper (see letter 559,
   note 1).
3 See letter 694.

685

To his wife, Merrion Square

[postmarked Ennis, 12 March 1817]

My darling Love,
   . . . There is a heavy dock, indeed a very heavy assizes at
the Crown side but very little in the record court, only six
records. I need scarcely say that I am engaged in them all.
I have, darling, changed my lodgings much for the better
and am very comfortably circumstanced in my new habitation.
I think I am in the very snuggest lodgings in Ennis. . . .

SOURCE : Fitz-Simon Papers

686

From his wife, to be forwarded by Charles O'Connell, Esqre., Ennis

[Dublin] 13 March [1817]

My dearest love,
   I know I need not make an apology for not writing to
you yesterday as Ellen[1] in her letter explained the reason why
I deputed her. It was a great indulgence to my poor Ellen,
and saucy Kate declares she must write to you very soon as
she longs very much to sign her name. I heard yesterday from
our dear boys. Maurice had not got the books and other articles
you sent to him but I presume before this they are arrived.
The poor fellows write in good spirits though much disappointed that you could not give them a call. However I
have promised on your return from circuit that we shall *all*

pay them a visit. Your going down specially to Galway is announced in this morning's *Freeman*.[2] You are attacked in the two last *Carricks* respecting the House of Industry.[3] I never read such ill-written trash and I regret exceedingly that the *Chronicle* took any notice of it and I am quite convinced, were you here, you would not allow it. Bric ought, I think, be more cautious how he writes and you ought to advise him on the subject. Your *friend*, Mr. L'Estrange, is the subject of every company in consequence of a *sermon* he delivered from the altar last Sunday, began by abusing Government, the ministers, the deputies from the Vetoists who are at present in Rome and he concluded by attacking the gentlemen who go to the side seats in Clarendon St. ' They go,' he said, ' for no other purpose than to admire the ladies, and let the ladies take care if they do not encourage *them*.' I hope what he did say was exaggerated. I was not at Clarendon Street on Sunday which indeed I do not regret. I hear Doctor Murray is quite displeased with him. Would to God you had not given him that letter from Mr. Hay. The altar at all events was no place for him to introduce politics. To please me, he is too fond of politics everywhere. . . . I expect to hear the horses will be taken from your carriage when you get near Galway. . . .

SOURCE : O'Connell Papers, NLI 13651

1   Their eldest daughter.

2   The *Freeman's Journal* announced that O'Connell was going to Galway for the assizes (*FJ*, 13 Mar. 1817).

3   At a Catholic meeting on 6 March 1817 Nicholas Mahon asserted that several Catholic ladies who had been in the habit of visiting the house of industry in Dublin for the purpose of catechizing the Catholic children there, had recently been refused admission by the governors (*DEP*, 8 Mar. 1817). The *Dublin Evening Post* claimed that the governors had resolved at a recent meeting to take this step ' in consequence of the great growth of Popery . . .' in the institution (*DEP*, 8 Mar. 1817). O'Connell had a resolution passed at the Catholic meeting stating that should the truth of Mahon's statements be ascertained, arrangements should be made to have the case raised in parliament (*DEP*, 8 Mar. 1817). *Carrick's Morning Post* expressed doubts as to the veracity of the statement made by Mahon and the *Dublin Evening Post* and questioned the wisdom of airing the case at a Catholic meeting (*CMP*, 10 Mar. 1817). It attacked O'Connell mainly on the grounds that he had criticized the viceroy at this meeting (*CMP*, 10, 11 Mar. 1817).

687

From his wife, Dublin, 19 March 1817, to Limerick

'Write to me when you arrive at Galway. I shall be so anxious to hear of your reception in that town. Was it you wrote the letter from Ennis to the *Chronicle*?'

SOURCE : O'Connell Papers, NLI 13651

688

To his wife, Merrion Square

Galway, 25 March 1817

My darling Love,

 . . . I have, darling, been quite successful here—got verdicts in both the causes which brought me. The first was for land and involved a good deal of law. I flatter myself that the good folks of Galway think I know a little on that subject. This may be vanity but I really do think I have made some character. I have also had the pleasure of concurring in procuring success for the widow Wilkins.[1] Philips[2] stated her case[3] in the most amusing and brilliant speech I ever heard. It was a most delightful exhibition. He had the court in a roar of laughter. I was just stepping into a chaise when another client appeared and handed me twenty-five guineas with another brief. I am therefore resolved to stay here for that cause also.

There was some attempt made to get up a dinner for me here but the poor slaves failed in getting any *sufficient* chairman as the great folks were too cold or too prudent to take a part in it.

Amidst my great professional triumph—for, darling, I have *triumphed*—I feel lonely and miserable at not having had a line from you, my *own, own* heart's dearest, tenderest treasure. . . .

SOURCE : Fitz-Simon Papers
1 Unidentified.
2 Charles Phillips.
3 Unidentified.

689

From his daughter Ellen to Tralee, c/o James Connor

Merrion Square, 27 March 1817

My dear Father,

Your expressions of pleasure at receiving a letter from me induced me to beg Mama's permission to write to you again though I don't think it is quite considerate of me to deprive you of a *sensible* letter from Mama by my *silly scribble.* I assure you, Kate is not a little vain of the letter she received from you. I am quite tired of looking at her *kissing* and *hugging* it. She even carries it with her to bed every night. . . .

SOURCE : Fitz-Simon Papers

690

To his wife, Merrion Square

Limerick, 29 March 1817, Saturday

[No salutation]

. . . I left Galway about five yesterday, slept at Gort last night and have come in here near forty miles before *this hour,* not yet one, and am dashing on to Tralee.

Darling heart, I succeeded in every cause in Galway.[1] Have left it in complete triumph and worked myself into an invitation to a public dinner by really not caring about the matter. You will see my reply in the *Chronicle*[2] and I may, sweetest, tell you without vanity that I made an impression in Galway as a working *tradesman.*

Darling, there will be a bill of mine due on Tuesday for £127. . . .

SOURCE : Fitz-Simon Papers

1 Only one of these has been identified. On 20 and 21 March 1817 O'Connell was counsel for the representatives and widow of one Roger O'Connor in an action to recover the amount of accounts for goods sold and delivered to Henry Kirwan, Esq., of Castletown-hackett. A verdict was found for the plaintiffs 'much to the satisfaction of all present' (*FJ,* 2 April 1817).

2 On 29 March 1817 O'Connell was invited to a public dinner in Galway by a deputation from the town headed by Major Anthony

James McDermott of Ramore. O'Connell declined the invitation
due to pressure of professional business. His reply expressed anti-
Orange and non-sectarian political principles (*FJ*, 2 April 1817,
quoting *Galway Chronicle*).

691

From his wife to Parade, Cork

2 April 1817

My own dearest Love,

. . . I am quite pleased with your answer to the
Galway gentlemen. The answer, together with the invitation,
appeared in this day's *Freeman* taken from the *Galway
Chronicle*.[1] . . .

Never was Dublin so high as at this moment as to bread and
potatoes. I don't know when *they* mean to stop raising their
price. Meat and butter are uncommonly high. It requires a
good fortune to live *now* in Dublin. . . .

SOURCE : O'Connell Papers, NLI 13651
1 See letter 690.

692

From his wife to Cork

[Dublin] 9 April 1817

My dearest love,

. . . I will lay my positive *commands* upon you not to go
in a *steam*boat while in Cork. I read this morning a melancholy accident which occurred in England by the bursting
of the steam boiler in one of these packets. I cannot help
feeling uneasy lest my letter may not arrive time enough to
prevent you from taking your favourite trip in a steamboat,
but as business, I know, prevents you from writing, *it* will also
keep you at home and *thus* I comfort myself. The briefs are
already coming in. . . .

SOURCE : O'Connell Papers, NLI 13651

142

693

From his wife to Cork

[Dublin] 11 April 1817

My dearest Love,

I wish to God you could contrive to get out of court for a quarter of an hour during the middle of the day to take a bowl of soup or a snack of some kind. Surely, though you may not be able to spare time to go to a tavern, could not James[1] get anything you wished for from the Bar mess at your lodgings, which is merely a *step* from the Court-house? Do, my love, try to accomplish *this* for really I am quite unhappy to have you fasting from an early hour in the morning until nine or ten o'clock at night. I wish I was with you to make you take care of yourself. I am quite sure there is not another barrister on your circuit would go through half the fatigue you do without taking necessary nourishment. If you dislike taking soup or cold meat, can't you take jelly? Do, darling, take something for my *sake*.

I sent a message to the *Chronicle* office by Roger[2] about the Kerry meeting. I was this day greatly amused with a *sketch* of *it* in the Cork paper. What a ridiculous fool Bobby Hurley[3] made of himself. I was greatly delighted with your remarks on *his loyalty*. It seems to me that the very *loyal* people wished only for a meeting of *their* own. They considered themselves of sufficient consequence and quite competent to express the sense of the county but, thank God, there are *some* to keep them *down*. I am all impatience to read the full report of *this* meeting.[4] . . .

SOURCE : O'Connell Papers, NLI 13651
1 His servant.
2 Roger O'Sullivan.
3 Rev. Robert Conway Hurly (1785-1849), High Street, Tralee; ordained, 1811; vicar of Kildrum, Co. Kerry, 1823-33; of Killiney, Co. Kerry, 1833-49.
4 A meeting of the gentlemen, clergy and freeholders of Kerry held in Tralee on 31 March 1817 at which an address was voted to the Prince Regent expressive of horror at the recent assault upon his person (*CMC*, 9, 11 April 1817). An altercation arose when Parson Hurly proposed that the meeting adjourn to enable the grand jury to attend. O'Connell, who had had some difficulty in persuading the high sheriff to take the chair, opposed the adjourn-

ment, declaring the meeting was already sufficiently respectable, and that he himself ' possessed a greater stake in the county, than many of the grand jury, and as great a stake as most of the rest ' (*CMC*, 9 April 1817). A full report of the meeting is not available.

694

From his wife to Cork

12 April [postmarked 1817]

My dearest Love,

. . . A notice came here from the Stamp Office last night informing you there was two months duty due at the Stamp Office by MacDonnell[1] and calling on you as one of the *security* to pay it. Should it be necessary for you to write to the office, the letter I got is signed R. Malins.[2] . . .

SOURCE : O'Connell Papers, NLI 13651
1 Eneas MacDonnell, editor of the *Dublin Chronicle*. See letter 684.
2 Richard Malins, 54 Prussia Street, Dublin, and Stamp Office.

695

To his wife, Merrion Square

Cork, 15 April 1817

My dearest Mary,

You excuse the infrequency of my writing when the Cork assizes are drawing to a close because the judges then always make an effort to terminate the business by an excess of hurry. Darling, it is now eight o'clock and Judge Mayne is still sitting. All the civil business is over even to the civil bill appeals, but Mayne has at least two days more of criminal business so that at worst, darling, I will be with you on Sunday at the very latest. To be sure, this assizes has lasted already half a century. It looks amazingly tedious when I look back though I did not feel the hours or days pass. I was in fact too busy to have leisure to mind anything but my trade.

Darling, in spite of all my labours I never was in better health or spirits. Do not be uneasy about my not eating in the middle of the day. The fact is I am grown too fat and should be quite a monster if I were to sit about devouring midday *meals* as you suggest to me, darling. You are fond of ruling me even in absence. You order me at once out of steamboats and into cook shops. Now the fact is that I like steamboats much and hate cook shops excessively. So darling, darling, sweetest love, let us compromise our quarrel and have neither the one nor the other. . . .

SOURCE : Fitz-Simon Papers

696

From his brother James to Merrion Square

Tralee, 18 May 1817

My dear Dan,

I delayed answering your letter of the 7th inst. until my Uncle Maurice and I came here when I expected to be able to give you a satisfactory account of the nature of his complaint. . . .

Need I tell you how sincerely I regret the necessity of your dear Mary's going to Bristol. God grant the waters may have the desired effect. . . . My Uncle Maurice desires me tell you your boys will be quite welcome to Derrynane. . . . I could not attempt to do anything for you with respect to getting a few hundreds to pay the expense of going to Bristol. *I gave strong hints* but have not succeeded. . . .

SOURCE : O'Connell MSS, UCD

697

To his wife, York Crescent, Clifton, via Bristol

Holylands Coffee Room, Strand, London, 31 May 1817

My darling Heart,

I arrived here about an hour ago after a very pleasant journey with a stupid companion and the *Quarterly Review*, but I feel very very lonely away from all that my heart prizes upon earth. It is an age since I heard of my *Irish* boys and my girls and you, sweetest and dearest love, are separated from me, God knows how long, but it is for the benefit of your health and anything that contributes to that cannot be irksome to me. Yet I really cannot get over the sensation of loneliness. Write to me, darling, every day till Thursday inclusive as I shall not leave this till after post hour on Friday. Tell me that you are getting daily stronger and stronger and give me news of my poor little boy Dan.

SOURCE : Fitz-Simon Papers

698

To his wife, York Crescent, Clifton

Holylands [Coffee House], Strand [London], 4 June 1817

My darling Love,

. . . Darling, I am a great rake and heartily tired of my raking life. I was at Drury Lane on Saturday. On Monday at Covent Gardens, yesterday at the opera and this night I go to Vauxhall after the popish dinner is over. Heart's love, this life would soon weary me, yet, being here and having nothing to do, I cannot keep myself from seeing whatever is to be seen.

Darling, I am just come in from my attornies. Do not be one bit uneasy about my recognizances.[1] You may well rely on it they will be just as you wish.

SOURCE : Fitz-Simon Papers

1 O'Connell appeared before the English court of King's Bench on 5 June 1817 to procure the discharge of his recognizances to keep the peace, following his attempted duel with Peel in 1815 (*Dublin Chronicle*, 11 June 1817).

699

To his wife, 2 Rodney Place, Clifton, 7 June 1817, from Enstone, near Oxford

' I was detained by twenty people yesterday evening in London till it was too late to leave town without risk.'

SOURCE : Fitz-Simon Papers

700

To his wife, No. 2 Rodney Place, Clifton, near Bristol

Holyhead, 10 June 1817

My darling Mary,

. . . The truth is, my heart *wants* you and my girls and boys in order to *fill* it. But, darling, I consider no *sacrifice* of any value when compared to the advantage of taking care of your health. Do, my sweetest Mary, promise me that you will be quite candid with me on this subject. Do, my own darling, give me your solemn promise that you will tell me the exact truth. You *never deceived* me save about your health and it now, I may say, corrodes my soul to think that you may still imagine you were doing me a kindness by concealing from me the exact state of your health. I do therefore require a solemn promise. Besides, darling, it would be so easy to try the south of France. The expense of the journey would now be just nothing for you would save it in one month. You could live perfectly well on five guineas a week in France. I would send my brother James instantly to accompany you there, and I would next spring, when every past transaction with others was completely forgotten (so that *even you* could not be alarmed), go for you myself, or if it was more *quieting* to your mind, meet you in England. I know I need not repeat my request to you to be candid. If you comply—as I am sure you will—you shall command, darling. Have you not always commanded every movement of mine?

I believe I gave you but an imperfect account of my London visit. On the Saturday of my arrival there I went to see Kean[1] at Drury Lane. It was a novelty to me to be quite alone and quite unknown in the crowd there. I do not *so* much admire Kean. He played Bertram. There was but once a burst to justify his fame. He certainly owes much of his success to a strange singularity of manner. On Sunday I was waited on by many English Catholics, amongst the first by Charles Butler. I returned his visit at his request instantly and was by him introduced to a great number of *their* Board. The Duke of Norfolk,[2] Sir John Trogmorton [*sic*],[3] Sir Harry Engliford [*sic*],[4] etc. I waited on Lord Fingall with Mr. Blake,[5] an Anglo-Irish lawyer who has been indeed very attentive to me. Lord Fingall had much conversation with me and punctually returned my visit but, as a *great secret,* I mention

to you that I do *not* think he will come back to the Catholics.
I will, however, try when I get to Dublin. On Monday I
attended the English Catholic Board as I before told you and
went that night to Covent Garden with Coppinger—Stephen[6]
—of Leemount. I saw Kemble[7] in *Cardinal Wolsey* for the
last time. On Tuesday I went to the House of Lords and
afterwards to the Opera with a Limerick lady and her husband, Col. Smith.[8] She was a Miss Dodd[9] and kept a school
in Limerick. With her I met *a flame* of mine, a Miss
Finucane.[10] So, darling, you ought to be quite jealous. They
are gone to France. On Wednesday I visited Major Cartwright
and Curran and the Duke of Sussex. I did not see the latter.
I was that day splendidly entertained by Blake at his house
with a large party of English Catholics of the first rank. And
the next day Lord Fingall and I were entertained in a similar
party at the Thatched House Tavern in St. James Street—
with that name it is one of the first taverns in the world. Our
feast was turtle—turbot, champagne, etc. On Thursday I had
to settle with my lawyer and attorney and paid and received
many visits. I could not tell you the lords and commoners to
whom I was introduced nor the attention I met with. Besides,
the truth is—and I would not say it to another human being
but you—I felt in our conversations that it was not difficult
to exceed in intellect and sound views men of high names.
I had, however, a great loss in not having seen Mr.
Brougham[11] who was too ill to be able to receive me. He, in
my judgement, is the very first man in England. Darling,
do not smile at my vanity, but your credulity with respect to
anything in my favour will easily make you believe that I
felt how cruel the Penal Laws are which exclude me from a
fair trial with men whom *I look on* as so much my inferiors,
but of this, darling, enough.

I saw the English Bar, darling, in its strength and be
assured, heart, they are just nothing to the Irish Bar. I felt
that easily and strongly. I spent almost the entire day on
Friday in the King's Bench and left my card for Sir Francis
Burdett after I came away from court that afternoon. The
diary of my journey is short. I came on Saturday to Stratford-
on-Avon, the birthplace of Shakespeare, 93 miles. The next
day to Llangollen and yesterday here. . . . As I am on the
vain topics, darling, you do not know that I shall fancy myself young and well looking. I will make you laugh, sweetest,
when we meet if you will remind me—*of the musician's wife*

—I will indeed and you will acknowledge I think that your husband, your doating husband, can be faithful even in temptation. Think, sweetest, of an old fellow of my kind having occasion to make this boast. I will make you smile at the story. Remind me of it, heart's treasure.

Sir Edward O'Brien[12] and his family are here. He has just paid me a visit of an hour. Darling, tell my Nell, and my Kate and my Bet how I love them. Tell my sweet John that he is my heart's darling. Tell them all that language does not contain words strong enough to convey the effusions of their father's heart and as to yourself, sweetest, how is it possible to say with what excess of tenderness and truth you are doated of by

Your fondest and most faithful

Daniel O'Connell

[P.S.] . . .

SOURCE : Fitz-Simon Papers

1   Edmund Kean (1787-1833), the celebrated Shakespearean actor. See *DNB*.

2   Bernard Edward (Howard), twelfth duke of Norfolk (1765-1842). See *DNB*.

3   Sir John Courtenay Throckmorton, fifth baronet (1753-1819), member of the English Catholic Board from 1808.

4   *Recte* Sir Henry Charles Englefield, seventh baronet (1752-1822), antiquary and scientific writer. See *DNB*.

5   Anthony Richard Blake (1786-1849), youngest son of Martin Blake, Hollypark, Co. Galway. Though a Catholic he was a member of the administration of Marquis Wellesley who appointed him chief remembrancer, 1823; described by a contemporary as ' the back-stairs Viceroy of Ireland '; author of *Thoughts upon the Catholic Question* (1828).

6   Stephen Coppinger (1795-1858), son of Thomas Stephen Coppinger, Leemount, Co. Cork; called to the bar, 1818.

7   John Philip Kemble (1757-1823), the well-known Shakespearean actor and manager of Covent Garden. See *DNB*.

8   Unidentified.

9   Unidentified.

10 Unidentified.

11 Henry Peter Brougham (1778-1868), Whig-radical; lord chancellor, 1830-34; created Baron Brougham and Vaux, 1830. See *DNB*.

12 Sir Edward O'Brien, fourth baronet (1773-1837), Dromoland, Co. Clare. M.P. for Ennis, 1795-1800; Co. Clare, 1802-26.

701

From his wife to Dublin

[postmarked 12 June 1817]

My own darling Love,

. . . Every hour, darling, I feel a change for the better.
Really the exertion I am obliged to make here is of infinite
use to me. The quiet, still life I lead at home cannot be con-
ducive to my health. Here I am obliged to be my own housekeeper with the assistance of Hanna[1] who is certain most
attentive. I am really quite surprised she gets on so well, her
memory so different from what it was at home. Having
something to think of and a good deal to do is equally as good
for her memory as it is for my health. I wish you could have
seen me yesterday setting off to market to Bristol in a donkey
gig with Betsey and John, Miss G.[2] and the girls walking by
the side of the *donkey*. On getting to town I discharged the
gig, paying a shilling, and sallied forth to the market where I
think I made for my first time some *bargains*. The best meat
is sold at Bristol for sixpence English a pound. Irish butter
so very good. Ducks three shillings a couple. Chickens half
crown. Vegetables much cheaper than in Dublin. Bread exceedingly good and cheaper than when I left home. Potatoes
are not so cheap as in Dublin but they are very good and the
best milk for three pence a quart. After sending Hanna home
with the marketing, Miss G. the children and myself went
to execute commissions and will you believe it *possible* that I
should be walking from 11 in the morning until four in the
evening without once sitting down except a few moments
in a shop. I was really surprised at myself and this morning
I feel as well, nay better, than if I had not walked half so
much. . . .

I returned the priest's visit on Tuesday. He is rather a
gentlemanly man, reserved in his manner and very handsome. I am to pay by the month for our accommodation at
the chapel. . . .

We see Captain O'Connell[3] every day. We met him yesterday in Bristol and he accompanied us home in a hackney
coach. He is most anxious to hear from you. He seems to
have a very general acquaintance in this neighbourhood.

Tomorrow I commence drinking the waters. The delicacy
of my eyes confined me a good deal but now they are almost

quite well. And how, darling, do you feel? I often think,
lonely enough. It is a new thing to you to be at home without
your family but I hope this time will be the last we shall be
so long separated. If I continue to improve in health as I
have since I came here, a journey to France will be unnecessary until the time arrives when it will be an advantage to
my boys and girls to spend some time in France. Then,
darling, you will be on the Bench and a *little* more your own
master than you are at present. . . . I beg of you, love, to
lock up my letters even at home. I do not like to have them
left in open drawers or on your writing table. . . . John is
very busy reading *Lalla Rookh*.[4] He admires it very much.
He says, 'When you come here you must sleep with Miss
G[aghran] and Ellen as their bed is larger than the one he
and I sleep in.' . . .

SOURCE : O'Connell Papers, NLI 13651
1 A maidservant.
2 Miss Gaghran, governess.
3 *Recte* Lieut. John O'Connell (died Feb. 1826), 67th Regiment, half-
   pay, 1816. Joined 7th Veteran Battalion, 1820.
4 Thomas Moore's poem, published 1817.

702

*To his wife, 2 Rodney Place, Clifton, near Bristol,
13 June 1817, from Merrion Square*

' I am . . . in this dismal, lonely barrack where the voice
of my own true love and of my children used to cheer me.'

SOURCE : Fitz-Simon Papers

703

To his wife, 2 Rodney Place, Clifton, near Bristol

Merrion Square, Wednesday, 18 June 1817
My darling Love,
   . . . Of public news there are none. The rioters are all
at peace, provisions very dear but no alarm, every effort making to procure more food and the prospect of the harvest
extremely good.[1] Indeed nothing can be better. So much,
darling, for public and private news.

Now let me thank you heart for your affectionate letter. I take it to bed with me and sleep with it in my bosom. . . .

Darling, the circuits I believe will be late. I think I will take an excursion to see you before they go out. Indeed I do, darling. . . .

SOURCE : Fitz-Simon Papers

1 There had been an outbreak of disturbances due to the prevailing distress in Kerry, Clare, Waterford, Cork and Limerick (*DEP*, 12, 14 June 1817). The lord-lieutenant issued a proclamation on 10 June 1817 appealing to the affluent sections of the population to refrain from the consumption of potatoes and urging them to sell their pleasure horses in order to conserve oatmeal (*Dublin Gazette*, 12 June 1817).

704

To his wife, 2 Rodney Place, Clifton, near Bristol

Merrion Square, 23 June 1817

My darling love,

I write this day at six o'clock to tell you on my sacred word of honour there is not the least ground in [the] world for your alarm. The fact simply is that I could not bring myself to write you a short letter and it has been *more than impossible* for me to write you a long one. Darling, the judges have for the first time made it a practice to sit from eleven till full five, and my being away for more than a week of term has thrown such a load on me as I certainly never before sustained. I will write a long letter to you tomorrow for my heart is restless and uneasy until I shall have disburdened it to you, sweetest love.

SOURCE : Fitz-Simon Papers

705

To his wife, 2 Rodney Place, Clifton, near Bristol

Merrion Square, 24 June 1817

[No salutation]

. . . I do not know which you will be, angry with me or laugh at me or pity me but I have been making myself very miserable about *your friend*[1] in Bristol or rather Clifton. Laugh at me, darling, it is what I deserve for being unhappy without any cause. Yet it will perhaps surprise you more when I tell you the absurdity of my reason. It was that in one of your letters you said he was very *respectful* and in another *very kind*. Now what train of thought was it that could put the word *respectful*? How could it be necessary to think of that! Thus, my own darling Mary, did I torture myself asking foolish questions—and then your consulting me about asking him to dine. Darling heart, you see what a very silly and foolish fellow your husband is, and indeed I am quite ashamed of my folly but could not get cured of it completely without thus exposing it to you. Do, darling, forgive me and I will try to forgive myself. . . .

Do you perceive that the *Freeman's Journal* is now directed in my handwriting? I get covers from the office and the paper is sent to me, and after I read it I make it up for you. . . .

I have said nothing of our Dublin riots because they were the silliest things imaginable. Women and boys plundering the bakers and a few butchers. In fact the distress and poverty is excessive but the people are as quiet as lambs and there will not be a reoccurrence even of those wretched squabbles. Judge Downes,[2] however, had half a company of riflemen to guard him. It amused me not a little to see how conscious the scoundrel was that everybody hated him. I could almost wish he had some reason to be terrified. . . .

Tell me whether you have had any attack of cold, cough or on the chest since I left you. Remember, darling, to answer this question minutely and tell me simply the truth. . . .

Forgive me, my own Mary, forgive me, my darling heart's treasure, for one passage in this letter. I would blot it out if I could but, darling, it has completely cured me to see how absurd my fears appear when written.

SOURCE : Fitz-Simon Papers

1 Capt. John O'Connell.
2 William Downes (1752-1826), justice of the king's bench, 1792; lord chief justice, 1803-22; created Baron Downes, 1822. See *DNB*.

706

To his wife, No. 3 Rodney Place, Clifton, near Bristol

Merrion Square, 29 June 1817

[No salutation]

. . . *This* instant I got your letter of the 25th. It made me
smile, darling, to find so much of it relate[d] to Capt.
O'Connell. Indeed I am angry, very angry, with myself for
what I wrote to you about him but, sweetest, the writing it
cured me by exposing to myself its absurdity.[1] Darling, I have
not written any pamphlet against or in reply to Peel though I
certainly intended to write one if I had leisure but it would
have been mild and gentlemanly in style whatever the argument might be. As to the aggregate,[2] all the causes of intemperance have gone by and it would only prolong our own
dissensions to be violent, besides, love, I easily and cheerfully
promised you not to be so. I pledge you my honour I will not
and I believe you know I never broke that pledge. . . .

Why, darling, do you not say more to me of your own
health? Are you able to walk out? *Have you had any attack
since you went to Bristol?* I underline this question in order to
get an express answer. . . .

I have Mrs. Shiel's little nephew and niece to run about the
house that I may hear the prattle and the little feet of children
going about. I sometimes take them and press them to my
heart but it does me no good and, darling, the tears come into
my eyes when I think of my own sweet ones. . . .

SOURCE : Fitz-Simon Papers
1 See letter 705.
2 A Catholic meeting which took place in Clarendon Street chapel on
3 July 1817.

707

*To his wife, 3 Rodney Place, Clifton, near Bristol, 5 July 1817,
from Merrion Square*

' This has been a busy week between the *nisi prius* trials
which, you know, detain me in court so late, and the aggregate meeting.'

SOURCE : Fitz-Simon Papers

708

To his wife, 3 Rodney Place, Clifton, near Bristol

Merrion Square, 11 [sic] July 1817 [postmarked 10 July 1817]

My darling Love,

I am not surprised you should wonder at my reply to Sir N. Conant as you did not see the rest of the correspondence. But if you had, you would easily perceive there was in it nothing to give you the slightest alarm, indeed quite the contrary, and to show you that I am convinced of that, I will put you in the way of seeing the entire. You have, love, only to inquire at the library for the file of the *Courier* newspaper, and I know they get the *Courier* at the library for I saw it there when I first subscribed for Ellen. Look out in that paper during the week after my departure from London and you will see the conversation between me and Sir N. Conant and his letter to which mine was a reply.[1] The whole will show you, what indeed I wrote to you from London, that it was impossible anything further could occur between me and Peel.[2] . . .

I will not leave this for circuit until Friday next. I then go by the canal boat to Tullamore and next day to O'Loghlen's brothers[3] in the county of Clare. . . .

I cannot avoid repeating my wish that you should spend the winter in France. I will tomorrow write to the General[4] about it. Darling, if I could see you spend one winter without illness I should quiet all my alarms for you. I will consult Dr. Leyne, however, on my arrival in Tralee. Your present change has been most propitious. I would fain make assurance doubly sure.

SOURCE : Fitz-Simon Papers

1 Sir Nathaniel Conant was the magistrate who had arrested O'Connell on his way to fight Peel in 1815. In an interview with O'Connell in London in June 1817 (see letter 698), he declared his intention of applying to have the latter's recognizances to keep the peace renewed, in view of his belief that O'Connell intended, in the event of the recognizances being discharged, to go at once to the continent with Peel to fight their delayed duel (*MC*, 9 June 1817). Conant contradicted some points in the account of the interview published in the *Morning Chronicle* from which it appeared that the authorities had been partial to Peel in the affair (Nathaniel Conant to the *Morning Chronicle*, 10 June 1817, *MC*, 11 June 1817). O'Connell claimed that the account of the interview was a true one

(O'Connell to the *Morning Chronicle*, 16 June 1817, *MC*, 25 June 1817; see also letter 588).

2   In his interview with O'Connell, according to the *Morning Chronicle*, Conant had made it clear that in the event of a fatal duel between O'Connell and Peel, the survivor would almost certainly be executed (*MC*, 9 June 1817).

3   The brothers of Michael O'Loghlen.

4   His uncle Count O'Connell.

709

From his wife to Dublin

Clifton [near Bristol], 14 July 1817

My own darling Dan,

. . . Nothing amuses Ellen and Kate more than reporting your expressions of affection for their mother who indeed feels most grateful for the manner you, my own darling, write and speak of me to our dear children. I assure you, my darling, you are our continual subject. When a kind husband or father is spoken of, Ellen and Kate will exclaim, ' Mamma, sure he is not so good a husband or father as our father?' You may guess, darling, what my reply is. You know what you deserve and you are aware that, in existence, I don't think there is such a husband and father as you are and always have been. Indeed, I think it quite impossible there could, and if the truest and tenderest affection can repay you, believe me that I feel and bear *it* for you. In truth, my own Dan, I am always at a loss for words to convey to you how I love and doat of you. Many and many a time I exclaim to myself, ' What a happy creature am I! How grateful should I be to Providence for bestowing on me such a husband!' and so indeed I am. *We* will, love, shortly be married fifteen years and I can answer that I never had cause to regret it. I have, darling, experienced all the happiness of the married state without feeling any of *its* misery, thanks to a fond and indulgent husband. . . .

You urge me to go to France for the winter. The idea of going so far from you and my boys is quite dispiriting and when I write the words the tears roll down my face. My health is not entirely so bad as to require a trip to France. My constitution will be always delicate but (as Doctor Barry of Mallow once told me) I may expect to live to a good old age. . . .

SOURCE : O'Connell Papers, NLI 13651

710

To his wife, 3 Rodney Place, Clifton, near Bristol

Merrion Square, 18 July 1817

My darling Heart,

. . . I write in the greatest hurry. I go off at four in the morning and post all the way to Limerick. I was totally unable to leave this in the Canal boat as I had proposed.

. . . Do you know that your saying nothing of your health in your two last letters alarms me not a little? You ought, my own love, to tell me in every letter the exact state of your health because nothing exceeds my anxiety whenever I fear any concealment. . . .

SOURCE : Fitz-Simon Papers

711

From his wife to Merrion Square redirected to Limerick

Clifton [near Bristol], 22 July 1817

My darling Love,

. . . How glad I am that you succeeded in carrying your motion at the Board[1] in spite of Purcell[2] and his revered uncle[3] but is it true that poor Mr. Hayes[4] is insane? I sincerely hope this report is merely the fabrication of his enemies. Poor man, how much I feel for his sufferings. It is truly melancholy and I must say a disgrace to the Court of Rome to allow so horrible a conspiracy to succeed. If the object was not a clergyman, there may be some excuse for the imposition practised on the Pope.[5] I fear, love, it will be an age before I can hear from you particularly from Ennis. Even in Dublin I did not get your letters from that *odious* place with the regularity I ought. . . .

You can't think how impatiently Betsey and John are expecting an answer to their *letter*. I know you will not fail to write to them. . . . The only thing that gives me any uneasiness at present is the fear of your making yourself unnecessarily unhappy about me. Believe me, my own Dan, I am not deceiving you. I have exactly told you everything respecting my present state of health. Are you very busy? I hope there is a good prospect this circuit for you. I hear the *times* are improving and I trust *it* is the case. . . .

My own heart, you can have no idea how constantly you are the subject of mine and my children's conversation, how we wish you were with us and how much we love you. In your children's opinion and in mine there is not such another man in the world as you are. When a handsome man, a good husband or a good father are mentioned, Ellen and Kate look with such anxiety for my answer to their question, ' Mamma, sure he is not half so handsome or so good as my father?' My reply is just what they wish, and it speaks the real sentiments of my heart.

SOURCE : O'Connell Papers, NLI 13651

1   See below note 5. The Catholic Association gave way to a new Catholic Board early in July 1817. At what appears to have been the last meeting of the association on 28 June 1817, some oblique comment was passed on the apathy alleged to have recently pervaded that body. A resolution was adopted for proposal at the impending aggregate meeting, inviting the seceders to return to the general body (*DEP*, 3 July 1817). At the aggregate meeting in Clarendon Street chapel on 3 July 1817 a resolution was passed to the effect that preparation of a draft of a petition for unqualified Emancipation ' be confined to the individuals who belonged to the late Catholic Board and Association, and of such others as they shall admit into their Body' (*DEP*, 5 July 1817). The first meeting of what the *Dublin Evening Post* called the reorganized Catholic Board, took place in Dublin on 12 July 1817 (*DEP*, 12 July 1817).

2   Nicholas Purcell O'Gorman.

3   Nicholas Mahon.

4   Rev. Richard Hayes, O.F.M., Franciscan College, Wexford, and Monck Street, Wexford. Author of controversial pamphlets on transubstantiation. Died in Paris 24 January 1824. See letter 571, note 3.

5   Richard Hayes, O.F.M., to whom the anti-vetoists had entrusted their remonstrate to the pope on the subject of the veto, was dismissed in May, and forcibly expelled from Rome on 16 July 1817 (see letter 571, note 3). At the first meeting of the reorganized Catholic Board on 12 July 1817 O'Connell moved ' That a sub-committee be appointed to prepare . . . a Letter of Complaint and Remonstrance to the See of Rome, upon the indignity offered by the Temporal Authorities of the Court of Rome to the very respectable delegate of the Catholics of Ireland, the Rev. Mr. Hayes, and demanding that he be immediately recalled' (*DEP*, 15 July 1817). O'Connell's motion was opposed by Nicholas P. and Richard O'Gorman (*DEP*, 12, 15, 19 July 1817) but was carried (*DEP*, 15 July 1817). Richard O'Gorman opposed several points in the draft of a very strongly worded remonstrance to the pope which O'Connell proposed on

18 July 1817. The draft was, however, adopted with 'some modifi-
cation' and the secretary of the Catholic Board was directed to
forward it to Cardinal Litta at Rome for presentation to the pope
(*DEP*, 19 July 1817).

712

To his wife, 3 Rodney Place, Clifton, near Bristol

Ennis, 23 July 1817

My darling Love,

. . . These were indeed miserable assizes. They are already
over, but four records to try. I was *of course* in them all. I
have not as yet set my foot within the Crown court and I
think I will not for the assizes. I shall not leave this for
Limerick until Friday as we are to have an aggregate here that
day. I think you will like the letters to the Bishops and Clergy[1]
because *it was I who* wrote them. I wrote also a considerable
part of the letter of remonstrance to the Pope. That Blockhead
O'Gorman, who is ever in the wrong, chanced as a matter of
course to stumble on the wrong side of this business.[2] He is in
truth a great dolt.

With respect to James O'Leary's bills, I am getting through
them constantly and fast. I see the end of them, and they have
long since ceased to fret or vex me. Indeed I do believe it was
well for me the thing occurred. Many applications have been
made to me to sign his certificate but I have peremptorily
refused. The women of the Rices put my brother John upon
asking. He promised to do so but has not as yet, and I will be
beforehand with him by telling him the moment I meet him
that I have pledged my most solemn promise to you not to
sign till I saw you again. The fact is I have no notion of
indulging the shabby cur to set up in any business again. His
conduct to me was so basely treacherous and fraudulent that I
ought not to let him again look on society. If, therefore, he
ever engages again in trade it shall be for the benefit of his
creditors. So much for that scoundrel, and a precious scoundrel
he is to be sure, but I ought to be ashamed of myself for feeling so envenomed against him, although it would, I think, be
allowed by anybody that I had *some* cause. God bless you,
sweetest, whom he was so near ruining and making a beggar
of with your children, but indeed it is your husband you
ought to blame. . . .

SOURCE : Fitz-Simon Papers

1 A circular was sent by the Catholic Board to all the Irish bishops
   expressing alarm at the dangers to the Irish church which the
   board saw in the expulsion of Rev. Richard Hayes from Rome.
   The circular objected to Catholic discipline in Ireland being submitted to Propaganda ' as if this were a mere missionary country
   without a national church '. It urged the Irish bishops to take steps
   ' to obtain the concurrence of . . . the pope in such a concordat as
   shall establish fully and forever that Domestic Nomination [in the
   appointment of bishops] which shall secure institution after each
   election, and confirm the Irish Church in her National Independence ' (DEP, 22 July 1817). In a separate circular to the Irish
   clergy, the expulsion of Hayes was similarly condemned and alarm
   expressed at the dispatch by the government to Rome of Sir John
   Cox Hippesley who, the board claimed, was an enemy to the independence of the Irish church. The circular also referred to the
   determination of the Irish Catholic laity never to submit to the veto
   (DEP, 19 July 1817).
2 See letter 711.

713

To Edward Hay

Limerick, 27 July 1817

My dear Friend,

I perceive ' the pliant Trojan '[1] has got Dr. Murray's support for the Veto. Their publication of their letter to you was
intended to intimidate other bishops from that zealous opposition to the Veto which the people look for and the times
require.[2] The person I am most surprised at is *you*. Why did
you not instantly counteract the poison by publishing all such
replies as you received reprobatory of the Veto and favourable
to Domestic Nomination? I presume you are waiting for more,
but as the war began at the other side, you ought at once to
have published every publishable letter.

I conjure you to let Dr. Coppinger's[3] and Dr. O'Shaughnessy's letter see the day as soon as possible.[4] Discretion will
injure, not serve us, on this point.

I am, I own, greatly shocked at the part Dr. Murray is
taking. I had the highest opinion of him and the greatest
respect for him. But I see he wishes, with Dr. Troy's see, to
inherit the patronage of the Catholic Church of Ireland. Oh!
it is melancholy to think of his falling off—he who compared
the Vetoists to Judas.[5] As to Dr. Troy, better could not be

expected from him. His traffic at the Castle is long notorious. But the sneer at the Board and the suppressed anger of those prelates would be ludicrous if the subject were not too important and vital. Are they angry because we urge not the *name* but the reality of Domestic Nomination? Alas, the fact is, that is just the cause of their ill temper and the source of their attack upon us.

You cannot conceive anything more lively than the abhorrence of these Vetoistical plans amongst the people at large. I really think they will go near to desert all such Clergymen as do not now take an active part on the question. The Methodists were never in so fair a way of making converts. Publish, my dear friend, publish.[6] The Ennis Aggregate[7] was the most numerous ever known. Send me by return the Address of *all* the Bishops.

SOURCE : FitzPatrick, *Corr.*, I, 49-50

1   Archbishop Troy.
2   To the address of the Catholic Board (see letter 712). Murray and Troy had returned on 18 July 1817 a joint reply (*DEP*, 24 July 1817) which the *Dublin Evening Post* described as '. . . cold . . . formal and equivocal ' (*DEP*, 24 July 1817).
3   William Coppinger (1753-1830), bishop of Cloyne and Ross, 1791-1830.
4   In their replies to the address of the Catholic Board (see letter 712) Drs. Coppinger and O'Shaughnessy, bishops of Cloyne and Killaloe, expressed their warm acquiescence in the sentiments of the Catholic Board (*DEP*, 24, 26 July 1817).
5   See letter 634.
6   The replies of many of the bishops were published (*DEP*, 26, 31 July; 5, 7, 19 Aug. 1817).
7   A meeting of Clare Catholics on 25 July 1817. Among its resolutions was one expressive of confidence in the reorganized Catholic Board and in support of domestic nomination of bishops (*CMC*, 1 Aug. 1817).

714

To his wife, 3 Rodney Place, Clifton, near Bristol

Limerick, 28 July 1817

My dearest Heart,

. . . The civil business is very small, the criminal calendar is very heavy. I shall, I perceive, have a dreary time of it. There however is no kind of fever in the gaol or I would *desert* that business altogether. The record against the Corporation of Dublin is come down at the suit of Mrs. Lyons. I shall let you know the result.[1]

Since I wrote the above I have come in from court after making a *great speech* and completely succeeding by a verdict of £1,200 for a poor man against the Barrack Board.[2] So *you know* I am in great spirits and I love you ten times better for being so, but is it possible for any circumstances to make me love you *better?* . . .

SOURCE : Fitz-Simon Papers

1 Mrs. Lyons of Croom sought to recover the amount of a city bond issued by Dublin corporation, which it had refused to pay her. A verdict was given in her favour of £1,000 damages and £150 costs (*DEP*, 2 Aug. 1817).

2 William Flattery sought damages of £4,000 from Messrs. Mackey and Ryan which he claimed was the amount of trespass sustained by him after abandoning his contract for building towers on the lower Shannon. He received damages of £1,275. The board of ordnance defended the action (*DEP*, 2 Aug. 1817).

715

From Rev. Peter Kenney, S.J., to Limerick

Clongowes Wood [College], 3 August 1817

My dear Sir,

. . . It is an invariable rule not to allow the college dress to be worn when the pupil is not under our care. This is made a matter of observance rather than of enactment for reasons of higher consideration than those of mere economy. You will easily conceive . . . that the pupil freed from the inspection of his guise may go, nay, even be very innocently brought by his parents to places where the *distinctive* uniform of a seminary conducted by clergymen could not with decorum appear. This observation is not, I am aware, applicable to many of our pupils, not at all in point in the present case. I trouble you with it because I value your approbation of the motives that originated the practice. In a crowd of pupils that may be dispersed in a city or through the country, many things, trifling in themselves, might occur that malevolence would visit on their teachers if their vest announced them pupils of a Jesuit.

Well aware, however, that the present case is quite out of

the sphere of these general reasons I have directed that the clothes in question should be immediately sent directed to you. . . .

Of Maurice I have everything good to say. His improvement in classical knowledge has been very considerable. If *you* and we can form him to steady habits of application, we shall get him to do anything. God has given him very ample talents. Exertion and cultivation will make him a solid and conspicuous scholar. Of good Morgan I cannot say so much. Less talented, he wants application which alone could supply for the deficiency. His dispositions are good: generous, bold and independent. If he had industry he would be no inconsiderable character. Let me entreat you, my dear Sir, not to indulge [them] too much.

SOURCE : O'Connell Papers, NLI 13647

716

To his wife, Clifton

Limerick, 5 August 1817

[No salutation]

Such, darling, is your son Morgan's epistle.[1] Need I tell you that it is genuine? He is always in great spirits. If I had space today, I would copy Mr. Kenney's account of my sweet boys. Maurice may, he says, be *anything*. I will write again this day to the General[2] to settle about our journey to Toulouse. We will go, darling, early in September that you may have fine weather. I shall again enjoy the unrestrained society of my darling children.

SOURCE : *Irish Monthly*, X (1882), 628
1   The above note was added to a letter from Morgan to his mother of the same date.
2   Count O'Connell.

717

From his wife to Merrion Square, redirected to Cork

Clifton, 11 August 1817

My darling love,

I easily perceived our dear Morgan's letter was his own production. He writes exactly as he speaks and always comically. He always reminds me of his Uncle James.[1] It was a great pleasure to you, love, to have your boys (of whom I perceive you are not a little *proud*) so many days in Limerick. I fancy I see you walking to the Catholic meeting, a son leaning on each arm. I should like very much to read Mr. Kenney's[2] account of the dear fellows. What a comfort to us, darling, that they should deserve the praise of such a man. I completely coincide in opinion with *him* respecting Maurice, but Morgan's great objection to apply himself will, I fear, be the means of rendering him unfit for any profession except the army which is the *last* I should wish for him. However if his inclination is in that way, there is little use in opposing him. When you go to Derrynane don't omit reading Mr. Kenney's letter for your uncle. He will be greatly pleased with it and with our dear Maurice who is already, I am told, a great favourite to him. My darling child ought to be a favourite to all his family. Would to God I could see him and my other darling boys before my departure for France,[3] but *this* is a wish in vain and I must be content and look forward to the hope that *this banishment* (if I may call it so) from you and my darling children will give me health and length of years to enjoy the blessings the Almighty has conferred upon me in giving me such a husband as you are and always have been, and such dear, dear children. May God of heaven protect and spare us to each other. And now, darling, I am going to make a request to you. It is that, if you have not fulfilled your Easter Duty[4] previous to your leaving Dublin, that you will do so 'before you leave Cork. I know, darling, you don't like to be spoken to on this subject but you will excuse your wife who idolizes you and who feels equally as anxious for the salvation of your soul as she does for her own and for her children's. . . . Ellen is very anxious I should become a pupil of hers to begin my French *grammar*. I fear she would *rather* be an impatient *governess* for, when she is deputed by Miss G[aghran] to hear the little ones their lessons, she can't bear to have them miss a word. *A propos,* darling, of Miss G[aghran], surely I said nothing on the subject of her not going with me to France in any of my letters to you? A thought of leaving her behind never entered my head. I should indeed regret very much that anything should occur to deprive the children of her. I assure you, love, I pass over many little unpleasant traits in her manners to me for my children's sake. I feel how competent she is to the charge she has undertaken, and I also am sensible how necessary it is for parents to overlook many little things in a governess when not injurious to the morals of their children. None of us [is] without our faults and therefore I make every allowance for the frailty of human nature but I must say this, that never was a governess so well treated by any person than Miss G[aghran] is by me. She is naturally haughty and, having authority at the early age of sixteen to this day, is the only way I can account for the very great opinion she has of herself. She has it to a fault.

Did you not say something to me in a former letter about not taking the carriage with me to France? I believe I replied to you to act as you thought proper about it but that, if you were to pay more than the sum you already paid, I advised you to return it. Consider you would have to pay duty for the carriage in France as well as you had to pay it in this country and then consider if the carriage is worth all this expense and if calculated for the French roads. Toulon or the neighbourhood of Toulon (and not Toulouse) is the part of France which Dr. Bernard recommends to me. . . . There is every fear the corn will be ruined by so much wet. Bread is much fallen. It is here the same price as in Dublin, every other article, fowl excepted, cheaper than in Dublin. I certainly think we would cost you more in Dublin than we will here for the time we shall remain, as nearly as I can calculate. Paying lodging money, horses and everything else (three months to Miss Gaghran included), grocer's and wine bill up to beginning of this month, I have laid out £162.2.0. I keep a regular account of every penny (even for *parsley*) that I lay out, paying all these bills which I mentioned above. I had money sufficient up to this day's expenses and tomorrow's. . . . I have fourteen guineas in gold. Shall I lose by keeping them? Say nothing, love, of what has passed between us respecting Miss G[aghran] to any person whatsover. . . .

SOURCE : O'Connell Papers, NLI 13651

1   O'Connell's brother.
2   Rev. Peter Kenney, S.J.
3   Mary did not go to France on this occasion.
4   The obligation on Catholics to receive Communion between Ash Wednesday and Trinity Sunday or as soon as reasonably possible thereafter.

718

*From his wife, Clifton, near Bristol, 1 September 1817, to
Merrion Square*

States her health is improving but she is still weak.

SOURCE : O'Connell Papers, NLI 13651

719

To Charles Phillips, Cheltenham

Rodney Place, Clifton [near Bristol], 26 September 1817

My dear Charles,

I just heard that you were going to be married at Cheltenham? Is it true? How long do you remain there? What do
you do with yourself next? Write to me and answer these and
as many other questions as will be sufficient to extract from
you *on the cross* all the facts respecting your *present destiny,
your future lot.*

I write in spirits because I have found my family in better,
much better health than I could have expected. Mary is daily
recovering and has not, the doctor assures me, one single
consumptive symptom.

I wish to God we could meet. I remain here near a week.
My family will then settle for the winter in a warm part of
Devonshire as it is too late to go to France and, for a better
reason still, that it is not necessary. What a refreshment it
would be to me to talk to you. I have seen nothing here but
stupid loyal slavish English, who for a rise of one per cent in
the funds would truck a republic for the government of slaves.
I left Ireland most wretched—fever—poverty—party spirit and
want of animation. Thank God the window tax[1] is throwing
a light on their understandings. With that miserable attempt
at something like a pun I console myself for the bitterness of
Irish miseries. . . .

SOURCE : NLI MSS 11489

1 A most unpopular tax levied on windows and hearths, June 1816.
The tax was abolished in 1822.

720

To Charles Phillips

Bath [Somerset], 16 October 1817

My dear Charles,

I got letters from both the Currans yesterday, containing the melancholy intelligence of their father's death.[1] I will go up to the funeral the moment I hear from you or them. William,[2] in his letter, promises to write again this day. What a man has Ireland lost! His utility, to be sure, was in his *very* latter days neutralized by illness and absence; but what a man was he! Of *all*—the *only* incorrupted and faithful. . . .

There is a loneliness and heaviness over me when I think of this great man whom we have lost. Charles, there never was *so* honest an Irishman. His very soul was Republican Irish. Look to his history· in 1778, in '82, in 1798—at the Union—at all times—in all places. Look to it, my dear friend —even for your own sake, but, above all, for his: you must erect a monument to both.

Write to me the moment you receive this letter and just say how long I can remain here and be *in full* time for the funeral. All the Irish in London, of all classes, must be invited. The upper ranks by cards—the lower, thus:—A printed bill must be sent to all the public houses resorted to by the working Irish to mention the hour when the funeral will commence and to request that all persons will fall in, two by two, as they arrive, at the remote end of the procession. I think it would be as well that all persons were required to wear a shamrock. Perhaps this may be said to be too fantastical, but I think it would be well. On *his* coffin should be laid a broken harp and a wreath of shamrock. I rather think there should be a committee formed to make arrangements.[3] Whether I go to town or not on Saturday or wait until Monday will depend on young Curran's letter of this date. It would affect you to see how sensibly my little girls feel *his* death. There have been some wet eyes, I promise you. Remember me most kindly to both the Currans.

SOURCE : FitzPatrick, *Corr.,* I, 51-2

1 John Philpot Curran. John B. H. Curran (1784-1832), second son of John P. Curran, and his brother, William, were both present at their father's death (*Dublin Historical Record,* XV, no. 2 [April 1959], p. 57).

2   William Henry Curran (1789-1858), son of John Philpot Curran.
    Called to the bar, 1816; author of *Life of John Philpot Curran* and
    Sketches of the Irish Bar. See *Boase*.

3   Despite O'Connell's suggestion of a public funeral for Curran, he
    was buried quietly at Paddington. In 1834 his remains were trans-
    ferred to Glasnevin, Dublin, where a monument was raised to him
    designed by Thomas Moore (Leslie Hale, *John Philpot Curran :
    His Life and Times* [London 1958], pp. 273-4; also *DNB*).

721

To his wife, 5 Millson St., Bath

Holilands [London], 20 October 1817

My darling love,

I got here at half after seven last night after a very
pleasant journey. I met in the coach six gentlemen at different
stages and was greatly pleased to find them all strongly disposed against the Administration. It was a treat I did not
expect. I got a great packet of letters this morning.

I saw the Currans and Phillips. No account as yet of the
father's[1] will but it is expected tomorrow or on Wednesday at
the latest so that, at the *worst,* I will be able to leave this on
Friday. Believe me, sweetest, I am most sincerely impatient
to leave this and be back with you and my own, own darling
children. I have spent half the day praising them to Phillips.
He and young Curran[2] inquired very particularly after you
all including, of all things, Rickarda.[3] Tell Kate I met Paine[4]
today. He looks fat and bloated and employs himself, I am
told, constantly abusing Ireland. I am the more ready to
believe this report because he could not refrain, even in my
presence, from throwing out more than a hint against the
poor country. I was even obliged to reprimand him. The
paltry cur, how I despise myself for taking such notice of
him. . . .

SOURCE : Fitz-Simon Papers

1   John Philpot Curran.

2   William Henry Curran.

3   Rickarda Connor (1796-1848), second daughter of James Connor and
    niece of O'Connell's wife. Married 1830 John Primrose, Jr.

4   John Howard Payne.

722

From his brother James to Merrion Square

Carhen, 9 November 1817

My dear Dan,

. . . It is not in my power to go to Dublin for this winter as I have a great many arrangements to make with my Uncle Maurice's tenants who have been abusing all his kindness to them. . . . There is, I thank God, a considerable improvement in the times, but I assure you it is very difficult to make up much money from lands in Iveragh. Your tenants, to do them justice, are behaving pretty well. . . .

SOURCE : O'Connell MSS, UCD

723

From his brother James to Merrion Square

Derrynane, 12 February 1818

My dear Dan,

I would have written to you before now but that I wished to be able to tell you that everything had been settled for my marriage with Miss O'Donoghue,[1] daughter to the late Charles O'Donoghue. This event will, I trust, take place in nine or ten days after Easter Sunday. In fact the only delay is the Marriage Articles not being written and Mrs. O'Donoghue[2] not wishing to have her daughter married in Lent. I need scarce tell you that this match meets my Uncle Maurice's approbation, and he with his usual kindness has consented to settle immediately on me a considerable part of the property he cut out for me in his will and to *bind himself* to give me the remainder on his death. Miss O'D[onoghue] is very young, not quite 17 years old, *but I think both amiable and handsome*. Her fortune is but £2,000 which I am to be paid on the day of my marriage. . . .

. . . I entreat of you on receipt of this letter to write to me and direct to Cahirciveen. If you put off doing so for a day or two you will not write at all and will then be excusing yourself from the hurry of business etc. . . .

I found my Uncle Maurice in very good health and spirits.

He is highly satisfied with your conduct, political as well as otherwise. The very flattering account John[3] gave him of your professional success both flattered and pleased him. We took care he should hear nothing of your row with Foster.[4] . . .

SOURCE : O'Connell MSS, UCD

1 Jane O'Donoghue (c. 1801-67), daughter of Charles, O'Donoghue of the Glens; married 31 March 1818 at Killarney James O'Connell, brother of O'Connell.

2 Mrs. Mary O'Donoghue (died 1845), widow of Charles, O'Donoghue of the Glens, and daughter of James Morrogh, Camden Quay House, Cork. As the spouse of the holder of a Gaelic title she should more correctly be addressed as *Madame* O'Donoghue.

3 His brother.

4 John Leslie Foster was spoken of offensively by O'Connell at a meeting of the Catholic Board on 4 December 1817 (*CMP*, 5 Dec. 1817). Foster demanded that O'Connell either disavow these statements or declare that they referred to him only as a public man. On O'Connell's declining a reply, Foster demanded a meeting with him. Due to O'Connell's being still bound to the peace in Ireland as a result of his attempted duel with Peel, this proved difficult to arrange. O'Connell finally agreed to a statement that his remarks only concerned Foster's public character, thus conciliating his opponent (see copies of statements and correspondence on the subject, *DEP*, 9 Dec. 1817).

John Leslie Foster (1781-1842), 13 Merrion Square, Dublin, eldest son of William Foster, bishop of Clogher. Baron of the exchequer, 1830-41; justice of the common pleas, 1841-42. M.P. for Dublin University, 1807-12; Yarmouth, 1816-18; Armagh, 1818-20; Co. Louth, 1824-30. See *DNB*.

724

To his wife, Merrion Square

Ennis, 3 March 1818, Tuesday

My heart's darling,

I am dying with anxiety to hear from you. I left you with a cough and such weather was never invented as we have had since. The horses were more than once stopped by the rain and sleet. . . .

Get Roger,[1] my love, to make out the last *Quarterly Review* in my study and to send it as a parcel by the Limerick coach to me in Limerick. . . . It contains a short review of *Mandeville* by Godwin[2]—a short review of Bentham's work on reform and a review of the expedition to the Poles, respecting polar ice. . . .

SOURCE : Fitz-Simon Papers
1   Roger O'Sullivan.
2   *Mandeville : A Tale of the Seventeenth Century in England* by William Godwin (Edinburgh 1817).

725

From his wife, Dublin, 6 March 1818, to Limerick

'Kate[1] is sitting for her picture and it promises to be like. There is no fear it will be too grave. She is so naturally gay that sitting so well *behaved* does not make any alteration in the expression of her countenance.'

SOURCE : O'Connell Papers, NLI 13651
1   His second daughter.

726

From his wife, Dublin 3 March 1818, to Ennis

'Kate is still sitting for her portrait which promises to be a much better likeness than Ellen's. Gubbins[1] says Kate has such marked features, it is easy to make a good likeness of her.'

SOURCE : O'Connell Papers, NLI 13651
1   John Gubbins, a native of Co. Limerick; practised as a portrait-painter in Limerick, Dublin and Belfast. See Strickland, *Dictionary of Irish Artists*.

727

To his wife, Merrion Square, 8 March 1818, from Limerick

'There is a good deal of business here. I did not get the *Quarterly Review*.'

SOURCE : Fitz-Simon Papers

728

To his wife, Merrion Square

Limerick, Monday, 9 March 1818

My heart's darling,

... I hope Kate's will be a better likeness than Ellen's for though he[1] has given a likeness of my sweet Nell's features, I do not think he has hit the character of her face. ...

Have you made any inquiries about the servant woman you sent to the fever hospital? If you could get her any extra comfort of wine etc., surely it ought to be done! At all events, darling, inquire for the poor creature. ...

SOURCE : Fitz-Simon Papers
1   John Gubbins.

729

From his wife to Limerick

Dublin, 10 March 1818

My own dearest love,

... Is it possible, love, that you *think* me so insensible as not to inquire about the maid that was sent to the hospital? How did you come to hear it? She was sent the day before you left this but I would not breathe a word of it to you lest it may alarm you. She was under O'Riordan's care,[1] was desperately ill but is now recovering fast. O'Riordan has every attention paid to her. She wants for nothing. ... Am I to give Mr. Gubbins any money until you return? ...

SOURCE : O'Connell Papers, NLI 13651
1   Dr. John O'Reardon.

730

To his wife, Merrion Square

Limerick, Thursday, 12 March 1818

My darling Mary,

... I got the *Quarterly Review* safe with the *Anti-Unionist*.

[P.S.] . . . We had yesterday a great triumph over that scoundrel Ingram from Cork.[1] . . . I write this letter in scraps whilst my worthy clients are teasing me. The fact is that it is a great pleasure to me to write to you but I am loaded with about twice as much business as anybody else. I have got no little credit for knocking up Ingram. I must however *now* run off to court. . . .

SOURCE : Fitz-Simon Papers

1 John Ingram, a Cork grocer, charged John Browder with assault. Ingram had come to Limerick from Cork to vote for the eldest son of Lord Gort, Major Vereker, in the by-election of July 1817. O'Connell, as counsel for Browder, maintained that Ingram had conducted himself offensively at the hustings and was a riotous character. Browder was acquitted, allegedly to the great delight of the populace (*The Interesting Trial of John Browder, at the Spring Assizes of Limerick, 1818, for an Alleged Assault on Mr. John Ingram, of Cork, Grocer* [Limerick 1818]; *LEP,* 12 Mar. 1818).

731

From his wife to Limerick

Dublin, 12 March 1818

My dearest love,

If I am to judge from your silence *these* two posts, the account I hear of all the business you are employed in must be true. Roger[1] told me he had a letter yesterday from Rice Hussey saying you were in *everything* in Ennis and very successful. That you would be concerned in all the business in Limerick, he wrote from Mr. Rice's[2] place near Limerick. . . . I have sent a good many bank notices to John Hickson since you left home which I suppose I was right in doing though you said nothing to me on the subject. . . .

SOURCE : O'Connell Papers, NLI 13651

1 Roger O'Sullivan.
2 Stephen Edward Rice, Mount Trenchard, Co. Limerick (father of Thomas Spring Rice, later first Baron Monteagle).

732

To his wife, Merrion Square

Limerick, 17 March 1818

My own sweet Love,

. . . I send this day a small remittance to John Hickson. Send to him for twenty pounds and, if you can, give two guineas out of them to Mr. Gubbins. If not, give him an order on John C. Hickson for four guineas. I will send you more money the moment I arrive in Cork. They are badly off for counsel in Tralee. Neither Gun,[1] Goold,[2] Pennefather[3] or your humble servant go there, at least I, who will actually arrive in Tralee, do not go for assizes business. . . .

I have given positive orders that all the Limerick papers withheld should be sent to you. I hope you have got them safe. I also threw in almost as good a *scolding* as you could yourself give for having detained them from you at all. But I believe the cock nose gives you an air of impertinence highly useful to set off your anger. . . .

SOURCE : Fitz-Simon Papers

1   Unidentified.
2   Probably Thomas Goold.
3   Either Richard Pennefather or his brother Edward.

733

From his wife to Tralee, c/o J. Connor

Dublin, 19 March [1818]

My dearest Dan,

. . . The trials you were concerned in are promised in a pamphlet, at least the principal one.[1] Roger[2] tells me every person is talking of you and I should like to read of you.

I got the money from Hickson. Mr. Gubbins did not wish for the money when I offered it to him but I gave him three guineas to pay for Ellen's *frame*. Kate is finished, a most excellent likeness. Betsey and John are now sitting. . . .

SOURCE : O'Connell Papers, NLI 13651

1   See letter 730.
2   Roger O'Sullivan.

734

To his wife

Cork, 23 March 1818

My darling heart's treasure,

. . . I earned from forty to fifty guineas in Tralee. . . .

I stopped about an hour in Killarney with James' fair one.[1] She was, of course, too shy to talk with me. She has a lovely countenance, as sweet an expression of face as ever I saw. She is in person large, indeed a good deal so for her age and, though not clumsy at present, she will, unless *the labours* of matrimony prevent it, be very likely to become a very large woman. . . . Write to her, love, to press her in the strongest terms to come to your house. Call her Jane and sister. . . . Do this for me, darling, in your best style, and seriously I know no woman, nor indeed any man either, who can write better than you, my first, my only love. Sweetest mother of my children, indeed I do not flatter you. . . .

[P.S.] . . .

SOURCE : Fitz-Simon Papers
1 His brother James's fiancée, Jane O'Donoghue.

735

From his wife to Cork

Dublin, 25 March 1818

[No salutation]

. . . I had a letter this day from Rick.[1] He mentions nothing new but tells me he never saw you looking better. He says I ought to lecture you well for being such a plague to young girls. He little knows how often I have *lectured* on *that* subject to no purpose. Really, darling, it is a shame to annoy the poor girls so much. My poor Ellen often gets a complexion from you. . . .

SOURCE : O'Connell Papers, NLI 13651
1 Her brother Rickard O'Connell.

736

To his wife, Merrion Square

Cork, 26 March 1818

My darling Love,

. . . I have had a great deal of criminal business in the city and there is an immense deal in the county. I never, my love, was in better health or spirits. The old gentleman at Derrynane[1] is, I hear, declining very fast. He has latterly lost his rest which I imagine at his time of life to be a very fatal symptom. The tenants in Iveragh are coming on right well and the death of the old gentleman would give us, exclusive of profession, full £4,000 a year between my present and *his* income. . . .

SOURCE : Fitz-Simon Papers
1   Hunting-Cap.

737

From his daughter Kate to Cork

26 March 1818

My darling father,

. . . We were amused at your joke on poor Uncle James. I thought he was not to be married until Tuesday. It seems he is in a great hurry. . . As to our pictures, Ellen's and mine are finished. You have seen Ellen's so there is no occasion to describe it to you. I am drawn with a sweet little dog in my lap and a basket of flowers on a table beside me.[1] Betsey and John are only just begun but I think we can already judge that they will be very like. . . .

SOURCE : O'Connell Papers, NLI 13645
1   These portraits are now on view at Derrynane.

738

From his son Morgan to Tralee, redirected to Cork

Clongowes, 27 March 1818

Dear Father,

My Mamma informed me in her last letter that you had left Dublin for circuit and told us to write to you weekly. . . .

I have not had the pleasure of a letter from my dear Father since last vacation twelvemonth for which reason, if it be possible, write me a few lines in return on receipt and you will greatly delight your affectionate son.

P.S. . . . Maurice[1] and Charles[2] unite in love to you.

SOURCE : O'Connell Papers, NLI 13645
1   His brother.
2   His cousin Charles O'Connell, later of Bahoss, Cahirciveen.

739
From his wife to Cork

Dublin, 27 March 1818

[No salutation]

Without consulting you, darling, I have this day written to engage Neligan's lodge at the *Spa* for three months commencing the first week in July. The terms are, I think, high—twelve guineas a month. However I could not get anything less and *this* lodge is by far the best one. . . . Kate gave you a full account of all the family yesterday. She was indeed greatly delighted with your letter. There are still two claims on your correspondence, Betsey and John. Do write to them, my love, for they are dear affectionate little creatures. . . . As a proof of Ellen's good health she this morning not only finished her own *allowance* of *stirabout* but half of Kate's. . . . I beg, my love, you will burn all my letters as you read them. I have a particular reason for making this request which I will tell you when we meet.

SOURCE : O'Connell Papers, NLI 13651

740
To Connell O'Connell

Merrion Square, 18 May 1818

My dear Connell,

Indeed, indeed you annoy me very, very much. Did I not tell you most explicitly that I was very grievously pressed for money this day? And surely, if I could do without it I would not draw on you.

. . . I had reckoned on you most confidently, and am sure, when you recollect the pressure that is on me, you will not refuse me. I therefore again beg of you to send me at least one of the bills accepted and the cash, or both bills accepted. Pray, pray, now do not disappoint me.

[P.S.] I again repeat that it is the actual want of the money makes me thus urge you. And I again beg of you to give me this lift.

SOURCE : FitzPatrick, *Corr.*, I, 54

741

To Stephen H. Rice

Merrion Square, 18 June 1818

My dear Stephen,

Will you be so good as to make the following calculations between me and the Knight of Kerry?[1]

The first rise—£13—quo. What is the Knight's proportion, the entire being charged on £584.11.0? He pays for £107.6.0 [one word illegible]. That is, we pay for £477.5.0 and he for £107.6.0.

The second rise is £68.5.0—quo. The Knight's proportion as before.

The third rise is £498.15.0—quo. The Knight's proportion as before.

The fourth rise is £105.0.0—quo. The Knight's proportion as before.

You will oblige me very much by making those calculations and sending them to me as speedily as you can.

SOURCE : Fitz-Simon Papers

1 This letter presumably refers to a property which O'Connell and the knight of Kerry held under lease from Trinity College, Dublin.

742

To his wife, Rathbeg, Rathmore, Co. Kerry

[Killarney] Wednesday morning [August 1818]

My darling Heart,

I need not tell you and I could not, how delighted I was at the account Dr. Moriarty gave me of you yesterday. . . . Darling, *that* is an excessively cold place and it would be a great object for you to be here. Do not require me to go out unless you want me as I am pressed for time. But do not spare me one moment if you have the least desire to see me. . . . I know nothing can exceed my sweet Kitty's[1] kindness. I doat of her for it but, darling, you ought to be here.

SOURCE : Fitz-Simon Papers
1   O'Connell's sister Kitty, wife of Humphrey Moynihan, Rathbeg, Rathmore, Co. Kerry.

743

To his wife, Rathbeg, Rathmore, Co. Kerry

Killarney, Thursday [August 1818]

My dearest darling,

. . . I have got Mrs. O'Donoghue's[1] carriage *in order* to bring you in . . . for, darling, unless Moriarty forbids it I will bring you in tomorrow. The place you are in is the coldest in Kerry. I feel a sensible difference of climate between that and this place. . . .

SOURCE : Fitz-Simon Papers
1   Mrs. Mary O'Donoghue, also styled Madame O'Donoghue.

744

To Michael Staunton

Killarney, 24 August 1818

My dear Staunton,

. . . For God's sake, who is Milesius?[1] An admirable writer at all events. I have been and am exerting myself to get your paper[2] into the clubs here. You are now the *longe et facile primus* of the Irish press.[3] I think you ought to encourage the painters to join in their petitions against the window tax.[4] If they act separately they will fritter away their strength. Besides, the *little Parliament*[5] is of infinite value, and will habituate the people to form an organ to express the public sentiment on affairs of greater moment.

SOURCE : FitzPatrick, *Corr.*, I, 54-5

1 The pseudonym of a writer to the *Freeman's Journal*, whose address appears as ' Slievedonard '. His letter consisted of a lengthy criticism of Robert Peel, who had lately vacated the office of Irish chief secretary (' Milesius ' to the *Freeman's Journal*, 9 Aug. 1818, *FJ*, 20 Aug. 1818).
2 *Freeman's Journal.*
3 O'Connell had quarrelled with his old allies of the *Dublin Evening Post*, which, he told a Catholic meeting at the end of 1819, was hostile to the Catholic claims.
4 In Ireland the window tax was in 1818 worth, according to the *Dublin Evening Post*, some £250,000 per annum (*DEP*, 18 Aug. 1818). A meeting of St. Michan's parish, Dublin, declared at the time that, notwithstanding a recent abatement of the tax, ' we are unable to pay it from the decay of trade, want of employment for our manufacturers, and the great increase of our absentees ' (*DEP*, 18 Aug. 1818). The *Dublin Evening Post* called for agitation against the tax which it termed the ' *Typhus Tax* ' (*DEP*, 8 Sept. 1818). Meetings took place in several parts of the country to petition for its repeal (*DEP*, 11, 18 Aug.; 3, 5, 8, 11, 15, 22, 26 Sept.; 1, 15, 22, 24, 27 Oct.; 7, 14 Nov.; 12, 29 Dec. 1818).
5 Probably the Catholic Board.

745

To his wife, Tralee

Carhen, 2 September 1818

My darling heart,

. . . Your boys are here in great spirits. They are extremely careful of their fire-arms though they are not a little proud of them. This trip to Iveragh will, you may depend on it, do them much service. They never quit their father while they can and I have the air of being proud of them. . . .

I came here on Saturday and found that the bishop[1] was at Derrynane. I therefore went off there to spend Sunday with

him and my uncle. The latter is greatly broken to my eye
though those about him do not perceive the change so distinctly as I do who have not seen him for two years except for
one day. Indeed, I think him extremely weak and feeble.

SOURCE : Fitz-Simon Papers
1   Charles Sugrue, bishop of Kerry.

746

From his wife to Derrynane

Tralee, 7 September [1818]

My dearest love,

. . . Mrs. *Bess*[1] never called upon me since I came here
though she was several times in town and yesterday she was
a quarter of an hour outside Mrs. Rice's[2] door in her carriage
and never sent even her servant to inquire for me. I saw
John[3] once and he called another time to ask how I did. This
is not the way you and I would act if *they* were in the
neighbourhood of Merrion Square but indeed darling, very
few of your family ever act by you as you do by them. . . .

SOURCE : O'Connell Papers, NLI 13651
1   Wife of O'Connell's brother John.
2   Mrs. Stephen H. Rice.
3   O'Connell's brother.

747

From his wife to Derrynane

Tralee, 9 September 1818

My dearest love,

I have received one letter from you since you went to
Iveragh. Were you in England I would hear more frequently.
I am quite satisfied you have written, and to neglect of those
to whom you commit the putting of your letters in the office
I impute my not hearing from you. Really, darling, it is quite
mortifying to me to be every day disappointed when I send
to the post office. . . . I saw my girls and boys[1] yesterday
quite well and as gay as possible. . . . The girls are most
anxious for your return and for their brothers' [return]. I

fear, love, it will be some time before you can be prevailed upon to quit your favourite spot. The boys, I suppose, will remain at all events until after the Cahir pattern. My poor fellows must enjoy themselves greatly, particularly as they are gratified in their wish of possessing a gun each. God grant no accident may occur. I must own I have my uneasy moments about them. Give them my tenderest love. Aunt Nagle is at present at our *villa* at the Spa. She came last night with Bess O'Connell[2] who had been in Killarney to see the stag hunt. From the latter I had a visit. The hunt, I believe, made her come. She made me some apology. I pity her for her whims but I really think she has a good disposition. How is your uncle?[3] Remember me in the kindest manner to him. Dr. Leyne is at present in the country attending Sir Rowland[4] who is very ill. . . .

SOURCE : O'Connell Papers, NLI 13651
1 O'Connell's children.
2 Wife of O'Connell's brother John.
3 Hunting-Cap.
4 Sir Rowland Blennerhassett, Blennerville, Co. Kerry.

748

To his wife at Capt. O'Connell's, Day Place, Tralee

Derrynane, 9 September 1818

My darling heart,

Your boys and I are quite well. They, poor fellows, are greatly delighted with this country and are, I am happy to tell you, no small favourites of their uncle. Indeed, darling, though they are *yours,* they are certainly sweet fellows. I need not tell you how pleased they were to read your letter for, like your girls with my letters, they were *imperative* in their commands on me to show them that letter. We are going for a couple of days to Coulagh to see an insurgent privateer.[1] The boys will write to you thence. We go off immediately but will be back for Cahir patron next Monday. Take care of yourself, darling, and rest assured that I will not build or throw down[2] without your approbation. . . .

SOURCE : Fitz-Simon Papers
1 Possibly a vessel from South America, part of Bolívar's naval force.
2 At the O'Connell home at Carhen.

749

To his wife, Day Place, Tralee

Derrynane, 16 September 1818

My darling Heart,

. . . We are only last night returned from Berehaven after spending a week there very merrily. Your boys enjoyed themselves very much in Berehaven. We went to see the Patriotic privateer[1] and there never was a sight better worth seeing. She contained men of no less than ten different nations. The Captain is a very intelligent, clever fellow. . . .

SOURCE : Fitz-Simon Papers
1   See letter 748, note 1.

750

To his wife, Day Place, Tralee

Portmagee [near Cahirciveen],
Wednesday night [23 September 1818]

My darling heart,

. . . We came down here by boat in a smart gale, firing at everything we saw. It would delight you to see your old blockhead of a husband and your pair of boys firing wildly. My own darling love, the joy of my youth and the sweet comfort of my maturer years, if you could enjoy Iveragh I should be really happy. It is surprising how I doat of the wild life I had here for a month or six weeks but I am growing so abominably fat that I hate and detest myself. Darling, what is the reason that my own girls do not write to me? I am as jealous with them as it is possible to be.

SOURCE : FitzSimon Papers

751

From his wife to Carhen

Tralee, 24 September [1818]

My dearest Dan,

Just as I had dined yesterday a welcome messenger presented me with a letter from you and another from our dear

Maurice together with a parcel containing £51.8.9 which I assure you was a most salutary relief as it has enabled me to pay my debts of which I had a *few*. . . . Tell my dearest Maurice with my love that his friends here are most anxious to see him. I know he will excuse my not answering his letter. . . . Tomorrow I shall be forty years of age. Will you and my boys drink my health? . . . The grouse are very acceptable. I should prefer a hare or two. . . .

SOURCE : O'Connell Papers, NLI 13050

752
To Owen O'Conor

2 November 1818

My dear Friend,

I have been all day at Green Street (Court House) defending a *Raper*. I have the pleasure to tell you that on Saturday you will find Lord Fingall *and his friends* at D'Arcy's.[1] For the sake of the cause be here on Friday. I have just heard from a credible person in London that Emancipation is certain. *I believe it.*

SOURCE : Clonalis Papers
1   D'Arcy's Globe Tavern of Essex Street, Dublin.

753
From Lord Fingall, Killeen Castle, Co. Meath, 21 December]818

21 December 1818

Apologizes for long delay in answering O'Connell's letter caused by his being in England and letters were not forwarded to him. Along with Jerningham[1] he has confidence in county meetings.

SOURCE : O'Connell Papers, NLI 13647
1   Edward Jerningham.

754

To Owen O'Conor

Merrion Square, 21 December 1818

My dear Friend,

I am just the very worst letter-writer in the world, and I cannot give a stronger proof of it than that I have left the letters of, believe me, one of the persons in the world for whom I entertain the most sincere regard and esteem, so long unanswered, and those letters too on a topic the most interesting. Pray excuse me. . . .

I entirely agree with you in your present view of Catholic affairs. We must do without Lord Fingall and, in truth, I am sincerely sorry for it because he is an excellent gentleman and personally as pure as gold but unhappily subject to some influence from less clean quarters. No matter, we must do without him. But we must not arraign his motives. I am decidedly for petitioning. If I petition alone, I *will* petition. The question seems to be how that can be done effectually. The [Catholic] Board is defunct.[1] *Honest Ned* Hay has outlawed us all.[2] He makes no distinctions. There are many debts due[3]—there is a great indisposition to *organize*. Yet there is not wanting among the people zeal and anxiety. But what is to be done? I am ready to concur with you in any plan you think best. I will join in anything you choose or set on foot any *system* as far as I can that strikes you as likely to succeed. In the meantime I have thrown together hastily a letter to the Catholics of Ireland. After I have cooled on my first impressions, I will print it in the *Weekly Register* of the 2nd of January and send you a paper. I mean to put my name to it.[4] This should not, however, suspend any plan you may form. Pray show you forgive my silence by answering this.

SOURCE : Clonalis Papers

1   The reorganized Catholic Board suspended its meetings at the close of 1817 though it did not become extinct, as the *Dublin Evening Post* maintained (*DEP*, 18 Jan. 1818). The board agreed on 29 April 1818 not to petition parliament (*DEP*, 30 April 1818). According to Fagan, the Catholics suspended agitation in 1818 because of their preoccupation with parliamentary reform (Fagan, *O'Connell*, I, 238-9).

2   A reference to Hay's having published an appeal to the Catholics to subscribe to the liquidation of debts which he claimed to have

incurred on their behalf since 1811. The *Dublin Evening Post* stated that Hay had been shamefully treated by the Catholics (*DEP*, 3 Dec. 1818).

3   It appears that the board was some £2,000 in debt (O'Connell to the *Dublin Evening Post*, 11 May 1818, *DEP*, 12 May 1818). The board were severely criticized for failing to pay £470 to the Rev. Richard Hayes, O.F.M., the balance of the expenses occasioned by his mission to Rome (*DEP*, 5 Feb. 1818). O'Connell had made arrangements to liquidate this debt at the board's meeting on 18 December 1817 (*DEP*, 20 Dec. 1817). In addition, Hay was left to pay a debt of some £260 which he claimed to have incurred as secretary (*DEP*, 3 Dec. 1818: Hay to the committee appointed for his relief, 5 Dec. 1818, *DEP*, 8 Dec. 1818).

4   O'Connell's address contained a long recitation of Catholic grievances. It appealed for an end to Catholic rivalries, for simultaneous petitions from every part of Ireland in favour of Emancipation and for the reconstitution of the Catholic Board. He declared: 'There is no man who may not be of some use in procuring Emancipation and if all can be roused to assist each other, . . . Emancipation will be certain' (O'Connell to the Catholics of Ireland, 1 Jan. 1819, *CMP*, 4 Jan. 1819). According to Fagan, 1819 was the year in which O'Connell commenced the practice of addressing annual letters to his countrymen (Fagan, *O'Connell*, I, 240).

755

From Henry Grattan

Stephen's Green [Dublin], 3 January 1819

My dear Sir,

I thank you for your kind communication and am happy that the speech[1] has given satisfaction. I hope it will produce good and reconcile all parties.

I enter into your sentiments on the state of this country. Ireland has ceased to exist as a nation, and I fear it is more likely that other nations will fall than that Ireland will rise. But of this I am certain that nothing national or useful can ever be effected without a cordial union of both classes in this country. Therefore it is that the speech seeks to unite us. The principle of our question being carried, such a useful discourse will tend to effectuate its final accomplishment.

As to the Society that you allude to—I had such an idea in my mind long ago. I attempted to lay the foundation of a club whose objects should be constitutional and patriotic.

Many of my friends know the efforts I made. I regret that they proved unsuccessful, and that the difficulties that were started caused its abandonment.

As to the one in question, perhaps during the lifetime of the individual it would be premature. That it should be connected with the period of '82[2] (the only period of Irish History), I am decidedly of opinion. From peculiar circumstances it would not be proper that I should be the mover of such a project; but whenever it should be effected, whether during the lifetime of the individual or after his termination, I trust I shall not hang back when the opportunity presents itself of upholding principles which I shall ever hold dear and which I conceive breathe attachment to the country and the constitution.

As to what you mention of poor Curran,[3] I quite coincide. Every honour should be paid to him. He loved liberty; he upheld it in the times of danger, and stood by his country when others sold her.

SOURCE : *Irish Monthly*, XIV (1886), 231
1 Unidentified.
2 The year in which legislative independence was procured for the Irish parliament.
3 John Philpot Curran.

756

To Owen O'Conor

Merrion Square, 6 January 1819

My dear Friend,

We are thinking of agitating again. All is arranged to wait on the Duke of Leinster[1] on Sunday next to beg his signature to a requisition to the Lord Mayor[2] for a Protestant meeting in our favour. Lord Charlemont,[3] Lord Cloncurry,[4] &c., &c., will sign. We hope Lord Fingall will be one of the party to the Duke. I wish to God you were here. Indeed we put the journey off till Sunday in hopes you may come up.

I enclose you the last letter I got from Lord Fingall. You see that he *would* come to meet a few of us. He will be in town in a few days. This would be an additional reason for your coming up but that, I fear, would be quite inconvenient at this season.

I got Staunton to send you a paper with my address.[5] I had but one object in writing it—to show that it was possible to call the Catholics together without introducing one irrelevant or irritating topic. I was as tame as Church music in order to achieve that purpose. But did you see how *your friend* of the *Dublin Journal*[6] attacked me?[7] Many a ludicrous and curious incident has occurred to me in the Catholic cause but anything so wanton and malignant as this miserable Scotch pedlar's[8] attack was never known. The barking of a cur dog is sense compared with it. I am perfectly right in everything he contradicts. The fellow told Lawless that he expected to increase the circulation of his paper by attacking me, even amongst the Catholics. Upon my soul I should not be surprised if he did; but that shall never make me relax. On the contrary, it puts me in spirits for further exertion.

SOURCE : Clonalis Papers

1 Augustus Frederick (FitzGerald), third duke of Leinster (1791-1874).

2 Thomas McKenny (1770-1849), lord mayor of Dublin, 1819: alderman from 1811; created baronet, September 1831.

3 Francis William (Caulfield) second earl of Charlemont (1775-1863), M.P. for Co. Armagh, 1798-1800; representative peer, 1806-63; created Baron Charlemont (UK), 1837.

4 Valentine Browne (Lawless), second Baron Cloncurry (1773-1853), United Irishman, 1795-98; imprisoned, 1798, 1799-1801, on suspicion of treason; created Baron Cloncurry (UK), 1831. See *DNB*.

5 See letter 754.

6 (*Faulkner's*) *Dublin Journal*.

7 The *Dublin Journal* described O'Connell's address (see letter 754) as a ' strange jumble of egotism and misrepresentation ' (*Dublin Journal*, 4 Jan. 1819). In his address O'Connell had maintained that Emancipation would give him the rank of king's counsel which, he declared, would ' add to my professional income probably more than one thousand guineas in the year, and . . . enable me considerably to diminish my personal labour . . .' The *Dublin Journal* taunted him with seeking Emancipation for his own ends.

8 Unidentified. FitzPatrick identifies this writer as John Giffard (FitzPatrick, *Corr.*, I, 59 n. 9; the name is also spelled Gifford), but this must be a mistake. Giffard had severed his connection with (*Faulkner's*) *Dublin Journal* in 1816 (Inglis, *Freedom of the Press*, pp. 179-80). In the late eighteenth century the term ' Scotch pedlar ' was applied in Dublin to agents selling imported British manufactured goods.

757

*From Owen O'Conor, Belanagare, Co. Roscommon
(Thursday), 7 January 1819 to Merrion Square*

Acknowledges O'Connell's letter of the 6th inst. and says he
will arrive in Dublin on Saturday or Sunday next.

SOURCE : Clonalis Papers

758

To John Primrose, Snr.

[Postmarked 9 January 1819]

My dear John,

I make it *a point* that your son John[1] shall be put into any
presentment in which I have any share on the new road, or
that goes through any part of my property. Neither of us
would interfere with Myles McSwiney and if it clashed with
him we would not insist on it. But with that single exception
it is my decided and anxious wish that John should be over-
seer. . . .

I hope I have given poor Maurice[2] *a lift* at Baltimore. I
suppose you heard from him by the same post I did. Emmet[3]
treated my letter as I expected but McNevin[4] behaved
very kindly. I expect to get for Maurice a good and very
eligible situation either from Bolivar[5] or Pueyrredon.[6] If you
have the poor fellow's present address, send it to me for I
could only get a general inquiry made for him by my friend
at Baltimore. . . .

SOURCE : O'Connell MSS, UCD

1 John Primrose, Jr. (c. 1796-1865), J.P., Hillgrove, Cahirciveen,
   Co. Kerry; cousin of O'Connell and land agent to him from 1822.
   Married 6 June 1830 Rickarda Connor, daughter of James and
   Betsey Connor of Tralee and niece of Mary O'Connell.
2 Unidentified.
3 Thomas Addis Emmet, M.D. (1764-1827), brother of Robert
   Emmet and United Irishman, 1795-98; exiled to Fort St. George,
   Scotland, on account of his revolutionary activities in 1798; moved
   to New York (1804) where he became a leading member of the bar.
   See *DNB*.
4 William James Macneven, M.D. (1763-1841). Delegate for Navan
   to the Catholic Convention, 1792; United Irishman, 1797-98.

Exiled to Fort St. George, Scotland, 1799-1802. In 1805 he moved to New York where he held several medical appointments. See *DNB*.

5 Simón Bolívar (1783-1830), son of a Creole aristocrat from Caracas, Venezuela; leader of revolutionary armies which gained independence for most of South America from Spanish rule and known as 'the Liberator'. He engaged the services of several thousand Irish and British soldiers. Died in exile in Spain, 1830, following civil war in Bolivia. See *Ency. Brit.*

6 Juan Martin de Pueyrredon, elected director of the United Provinces of Rio de la Plata for a three-year term commencing July 1816. Supporter of Bolívar.

759

From Lord Fingall to Merrion Square

Killeen Castle, 10 January 1819

Dear Sir,

I am this week under an engagement for some time past to go to Lord Gormanston's and the ensuing one particularly obliged on account of the new road act[1] to attend our Quarter sessions. . . . I should be sorry to appear wanting in respect to the Duke of Leinster or insensible to the kind and flattering wish expressed that I should join the deputation to his Grace tomorrow,[2] however differently we may view the subject, and shall ever feel most grateful for the kindness and partiality of those who wish my interference though convinced they much overrate any services I could render. I was for a long time, when better fitted to take a part, a very unsuccessful partici-pater in our political proceedings.

SOURCE : O'Connell Papers, NLI 13647

1 57 Geo. III c. 107 (July 1817) entitled *An Act to provide for the more deliberate Investigation of Presentments to be made by Grand Juries for Roads and Public Works in Ireland, and for accounting for Money raised by such Presentments,* whereby magistrates of a certain property qualification were required to assemble at the spring quarter sessions to consider the propriety of executing the roads and public works proposed in the presentments of the grand juries. Investigation of grand jury presentments was further regulated by 59 Geo. III c. 84 (July 1819).

2 See letter 756. The deputation, which consisted of 'highly respectable Gentlemen', waited successfully on the duke of Leinster on 11 January 1819 (*DEP*, 9, 12 Jan. 1819).

760

From George Silvertop[1] to Merrion Square

Rue Bleue 15, Chez Mons. Callaghan, Paris, 12 January 1819

Dear Sir,

In venturing to trouble you with this letter I feel apology almost unnecessary because the real Friends of Religious Freedom throughout the world ought to be inspired with a common enthusiasm and because I know no man who has exerted himself more warmly for the promotion of that sacred cause than yourself. Valuable, however, as every moment of your time must be, I really do feel that I am taking a great liberty in the request I am about to make and therefore under that plea I look forward to the kindness of your indulgence. Since I have been on the Continent I have read partial accounts of three very extraordinary facts. 1st, a dreadful affray in the County of Tyrone between Orangemen and Catholics in which several of the latter were killed and wounded, the Orangemen being armed with firearms, the Catholics having none. 2nd, a most extraordinary scene at a dinner given by the Lord Mayor of Dublin to the Lord Lieutenant and Chief Secretary in which an Alderman Archer[2] (the Mayor not having proposed any) insisted upon a toast highly irritating to the Catholics being proposed and in consequence of its [one word illegible] proposal a great uproar and disturbance took place in this [? room] of hilarity and feast. 3rdly, an application to the Lord Chief Justice requesting him to appoint a chaplain for the Catholic prisoners in Newgate, they having been without one of regular appointment for four years in consequence of the Grand Jury, in whom is vested by law the nomination, having appointed three persons at various intervals each of whom were evidently persons highly improper, and the nomination of these three persons having been executed in a spirit of determined hostility to the Catholics extending itself even to the dungeons of Newgate. Every particular respecting these three facts I most particularly request the favour of you to furnish me with and of as many others of the same nature as your time will permit you to give me.

I write this letter in complete confidence and therefore must request you to be so good as to communicate it to no person whomsoever. You will now give me leave to state to you the reasons why I venture to trouble you. In the first conversation I had about a week ago with the celebrated Abbé Grégoire,[3] formerly Bishop of Blois, the conversation turned much upon religious freedom of which, in its most pure sense, he is a sincere advocate. In stating to him the outline of the above circumstances, he was all fire and eagerly requested me to furnish him with the particulars in order that such conduct might be exposed to the whole of Europe and thus try the power of shame to make Great Britain alter her laws. Nothing, as he said, is so ' piquant' as anecdote and therefore that these three facts would furnish abundant foundation either for a pamphlet or for some letters in the different newspapers of France and Germany.

I saw him again yesterday and on reflection both he and I are convinced that their general publication together with remarks from a Catholic bishop (a most virtuous and holy man though a great enthusiast for liberty) may produce a great sensation and, appearing before the world with proper observations, may tend in England to produce considerable sensation. . . .

Permit me to observe, nothing could be more useful to the general cause than having in London a prudent person always possessed of a sufficient command of money to seize every occasion to insert in the London and provincial papers articles favourable to the cause. I am not aware that the people of Ireland have or have ever had such a person. Our little Board[4] has done much in that way but we ought to have done much more. This, however, is no excuse to your countrymen whose number, talents, riches, etc. give them every facility to command such means. I hope petitions are preparing from all parts of Ireland and that they are framed on the true basis of religious freedom. The King of France has only one way to keep the throne for himself and the Bourbon race. It is to be ' the most liberal of the liberal'. So with us, friends of religious freedom, our duty and our policy is to liberalize illiberality.

Things are going on very well here which is certainly the freest country in the world. The new ministry is extremely popular and, what is very fortunate, are understood to be completely united.

I shall remain here for five or six weeks. . . . I wish you to be so good as to send me the resolution of your Board[5] at the time the Protestants of France were threatened with persecution.[6] In Dublin, Cork, Limerick, Waterford, Wexford, are not the Catholics among the greatest capitalists and are they not excluded from any discretion in the Bank [of Ireland] though by far the largest portion of the capital of Ireland is the property of Catholics? Is education making rapid strides and do the priests encourage it? What may be the Irish population and the proportion of Catholics? Do the Methodists make many proselytes among the Catholics? . . .

SOURCE : O'Connell MSS, UCD

1 George Silvertop (1775-1849), Minster-acres, Northumberland. Educated Douai College, 1784-5 May 1792. Took a prominent part in Catholic Emancipation movement in England; opponent of Milner. Acted as medium of communication with Rome for Lord Liverpool's cabinet. See *Gillow*.

2 William Henry Archer, merchant, 9 Gardiner's Place, Dublin. Lord mayor of Dublin, 1812. Elected alderman, 16 March 1804.

3 Henri Baptiste Grégoire (1750-1831), prominent French revolutionary, polemicist, Jansenist, upholder of the Enlightenment. Consecrated constitutional bishop of Blois, 1791. Refused to abjure his tenets when dying and was refused Christian burial.

4 The English Catholic Board.

5 On 5 March 1816 the aggregate Catholic meeting in Clarendon Street chapel resolved: ' That viewing with indignation and abhorrence the unmerited and unchristian-like persecution of the French Protestants, we feel ourselves imperatively called on thus publicly to protest against the violation of what we deem the most sacred of all Rights, the Right which every man has to worship God according to the dictates of his conscience.'

6 Much indignation was aroused in England at the persecution of Protestants alleged to have occurred in Lower Languedoc, 1814-16 (Mark Wilks, *History of the Persecutions Endured by the Protestants of the South of France* . . . , 2 vols. [London 1821]; Helen M. Williams, *On the Late Persecution of the Protestants in the South of France* [London 1816]; John Evans, *An Address on the Persecution of the Protestants in the South of France* [London 1816]) Silvertop was prominent at an English Catholic meeting in Newcastle in January 1816 which condemned the alleged persecutions (*CMC,* 15, 17 Jan. 1816).

761

From Myles McSwiney to Merrion Square

Killarney, 13 January 1819

My dear Dan,

I am truly obliged by your kindness in accepting poor Roger's[1] bill which necessity obliged him to draw on you to pay his law adviser on a General Court Martial before which he was brought by his colonel on three different charges. The trial lasted 36 days, and I am sure you will be pleased to hear that he was *honourably* acquitted, the charges being considered frivolous and vexatious. The colonel is now *in arrest* by order of Sir Thomas Maitland,[2] the Governor of Malta, and the Adjutant of the Regt. ordered to England with dispatches relative to this business. The whole business will be published.[3] . . . I am here at present attending the sessions relative to the new Drung road,[4] the money is to be advanced from the Consolidated Fund. . . .

SOURCE : O'Connell Papers, NLI 13646

1 Roger McSwiney, son of Myles McSwiney and Bridget O'Connell, nephew of O'Connell. Lieutenant, 8th Foot, 1809; placed on half-pay, 1819.

2 Sir Thomas Maitland (1759?-1824); governor of Malta, 1813-24; lieutenant-general and commander in the Mediterranean, 1815-24. See *DNB*.

3 Unidentified.

4 See letter 853.

762

From William Drennan

Belfast, 30 January 1819

My dear Sir,

Or rather, let me say, dear O'Connell, in the familiarity of friendship, and writing to you about our common country and a mutual friend. I allude to John Lawless, through whose zeal, activity and intelligence you have been principally indebted for the Protestant meeting at Belfast[1] which has given an impulse to the inert mass of public mind and which promises a happy result throughout the country and particularly in the capital, owing, I believe, in no small degree to the alacrity and promptitude of the very same individual who knows the value of the moment and shoots it on the wing. He knows and you know, both by profit and loss, the importance of the periodic press, not merely in its being a lever to raise a public mind to its just and natural elevation but to counteract in a degree the dead weight of the ministerial prints which, by open hostility or as dangerous neutrality, would close up every aperture of communication with the vital air of liberty, either civil or religious. A newspaper on the principles of such a holy alliance is certainly much wanted in the North which, like other bodies of human nature, is quick in its fits of heating and cooling, patriotism too often beginning with a feverish flush and ending with a shudder. Catholic Emancipation to its full extent and a reform in Parliament to its practicable extent are the subjects on which the best information is still required for a full and free development of the public mind in both countries. And I know of no person in this vicinity better qualified to conduct a paper on such grounds than Mr. L[awless], provided he had the means! The town of Belfast has, however, contributed the sum of £500 to the undertaking, and there is a confidence, I know not how well founded, that 25 shares of £20 each might be collected in Dublin from Catholic or Protestant nobility or gentry who may see and feel the value of the object principally in view and, I may add, the merits of the agent who is to carry it into execution with the certainty of security and permanence by such a capital £1,000 and by *that only*. Mr. L[awless] proposes, I believe, to go to Dublin in some days, when he can no doubt give a fair and honest report on this subject[2] if mentioned to him, but there is a painful awkwardness in every ingenuous mind in speaking *first* on a matter of this nature even to Daniel O'Connell.

I have been just reading Scott's ' gathring ' of Clan-*Connell*.[3] *That* was a war-cry but your voice is only raised for harmony and peace. God grant it, and yet I fear every attempt will be made to instigate and goad into intemperance by the recrimination of anti-Catholic petitions while administration looks on with passive neutrality. If this be, to hear the impartial verdict of public opinion and from a fear of revolting the religious as well as civil corporations in *England* as well as Ireland, there may be prudence in the forbearance of any prejudgment on the case but, at all events, *now* is the time to

Protestants

sound forth the general opinion. I hope the Protestant meeting in Dublin[4] will speak *ore rotundo*, for the Catholics in their meetings mean, I suppose, to act chiefly by their auxiliaries.

I have read with attention your two last productions. They are worthy of you and I think Mr. E. MacDonnell's well worth the perusal.[5] They both make great developments and, though I think you have explained the prudential motives for blinking the Veto at this *combining* juncture, yet I think the bishops (if they conform) will have to repair to the confessional of their own consciences or, mayhap, to the plenary absolution of the Pope. My maxim was No Pope in the King and No King in the Pope but their alliance answers the end. Well, I see the whole matter is settled. The Veto in operation already. Well, you must balance the *much* you may receive against the *comparatively* little you lose. The Catholic *regium donum* will follow the Presbyterian *regium donum*, but the love of laymen for liberty will overcome and quench the ecclesiastical proneness to prostration. Take what you *can* get and trust to the future, nor cast away your civil rights in compliment to those who degrade the dignity and sanctity of the latter. The truth is, I believe, that government is endeavouring by every means to pension the R.C. prelacy as well as the Presbyterian clergy and to supply their stalls with a well fitted rack and manger. Poor human nature! What will become of the divine?

You will always act the honest part, not the poor spirited and aspiring character of the day. I would not condescend to compliment you or anyone without grounds, but I sincerely think you possess many of the characteristics of Charles Fox, his manly spirit, his openness and candour, his ability and perhaps a little of his gullibility, the weak part of an otherwise impregnable stronghold of honesty and honour. I was going to say to you, as I would have said to him, oddly as it may sound, ' Beware of the goodness of your heart. Your paper,[6] which blinked the Veto, called for an answer and got it. Eneas[7] fought with Achilles. Your reply has vindicated your consistency and politically accounted for your omission.' I have known in my time many Catholic leaders, from the profligate and prostitute [? Mc] K—a[8] up to the honest man I write to. It is a ticklish station but with moral integrity that disdains the juggling and *leger-de-main* of speculating politicians, your object will be obtained and your name be recorded in History.

SOURCE : O'Connell Papers, NLI 13647

1 A petition in favour of unqualified Catholic Emancipation, drawn
up by Dr. William Drennan, the Belfast radical (*DEP*, 3 Dec. 1818)
was adopted at a meeting in Belfast on 2 and 7 December 1818
(*DEP*, 3, 10 Dec. 1818). The chairman declared that ' the party
interested in the continuance of Catholic disqualification was small,
poor and contemptible ', and that the purpose of the meeting was
to rouse the Irish Protestant community to petition for Catholic
Emancipation (*DEP*, 10 Dec. 1818). Jack Lawless took a prominent
part in this meeting (*DEP*, 3, 10 Dec. 1818).

2 Lawless founded the *Irishman* in 1819.

3 This is a flippant reference to Sir Walter Scott's ballad ' MacGregor's
Gathering ' written in 1816. The writer obviously substitutes ' Clan-
connell ' for Clan Gregor.

4 See letters 756 and 759. The requisition to the newly elected lord
mayor of Dublin, Thomas McKenny, in favour of a Protestant
meeting for Catholic Emancipation, was signed by Leinster, Down-
shire, Meath, Charlemont, Donoughmore, Clifden, Cloncurry and
Cremorne, and four M.P.'s: Henry Grattan, Luke White, Richard
W. Talbot and Richard Martin (*DEP*, 9 Feb. 1819). The meeting
took place in Dublin on 11 February 1819 under the chairmanship
of the lord mayor. Leinster, Charlemont, Meath and Cloncurry
attended, together with Sir Marcus Somerville, M.P., and William
Parnell, M.P. Attempts by Lord Frankfort to prevent the meeting
proved a failure. It was agreed that petitions be sent to parliament
in favour of Emancipation and a call made on the Protestants of
other parts of Ireland to follow this example (*DEP*, 11, 13, 16
Feb. 1819).

5 See letter 754. McDonnell published a long reply to O'Connell's
address, apparently criticizing his omission of reference to the veto,
and his earlier contention that a section of the hierarchy were
favourable to the veto and the people apathetic to it. In reply
O'Connell sought to demonstrate the truth of his contentions and
condemned Archbishop Troy, in particular, as a vetoist (*DEP*,
2 Feb. 1819).

6 O'Connell's address to the Catholics of Ireland (see letter 754,
note 4).

7 Eneas MacDonnell, ex-editor of the *Dublin Chronicle*.

8 Very probably Theobald McKenna (died 31 Dec. 1808). An Irish
Catholic pamphleteer, he supported Emancipation in the 1790s but
accepted government payment to write against radicalism and in
favour of the Union. Later, he attacked the government for not
having granted Emancipation with the Union.

763

To Owen O'Conor

Merrion Square, 11 February 1819

My dear Friend,

Are you not delighted that you did not stay in the country and plead, as you might, business &c. &c.?

Get the signatures[1] you mention and as fast as you can.

Could you not contrive to make me and the Grattans acquainted? It was a Grecian patriot that said, 'Strike, but hear!' I was going to swear that Ireland has as true patriots. I would cringe to no man, but I would join every man who wishes well to Ireland. See whether, without derogating, we could *all* join.

I return your congratulations on the day.

SOURCE : Clonalis Papers

1 To the Protestant petition to parliament in favour of Catholic Emancipation (see letter 762, note 4).

764

To his wife, Merrion Square

Ennis, 7 March 1819

My own darling, darling heart,

You were ill, I thought, when I left you. You had symptoms, I think, of your former complaints. Indeed, sweetest love, I am truly miserable about you. If it be *but* breeding I will be as gay again as a lark with the hope of one more sweet darling such as our Dan. . . .

I forgot, my dearest heart, a *penhandle* in my inkstand. It is of blackest wood with a small silvery machine to receive the pen part of a quill. Send it to me by the first possible opportunity. . . .

SOURCE : Fitz-Simon Papers

765

To his wife, Merrion Square

Ennis, 9 March 1819

My heart's darling love,

. . . Speak to my little boy about me often. Tell him again and again of what a doat he is to his father. Remind him of me. I saw his foster father yesterday. His nurse is well with a fine boy of her own. Would to God, sweetest, dearest life, I could promise the occasion for *her care*. Do say to me whether I have any present chance of giving the nurse another employment. . . .

Darling, I write to you in great spirits. I never was in better health or so high in professional *glory*. . . .

[P.S.] . . . I cannot tell you how I rejoice in Lord Trimleston's verdict.[1] It is in itself a great triumph. I do think Popery is winning its way daily. I wish you could hear *how* Burton as judge spoke of me a while ago to a jury.[2] . . .

SOURCE : Fitz-Simon Papers

1 In a case to try the validity of the will of the fourteenth Lord Trimleston (*FJ,* 12 June 1818). He left a considerable estate to his second wife, who was a Protestant, to the exclusion of his Catholic son, the fifteenth baron. See *Maj.-Gen. Evan Lloyd and Alicia Dowager Baroness Trimleston versus Thomas Lord Baron Trimleston* (Dublin 1819); *Lloyd and Wife versus Trimleston* (Dublin 1819).
2 Case unidentified.

766

To his wife, Merrion Square

Limerick, 14 March 1819

My own love,

. . . There is a great share of business in this town, more indeed than three judges can by any possibility finish as Baron Smith is seldom in court till near three o'clock. Burton is doing his part of it extremely well but very slowly. I shall leave this on Saturday next for Ballinrobe. I go there by Gort and Galway. . . .

SOURCE : Fitz-Simon Papers

767

To his wife, Merrion Square

Ballinrobe [Co. Mayo], 23 March 1819

My darling Love,

I am just leaving this and have but time to write you one
line. I came here on Sunday early enough to hear Mass and
was so engaged all the rest of the day that I had not time to
write even one line. The trial[1] occupied all day and a great
part of the night, from nine yesterday till *two* o'clock this
morning. I fasted the entire time and, what was worse, our
case was very *badly* proved. The jury are still in and no likelihood of a verdict. I am just starting for Tralee where I shall
certainly reach early tomorrow. . . .

SOURCE : Fitz-Simon Papers

1 An action brought at Ballinrobe on 22 March 1819 by a Capt.
   Fitzgerald against a Capt. Kerr. Fitzgerald charged Kerr with
   holding a criminal conversation with his wife and claimed damages
   of £20,000. O'Connell was counsel for Fitzgerald, who received
   £1,500 damages (*DEP*, 30 Mar. 1819).

768

To his wife, Merrion Square

Cork [postmarked 13 April 1819]

My own dearest darling,

. . . My vanity, heart, was never so much *pampered* as
it has been since these assizes began. I have been remarkably
successful, especially in bothering parsons. The Rev. Horace
Townsend,[1] a celebrated wit and a kind of *star of the west*,
passed through my hands in a cross-examination which made
him appear both ludicrous and dishonest. He attempted to be
impertinent but *you know,* love, there is no beating me at
that and I got the laugh completely against him. I greatly
gratified all the auditors.[2] In short, love, I am quite *spoiled*
by success and adulation. . . .

SOURCE : Fitz-Simon Papers

1 Rev. Horatio Townsend (1750-1837), Derry, Rosscarbery, Co. Cork,
   author of a number of statistical and agricultural works on Co.
   Cork. See *DNB*.

2 The case heard on 9 April 1819, *Roche* v. *Rev. Robert Morett*, rector of Castletownshend. Morett, a magistrate, had recently tried a case between Roche and a shoemaker. He had found in favour of the shoemaker and was alleged to have called Roche's honesty into question. Roche took an action against Morett for defamation. Rev. Horace Townsend appeared as witness for Roche. O'Connell was counsel for Morett whom he stated in court to be a notably benevolent magistrate. A verdict was returned in Morett's favour (*Cork Southern Reporter*, 10 April 1819).

769

To Daniel O'Connell of Kilgorey, Co. Clare, c/o John Howley, Esq., Limerick, 27 April 1819, from Merrion Square

Concerning £350 owed to the recipient.

SOURCE : MSS 5759, NLI

770

From Myles McSwiney to Merrion Square

Carhen, 7 May 1819

My dear Dan,

. . . There is nothing doing with respect to the building[1] for want of any directions from you. You may recollect at the last March twelve month assizes in Cork that James[2] mentioned to you that Carhen Demesne being so confined that he recommended to you to add the two fields in Primrose's hands to it which you desired to have done but Primrose refused to give them up to me. . . .

SOURCE : O'Connell Papers, NLI 13646
1 At Carhen.
2 O'Connell's brother.

771

From Ellen Connor to Dublin

Bayview Cottage [postmarked Tralee], 12 June 1819

My dearest Uncle,

I will rouse myself, I am roused, I will do all and everything you wish me. Do not think I indulge sinfully in regret for my grievous misfortune. Oh no, I do everything in my power to lessen that regret but it is impossible; whilst I live that darling Father, though gone, will still hold first place in my heart. Oh my Uncle, you know not half of what that father was to *me* but if I go on this way I shall only take up your precious time of which there has been so much already given up to my unhappy family. May God forever bless and protect you. What would become of us but for you? . . .

Richard Leyne[1] told me he mentioned that Killarney school was a good one. I conjure you, my Uncle, if the two little boys are to go anywhere, let it be to Clongowes. Let what will be done to guard against it, those inferior schools will in the end be more expensive than Clongowes, and poor Maurice,[2] with whom strictness is so necessary, will return home to us a dunce. As I wrote to Colonel Crosbie, would you approve of my writing to Judge Day who is at Tralee, and to Sir Edward Denny? If so, tell me what to say and I shall write. Still, your having done so is of much the greatest importance. . . .

SOURCE : O'Connell Papers, NLI 13651

1   Richard Leyne (1790-1864), son of Maurice Leyne, M.D., J.P. Captain, 73rd Regiment. Led his regiment into Paris after his senior officers had been wiped out at battle of Waterloo. Married 1817 Elizabeth, daughter of James Connor and niece of O'Connell's wife. Appointed R.M., 1841.

2   Maurice Connor, M.D. (c. 1809-1839), son of James Connor, Tralee, and nephew of O'Connell's wife. Educated Clongowes Wood College, 1819-22; resident medical officer at Westcove, Co. Kerry. Married 1833 Johanna, daughter of Darby Murphy, Listowel, Co. Kerry.

772

To Owen O'Conor

Merrion Square, 15 June 1819

My dear Friend,

I am the worst letter writer in the world or I should have written to you from circuit. Allow me now to ask whether you can, without inconvenience, come to town before Saturday next? We have wanted you for some time, but I was unwilling to be instrumental in bringing you from home until the utility of your honesty, conciliatory temper and admitted respectability became obvious. If you can come up, you will, I think, be the means of a perfect union. It seems to many honest men necessary so to recommence operations as to be *certainly* before the next meeting of parliament the very first week in November or at least in the first week of their sitting. We have been materially injured by the late period in which the question[1] has always come on.

SOURCE : Clonalis Papers
1   The Catholic question.

773

From his brother James to Merrion Square

Killarney, 12 July 1819

My dear Dan,

. . . Let me, my dear Dan, beg of you to bring me to the assizes the mortgage deed of Bolus with a regular assignment of it to the General.[1] Rice Hussey has repeatedly called on you for those papers. It is indeed very painful to my feelings to be obliged *again and again* to write to you on this subject, but when I show you a letter I received from the General written the 6th of last month, you will, I am sure, see the necessity of giving me those papers on the faith of which I gave you eight hundred pounds of our Uncle's property which he had committed to my custody. It is now two years since you got this money, at a moment when you had *Bills or Notes* coming to maturity for a large amount and, though my brother John had an equal control over the General's property with me, *I took all the responsibility on myself* of not only giving you that sum but also seven hundred pounds more which you secured by a mortgage on the College lands. It was in a great measure at my request the General consented to advance £3,600 to redeem O'Leary's annuity for you. . . . He very naturally looks to John and to me for an account of the ten thousand pounds he placed in our hands and surely nothing can be more reasonable than he should. The General's letter to me is *rather a sharp one,* coming from such a man as him who has made such sacrifices for his family and indeed most generously gave up the savings of a long and honourable life for *the sole purpose* of serving the younger sons of his nephew. In his letter to me he mentions an application of yours to be allowed to receive the interest you pay on the £3,600 for some years. This, he says, he positively refused to do as it would break in on his plan of allowing the interest of the £10,000 to accumulate until the entire accumulated to £20,000 which was then to be disposed of as directed by his will. The annuity the General allows his sister, Mrs. Segerson,[2] thirty pounds British, he remits out of his pay, but even that small sum may delay the object he has in view. . . .

SOURCE : O'Connell MSS, UCD
1 His uncle Count O'Connell.
2 Alice Segerson (c. 1728-1820), aunt of O'Connell, sister of Hunting-Cap; married c. 1750 John Segerson, The Manor, Ballinskelligs, Co. Kerry.

774

To his wife, Merrion Square

Ennis, Monday, 26 July 1819

My darling Love,
. . . I got before eleven to Maryborough and left it next morning at five. I was in Limerick shortly after one, stayed there near two hours recruiting for the patriot service.[1]

We have had a busy day of this. I spoke to evidence in two cases and stated one besides examining witnesses. This is one of the best assizes I have known for some years. . . .

SOURCE : Fitz-Simon Papers
1 The Irish Legion to South America organized by John Devereux. See letter 778, note 1.

775

To his wife, Merrion Square

Ennis, Thursday, 29 July 1819

My darling Heart,
Baron Smith keeps such shocking hours that I have not had one moment to write to you yesterday. It is now near eight o'clock and I have just come in from court in the interval

between two trials in order to send you one line. . . . I never was in greater professional *glory*.

Darling, I am again called back to court.

SOURCE : Fitz-Simon Papers

776

From Count O'Connell

[Original in French[1]]

Paris, 30 July 1819

[No salutation]

It is more than time, my dear nephew, to inform you of the receipt of your two letters. . . . I could not accede to the request you make of me without breaking an almost religious resolution which I had taken in the interest of your younger sons and of those of your brothers, and I felt an extreme repugnance in refusing it. It is to this conflict between my heart and conscience that I must impute the hurt I have caused you, and it is to this factor that I turn for my justification.

And now for some details. One of the motives which determined me to visit Ireland in 1814 [*recte* 1815] was to see with my own eyes the situation of my family. I was not able to see your children and those of John without feeling the most tender emotions for them and the most ardent desire to contribute to their welfare. As my fortune was too modest to share between the boys and girls I resolved to give it solely to the younger sons in equal parts. As soon as I had come to this determination I got rid of my carriages, horses etc. and restricted myself to only one domestic servant, doing without everything not strictly necessary for my situation in life. This, my dear nephew, is the literal truth. Nobody knows this except you and me. Others could gain some merit from such a sacrifice but I gain none. It yields me more delightful gratifications than those of vanity, and I beg of you to tell no one. Having also renounced for my personal needs the only property which I possessed, I have only my pension from the English Government—£500—and six thousand francs (£250) from the King of France. It is with this income that, thanks to the spirit of order, of regularity and of economy that I have invariably practised on the restless stage of the world, I still find means not only to support myself with all the decency which my rank in society demands but to do by the by some good works. In my opinion such is entirely the power of the spirit of order.

After this exact explanation of what concerns me personally, let us dwell a while on what concerns you. Now here is the picture of your financial situation which I have formed. The income from your lands which was more than £2,000 has presumably fallen to £1,500. Your professional income could not be more than £3,500, thus a total income of £5,000. Let us see now what your expenses are. For the interest on your debts, £1,000; for your living expenses, £2,000; for paying off the principal of your debts, £2,000. The total is £5,000. If this calculation is not too far from the truth, you should be able to pay off your debts in five or six years[2] by limiting your living expenses to £2,000 a year and making it a rule not to contract any new debts under any circumstances.

£2,000 is a decent income, and it would ill become the good father of a family not to be content with it. Consider what would happen to your family if they had the misfortune to lose you. Listen to your heart which is naturally so good, so feeling, so loving, and reject ill-intentioned and frivolous suggestions of vanity. Providence attaches to different ranks of society different duties: those of a father are common to all because they are the most sacred. Therefore, my very dear nephew, apply your good fortune and your glory to doing them well. Do not indulge the restless and often dangerous ambition to leave the station in which it has pleased God to place you. He has deigned to give you every talent necessary for your distinction and for assuring your children an honourable living. Profit from his gifts. Try to be equal to them by your feelings and your actions, and leave to his Providence the care of conducting yourself in the short passage of this life. Put less effort into Emancipation, not abandoning it, however, but only using as much effort as is consistent with prudence, honour and virtue. Believe, moreover, that nothing can advance by even a day the time marked out by Providence. *Nisi Dominus aedificaverit domum, in vanum laboraverunt qui aedificant idem.*[3] Give me in your first letter the true and exact list of your debts, of all your expenses, the net income from your property and the amount which your profession brings you. Believe me, I will be ready to share with you the income which I have reserved for myself if your situation demands the help of your friends, but I have the right to demand from you every economy and the sacrifices which the ordering and arranging of your affairs will necessitate. . . .

. . . Your idea of putting Morgan into the French service is neither practical nor desirable. If he has a definite vocation for an army career he must learn mathematics, drawing, fortification and geography and in four or five years he will have to buy a commission. . . . He must learn to dance and fence and of course must know how to speak and write French well. . . .

SOURCE : Fitz-Simon Papers

1 Count O'Connell wrote in French because he did not wish O'Connell's wife to know the contents of the letter.
2 O'Connell's debts were greater than Count O'Connell thought. At this time they totalled £20,000 or more.
3 Unless God builds a house, they labour in vain who build it.

777
To his wife, Merrion Square

Limerick, 1 August 1819

My darling Love,

. . . We finished the business at Ennis early on Friday. I was the only counsel in all the records. The business here is not heavy, and I have strong hopes of being in Tralee on Saturday. We go to Tarbert in the delightful steamboat. She is a noble vessel and the scenery splendid and infinitely less risk in travelling in that way than in going in a chaise or *riding a horse.* . . .

Did you read the address from the London meeting to the Catholics of Ireland?[1] It is a most powerful paper and ought to make a great sensation. We abstain from public meetings this circuit least we should commit ourselves *too soon* on the subject.[2] My *political spirits,* darling, are reviving fast. . . .

SOURCE : Fitz-Simon Papers

1 An address to the members of the Irish Catholic Board had been drawn up at a reform meeting in Smithfield on 21 July 1819 under the chairmanship of Henry Hunt (*DEP,* 29 July 1819). It called for an end to the unprincipled policy of sowing dissension between the peoples of Britain and Ireland and proposed a ' Political Union in the Cause of Civil and Religious Liberty ' urging that for this purpose ' the oppressed Protestant People of England, the oppressed

Dissenting People of Scotland, and the oppressed Catholic People of Ireland, unite, as becomes brethren and Britons' (*DEP*, 27 July 1819).

2 It had been requested by the participants in the above Smithfield reform meeting that their resolutions and address be submitted by the Catholic Board to 'the Catholic meetings throughout Ireland' (*DEP*, 29 July 1819).

778

From John Devereux[1] to Limerick

Dublin, 3 August 1819

My dear Sir,

As I am about to leave the country and feel some anxiety about the law case you are directing, I shall feel particularly obliged by your transmitting the drafts of the two bills as early as possible for I find it is of the utmost importance that they should be filed immediately.[2] Be good enough to let me know by return of post when I may expect them.

Captain O'Connell[3] has just presented me your esteemed letter in favour of his nephew.[4] . . . I have only to assure you, my dearest Sir, that whenever he joins the Legion, I shall select and appoint him near my person so as to watch and take care of him with a father's care—and believe me, I do feel most highly complimented and flattered that you should think me worthy of so sacred a trust to one so near and dear to you as this youth. As I thought it would be a little complimentary to the father, I told him that I would order a commission to be made out for the youth in the Regt. of Fusiliers which I am now forming as 'my own Regt.' under Col. Lyster[5]—and which the youth can keep by him so as to serve in the event of his joining us hereafter. This Regt. will be the choicest of the whole and it is already joined by some of the first youths both from Scotland as well as Ireland.

A similar document you'll permit me also to leave for your son[6] whom I shall name as on my staff although it may be no other than a mere compliment yet it will serve to record that affection and respect for you—and for virtues and merits which I feel too strongly to express by words.

Accept, my very dear Sir, my warmest wishes,
        Ever your most attached and respectful friend,

John D'Evereux

[P.S.] I am rejoiced to learn that your [sic] recovering so well from the effects of that unfortunate accident that happened to you on the day of the great dinner.[7]

SOURCE : O'Connell Papers, NLI 13647

1 John Devereux (he spelled it D'Evereux) was born in Co. Wexford in 1778 and died in London in 1860. He took part in the 1798 rebellion at New Ross and was hidden by Fr. William L'Estrange, O.D.C., before going into voluntary exile in the U.S.A. Becoming involved with a group of Latin-American emigrés in Baltimore, he went to the republics of La Plata and Nueva Granada to offer help. These efforts coming to nothing, he wrote to Bolívar from Haiti on his way back to the U.S.A., offering to raise a volunteer force in Ireland for service in Venezuela. Bolívar accepted, and Devereux was back in Ireland at the end of 1818 to organize. His legion reached Venezuela in the latter half of 1819, but Devereux himself did not arrive until June 1820, by which time his legion had mutinied and the greater part had been packed off to Jamaica. He went on to Colombia to claim his expenses and in 1824 returned to England having, as he himself admitted, made a considerable fortune. Tall, handsome and vain, he was given to intrigue and boastful statements and was not averse to forging and altering documents to suit his purpose. He won the confidence of O'Connell who stood by him even after charges had been made, probably with much truth, that he had organized the Irish Legion for his own financial benefit. (This note is supplied by Eric T. D. Lambert.)

2 About this time Devereux was involved in litigation with Liverpool ship owners in connection with debts incurred in sending troops to South America.

3 Capt. Rickard O'Connell.

4 *Recte* 'your nephew'. Thomas O'Connell (born 1801), son of Rickard O'Connell and nephew of O'Connell's wife. Sometime clerk of the Tralee Union. Appointed captain in Col. Lyster's regiment of Devereux's Irish Legion but never went to South America.

5 William Lyster, son of John Brabazon Lyster (commissioner of wide streets); lieutenant in 100th Regiment, 1811-18; colonel in the Regiment of Fusiliers ('Devereux's Own') in Irish Legion.

6 Morgan.

7 On the morning of 19 July O'Connell injured his leg when his horse fell under him in the Phoenix Park. On that evening he attended a public dinner at Morrison's Hotel in honour of Devereux and South American freedom (*CMP*, 21 July 1819). O'Connell acted as secretary in organizing the dinner (*CMP*, 19 July 1819).

779

From his wife to Limerick

Lanesville [Monkstown, Co. Dublin],
Thursday morning, 4 August [1819]

My dearest Dan,

Mr. O'Kelly[1] came here to spend the day and he begged of me to tell you a friend of his was shown a letter by Neddy Hay from the Bishop of Norwich[2] on the subject of the Witchery Resolutions,[3] strongly pressing the necessity of contradicting and clearing the Opposition from the charges brought against them in the [*Dublin*] *Evening Post*[4] as *he,* Norwich, was quite certain Lord Grey would not do anything for the Catholics until this charge was publicly contradicted. Why don't *those* concerned come forward as you did?[5] I was greatly pleased on reading Mr. Ponsonby's[6] letter[7] in the *Freeman* of yesterday and the remarks on your conduct respecting these resolutions. What a pretty fellow is this Neddy Hay! and what a shame to have him any longer a secretary to Catholics of Ireland. Surely there can be no dependence placed upon such a fellow. . . .

SOURCE : O'Connell Papers, NLI 13650

1 Mathias J. O'Kelly.
2 Henry Bathurst.
3 The resolutions passed by the Catholics in June 1812 in which it was hinted that the hostility of the prince regent to the Catholic claims arose from the influence of one of his mistresses (*FJ*, 20 June 1812; Fagan, *O'Connell*, I, 158).
4 On 29 June 1819 the *Dublin Evening Post* stated that the witchery resolutions had been drawn up by the Whig opposition in England and conveyed to Dublin by a relative of George Ponsonby; and had then been passed by a Catholic meeting not fully conscious of their import.
5 At a Catholic meeting in Dublin on 1 July O'Connell stated that he himself had sponsored these resolutions and that the charge that a relative of George Ponsonby had been involved was a gross falsehood. At this (1 July) meeting Edward Hay admitted that he had supplied the information for the article in the *Dublin Evening Post* of 29 June (*DEP*, 3 July 1819).
6 William R. Ponsonby, son of George Ponsonby who was leader of the opposition 1808-17.
7 Ponsonby published a denial that he, his father or any of his relatives had taken any part in the resolutions (William R. Ponsonby to Edward Hay, 16 July 1819, *DEP*, 3 Aug. 1819).

780

To his wife, Merrion Square

Limerick, ¼ after 4 in the morning, 4 August 1819

My darling love,

. . . My darling Dan's nurse was here yesterday with a very lovely boy of her own. . . . The nurse was greatly morti-fied at hearing you would not give her another chance of a nursing. I assured her all the blame ought to be attributed to me. *Is it not so,* darling?

She is really a most respectable woman and inquired for the family with as much tenderness and propriety as the person of the highest education and best heart in society could do. . . . May I beg of you, love, to write to the poor woman? . . . Do, darling, take the trouble of writing to her and of course pay the postage. She really deserves this attention. Oh, how I wish you were *preparing* another nursing for her! . . .

SOURCE : Fitz-Simon Papers

781

From his daughter Ellen to 2 Day Place, Tralee

Merrion Square, Tuesday, 10 August [1819]

My dearest Father,

I am delighted at getting permission to write to you as it gives me a claim to a letter from you in return. . . . We drank your health on Friday last (your birthday) with *three* times *three* and I scarcely think it was ever drunk at any public dinner with more enthusiasm. We were to see Miss O'Neill[1] the other night in the character of Evadne in Mr. Sheil's new tragedy.[2] We were enchanted with her. I think she is the sweetest creature that ever appeared on the stage. . . .

SOURCE : O'Connell Papers, NLI 13645

1 Eliza O'Neill (1791-1872), celebrated Shakespearean actress. Married December 1819 William Wrixon Becher, M.P. See *DNB*.
2 *Evadne; or, The Statue,* a tragedy in five acts by Richard Lalor Sheil (1819).

782

From his wife to Tralee care of Capt. O'Connell, Day Place

Lanesville [Monkstown, Co. Dublin], 12 August 1819

My dearest Dan,

... Tom[1] is quite well. ... Neither he nor Morgan
has as yet got *their* commissions. What does your uncle[2] say on
the subject of Morgan's going to France? I was greatly disappointed I could not read his letter. Probably he wrote in
French with *that* intention. Perhaps he has as contemptible
an opinion of ladies' sense as the old gentleman.[3] Notwithstanding that opinion I must say that I love and respect him
very much. He is a charming old man. *It* would be quite impossible not to like him. ...

SOURCE : O'Connell Papers, NLI 13651
1   Tom O'Connell, her nephew.
2   Count O'Connell.
3   Hunting-Cap.

783

From his daughter Kate to Cork

[Lanesville, Monkstown, Co. Dublin] 13 August 1819

My dearest Father,

.... We take delightful long walks every day to Dunleary
[now Dún Laoghaire], Killiney, Cabinteely, etc. We don't
forget your promise of taking us on excursions to the Dargle
and other beautiful parts of the County of Wicklow when you
return after the Cork assizes. Bray is only four miles from
here so that we are in the neighbourhood of all those places.
Mr. L'Estrange comes to us sometimes for a few days. ...

SOURCE: O'Connell Papers, NLI 13645

784

From his wife to Parade, Cork

Lanesville [Monkstown, Co. Dublin], 16 August [1819]

My dearest love,

You will be surprised to hear I have parted with William[1] and you will believe I should have not done so were I not provoked by receiving the greatest impertinence (I ever experienced) from him because I refused to pay a helper which he, without asking permission, brought out here. In truth, William thought he could do anything he pleased, that he would not be parted with, and since his last engagement his stubbornness knew no bounds. The conclusion of his *address* to me was to the following effect: ' The devil mend me for coming back to you, and when my two years are up I will leave you there.' This happened in the hall of our house in town in presence of my children and other servants. Immediately on my coming home here I sent Morgan[2] to tell him to give up his things, that he should never drive my carriage again, that I was ready to pay his wages when I got the clothes from him. He sent me word he would not leave me nor give up his things until he was paid up to the 20th February next, the end of his two years. This I of course refused to pay, and Morgan told him I would pay him four guineas which was coming to him, that the law was open to him, that if he was entitled to be paid the two years in full he knew his remedy. He still persevered in refusing to give up the things and insisting on the two years' wages. In short, love, I should write a volume to give you any idea of his conduct. Yesterday morning he gave up the things but went off without taking his money. His boast was his master would pay him what he demanded. I cannot tell you the state of agitation his conduct threw me into. The ingratitude of the fellow I felt more than anything else. I am truly sorry I ever took him back and I hope, heart, that nothing will induce you to ask me to take him again. The helper is taking care of the horses and drove me to Mass yesterday. This man I will keep until I can get a good coachman. T. O'Mara[3] and Mrs. O'Mara[4] came yesterday to return my visit. . . . Both Mr. and Mrs. O['Mara] admired this place very much. The former expressed a wish that you would purchase it as it is just the place for me. . . . I am

greatly pleased with your letter to Staunton and to the
[*Dublin*] *Evening Post*. The latter, I think, is in a hobble.
The truth must now come out.[5] . . . Miss O'Neill[6] has left
town without returning my visit. Strange conduct. She returned every other visit. . . .

SOURCE : O'Connell Papers, NLI 13651

1 Their coachman.
2 Their son.
3 Thomas O'Mara (died 1843), 3 Bachelor's Walk, Dublin, and
   Lisanisky, Blackrock, Co. Dublin, and Glencullen, Co. Dublin.
   Married 1806 Margaret, widow of Thomas Fitz-Simon of Glencullen. A prominent and wealthy attorney, noted as a duellist, he
   helped to effect a reconciliation between O'Connell and Richard
   Lalor Sheil in 1823.
4 Margaret O'Mara (1771-1854), widow of Thomas Fitz-Simon of
   Glencullen and wife of Thomas O'Mara, daughter of Bartholomew
   Callan, Osberstown House, Co. Kildare.
5 The *Dublin Evening Post* of 7 August 1819 called on O'Connell and
   Denys Scully to deny that they had had ' several communications
   with a confidential agent of the Opposition ', previous to the passing
   of the witchery resolutions (see letter 779). In a letter from Tralee
   dated 10 August 1819, to the *Dublin Evening Post* O'Connell denied
   that he had had ' any confidential communication with any confidential or other agent of the Opposition ' on these resolutions, and
   he was thoroughly convinced he could say the same for Scully.
   He called on the newspaper to produce proof of its allegation
   (*DEP*, 17 Aug. 1819). In reply the *Post* said it could not produce
   legal proof since its allegation was based on verbal statements by
   persons, who could not be compelled to give evidence in a court of
   law, and on a consideration of the events of 1812 (*DEP*, 17 Dec.
   1819).
6 Eliza O'Neill, the actress.

785

To his wife, Merrion Square

Cork, 18 August 1819

My heart's own darling,

I have this moment got your letter of Monday (16th inst.)
and am shocked to hear of William's[1] impertinence to you.
You did quite right to part with him instantly. What an ungrateful rascal you have found in him after all. I wish I had
been at home to have flogged the scoundrel. But, sweetest,
how could you entertain the slightest fear that I would give

him any countenance whatsoever? Indeed, darling, I do not deserve that you should think so. On the contrary, I am quite convinced that I am much more angry with him than you can be. He is entitled to be paid to the end of the current quarter but no more. You may be sure I will not give him a single shilling or even the smallest countenance but directly the reverse.

I have ordered you both the Cork papers since the beginning of the Kerry assizes that you may see how busily engaged I am in all the trials. . . .

I have just had a very flattering communication from Lord Donoughmore on the subject of ' the resolutions of 1812 '. He seems actually delighted with my conduct and is certainly inflamed with great rage against ' honest Ned Hay '. That scoundrel can never again show his ugly nose and dirty person in Catholic affairs. . . .

I am glad you have seen Mrs. O'Mara. Her husband is a very sincere friend of mine. I should be glad if you had occasion to cultivate her acquaintance. The neglect of Miss O'Neill[2] is impertinent but of course only to be laughed at. I suppose she connected your visit in some way with Phillips'.[3] But she was greatly mistaken. It is not worth a single thought. . . .

SOURCE : Fitz-Simon Papers
1   Coachman.
2   Eliza O'Neill.
3   Charles Phillips.

786

To his wife, Merrion Square

Cork, 23 August 1819

My sweetest darling,

. . . Baron Smith has kept us all quite idle today. I was afraid to sit down to any kind of business or even to write to you least I should be called off at a moment's warning to court. And he has only now announced that he would do nothing until tomorrow. . . . I am quite uneasy least I should not be able to go up to you. I will wait here for your answer. Going up will leave me hardly any vacation . . . and if I go up I must pass a day at Knocklofty with Lord Donoughmore. Then

I must have another delay in Tralee. . . . Decide for me, sweetest, but there is no use in putting the question to the poll in the house as I believe all votes would concur in deciding for my return.

I had a most delightful day yesterday on the river in the steamboat. I never enjoyed a day more. I laughed an immoderate deal. . . .

SOURCE : Fitz-Simon Papers

787

To Daniel O'Connell, Kilgorey, Tulla, Co. Clare

Cork, 24 August 1819

My dear Dan,

I find that I shall not be able to meet the £300 bill without your assistance again. I wish to break it down by instalments and enclose you my note for £250. . . . The original bill was £350. I will thus have reduced it £100 and I shall feel no inconvenience whatsoever if you can allow me to continue this scale of reduction. At all events *do it* this time. . . .

SOURCE : NLI, MSS 5759

788

From his wife to Parade, Cork

Lanesville [Monkstown, Co. Dublin],
Thursday night, 26 August 1819

My dearest Dan,

You ask me to decide whether you will return to your family previous to your journey to Kerry. Never in my life, darling, did I feel half so much at a loss what to say. The subject is a trying one and if I were to act from my own feelings and those of our children I would say do not go to Kerry without giving me and your family the happiness of seeing you. After maturely considering everything for and against my wishes on the subject I think you had better go on to Kerry, finish your business *there,* three weeks at the utmost you said in a former letter would suffice, three weeks more between Carhen and Derrynane *ought* to be a sufficient time for you to spend, but the dread is that when once you put your foot in *that* country it will be a hard matter to prevail upon *yourself* to quit it. How you would love grousing and any other country amusements you could wish for. O'Mara was expecting you to his part of the world and was determined to preserve *the game* for you, but all our plans are *now knocked* in the *head*. *It* would be impossible for me to give you an idea of the gloom that spread o'er the face of your family when I communicated the subject of your letter to me yesterday. My poor Nell and Kate wept and wished Iveragh was out of the world, ' every barrister returns to stay with his family (but our father) when circuit ends '. However, after arguing with them for some time I brought them to join me in thinking as you could stay only three or four days here it was better you should go first to Kerry by which means you would be able to return to us early in October. On these *conditions* and *no other* will we hear of your going to Tralee without paying *us* a visit. And we must have a *certificate* under your hand to that effect. I well know what a disappointment it is to yourself not to be able to spend some time with me and with your children. Indeed, my own love, I am certain you feel the disappointment as much as we do and, if I have said anything to hurt your feelings, be assured I did not mean it. No, my dearest Dan, you are dearer to me than my existence and I would not intentionally give you a moment's pain. Write to me as regularly as you can. I suppose you will have the papers forwarded to you while you stay in Kerry. What will you do with your circuit *carriage*? Perhaps one of the barristers coming direct to Dublin would take charge of it for you. . . .

[P.S.] . . .

SOURCE : O'Connell Papers, NLI 13650

789

From his son Morgan to Cork

Lanesville [Monkstown, Co. Dublin],
Friday, 27 [August] 1819

My dear Father,
. . . Mr. L'Estrange was here last night and showed me *my* Commission as Captain in Colonel Lyster's Regiment of

Fusiliers and aide-de-camp to the General. You will be a little
surprised when you hear this and also when you hear that
I was enrolled on the staff the 27th of June last, when the
General was in Liverpool. Tom O'Connell has also got a
commission of Captain in the same corps. . . .

> I remain, your very affectionate son,
> Morgan O'Connell.

> Captain, 1st Regt. of Fusiliers and
> Aide-de-camp to General D'Evereux, Irish Legion

SOURCE : O'Connell Papers, NLI 13645

790

To his wife, Merrion Square

Killarney, 1 September 1819

My dearest love,

I left Cork late on Saturday evening and travelled in a
gig with old Mr. Coppinger,[1] the Counsellor's father, eleven
miles to Leemount, his place. It is a sweet spot but embittered
to him cruelly by the loss of his only daughter. I remained
there on Sunday and Monday in continual rain. But I had
Father England[2] and a delicious dish of politics. I never was
in half such spirits on political subjects at least since the last
triumph of legitimacy.[3] I begin to entertain strong hopes that
the dominion of the good and the wise is not eternally to
belong to the greatest scoundrels in the creation. . . .

I wish, darling, you would gratify me by not bathing my
poor John any more as he does not like it. A violent dislike
to bathing is a kind of warning nature gives against the use
of the bath. . . .

SOURCE : Fitz-Simon Papers

1 Thomas Stephen Coppinger, Leemount, Co. Cork, father of Stephen
  Coppinger, B.L.

2 Probably Fr. John England, P.P.

3 A reference to the fall of Napoleon and the restoration of the old
  order which O'Connell regarded as disastrous for liberty. See
  letter 562.

791

To his wife, Merrion Square

Tralee, 4 September 1819

My darling Heart,

. . . Both John[1] and you have heard from me before now. You see I am anxious about his not bathing. In fact he has a very large head and the cold bath is dangerous for persons of that configuration. But you, my sweetest love, are the best judge, and I am sure of your anxiety for his health.

I will write by the next post to my darling Morgan. He is no small favourite of mine. I suppose he takes up his title of Major to which as Aide-de-Camp he is entitled. My poor fellow. . . .

Will you call at Hodges and McArthurs[2] and ask them when they can send me the *Edinburgh Review* which I see just advertised in the London paper. You know how impatient I always am for the *Review* so that I am quite sure you will not delay making the inquiry. . . .

We have races here if you please. I went yesterday as they were near the bath. Such a miserable attempt at a race was never made. . . .

SOURCE : Fitz-Simon Papers
1 His son.
2 Booksellers and stationers, 21 College Green, Dublin.

792

From his wife to Cahirciveen

Dublin, 4 September [postmarked 1819]

My dearest Love,

On my arrival here this morning I was most agreeably surprised to find a letter from you to me and another to John. I was really quite uneasy about you. I neither knew where you were nor how you were. How I do abominate the County Kerry. As for your children, they never cease abusing *it*, at least the female part. Indeed, my own love, it is a cruel disappointment to your family to have you stay away so long but we are satisfied you feel equally as sore on the subject and we

console ourselves in the certainty of seeing you *early* in the
next month. . . .

I send you through Maurice a *Clare Journal*[1] [which] came
yesterday with a letter which I now forward to you. I don't
know for what but I feel most uneasy about Mr. Staunton's
publication in the Ennis paper. Tell me what it is about. At
the other side of this letter I will send you a list of the bills
that are due. You always settled them previous to the summer
circuit. I told you in a former letter that I forged your name
for [? Nowlan], the carpet man. Mr. Hickson, who I saw
this day, seemed to be quite in a puzzle about a bill of yours
to a large amount which he knew nothing of until the notice
was sent him. . . .

Burn all my letters while you are in Kerry.

[overleaf]

Darcy Ayre, Grocer	£192.	5. 5
William Keane, Chandler	68.	8. 6
Samuel Kelly, Painter	78.	13. 8

The grocer's and chandler's bill are for a year up to the last
day of July 1819. *They* want a settlement very much. Kelly's
is for painting and papering the house last October. Burn this
letter, I again entreat of you.

SOURCE : O'Connell Papers, NLI 13651
1 Not extant.

793

From his wife to Derrynane

Lanesville [Monkstown, Co. Dublin], 7 September [1819]

My dearest Love,

. . . My poor fellow [John] joined his entreaties to your
request of not bathing him. I should at once accede, only
O'Riordan[1] recommended the cold bathing to John in particular to strengthen him after his long and severe illness. . . .
The boys have not bathed since they came here. They are at
present grousing at Glencullen. I hope to prevail on *that*
family[2] to dine with me on Sunday next to meet Mrs. Mahon[3]
and the O'Gormans.[4] I thought you would wish me to pay a
compliment to Mrs. Mahon and I therefore asked her. I shall

ask Finlay[5] and his wife to dine with me. I will depute Mr.
O'Mara to *act* for you. He is such a pleasant man. I think he
is the very best substitute I could give my friends for the loss
of your society. You will say *it* is a *bold* thing for me to ask
company in your absence. I assure you I would cheerfully give
up the pleasure except for the above mentioned motive. I
get hares and grouse constantly from Mrs. O'Mara. . . .

I hope, my heart, you will not leave Tralee without finally
settling poor James Connor's affairs. . . . Your letter this
night has decided John's bathing. He shall not again venture. . . .

[P.S.] Burn this letter and every other you receive from me
while you stay in Iveragh.

SOURCE : O'Connell Papers, NLI 13650
1   Dr. John O'Reardon.
2   The O'Maras of Glencullen.
3   Probably the wife or mother of Nicholas Mahon.
4   The Purcell O'Gormans.
5   John Finlay.

794

To his wife, Merrion Square

Carhen, 8 September 1819

My darling love,

. . . Do not, love, forget to call about the *Edinburgh
Review* and do not detain it one hour for the purpose of sending it by a safe hand. *Safe hands* never send anything forward in time. . . .

The Knight of Kerry is making a fortune of slates. I
believe I will soon become a great slate merchant. . . .

SOURCE : Fitz-Simon Papers

795

From his wife to Carhen

Lanesville [Monkstown, Co. Dublin],
Friday, 10 September [1819]

My dearest love,

. . . Mrs. Mahon, the O'Gormans, O'Maras and Finlays

are to dine with me. Would to God, darling, you were to make one of the party. I feel quite awkward at the idea of entertaining company without you. . . . You know, darling, how little of your company we enjoy during term. Do then try to arrange your business so as to give us the happiness of having you *here* free from care and business for three weeks. I am quite satisfied you feel as anxious to be with your family as they feel to see you, but the fear is that *this* person and the other will be detaining you with their business. Leave it to Stephen Rice and I *promise* you that here you will get as much to do, at least as much emolument by business, that you could do at your leisure, as you would get in Kerry by being chained to the *desk* from morning until night. . . .

Friday night. 11 o'clock.

. . . I am in very bad spirits since I learned from my mother you would not be in Tralee until the 10th of October. This gives *us* no chance of seeing you until the latter end of *that* month as you will be detained again in Tralee. I may expect to be disappointed when you go to Kerry. How I do *hate* Kerry. . . .

SOURCE : O'Connell Papers, NLI 13650

796

To his wife, Merrion Square

at Cahir[civeen], Sunday, 12 September 1819

My darling Love,

. . . I spent the last three days at Derrynane. The old gentleman is in good health and excellent spirits. I spent my three days very pleasantly with him. I left Derrynane at five this morning, breakfasted with Butler, killed a fine hare and came here quite in time for Mass. We begin our grouse shooting tomorrow. The weather is become fine again and we have a prospect of great sport. . . .

SOURCE : Fitz-Simon Papers

797

From his wife to Cahirciveen

Lanesville [Monkstown, Co. Dublin], 13 September [1819]

[No salutation]

. . . I hope, my heart, you have no intention of building at Carhen. I really think it would be throwing your money away, at least for some years. Only think of the short time you have to spend out of Dublin and would it be worth your while to build? Consider well before you involve yourself. I am led to write on this subject from having heard you were determined to begin your house in Iveragh before you left the country. I thought you had given up every notion and I still hope you would not do anything in this way without first mentioning your intention to me. . . .

[14 September 1819] . . . I assure you, love, this house often reminds me of what Carhen was. Not a week passes without visitors of some kind. Maurice, just like yourself and your poor father, cannot see any friend without asking them to spend a day or two in the country with him. . . . Burn this I beg of you as well as my other letters.

SOURCE : O'Connell Papers, NLI 13651

798

From his wife to Carhen

Lanesville [Monkstown, Co. Dublin],
16 [and 17] September 1819

My dearest love,

. . . The conclusion of the next patron will, I hope, see you on your way out of the country. . . .

Friday [17 September 1819]

. . . I suppose you have heard of the second *conversion* of Lord Dunsany.[1] During the assizes of Trim he took the oaths of allegiance as a Catholic and went publicly to Mass to the great annoyance of some of the members of his family. Report

says that the second Miss Byrne[2] of Cabinteely is to be married
to Lord Gormanston's eldest son.[3] It is whispered that the
eldest Miss B. is a little out of her mind. . . .

SOURCE : O'Connell Papers, NLI 13651

1 Randall (Plunkett), thirteenth Baron Dunsany (1738/9-1821), Dunsany Castle, Co. Meath.
2 Georgiana Mary Byrne (died unmarried 1850), second daughter of
   Robert [O']Byrne (1746-99) and Mary Devereux.
3 Hon. Edward Anthony John Preston (1796-1876); high sheriff,
   Co. Meath, 1831, and Co. Dublin, 1845. Succeeded as thirteenth
   Viscount Gormanston, 1860. He married in 1836 Lucretia, eldest
   daughter of William C. Jerningham.

799

To his wife, Merrion Square

Portmagee [Cahirciveen, Co. Kerry], 18 September 1819

My darling Love,

I will *not* burn your letters. I could not do it even now,
but the moment I get to Derrynane I make them up in sealed
parcels and lock them up so that no person can possibly get
at them. Be assured that I keep them with the utmost safety.
On that you may implicitly rely.

The Dublin post days for this country are Tuesdays,
Thursdays and Saturdays. Letters arrive here, that is, in
Cahirciveen, the morning of the third day. The post appears
to be very regular and correct.

I go off in the morning to Derrynane where I shall spend
the entire of the next week working at my trade. I spent this
week *sporting* and never in my life was in better health or
spirits. The weather is delightful and game in the greatest
plenty. The house at Carhen I am not building. I am only
raising stones there to build one time or the other, and it is
impossible to attempt it until next year, nor even then without
your permission unless indeed the old gentleman[1] was to give
me the money for doing it. You may be sure I will do nothing without your perfect concurrence. It may yet tempt you
to spend a summer in Iveragh if you had—as there shortly
will be—an excellent road quite level *over* Drung. Myles
McSwiney and a Mr. Meredith[2] have contracted for making

the road[3] and are actually employed in the work. They will certainly clear from three to four hundred pounds each by the job. . . .

SOURCE : Fitz-Simon Papers

1   Hunting-Cap.
2   Unidentified.
3   See letters 761 and 853.

800

To his wife, Merrion Square

Derrynane, 22 September 1819

My darling love,

. . . I *promise* you, love, to leave this as soon after the *pattern* as possible. The weather has *been* and is delightful. The last week I was every day on foot. This is a week of comparative quiet. I devote only Friday and Saturday to shooting and hunting. On Sunday I go to Carhen. We spend Monday at Primrose's and the Pattern begins on Wednesday and now continues three days.

I got a letter by the last post also from Maurice. O'Mara has offered him a horse and he, poor fellow, feels a natural anxiety to be master of it. I do not know what to say to him about it. The expense of keeping another horse would be considerable and would totally preclude me from having a horse for my own riding. Besides it would create a great jealousy unless we had a horse for Morgan too. In fact there are, therefore, such difficulties in the way that I do not know how to comply with the poor fellow's request and yet I do still less know how to refuse him. It will certainly preclude me from thinking of getting a horse for myself much as that is wanting to the preservation of my health. I will not answer his letter till I hear from you and do you speak with him about it and *in short* do just as you please. I refer it to you. . . .

SOURCE : Fitz-Simon Papers

801

*To his wife, Merrion Square, 26 September 1819, from
Carhen*

' On second thoughts I think you had better allow Maurice
to take the horse from O'Mara as *a loan* not as a gift. This
will enable us to send him back if necessary, and to gratify
my dear Maurice.'

SOURCE : Fitz-Simon Papers

802

To his wife, Merrion Square

Killarney, Monday, 11 October 1819

My darling Heart,
    You will be glad to find me clean out of Iveragh and will
now be sure that I will soon be with you. . . .
    I have had a very flattering letter from General D'Evereux.
He very cheerfully accedes to taking Tom O'Connell out in
his own vessel with himself. She is a sloop of war elegantly
fitted up, and he promises Tom a good berth. He must be
immediately ready as D'Evereux will be in Dublin as soon as
me.

SOURCE : Fitz-Simon Papers

803

To Owen O'Conor

Merrion Square, 21 October 1819

My dear Friend,
    Whose fault will it be if we are not emancipated this
season? I think our own. One grand effort now ought to
emancipate us, confined, as it would be, exclusively to our
own question. After *that* I would, I acknowledge, join the
reformer's hand as well as heart, unless *they* do now emancipate. By they, of course I mean the Parliament.
    I intend instantly to set the cause in motion. This great

experiment is worth making. I think you will let me have your assistance. I write by this post to Lord Fingall. I am strongly prompted by our friends in Parliament. I wish to God you could come up *at once* to help me. If we *show out* before the Regent's speech is prepared, perhaps we may be remembered in it. If you agree with me that this time requires a sacrifice, you will come up. My own opinion is that we will be emancipated *now or never*.

I came to town only yesterday, and already I have many irons in the fire to raise the blaze which should lead us to victory. I want you much, and the cause wants you more.

SOURCE : Clonalis Papers

804
To ———?

21 October 1819

[Extract]

The period is at length arrived when we may ascertain and place beyond any doubt whether it be determined that we are for ever to remain a degraded and inferior class in our native land, and so to remain, without any one rational cause or even any one avowable pretext. We may now reduce the enemies of liberty of conscience to this dilemma—either now to grant us Emancipation or to proclaim to us and to the world that as long as the Parliament shall be constituted as it is at present, so long all hope of Emancipation is to be totally extinguished.

To this dilemma our enemies may be reduced, and it is a precious advantage to be able, for the first time in the history of Catholic affairs, to place them in a situation in which emancipation cannot be refused without an avowal of stern, unrelenting and inexorable bigotry; or of worse, of a disposition to make use of bigotry as an instrument to perpetuate the divisions, dissensions and consequent degradation and oppression of Ireland.

SOURCE : FitzPatrick, *Corr.*, I, 62

805

To Lord Cloncurry

Merrion Square, 4 November 1819

My Lord,

I suppose you heard of the adjournment of the meeting at Humphries[1] until the 1st of December. A pail of cold water could not have been half so chilly. Peter Burrowes, the mover, is just gone off, I am told, to London on a political mission. I suspect—but may be wrong—*wheels within a wheel*.

But it will not do. The people insist on an immediate dinner.[2] Instead of retarding the subscription, it will much promote it. In fact, if the dinner be not got up properly, it *will* be got up badly: for there is no restraining public feeling on the subject. I wish I had the favour of ten minutes' conversation with you. I see that the Duke of Leinster is in town; let me but be able to procure his assistance and yours, and everything will be as you could wish it. I repeat that the dinner should be one of the stimulants to the subscription because I know that it would be the most powerful in its effects. The committee for the subscription at Humphries' are Protestants. The dinner should be given by Catholics and Protestants (oh, how I hate these distinctions!) that is, by Irishmen.

We want also a parish meeting in this *most loyal* parish to thank and address McKenny. I will leave the requisition at your house in town for your signature and for any other you can procure. I do entreat of you to *step out* about the dinner as the very best source of promulgating generous and patriotic sentiments.

There was a handsome sword bought for General Devereux with the surplus produce of the tickets for his dinner after paying for the entertainment. I know that it would be taken very kindly if you would have the goodness to present it when he arrives.

Let me return you my most hearty thanks for your letter[3] to Hunt.[4] Perhaps the thanks you receive from the honest will be almost as flattering as the abuse of the venal and the servile.

SOURCE : Cloncurry, *Personal Recollections,* p. 265

1   At a meeting in William Humphrey's, 15 Fownes Street, Dublin, the committee of the Protestant Friends of Catholic Emancipation resolved that a general subscription be raised 'for paying some distinguished mark of public . . . gratitude to Alderman Thomas McKenny, the late Lord Mayor, for his virtuous and independent conduct in calling and presiding at the Meeting of the Protestant Friends of Roman Catholic Freedom . . . in February last' (*DEP,* 30 Oct. 1819; see also letter 762, note 4).

2   A public dinner to McKenny, at which it was stated the duke of Leinster would preside, was advertised in the *Dublin Evening Post* (*DEP,* 13, 20 Nov. 1819). It was stated that the dinner would be delayed pending McKenny's recovery from illness.

3   In reply to a circular letter from the English reformers addressed to persons in Ireland possessing influence with the Catholics. Cloncurry's reply expressed support for parliamentary reform, annual parliaments and universal suffrage (*DEP,* 28 Oct. 1819).

4   Henry Hunt (1773-1835), the celebrated radical, reformer and orator who spoke at St. Peter's Fields (Peterloo) in 1819; imprisoned, 1820-22; M.P. for Preston, 1830-32. See *DNB.*

806

To his wife, Merrion Square

Cork, 1 January 1820

My darling Heart,

. . . There is a kindliness in my own Mary which renders her society most endearing to her husband. I am beginning a new year and I can well say that you have constituted the sweetness and happiness of the past. The season of compliments is over between us, but I can say in perfect sincerity that during this last year as during many preceding ones there was not one single action, word or thought of yours but what was directed to the comfort and happiness of your husband and children. Darling, I am truly and most cordially grateful, and believe me, I prize and cherish you with all the fondness and the pride of one who has made the best of all human selections. . . . Indeed, darling, I love you with more of tenderness and truth than ever woman was loved before. . . .

SOURCE : Fitz-Simon Papers

807

From his wife to Tralee

Dublin, 4 January 1820

[No salutation]

The tenderness and affection of your letter, my own darling, added considerably to the happiness of hearing of your safe arrival in Cork. . . . To you, darling, I owe everything. *It* would be quite impossible for any woman married to you not to be happy, but never could woman love you as well or as truly as I do. You are dearer to me than existence. This I am satisfied you will believe as you know me incapable of thinking one way and speaking another. Your children talk of you with absolute adoration. The days that must intervene before your return are counted over every day. . . . Morgan is as sanguine as ever in the Patriot cause. He minds no reports or published letters. The papers will tell you all. The poor General[1] is cut up everywhere but I cannot bring my mind to believe he could be a *second Judas*.[2] . . . I purpose sending the carriage to the *funeral* of Lady Talbot.[3] I am sure you will have no objection. *She* was an Irishwoman, a good wife and mother, and Lord Talbot[4] is not a bad man.

SOURCE : O'Connell Papers, NLI 13651

1 John Devereux.
2 Disaster had overtaken the first contingent of Devereux's Irish Legion which had landed on the island of Margarita in August 1819. Reports of the disaster for which Devereux was blamed were beginning at this time to arrive in Dublin (*DEP,* 14 Dec. 1819; *CMP,* 30 Dec. 1819; 5, 7, 8, 12, 13, 14, 15, 24, 28 Jan. 1820).
3 Frances Thomasine (1782-1819), wife of the second Earl Talbot and daughter of Charles Lambart, Beau Parc, Co. Meath. She died 30 December 1819 in the Viceregal Lodge, Dublin, and was buried at Ingestre Hall, Staffordshire.
4 Charles Chetwynd (Chetwynd-Talbot), second Earl Talbot of Hensol (1777-1849), lord-lieutenant of Ireland, 1817-21. An opponent of Emancipation but regarded by O'Connell as impartial. See *DNB.*

808

To his wife, Merrion Square

Killarney, 11 January 1820

My darling love,

I will be at home with you to dinner on Monday the 17th,
that is positive. . . .

I am also on the thorns about Maurice. I hope, love, you
speak to him *every day.* His missing the study of one single
day would most probably throw him out of the premium.
Tell him, heart, that I most anxiously entreat of him to attend
to his Latin. He may think that he can get off on that easily
but he is mistaken. If he does not study every day he will be
defeated. I wish he would share my anxiety for his
success. . . .

SOURCE : Fitz-Simon Papers

809

From John Devereux[1]

[Probably c. 31 January 1820]

[Extract]

I omitted to mention in my defence or statement that on the
arrival in London of the commissioners of Venezuela and
New Granada,[2] they generously marked my exertions in the
cause of their country by a proposal to make me the usual
allowance by contract. Actuated by no motive of selfishness
I declined their well-meant proposition and in reply assured
them that I looked to no compensation beyond the glory of
the achievement.

[Extract]

Enclosed, my dear Sir, is a letter from Colonel Blosset[3] next
in command to English of the British Regt. or Legion as they
now term it after *ours,* dated Maturin the 27 Octbr. [1819].
It is only brought me this instant by Mr. Blennerhassett whose
son[4] is at Margarita. As I think it of importance, you'll please
to take care of it with the *Orinoco Courier*[5] or rather after
you have perused it with the *Orinoco Courier* you'll please

hand to Hamilton[6] who will wait upon you for them. Quiet
poor old McNally.[7] In a pecuniary point of view I will be
happy to satisfy him and indeed I have made arrangements
to satisfy *all* if they will only give me a little time.

SOURCE : Fitz-Simon Papers

1　These two extracts are from the same letter, the first part of which
　　has been torn off. They are probably postcripts to letter 810.
2　Penalver and Vergara, who were sent to London by Bolívar in
　　connection with the raising of a loan.
3　Colonel Blosset was second-in-command to Brig. Gen. James T.
　　English who had returned to Margarita leaving Blosset in command
　　at Maturin.
4　Lt. Henry Blennerhassett, son of Capt. Thomas Blennerhassett
　　(formerly of the Kerry militia). He died in Margarita in August
　　1819.
5　*Correo del Orinoco* of 2 October 1819 which contained O'Connell's
　　invitation to the dinner (see letter 810, note 3) and the *Morning
　　Chronicle's* report on the dinner.
6　W. H. Hamilton, one of the two editors of the *Dublin Evening Post*.
　　He died in Nueva Granada on 26 December 1825.
7　Leonard McNally (1752-1820), barrister. Member of committee set up
　　to examine charges against Devereux, the first meeting of which
　　took place on 29 January 1820. See *DNB*.

810

From John Devereux

London, 7 February 1820

My dearest Sir,

I am now on my legs and shall positively set out on Wednesday next. I can never sufficiently acknowledge the debt
of gratitude you have laid me under by the kind, the generous
part you take in my present situation.[1] But, please God, with
your generous protection I shall soon stand higher than ever.
I have reason to know, though I never gave him cause, that
the Reverend Mr. L'Estrange is my secret enemy—and this
with a view to save his brother.[2] Now I assure you most
solemnly, my dear Sir, I have never given Mr. L'Estrange
cause to act this ungenerous part but, on the contrary, I have
prevented many things coming to a knowledge of the public
that would disgrace his brother for ever and which I can
prove to you by documents now in my possession. You might

therefore influence him to soften down Carrick's paper, where I understand he exercises in secret his crafty influence against me.

Enclosed is the *Orinoco Courier* which is under the immediate direction of the Secretary of State, Sr. Don J. German Roscio, and in which nothing can appear but with the approbation of the Government. You'll perceive in it the note of invitation you honoured me with for the great dinner,[3] and my answer, by which you'll perceive also by the heading of my answer, that there is no question of my rank in the service.[4] This you had as well keep by you as it is at least a collateral evidence of my rank and authority being fully recognized. I hope you'll manage Phillips, on whose friendship and goodwill I count. With best compliments to Mrs. O'Connell and best wishes for your most interesting family.

[P.S.] . . . You can give out that you have seen it in the *Orinoco Courier*—my name announced as far back as the 2nd of October, headed with the order and rank I hold in the Republic.

I am glad to see young Curran's name on the committee[5] as I flatter myself that he cherishes a friendly feeling towards me. I am rejoiced to find the worthy Mr. Burrowes's name also of the number.

SOURCE : Fitz-Simon Papers

1 On 29 January 1820 a meeting was held in Dublin ' for the purpose of investigating the circumstances which had led to the calamities that have befallen our Countrymen in the expedition to Margarita ' (*CMP*, 28 Jan. 1820). To the annoyance of several of the participants, O'Connell spoke at length in Devereux's defence, and at his suggestion a committee was appointed to investigate the very damning charges against Devereux (*CMP*, 31 Jan, 1 Feb. 1820). On 5 February a number of the members, led by Charles Phillips, withdrew from the committee asserting that they were being browbeaten by disreputable witnesses who seem to have favoured Devereux (*CMP*, 8 Feb. 1820).

2 Maj. Anthony L'Estrange, who took out the first contingent of the lancers of the legion. They arrived in Margarita 11 August 1819 on the *William*. He was accused of disloyalty to the legion and of selling their provisions in Margarita on landing. He died of yellow fever in Margarita sometime before December 1819.

3 A dinner held by the ' Irish Friends of South America ' which took place on 19 July 1819 (*CMP*, 20, 21 July 1819). O'Connell had

composed the published invitation to Devereux to attend this
dinner (*MC*, 20 July 1819).

4 Devereux's reply to the above invitation is published in *Carrick's
Morning Post*, 19 July 1819. It is headed ' Juan D'Evereux, De la
Order del Libertador Mayor General del exercito de la Republica
de Venezuela y Nueva Granada; y Commandante de la Legion
Irlandesa, etc.' He was not made a *general de division* (major-
general) until 14 December 1819 (D. F. O'Leary, *Memorias del
General Daniel Florencio O'Leary*, 3 vols. [Caracas 1952], II, 24).

5 William Henry Curran.

811

From John Devereux to Merrion Square

Liverpool, 18 February 1820

My dear Sir,

My heart is too full to express to you all I feel for the
generous, the superhuman part you have acted by me—
actions and not words must prove the gratitude of my heart.

I am now, my dear friend, secluded from public view
under the roof of a kind friend, there being a Government
warrant issued for my arrest. If I show myself in Ireland
nothing can save me from arrest, for the Spanish Minister
has laid his plans so profoundly that the Government must
in its own defence prosecute me. Depend upon it that all this
uproar against me is got up by the able management of San
Carlos's[1] agents. Why therefore expose myself to inevitable
ruin?[2] My best vindication will be acting with my troops at
the point of the bayonet by the side of Bolívar[3]—and the first
blow that is struck will be my best reputation. In a word,
my dearest friend, you must yourself see that there is an
organized conspiracy formed to put me and the Legion *down*—
at the bottom of it *all* is San Carlos—and Spanish dollars with
promises (never to be performed) to any amount. As a *secret*
I tell you, that San Carlos boasted to the Marquess of Headfort[4] how well he laid his plans to crush me and all future
expeditions from Ireland—and this I assure you a fortnight
or three weeks before the storm burst upon me. He moreover
declared that these armaments going from Ireland gave his
court infinitely more uneasiness than the taking of Santa Fé
by Bolívar. Hence, my dear Sir, you may judge how important
they deemed my overthrow. Oh! that wretched Phillips—

to give in to the conspiracy!⁵ But I leave him to himself and his own reflections—as his best punishment.

Unless you counteract me, it is my present determination to go by the packet to Granada and take with me your son⁶ and a part of my staff—and let the expedition, which is now prepared, follow. But to go to Ireland to sulk I would prefer being put under ground at once—a detention of six or seven months would be as bad to me as seven years at this moment-ous crisis of my affairs. It *would* be a most gratifying cir-cumstance to me, my dear Sir, to have it in my power to present your dear son to Bolívar. I would deem it the proud-est honour of my life. After the shameful conduct of the com-mittee in prejudging and condemning me,⁷ I really think a statement made to be published as I am *off* would be my best defence to the nation [about one word missing] cause and assign as a reason for not coming before the [about three words missing] in consequence of the Enlistment Bill,⁸ and that I could not attempt while in the Kingdom to combat my enemies without committing myself and the best interests of the cause.

J. D'Evereux

[one word missing] letters must now be addressed to me under cover to Messrs. Wm. & James Brown, Liverpool.⁹

SOURCE : Fitz-Simon Papers

1 Duke de San Carlos, Spanish ambassador to Great Britain.
2 Devereux apparently feared the outcome of attempts in Dublin to organize an investigation into his conduct (see letter 810). On 13 February 1820 a letter was published which purported to be from the field officers of the Irish Legion and which expressed the determination of the latter to have the interrupted investigation into Devereux's conduct resumed on his returning to Dublin (*CMP*, 13 Feb. 1820).
3 Simón Bolívar.
4 Thomas (Taylour), first marquis of Headfort (1757-1829).
5 Charles Phillips led the secession of members from the Dublin committee set up to investigate Devereux's conduct (see letter 810, note 1).
6 Morgan.
7 Whether the Dublin committee issued any formal condemnation of Devereux has not been ascertained.
8 An act which came into force on 3 July 1819 (59 Geo. III c.69). It prohibited British subjects from enlisting in foreign armies, but proved largely ineffective.
9 Of 34 Strand Street, Liverpool, merchants.

812

To Denys Scully

Merrion Square, 27 February 1820

My dear Scully,

I enclose you the account between us signed. Send me a counterpart signed by you. Many, many thanks, my very kind and good friend.

I also enclose you the papers on the B——[1] controversy. The charge was given me yesterday by Daniel.[2] I return it with my reply. Poor B——. How sincerely I feel for his *exposure*. In truth there is as little talent as good feeling in this composition. It is after all the remote holding out of an uncertain pistol in order to extort money.

SOURCE : Scully Papers

1 Perhaps Richard Newton Bennett. Nothing is known of this controversy.
2 Unidentified.

813

To his wife, Merrion Square

Limerick, 6 March 1820

My darling Heart,

With my usual rapidity and, of course, safety I arrived here at half after nine last night without the slightest accident or disappointment. I will not go on to Ennis till after breakfast, and the worst is that there is very little to be done in that famed city.

I have thought of nothing but my poor friend Devereux and his triumph[1] since I left Dublin. I am amazingly impatient to see honest *Carrick*. The scoundrel has no recourse but to call it a forgery.[2] I write by this post to Colonel Hall.[3] Let Morgan have everything ready. I will get James Sugrue to make all the arrangements for his sea store etc. Short as his stay in Ireland may be, let him learn as much arithmetic as possible. Set him about it the moment you receive this letter. Even the knowledge of compound addition or subtraction would be better than total ignorance. Tell him it is my anxious request that he should devote a couple of hours a day to that exclusively. Let him not delay getting the multiplication table by heart, but let him apply as much to the practical part as can be done.

. . . My Maurice, my noble boy. Oh how triumphant he would make me if he would but exert himself. I declare to God I am sure he could go through his entire examination in a week if he pleased. Tell him his father entreats of him to take his natural place at the head of his class. He *can* do it if he *will,* but what does that signify if *he won't?*

SOURCE : Fitz-Simon Papers

1 The triumph refers to the publication of an address purporting to be from Simón Bolívar ' to the Brave Soldiers of the Irish Legion ' dated 14 December 1819. It declared that ' the promises which the virtuous and brave General Devereux has made you as the groundwork of your incorporation with the Liberating Army shall be religiously fulfilled on the part of the Governor and people of Venezuela ' (*CMP,* 6 Mar. 1820).

2 *Carrick's Morning Post* did claim that the above address was a forgery and that it had originated in Trinidad (*CMP,* 6 Mar. 1820). Eric T. D. Lambert, the historian of the Irish Legion, states that the address was genuine.

3 Francis Hall, lieutenant in 14th Regiment Dragoons, placed on half-pay, 1817. Philosopher and supporter of Jeremy Bentham. Colonel in Irish Legion, accompanied Devereux to South America. Assassinated in Quito, Ecuador, 19 October 1833. Defended Devereux in pamphlet, *An Appeal to the Irish Nation on the Character of General Devereux* (Dublin 1820).

813a

To John Finlay, Dublin

Limerick, 6 March 1820

My dearest friend,

Was I right when I said to you and Foley[1] and left you to translate the phrase for him, *Durate et vosmet rebus servate secundis.*[2] The favourable turn has arrived and the tide of good fortune should now be taken at its flow. You know well that it was ' the cause ' which first attached us to Devereux. I confess I soon liked the man. There is an unsophisticated flow of heart about him which caught my affections and mingling his mighty cause with his kindly self I became and in the worst of times continued and am his friend. But I repeat

it, ' the cause ' is the first great object. One more land of
liberty is a conquest over despotism and over legitimacy which
they cannot afford. Let us push the victory as far as we can.
I think you may well now do something either with your
name or at least anonymously in the papers. I believe the latter
is preferable because I have no idea of allowing you to commit
yourself with the raw and unfledged youths who have
returned for more of their mothers' breast-milk!! But your
pen is vigorous, and this is the time to have every pen in the
cause. The press is either bribed or seduced against us. There
was besides all the *vis inertiae*[3] of the constant hatred to liberty
and to her friends in full play against us. Write the cause
up again, my dear friend, or at all events help to do so. If
you even fail you will have the pleasure of having made the
exertion and of knowing that you have on this as on all other
occasions done your duty. Surely Ireland could supply ten
legions instead of one, and if there were such a man as
Colonel Hall at the head of affairs *to regulate* all the details,
a regiment a week may be sent out.

Colombia—I love the name—Colombia wants soldiers and
colonists. And there are the mighty realms of Mexico to be
freed and [? to be] peopled to five times their present number.

Let us work for liberty abroad since powerful oppression
in the upper classes and turbulent insubordination in the lower
preclude the possibility of working for liberty with either
at home.

SOURCE : Harvard University Library.
1 Either Matthew Foley or Patrick Dempsey Foley.
2 *Persevere and make use of more favourable opportunities.*
3 *The force of inertia.*

814

From his wife to Ennis

Dublin, 7 March 1820

[No salutation]

. . . The boys did not leave the General[1] until near twelve
last night. Besides the priests belonging to the house,[2] Colonel
Kenny[3] and a Mr. Young[4] dined with him. After Bolívar's
health and the Irish Legion, the General, after a beautiful
panegyric on you, proposed your health, styling you his God-

like friend. This toast, you will believe, was drunk with enthusiasm. The General was in great spirits, received your boys with the greatest affection. This time two-and-twenty years his friend, the Rev. Mr. L['Estrange] was *hiding* him previous to his getting off to America. Morgan breakfasted with the General this morning. He is not yet come home. I shall be no time in procuring a master for Morgan though. I fear he will not be able to attend him as he ought. What between sitting for his picture and going to you, the short time he has to stay here will be nothing. Carrick in his paper yesterday asserts the Proclamation[5] is a forgery fabricated at Trinidad, and Mr. Phillips said it was fabricated in London. There is no minding what such characters say. I was at Finlay's yesterday. Mrs. Finlay told me that Finlay was greatly delighted and in high spirits about the General. He was quite amused at the idea of the forgery. Colonel Hall was to dine there yesterday. . . . You will be surprised when you read an article on the Education Society in the *Freeman*.[6] Conway of the [*Dublin*] *Evening Post* waited on the General on Sunday [one word illegible] expressed his regret that his paper had not taken up his cause as it should have done, that it would do so now to the fullest extent and that he may command it. *This* is the paper that the good people said was bribed by the poor General. I shall wait Morgan's return from breakfast to conclude this letter.

Four o'clock. Morgan is this moment come in. The General recommends to him not to take any servant out as he can easily get one when he arrives and that his servant will attend him on the voyage. . . .

SOURCE : Fitz-Simon Papers

1   John Devereux.

2   The Carmelite monastery, Clarendon Street, Dublin.

3   John Kenny, colonel and acting adjutant general of the Irish Legion. He never went to South America. A strong supporter of Devereux when he was attacked in 1820.

4   Either Lt. Col. Brooke Young, lieutenant in 8th Foot, 1813-17; became colonel of Rifles in Irish Legion: sailed to South America with Lyster in March 1820; gave evidence in Dublin before committee set up to investigate charges against Devereux. Last heard of near Cartagena, probably making for home, 11 July 1826. Or Robert James Young (died 7 Aug. 1827 in Ireland), son of Robert Young, Culduff, Co. Donegal. He sailed on the *Laforey* in

July 1819 from Dublin and returned from South America immediately on arrival.

5   See letter 813.

6   On this day, 7 March, the *Freeman's Journal* stated that the *Dublin
    Weekly Register* of 26 February had published a letter from
    O'Connell to the Irish Catholic hierarchy asserting that the duke
    of Leinster and Lord Fingall intended to resign from the Society
    for Promoting the Education of the Poor of Ireland (otherwise
    known as the Kildare Place Society). The *Freeman's Journal* added
    that it was authorized to deny this assertion. In this letter to the
    Dublin Weekly Register O'Connell referred to the rejection by the
    meeting of the Kildare Place Society on 24 February 1820 of his
    proposal that a committee be appointed to report ' whether the
    means hitherto adopted by the Society were calculated to carry into
    effect in a fair and candid manner its avowed leading principle ',
    namely, equal facilities to persons of all religions. The rejection
    of his proposal, he argued, showed that the society was not sincere
    in its profession to afford such equality and, as a result, Leinster,
    Fingall and Cloncurry had indicated their intention to resign from
    the society. O'Connell then proposed the formation of a national
    association for education for ' the education of all classes of Chris-
    tians, conjointly and without interference with their religious tenets '
    letting ' each child be separately and apart instructed in the religious
    tenets of its parents by persons of its own religion '.

815

To his wife, Merrion Square

Ennis, Wednesday, 8 March 1820

My heart's own darling,

We have had very little business here and that little is now
quite over. I feel, however, a good deal fatigued as one of the
records lasted yesterday in part and nearly the entire of this
day. I spoke to evidence in it for near two hours and I fancy
contributed to get my client a verdict. At all events he has
got one and expresses great gratitude to me.[1] My vanity may
supply the rest.

. . . Do not send me any more newspapers until you hear
from me again as I pay one and eight pence a pair for them.
I believe it is occasioned by the dissolution of parliament.[2]
Send to inquire from Staunton and learn whether if it be not
attributable to the dissolution he could do anything in the way

of folding to have them come to me safe. Perhaps your seal-ing-wax occasions the postage. . . .

SOURCE : Fitz-Simon Papers

1 Court case not identified.

2 The dissolution was occasioned by the accession to the throne of George IV. The connection between the dissolution and the pay-ment of postage on newspapers is not clear.

816

To his wife, Merrion Square

Limerick, 10 March 1820

Darling Heart,

I came here yesterday about eight in the evening having completely dispatched all the business in Ennis. That all was very little, you may imagine how wretchedly little when I tell you that I who was in every cause received but thirty guineas. Indeed it little deserved the trouble of coming down for, and if there were not better times in prospect I would pitch Ennis to the dogs and not go there any more. As a con-solation, however, there is a great harvest in this town and the key-note of politics is high indeed. Rice[1] enters the field for the first time with hope of success even at the election itself. We give him a grand dinner on Monday next which will give a fillip to political feeling through the County.

I left Ennis too early to get the papers and letters of yester-day. I hope, darling, you have sent to inquire the reason why postage was charged on newspapers.

I am not surprised about the Duke of Leinster[2] for I was aware that to a certain extent I had been mistaken, but I think I will be even with the association and turn this very thing to their discomfiture.

I was much amused by the impudence of that base rascal Lonergan.[3] It was quite consistent with his audacity to allege the Proclamation to be a forgery.[4] In fact he had nothing else for it, and his saying *so* only proves that he is not acting from principle, a thing indeed that would have been easily believed of him beforehand.

There are several young men ready to *buy* commissions. Let Morgan inquire whether they can be taken out on paying their money and equipping themselves. I find that it is quite essential that Morgan should wear flannel next his skin, flannel and temperance are the two great secrets which ensure health in the West Indies. . . .

SOURCE : Fitz-Simon Papers

1 Thomas Spring Rice (1790-1866), M.P. for Limerick city, 1820-32; Cambridge, 1832-39. Under-secretary to the home office, 1827-28; secretary to the treasury, 1830-34; chancellor of the exchequer, 1835-39. Created Baron Monteagle, 1839. See *DNB*.
2 See letter 814, note 6.
3 Richard Lonergan (c. 1782-1827), proprietor of *Carrick's Morning Post*, 1819-27, of 11 Prussia Street, Dublin.
4 See letter 813, note 2.

817

From his son Maurice to Limerick

Merrion Square, Saturday, 11 March 1820

My dearest Father,

It is with very great pleasure that I claim my privilege from my mother of writing to you first of all the flock. To come at once to what I know you feel most interested in— we will conclude *the Locke*[1] with Sandes[2] on Monday next for the first time, and before this day week I think I may pretty confidently promise you to be master of my whole examination—Science and Classics. I have attended every lecture punctually since you left town except on Tuesday when a violent headache detained me at home all day. However I have since made up for it. . . . We dined with the General[3] on Monday last. . . . They are going to purchase a bust of Curran[4] at the Library.[5] Of course it will have your aid and support. . . .

SOURCE : Fitz-Simon Papers

1 Probably a work written by or about the political philosopher, John Locke.
2 Stephen Creagh Sandes, D.D. (1778-1842), F.T.C.D., 1807; bishop of Killaloe, 1836-39; bishop of Cashel, 1839-42.
3 John Devereux.
4 John Philpot Curran.
5 The Law Library, Four Courts, Dublin.

818

To his wife, Merrion Square

Limerick, Tuesday, 14 March 1820

My dearest Heart,

. . . I will certainly write to Maurice and to you tomorrow. The fact is we gave a great dinner to Rice[1] yesterday and though I drank only water yet having stayed up until one I could not rise until after eight, and then my clients were like a pack of hungry beagles after me. . . .

SOURCE : Fitz-Simon Papers
1   Thomas Spring Rice.

819

From his wife to Limerick

Dublin, 14 March [1820]

My dearest Love,

. . . We are greatly delighted with Hall's defence of our friend.[1] It is very well written, not unlike the way you would write. What a pity Hall was not with the General when he first commenced raising the Legion. I don't know what Carrick says now[2] but I will buy his paper of this day and forward it with the others to you this night. I must contrive to send Rick[3] one of Hall's pamphlets. He will rejoice at Devereux's triumph. Our children, my darling, are all as well and as happy as they can possibly be in your absence. I read for them always that part of your letters concerning them. *They* exultingly look at each other as much as to say, ' my father loves me as much as he does you.' . . . John, a sweet boy, is quite an enthusiast about the General. He begs of me to ask you, love, for him to take the name of Devereux in Confirmation. He always writes John Devereux O'Connell. He was walking the other day in the Square with a very nice boy. Ellen asked him when they came home who he was. ' I assure you, Ellen, he was a very great enemy of the General's but I talked to him and convinced him and when we parted he was the friend of General Devereux.' . . . Morgan is the gayest of the gay, getting on famously with his arith-

metic, mathematics and astronomy. He has got notice from
the General to be ready at a day's warning. However, I think
you will be home before *they* will be ready to leave this. . . .

Today's *Carrick* contains not a word on the South
American business. I believe all *his ammunition* is out. . . .

I am prouder of you than ever. Thank God, you acted so
nobly by your friend[4] in the hour of need. . . .

SOURCE : Fitz-Simon Papers

1 A pamphlet by Col. Francis Hall entitled *An Appeal to the Irish
   Nation on the Character and Conduct of General Devereux* (Dublin
   1820).
2 Observing that Hall's pamphlet was selling at 1/8d per copy,
   Carrick's Morning Post commented, ' One should think the poor
   simpletons of Irish had already paid dearly enough for an acquaintance with the General and his retainers, without being required to
   pay for his *vindication* also' (*CMP*, 13 Mar. 1820).
3 Her brother Rickard O'Connell.
4 John Devereux.

820

To his wife, Merrion Square

Limerick, 15 March 1820

My darling Heart,

. . . This is a *good* assizes. You will, however, be surprised to hear that I had a client convicted yesterday for a
murder for whom I fought a hard battle, and yet I do not
feel any the most slight regret at his conviction. It is very
unusual with me to be *so* satisfied, but he is a horrid villain.
In the first place he got a creature, a lovely creature of fifteen,
to elope with him from her uncle who brought her up an
orphan and to rob him of his all, 100 guineas, and in three
weeks after he contrived to get her into a boat on the Shannon
with his servant, said when he returned to Glin that he left
her at Kilrush, then reported she had gone off with a sea
captain, and she was not heard of afterwards for near two
months when a mutilated carcase floated on shore, or rather
was thrown, which was identified to be hers from some extremely remarkable teeth. He will be hanged tomorrow unless
being a gentlemen prevents him.[1]

I have agreed to go to the Mallow election for Becher
Wrixon. I leave this late on Friday or early on Saturday if

the contest goes on. There are but 300 freeholders so that I shall be in Tralee to Breakfast on Wednesday.[2] . . .

I got last night Hall's pamphlet.[3] I have not had time to read it yet. . . .

SOURCE : Fitz-Simon Papers

1 John Scanlan, hanged in Limerick on 16 March 1820 for the murder of Ellen Hanley, his body being given for dissection (*Ennis Chronicle*, 18 Mar. 1820). It was on this case that Gerald Griffin based his classic, *The Collegians : A Tale of Garryowen* (1829), which in turn provided Dion Boucicault with his material for *The Colleen Bawn* (first performed 27 Mar. 1860).
2 O'Connell was to assist as election agent William Wrixon Becher, a Whig-Liberal candidate for the Mallow seat in the general election. Born 1780, died 1850, he assumed the additional name of Becher, his mother's name. Created baronet, 1831; married 18 December 1819 Eliza O'Neill, the celebrated actress.
3 See letter 819; note 1.

821

To his wife, Merrion Square

Limerick, 16 March 1820

My darling Heart's Love,

. . . I am not as yet quite sure whether I shall be obliged to go to Mallow. I shall learn during the day. I should prefer not going there, as I would otherwise have two or three days of leisure to attend to other business between the two assizes, for nothing will be done in Tralee before Wednesday next. . . .

[P.S.] I *must* go to Mallow.

SOURCE : Fitz-Simon Papers

822

From his wife to Mallow

Dublin, 18 March 1820

My dearest Dan,

. . . Most fervently do I pray that our friend may be delayed for at least six weeks more and, indeed, I think there is every likelihood of his not being able to go out as soon

as he expected.[1] Up to yesterday there was no account except
of his safe arrival at his destination for the present. Our
dear Morgan is in great spirits, anxious to be off.[2] . . .
There was an idle report prevalent last night that a *body* of
Ribbonmen were to march to Dublin and take down the
statue in College Green. The police were parading the streets
all night. For the first time this year, I went to Chapel yesterday to Townsend Street. A young gentleman of the name of
McCabe[3] preached a beautiful panegyric on St. Patrick and
at the same time gave the Education Society a great dressing.
He called upon the rich and the middling classes to lose no
time in uniting to do away the danger that was abroad.
Proselytism was the Bible hawkers' view and not the religious
education of the poor of Ireland. I am quite anxious to know
the answer you got from his Grace and his Lordship.[4] There
is a very good article in the *Irishman* of this day respecting
the contradiction which appeared (in the papers) of what
everybody understood had fallen from the Duke of Leinster.
This Lawless[5] in my opinion is the only proprietor of a paper
that had any public spirit. We don't hear a word on South
America at present. . . .

SOURCE : Fitz-Simon Papers

1   A reference to Devereux whose expedition to South America sailed
    from Liverpool on 27 April 1820.
2   Morgan sailed with Devereux from Liverpool on 27 April 1820.
3   Rev. P. A. McCabe, curate of Townsend Street chapel.
4   Presumably O'Connell had written to Leinster and Fingall concern-
    ing his statement that they had resigned from the Kildare Place
    Society. See letter 814, note 6.
5   John Lawless, editor of the *Irishman*.

823

To his wife, Merrion Square

Mallow, 19 March 1820

My darling Heart,

I left Limerick on Friday at half after five and slept at
Charleville. I was here yesterday at an early hour. The
election commenced at about one o'clock. Mr. Becher made
an excellent speech, indeed, one of the best I ever heard. It
was full of excellent principle and admirably well delivered.

His antagonist is an unfledged boy of twenty[1]—quite an
English boy—confident and shallow—a man in his own
opinion but not in that of others. He said simply that he was
of no party and had no *political principles,* a most precious
avowal. His ancestor,[2] who proposed that Cromwell should
be King, *had* principles though they were not good ones.

The polling commenced and each party, after tendering
ten votes each, closed for the day. I had the good luck to
strike off the first vote tendered for Jephson—a very zealous
partisan, a Mr. Crother,[3] who had a speech ready too. There
remain about 250 voters to be polled, and as we must begin at
nine tomorrow and must continue until five I should expect
that we will either close the election altogether or at least get
so far forward as to be certain that I shall be able to leave this
on Tuesday by twelve or one o'clock.[4] I shall, beyond a doubt,
be in Tralee before the court sits on Wednesday and not lose
either a brief or fee. I am very well pleased that I came here
as I have been of considerable use to Becher. I am going out
to his house to dinner and will return again this night. The
fact is, heart, that I go principally to see *the O'Neill*[5] on a
new stage. I will, if possible, tell you tomorrow what I think
of her. At all events I will not leave this without writing. I am
in great spirits. The complete revolution in Spain is so
auspicious a circumstance that I hail it as the first of a series of
events useful to human liberty and human happiness.[6] Until
the last papers I was not without my fears of a failure, but
now my mind is quite at ease and I enjoy this revolution as all
the scoundrels of society enjoyed the battle of Waterloo.

SOURCE : Fitz-Simon Papers

1   Charles Denham Orlando Jephson (1799-1888), Mallow, Co. Cork;
     Whig-Liberal; M.P. for Mallow, 1826-59. Created baronet, 1838.
     Assumed in 1838 additional name of Norreys, thereafter known as
     Sir Denham Jephson-Norreys.
2   William Jephson (1615?-1658), member of Long Parliament until
     ' Pride's Purge '. See Jephson, *Anglo-Irish Miscellany,* pp. 16, 37-51.
3   Unidentified.
4   Polling commenced on 18 and ended on 23 March, the final result
     being 109 votes for Becher and 76 for his opponent, Jephson (*DEP,*
     21, 30 Mar.; *FJ,* 21 Mar. 1820).
5   The actress Eliza O'Neill, who had married William W. Becher in
     December 1819.
6   The *Liberales* had revolted and forced Ferdinand VII to restore the
     liberal constitution of 1812.

824

From his daughter Ellen to Tralee

Merrion Square, 20 March 1820

My dear Father,

. . . I was delighted to hear that you had gone to Mallow
as I suppose you saw the fascinating Mrs. Becher,[1] and I long
to know your opinion of her in private society. I am sure you
were greatly pleased with Col. Hall's pamphlet.[2] For our parts
we were *delighted* with it. I think it would convince any
unprejudiced person. Of course Mama has told you that we
have got the General's picture.[3] It is, I think, the strongest
likeness I ever saw. We are all as great advocates of his as ever
but we have not many to oppose us at present as most of our
former opponents are coming round to our opinion. John had
a great argument about him the other day in the Square with
a little boy whom he *at last convinced*. ' He came in an
enemy ', said John, ' and he went out a *friend*.' . . . Little
Dan is as bold as ever. Mama *says* she whipped him the other
day but I don't think either you or I will attach much credit
to that assertion, that would be in her the height of *magna-
nimity*. To say the truth he is a most bewitching little darling,
and I don't wonder he should be a *little* spoiled. Morgan's
picture[4] is almost finished. I did not see it yet but Mama says
it is extremely like him. He is drawn with the pelisse of the
hussars according to the General's recommendation to Mama.

SOURCE : O'Connell Papers, NLI 13645
1   See letter 823, note 5.
2   See letter 819, note 1.
3   Whether Devereux's picture still exists is not known.
4   This portrait is now on view in Derrynane.

825

To his wife, Merrion Square

Tralee, Thursday [23 March 1820]

My darling Love,

I could not possibly write either Monday or Tuesday. I
left Mallow at six on Tuesday evening and got to Killarney by
two in the morning. I came off here at half after five and

spent the day in court. Yet I never was in better health or spirits.

I cannot write more today, darling. We have a great dinner *tonight* for the Knight of Kerry. I believe I will be in the chair. With a thousand loves to all *ours*.

SOURCE : Fitz-Simon Papers

826

To his wife, Merrion Square

Tralee, Saturday [25 March 1820]

My darling love,

. . . We had a grand dinner[1] on Thursday for the Knight. I was in the Chair and we had a very delightful evening of it as ever I spent. I made a vast variety of speeches and the Knight also spoke often and he spoke well. Your health was drunk and I said something of the turning all the gall of human existence into honey which brought a tear of affection into my eye and delighted everybody.

SOURCE : Fitz-Simon Papers
1 Not reported in newspapers.

827

From his wife to Parade, Cork

Dublin, 27 March 1820

My dearest Dan,

. . . Believe me, Dan, it is the first wish of my heart to make you happy and *that* wish is the result of the sincerest and truest affection that ever woman bore for man. I am really, darling, flattered when I think and know that I still possess your affections. You have often told me you loved me as much *this* day as you did during the first year of our marriage and I have no reason to doubt you. On the contrary I have every reason to know there is not nor cannot be a woman on earth more blessed in the affections of the best of husbands than I am. I wish, darling, I had been listening to you on Thursday night.[1] Shall we see any of the speeches published? . . .

I believe you may reckon on seeing Morgan by this day
week. Hall expects to leave this in less than a fortnight. I got
a letter from the General[2] on Saturday. He says nothing of the
time he expects to be able to leave England. *He has sailed with
Lyster from Belfast.* I shall send you his letter this night with
some papers, also a note which I got from him. Perhaps you
may hear in Cork of young gentlemen ambitious of going out
to South America. Recollect *they* must be gentlemen. Morgan
is in the highest spirits, the hope of being off soon, while I am
just the contrary. As the time approaches for parting with my
fine boy, my heart fails me and I regret having ever given my
consent. God grant I may not have cause to repent my compliance. Will not *this* business in Spain[3] injure the cause of
South America? Ferdinand can now send Morillo[4] troops and
that is all the latter wants. Would to God you could be home
before Morgan left this. It would be such a consolation to me.
I yet have hope you will. Maurice was yesterday with Mr.
L'Estrange. He read the greater part of his brother's[5] letter for
him written August last. He gives a very different account of
his conduct to what the *runaways* did and desires to be
remembered to the General and to you. It is hard to believe
anything these times. We are all anxiety about Colonel
Talbot.[6] Mr. O'Mullen[7] who is exerting himself for him told
us last night *he* would be returned. The ninety Catholics,[8] how
they have behaved! Surely, darling, it is not worth-while ever
more to advocate the cause of such heartless wretches! Believe
me, they are more content with their chains than they would
be if Emancipation was granted to them tomorrow. . . .

[P.S.] . . . Hickson has sold his house and establishment.
He is going to reside entirely in the country.

SOURCE : O'Connell Papers, NLI 13651

1 At the public dinner in Tralee on 23 March.
2 John Devereux.
3 A reference to the recent acceptance by King Ferdinand VII of the
   constitution of 1812 (see letter 823).
4 Pablo Morillo (1777-1838), field-marshal, a native of Spain and a
   veteran of the Peninsular War. Brilliant commander of the Spanish
   expeditionary army to the South American colonies, 1815. The 1820
   revolution in Spain was responsible for his return home.
5 Major Anthony L'Estrange.
6 Richard Wogan Talbot (c. 1766-1849), Malahide Castle, Co. Dublin;
   M.P. for Co. Dublin, 1790-91, 1807-30; sometime colonel in the army;

succeeded 1834 as second Baron Talbot of Malahide; created 1839
Baron Furnival (U.K.). In March 1820 he was defending his Co.
Dublin seat in the general election.

7   Rev. Cornelius O'Mullane.

8   Presumably electors who had voted against Talbot (*FJ*, 20-30 Mar.
1820).

828

From his wife to Cork

Dublin, 28 March [postmarked 1820]

My dearest love,

. . . I hope James takes care of the *Irishman*.[1] *It* is my
favourite paper. Poor Lawless is the real Patriot. Don't you
approve of his reply to Mr. Stewart?[2] Our darling Morgan is
making all his arrangements for joining the General. I hope
in a few days we shall know exactly the time he will be leaving this. May something interfere to keep my child until your
return! Maurice O'Connell[3] means to go out as a cadet and is
getting the undress of the Hussar Guards. . . . Twenty
pounds is the least sum for the undress suit. . . .

Mr. L'Estrange dined here yesterday. He told me that so
far from the General's authority being questioned at Margarita
his brother[4] mentions ' as we were sailing into the harbour a
South American vessel met us and was preparing to attack
our vessel, thinking it was an enemy, but when told we were
troops belonging to General Devereux, they gave him three
cheers and welcomed the troops. We were kindly received on
shore by English[5] and Brion[6] who expressed their regret the
troops had not arrived in time to aid in the attack on Cumana.'[7]
Mr. L'Estrange is in the greatest spirits. He purposed taking
the letter this day to Colonel Hall. Would to God *he* had
been more guarded and kept his mind to himself. The General
seems greatly hurt at the part Mr. L'Estrange took against
him.[8] . . . God be praised you have the best of constitutions
and you have a temper that enables you to get through every
difficulty and fatigue. I often boast of the sweetness of your
temper. In my life, darling, I never met with such a disposition and so placid a temper as you possess. I saw Mr. Hickson[9]
this day. He does not intend parting his establishment until
your return though in my mind he could never make a bad

or a foolish bargain. Mr. Keough[10] preached last night in Church Street Chapel and gave the Bible *hawkers* and the Education Society[11] a great dressing. What are the bishops about, not even Dr. Sugrue? Perhaps he is one of the *cautious*.

SOURCE : O'Connell Papers, NLI 13651

1   The *Irishman* (Belfast), owned by 'Honest Jack' Lawless. Not extant.
2   Unidentified.
3   Maurice O'Connell, probably son of Maurice O'Connell, Moyresk, Co. Clare, a cousin of O'Connell; went to South America with Devereux. Joined Sandes' Rifles as lieutenant with seniority from 23 August 1820. Took part in the campaign at the battle of Carabobo which liberated Venezuela. Died of yellow fever 2 April 1822.
4   Major Anthony L'Estrange.
5   James Towers English (c. 1775-1820), a native of Dublin, recruited and organized the British Legion, 1818-19; died of fever in Margarita, 1820.
6   Pedro Luís Brion (1782-1821), a wealthy Jewish merchant from Curaçao: admiral of Bolívar's naval forces, 1816-19.
7   A town on the Caribbean. It was attacked on 6 August 1819 by troops under Gen. James T. English.
8   See letter 810.
9   John C. Hickson.
10 Rev. Michael Bernard Keogh, O.F.M.Cap. (died 9 Sept. 1831). A popular preacher, he was parish priest of Howth from 1818 until he retired owing to ill-health early in 1831.
11 The Kildare Place Society.

829

To his wife, 30 Merrion Square

Cork, Saturday, 1 April 1820

My darling Heart,

I am just come in from court after a day of much toil and fatigue, but after having got rid of both in the warm bath. . . .

I am afraid Maurice will think I wrote to him too harshly. Indeed, sweetest, I did not mean to do so. Tell my own boy that I did not mean to do more than to stimulate his industry. Tell him that whether he wins or loses he will be equally dear to his father.

I must run to get *my fish* for this week; I am a great papist.

SOURCE : Fitz-Simon Papers

830

From his wife to Grand Parade, Cork

[Dublin] 1 April 1820

My dearest Dan,

By the evening mail of yesterday Maurice received your letter which I trust will have the effect of stimulating him to exertion. I certainly think with you that Maurice wants only application to succeed. . . . Your example of early rising and close study has the best effect upon him. He is very young and we must make allowances for him. . . . He [John] shall never go to Clongowes. What nice mannered boys Maurice and Morgan were when they went to Clongowes. Indeed they may now well deny it. It is almost impossible to get them to divest themselves of the vulgarity they acquired at *that* college. . . . Poor Ricarda[1] seems quite flattered at your not dining out from *them* while you were in Tralee. She tells me you used to sit chatting with *them* for near three hours every day after dinner. I really think *they* feel the same affection for you that they did for their poor father.[2] . . .

Morgan requests with his best love to let him have immediately what answer he is to give the General[3] about O'Neill.[4] He has just seen Hall. No further orders for *their* departure. . . .

Darling, I do regret not having you at home on Thursday last. What a happy and a proud group you would have round you in the balcony. I never witnessed such enthusiasm as when the procession[5] came in view of *this* house.

SOURCE : O'Connell Papers, NLI 13651
1 Her niece Ricarda Connor.
2 James Connor.
3 John Devereux.
4 Henry O'Neill, surgeon with the Irish Legion in South America.
5 On Thursday, 30 March, Col. Richard Wogan Talbot was chaired in procession through the streets of Dublin, including Merrion Square, to celebrate his electoral victory in the county (*FJ,* 31 Mar. 1820).

831

To his wife, Merrion Square, 2 April 1820, from Cork

' It was at all times worth a man's while to be honest but now
and since the completion of the Spanish revolution,[1] it is
likely to be the most interested policy to be faithful and true
to the people.'

SOURCE : Fitz-Simon Papers

1   See letter 823, note 6.

832

From his wife to Parade, Cork

Dublin, 3 April 1820

[No salutation]

. . . You can't think how proud my John is of the *noise* he
made last Thursday.[1] Had *they* known whose son he was at
first, *they* would have put him into the Chair with the
Member. When he was known the people called for champagne to give him, and many of them said they would *fight*
for ever under O'Connell's banner. . . . Have you consulted
your uncle[2] lately about Morgan's going with the General?
I am sorry to tell you your friend Mr. L'Estrange is *wheeling*
round again against the General and the cause. *He* is in my
mind a complete weather-cock. Last week he was favourable
to us, but yesterday he was saying everything to Morgan to
disgust him against the business. I think it is very unnecessary
for him to interfere with you and me in anything concerning
our children. *He* advised Morgan to go to a military college
in France or ' would he not prefer joining the Spanish Army?'
Mr. L'Estrange is too fond of meddling and wishing to put
himself forward on every occasion. His behaviour[3] about
D'Evereux has not served him even with the enemies of *that*
man. As to my part I can never feel the same esteem for him
that I did. James Sugrue's Mr. Smith[4] is come to Dublin with
the same story. Sugrue seems as much incensed against our
friend as anybody else. I wish you were here to keep them all
in order. I would not be a bit surprised if Morgan changes
his mind. *He* is so beset. *They* really speak to him on this
subject as if they thought his parents were anxious to get rid

of him. I wish from my heart Morgan never determined on going to South America. . . .

source : O'Connell Papers, NLI 13651

1   See letter 830, note 5.
2   Count O'Connell.
3   See letter 810.
4   Unidentified.

833

From his wife to Parade, Cork

Dublin, 4 April 1820

[No salutation]

It delights me very much, my own love, that my letter of Friday afforded you such happiness. . . . Our children felt very proud of their father. My Kate was overcome to tears but the unanimous wish was for your presence in the balcony. The people however were aware of your absence so that the compliment of passing your door was greater.[1] *We seldom disagree,* darling, on any *subject* either domestic or political. *It* is therefore unnecessary for me to say that I coincide with you in the necessity of honesty towards the people nor can the scene of last Thursday be forgotten by me and I felt proud that your abilities, exertion and honesty in your country's cause called for such a burst of applause and gratitude from so respectable an assemblage of your countrymen. . . .

You don't say, love, what you think may be the effect of the Revolution in Spain[2] on the South American business. I perceive by the papers there is an armistice proposed to the Government of Venezuela. I pray most sincerely *it* may be granted and the independence of South America established without further bloodshed. Morgan will not agree with me on *this* point. He wishes to have some of the glory but I prefer having everything settled before him. . . .

. . . An answer is promised to Sheil's pamphlet[3] but it is not forthcoming.

source : O'Connell Papers, NLI 13651

1   See letter 830.
2   See letter 823.
3   Unidentified.

834

From his wife to Parade, Cork

Dublin, 6 April [1820]

My dearest Dan,

. . . Colonel Hall sailed for Liverpool with Major Bennett[1] last night. *They* were ordered *there* by the General to make preparations for their embarkation from Liverpool for Angostura when all is ready. Morgan and those who are to go with the General are to go from this in the Liverpool packets and sail with him from there. *His* being *there* is kept *secret. This* intelligence I got from Finlay. . . . As I have got my wish of Morgan's waiting your return I am quite satisfied. . . . I am told there are very satisfactory letters in town from several officers belonging to the Lancers. Mr. Somers,[2] the brewer, got a letter from a nephew of his written the last day of December. He says he is as happy as he can wish, that the Irish Legion are greatly liked, the greatest difference between the attention paid to them and to the British Legion, particularly by Admiral Brion. *This* young man encloses a copy of Bolívar's Proclamation[3] to the Legion. I saw a letter yesterday written in January from a private of the Lancers. He distinctly says the officers who came home were cowards. The whole of McDermot's[4] officers with the exception of eight returned.

SOURCE : O'Connell Papers, NLI 13651

1 Probably Bryan O'Donnell Bennett, lieutenant, 101st Foot, 1816; placed on half-pay, 1817; sailed with Devereux on 27 April 1820. Died of yellow fever at Santa Marta, Colombia, in December 1820.

2 Alexander Somers, 1 Upper Mount Street, Dublin.

3 Presumably that which had been published in Ireland in March 1820 (see letter 813, note 1).

4 Anthony James McDermott, Ramore, Co. Galway, an officer in the Austrian service. He raised a regiment called Cundinamarca for Devereux. He did not go to South America but his unit did.

835

To his wife, Merrion Square, 10 April 1820, from Cork

' I got the *Monastery*[1] safe but will not be able to read one
line of it before I start for Dublin. I mean to read it in the
coach going up.'

SOURCE : Fitz-Simon Papers

1   *The Monastery*, by Sir Walter Scott, which had just been published
for the first time.

836

From his wife to Parade, Cork

Dublin, 10 April 1820

My dearest Dan,

I read with great regret the result of a duel[1] between
Hutchinson and Callaghan[2] in the Cork papers this morning
and cannot divest myself of a dread that a man of so delicate
a constitution as Mr. H[utchinson] will fall a victim to the
illness which must proceed from the amputation of his finger.
What on earth was the cause of this unfortunate business?
The stupid papers give no detail. If it was Colthurst[3] and
Callaghan that fought I should not be so much surprised. I
hope, darling, your letter *this* evening will give me a more
satisfactory account of our patriot. I could have cried to think
he should lose even a finger by the hands of such a *fellow* or
that he should be obliged to meet him. Hutchinson is honest
and that is his fault. *They* would wish to put him out of the
way. I wish to goodness you were out of Cork. I anxiously
entreat of you, my own love, to take care of yourself. I know
your friendship for Hutchinson. I also know that you love
your wife and family and for their sakes you will not involve
yourself in any party business. . . .

I got a letter for you last night from Lord Cloncurry
requesting of you to lose no time in getting up the dinner for
the late Lord Mayor.[4] *This* was the purport of the letter. . . .
You perhaps will be surprised at my having occasion for
more money. All I can say [is] that I practise economy to the
fullest extent. Not a shilling is spent that can be avoided. . . .

SOURCE : O'Connell Papers, NLI 13651

1 On 7 April this duel was fought near the Lough, Cork, between
   Hon. Christopher Hely-Hutchinson, M.P., and Patrick W. Callaghan, the former attended by Sir William A. Chatterton, Bt., the
   latter by Denis Richard Moylan (*Southern Reporter*, reprinted in
   FJ, 11 April 1820).
2 Patrick W. Callaghan (died c. 1840), fourth son of Daniel Callaghan
   (a rich merchant), Lotabeg, Cork, and Mary Barry, Donnalee.
3 Sir Nicholas Conway Colthurst, fourth baronet (1789-1829), M.P. for
   Cork city, 1812-29.
4 Thomas McKenny. See letter 805, notes 1 and 2.

837

To General Bolívar

Dublin, Ireland, 17 April 1820

Illustrious Sir,

A stranger and unknown, I take the liberty of addressing
you. I am encouraged to do so by my respect for your high
character and by my attachment to that sacred cause which
your talents, valour and virtue have gloriously sustained—I
mean the cause of Liberty and national independence.

Hitherto I have been able to bestow only good wishes upon
that noble cause. But now I have a son able to wield a sword
in its defence, and I send him, Illustrious Sir, to admire and
profit by your example, and, I trust, under your orders and
auspices, to contribute his humble but zealous exertions for
the success of the arms of the youthful but already renowned
Republic of Columbia [*sic*].

The delusions of paternal affection may well cause me to
appreciate beyond their value the services which are now
offered to you. But even I may be permitted to say that those
services are disinterested and pure, and that they originate in
sentiments of which you could not but approve because they
are congenial to those which have actuated your high and
mighty soul in all your exertions and sacrifices for the independence of your native land.

To such sentiments of love of liberty are superadded two
other powerful motives. The first is, that I feel I owe it to the
cause of liberty to give you the best proof in my power of the
devotion with which your fame and character are admired

and cherished in remote regions. The second is, that my son may be enabled to form one link in that kindly chain which will, I hope, long bind in mutual affection the free people of Columbia [*sic*] and the gallant but unhappy natives of Ireland.

Actuated by these views, my son tenders to you his services. Deign to accept of them in the spirit in which they are offered. He accompanies to your shores my gallant and honourable friend General D'Evereux, under whom he will always be proud to serve.

That you, Illustrious Sir, who imitate the virtues of Washington—may, like him, live to see all the enemies of your country confounded and defeated and to enjoy the heartfelt triumph of beholding your native land perfectly free; that in life you may be honoured and revered like Washington, your great prototype; and that after a long, useful and glorious career upon earth your fame and your memory may be embalmed in the tears and affections of the wise, the good, and the patriotic of all nations, is the fervent prayer of

Your Excellency's most obedient, most faithful,
humble servant,
Daniel O'Connell

SOURCE : Biblioteca Luís-Angel Arango

838

From John Devereux to Merrion Square

Liverpool, 23 April 1820

My beloved friend,

Mr. MacSweeny[1] handed me your dear letter and I have satisfied his views as well as yours I trust—at least I have to the utmost extent in my power—namely—I have placed him on my personal staff with the rank of Major—and if the Liberator[2] can but meet my views, namely, that he advances even enough to provision the ships, I engage to furnish them —as well as arms and clothing for any number of troops for the new war which is to be entered on for the liberation of the Mexican provinces. After the close of the present campaign Major MacSweeny can return a full colonel and form a regiment in three months with the means I shall place in his hands.

Your darling boy shall accompany him if you desire it as
Captn. for I shall have him drilled sufficiently in this campaign to head a company. He is really a sweet fellow—and I
find in him what I delight in a youth—that he is full of
humour and spirit. I am so proud, my dearest friend, of this
pledge you have given me of your regard and confidence that
I have already adopted him as the son of my heart—and my
precious darling, my betrothed wife, will love him no less. In
short if I succeed in my present undertaking he shall one day
show himself and shine to his country, as his patriot father
does so gloriously before it—noble and generous and magnificent!

Will you, my dear Sir, have the goodness to see Col.
Kenny in respect to a power of attorney I have sent on to
Dublin to sell a small property to meet Colonel Lyster's bail—
and as the proceeds will much more than cover it—I beg of
you in the meantime to satisfy Mr. Reilly[3]—his proportion
is fifty pounds—which, if you could advance will greatly
relieve me—and you can reimburse yourself when Murphy[4]
effects the sale to whom I have sent the power of attorney, he
having the lease in his possession. Mr. Reilly lives in Stephen's
Green. Only that the post is about to close and too late to
send out for a stamp I would send you my note on Mr.
Herring[5] of London at three months for the amount but I
shall do it by tomorrow's post. I have everything ready to
embark on board—and should have sailed this day but for
Morgan who came forward as *spokesman* for his brother
officers and pleaded that it would [be] a great inconvenience
to embark until tomorrow evening when, please God, we shall
be all embarked. Hall I leave behind as he is yet, it appears,
in London and as the wind is fair—and a single day might
lose me the loss of my *fame,* I do not wait for him.

Ever Ever Yours!

J. D'Evereux

[P.S.] I wish, my dear Sir, that you would temper poor
Kenny[6] to a little forbearance until we redeem ourselves on
the other side—for they will believe nothing on this, I mean
my enemies.

SOURCE : Fitz-Simon Papers
1   Roger McSwiney.
2   Bolívar.

3 William Reilly, 87 Stephen's Green, South.
4 Unidentified.
5 Herring and Richardson, Copthall Buildings, London; one of the
   main London financiers of the various expeditions including those
   of Devereux to some extent.
6 Probably Lt. Col. J. Kenny.

839

To Owen O'Conor

Merrion Square, 5 May 1820

My dear Friend,

I wish it were your convenience to come to town. We are
getting up another *struggle* and we of course want you. Besides, there is the dinner to Alderman McKenny for which I
have reserved for you the ticket No. 1. There are so few who
honestly and with a clear conscience labour for ' the ancient
Faith ' that I feel very lonely when you are not with us. Be
so kind as to say whether you expect to be in town.

SOURCE : Clonalis Papers

840

From his brother James

Killarney, 9 May 1820

My dear Dan,

. . . I perceive by a letter Roger McSwiney wrote from
London he did not go out *with Devereux,* he could not procure leave of absence and would have lost his half-pay. Under
these circumstances he acted (in my mind) quite right in not
risking his all on so precarious an undertaking. He says poor
Morgan was in high spirits.

Our friend the Knight of Kerry is yet at Ballinruddery.
Report says he is coming into office with Mr. Plunket. I hope
so as the poor fellow has a large family and a very small
fortune much encumbered, and he has been *a Patriot long
enough, God knows.*

SOURCE : O'Connell MSS, UCD

841
To Lord Cloncurry

Merrion Square, 14 May 1820

My dear Lord,

I am *so* delighted that you had an opportunity at the dinner of seeing the manner the people cherish you because you are honest. It really is better to be so than to take part with the enemy. But now you see that you owe us a debt in return; and I call on you to pay it on the double.

In the first place, there is the 'Irish National Society for Education'.[1] I enclose you a prospectus, first, for your own advice and correction and then, when you have made it conform to your sentiments, to entreat that you will lay it before his Grace the Duke of Leinster, for his approbation and sanction. I am winding up the Roman Catholic prelates, and making every arrangement to have a public meeting as quickly as possible. We have not an hour to lose because we should be before Parliament if possible to share the grant. I pray your most speedy attention to this subject. If we can have the Duke as patron and you as one of the presidents, we shall get on rapidly. I mean to solicit your vote for the office of secretary. But time presses.

The second thing I would submit to you is our 'Society for Parliamentary Information'.[2] Let us, if you please, begin it. If you will put your name to it and get me one half-dozen Protestants I pledge myself to get you a batch of Papists of the first water. If it were once on foot it would accumulate rapidly and when we were strong enough, we would call in the aid of the excellent Duke, the finest fellow that ever bore 'the noble name of Fitzgerald'. Let us not postpone making some efforts for Ireland. We may be calumniated but do we not deserve reproach if we tamely crouch beneath our miseries and leave this ' *loveliest land on the face of the earth* ' a prey to faction and the victim of unopposed oppression? Reflect on this, and let us make an attempt to combine good and honest men in an exertion for the country.

SOURCE : Cloncurry, *Personal Recollections*, p. 269

1   According to a letter from William Coppinger, Catholic bishop of Cloyne and Ross, to his clergy, published in the *Freeman's Journal*, 20 March 1820, O'Connell was attempting to form a new education

society which would implement the plan of Bishop Doyle of Kildare
and Leighlin ' for educating children of the different religions, in
the same school, without any reference to religious subjects, which
may more properly be treated by their own clergy in their respective
places of worship '. The society was founded but passed out of
existence when it failed to obtain a state subsidy (FitzPatrick, *Dr.
Doyle*, I, 228-9).

2 This society does not appear to have been founded.

842

From his son Morgan

Head-Quarters Margarita, Government House,
Wednesday, 14 June [1820]

My dear Father,

Here we are at last, ' in the sandy oven of Margarita ',
where we arrived about six o'clock on Monday evening last,
and where we were received with every demonstration of
joy and satisfaction. On our arrival here, Col. Hall and Major
Bennett went ashore but in a short time the latter returned
along with Col. Low,[1] Aide-de-Camp to the President, and
Col. Richards,[2] deputed to wait on the General from the
constituted authorities. They hailed the General with all the
respect due to his rank as Lieutenant-General of the Armies of
the Republic, to which high rank he was promoted as one
of the first acts of the President on his triumphal entry from
Angostura into Santa Fé. . . . In the course of the evening
some of the officers who had been left behind sick by Alymer[3]
but who go on at present with us, came on board.

O'Kelly's[4] nephew is here, I know not why. The officers
said that the Legion mustered about 1,000 men, before leaving
this, but only about 800 went, the rest being either in a bad
state of health or having misconducted themselves. . . .
Young Sexton[5] from Ennis, Maurice O'Connell's friend is
gone on; he fought a duel coming out but was not wounded.
There are at present in the stores here and at Angostura,
18,000 stand of arms, etc., all provided by the General.

I never enjoyed better health in my life than I do at
present. This place is not near as hot as I have heard reported.

Mr. O'Mullan[6] has just bid me tell you that you had better
send your letters to me through the hands of Col. Kenny, who
will send them on along with the General's, and we will

direct ours through the same channel. The General is named
by Bolívar in his dispatches as the senior Lieutenant-General
in his service, as I mentioned before, and the government
of this island is given up to him during our stay here. He and
his staff, of whom I am a member, dine every day at the
expense of the Government. General Bolívar sent a beautiful
white charger for the General's use . . . [which] originally
cost 500 guineas. The Legion at the taking of Rio de la
Hacha lost not a man, the town having surrendered without
firing a shot. The time the Legion were here, they got regular
rations and pay. Everything is going well on the Main; one
of the expressions of the Supreme Chief in his dispatches to
the General was that the Irish Legion had contributed greatly
to the liberation of New Granada, and that he complimented
him for his former [sic] love of liberty. . . .

SOURCE : *Carrick's Morning Post*, 23 August 1820

1   George Augustus Low, formerly of Athlone.
2   Lt. Col. Thomas Richards, secretary to Admiral Brion. Married a
    Venezuelan, and they had thirteen children. Died in poverty,
    6 September 1840, in Caracas.
3   William Aylmer (died 1820), son of Charles Aylmer, Painstown,
    Kilcock, Co. Kildare. United Irishman and a leader in the 1798
    rebellion, he was amnestied and did well in Austrian army. Joined
    Devereux's Irish Legion in 1819. Wounded at Laguna Salida (Rio
    Hacha) 25 May 1820. Died 20 June 1820.
4   Probably Mathias J. O'Kelly.
5   Lieut. M. N. Sexton, who died of wounds 26 May 1821.
6   Rev. Cornelius O'Mullane who accompanied Devereux to South
    America as his chaplain. They later quarrelled.

843

From his son Morgan

Head-Quarters Margarita, Government House,
Thursday, 15 June [1820]

My dear Father,
    . . . I had scarcely finished my letter [to you of yester-
day] when an order from the General came, saying, that as
he dined that day with General Arismendi,[1] he desired that I
should come ashore in my full uniform when I should find
a horse ready for me to go to Arismendi's. On my landing I
went to the Governor's house, where having found my horse,

I rode off along with Col. Low's young son, a fine boy not eight years old. . . . On alighting I was met by Arismendi, General Devereux, Col. Low, Col. Hall and Major Bennett.

General Devereux then presented me to General Arismendi, at the same time telling him who I was and what you had done for the cause. Arismendi answered in Spanish that he felt truly happy in seeing the son of such a man as you joining the cause. . . . His power, I must observe, is very great, and I must also remark that he is the second in command to Bolívar, being Captain General of the Armies of Colombia. . . .

. . . Arismendi is a small, active, thin man with large black *mustachios,* and is very like the picture[2] you have of Bolívar but his face is a little wrinkled. I never in my life saw such a dinner before. We began by turtle soup, then came all sorts of fowl, fish, yams, bananas, game, etc., and the largest turkey I ever beheld, I am sure it was as large as a sirloin of beef. There were all sorts of spiced and forced meats, with bottled porter, etc. After dinner a most sumptuous dessert was introduced, such a one I might challenge all Europe to produce—pineapples, melons, both water and musk, bananas—I can't remember half of their names nor did I at the time know them, it may be enough to say that all the fruits you ever read of are here in abundance. Immediately after the dessert they gave toasts . . . they then gave Admiral Brion, General Devereux, and the glorious strangers who had left their native land to give the South Americans Liberty . . . Col. Hall then got up, and having returned thanks in the name of the Legion, he gave 'a strict and lasting friendship between England, Ireland and Colombia'. The next toast that was proposed was 'Daniel O'Connell'. It was given by Col. Low, a fine fellow and an Irishman. He proposed you as 'the most enlightened, the most independent, and the most patriotic man, not only in Great Britain but in all Europe'. This was drunk with great acclamations, and Col. Low's son, standing up on his chair, shouted: 'Viva el Counsellor O'Connell.' But I forgot to tell you that as soon as Col. Low had given you, the General stood up and . . . expressed his gratitude to you for all you did for him, and said that without you the Irish Legion could never have existed, that to you it owed its origin and that you, by preparing the minds of the people of Ireland through the public prints for the cause of South America, had raised up in their breasts a sensation till that time unknown amongst them. . . . The last toast that was given was one from Low's little son who quite spontaneously getting up on his chair, gave: ' May the first man that deserts his colours have a sword through his body.' . . . After dinner we had coffee, and Arismendi, taking me and the General by the hand, said (Col. Low was interpreter) ' that as my father had evinced such friendship and such enthusiasm for the cause of Colombia as to send out his son, and as he had done such an essential service to the Republic by his efforts in assisting the General, that if anything happened General Devereux, that he (Arismendi) would consider me as his son. . . .'

SOURCE : *Carrick's Morning Post*, 23 August 1820

1 Juan Bautista Arismendi (born c. 1780), captain general of the armies of Colombia.

2 Whether this picture still exists is not known.

844

To his wife, Merrion Square

Westport, 1 August 1820

My darling Love,

Here I am at another extremity of this poor Island. This is, however, a lovely spot. I got a verdict yesterday easily and am bound for Galway. I think I got some *fame*. I certainly laughed a good deal at the archbishop[1] and made others laugh at him not a little. The Beresfords are greatly pleased with me. . . . If they had not resolved to take me to Galway do you know that I was determined to have made Dublin my way to Cork. . . .

SOURCE : Fitz-Simon Papers

1 Obviously Hon. Power Le Poer Trench (1770-1839), second son of first earl of Clancarty; bishop of Waterford and Lismore, 1802-10; bishop of Elphin, 1810-19; archbishop of Tuam, 1819-39. See *DNB*.

845

To his wife, Merrion Square

Galway, 3 August 1820

My own darling,

. . . The *Lord of the Soil* at Kilrush is Mr. Vandeleur,[1] the Commissioner of the Revenue. He got the place by selling the country at the Union. I hope he will live to be fined for that offence. He is as white-livered and as bigoted a dog as you could wish to see. You will not therefore wonder that he should dislike me. It mortified him I believe not a little that *his* people should testify kindness to a popish agitator, and do you know that I think I have consumed too much of my paper in writing to you about him but, darling, it was in answer to your question.

. . . I hope to leave this on Sunday, that is, darling, *after Mass.* I really would not lose Mass for any consideration. No man has so much right to be grateful to Providence as I have. I wish I was as grateful as I ought to be. You are, my Love, one great cause of my gratitude. . . . I would not, darling, now be unfaithful to you even by a look for the created universe. . . .

Mr. Kenny[2] was right in saying it was the Archbishop of Dublin [Lord John George Beresford] who is substantially my client here, because both he and Mr. Hume[3] of the Treasury are the executors of the late Archbishop of Tuam.[4] It was at their instance or at least with their full approval that I was employed and hitherto, at least, they are quite satisfied. The Hon. Mr. William Beresford[5] attended the trial. He met John Guthrie[6] here and talked a great deal to him in praise of Mary's husband. He said that he wished to God the King knew that he had a Roman Catholic subject of such talents! He said this when he thought I never would hear of it, and I repeat it because I wish my Mary should know what is said in her husband's favour. . . .

Do you know that Charles Phillips has prepared for publication a most furious defence of the Queen and attack on the King!!! a certain fact.[7]

SOURCE : Fitz-Simon Papers

1 John Ormsby Vandeleur (c. 1766-1828), Kilrush, Co. Clare; eldest son of Crofton Vandeleur and brother of Judge Thomas Burton

Vandeleur. Commissioner for customs for Ireland, 1799-1801, 1809-10, 1814-22.
2 Unidentified.
3 Arthur Hume, deputy cashier of the exchequer.
4 William Beresford (1743-1819), archbishop of Tuam from 1794; created 1812 Baron Decies. Brother of first marquess of Waterford.
5 Rev. Hon. William Beresford (1780-27 June 1830), son of archbishop of Tuam, first Baron Decies.
6 John Guthrie (died 1845), Gardiner Street, Dublin; called to the bar, 1794. A Protestant supporter of Catholic Emancipation.
7 *The Queen's Case Stated* (London 1820), by Charles Phillips, of which at least twenty-two editions appeared in 1820.

846

To his wife, Merrion Square

Galway, 5 August 1820

My darling Heart,

I have the pleasure to tell you that we have *again* succeeded.[1] There remains but one case more and that will be on this day. We upon that also expect success. . . . I should be ruined horse and foot but for these special cases. Blessed be God for all his goodness. They have come in these bad times quite opportunely and I rather think they will arrive again for I believe I have made *an impression*. This may be vanity but, heart's darling, *you* will excuse it and *you* will believe even more than I say because your love for your husband deceives you. . . .

I will remain with you after the Cork assizes at least a fortnight and will not spend more than a month in Kerry. . . .

SOURCE : Fitz-Simon Papers
1 Court case unidentified.

847

To his wife, Merrion Square

Cork, 7 August 1820

My darling Heart,

The third cause of Beresford's was just called[1] on last Saturday and then a compromise took place quite to their satisfaction. So that the result has been every thing I could desire. . . .

I left Galway before two in the afternoon of Saturday and reached Newmarket near Ennis with great ease. I left that early yesterday, heard Mass and breakfasted in Limerick and arrived here about nine last night. . . . My special retainer was *a triumph.* . . .

SOURCE : Fitz-Simon Papers
1   Unidentified. It was called at Galway.

847a

To William Conyngham Plunket, House of Commons, London, redirected to Stephen's Green, Dublin, redirected to Bray [Co. Wicklow].

Cork, 7 August 1820

Private

My dear Sir,

I hope and believe you will pardon the liberty I take in obtruding on you with this letter when you consider my motives for doing so. I would not yield to these motives, powerful as they are, if I was not convinced that you feel a deep interest in everything connected with the administration of justice in Ireland—and there is every reason why you should do so. Besides, you are the natural representative of the *unattached* portion of the bar, and I think that Kerry and Kerrymen have some claims upon you.

After all these *excuses* I come to the point. *Our* chairman,[1] Mr. Stephen Rice, is dangerously ill and will probably be no more before this letter leaves Cork. There never lived a more worthy man, and his loss will be long deplored not only by those who knew the simplicity and singleness and affectionate goodness of his heart but by every individual in that extensive and populous county—Kerry—where he has for more than twenty years decided annually many thousand causes, I should suppose upon an average from seven to eight thousand. This will give you an idea of how important it is that he should have for his successor a man competent to do the duty of the office. Indeed, the peace of the county as well as the property of the lower classes depend on the proper selection of the chairman or are at least involved to a very great degree in that choice. I ought to be extremely anxious that the choice should be a good one as my *present* property and my *future* expectations centre in that county, and I have the best reasons for knowing the qualifications of the candidates or, perhaps I should say, their want of qualifications.

Colonel Crosbie votes with the ministry and has the patronage of the county, the more especially as the Knight of Kerry is, you know, a *decided* oppositionist. The object of Col. Crosbie would probably be to place a Mr. Fitzgerald[2] in the situation—a retired barrister who only remained at the bar long enough to ascertain his own unfitness and incapacity and who certainly does not and has not for many years answered the description of a practising barrister which is the description given to eligible persons by the statute. Indeed, he is more unfit for the office than I choose to describe, the more especially as I have no kind of personal ill-will to this gentleman and hate to *defame* anybody, but he is in truth quite unfit. There are also one or two persons connected with Judge Day and with the borough of Tralee who may have some chance. The one is *his* nephew, Mr. Robert Day,[3] a retired barrister totally unfit for the office. Mr. William Rowan,[4] another retired barrister, [is] if possible still more unfit. He has not been in profession these twenty years. It would be a cruel violation of the trust reposed in the Irish government if it were *knowingly* to appoint any such person.

There is indeed one connection of Judge Day's who would be in every respect qualified. You know him I believe—well— John Franks.[5] I need not tell you that he is as pure and as amiable a gentleman as any alive. He is also a barrister in considerable practice and with a mind not only stored with legal learning but possessing that discrimination and firmness which are so essential to the judicial character. It would be a great blessing to the county to have such a man entrusted with the office of chairman, the only office that brings the law for any purpose beneficent to the Irish peasant, in contact with him. His appointment would give universal satisfaction.

I need not add that I write this letter under the seal of most confidential secrecy. I write it too in the chance that you may have some occasions to represent the facts which I state to you in quarters to which I have no access, and this trouble I readily suggest because its result may be so very useful. It is superfluous to say that as to myself I have not and cannot have any other motive than those that arise from my local connection with Kerry and my fervent wish to have justice administered fairly and impartially and attachment to the laws preached in a manner not over frequent in Ireland by showin[g] the people the advantage of those laws. Besides, it would not be worth my while to accept any such office, and if it were, I am perhaps mistakenly but indeed honestly too much of a reformer to be within the reach of any office, my popery entirely out of the question.

Pray pardon me for this volume of an epistle. I believe you know Franks well enough not to be surprised that his friends should be zealous about him, and when to friendship is added a zeal for public utility they both carry with them the claim for pardon notwithstanding any intrusion.

SOURCE : Papers of Mrs. Nicholas Shorter

1 The chairman of the quarter sessions, the official title of which at this period was assistant barrister. Incidentally, Stephen H. Rice lived until 1831.
2 Unidentified.
3 Robert Day, second son of Rev. Edward Day of Beaufort, Co. Kerry. Called to the bar, 1802.
4 William Rowan, High Street, Tralee. Called to the bar, 1790.
5 John Franks (1769-1852), born at Lohercannon, Tralee, Co. Kerry; nephew of Judge Day. K.C., 1822; one of the judges of the supreme court, Calcutta, 1825-34; knighted, 1825. See *Boase*.

848

To his wife, Merrion Square

Cork, 11 [and 12] August 1820

My own darling Mary,

. . . I perceive my Morgan did not write from Margarita. His letter is dated at Granada. In every other respect the letters are most satisfactory. That scoundrel Carrick[1] may say what he pleases. . . .

[12 August 1820]

. . . I fear too I shall have a day's delay at Clonmel on my way up to do business for Connell O'Connell. . . .

. . . The accounts this day from poor Stephen Rice are

more favourable. I suppose the poor fellow will work his way through his illness. He certainly was always the *best* of his family. I have ever entertained a great affection for him.

SOURCE : Fitz-Simon Papers

1 *Carrick's Morning Post* continued to denounce Devereux.

849

From his son Morgan

Extract

Head-Quarters Baranquilla,
Monday, 13 [recte 14] August 1820

My dear Father,

. . . After a few weeks' tedious passage from Jamaica, we anchored in the Bay of Savenella and none but the General[1] was allowed to land, accompanied by two aides-de-camp. Your humble servant was one of those, but the General not being able to procure horses enough for us, I was left behind. As soon as the General saw Admiral Brion he solicited permission for all of us to land, which the Admiral granted, and sent down a large *bengo* or boat for us to come up from Savenella to Baranquilla 22 miles distant. The *bengo* came down but the crew never mentioned a word of the message. They loaded her from several vessels with different articles, went up the river, and we never knew she was for us until she was gone. The passage up the river always occupies from 24 to 30 hours for large boats in consequence of the strength of the current running down. As soon as the General saw we were not come, another large boat was dispatched, and after lying at Savenella for a near week we came up here after 24 hours passage. On our arrival here the officers and soldiers were billetted on the inhabitants and supplied with excellent rations, of beef 3 lbs. each, of bread a good loaf, and rice, candles, etc. I being on the General's staff stop at the same house with him. The Admiral behaves very well to the General, and indeed we are all treated here with the greatest respect.

It seems that Montilla[2] has refused to give up the command of the Army to the General, in consequence of which the General has dispatched Hall and Bennett to the President to lay the matter before him. . . . Bolívar is at present with-in ten days journey of this.

I rode yesterday with Mr. Burke[3] to Soledad, about 7 miles off, where 400 Creoles are stationed. I was presented to Admiral Brion and to Madame ——, a superannuated old Duchess. You will be surprised to hear, and no doubt re-joiced, that I have got Thady O'Sullivan as servant who came out with Palmer[4] of the Lancers. My dear Father, I'll write again to you before I leave this.

Morgan O'Connell

[P.S.] . . . Mr. O'Mullen,[5] Maurice O'Connell, etc. are all well. We are to attack St. Marta in a few days.

SOURCE : *Dublin Evening Post,* 11 November 1820

1 John Devereux.
2 Mariano Montilla, a wealthy aristocrat from Caracas. Sent by Bolívar to command the Irish Legion in Margarita, December 1819; general of the army, 1827-28.
3 A member of Devereux's Irish Legion. Probably Sgt. Maj. William Burke (sergeant-major in those days was a superior rank to major). He was the father of Alexander and John Burke who were at school in Clongowes Wood College.
4 Capt. Palmer died of dysentery, 1820.
5 Rev. Cornelius O'Mullane.

850

To his wife, Merrion Square

Cork, 16 August 1820

My dearest darling,

I got my Morgan's long letters[1] this morning for *one* penny and I would have given many pounds to hear from him. They have set my heart at ease. He is a sweet fellow and will I trust be yet a comfort to us both. I will publish his letter because you suggest it and because it does Devereux so much justice. . . .

SOURCE : Fitz-Simon Papers

1 Obviously letters 842 and 843 which were published in *Carrick's Morning Post* 23 August 1820.

851
From his son Morgan

Head-Quarters Baranquilla, 25 August 1820

My dear father,

Great and glorious news! On Monday last dispatches arrived saying that Bolívar would be down here in a few days. Immediately everything was got ready for his reception, and on the morning of Wednesday word was brought that the President had arrived in Soledad, six miles off. The Admiral[1] immediately mounted his horse and went off to meet him and in a few minutes the General,[2] Col. Stopford[3] and I followed in full gallop. We had not ridden far when we met his Excellency. The President wore a splendid red uniform and was surrounded by a splendid staff. We immediately took off our caps to salute him and I rode in the rear of his staff where I was accosted by a young man in uniform who asked me if I did not remember him. I answered no. He then said, ' I am Dan Leary '.[4] We then shook hands and were as good friends as if we had been together for twenty years. He is aide-de-camp and Military Secretary to Bolívar.

By this time we had arrived at the house destined for the reception of the President where we all dismounted and entered. We had not been there two minutes when O'Leary introduced me to Dr. Foley,[5] Bolívar's Staff Surgeon, a Kerryman. The President was dressed in a Light Dragoon's cap and white feather, scarlet coat, beautifully laced all over, and which was made in Santa Fé. We had hardly been seated when the President intimated to the Admiral his wish to inspect the stores and gun-boats. Well, off with us down to the Navy Yard, through all the stores etc., then to the Admiral's where there were refreshments prepared for us, then to the Chapel to hear *Te Deum,* and then to the President's where we took leave of him.

That day we all dined with the Admiral, and in consequence of the great crowd who were invited, the General could not bring all his staff and so only brought me which was far the greatest honour as being the first day.

The first toast the President gave after dinner, immediately after the Admiral's giving his, was ' General Devereux and his brave Companions '. In the evening there was a grand

ball. The President's staff are all very finely appointed, being
dressed in a beautiful dress made at Santa Fé. . . . At the
Admiral's we were all introduced to him [the President]. As
soon as he came up to me, O'Leary told him that I had a
letter for him,[6] upon which I presented him with it, and he
and O'Leary retired into another room. When he had read it
he sent me word ' that I might always command him as my
friend and protector and that he should be always happy to
do anything for me that lay in his power '. He is a thin spare
man about the height of my uncle Rick,[7] very fine forehead,
dark eyes and a very mild melancholy cast of countenance.
He is a man of very reserved manners but, when he wishes,
can be as merry as another. There is but a faint resemblance
of him in the picture which you have at home. When he met
the General he told him that his affection for him was not in
the least diminished by the loss of the Legion,[8] that was not
his fault, and that he knew how great the shock must have
been for he himself knew what adversity was, and that his
love for him was as great as ever for he was his friend when
unfortunate and had endeavoured to serve him by doing great
things. When the General asked him to take me on his personal staff, he said, ' Let the excellent young man stay with
you for six months. By that time, I will have a regular
organized staff, and his place shall be kept for him. He will
then speak the language, and, moreover, I have numberless
hardships to go through which I would not bring him into
for the character of his father is well known to me.' He went
away that night and is expected here in a few days again
when we will meet him at Cucuta and will be joined, I
believe, to his own army. He is very fond of the British, and
all these troops at present in the service are to be given to the
General, and to every hundred British four hundred Creoles
are to be added, which will make a very fine army. All our
boats must be ready against tomorrow night. Cols. Hara[9] and
Montilla have just rode into town, I suppose to hurry on the
expedition against Santa Marta.

   . . . The expedition for Santa Marta leaves this the day
after tomorrow and there will be a great show of boats and
flags and men. The Admiral's own boat mounts three guns,
one eighteen-pounder in her bow, a six-pounder in the middle
and a four-pounder near the stern. Most of the other boats
mount two guns.

   . . . I must not forget to tell you that Mr. O'Mullan[10] wore the stole ornamented with shamrocks, made by ————, on the day the *Te Deum* was sung when Bolívar was present, and of which he is very proud. . . . The rain here has made most prodigious channels in the streets and swept away a great quantity of sand and dirt. There is no such thing as carrying any luggage further than Cucuta except a couple of small valises, one of which your servant carries and the other you take yourself behind on your saddle. It will be very pleasant that we are going up to Head-Quarters and that I will be along with O'Leary who inquired most affectionately after you all and desired to be remembered to every one of you. Mr. O'Mullan and the General desire to be remembered most affectionately to you all.

SOURCE : *Dublin Evening Post,* 28 November 1820

1 Admiral Brion.

2 John Devereux.

3 Edward W. Stopford, lieutenant, 72nd Foot, 1815; placed on half-pay, 1818; colonel in English's Legion; chief of staff to Montilla at Margarita. Founded and edited *El Colombiano* in Caracas, 1823, which supported the revolutionary cause and was printed in Spanish and English.

4 Daniel Florence O'Leary (c. 1800/01-1854), son of Jeremiah O'Leary, merchant, Patrick Street, Cork, and grandnephew of Fr. Arthur O'Leary, O.F.M.Cap. Joined the British Legion under Col. Henry Wilson, 1817; served as A.D.C. to Bolívar, 1819-27; General of Brigade, 1821-27; commanded Bolívar's army in southern Bolivia, 1830; British chargé d'affaires and consul-general in New Granada, 1843-54. Author of *Memorias del General Daniel Florencio O'Leary* (published in Caracas, 1952).

5 Thomas Foley, M.D., inspector of hospitals of the ' patriot ' armies under Bolívar. Staff surgeon to Bolívar, 1820.

6 That is, letter 837.

7 Capt. Rickard O'Connell.

8 There had been much discontent among the first contingent of Irish troops recruited by Devereux who arrived in Margarita under Aylmer in the second half of 1819. This discontent led to open mutiny on 1 June 1820. Devereux himself did not arrive until the end of June of that year.

9 Edward [O']Hara of South King Street, Dublin.

10 Rev. Cornelius O'Mullane.

852

To his wife, Merrion Square, 6 September 1820, from Cork

' I am making an arrangement to have a great dinner given
to Dr. England[1] on the 10th of October.'

SOURCE : Fitz-Simon Papers

1 John England (1786-1842), president of St. Mary's Diocesan College,
   Carlow, 1812-17; P.P. of Bandon, Co. Cork, 1817-20; bishop of
   Charleston, South Carolina, 1820-42. Author. See *DNB*. Joint proprietor or editor of *Cork Mercantile Chronicle* during the veto
   controversy, c. 1813-c. 1815.

853

To his wife, Merrion Square

Carhen, 12 September 1820

My darling Heart,

. . . I travelled the lower road along Drung.[1] It is really
a noble work excellently well executed and makes the access
into Iveragh as level as the mail-coach road to Dublin. To
you, my love, who experienced the miseries of the upper road
it would be astonishing if ever you condescended to visit this
wild land again to find yourself arrive without a single *hill-
ock*. But *that* is a happiness I cannot expect. . . . The Dublin
mail reaches us in 48 hours. . . .

I will remain here until the *Pattern* of Cahir [civeen] on
Thursday, but I will not remain to dine at the pattern as I
go on to dinner to Derrynane that day. I was out this morning with a nice little pack of hounds and killed a hare and
was in to breakfast as I was obliged to send an express with a
Cork marriage settlement. I never saw this country look so
well. It would astonish you to see how the trees are got up
here. It will soon be a little forest. . . . Everybody *wild* in
favour of the Queen except the *Palatines*.[2] I will not have
races this year but I will institute a prize *for you* for girls in
Cahirciveen and one for myself for boys. This you will be
as well satisfied with as if I had races. . . .

SOURCE : Fitz-Simon Papers

1 The new section of the Cahirciveen-Killorglin road between Kells
   Bay and Glenbeigh, a considerable feat of civil engineering for the

day, was constructed in partnership with another by O'Connell's brother-in-law and land agent, Myles McSwiney of Carhen, from funds allocated under the Poor Employment Act (1817).

2 The Queen Caroline affair was reaching a climax with the return to England on 5 June of Caroline of Brunswick, the estranged wife of George IV, and the introduction by Lord Liverpool on 5 July of a bill to dissolve her marriage and to deprive her of her royal title. Popular opinion was enthusiastically with the queen. The Palatines were Protestant tenant farmers in Co. Kerry, descendants of early eighteenth-century German immigrants. O'Connell in this instance probably used the term to denote Protestants generally.

854

From his son Morgan

Head-Quarters Baranquilla, Tuesday, 12 September 1820

My dear father,

I take the opportunity of sending you another letter as an embargo has been laid on all the vessels in the harbour until the expedition for Santa Marta shall have sailed. Mr. Burke is, of consequence, delayed. . . . I mentioned in my very last letter that Turbaco was the head-quarters of Col. Montilla's army amounting to, I believe, twelve or thirteen hundred men, 75 Irish. Montilla was for a long time down in this part of the country, getting everything ready for Santa Marta, thinking all safe at Turbaco, but on the morning of Friday, 1st of September, between the hours of 7 and 8 or thereabouts, the town was attacked by near 400 Spaniards from Cartagena. The Patriot troops under the command of old Col. Ayala[1] in Montilla's absence formed in the square, and the enemy coming up through the side streets opened a heavy and destructive fire upon our troops who, with Ayala and Garcine[2] at their head, went off at full speed into the wood, leaving only the Margarita Creoles, 100 men and the Irish under Capt. Du Verney,[3] amounting to 25, the rest being out foraging with the cavalry. As soon as the Spaniards entered the town they made for the quarters which the President had occupied (which shows plainly there was treason in the business) but Bolívar had left it three hours before! . . . On entering the President's quarters they killed two men they found there. The Irish stood the enemy's fire for a long time but at length were forced to leave the town. It was, however, reoccupied by our cavalry in half an hour, who drove the enemy out.

Dr. O'Reilly[4] of the Lancers has come down here wounded from Turbaco, and his account I now give: he is himself, however, sending home an account. He says they were drawn up in line and he was standing by a Creole who, during the action, was shot through the head. O'Reilly says that the Creole was hardly down when a ball struck him on the side of the neck and went through one of his cheeks, taking a couple of teeth with it. When he came to himself, the first thing he heard was Du Verney crying out to the men, ' Well, boys, they are all gone, I believe we had better make our retreat.' ' Well, then,' says O'Reilly to himself, ' I'll make off if I can.' So he got up . . . and made off. Young Sexton from Ennis is wounded and Col. Barnes' son[5] is badly hurt. He was in the act of firing a three-pounder on the Spaniards when he was cut down by a Spanish captain who came behind him. The Spaniard immediately rode on to the other gun but a couple of the Irish shot his horse, and before he could rise he was bayonetted by the Creoles. Tell Maurice his friend John Byrne[6] is alive and merry. The Dr. O'Reilly I mentioned is the son [? recte brother] of Dr. O'Reilly of Thomas Street who came out with a Captain's commission in the Lancers. He is also the young man whose letters, along with Col. Minchin's,[7] turned the laugh against the runaways in Dublin.[8] On his arrival at Margarita he inquired for the cake shop, and it is supposed that his disappointment at not finding one was the principal cause of his returning home.[9] The poor General is just recovering from a very severe illness but, thank God, he is now in a convalescent state. He owes his life to Dr. O'Reilly next to God for there never was a man so near going as the General was.

Tell the girls that Maurice[10] is desperately in love with a young lady from Carthagena . . . of the first families there; and she, her brother and uncle with the rest of the family fled from Carthagena on the breaking out of the siege. She is niece to General Costello[11] who was Bolívar's enemy. However, his brother is at present one of his greatest friends. . . . When we go there in the evening I generally let her and Maurice make it out together as he is teaching her English, and her brother and I have a conversation on tactics which you must suppose to be very learned. Capt. Palmer, the gentleman with whom Sullivan[12] came out, is dead—he died of dysentery. He is much regretted. He was, I am told, a brave and worthy man but he neglected his health sadly. We buried him the other morning and we all marched home to the tune of Patrick's Day.

Morgan O'Connell,

Lieutenant and Aide-de-Camp

SOURCE : *Carrick's Morning Post*, 29 November 1820

1 Juan Pablo Ayala, son of a Creole aristocrat; active in the revolutionary movement in Caracas from 1810; colonel in Bolívar's army, 1819.

2 Possibly Col. Garcin, a native of France and a veteran of the Napoleonic Wars. Joined the army of Bolívar, 1820.

3 Unidentified.

4 Michael O'Reilly, M.D., son of Joshua O'Reilly, Thomas Street, Dublin. Arrived Margarita September 1819 in Aylmer's Lancers. Joined the Rifles after the mutiny of the Irish Legion, 1820. Died of yellow fever, 1821.

5 He was killed at Turbaco defending his gun.

6 John Edward (Edmund?) Byrne; went to South America in Aylmer's Lancers. Captain and A.D.C. to Montilla, who commanded the force in which the Irish Legion originally served. He did not mutiny in 1820 and went with Montilla to Santa Marta.

7 Unidentified.

8 The officers who went out to Margarita in 1819 under Aylmer and for whom Devereux had made no proper arrangements for their arrival. They had arrived in Margarita August 1819, but the first of them was back in Dublin by December 1819.

9 The person being criticized by Morgan O'Connell for having ' inquired for the cake shop ' is obviously not Michael O'Reilly. It seems as if *Carrick's Morning Post* copied the letter erroneously.

10 Maurice O'Connell, Irish Legion.

11 *Recte*, Castillo.

12 Thady O'Sullivan.

855

To his wife, Merrion Square

Derrynane, 15 September 1820

My darling Heart,

    . . . I found my uncle astonishingly stout and well and as kind as ever I knew him. Indeed his affections seem to increase with his old age and his *harshnesses* to diminish. He asked for you very affectionately, but I was this day a good deal afflicted at his telling me that he had heard that my Maurice, or rather, his *namesake,* as he called him, showed a disposition to idleness. It stung me to the heart—my poor Maurice—how little does he think of all the miseries which his unhappy listlessness inflict[s] on his fond father. The fact is that he intends and resolves to be diligent, but then his diligence is to commence ' tomorrow ' and, of course, ' tomorrow ' never comes. Would to God he would once resolve to be diligent ' *this day* '. . . .

. . . I promise you, however, that you shall never again see the least coldness of manner from me to my poor Maurice. I bitterly regret that I was ever cold with him. It is my duty to bear with him with affectionate tenderness, and it is my inclination also. . . .

SOURCE : Fitz-Simon Papers

856

To his wife, Merrion Square

Derrynane, past 6 o'clock, 18 September 1820

Darling heart,

I am just going out to hunt. . . .

Darling, I myself was never better in health or spirits. Nothing but the unfortunate idleness of my poor Maurice to grieve or afflict me. You are mistaken, darling. I was not *idle* at his age. I loved a play day certainly but on all other days I *worked* fervently. My Maurice does nothing but what O'Donoghue[1] does for him. He ought, if he had *my spirit,* get through his Euclid of himself. . . .

SOURCE : Fitz-Simon Papers
1 Private tutor.

857

From his wife [summer residence outside Dublin], 19 September 1820, to Derrynane

' Tell me how you approve of Bric's letter[1] and what answer you purpose giving. I did not of course mention the subject of the letter to any person.'

SOURCE : O'Connell Papers, NLI 13651
1 Unidentified.

858

To his wife, Merrion Square

Waterville [Co. Kerry], 20 September 1820

My darling Love,

Here I am at your old *favourite* spot. I spent yesterday
with Butler on the mountain. We had a most delightful day
of it. Indeed as much so as ever I remember. We shot four
brace of grouse and I shot by far the greater number, five
out of the eight. I wish you were within *reach* of them. It
would be *some* pleasure to me to help you to them. I had
what to me is no small gratification—liberty to tire myself
heartily, and I did tire myself on the mountain and then had
to walk here about three miles. I was deliciously fatigued
when I came in. It would do me the greatest good if I could
have such a day once a month. . . .

Oh, darling, were you not delighted with the Portuguese
revolution?[1] It is coming home to our own oppressors, and I
am collecting health in these wilds to live to see Ireland free
and independent. What is most consolatory is that all these
great changes are taking place without bloodshed. Not one
human life sacrificed, no plunder, no confiscation, nothing
but what every honest man must approve of. Darling, it fills
me *with hopes*.

But when did I write to you such a dissertation on
politics! . . .

SOURCE : Fitz-Simon Papers
1 In August a constitutionalist revolution began in Portugal, resulting
in the expulsion of British officers from the army and the return of
John VI from thirteen years of residence in Brazil.

859

From his wife to Derrynane

[Summer residence outside Dublin], 21 September 1820

My dearest Love,

. . . God be praised we have again heard of our darling
Morgan. That he was well and happy when *this* letter was
written, the 24th of July, you will perceive. Maurice[1] forgot

to date *it* but on the envelope was in his handwriting July the 24th. . . . Strange [that] my dear child did not write. He waited, I suppose, to give us an account of his reception by Bolívar. By this time I trust he is with him. How truly unfortunate is our poor friend, the General. His persecution can only be equalled by that of the Queen's.[2] Gracious Providence, who was the incendiary that told your uncle[3] of Maurice's dislike to study? It could serve no end to make such a communication to the old gentleman but those who made it had a bad motive in doing so. It is not the first time he has been told matters that should have been kept from him but let them go on, it will all recoil upon themselves long, very long, before either you or I would tell your uncle anything that would prejudice him against *their child* or *children*. . . .

Mr. L'Estrange is with us still and I have had the happiness of hearing Mass three times this week. . . .

SOURCE : O'Connell Papers, NLI 13651
1 Maurice O'Connell, Irish Legion.
2 Queen Caroline.
3 Hunting-Cap.

860

To his wife, Merrion Square

Derrynane, 22 September 1820

My darling Heart's love,

I did not mean you any *slight,* sweetest, when I spoke of your condescending to come to Iveragh. I well know that the society of your husband is dear to you and indeed, my Mary, it ought for that husband loves you with a tenderness and a sincerity which words cannot express and which can only be conveyed in the unutterable language of the heart. . . . It is true my dear Maurice grieves me excessively but, poor fellow, he is not the less dear to my heart. What I would want of him is to *work* by himself but you perceive, darling, that he will not work even with O'Donoghue without your presence. Good God, how different from his father. . . .

SOURCE : Fitz-Simon Papers

861

To his wife, Merrion Square

Carhen, 26 September 1820

My darling Love,

We are just setting off for Portmagee to Dick Mahony's. He goes with us by boat and we carry the hounds to him in Valentia as this is the only tolerable day we have had for a week or ten days. . . . I will not go to the *Patron* but spend that and the ensuing day at Derrynane. . . . You will do what you please about leaving the country place. Whatever you do, stay or come to town, I will *strongly* approve of it. Indeed, darling, I have no merit in doing so because you always act right. . . .

SOURCE : Fitz-Simon Papers

862

To his wife, Merrion Square

Killarney, 4 October 1820

My darling Heart,

. . . The weather has changed and *was* very *tempting* but I was afraid my girls would actually beat me if I neglected their *fierce* commands. I had some very delightful hunting but I am now sat down to attend most carefully to my trade. I do not mean to throw away one other moment. . . .

Kean Mahony[1] is holding the sessions here and is doing the business perfectly well. Indeed the contrast between his mode of discharging the duty and poor Stephen's[2] is very striking. I hope it will be of great use to him to have his capabilities known and that it will be the first step to professional employment. . . .

SOURCE : Fitz-Simon Papers

1 Kean Mahony (1789-1846), Castlequin, Cahirciveen, Co. Kerry; only surviving son of Myles Mahony and Mary, daughter of Charles Geoffrey O'Connell, Portmagee, Co. Kerry. Called to the bar, 1814; J.P. for Co. Kerry, 1820.
2 Stephen H. Rice, assistant barrister for Kerry.

863

From his wife to Tralee

[Summer residence outside Dublin], 5 October [1820]

My dearest love,

. . . You have seen our darling Morgan's letter to Ricarda Connor. Would to God we knew where he is at present. Admiral Brion's letter[1] which appeared in the *Freeman['s Journal]* of yesterday distinctly says there will not be any more troops received from Ireland. He calls them a banditta. In my opinion that gentleman has not behaved by the Irish troops as he should have done. I hope he will be made to suffer for his conduct. What a misfortune to Devereux to have anything to do with Aylmer! The unfortunate man was in a state of intoxication from morning until night which gave O'Connor[2] full opportunity to wreak his vengeance[3] upon the poor General. . . .

SOURCE : O'Connell Papers, NLI 13651
1 A letter signed Admiral Louis Brion to Duncan McIntosh, merchant, Aux Cayes, Haiti, dated 8 July 1820. Along with other observations it maintained that the South American natives would rather serve the Spaniards than the disorderly foreign troops, and that Devereux's force of 4,000 men would not be received by Bolívar's forces at Baranquilla (*CMP*, 4 Oct. 1820).
2 Francis Burdett O'Connor (known as William O'Connor) (1781-1871), brother of Feargus O'Connor, the Chartist leader, of Connorville, near Manch, Co. Cork. Sailed from Dublin July 1819 for South America; commissioned as lieutenant-colonel, 10th Lancers. General in the army of Bolivia, 1825.
3 Presumably in the letters and personal narratives which stirred up the controversy in Dublin and led to Devereux's being charged under several heads, including that of organizing the legion as a mere speculation to make money.

864

To his wife, Merrion Square

Tralee, 9 October 1820

My darling Heart

. . . I have been every moment busy in order to get to you, and still, heart, my business multiplies. I never would get

through it if I were to wait to finish it but I will not. This
week I *must* devote to Kerry but the next will certainly take
me to Dublin, please God. . . .

. . . Will you, darling, write to Jane O'Connell,[1]
Killarney, to say that I mentioned to you an intention on the
part of James to visit Dublin this winter and entreating of
her to accompany him? Do this, sweetest, in your best style
and take care to write to her as *a sister*. My James is indeed
a brother and was always so to you. I am writing this letter
in the midst of an arbitration. . . .

SOURCE : Fitz-Simon Papers
1   Wife of O'Connell's brother James.

865

To his wife, Merrion Square

Tralee, 11 October 1820

My darling Heart,

. . . Darling, what a town this is! No Dublin post from
Monday until Thursday. It is really vexatious that somebody
does not *vindicate* the town. There is a daily Dublin post to
Listowel because the Knight of Kerry exerts himself. I am,
you see, in a passion on this subject. . . .

. . . Are you not delighted with the Queen?[1] How she
will *flog* the scoundrels *every one*. . . .

SOURCE : Fitz-Simon Papers
1   Queen Caroline.

866

To his wife, Merrion Square

Tralee, 12 October 1820

My darling Love,

Why will you make yourself uneasy about our darling
boy? He is as likely to do well in his occupation as any person
that ever lived. There is nothing to alarm you in the newspapers. Bolívar will not attribute to Devereux the miscon-
duct[1] of men in his absence and still less could he resent it to
our gay and gallant boy. Besides, surely he knows he has his

own happy home to come to when he pleases and his father's *heart* and his mother's *arms* open to receive him! . . . I yesterday saw a letter from Father Houlihan[2] who was *unfortunate* in Iveragh. He is at Jamaica under the name of Blake. He gives a long and most satisfactory account of our sweet boy, dined with him and spent many hours chatting with him. He describes his health as excellent, and in every respect his letter is comfortable. It is dated the 18th of July. . . .

I am detained here, my heart, not only by business but in order to settle my accounts with Myles McSwiney. I could not bring him to settle while I was in Iveragh. . . .

SOURCE : Fitz-Simon Papers
1 Part of the Irish Legion had mutinied.
2 Unidentified.

867

To his wife, Merrion Square

Tralee, 13 October 1820

My darling Mary,

. . . I have just gone through McSwiney's account and have gone through them to my great consternation. You may imagine, heart, how grievous it is to me to find that he stands in my debt for my monies actually received by him from £600 to £800, a sum that would make me *actually* rich. It is very, very cruel of him to treat me thus. I have put my property in the hands of my brother James in future so that I have at least the comfort to know that I cannot suffer any further loss whatsoever. I do not indeed know how Myles McSwiney will ever repay me. Some of my money I will get, I hope, out of the road, for there is still a £1,000 due to him and his partner on that account of Government. There is, after all, no use in fretting, but I must look more carefully to the time to come.

. . . Make your mind easy about my darling Morgan. His share of the evils[1] which befell the Irish Legion are small indeed. He has means to supply his wants and can return when he pleases. . . .

SOURCE : Fitz-Simon Papers
1 The hardships which the legion endured in Margarita due to the lack of organization to receive them.

868

From his wife to Cork

[Summer residence outside Dublin],
15 [16 and 18] October 1820

My dearest love,

. . . I shall not in future, my own heart, give way to unhappiness about our darling Morgan. You have convinced me of the folly of minding newspaper reports. What you say relative to Devereux and Bolívar is very just and, should my child find it necessary to quit the service, he has a happy home to return to. I wish he was gone from Jamaica. Before now, I suppose he is. . . .

16 October.

. . . I cannot tell you, darling, how much it frets me to have you treated so unhandsomely by Myles McSwiney but I don't see why the gentleman should not be obliged to pay it. Surely, darling, he has a property? Could he not pay you by a hundred a year? I should be sorry you distressed him but you must consider for your own children and not throw such a sum away. . . .

[18 October 1820]

. . . I have got an answer to my letter from Jane O'Connell. She will come up with James about Christmas. . . .

SOURCE : O'Connell Papers, NLI 13651

869

To Thomas Spring Rice, House of Commons

Merrion Square, 16 November 1820

(Private)

My dear Sir,

I am become a place hunter and want to press you into *such* a service. Do not be alarmed, I do not want anything with a salary as inconsistent with my principles.

The fact is just this. I have ascertained the right of the

Queen to have law officers in Ireland and I am anxious to
be her Attorney-General here. It would be of great use to
my clients that I should not be flung into the back row, and
I believe I have as many clients as any person who has been
at any time selected for a law office even by the King. The
Penal Laws do not exclude a Catholic from being Attorney-
General to the Queen, and it would be no small mortification
to her worst enemies in this country to have me selected. . . .
[Would you] deem it *quite right* to hand a letter from me to
Mr. Brougham? . . .

SOURCE : Monteagle Papers, NLI 13367(2)

870
To Lord Cloncurry

Merrion Square, 16 November 1820
My dear Lord,
    I want a place, and what is more, I want you to help me
to get it; but it is a place fit for a Radical, which I am, and
ever shall remain.
    Will you allow me to ask you whether you deem it wrong
to write for me to the Duke of Leinster to solicit his influence
with the Queen to appoint me her Attorney-General in Ireland? She certainly has a right to such an officer, and I have
a right to fill the office if she condescends to appoint me.
There is not one shilling of public money attached to it; nor
is it in any sense inconsistent with my principles which are,
and ever shall be, favourable decidedly to a complete—say,
a radical reform.
    I feel I am taking a liberty with you in asking your
assistance, but I do hope you know me too well not to believe
I would not, for any consideration, ask you to do anything
which I was conscious was in any respect inconsistent with
your feelings. If I be wrong in my request, pray excuse me,
and do not think the worse of me. I know of no event which
would afflict me more than to lose any way in your good
opinion.
    The truth is that my leading motive in looking for this
office is to annoy some of the greatest scoundrels in society
and, of course, the bitterest enemies of Ireland.

SOURCE : Cloncurry, *Personal Recollections,* p. 270

871

From James O'Connell

Killarney, 16 November 1820

My dear Dan,

You have before now heard of my sweet babe's death, an event which you may well suppose has left us all in the greatest misery. My darling Jane has not yet left her room and is wasted to a perfect shadow . . . but God's will be done.

. . . I was only prevented by the illness of our family from going to Iveragh to look after your business but will, please God, do so in two or three days. The ride will be of use to me. I should suppose any part of the balance Myles [McSwiney] owes you that he *can ever pay,* he will before the first of next month when you expect a considerable remittance and indeed have every right to expect it. . . .

O'Brien[1] and Myles[2] have disposed of the greater part of their cargo but for their luck in this way and the Drung road,[3] you would indeed be badly off. . . .

SOURCE : O'Connell MSS, UCD
1 Unidentified.
2 Myles McSwiney.
3 See letter 853.

872

From Myles McSwiney to Merrion Square

Carhen, 17 November 1820

My dear Dan,

I received your second letter last night. . . . I got since I saw you out of your May gale only about £120 which I paid off for your account £66 to James Lawlor, a year's interest to Ellen[1] and some other small payments. The reason why so little was received was that I was waiting for James[2] to regulate the abatement necessary to be made to the tenants which, I am grieved to say, he cannot now attend to as no doubt you have ere now heard of the death of his sweet and only child by the measles. . . . You may rest assured as fast as I can get in any of your rents I will remit to you together with anything I can add out of my own means, and should wish to hear from you relative to the abatements necessary to be made as, until these are regulated, the tenants will not willingly pay what they have in hands. I am sorry there is no tea at present here worth sending to you. The brandy I have kept and will send it as you direct.

I cannot possibly be as particular as you wish at the present moment in copying off the accounts. They are voluminous but consider that I have to account with you for about £350 over the balance struck in Tralee. The latter sum is out of your last March and May gale. . . .

SOURCE : O'Connell Papers, NLI 13646
1 O'Connell's sister.
2 O'Connell's brother.

873

From Alexander Wood to Merrion Square

Strictly confidential

Traveller Office, London, 17 November 1820

Dear Sir,

I did not receive your letter yesterday in regular course for an Irishman's reason—that the Irish mail did not arrive. I lost not a moment, however, on receipt of it in making such inquiries on the subject respecting what you have written as I considered at the present time prudent—for I doubt if the Queen or her friends know that she can appoint an attorney-general in Ireland. This will prevent me from saying anything here on the subject until I have again the pleasure of hearing from you. The best mode, in my opinion, to make the application will be through Mr. Brougham. In the first place I am convinced that her Majesty will not nominate to the situation in question without his approbation, particularly as it is a legal appointment. In the next place Mr. B[rougham] is at present what he was not some time ago—in very great favour with the Queen. He exercises a control over all she does and to a certain extent over the conduct of all those about her. Perhaps, too, if the first application were made through any other channel it might displease him and you know human nature. If you are not personally known to Mr. B[rougham] or whether or no, Sir Henry Parnell is the best person in my opinion to make known your wishes. He is, I have good

authority for saying, on more friendly terms with Mr.
B[rougham] than any other Irish member, and I need not
say how he and you stand both as to the past and future.
Lord Darnley[1] too is a fast friend of the Queen, and Earl Grey
and Mr. B[rougham] are most intimate. You will be able to
judge of such others yourself in both Houses as might be
useful for your purpose from the part which they have lately
acted and the influence that you may be able to bring to bear
on them. I doubt if Mr. Hutchinson (the Cork member) could
do much for you for many reasons, but you will of course
be easily able to sound your way in this respect whereas I can
only give you conjectures.

So much for our part of the Queen's friends. As to the
other, Alderman Wood is the person to move through. The
Queen has deservedly the first confidence in him *but* he should
second Mr. Brougham for when two great orbs spin in the
same direction, there is, you know, an eclipse of one!! In
plain terms these men do not on any subject draw together.
The alderman, however, is a good liberal and honest man and
will always pursue a straightforward course, the circumstance to which he principally owes his popularity and
weight. From all I know of the English they hate chicanery
of all sorts—and by the way if the opposition had the confidence of the people they might bear all before them. At least
so I think, but they are suspected. On no account should you
on the point you allude to neglect the alderman. I am not
aware of any other information which today I have it in my
power to give but, as I shall keep a look out whatever may
arise to me, I shall communicate without delay.

There is one thing which I must beg leave to remark to
you. The silence of the Catholics, I can assure you, was *felt* by
the Queen, and Alderman Wood mentioned it to me more
than once. I trust it will not, for the honour of our country,
continue longer, but you may judge whether their now joining in the song of triumph will come with so good a grace
as if they had also joined in [the] fight that preceded the
victory. Besides, their accredited organ [Donoughmore] was
so outrageous an enemy of the Queen that it gave a sort of
authority to the report of their neutrality being purchased by
promises. I will also candidly say that Lord Donoughmore is
no credit and little support to any cause for, believe me from
observation, he is a laughing-stock to the House. There is
another consideration which appears worth mentioning,

namely, whether the Queen will think it prudent to make any appointment such as you speak of till after the Commons have settled her establishment, at least whether she will not be cautious how a division may be created among her friends there [?or the] feelings of the people here towards her in any way affected. Excuse me for these hints.

I beg leave to return you sincere thanks for the information respecting my family. I am, dear Sir, with great satisfaction to think that I can do anything obliging to you. . . .

[P.S.] The best way, in my opinion, to move the Alderman is through mercantile houses in the ' City ' having influence during the elections.

SOURCE : O'Connell Papers, NLI 13647
1   John (Bligh), fourth earl of Darnley (1767-1831).

874

From John Bric to Merrion Square

[postmarked 24 November 1820]

My dear Sir,

You are the attorney-general of Ireland for her Majesty.[1] I write this *at your friend* Power's[2] lodgings. Cobbett[3] was with him at eleven o'clock last night and gave him this information. Alderman Wood gave the information direct to Cobbett, and Mr. Brougham has interested himself for you as much as any man could. Until we have official information we will not talk in public. You shall hear from me tomorrow. This in haste.

SOURCE : Fitz-Simon Papers
1   Bric was mistaken in thinking that this appointment had been made.
2   Probably Richard Power, Clashmore, Co. Waterford, nephew of Sir John Newport. M.P. for Co. Waterford, 1801-02, 1806-30.
3   William Cobbett (1762-1835), celebrated journalist and political radical; proprietor and editor of the weekly *Political Register,* 1802-35.

875

From Henry Brougham

Private

44 Lin[coln's] Inn Fields, London,
25 November 1820

Sir,

I had the honour of receiving your letter yesterday, having before received one[?] from my much valued friend, the Knight of Kerry. I have communicated upon this subject with her Majesty who has been graciously pleased to desire that I would act in the matter according to the best judgement which I can form.

In order to assist me I must request you to let me know what precedents there are of Queen's consort appointing attorneys-general and how those appointments were acted upon and whether they were disputed or were admitted by the courts. Be pleased also to state if the precedents extend to solicitors-general and whom among the *Protestant* barristers of proper standing you would be inclined to recommend for that office in the event of your holding the other?

I beg to add that if this correspondence shall end in your holding it, nothing will give me more entire satisfaction than to have been the instrument of mitigating in one instance the severity of the Penal Laws respecting Catholics, which I really deem as prejudicial to the interests of the Establishment as of the country at large. In such questions the Queen of course takes no part but, having been permitted to exercise my own discretion, I cannot avoid stating one of the views which will certainly regulate it.

P.S.   I have to add that I am happy in having the concurrence of my colleague, Mr. Denman,[1] in this proceeding.

SOURCE : O'Connell Papers, NLI 13647

1   Thomas Denman (1779-1854), M.P. for Wareham, 1818-20; Nottingham, 1820-26, 1830-32; chief justice of the King's Bench, 1832-50; knighted, 1830; created Baron Denman of Dovedale, 1834. See *DNB*.

876

From John Bric to Merrion Square

Morning Chronicle Office, London,
25 November 1820

My dear Sir,

I sent a hasty note to you last night. I waited (as I thought I might) on Mr. Brougham this morning. I do not find that the appointment[1] has actually taken place, but Mr. Brougham informed me that it will if circumstances admit. Those circumstances he detailed to you in his letter which doubtless you have received before now. Mr. Brougham says he expects your immediate answer with the result of your inquiries. The thing I look on as done. I therefore have suspended future operations. I was about to send out to Doctor Parr[2] with a letter from Hone.[3] I also would try what the present Lord Mayor[4] would do as well as Mr. Bennett,[5] but the matter is in the hands of Mr. Brougham whose influence over the Queen is absolute.

With respect to the political movements in Dublin—those your own views and wisdom will regulate. In case of an address I certainly think you ought to come over here to present it. Is Donoughmore to have the Petition? He is estimated in this country according to his merits. He is the most despicable and the most despised of men. I hope the cause of the Catholics will be rescued from the disgrace and misfortune of his friendship.

The Queen and her friends I should think would be delighted to see this fellow degraded. Really he is an object of abhorrence.

I hope you will let me know as soon as possible the result of your inquiries and, now that you are fairly *in for it,* that not one moment will be lost by you. We will have a delightful triumph over all that is base and vile in Ireland. I have nothing more to add. . . .

SOURCE : Fitz-Simon Papers

1 See letter 874.
2 Rev. Samuel Parr (1747-1825), curate of Hatton, Warwickshire, 1785-1825; pedagogue and political writer; appointed chaplain to Queen Caroline, 1820. See *DNB.*
3 William Hone (1780-1842), pamphleteer and bookseller. See *DNB.*
4 John Thomas Thorpe, elected lord mayor, 9 November 1820.
5 Richard Newton Bennett.

877

To Lord Cloncurry

Merrion Square, Sunday
[probably 26 November 1820]

Her Majesty's Attorney-General[1] will have the honour of
accepting Lord Cloncurry's kind invitation for tomorrow. If
he has delayed his *written* answer until he could call himself
by that name, he has not forgotten for one moment, and
never will forget, the respectful and very sincere attachment
and regard he bears to his Lordship.

SOURCE : Cloncurry, *Personal Recollections,* p. 270
1 See letter 874.

878

From the Knight of Kerry to Merrion Square

Carnarvon [N. Wales], 29 November 1820

My dear O'Connell,

Before this reaches you, you will have received Mr.
Brougham's letter and nothing indeed can be more liberal
and kind than his feelings. I only fear from a passage in his
letter to me, which was written after that to you, that he may
think himself in a scrape by giving a Catholic *precedence. If
so,* I am sure you would construe him generously and take
the solicitorship.

[P.S.] Brougham transcribed for me the substance of his
letter to you.

SOURCE : O'Connell MSS, UCD

879

From Alderman Matthew Wood

Wednesday [probably December 1820]

Dear Sir,

I was favoured with your letter yesterday and I went to
Brandenburgh House [residence of Queen Caroline] expressly

to communicate its contents to Her Majesty, and I can assure you she received it most graciously. She had not the least objection to the appointment if it meet with the approbation of Mr. Brougham. Her Majesty received a letter from Mr. B[rougham] to say he would see her this evening. It is probable you will hear in the course of another post something more on the subject. I assure you, Sir, it will give me great pleasure if you succeed according to your wish as I have long admired your public-spirited conduct on many occasions, and I am quite sure the people of Ireland will rejoice at such an appointment.

SOURCE : O'Connell Papers, NLI 13647

880

From his brother James to Merrion Square

Cork, 7 December 1820

My dear Dan,

. . . I was in Iveragh last week and will, please God, go there again before *Cahir*[civeen] *fair, the 13th inst.* Your tenants seem well satisfied with the abatements I promised them for *this year only* and will, I am convinced, make every effort to pay their rents. I will write to you again after the fair and tell you what money you will be likely to get in this and the next month when any shilling they have to pay for the year will be got in.

I spent four days at Derrynane. My uncle is quite well. He showed me your letter in which you mention your being involved with Goold[1] for Buncar. This annoyed my uncle very much as what I told him was that *Pearse*[2] executed a lease to James Connor in which your name was not mentioned, and again last August when I proposed to buy this property from Goold, in talking to my uncle about the value, I never of course pretended you were at all interested. . . .

I regret to see by the Dublin papers of Wednesday that your appointment as Attorney-General to the Queen has not yet been confirmed.

SOURCE : O'Connell MSS, UCD

1 Unidentified.
2 Possibly Daniel Pierse of Ballynoe or Thomas Pierse of Meenago-hane, both of Causeway, Co. Kerry.

881

To Henry Brougham

Merrion Square, 15 December 1820

Sir,

I had the honour of receiving a verbal communication from you by Sir Henry Parnell. He was kind enough to call on me near a week ago but the sittings at *nisi prius* have precluded the possibility of my sooner acknowledging the honour of that communication.

I dare say I have supposed that you were better acquainted with the state in which public documents are in this country than you could have had any occasion to be and, therefore, I neglected to inform you of the impossibility of tracing any such appointment as that which I seek. You may learn with surprise that there is not a single trace of the appointment of a King's Counsel in Ireland amongst any of our records before the year 1720 although historic documents mention an immense number of persons in that station. Ever since 1720 the list of King's Counsel could not be made out without many omissions nor at all but by means of the rolls which show the persons who took the oaths required by the Popery Acts of Queen Anne's reign. The practice in this country is to admit King's Counsel in Chancery only. There alone the ceremony of admission takes place and the individual admitted takes his station as a matter of course in all the other courts. There cannot be any evidence of the admission within the Bar in the law courts, and even in our court of Chancery the register's book contains no entry of it. At least the books in the reigns of the two first Georges do not contain any such entry, and at this moment one could not ascertain from public documents who was or not a King's Counsel but for the preservation of some warrants with certificates of 'the Oaths' having been taken.

The Statutes of Anne do not touch the case of any appointment by a queen consort. They require 'the Oaths' from persons only who hold under the grant of the King, that is, of the Crown, and any grant by the King of an office under the Queen or in her service has it appears been held to be void.

To return to the state of our public records, they have all been most slovenly kept, not preserved. There are chasms of years within the last century in the *recovery roll* and I need not instance any other when so important a public document is defective. The Irish Parliament have been compelled to pass a law to render a fraction of a recovery accompanied by possession as effectual as if the entire record existed. Lord Redesdale has more than once remarked that in Irish causes there were always some deeds lost and it is our daily experience to find it impossible in any case to get all the deeds of any estate. We are in fact a slovenly people, *the causes* of which are obvious.

Under those circumstances it is impossible to find precedents of this appointment, but the principle is perfectly clear and the tradition of the Bar accompanies and sanctions that principle and the occurrence which Mr. Fitzgerald[1] *can prove* shows beyond controversy a modern recognition of the right to make this appointment.

My own opinion accords very decidedly with this view of the case and should you, Sir, advise her Majesty to honour me with this appointment, I will *enforce* (if *force* be necessary) her Majesty's right without allowing a thought of the expense of the contest coming from any other person than myself. My opinion is that I should be entitled to a *mandamus*. A barrister in this country is not a mere creature of courtesy as in England but is called to the Bar by force of a Statute of the reign of Henry VIII and, having that legal capacity, I consider that I should, by her Majesty's appointment, be enabled by a *mandamus* to compel the Chancellor to admit me. I may be wrong but, if so, I am wrong very *premeditatedly*. I may be sneered at for giving myself a wrong opinion though, whether right or wrong, I fancy I do at present give as many—probably more opinions—to others than any Irish barrister. I cannot except one.

I believe I forgot in my last letter to say that my friend, Mr. Bennett,[2] is a Protestant of the Established Church.

It is said here—for we live as in a village—that Mr. Plunket is not pleased and, *they say,* has taken measures to prevent, if he can, this appointment. If he could influence the choice, I should withdraw my claim—not on any professional grounds for in that respect he is more than civil—but because I totally differ from him in politics, and he knows well that I am dissatisfied with his having got the Catholic petition. He got it *by accident*. It will be taken from him by design. I recognize in this country no political party but that of which the Duke of Leinster is the head. I have not room to apologize

for this long but hasty letter. Do not, however, imagine that
I anticipate opposition should her Majesty honour me with
this appointment. I am only ready for it, but I have the
strongest reason to believe that no opposition will be given.

Delay is inconvenient to myself personally but I shall urge
nothing on that account.

SOURCE : Brougham MSS, University College London
1 The Knight of Kerry.
2 Richard Newton Bennett. This letter is not extant.

882

From his brother James

Killarney, 22 December 1820

My dear Dan,

I yesterday on my return from Iveragh received your letter
of the 19th inst. and sent Charles Sugrue by this day's coach
£220 with directions not to *lose a moment* in forwarding it to
you to Dublin. £20 of this is the money you paid for the
piano for Kitty [presumably O'Connell's sister, Mrs.
Moynihan] and the remaining £200 is money of my own. . . .
These are indeed, as you justly observe, dreadful times and
there is no getting a guinea in Iveragh as all the tenants'
resources are completely exhausted in paying off the May gale.
Pigs sold at Cahir [civeen] fair the 13th inst. for about 17/-
the hundredweight and everything else equally low.

I have no doubt you have at least a balance of £400 due to
you of Myles McSwiney. . . . I know the poor man is now
straining every nerve to pay this off. . . . Do not suppose for
a moment that I mean to excuse him for spending a guinea
of your money, but consider that *this large balance* became
due in the course of five years, and indeed, my dear Dan, you
are yourself much to blame in not having devoted a few hours
once a year when you came to Iveragh to look into your
affairs. Surely but for the Drung Hill road and *the tobacco*
business the large balance due to you would never produce
2/6 in the Pound. . . . I am quite certain he has not since last
October of course misapplied a shilling of your money, and I
am decidedly of opinion the accounts and receipts of your
rents had better remain with him until then when you *can
finally close and* wind *up all* pecuniary transactions. If I sup-

posed Myles McSwiney was now misapplying one penny of your property I would at once suspend him, but I again repeat he is not doing so.

. . . It is of course unnecessary for me to say that I will undertake the management of your property in Iveragh. . . .

SOURCE : O'Connell MSS, UCD

883

From Henry Brougham to Merrion Square

23 December 1820

Sir,

I have been honoured with both your letters and I should have had many apologies to make for not answering the first, had I not explained the reason through our common friend, Sir H. Parnell.

I need hardly renew the assurances which I before gave how satisfactory the appointment will prove to me, if it takes place, but I beg leave to state for your consideration how awkwardly I feel situated in advising upon it. I am bound (together with my colleague) to report to the Queen an opinion upon H.M.'s right to make the appointments. We must endeavour, therefore, first of all to satisfy ourselves of the grounds of the right.

Now none can be so satisfactory as the practice in former cases, and I trust you will see the necessity of applying yourself as speedily as possible to the inquiry whether or not any instance exists of a Queen *Consort* naming an attorney- or solicitor-general in Ireland and of any of the courts admitting the rank of the officer nominated. If the inquiry prove unsuccessful, you may state the reasons why no distinct answer to the question can be given. But if it is possible to answer it either in the affirmative or negative, a very material fact will be gained by such answer.

Should it either appear that no appointment has been made or that, though made, it has been inoperative in point of precedence; or that for any reason it is impossible to ascertain the matter either way, then I should request you to state the grounds upon which, *independent of precedents,* you deem the right maintainable. Perhaps the best way will be for you

to draw up a case fully as if it were to be laid before counsel
for opinion because, in fact, that is the first step to be taken,
and I am sure you will at once acquit me of the least disrespect
towards you or doubt of the soundness and value of your own
opinion when I add that *our* reporting upon the case here, in
our official capacity, is quite a matter of course. It is scarcely
necessary to add that *your* opinion will have the greatest
weight with us in forming our own. When we shall have so
reported, even should it appear that the right is doubtful, it
will still be a question whether it ought not to be claimed and
exercised by making the appointments.

But first of all it is necessary to make our report upon the
right, and such a statement as I have above described will
enable us immediately to do so.

P.S. In reference to what you say of Mr. P[lunke]t[1] I beg
leave to assure you that I have had no communication whatever with him upon the subject nor indeed with any person
except yourself and Sir H. Parnell in Ireland.

SOURCE : O'Connell Papers, NLI 13647
1   See letter 881.

884

From John Bric to Merrion Square

[postmarked probably early January 1821]

[No salutation]
Nine o'clock. I have just read your admirable address.[1] I will
have it printed by Hone tomorrow. This will spread it about
the town like wildfire.

We are labouring to get up a meeting here. You shall have
your share of it. I think it would be well if you would write
to Brougham offering to assert the right[2] in Ireland should
that right be disputed. This would leave him without an
excuse.

SOURCE : Fitz-Simon Papers
1   O'Connell's very vigorous letter to the Catholics of Ireland of 1
    January 1821.
2   The right for Queen Caroline to appoint an attorney-general for
    Ireland.

885

From John Bric to Merrion Square

London, Friday [5 January 1821]

My dear Sir,

I congratulate you from my soul. You have acted a part that places you higher if possible than you have been in Ireland and brings you forward in this country in a new character. Look at the *Morning Chronicle*. I am sorry I cannot send you one as *every paper in our office has been sold*. I went immediately after I read the account in the *Globe* of last night to the editor of the *Chronicle*[1] and requested that he would place you in the foreground. You see he has done so in a kind manner.[2]

If you think it fit, write a letter of thanks to Mr. Perry. He is fond of attention. I think you ought to do so but you are the best judge. The impression here is great [that] the *thing* will lead to further consequences. I shall write to you tomorrow. I am happy always to see your name placed in the front of independence. I write this merely to express my delight.

SOURCE : Fitz-Simon Papers

1 James Perry.

2 The *Morning Chronicle* of 5 January dealt at length with the meeting of Co. Dublin freeholders on 30 December convened by the high sheriff for the purpose of passing an address of loyalty to the king. On the previous day a meeting had taken place at D'Arcy's Tavern where it was decided to add to the address a condemnation of the conduct of the government in regard to Queen Caroline (*FJ*, 30 Dec. 1820). At the county meeting the sheriff's attempt to have the address pass without the condemnation was vigorously opposed by O'Connell and others who accused him of conducting the meeting in an illegal manner. When he dissolved the meeting Lord Cloncurry was voted by those present into the chair and, having taken it, was removed by the military. He and his supporters then met across the road at a tavern. There they passed an address to the king which contained a denunciation of the government for its treatment of Queen Caroline (she was mentioned by implication). On O'Connell's proposal it was unanimously decided to appoint a committee to ' lay before the Lord Lieutenant the outrageous and illegal conduct of the sheriff ' (*FJ*, 1 Jan. 1821).

886

From John Bric

Thursday, 9 [and 11] November, 1820[1]

My dear Sir,

I received your letter this morning. . . . I perceive that you did not receive my letter written on the arrival of the important news[2] from Dublin. That intelligence has created a strong sensation here and you see the [*Morning*] *Chronicle* and the *Traveller* have acted well. Wood,[3] an honest, clever, good-hearted Irishman, has the merit of the *Traveller*. The *Morning Ch*[*ronicle*][4] really deserves much credit for the part it has taken. It deserves our thanks for the manner in which it has put you forward. I think you ought to write a letter of thanks to Perry.[5] The gentleman who writes most of the leading articles is a Scotchman, a Mr. Black.[6] He received a request of mine on this subject in the kindest manner. Should you write shortly to me, mention his name. Those little attentions are grateful and are valued. The Government press, the *Courier,* in a shy manner, evidently afraid of the business (it is not ashamed of anything), and the *New Times* in a more open manner labour to excuse the outrage. So much the better. The honest men here deprecate the proceeding of course and are unanimous in their praise of the wisdom and spirit displayed[7] at Kilmainham and afterwards by the friends of freedom.

A parliamentary proceeding is the thing. Of course we are not so simple as to hope for redress or to expect the punishment in any way of the sheriff[8]—no. If the sheriff's soldiers ran you and the Mr. Hamilton Rowan[9] and Lord Cloncurry through the body, not a hair of the sheriff's head would suffer for it. We have really come to this. But then a parliamentary inquiry will be of great use. It will agitate the affair in this country, it will enable the honest Members to hold up those miscreants to public odium. If we cannot punish the fellows let us at least have the consolation of abusing them, a poor consolation certainly but the only one at present within our reach. The outrage was opportune. It shows what gentlemen the loyal addressers are and it has brought you out in the most favourable and the most forceable way. If the Queen have any real friends about her, if it be the object of her advisers to strengthen her interests, to increase her power of resistance against future oppression, they must see your value and will yield to your request. Why the appointment[10] was not long since made, I am really unable even to conjecture. Is Mr. Brougham sincere? If he be, it would appear to a simple mind that nothing could be more easy than to make the appointment. Whether in point of law that appointment could be sustained is another consideration.

Saturday morning

I have not been able to finish this letter. The foregoing part was written on Thursday. The legal question you would agitate—and it requires not a great sagacity to conclude that agitation is the interest of the Queen. She is before the wind and should sail on. Opposition will serve her. The opposition of her enemies will only [render them] more odious and less able to injure her. Even in the present case their refusal to ratify your appointment, that is, to swear you into office would furnish an excellent topic for invective. I confess to you I feel the utmost disgust at the conduct of Brougham. The miserable paragraph[11] which he dictated for the *Traveller* was worse than nothing. This is the moment to command him. You have already paid the purchase; there is no excuse for not making the appointment. *Delaying* it I will take as refusing it. You ought certainly not to sleep over this matter. Perhaps it would be of some service if you by letter authorized me to call on Brougham. Write a line to Alderman Wood[12] and mention my name in it so that I may call on him as your agent. I have been informed I cannot, however, say whether it be true or false that Brougham's influence at Brandenburgh House[13] is not so powerful as it has been. Wood, honest and consistent, remains the same. I have been told that Wood can do a great deal and, *if you let me at him* as your agent, I think that *now* we will bring it to an issue. It is really enough to make one vexed to death to see it delayed in this paltry and selfish way. What a subject for jest is it with the base Orange Bar. The appointment, I should think, is all you want even though it should not be ratified, still your object is in a great measure served. You see how admirably the press is keeping up the cry. Now you are talked of here and in a little time you will be universally known and admired [remainder of letter is missing].

source : Fitz-Simon Papers

1 The correct date of this letter (from internal evidence) is 11 and
  13 January 1821.
2 See letter 885, note 2.
3 Alexander Wood.
4 The *Morning Chronicle* published secondary leading articles on the
  subject on 5, 6, 8, 9 and 11 January.
5 James Perry (1756-1821), proprietor and editor of the *Morning
  Chronicle,* 1789-1821. Under Perry's editorship the *Morning Chronicle* was the organ of the Whig party. See *DNB*.
6 John Black (1783-1855), journalist for the *Morning Chronicle* from
  1817; editor, 1821-43. See *DNB*.
7 See letter 885, note 2.
8 Sir Richard Steele, third baronet, Hampstead, Co. Dublin. Married
  1798 Frances Mary Colette, daughter of Lieut. Gen. Edward Count
  D'Alton of the Austrian army.
9 Archibald Hamilton Rowan (1751-1834), United Irishman and secretary to the Dublin Committee, 1792-94; imprisoned, 1794, and escaped
  to France; moved to Philadelphia, 1795; returned to Ireland on
  pardon, 1804. See *DNB*.
10 The proposed appointment of O'Connell as the Queen's attorney-
   general for Ireland.
11 This appears to be a news item in the *Traveller* of 1 December 1820
   which is stated to be taken from the Dublin newspaper, *Carrick's
   Morning Post*: 'APPOINTMENT OF HER MAJESTY'S
   ATTORNEY-GENERAL FOR IRELAND. We believe we may
   announce with certainty that Mr. O'Connell will be appointed
   Attorney-General to the Queen for Ireland, if that appointment has
   not already taken place. We understand that Mr. Brougham has
   received her Majesty's commands to make the necessary arrangements for expediting the appointment of Mr. O'Connell, and that
   Mr. Brougham has undertaken it with alacrity. The next post may
   bring intelligence of its completion. There is no legal obstacle to
   this office being filled by a Catholic lawyer.' This quote is from
   Carrick's Morning Post of 27 November 1820.
12 Matthew Wood.
13 London residence of Queen Caroline.

887

From John Barclay Sheil[1] to Merrion Square

Edinburgh, 17 January 1821

Dear Sir,
   Although personally unknown to you . . . as an Irish
Catholic I have ever esteemed and loved you almost from my

boyhood, and as the son of Dr. Sheil[1] of Ballyshannon and the relation of Owen O'Conor, I have been taught by my best friends to confide in your sincerity *and fidelity to my country*. . . .

Since the year 1808 I have enjoyed through the liberality of my father the most extensive opportunities of education that could be imparted under the disqualifications of the Penal Code to an Irish Catholic. My classical education was completed in the college of Stoneyhurst in England and subsequently I was a student for four years in the University of Dublin. Since my departure from Dublin College I have resided four winters in Edinburgh and have been elected President of the Royal Medical and Royal Physical Societies *in the same year,* an honour which no Irishman except the celebrated *Thomas Addis Emmet* ever before enjoyed and which was only attained by him and myself in the last century.

[He praises O'Connell's letter of the 1st January[2] which had made such a favourable impression in Scotland particularly among members of the Scottish Bar. He encloses a letter he lately received from Lord Erskine, who expresses such pro-Irish sentiments, and Sheil gives O'Connell permission to make any use of it he wishes.]

 . . . If petitions on behalf of Catholics are to be sent forward to Parliament, let them be confided to *Erskine* or to some man who detests corruption and not to *Donoughmore* or to sycophants of his description. . . .

I wish Counsellor Phillips would come over *here* even for a few days. Pray tell him I am confident that nothing could so much serve his fame as an appearance in Edinburgh just now. . . . Why should not *Mr. Jeffrey*[3] and he be friends? I wish it ardently. . . .

 . . . I could not restrain my feelings when I read your Printed Letter. . . . I send you also a letter I had from *Emmet a year ago.* He lives in another clime but are his principles changed by vicissitude? Why cannot the youth of Ireland yet imitate his independence? . . .

 . . . I have read Richard Sheil's letter lately published in reply to your address to the Irish Catholics[4] and regret to see that his vetoistical folly is unchanged. If he knew how little is thought of such qualifying measures by men of talent here he would, I think, become an apostate from his present political creed and be forgiven. I suspect the Primate, Dr. Curtis,[5] is a vetoist. I met his Grace at Ballyshannon last September and proposed your health in his company. Dr. McLaughlin[6] could tell you what occurred. His Grace did not seem to relish your politics but *five* other bishops who were present declared they considered you the most sincere Catholic in Ireland. Dr. McNicholas[7] is a zealous friend to you and to truth.

SOURCE : O'Connell MSS, UCD

1   John Barclay Sheil, M.D. (born c. 1797), son of Simon Sheil, M.D., Ballyshannon, Co. Donegal, by his first marriage, and author of *History of the Temperance Movement in Ireland* (Dublin 1843). Simon Sheil's second wife was a sister of Owen O'Conor.
2   For text see *Freeman's Journal,* 8 January 1821. The letter put the case for Catholic Emancipation but argued that ' it is hopeless' to continue our Petitions to an unreformed Parliament '.
3   Francis Jeffrey (1773-1850), advocate and critic; one of the founders (1802) and editor (1803-29) of *Edinburgh Review*; M.P. for Malton, 1831-32; for Edinburgh, 1832-34. Received a judgeship in 1834, becoming Lord Jeffrey.
4   For text see *Freeman's Journal,* 11 January 1821.
5   Patrick Curtis (1747-1832), archbishop of Armagh and primate of all Ireland, 1819-32.
6   Peter McLaughlin (c. 1760-1840), bishop of Raphoe, 1802-18; bishop of Derry, 1818-40.
7   Patrick McNicholas (c. 1781-1852), bishop of Achonry, 1818-52.

888

From Alexander Wood to Merrion Square

London, 22 January [1821]

Confidential

My dear Sir,

   Bric's letter of Saturday has informed you of his absence from town and you will thence have judged the cause of my not writing sooner. I have with as much discretion as possible made all the inquiries I could on the subject of your last letter. One consideration has been suggested to me which I think decides the matter. Professionally Mr. B[rougham] as Queen's Atty-G. could not give an opinion *against* his right, and therefore no case could be submitted to him professionally.

   For my own part I wish it were otherwise, for I know it

must be unpleasant for you to be under any obligations in that quarter. However, if any passage of Mr. B[rougham]'s letter to you requires a statement of his right, there can be no hesitation in laying the one you have sent before him. But it will be necessary for you to write a letter to Mr. Brougham which with the statement I shall enclose and forward. Would it not be advisable to alter the statement a little in *tone,* that is, merely to submit the case without formally *demanding* an opinion? Your letter will, of course, be answered and an opinion given, but the obligation will be the less. If you approve of this suggestion, I shall copy the statement in that shape before submitting it. The *right* appears to myself well made out and at all events the least that ought to be done is to make the appointment. Your letter[1] to the Catholics has broken down a great deal of prejudice here and was an excellent stroke of policy. At the meeting of the Common Council on Thursday there will be a motion for a petition in favour of Catholic Emancipation.[2]

SOURCE : Fitz-Simon Papers
1 See letter 887, note 2.
2 In the report of this meeting in the (London) *Morning Chronicle,* 26 January 1821, there is no mention of the petition.

889

From his brother James to Merrion Square

Killarney, 24 January 1821

My dear Dan,

You have before now heard that all idea of a county meeting in Kerry to address his Majesty is given up. The friends of *Lord Castlereagh & Co.* were well aware that they would *be met at the* County Court-house by a number of independent freeholders though the wretched aristocracy of Kerry to a man would support any measure that had the appearance of loyalty without once considering that the King and his *ministers* were quite distinct and, in fact, that they are the only real enemies his Majesty has in Great Britain.

I regret to tell you that Colonel McCarthy and Jerry Mahony are likely to be put into the King's Bench. McCarthy and Pierce Mahony,[1] the attorney, had some difference of opinions.[2] Jerry Mahony called on Pierce who refused to make the necessary concession, and Jerry delivered a message but no person was present but Pierce and Jerry. You are therefore on receipt of this letter to consider yourself retained, and let me beg of you also to retain Richard Pennyfather[3] for them.

Jerry Mahony has written a long letter to their law agent and one nephew agrees and gave him all the particulars. Pierce Mahony has by his conduct proved himself a most consummate coward nor do I think a criminal information under all the circumstances will be ever granted against McCarthy or his friend. Do not delay retaining Pennyfather as I fear Pierce may be beforehand with you.

SOURCE : O'Connell Papers, NLI 13647
1 Pierce Mahony (1792-1853), attorney, Woodlawn, Killarney; Kilmorna, Listowel, Co. Kerry, and Dublin. M.P. for Kinsale, 1837-38; parliamentary agent to the Catholic Association, 1828-29.
2 See letter 920.
3 Richard Pennefather (1773-1859), baron of exchequer, 1821-59. See *DNB*.

890

From S. M. D'Esterre,[1] Guernsey, Channel Islands, February 1821, to Merrion Square

Asks O'Connell to send him a copy of the will of his deceased father, Norcot D'Esterre of Limerick city, and to procure for himself a situation in Dublin.

SOURCE : O'Connell MSS, UCD
1 Samuel Martin D'Esterre, brother of John N. D'Esterre whom O'Connell killed in a duel in 1815.

891

From his wife

19 March 1821

[incomplete copy of letter]

My dearest love,

. . . I fear you will be disappointed at not getting the *Catholic Advocate*. . . . There is a letter in *Carrick*[1] from a Catholic addressed to you, in my mind a very silly one and evidently written by a Vetoist. I am really astonished how anyone can think themselves equal to answering any letters coming from you, they only make themselves ridiculous, and the only wisdom they show is not putting their signature to such trash.

SOURCE : O'Connell Papers, NLI 13651
1   *Carrick's Morning Post*, 14 March 1821.

892

To his wife

Limerick 22 March 1821

My dearest darling,
      . . . At all events do not touch the bill money. It would set me quite astray if you were to do that. I left you £130 for bills out of which you paid on the 21st £69 some shillings leaving in your hands £61 or, rather £60 because of the shillings, call it exactly £60. I am sure Mr. Mahon took up the £35. There will be due on the 25th a bill for £58.10.0 which you thus have and £1.10.0 over. There will be another bill for £50 due on the 28th, that is, Wednesday next. Make a memorandum, darling, of those bills, and I now perceive that I shall in the interval, please God, be able to send you at least £20 on account of the house, etc., that is exclusive of bill money. Say to me in your answer to this the exact balance of bill money which you have with a promise not to touch it and then I am quite safe. Indeed I am quite safe even without such promise because I am blessed with a darling wife who only consults my wishes. . . .

SOURCE : Fitz-Simon Papers

893

To his wife, Merrion Square

Limerick, 23 March 1821

My darling Heart,
      . . . And now I think of it you can answer this letter to this place by writing on Saturday and I will get your letter on Sunday. I therefore enclose only half the £50 note as I *know* money will *make* you write. There is a pull by the cock nose for you.

Fasting agrees perfectly well with me, if fasting it can be called.

The Catholics here meet tomorrow. I will, please God, give them a flaming harangue. I hope the Catholics in Dublin will bestir themselves.

SOURCE : Fitz-Simon Papers

894

From John Barclay Sheil to Merrion Square

Edinburgh University, 1 April 1821

Dear Sir,

. . . Your letter to the *Dublin Evening Post* from Limerick to the Roman Catholics of Ireland[1] has been read with deep attention by some of the most talented and disinterested friends of *the Catholic cause in Edinburgh*. It is a cause which has long been advocated with fidelity and constancy by the gentlemen who write in the *Edinburgh Review,* and if I do not assert an untruth in declaring my own opinion, I should say candidly that I impute in no trivial degree the change which has of late years occurred in the Protestant mind to the admission of Catholics to political equality as attributable to the arguments and to *that effect* which the *Edinburgh Review* has produced in its extensive and extending circulation throughout Scotland and England.

I have the honour of being intimately acquainted with the principal conductors of that review.

Your letter of the 17th from Limerick[2] is considered warm and impetuous, your attack on Plunket deemed ungenerous as he must be *considered disinterested,* consequently your error entitled to indulgence.

By letters from London I find the bills will positively pass the Commons. The English Catholics are unanimously for them even with the securities. In reality, what peril to our religion can it generate if these bills pass? You may refer me to your printed argument but *I doubt* the fact that spiritual and conscientious communications on matters divulged in Confession to the parish priests would be subjected to scrutiny of that Board which it is proposed to nominate. The very attempt would be monstrous and awaken public *execration,*

and as to the government having a negative on the appointment of bishops, what evil could it cause? Are you not sensible that nothing can exceed the scene of *intrigue* which has
been carried on for years amongst the Catholics in Ireland
as well priests as laymen about the appointment to mitres?
Did not the clergy of my own county, the Co. Donegal, just
sign the postulation for Bishop MacGettigan and then retract
their signatures and write letters against him to Rome and,
even when Dr. Curtis came down to Ballyshannon to con-
secrate him, did not some clergymen from the Diocese of
Derry, who were in chase of the mitre of Raphoe, apply to his
Grace the Primate to *suspend the consecration*? While such
a system is going on, is it not even desirable that an authority
should be vested somewhere at home to control such chicanery? In short, my dear Sir, it is the wish of the friends of
liberty [in Scotland] . . . that Ireland should now *accept* the
chance which fortune presents to her of a more honorable
rank in the constitution.

SOURCE : O'Connell MSS, UCD

1 *Dublin Evening Post,* 22 March 1821. The letter was in opposition
to the two bills Plunket introduced into the Commons on 7 March,
one to grant Catholic Emancipation and the other—intended to
qualify the first—to concede to the government a right to veto
appointments of Catholic bishops and deans. On 26 March the bills
were consolidated into a single measure which finally on 17 April
was defeated in the Lords by 159 votes to 120.

2 The above-mentioned letter.

894a
To his wife, Merrion Square

Cork, 2 April 1821

My darling Love,

First you will be not a little pleased to hear that everything
is settled for Ellen Connor's wedding immediately after
Easter.[1] I had fixed to go back next week to Tralee but on
reflection—and keep this to yourself—I find that I will be
able easily through my brother James to arrange everything
without going there—or, what is more material, staying away
from my family. Do not, however, say one word about it to
anybody as *they* would fear some fresh obstacle which, how-

ever, *shall not* exist. I will, I promise you, my own love, arrange everything satisfactorily without going back—and you and my children will be annoyed by my presence a week sooner by that means.

I now enclose you the other half of the fifty pound note of which I sent you one half from Tralee. . . .

I do not think I was ever so constantly busied as I was in Tralee at these assizes. The moment I left court I was always surrounded with arbitrations etc. so that I was compelled to get Rickarda[2] to write to you on Saturday and I now perceive that since Wednesday last I did not write you a line.

Darling, I enclose the present notes on *my way* because I pay the postage to insure a safe and prompt delivery.

I travelled from Tralee yesterday with great expedition. My hurry was to be in time for the aggregate meeting which takes [place] this day. We shall have a great meeting of it and put to shame the wretched Vetoists of Dublin. We met in Kerry on Saturday and of course did what we chose. I will this day touch upon the scholarships of Trinity College.

How idle it is, darling, for people to talk about fasting being injurious or dangerous to a strong constitution. I wish you could know in what excellent health your husband is in, a little thin certainly but, instead of being the worse, I am very much the better for that. . . . Best love to your mother.

SOURCE : O'Connell School, Dublin
1 Ellen Connor never married.
2 Rickarda Connor.

895
To the Knight of Kerry

Cork, 8 April 1821

My dear Sir,

The information you have hitherto given me respecting *the Bill*[1] has been very satisfactory and correct. It is not your fault if it has passed in its present shape. There are, indeed, some of *our friends* who surprised us a good deal. Young Rice[2] cannot well escape imputations which I should be truly sorry to countenance. But the Catholic Clergy in Limerick told me early that he would take the precise part he did. The truth is, some people imagine that *we* think as little about our religion as *they* naturally do.

If the Bill passes in its present shape it will tend to exasperate and render matters worse in point of popular tranquillity than they are at present. But I strongly suspect that the re-establishment of Legitimacy in Italy will do more to throw out the Bill in the Lords than the eloquence not only of a Master in Chancery[3] but of the Chancellor[4] himself, pathetic as well as poetic although his Lordship be.

I see there is an Assistant Barrister[5] Bill in agitation for England, leaving the trial by jury. I think the plan promises well, and that with modifications it would be highly useful in Ireland. The present Irish system is productive of the vilest perjury, and does more to demoralize our peasantry than all the details of Law and Religion can be calculated to prevent.

SOURCE : FitzPatrick, *Corr.*, I, 70-1

1   See letter 894, note 1.
2   Thomas Spring Rice.
3   Thomas Ellis (1774-c. 1832), eldest son of Richard Ellis, Youghal, and Mary Hilliard. M.P. for Dublin city, 1820-26. Master in chancery, 1806-32. In the Commons on 2 April Ellis opposed the bill and made a hostile reference to O'Connell (*DEP*, Supplement, 7 Apr. 1821).
4   Lord Eldon.
5   In Ireland assistant barristers, though originally appointed as salaried assistants to justices at quarter sessions, by this time exercised powers to determine civil suits involving less than £20. See R. B. McDowell, *The Irish Administration*, 1801-1914 (London 1964), p. 113.

896

To Cornelius MacLoghlin,[1] Merchant, Usher's Island, Dublin

Cork, 10 April 1821

My dear and exalted friend,

Get as many honest names to the enclosed[2] as you can for some day next week. I have sent one to Dr. Sheridan. Let us do the best we can. Do not despair. The people are honest. I expect to be in Dublin on Saturday night.

SOURCE : O'Connell MSS, UCD
1 Cornelius MacLoghlin (1761-1851), 13 Usher's Island, Dublin. Catholic merchant; a trustee and treasurer of O'Connell testimonial, 1829, and O'Connell tribute in succeeding years. A member of the United Irishmen.
2 On the back of the letter O'Connell has drafted the address to which he wishes to have the signatures attached. It is a request to have a meeting of the Catholics of Ireland called in Dublin to consider matters vital to the Catholic religion, the date in April to be announced.

897

From his daughter Elizabeth to Post Office, Cork

Merrion Square, Tuesday
[postmarked 10 April 1821]

My dearest Father,

It is a long time since I had the pleasure of writing to you and I assure you I feel very happy to be again able to do so. . . .

Ellen[1] received a delightful long letter from you on Saturday which made her so happy and *conceited* that I think you will spoil her if you write her many more of that description. I wish *I* had any chance of such a letter, but I know I don't yet deserve all the fine things you said of Ellen so I must content myself for two or three years more. I wish I had some news to tell you but I have not one word. . . .

SOURCE : Kenneigh Papers
1 O'Connell's eldest daughter.

898

To his wife

Cork, 14 April 1821

My sweetest Mary,

. . . I wish with all my heart that the present rascally Catholic Bill[1] was flung out. While I am travelling on Monday morning the rascals will be debating.

SOURCE : FitzPatrick, *Corr.*, I, 71
1 See letter 894, note 1.

899

From Lord Donoughmore

Bulstrode St. [London], 19 April 1821

Copy

Dear Sir,

Your letter to me needed no apology. To your opinion and suggestions on any public subject it would be my duty to hearken with attention and respect more especially, however, upon the present occasion when you are yourself amongst the parties for whom Parliament had undertaken to legislate and when there is no other person in the country in which you reside more likely to become an immediate gainer by the provisions of that bill respecting which you so strongly remonstrate against its passing into a law.

With what you say respecting the advantages held out to the Catholics by the measure which was disposed of on Tuesday last[1] compared with the actual state of that country to which they belong (it is of our own countrymen of course that I intend to speak). I entirely agree in opinion. The bulk of the people have obviously nothing to gain by any relaxation of the existing code of disabling statutes. To the manifold privations under which they are pressed down to the ground it is a far different system of remedies which ought to be administered. And I also perfectly coincide in the sentiment which you express, viz., that the measure having been construed by the R. Catholic clergy as a bill of pains and penalties against them, such and precisely in the same point of view will it be received by the whole body of the laity of their religious persuasion however entirely uninterested themselves in any one of the enactments of the bill. I am also quite sure that any attempt to put such provisions into execution would create irritation and resistance. Indeed, a more certain and fruitful source of mischief I cannot well conceive to myself than the bill would have proved to be if it had passed into a law in the shape in which it had reached our House from the other House of Parliament.

Accordingly I had declared against having anything to say to it on its arrival from the Commons excepting only as an avowed enemy till its supporters in the other House had acquiesced in important amendments to meet the objections which I had stated in every case excepting that of the royal negative only and to this I persevered in the same hostility which I had expressed on all former occasions.

It is, however, not the less my conscientious opinion that from this negative would never have arisen any sort of influence to the minister of the Crown or any obstruction or annoyances to the Catholic clergy in filling the important situations in their church.

With the exception of all cases relating to the confessional I cannot discover any reasonable objection as proceeding from the side of the Catholic to that provision which would have passed all the other correspondence from the Pope through the Board which the bill sought to create. . . .

But what stared me in the face at once . . . was the compulsory oath which it intended to impose upon the whole mass of the Roman Catholic Clergy. . . . Against this barbarous and wild attempt I raised my voice at once and the parliamentary friends of the measure in the Lords, and amongst them two of his Majesty's Cabinet ministers, fully acquiesced in my objections and authorized me to say in my place that this provision was not to stand part of the bill. . . .

The decision of the House was obviously against the whole weight of the arguments. The Chancellor[2] and Lord Liverpool[3] never having exerted themselves upon the subject with less effect and that too in the face of an almost unequal display of reasoning and of talent. The number of the Catholic laity who have any sort of prospect of profiting by what is called Emancipation being so very small and as it can advantage the Catholic clergy in no degree whatsoever . . . how improperly has this been always considered as the great leading Irish question. . . . And is it quite certain that the Catholic clergy feel any interest whatsoever in any further relaxation of the disabling statutes . . . ?

My brother[4] will accompany the delivery of this letter with a copy of a late communication[5] of mine to Dr. Troy.

SOURCE : Donoughmore Papers
1   See letter 894, note 1.
2   Lord Eldon.
3   Robert Banks (Jenkinson), second earl of Liverpool (1770-1828); prime minister, June 1812-April 1827; opponent of Catholic Emancipation.
4   Francis Hely-Hutchinson, M.P.
5   Unidentified.

900

From his brother James to Merrion Square

Killarney, 19 April 1821

My Dear Dan,

. . . Indeed, circumstanced as you are with James Connor's family, I did not think it possible you could avoid being in Tralee before *Easter Sunday,* and perceived by Edward Connor's[1] manner when I asked him for you, that he was cruelly disappointed. The fact is, my dear fellow, unless you can *at once* close your accounts with the Connor family, your character as a man of honour and integrity will suffer.[2] Several reports of an unfavourable nature have already gone abroad about the manner you have disposed of the money of your wards. God knows, my dear Dan, what pain it gives me to be obliged to write to you in this way. Nor would I do so if I did not know that this business was very generally spoken of both here and in Tralee.

. . . John Murphy[3] will lend you £200. . . .

Myles McSwiney has at length closed his accounts to this day and I will take them to Dublin. He has paid up any money of yours he received but I candidly confess he has been a very unsatisfactory agent but, my dear Dan, I perceive you never said a word to him about your taking your affairs out of his hands, and, until you call on him *either by letter or otherwise* to hand me over his books, I cannot think of calling for them. Did I do so, the entire odium of removing him would be thrown on me which you must admit is not fair or reasonable. . . . No consideration will induce me to ask for Myles' books until he offers them to me. . . . Why you allowed Myles McSwiney to run such a course, I am at a loss to imagine. However, from his success *in trade,* you have been very lucky in being paid the large balance due to you last October. . . .

SOURCE : O'Connell MSS, UCD

1   Edward James Connor (died 19 Nov. 1827), third son of James and Betsey Connor, Tralee, nephew of O'Connell's wife. Attorney.
2   Subsequent letters show that O'Connell behaved generously to the Connor family, particularly to Charles Connor. James Connor's eldest child, Ellen, said in a letter to O'Connell on 14 June 1837: ' I can *repeat in sincerity* that I am shocked and grieved at the immense sums you have advanced for our family.'
3   John Murphy, Valentia, Co. Kerry.

901

To O'Conor Don

Merrion Square, 23 April 1821

My dear Friend,

What is to be done now?[1] That is the question. Everyone agrees that we should meet. Some are for addressing the King, some for declaring against any further petition, some for proclaiming reform. But I think *all* agree to meet. It would be desirable to heal the miserable little schism which has arisen amongst ourselves. It can be done only by coming together. Even the Vetoists must admit that *securities* do no good because we are kicked out as unceremoniously with them as without them.

I send you a copy of the requisition[2] at the other side, and entreat of you to allow me to put your signature to it. I hope, too, it will be your convenience to attend the meeting. I think there is no person who could contribute so much as you to prevent the collision of parties. The fact is you are respected and loved by everybody, and your unaffected kindliness of heart and soundness of understanding may, I think, help us out of our present dilemma.

We are cast down by our enemies, and we may make ourselves despicable by either a stupid acquiescence or by absurd dissension. I care not, however, what quantity of abuse they may fling on myself. I console myself in my honesty.

SOURCE : Clonalis Papers

1 See letter 894, note 1.
2 It requested 'a meeting of the Catholics of Ireland at Dublin on Monday, the 7th of May 1821, to take into consideration the present state of Catholic affairs, and the measures best suited to the wants and wishes of the Catholics of Ireland'.

902

From John Cartwright to Merrion Square

Burton Crescent, London, 25 April 1821

Dear Sir,

As Chairman of the late Meeting[1] of Friends to Civil and Religious Liberty, it is particularly due to you, as the great champion of their cause in Ireland, to assure you that I am persuaded the resolutions[2] which that meeting came to express the sense of the far greater part of the genuine reformers of England, and only want to be made familiar to the public mind to become general. Considering the fallibility of mortals, it must ever be in vain to hope for perfect unanimity in any religious opinions or, rather, political opinions touching men's rights to religious freedom.

[Cartwright says he would have written the results of the meeting sooner, as O'Connell was on circuit at the time, but for the fact that the resolutions were published in at least nine newspapers which he lists.]

As an enlightened advocate for radical reform in the national representation without which liberty, either civil or religious, is a word without a meaning, we may confidently trust you will not fail to notice the resolutions above adverted to at the aggregate meeting of the Catholics which I understand will shortly be held in Dublin.

What can I say of the late failure of Mr. Lambton's[3] motion[4] for what, by a misnomer, it is the fashion to call moderate reform? I will neither give it a name nor speak of the treatment it received? Hoping only that the result will furnish instruction which will lead to better things, namely, that it will tend to establish the opinion that the reform which is most perfect, will, for that very reason, be found most practicable.

SOURCE : O'Connell MSS, UCD

1 This meeting took place at the Freemasons Tavern, London, on 18 April 1821, Cartwright in the chair (F. D. Cartwright, *The Life and Correspondence of Major Cartwright*, 2 vols. [London 1826], II, 208-9).

2 The two resolutions passed condemned Plunket's bill to grant the government a veto in the appointment of Catholic bishops and deans (see letter 894, note 1) and called for the disestablishment of the Church of England, Church of Scotland and Church of Canada (Cartwright, *Major Cartwright,* II, 208-9).

3 John George Lambton (1792-1840), Radical-Whig; created 1828 Baron Durham; 1833 Viscount Lambton and earl of Durham. See *DNB*.

4 This motion, proposing the limitation of parliaments to three years' duration, the enfranchisement of all possessing taxable property and the abolition of rotten boroughs, was introduced into the Commons on 17 April but defeated the next day by 55 votes to 43.

903

To Connell O'Connell, Cashel [Co. Tipperary]

Merrion Square, 28 April 1821

Sir,

I have seen your letter to my brother James and with respect to the statement you sent, it is in vain to ask for it as if it were in my power you should have had it long since. But I have it not which I much regret. Yet as it did not contain any original paper whatsoever I am quite ready to pay for having as many copies as you choose made from the original draft if in your possession. I cannot do more.

With respect to money matters I distinctly deny that I owe you any money. I lent you a large sum about three years ago. I took up the bills you accepted for me for former fees and had a long account of fees against you when you gave me on my most pressing solicitation £300. Indeed, I was obliged to have recourse to an urgency of which I ought to be ashamed but without which I could not have got payment. I am now ready to go into the account with you and if the balance be against me, I will instantly pay you, but it must be on the terms of your doing the same should the balance be against you as I hope to be able easily to show it is.

Now ask yourself if you choose what favour you have ever done me. I know that I may have in the warmth of my heart written to you in terms which my regard for you made me *imagine* you deserved from me but what real favour did you ever do me. *You gave me business to be sure* but I *did* that business for you, and you certainly all your life paid me as badly as any other attorney ever did, indeed, I think, worse. *You gave me advice* but that was a compliment I returned you, and I am sincerely glad I did not take your advice. I would not now have followed the course you advised for the wealth of Ireland. Whether you are as satisfied with neglecting mine is your own affair. Upon the whole, therefore, I have only to express my regret at not having your statement forthcoming. If I can in any way repair that loss I am ready to do so. I wish to part with you without asperity or anger and feel no resentment at your (to say the least of it) most unkind letter to my brother. Whatever harshness you may use shall be forgotten instantly by me and I only regret that your letter to my brother should have called for this reply.

SOURCE : Property of Arthur Guinness Son & Co. (Dublin) Ltd.

904

From Henry Brougham

London, 8 May 1821

Sir,

I am extremely sorry for not having answered your former letters as my omission seems to have given you some doubt of their having reached me. This delay was owing to my expectation that I should soon be enabled to give you a satisfactory answer, and I put off writing from day to day in this hope.

Mr. Denman and [?myself] fully considered your reasons and, though we have not made any formal report to the Queen, yet we are both of opinion that the right in question is not sufficiently established by those reasons to authorize us to give our advice to H.M. in favour of trying it. Whether H.M. may be [about two words missing] raise the question for the purpose of having it settled or not, I am at present unable to say, but I shall inform myself upon this point immediately and let you know.

Should it appear that the appointment cannot take place or that, being made, it is not admitted by the courts, I need hardly say how much I shall regret it.

SOURCE : O'Connell Papers, NLI 13647

905

From John Bric to Merrion Square

London, *Morning Chronicle* Office, 26 May 1821

My Dear Sir,

I had great satisfaction in receiving your letter. I feel truly gratified at the manner in which you address me, but I must be excused for saying that I cannot depart from that ' deferential tone ' which is due from me to you and which is not incompatible with the warmest feelings of gratitude and of devoted and disinterested friendship. Having other matters to say I shall not now go into the subject of your letter. I shall only say that the Bill[1] is as good a bill as you will get, that the measure must be set at rest in some way or other before any-

thing can be done to amend the condition, to raise the character, to combine [sic] and animate the mind or to achieve
the independence of Ireland, that real independence which
I agree with you consists not in C. Emancipation, which has a
broader basis, an appearance in every way more glorious, without which Ireland can be nothing and to which the heart of
every true patriot is directed with a fond though distant hope.
In this view of the case I attached great importance to the bill.
I lamented the opposition that came from the Catholics and I
heard of its loss with sincere sorrow. My country is my dearest
object, my religion an object of respect. I cannot to the apprehensions of the clergy, which I think unfounded and prejudiced, sacrifice the hopes of Ireland's independence. You say
the bill would make them parish spies. I do not think so but,
if it did, they would cease to be parish priests. The people
would act for themselves and think for themselves. The country
would advance in spite of every combination. But I shall say
no more for the present.

Wood[2] (though not, I believe, authorized) informed me
that you received a letter from Mr. Brougham[3] deciding against
your claim. Now the question appears to me to be this. Is
there in law a fair and reasonable chance of success? If not, he,
I think, is right in not wishing to agitate the claim. If there be,
he is sacrificing the interests and rights of the Queen possibly
for the purpose of evading your object. It is, I think, impossible
to view his conduct with any other sentiment than that of disgust. If your mind be made up as to the law of the case and
that you should think it worth your while to make a second
effort, I confess I should wish you to do so and to triumph
if possible over Brougham and his friends. I think in that case
you should come to London. If you had come over before, I
am sure you would have had the office. Bring with you letters
to Burdett and to Denman and Lushington.[4] You know Wood[5]
and the Duke of Leinster. The best course would be to make
one application to the Queen herself. I really feel that I have
a claim on her Majesty myself, and certainly I would make
that claim on your behalf in the most decided manner. You
would have time to run over now. Few need be made
acquainted with the object of your journey, and you might in a
few days put the matter to rest. I feel [one or two words
missing] this matter perhaps more strongly than you do yourself. Let me know what you intend to do, if possible by return
of post. McNamara[6] has arrived here from Angostura. A few

days before his departure he saw a gentleman that arrived from Devereux. I am happy to inform you that the gentleman gave the best account of Morgan. He left him in a state of perfect health.

SOURCE : Fitz-Simon Papers
1   See letter 894, note 1.
2   Alexander Wood.
3   Letter 904.
4   Stephen Lushington (1782-1873), Whig M.P. for various boroughs, 1806-41; counsel for Queen Caroline, 1820; judge of high court of admiralty, 1838-67. See *DNB*.
5   Alderman Mathew Wood.
6   Mathew McNamara, South Cumberland Street, Dublin; commissariat officer for the Irish Legion to South America. He had a son, two brothers, two cousins and two nephews in the legion.

906

From his brother James to Merrion Square

Killarney, 26 May 1821

My Dear Dan,

I only returned from Derrynane this day. I left my uncle quite well. He was greatly pleased at the account I gave him of Maurice[1] and, indeed, the more so as he had not a favourable opinion of his diligence.

I found no less than three letters before me from Tralee all about *Ellen Connor's* match with Mr. Neligan,[2] one from her, one from your brother-in-law, Rick O'Connell, and another from George Rowan.[3] *They all think* you have placed a £1,000 in my hands to be handed Miss Connor. . . . I have not answered any of the letters yet, nor will I do so, with the exception of Ellen Connor's and I will, of course, be as guarded as I can in my letter to her. I regret to say I have not been able to procure the £400 for you in Iveragh. As to expect anything from Myles McSwiney, it is absurd to do so, and no money can be had from your tenants before the latter end of August or rather the 15th of September. . . .

SOURCE : O'Connell MSS, UCD
1   O'Connell's eldest son.
2   William J. Neligan, attorney, Tralee.
3   George Rowan, Ralanny, Tralee; collector of excise for Tralee area, 1803-17.

907

To O'Conor Don, Belanagare

Merrion Square, 16 June 1821

My dear friend,

Your opinion had great influence over my judgement in deciding me to postpone the aggregate meeting but the time is now arrived when we *must* meet. The above is the requisition[1] to which in consequence of your former authority I have put your name but it will not be published until I hear from you again. It is intended to get as many signatures to it as possible from all parts of Ireland and if you will do me the kindness to send me up as many Roscommon names as you can you will oblige me by doing it as speedily as possible, with the residences. We will I think cover an entire page of newspaper with our requisition.

Some people suggested that the requisition should be confined to the address to the King but, as that would throw us into two aggregates instead of one and as the Corporations of London and Dublin do their other business the same day on which they address the King, it would be absurd, I think, for us to be more squeamish. Besides, when the people come together they would certainly be for an expression of public sentiment and it would appear to bear an air of treachery if we were not to control that *which* we would not have the power even to check. So it is determined to do all our business at once.

I hope you will be able to come up some days before the meeting. We shall want you much to assist in the arrangements as to resolutions, address, etc. I have at present hopes that all parties may come together on the present occasion notwithstanding any exertions to the contrary *to be made* by the King of Smithfield.[2]

Let me entreat of you to make an exertion to be in town for at least a week before the meeting. Nobody knows better than you do how much is to be done on those occasions before we are ready to meet the public.

Lord Cloncurry, Alderman McKenny and some others have formed an Irish Club. In putting down the names of the original members I took the liberty of putting down yours. We dine together eight times in the year, as many as are in town and I think we are already doing some good. . . .

SOURCE : Clonalis Papers

1   This was for an aggregate meeting in Dublin to consider presenting
    a loyal address to the king in anticipation of his coronation and visit
    to Ireland and, in addition, to consider making a statement on the
    Emancipation question. It eventually appeared as an advertisement
    in *Dublin Evening Post*, 28 June 1821.
2   ' Billy Murphy of Smithfield ' of Messrs. William and James Murphy
    & Co., 48 Smithfield, Dublin, a rich salesmaster who had taken
    part in the 1798 rebellion (see O'Keeffe, *O'Connell*, II, 309-10). He
    died 2 September 1849.

908

From O'Conor Don

18 June 1821

My Dear O'Connell,

I was favoured with your letter of the 16th instant last night.
You know that I have always relied more on your judgement
in Catholic politics than on my own and that it would distress
me to differ in opinion with you in any instance, but from the
part I have taken in Catholic affairs you will find that I have
in every instance sought the unanimity of our body, conceiv-
ing that our disunion has been in a great degree the cause of
our defeat hitherto.

I think the meeting should be to address the King alone.
To couple it with other business would lessen the compliment
to him and that having the Duke of York[1] a declared and
decided enemy, we should do everything possible to gain his
Majesty's support. If the requisition was confined to this I
think we would all go together but I fear that if it be not we
shall be again split into parties and consequently weakened.
I hope you will excuse my writing my sentiments so fully on
this subject and request to hear from you again.[2]

I am extremely obliged to you for having put down my
name amongst those who have formed an Irish Club. . . .

SOURCE : Clonalis Papers

1   Frederick Augustus, duke of York and Albany (1763-1827), second
    son of George III and close companion of George IV. Active
    opponent of Catholic Emancipation. See *DNB*.
2   Further correspondence is wanting. O'Conor Don's name headed
    the requisition published on 28 June 1821 (see letter 907, note 1), but
    on 3 July the *Dublin Evening Post* published another requisition,

signed by O'Conor Don and others, for a meeting which would confine itself to voting a loyal address. The aggregate meeting on 19 July—the day of the king's coronation—refrained from touching on the Emancipation issue (*DEP*, 19, 21 July 1821).

909
To Joseph D. Mullen[1]

18 July 1821

My dear Mullen,

I am just told that Sheil has prepared an address for the aggregate meeting full of the worst politics, rejoicing at the downfall of the spirit of democracy, a kind of ode in prose in favour of the Pitt system.[2] I entreat of you to exert yourself to bring as many honest men as possible to the meeting to enable us to control any political rascality. Perhaps we are in more danger than you imagine.

SOURCE : FitzPatrick, *Corr.*, I, 73

1 Joseph Denis Mullen, trimming manufacturer of 146 Francis Street, Dublin; sometime governor of the Four Courts Marshalsea; a prominent member of the Catholic Association. A director of the Royal Canal Co. from c. 1821.
2 Sheil's address as *amended* and adopted by the aggregate Catholic meeting on 19 July does not bear out O'Connell's comment though its language is flowery (*DEP*, 21 July; *FJ*, 20 July 1821).

910
From his brother James to Merrion Square

Killarney, 25 July 1821

My dear Dan,

. . . I regret to find you did not draw up the necessary deed from the General[1] to John and me. Whether it is to be a release or a deed of free gift, I of course do not know. I merely wrote to the General to say that the deed necessary to carry his intention into effect would be very soon forwarded to him. Should you not have leisure to do this business, Roger[2] must at once employ some other lawyer. You, my dear Dan, are more interested than John or I as, should any accident happen the poor General before *this deed is executed* or Government establish their claim against him, your situation would be very bad. I can say for myself with the greatest truth, if I were to consult my own individual interest I would much rather the General insisted on the monies being allowed to accumulate until it amounted to twenty thousand pounds. You had, I think, better not write to the General until you first acquaint me with what you intend to say on this subject. I am determined candidly to tell him that I intend applying my share of his bounty in whatever way I think it will be of most advantage to my family. Let me again beg of you not to delay giving Roger O'Sullivan the draft of whatever deed you think necessary. Should you not do so *at once,* I must get it prepared by some other lawyer.

SOURCE : O'Connell MSS, UCD
1 His uncle.
2 Roger O'Sullivan.

911

To the Earl of Donoughmore

Saturday, 4 o'clock [25 August 1821]

Mr. O'Connell had the honour of waiting on Lord Donoughmore from several Catholic gentlemen respectfully to solicit his Lordship's kind counsels (which have always been so readily and usefully bestowed) on the subject of the ' outrage' committed on their feelings by Mr. Alderman Darley[1] having *revived* the obnoxious and insulting toast at the Mansion House.[2] The Catholics apprehend much jealousy on the one hand, and great encouragement to dissension on the other, if the Government shall continue in office and leave unpunished a person who has thus a *second* time *violated* the good understanding between all parties. At the same time they are unwilling to take, *unadvisedly,* any such public proceeding as may increase the interruption of harmony. Mr. O'Connell will have the honour to call again at any hour Lord Donoughmore will be so good as to signify by a line through the penny post or otherwise.

SOURCE : Donoughmore Papers
1 Frederick Darley (died 1841); chief police magistrate, 1813-41.
2 At the end of a dinner in honour of King George IV, then in Dublin

on a conciliatory visit, a toast was proposed to 'the glorious and immortal memory of King William the Third'. See *FJ*, 25, 27 August 1821.

912

From Lord Donoughmore

Saturday Night, 25 August 1821

Copy

Lord Donoughmore regrets very much that he was not at home when Mr. O'Connell did him the honour of calling at his brother's.[1] . . .

In the celebration of the treaty of conciliation[2] between the Corporation of this city and some very respectable persons of the R.C. body and at which kind mention was made both of the living and of the dead who had the honour of being selected as their parliamentary advocates, though Lord Donoughmore was thrown overboard altogether or perhaps placed by common consent as the first offering upon the altar in token of the entire oblivion of all inconvenient recollections on both sides, Mr. O'Connell is quite justified in considering Lord Donoughmore's best counsel and most zealous exertions at all times the property of his R.C. countrymen whenever occasions shall arise to call for either the one or the other for their service.

Under what has so recently passed and under all the circumstances of the present moment and at an entertainment on so high and solemn an occasion and to which the Earl of Fingall, who had been so justly distinguished by the King, was invited as a guest, the toast to which Mr. O'Connell's note alludes as having been given from the chair does certainly not appear to have been a due execution of the treaty so very lately entered into of conciliation and brotherly love and which was accompanied at its inauguration by so many warm and gratifying professions on both sides, and if the denunciation against the whole Roman Catholic body proceeded, as Mr. O'Connell's note represents it to have done, from high official authority in the administration of justice in this city and under the immediate appointment of the Government, these circumstances cannot be expected to soften down the feelings of the insulted body under the provocation which they appear to have received.

With the circumstances which took place on the occasion of this dinner Lord Donoughmore must necessarily be entirely unacquainted as, no seat having been provided for him at any of the tables though he had received the honour of an invitation, he had been obliged to retire before the commencement of dinner but not till he had received the high honour of the most condescending notice from his most gracious sovereign. . . .

SOURCE : Donoughmore Papers

1   Either Christopher or Francis Hely-Hutchinson.
2   A Catholic meeting at D'Arcy's Tavern on 10 July to prepare the proposed congratulatory address to the king was approached by an envoy from the lord mayor with a proposal that the Catholic body and the Dublin corporation should come together to celebrate the king's coronation on 19 July. The Catholics are reported as having welcomed and accepted this proposal in a conciliatory spirit (*FJ*, 11, 12 July 1821; *DEP*, 12, 14 July 1821).

913

From Lord Donoughmore

Henrietta St., Monday Night, 27 August 1821

Copy

Lord Donoughmore hastens to correct an inaccuracy of which he has been but this moment apprized in his reply to Mr. O'Connell's late letter.

In alluding to the toast which was the cause of Mr. O'Connell's writing, Lord Donoughmore stated it according to his then conception of the matter as given *from the chair*. As Lord Donoughmore has since learned, this was *not* the case, but the person presiding at the time having, on the contrary, *refused* to give the toast, it was given by a gentleman high in official situation in the Corporation and under the Government.[1]

This correction of his own misapprehension Lord Donoughmore thus states for the sake of accuracy alone, not as tending in the slightest degree to remove or to soften the feeling which this aggression appears to have created in the minds of his Roman Catholic countrymen.

source : Donoughmore Papers

1 Later on in the evening Abraham B. King, who as lord mayor had been presiding, vacated the chair to Alderman Beresford. The latter received a request for the 'Glorious and Immortal Memory' toast but declined it. Thereupon Alderman Darley, the head of the police force, proposed it, and it was reiterated from the chair 'amid loud clamour' (*DEP*, 25 Aug. 1821; *FJ*, 25, 27 Aug. 1821).

914

From Lord Donoughmore

Henrietta St., Monday, 3 September 1821

Copy

Dear Sir,

Though my reply to your communication upon the subject of the offensive toast at the late Corporation dinner at which the King had condescended to be a guest[1] recommended the necessity of perfect quiescence on the part of the Catholics themselves, I did not think it less the duty of their friends and who were the friends of internal harmony and conciliation at the same time to express to those in authority, and if it should be necessary so to do in the highest quarter, how indispensable it was that his Majesty should not leave the country till effectual steps should first be taken to prevent the recurrence again of so certain a provocative to mutual hatred and perpetual division.

Impressed with these feelings I waited upon Lord Sidmouth for the purpose of urging the indispensable duty of the Government under all the circumstances to express their strong disapprobation of what had taken place, and I came prepared to communicate to his Lordship a mode by which this disapprobation on the part of the Government might be sufficiently marked to prevent a similar occurrence in future without bearing with too much severity upon the individual, any idea of which I am sure you would have condemned as much as myself. And I had solicited the honour of a private audience from the King for the purpose of pressing this point upon his Majesty if it should have become necessary. The good sense and just feeling of Lord Sidmouth rendered any such interposition on my part quite unnecessary as I was given to understand that such a communication was made, though not in the form which I had suggested, but so as to make it equally effectual for every good purpose, and I had further the happiness of learning from the same authority that a communication would be or had already been made to Lord Fingall as at the head of the Catholic body from the proper quarter which ought to prove and which would accordingly and of course prove entirely satisfactory.

Having received this information before I was admitted into the Royal presence on Sunday, it became unnecessary for me to enter at all into that subject except perhaps to express my gratification at the conciliatory counsels which had so happily been adopted. . . .

SOURCE : Donoughmore Papers
1   See letters 911, 912 and 913.

915
To Lord Donoughmore[1]

Merrion Square, 9 September 1821

My Lord,
    I delayed acknowledging the receipt of your letter until I could have the honour of informing you that I had transmitted it to the Earl of Fingall as the proper channel to communicate its contents to the gentlemen who conferred with him on the occasion which induced my visit to your Lordship. The advice you, my Lord, were pleased to give was that which everybody recognizes now to have been the most suitable to the occasion. Allow me to return your Lordship most respectful thanks not only in my own humble name but in the names of all the gentlemen who acted with me on that occasion. Indeed, the Catholics must always feel the deepest sense of gratitude towards your Lordship although they may find it *impossible* to evince that gratitude in particular circumstances. For myself personally, I am under obligations to your Lordship and your family which no time can weaken nor can any opportunity ever occur to enable me sufficiently to testify my sense of the favours which I have received. Believe me, my Lord, that no event has taken place to give your Lordship just reason to suspect any portion of the Catholics of neglect, and if I were not unwilling to trespass

on your time by going into details I would, I think, satisfy your Lordship on that subject.

source : Donoughmore Papers

1 On the letter is noted on behalf of Lord Donoughmore the following: 'A most satisfactory and indeed a particularly kind letter in reply to my letters of 25 August and 3rd inst.'

916

To his wife, Merrion Square

Ennis, 11 September 1821

Copy

My darling love,

I came here too late to write to you before dinner yesterday, and as I dined at Giles Daxon's,[1] I could not leave in time to write before the closing of the office. . . . I do indeed look forward to the happiness of seeing you in Limerick. . . . Really, I think that the journey would do you good instead of being any nervous risk. . . . Thank God! I have contributed to get an *honest* verdict in a case,[2] a doubtful case of great importance, by a speech.

source : Fitz-Simon Papers

1 Of Stamer Park, Ennis. Treasurer of Co. Clare.
2 Unidentified.

917

To his wife, 13 September 1821, from Ennis

'. . . So now I have given you all my commissions except to tell yourself that there never was a wife more sincerely respected and loved at the moment as you are by a husband who owes you more happiness than any woman ever bestowed on man. . . .'

source : Fitz-Simon Papers

918

To his wife, 15 September 1821, from Limerick

' . . . I give up with great regret the idea of seeing you here but, believe me, my heart's love, you have not the least reason to be alarmed about our darling Morgan from the accounts. Comparing the dates and position of the troops, the success, I may say the final and complete success, of Bolívar is quite, quite manifest. We shall, please God, hear from our sweet fellow by the next Jamaica mail. A Jamaica mail ought not to be far distant as the wind has been so long southerly but then there is no judging of that by our climate. You mistake in saying that the city of Caracas ultimately' remained with the Royalists. It was with the patriots. . . . '

SOURCE : Fitz-Simon Papers

919

To his wife, Merrion Square

Limerick, Saturday, 22 September 1821

My own dearest Love,

. . . I am a little amused by the sweet sauciness which I think made you imagine by one letter of mine that I was careless whether you came to Cork or not. Oh, my Mary, how you wrong me. I could not trust myself to attempt to express how anxious I am that you should meet me in Cork or to describe how delightful you would make my stay in that city which is always an odious place to me without you. . . . You are everywhere the solace of my existence and in Cork I would feel a double relish of your sweetness. . . . You could, I think, with perfect propriety come with your maid and Finn[1] in the public coach to Kilkenny and then you could post. . . . So that you *might* leave Dublin this day week, go that day to Kilkenny, hear Mass there next day and afterwards post at your ease to Clogheen; sleep at Clogheen on Sunday and come on the next day to Cork where I should be before you to press you to the fondest heart that ever cherished purity, good sense and tenderness. . . .

SOURCE : Fitz-Simon Papers
1 W. F. Finn, his brother-in-law.

920
To his wife, Merrion Square

Tralee, 26 September 1821

My darling Heart,

. . . I have the happiness to tell you that we succeeded for Col. McCarthy and Jerry Mahony in the prosecution instituted against them by honest Pierce Mahony the attorney.[1] The triumph is attributed in a great degree to your husband although *you* may think him incapable of such an exertion.

I feel quite *nervous* at your letter which I got this moment. You *will* believe that it gives me exquisite delight that you should come down and I think it will serve, not injure, your health. But I cannot divest my mind of a tender apprehension for your safety. The weather is so very bad and the way so long. I cannot express to you the misery I would feel if you were to be taken ill. However, with the blessing of God matters will be all for the best, and need I again say that my heart is full of delight at the prospect of seeing you? . . .

SOURCE : Fitz-Simon Papers

1 The case tried in the record court at Tralee on 25 September arose out of a challenge to a duel. O'Connell's cross-examination of Pierce Mahony brought an agreement between the parties to drop the case, each to pay his own costs (*DEP*, 4 Oct. 1821). See letter 889.

921
To his wife

Cork, 12 October 1821

My Heart's Darling,

. . . The assizes are now quite over, and I spent this day *arbitrating*. Tomorrow I will be busy writing one thousand things but I will, please God, write to my sweet Betsey,[1] and you may expect a letter from me every day while I am here.

I had a *great* and *glorious* assizes. I believe I am at the top of the wheel for which I thank God. . . .

[P.S.] I had great fun at the county meeting.[2] You never saw or heard of anything that took better than my hit at Mahon[3] in reply to his attack on my cap. I concluded by saying ' I would call my cap[4] the cap of unanimity, but then the cap would not fit Mr. Mahon '.

SOURCE : O'Connell Papers, NLI 13645

1 His daughter.
2 Unidentified.
3 Nicholas Mahon.
4 A London paper of the day gave prominence ' From our own Correspondent ' to the following: ' Dublin 16 September 1821: Counsellor O'Connell is now travelling on circuit, with a fur cap and a gold band, which he says is a present from the King, who certainly wore such a cap on his landing in Ireland ' (FitzPatrick, *Corr.*, I, 75 n.).

922

To his daughter Ellen, Merrion Square

Cork, 16 October 1821

My dearest Nell,

I owe you an apology for writing *this* letter to you. Do not be *very* angry with me for doing so. The fact is that I have a foolish notion floating in my mind that your mother is on the road coming down and yet, my sweet Nell, it is the most silly thing in the world for me to think so because it is so very, very late in the Vacation. . . . However this floating notion makes me unwilling to write to her because, Nell, I do not like to write what I am not sure would be read by the person to whom it was written, and I love that person so tenderly that I could not bear to write for any other eye what I intend for her. . . .

SOURCE : Fitz-Simon Papers

923

To his wife

Tralee, 30 October 1821

My own Love,

. . . Darling, your son[1] and I arrived here yesterday from Carhen. We had a delightful day of it riding to Killorglin; then we were jumbled in a carriage over the worst of all possible bad roads. Your son was exceedingly tired, as he had been dancing the night before at Primrose's[2] until two in the morning in great spirits but to a most miserable piper. . . .

I am extremely hurried here, as you may imagine, and am now on the point of going into the Connors'[3] affairs. . . .

SOURCE : FitzPatrick, *Corr.*, I, 77-8

1 His eldest son, Maurice.
2 Hillgrove, near Carhen.
3 The family affairs of James Connor deceased.

924

From Daniel McCarthy[1] to Merrion Square

Cork, 22 November 1821

My dear Counsellor,

I have been often embarrassed in mind but never so much so as since the receipt of your letter of the 28th ult. handed me only a few days ago by Mr. Henry Orpen.[2]

How to bring myself to refuse any application, however injurious to my interest, from the man whom of all others I would be most willing to oblige, and whose friendship I most value, is a task truly difficult. It is one which I had hoped would never be imposed upon me by so estimable a friend in as much as that he ought to have conjectured the utter impossibility of complying under existing circumstances with the tenor of his letter. You, my dear Sir, are aware that I am in possession of Clountoo[3] near two years and that up to the last day of the last Cork assizes you never suggested to me either the intention or possibility of disturbing my title to that concern. . . . [McCarthy has tenants on the Clountoo property.] I shall conclude this letter with a fervent hope that nothing can arise on the present subject to estrange from me the friendship of a man to whom upon every occasion I should like to be attached and whom it has been my pride and boast to call my friend.

SOURCE : O'Connell Papers, NLI 13647

1 Unidentified.
2 Henry Orpen, port surveyor, Killowenmore, Kenmare. Died 1838.
3 Clountoo, Kenmare, Co. Kerry.

925

From John Devereux

Caracas, 24 November 1821

My dear friend!

This makes my third letter to you since my arrival in Caracas, so that I have little to say referring you to my last for the state of things here. The affair[1] between me and the wretched Nariño[2] of which I wrote you a full account in Sept. last has been submitted to the High Court of Justice in this city of which the following is the sentence: —

'They decree Lieut. Genl. Jno. D'Evereux to be fully acquitted from every charge declaring his reputation and fame to be perfectly unsullied by this affair.'

You will, my dear Sir, perceive from this that Nariño's arbitrary conduct has met with the same condemnation in a court of justice which it had previously received in the bosom of every independent and liberal minded man in the country. All the principal military, as well as civil chiefs of the Republic, have been my staunch supporters throughout the whole proceeding and join most cordially with the public in the satisfaction which the decision has created.

I am only anxious now, my dear friend, to learn of the safe return of your gallant son, my dearest Morgan, whom I find went by the way of the United States. I regret exceedingly that things here did not answer his expectations and for myself I assure you I am most anxious to quit the service and, but for the desire of rendering all the good in my power to the brave fellows who adventured with me in it, I would leave the country tomorrow.

Now that General Marino[3] has no longer any command, I have written to Maurice[4] to know if he would like to take the same situation on the President's staff, and if he has no objection, I am confident that his Excellency will have no hesitation in receiving him in Morgan's place.

I am now on the point of setting out for Santa Fé and from thence to Quito. As the war to all appearance must terminate with the close of this campaign in the South, I shall return and lay before you my colonizing plan[5] in which I wish to give you an interest that may be worthy of your acceptance.

Having written to you and Morgan four or five letters since my arrival in this capital, I have no news at present worth communicating. When I reach Santa Fé I hope to be able to write to you and our common friend Finlay more distinctly on my land project. Tell Morgan that I have attached his friend French[6] to the Orinoco Battalion which is now commanded by Majr. Boyd,[7] formerly captn. in the 1st Rifle Regt. of the Legn. and that I leave behind me here Col. Lyster taking his pleasure as chief of the Vice President's staff of Venezuela, and Lieutenant Col. Brook Young, Town Major and Commandante of Caracas. Col. Hall, Chief of the Topographical department of the Republic and Col. the Baron de Reinboldt[8] in command of the finest Regt. in the service— the Tiradores—Majr. Heise[9] as a cavalry officer was offered the command of a corps of cavalry that is about to be raised in this section but he declined it and preferred going on a confidential mission from me to Mexico. The war being at an end on the coast, he saw there was nothing to be done in the way of actual service, and therefore wished to change his ground for a quarter that opens a wider field to the enterprising soldier.

Poor O'Mullan[10] who is now no more has my forgiveness. On his deathbed it appears he positively denied the charge brought against him by Captn. King of the Navy[11] and no doubt he was innocent.[12] His fault, poor man, lay in that of a turbulent restless disposition of mind that did not know well what to be at to gain some distinction or notoriety in life. I assure you, my dear Sir, I regret much the misunderstanding which took place between the poor man and myself so recently before his death, but the hostility and rancour which followed was provoked by himself, and which I felt lest you might think from his misrepresentations that I acted harshly by him. But the poor man is for ever gone and peace be with him in a better world.

Is it not cruel that I have never received one single line from Ireland since I set sail from Liverpool? I long most heartily to hear from you and your dear Lady, to whom and your charming family I beg to be affectionately and respectfully remembered—and assure yourself my tried and noble friend of the constancy and gratitude,

of your ever devoted and affectionate

J. D'Evereux.

I pray you my dear friend to recall me very kindly to Counsellor O'Gorman[13] and his brother, and to Mr. Wm.
Murphy. . . .

SOURCE : Fitz-Simon Papers

1   Devereux had attempted to fight a duel with Nariño who was then
     interim vice-president of the combined republics of Nueva Granada
     and Venezuela, later known as Gran Colombia, and who is said to
     have insulted the widow of General James T. English. Devereux
     was imprisoned by Nariño, allegedly under very severe conditions.
     He was later sent for trial to Caracas in November 1821 where he
     was acquitted (Salvador de Madariaga, *Bolívar* [London 1952],
     pp. 414-15).
2   Antonio Nariño (1765-1823), interim vice-president of the combined
     republics of Nueva Granada and Venezuela in 1821. A former
     civil servant and, later, opponent of Spanish rule.
3   General Marino, one of the patriot generals.
4   Maurice O'Connell of Sandes' Rifles.
5   This plan never came to fruition. Eric Lambert believes it was
     probably another attempt to raise money under false pretences.
6   Charles French of New Ross, Co. Wexford; went to South America
     with Col. William Lyster's regiment (' Devereux's Own ') in 1820.
7   Charles H. Boyd went to South America with Col. Lyster's regiment
     in 1820.
8   Col. the Baron de Reinboldt, Hanoverian, formerly of the King's
     German Legion. Went to South America with Lyster's regiment,
     1820. Became a brigadier-general; married in Venezuela.
9   Major Heise (also Haise and Heisse). Went to South America with
     Col. Lyster, 1820. He killed Staff-surgeon Compton in a duel on the
     way out.
10   Rev. Cornelius O'Mullane.
11   King had been a long time in the ' Patriot ' navy.
12   Unidentified.
13   Nicholas Purcell O'Gorman and his brother Richard.

926

From his son Morgan to Merrion Square

Spithead, Saturday, 22 [December] 1821

Copy

My Dear Father,
    When I dispatched my letter to you on Thursday I was
just going on board as we expected to sail that evening, but on

coming on board a violent gale of wind sprung up and continued until this morning at 5 when it abated. In consequence
of this we are now almost ready to sail for Chatham. As soon
as you receive this, write to me and direct to Mr. M.
O'Connell, H.M.S. *Raleigh,* and direct to Portsmouth. . . .
[Morgan relates that his watch was stolen.]

[Morgan apparently wrote a second letter on the same day
to his father as follows (it is written on the same sheet of
paper as the above letter and in the same hand)] :

H.M.S. *Raleigh,* Spithead, 22 December 1821
(Private)

My Dear Sir,
[Morgan says that purchasing clothes at Spithead has nearly
exhausted his supply of money. He sends love to his family.]

P.S. Tell Maurice to remember me to Roche,[1] Therry[2] and all
our friends. Tell him also that John Byrne,[3] who was an aide-
de-camp of Montillo's, has left him in disgust and turned
merchant with Burke. Montillo did not behave properly towards him, for Byrne was his oldest aide, still Montillo recommended his two other aides for promotion and never said
a word in favour of Byrne, so I think he was perfectly right
in leaving him. . . .

SOURCE : O'Connell Papers, NLI 13645
1   Probably John P. Roche, Dublin, student at Clongowes Wood
    College, 1814-19.
2   Probably Roger Therry (1800-74), Dublin, a student at Clongowes
    Wood College, 1814-18. Barrister. Lived in Australia, 1829-59, where
    he became a judge. Knighted, 1869; died in Dublin, 1874.
3   John E. Byrne.

927

From Myles McSwiney to Merrion Square

Carhen, 25 December 1821

My Dear Dan,
    As I must suppose you will have heard ere this reaches
you of an outrage which was committed in this neighbourhood at *Gurranebane* the night before last, I think it right to
give you the particulars so far as I have yet heard them. There

is on that farm, Primrose's part, a process server and tithe valuator of Dowling's,[1] a very bad character, and it appears a number of processes were served for the next session. On the night before stated a number of persons broke into his house, took away the original processes and, he says, tithe notes and beat the man, I am told, severely. Report says there were 200 persons, which I don't believe. However, I have been informed they called at some other houses, *four I know of,* and administered oaths of the nature of which I am yet not informed of, but think I shall in the course of a few days as the persons sworn are tenants of yours at Gurranebane and Letter. John Connell, Driver, tells me one man on horseback called and required admittance into his house that night which was refused by his son, on which the person said they would call on another night. Connell was not at home that night. He says he slept at *Dirreen.* I know of no occasion he had to be away and, though I have the best opinion possible of the man, I will inquire what made him from home. Dowling's exorbitant charges for tithes, every person will allow, may provoke the people to such an outrage, but it will be reported in such a way as would lead the public to believe that this heretofore peaceable Barony was in a state of open insurrection. . . .

SOURCE : O'Connell Papers, NLI 13646
1   Rev. Michael Dowling.

928

From his brother James to Merrion Square

Paris, 28 December 1821

My Dear Dan,

I would have written to you since my arrival in Paris the 13th inst. but that I expected to be able to leave it for home ere now, but as I must stop here another week I thought you would be uneasy at not having heard from me. I found the poor General[1] looking very well indeed, quite as well as when you saw him last.

I laid before him the statement of his property which you saw in Dublin, and I regret to add it did not answer his expectations as he thought it ought to amount to more but what annoyed him most was that there was no part of the principal of the money given to reduce Hickson's annuity paid, as had been promised by *John and me as his agents would be done by £500 a year* but that over three years' interest *on that principal sum was also due.* The General asked me under these circumstances when the plan he laid down for the benefit of your younger sons was defeated, what he was to do and I had no hesitation in recommending to him to allow me to call in the eight thousand pounds of his money that remains due to him over and above what was paid for Hickson's annuity and to place it in the French Funds for his own use. This he refused to do but, after some time, said he would release you and your property from Hickson's annuity, both principal and interest, and let John and me divide the remainder, share and share alike, and manage it in the best way for our families. Indeed, for myself, I can solemnly declare I bitterly regret I was in any way accessory to his disposing of his property in the English Funds as I was not able, *as one of his agents,* to manage it in a manner that would give him satisfaction and that he no doubt from his noble and disinterested conduct had every right to expect. God knows I was not to blame. The General executed the different deeds I brought over.

Paris *far far surpassed* any idea I formed of it. The public buildings are magnificent. It is to be sure the most delightful place *a bachelor was ever in.* Had I come here an unmarried man I would not leave it while I had a guinea. My friend, John Bernard,[2] lives near me. He has been in Paris for the last six months so that I have an excellent guide in him. I hope to be in Dublin about the 14th inst. [*sic*] as my concerns in Kerry need my presence much.

SOURCE : O'Connell MSS, UCD
1   Count O'Connell.
2   Of Ballynegar, Lixnaw, Co. Kerry.

929
From O'Conor Don

Belanagare, 30 December 1821

My dear O'Connell,
    I find by the newspapers that the Marquis of Wellesley is arrived, that Saurin is removed and W. C. Plunket

appointed Attorney-General in his place. Does the Marquis not therefore carry the olive branch with him and, if he does, should not the Catholics address him as a conciliator and peace-maker without delay? I put those questions to you as one who I know will consider them with judgement and act accordingly.

When I was last in Dublin I was so occupied with the business of others that I could not visit some of my nearest and best friends, and I assure you regretted much that I could not have a few minutes' conversation with you nor visit Mrs. O'Connell.

SOURCE : Clonalis Papers

930

To Hunting-Cap, Derrynane

Merrion Square, 5 January 1822

My dearest Uncle,

Since I got your letter of the 19th of December events both of a public and private nature have crowded on each other so fast that I have materials for a long letter without being able to tell you *all,* especially *all* that a few days more may enable me to do. . . .

I am happy to tell you that my son Morgan is in England, safe and well. The war is over in Colombia and, as he never intended to remain there unless with the chances which a continued warfare would give of exalted promotion, and especially as land, not money, is the mode of remunerating all services, he determined to come home. He had at the close of his campaign a fever and ague and left Maracaibo on his health being perfectly restored in September last. He sailed for New York but, after passing Cape Maize, the eastern extremity of Cuba, the ship was put so much out of her course by the current setting north-west that she went in on breakers off an uninhabited island called the Green Island, about the centre of the Great Bahama Bank. She struck at night and the sea went constantly over her till day when she held so long together that the crew were able to get out their boats and get on shore on an island on which there was no water. The wreck, however, kept together till they got provisions, water

and the entire cargo out of her. He and the captain and three
of the seamen then set out in the boat for Cuba. They were
out four days and three nights and, after encountering another
gale, were ' boat wrecked ' on the coast of Cuba. The boat
was hurried in on an ironbound shore amidst tremendous
breakers and the chance of getting on a solitary sand strand
of forty paces alone preserved their lives. Thence they got to
St. Iago de Cuba. An American captain invited Morgan into
his vessel and was disposed to act kindly towards him. When
the captain of a very fine schooner from New York then lying
at St. Iago came alongside and, having inquired for the young
Irish gentleman and found out his name, he asked if he was
son to Counsellor O'Connell and being answered in the affirmative he immediately told Morgan that his name was Charles
O'Connell,[1] that he owed his education to your kind care and
spoke of you in terms of the kindest affection and gratitude
and gave Morgan a sketch of his early life, the number of
years he lived at Derrynane and his mother's having lived in
the house. *He did not say in what situation* but from the
description you easily recognize that he was that little Charles,
the son of Nell Real. He insisted on Morgan's coming to live
with him in his vessel and treated him with the utmost kindness and attention. His vessel was about 200 tons, his own
property, was then delivering her out cargo and had a freight
engaged to New York to sail in less than three weeks and he
declared he would not only take Morgan to New York but
would there engage a freight to Ireland or England and bring
him home. In short, he showed a paternal kindness to Morgan,
saying he could not do less for so near a relation of yours.

My poor Morgan thought his troubles were now at an end
and resolved, of course, to remain with Charles until the
return of his former captain who had hired a schooner to
go back to the Green Island for the remainder of his crew
and the cargo which, as I told you, was saved out of the
wreck. During his absence Morgan lived with poor Charles
and was treated by him as a son, wanting for nothing.

But Charles or Charley, as we used to call him, had a
boatswain, an Italian, whom he struck one day. Soon after
Morgan's arrival the fellow rushed at him with a knife and
cut him severely on the head, knocked him down, jumped
on his chest, hurt him excessively and then jumped himself
overboard. Charles came ashore and, while Morgan and a
party of the country police were going in pursuit of the boat-

swain who was supposed to have swam to another vessel, poor
Charles was taken very ill. Morgan went off for an English
doctor, sat up with Charles all night but towards morning
the poor fellow expired.

This most afflicting incident shocked poor Morgan excessively as I am sure it will everybody who hears of it. It was
strange enough that he whom you so many years ago brought
up should thus have expired in Morgan's arms in a foreign
land and after such a meeting.

My poor Morgan was thus thrown on the world again.
He had then *no* friend in the country, but fortunately a vessel
under Danish colours came in commanded by an Irishman
of the name of Wood. He had been in the British navy but
lost his lieutenancy because, as a Catholic, he refused to take
the oaths. He was from Cork and knew our family perfectly
well. He behaved in the handsomest way to Morgan and
took him with him to Kingston in Jamaica where I had
established a credit for my poor fellow in case of accidents.
There Morgan met a Lieut. Achmuty,[2] an Irishman belonging to the *Raleigh* Sloop of War, who offered him a passage
home, of course without any charge, and Morgan accordingly
came home in her. They have arrived at Chatham whence
I heard from my sweet fellow two days ago. I wrote to him to
go up immediately to London where I trust he will meet
James[3] this week on his return from Paris. Morgan is in excellent spirits. His letters are full of lively and animated
description. His trip to South America has done him nothing
but good as it would otherwise have been difficult to tame
him down to the sobriety of business. He retains his rank of
Captain and can go back at any time he pleases with that
advantage whatever it be. He is very prudent in money
matters.

I have scarcely courage after so long a letter on private
affairs to talk to you of political subjects but the times are so
pregnant that one overflows. I trust we have lived to see something done for the Catholics. Mr. Plunket and I have had
many meetings. I have got him to give up much of his
obnoxious securities and I strongly hope that he will completely accede to our wishes and allow us to be emancipated
without any of those restraints on our religion for which no
civil rights could afford any compensation. He is to be
Attorney-General immediately. Saurin, our mortal foe, is I
trust extinguished for ever.[4] He *has* refused the Chief Justice-

ship with a peerage. He thinks that the liberal system will not last six months. Bushe,[5] the Solicitor-General, was promised yesterday to get the place of Chief Justice. Downes must retire. He has been long incompetent. Mr. Blake, the Catholic barrister who came over with Lord Wellesley, is a very particular friend of mine and is to introduce me on Tuesday to his Excellency. I mean to attend his levées as it will cost me nothing and will afford me perhaps some advantages. Lord Wellesley is, I conceive, the harbinger of Emancipation and is determined to put down the Orange faction. Indeed I may be easily deceived but I have reason to entertain most favourable hopes and, if the Catholics shall be emancipated, I do expect that I shall get *fair play* in my profession.[6] Perhaps I may have something confidential to tell you on this subject, perhaps not, but if I have I will write again in a few days.

Be so good as to send me up the receipt for the last volume of the *Statutes*.

SOURCE : Fitz-Simon Papers
1   A member (obviously illegitimate) of the O'Connell family of Bally-brack, Waterville, Co. Kerry, and thus a distant cousin of O'Connell.
2   Robert Ross Achmuty (died 1844), son of Robert Achmuty, Dublin. Married 1822 Alicia Jane, daughter of Arthur Auchmuty, M.D., Kilmore House, Roscommon. See William R. O'Byrne, *Naval Biographical Dictionary* (London 1849).
3   O'Connell's brother.
4   On 15 January 1822 Plunket succeeded Saurin as attorney-general.
5   Charles Kendal Bushe (1767-1843), a leading opponent of the Union; solicitor-general, 1805-22; chief justice of the king's bench, 1822-41. See *DNB*.
6   That is become a K.C. (king's counsel). As a K.C. O'Connell would be able to earn at least as large a professional income as heretofore and with less physical exertion, especially less travelling on circuit. A Catholic could not become a K.C. until the Emancipation Act of 1829.

931

From Myles McSwiney to Merrion Square

Carhen, Sunday, 6 January 1822

My Dear Dan,

I regret to have to inform you of a horrid murder[1] which took place the day before yesterday at the Glynn [Glen].

That firebrand, *as you justly call him,* Dowling[2] sent three
men, one armed with a case of pistols, to execute a decree on
the effects of William Casey of Aghort. They succeeded in
taking one or two cows but it appears there was a rescue by
women and boys principally, among whom was a son of
Casey's aged about 18, at whom one of Dowling's party,
named Sugrue, snapped a pistol which missed fire. This man
was a pensioner of very bad character and for that reason was
employed by Dowling. This party then retired to a neigh-
bouring house where they got some whiskey. While in this
house an elder son of Casey's went to them and told them he
had not the money then but assured them it should be paid on
Sunday, this day, with which they seemed satisfied. This
occurrence collected a number of persons about the place and,
on leaving the public house, the party went up to them, and
out of their way, on which a woman said this Sugrue ought
to be deprived of his arms, on which he deliberately went up
to the younger Casey and shot him through the head of which
he shortly after died. An immediate attack was made on them
and this Sugrue was killed on the spot, and the two others
severely beaten. This debt, I understand, was due for the
service of a *bull* and the decree obtained in consequence of
the different partners in the farm not co-operating in the
payment. I should be glad to hear from you on this subject
and to know whether the parties who may be charged with
the death of Sugrue can be bailed, also whether the two others
who accompanied him ought not be prosecuted for aiding in
the murder of Casey and, *if so,* how the information should
be drawn. Dowling wants to make this a Whiteboy transaction.

   We all here were quite happy to hear of Morgan's safe
arrival in England.

SOURCE : O'Connell Papers, NLI 13646

1 In the *Dublin Evening Post* of 10 January 1822 appeared an unsigned
   letter dated Cahirciveen, 6 January, containing an account of the
   Glynn affair very similar to the above. Its author was evidently
   Myles McSwiney. A denial of the main allegations in this letter was
   made by Dowling in a letter dated 15 January 1822 in the *Dublin
   Evening Post* of 22 January 1822.

2 Rev. Michael Dowling.

931a

To William Conyngham Plunket

Merrion Square, 10 January 1822

Dear Sir,

I take the liberty of sending a parcel of papers which have been transmitted to me from Nenagh[1] in order to have them laid before Government, and if you should be pleased to read them you would perhaps also read the letter of Mr. Dillon[2]— a gentleman of the Bar who sent them to me. This young friend of mine is certainly a man on whose veracity every reliance can be placed.

I have already communicated the substance of these papers through the Knight of Kerry to Mr. Holmes,[3] the captain of the Nenagh Corps.

I cannot venture to trespass on you so far as to ask your advice how I should now proceed with respect to those papers, but any suggestion you may be so good as to give me will be carefully attended to by me and I may say at once obeyed. My objects are 1st to put the outrage committed in regular course for a trial by jury in the ordinary way, and 2ndly if possible to lay the foundation for converting the Nenagh Corps into a body of loyal Protestants and Catholics without any *regular* Orangemen at all.

Be so good as to leave these papers out so that when I call at two this day I may get them unless you see reason to detain them longer.

The Rev. Mr. Dowling, the curate and magistrate in my neighbourhood in Kerry, has since I saw you last been the unfortunate cause of the deaths of two men.[4] They were killed on the occasion of executing a civil bill decree at his suit. It was for ' *the services of a bull'*, rather an unclerical species of industry.

SOURCE : Papers of Mrs. Nicholas Shorter
1 Three members of the Nenagh Yeomanry Corps, Robert Charles, Richard Charles and Michael Doolin, were charged with shooting and wounding John Ryan, outside Nenagh, 21 December 1821. The case later came up before Clonmel assizes on 5 April 1822. A verdict of not guilty was returned.
2 Probably G. Dillon, 42 Gloucester Street, Dublin; called to the bar, 1818.

3 Perhaps Peter Holmes, Killedernan, near Borrisokane, Co. Tipperary,
   landowner.
4 See letter 931.

932

From Hunting-Cap to Merrion Square

Derrynane, 15 January 1822

Dear Dan,

I last post received yours of the 10th inst. and agreeable to
your desire take the earliest opportunity of answering it. I am,
extremely happy to hear the kind reception you met with at
the Castle.[1] The more so as I hope it augurs favourably for the
Roman Catholics. With respect to your applying for a
yeomanry corps in Iveragh I am of opinion it is better to postpone it for the present. First, because there seems to be no
necessity for a second corps in that barony, that granted to the
Knight of Kerry being sufficient for anything that appears at
present for the duty there, and next and chiefly least your
corps, as neither John nor James could attend in the barony,
may be made use of to obstruct and oppose the Revenue and
Water Guard and to protect and cover the smuggling of
tobacco, is a circumstance which speedily would be represented to Government and would of course bring a blemish
on you and on the corps. I therefore recommend that you will
not apply for one and I think James, when he arrives with
you, will concur in this opinion. Whatever the other object
may be, which you hint at, I wish you may succeed in it but
trust that your conduct in general will be guided by prudence,
calm and moderation and will be such as to merit a continuance of the approbation and confidence of his Excellency.

P.S. Mr. Finn came here yesterday morning and has left me
this day, being obliged as he said to proceed directly to
Killarney. I showed him your letter and he seemed highly
pleased at the reception you met with at the Castle.

SOURCE : Fitz-Simon Papers
1 At a meeting of Catholics at D'Arcy's Tavern on 7 January a
   congratulatory address to the new lord-lieutenant, the Marquis
   Wellesley, was adopted on O'Connell's motion. Presumably
   O'Connell was one of the delegation which presented the address
   (*FJ*, 8 Jan. 1822).

933

From Myles McSwiney to Merrion Square

Carhen, 16 January 1822

My Dear Dan,

I have been favoured with your letter of the 10th inst. relative to the yeomanry corps etc.[1] and immediately forwarded your letter to your uncle an answer to which you will receive by this post. I understand from Finn, who is here and returned from Derrynane yesterday, that your uncle does not approve of it, but am sorry to say your intentions have been made *quite* public by Paul Jones[2] who returned from Dublin and said he was told of your intended application by yourself and the Knight of Kerry. Until *his* report I did not mention the subject to any person except Kean Mahony, not even to John Primrose whose name was mentioned in your letter. Kean Mahony seemed to hesitate as to consenting to be an officer but this day has changed his mind and is now ready to accept of a commission if the corps should be established, from a conviction that the appearances to disturbance have appeared to increase in this barony. *Swearing* has taken place to a great extent in the parishes of Cahir[civeen] and *Filemore* principally, and extended to Dromid where they were out last night about Waterville, Spunkane etc. A notice was posted a few nights back on James Butler's door *advising* him to discharge his steward, who lives at Baslicon and is in charge of a dairy there, in *ten* days and, if not, that the steward and cattle would be disposed of by a powerful force. We had an adjourned meeting here yesterday and the day before to consider of the causes of the disturbances which have taken place, which appeared to us to be principally if not entirely caused by the exactions practised in the valuation and collection of tithes in those parishes, but for particulars I refer you to the *Knight* to whom K[ean] Mahony has given a full statement. He has taken great pains to ascertain the annual increase, as the produce of lands fell off, and defied Dowling to say he was not moderate in stating the increase at 75% since the year 1815, and referred to *his* (Dowling's) books, which he would not produce. I regret John[3] did not attend the meeting though he promised to do so. There was a mistake in the statement of the execution of the decree by Dowling and which led to the

loss of two lives in the Glyn[Glen], it having been said that
the decree was obtained for the service of a *bull* which
Dowling denied, saying *truly* it was for tithes, on which I
sent for Casey, the father of *the deceased,* who admitted that
the decree which led to the murder of his son was obtained
for tithes, *much overvalued,* as I proved satisfactorily to the
meeting that they were increased, *two thirds* in two years, this
decree being for the year 1820, £2.12.9; in the year 1819,
£1.5.0, and in the year 1818, £0.17.0. But Dowling some time
before obtained a decree against the said Casey for the service
of a bull *and which* was executed by taking some of the stock
of Casey and lodging them in Keel pound, but as there
appeared a difference of opinion occurred as to what *the
owner* of this parish bull should be paid, the cattle were
liberated, referring the matter to John Primrose. I am *now*
correct, having the admission of Dowling and John Primrose
publicly to these facts. But at the same time I have reason to
believe Dowling will make a contradictory statement, knowing that *this decree* was *not* obtained for the service of a *bull,*
thereby endeavouring to have the entire statement discredited.
I refer to you whether this should not be so far admitted in the
same paper, the [*Dublin*] *Evening Post.* Our meeting here was
attended by J[ame]s Butler, *Chairman* Whitwell,[4] J[ame]s
Hickson,[5] Fitzmaurice,[6] Fitzgerald,[7] Geoffrey O'Connell,[8] the
Primroses, Flaherty[9] and Murphy,[10] Kean Mahony, Dowling
etc. I have now to call your attention to a circumstance which
occurred in this neighbourhood about a fortnight back, which
was that Kean Mahony had received information that a party
were to be out that night in his neighbourhood for the purpose
of swearing in the people there, on which he appointed with
ten or twelve of his tenants to meet him at a certain hour and
place for the purpose of apprehending some of them. They
accordingly met and fell in with four of the water guards who
told him the Whiteboys had passed and offered *him* their assistance, but one of them said their number was too few and
went to the shore and brought on more of their number
amounting to ten persons who, under Mahony's directions,
made four prisoners. On their return from Kimigo the entire
party appeared quite unarmed, these persons Mahony kept
prisoners until the following evening and then discharged
them on the assurance of one or two substantial farmers that
they should be forthcoming when called for, which they were
told would not be required if the neighbourhood was after

quiet. This I know has had a very good effect in that district.
But Dowling has made a representation of the matter to Col.
Crosbie, stating that they were taken in the act of swearing in
persons and calling on him to represent the matter to Government which he did by forwarding Dowling's letter. Mahony
gives a full statement to the Knight to which I again refer
you. . . .

SOURCE : O'Connell Papers, NLI 13646
1   See letter 932.
2   Unidentified.
3   O'Connell's brother.
4   Whitwell Butler, brother of James, of Waterville, Co. Kerry.
5   Probably James Hickson of Lansdowne Lodge, Kenmare, agent to
    the marquis of Lansdowne, 1815-22.
6   Unidentified.
7   Edward Fitzgerald, Kenneigh, Waterville, Co. Kerry. Married
    6 May 1813 Alice Hayes, daughter of William Hayes of Kenneigh.
8   Probably of Ballybrack, Waterville, Co. Kerry.
9   Probably Rev. Edward Flaherty, Inchalough, Cahirciveen, Co. Kerry.
    P.P. Cahirciveen, c. 1800-25. Died as chaplain to the Mahony family,
    Castlequin, Cahirciveen, in 1838.
10 Possibly John Murphy of Valentia, Co. Kerry.

934

From John Bric to Merrion Square

London, 18 January 1822

My Dear Sir,

I have had the pleasure of receiving your letter. You have
doubtless received more than one letter from Morgan[1] and
it is now altogether unnecessary for me to renew assurances
of his health. In compliance with your wishes he intends to
leave this on Monday morning for Oxford and from thence
to proceed to the Head by the stages you have pointed out.
It would indeed be to me a source of proud and happy satisfaction to have it in my power to do anything worthy your
thanks and those of Mrs. O'Connell, but surely in the present
case I have done nothing to deserve those flattering [remarks]
which you have been pleased to make. I should be a base
fellow if my heart did not burn within me in any case where
you or yours may happen to be concerned.

I have read with undiminished satisfaction your admirable

letter.[2] It is spoken of here by everyone and praised by everyone that speaks of it. I have no doubt whatever but that you will steadily pursue the same path. If it lead not to freedom it is sure to lead to character and to that moral power which springs from firmness blended with wisdom. Those wretched Corporators are only objects of compassion. They, thank God, have not the power to decide on the fate of Ireland. I think they are alike unworthy of provoking or conciliating.

We have it here that you and Mr. Plunket have been discussing the principle of a bill. It certainly is a nice point, or rather, embraces many nice points. I shall merely take the liberty of observing that, as we have to get everything, we should not refuse to give all that rational and honest men would require for the satisfaction of this country. This is a moment peculiarly auspicious, but if the King died tomorrow what would be our state? True moral causes must ultimately work out [to] our salvation, but power and bigotry [? may be able] to keep Ireland for many years in [one or two words missing] in faction and in chains. Mr. Black, the [? editor] of the *Morning Chronicle,* begs me to convey to you his assurance that he will be happy to attend to any communication of yours, exercising over it that discretionary power which the *Morning Chronicle* has always exercised over the communications of all correspondents. . . .

SOURCE : Fitz-Simon Papers
1   O'Connell's son.
2   Unidentified.

935

From his brother James to Merrion Square

Killarney, 18 January 1822

My Dear Dan,
    . . . I sent an express to Iveragh this day and if any money of yours has been received, it will be remitted with as little delay as possible. . . . I regret to add you have very little to expect from that quarter as *every peasant in the Barony of Iveragh is a Whiteboy* and, as such, are determined neither to pay *rent, tithes or taxes.* This information I had from a priest who lives there and whose name I cannot even tell you. Some of the gentlemen there expect a cargo of tobacco, but I am

determined to stop that vile traffic in Iveragh which has con-
verted the most peaceable peasantry in Ireland into an armed
banditti. I will go to that country in a few days and easily
obtain such information as will enable me to *lay hold on some
of the leaders* who [*sic*] I will lodge in Tralee jail. Rest
assured I will take care to act with moderation and firmness.
Those nightly legislators profess great respect for the
O'Connell family and I hope soon to be able to *prove* to some
of the leaders by lodging them in Tralee jail, how well I wish
them.

SOURCE : O'Connell MSS, UCD

936

From John Bric to Merrion Square

London, 25 January 1822
[on mourning stationery]

My dear Sir,

(The paper is in mourning though I am not.) . . .

Now with respect to the 'Great Council'[1] I beg of you to
answer by return of the post the following questions:

What may be the highest price your friend[2] will give for
a seat for six weeks?

What for the whole of the Session?

What security can be given to the party here that he'll
vacate at the expiration of the stipulated time. How is the
money to be paid (through what channel)?

I am most anxious to hear distinctly from you on this
subject and without an hour's delay.

The Resolution[3] signed ' R. Therry '[4] is applauded by
many. Others think that it gives to the base faction an importance, the less they are mentioned the sooner I believe will
they fall into oblivion and contempt.

Is Plunket Atty-Genl? I understand that he and you are
good friends. I hope nothing may interrupt your connection.
He is all powerful here.

SOURCE : Fitz-Simon Papers
1   Unidentified.
2   Unidentified.
3   This resolution embodied a statement by ' the committee appointed

to make arrangements for the celebration of his Majesty's accession '
that the proposed dinner would be postponed until ' a more favourable opportunity of attaining all the purposes for which it is
intended ' (*FJ*, 21 Jan. 1822). It also contained an allusion to the
anti-Catholic spirit which had recently been manifested by the
guild of merchants at their quarterly meeting on 14 January in
refusing membership to a Catholic, Hugh O'Connor of Mountjoy
Square, Dublin (*FJ*, 15 Jan. 1822), and at the Dublin corporation
dinner on 15 January where this act was applauded (*FJ*, 16 Jan.
1822).

4   Roger Therry.

937

From his brother James to Merrion Square

Carhen, 17 February 1822

My Dear Dan,

On the 12th inst. I received your letter directed here. I
confess I was much surprised at your not answering either of
my letters from Killarney before, circumstanced as I was here,
surrounded by *Whiteboys whose resentment I had incurred.*
I did expect you would at least have told me you made the
application to government for me I required you to do but
three weeks elapsed before you wrote *me one line.* I of course
could not blame you for not succeeding in getting a military
party but, I again repeat, your silence both surprised and
annoyed me as it appeared you seemed quite indifferent of
what was to become of me who, I will say, at no small personal risk left my family in Killarney, took up my residence
in the centre of your property and by prompt and energetic
measures, I trust, have restored the barony to peace and order.
Most of your tenants in this parish were not only affected
with the wicked spirit of insubordination now unfortunately
so general in the South of Ireland but were actually leaders
and principals among the infatuated wretches who composed
Captain Rock's Corps.[1]

The papers have I presume informed you that seven of those
deluded wretches are now in Tralee jail. Jack Douley's son
is one of them. Honest Frank made his escape and I candidly
confess, though I do not regret his having done so, if he was
now in custody I would prosecute him in the same way
I will *his friends* that are in jail. I know in times like the

present that any man who takes a part in putting down an atrocious blood-thirsty rabble who have combined against everything that is respectable in the country, must calculate on the probability of meeting the fate[2] of poor Major Hare, but with respect to myself I am determined at any risk to do my duty. At present all seems quiet in this Barony. No meetings of Whiteboys either by day or night. The panic produced by the arrest and committal of these men I before alluded to is very great. Confidence too, I hope, is restored as I have promised at the Chapels to have no further arrests made provided there are no more meetings of Whiteboys so that without being too sanguine I think I may almost promise that the *mania of Whiteboyism* is over in Iveragh. All the landed proprietors are determined by making such abatements as the state of the times absolutely require not to drive the people to despair but by a firm and humane conduct to show them it is only by a peaceable and proper demeanour for the future they can expect any redress. The people on *some farms,* who were most forward as *Whiteboys* will and must feel the displeasure of their landlords. No military party has yet come to Cahirciveen. I should certainly be glad they came but I fear they cannot be spared. My Uncle Maurice was quite right in preventing you from asking government for a yeomanry corps.[3] Had you got one, who in the name of God were *to compose it?* . . .

I will scarce be able to make up between this and the assizes your head-rents. Your tenants as well as every other gentleman in Iveragh ate the pigs and beeves and laid out any money they received since the 10 of November last (when Captain Rock first made his appearance in Iveragh) in buying clothes and whiskey. There is no use in distraining their stock as they really *now have no money to pay* and unless the rest of the spring becomes very fine, half the cattle in this barony will die before the first of April and, to add to this, potatoes are now 6/8 a peck and not near enough of them in Iveragh so that I regret to add there will be almost a famine in the country. The insurance paid on your life, £91 a year, will be due next month, I mean that effected for account of the General. . . .

This I mention lest you may wish to have it still kept up though I am far from thinking you ought. My Uncle Maurice is quite well. . . .

SOURCE : O'Connell MSS, UCD
1 ' Captain Rock ' was the fictitious commander of the Whiteboys,
   the predecessor of ' Captain Moonlight ' of the later part of the
   nineteenth century.
2 Major Thomas Hare was shot dead at his home, Mount Henry,
   near Rathkeale, Co. Limerick, on 31 January 1822 (*DEP*, 5 Feb.
   1822). One of the culprits, Oliver Fitzgerald, was eventually traced
   to America and extradited back to Ireland, where on 6 August 1824
   at Limerick assizes he gave evidence against three accomplices
   leading to their conviction and execution (*Patriot*, 10, 12 Aug. 1824).
3 See letter 932.

938

To his wife, Merrion Square

Ennis, 11 March 1822

My darling Love,

. . . I came on here rather slowly after eating a most
hearty meal *after* twelve in Limerick of beef-steak and broiled
turkey.

. . . Now, darling, you must become a complete woman
of business and nobody living—without flattery—is fitter for
it. Finn[1] when in town called on the proprietor of *the Dorset*
but was squeamish about telling him for whom he wanted
the passage. That is not the way to act. I think, my Love,
you had best call on him.[2] . . . I would not consent to your
sailing *sooner* than the fifteenth of April or indeed I would
prefer your not going before the 20th say the 18th of April
precisely. When you have so many he ought to take a lump
sum and, darling, take care that there is to be no charge for
either shipping your baggage in Ireland or landing it in
Bordeaux. . . .

You have £150 for bills. There is one for £150 to be due
the 13th or 15th. Write to James Sugrue the moment you get
this letter for £100 to meet it. *That* will leave you the £100
clear for the next bill which will not be due before the 23d.
There will be a college bill for £138.10.0 due the 22d but that
I will send you provision for. There is also a bill for £300 due
this week. . . .

The reference for the house[3] should be to Jerry McCarthy.[4]
Send for him and let him not say whose the house is unless
he finds somebody *seriously* intending to deal. I have an

objection to allow you to leave it whilst you are in Ireland. . . . Reserve however my study until my arrival and
the standing and writing desks and movable chests of drawers
altogether.

SOURCE : Fitz-Simon Papers

1 William F. Finn.
2 Mary and their five youngest children were just about to go to
   reside in France for the sake of economy.
3 O'Connell was attempting to sell or let his house in Merrion Square.
4 Tailor and draper of 62 Dawson Street and 44 William Street,
   Dublin. Died 1840.

939

To his wife

Ennis, 12 March 1822

My darling Love,

I wrote two letters to you yesterday. Serjeant Lefroy[1]
arrived here about one o'clock this day and tried one record.
Tomorrow a great case of a priest, a friend of mine, comes
on for defamation.[2] And the next day another great cause,
after which I will, please God, go to Tipperary on my way
to Wexford. I mean to be back in Limerick early on Monday
morning, before the jury can be sworn. I should be very grateful to Providence which has given me so strong a constitution
as to enable me to resist *all* fatigue. Blessed be His holy name!

Your alarms about the county of Limerick are greatly
exaggerated—the people attack only their enemies. Besides,
darling, I travelled at hours in which they never attack anybody. And the military force is immense. You need, in truth,
be under no kind of uneasiness for me.

SOURCE : FitzPatrick, *Corr.*, I, 78

1 Thomas Langlois Lefroy (1776-1869), K.C., 1806; M.P. Dublin
   University, 1830-41; baron of the court of exchequer, 1841-52; chief
   justice of queen's bench, 1852-66. See *DNB*.
2 Matthew Canny of Drumline, Newmarket-on-Fergus, versus the
   Rev. Francis Stenson, P.P. of Newmarket-on-Fergus. This was an
   action for defamation resulting in a verdict for the plaintiff, £20
   damages and 6d. costs (*Limerick Chronicle*, 16, 20 Mar. 1822).

940

To his wife, Merrion Square

Ennis, 13 March 1822

My darling heart's love,

. . . I think with you in everything especially as to the sale of the horses and carriage. I wish we had £200 for them *once* paid. I fear we will not so soon. . . .

This is not a *Lent* at all the way you have made me go on. I am afraid, heart, *we* have been too tender of my body. Alas, darling, I ought to be too grateful to God to neglect any of my duties. May his holy name be blessed.

SOURCE : Fitz-Simon Papers

941

To his wife, Merrion Square

Wexford, 17 March 1822

My darling Heart,

. . . The trial which brought me here came on about ten yesterday morning and lasted until past seven but was not, I am sorry to say, concluded. The Chief Justice[1] was kind enough to endeavour to finish the trial[2] on my account but it became plainly impossible. He invited me to dine with him and I spent a very pleasant evening. He is a delightful companion and it is impossible to have any man fill his station better than he does. . . .

Darling, I will not dwell on the pain our separation gives me. It is indeed heart-rending but it cannot be avoided or at least the advantages to our family are so great that we must endure it with resignation. . . .

SOURCE : Fitz-Simon Papers

1 Charles K. Bushe, who had become chief justice of the king's bench only the previous month.
2 Unidentified.

942

To his wife, Merrion Square

Limerick, 21 March 1822

My darling Mary,

. . . Why do you delay to close any bargain you think prudent? Do not, my first and only love, pay me so bad a compliment as not to be convinced that whatever you do I shall approve of. Indeed I should feel extremely happy to get £400 a year for the house and any thing like £100 for the horses. . . . You would delight me even if you made a bad bargain because I would then show you how sweet it was to me to have something to forgive you. But, darling, £400 a year for the house and £100 for the horses is more than you *will ever* get. In future only let me know what you *have done*. Do not delay to consult me as to what *you are to do*. . . .

I sent you £118.15.0 Wexford money. . . . There is another bill due tomorrow to Dr. Wilson[1] of the College. James Sugrue will call on you about it. Give him the £65.15.0 if he asks for it to take up Dr. Wilson's bill. I write both to Dr. Wilson and to Sugrue. If my brother James was not behaving cruelly by me this money would be long since in Dublin. I cannot help it, darling.

SOURCE : Fitz-Simon Papers

1 James Wilson, D.D., F.T.C.D., rector of Clonfeacle, Co. Tyrone, 1825.

943

To his wife, Merrion Square

Limerick, 22 March 1822

My darling Love,

I am not surprised to find that you could not get the money you expected for the horses or house. It cannot be helped, darling; do not however be impatient. We have time enough to think of taking less. . . . The times are dreadful and I wish we had £365 a year for the house over taxes and well secured. Send to O'Mara and let him know I will sell my own horse for £40 if possible, if not for thirty guineas. . . .

I am sure, darling, we are doing right to separate thus for a short time. I am hoarding gold for your journey. Only think, darling, how splendidly independent we shall, please God, be if we survive the old gentleman and in his lifetime see all my debts paid, an event highly likely under the present circumstances. I wrote yesterday fully to James Sugrue about the vessel he proposed to hire. . . . I think he can get one of the first class for £60 and your seat, love, will be very inconsiderable in expense. You should carry your own wine, spirits, porter, soda water, milk, brandy etc. even if you sailed in the *Dorset*.

I have also written to John Hickson[1] for information and intelligence although he is very remote from where you are going and I am not sorry for it. He may however give me some useful hints for economy of which he is master. This journey already gives me a feeling of independence which my brother James' conduct renders doubly necessary. . . .

SOURCE : Fitz-Simon Papers
1 John C. Hickson, late of College Green, who had sold his business in 1820 and taken up residence in France.

944

From his brother James to Merrion Square

Killarney, 28 March 1822

My Dear Dan,

I last night received your letter of the 22nd inst. It was sent me by express here from Cahirciveen as I came to Tralee to attend the meeting of magistrates on Monday last when *we unanimously agreed to have the entire of Kerry put under the Insurrection Act,*[1] and I presume before Sunday next the Proclamation will come from the Castle for that purpose.

. . . Your income by lands is so cut up by interest of money, annuities to poor relations and to fosterers that, in the best of times, you have but little *to actually touch,* and, as you ought not to have owed more than the last September gale to the College,[2] it was in my opinion highly imprudent of you to accept a bill for the College fines of Mr. Blennerhassett[3] until that gentleman put funds into your hands, and surely the College would *give in those times* a little more time for the last November gale. It is, I am convinced, absolutely necessary you should at once diminish your establishment. Indeed, had you £5,000 a year paid quarterly out of the Bank of Ireland, you could not avoid getting into debts. Whether you will better your situation much by taking J[ames] Connor's house and fixing yourself in Tralee where *you must keep an open house for all your family,* I will not attempt to decide but I trust you have made your entire family acquainted with your real situation. If they and you are serious in wishing to conform yourselves to your embarrassed circumstances, the South of France would in my opinion be the place to fix them. However, of this ye are the best judges. If you continue to manage the affairs of James Connor's family, which contrary to my earnest request you undertook, you will be involving yourself much more every day.

SOURCE : O'Connell MSS, UCD

1   An act to suppress insurrections and prevent disturbance of the public peace in Ireland (3 Geo. IV, c.1) until 1 August 1822. It received the royal assent on 11 February 1822. It enabled magistrates to have a district declared in a state of disturbance and thus subject to special regulations including a curfew.
2   Trinity College, Dublin.
3   The representative of Sir Rowland Blennerhassett, deceased.

945

To John Primrose, Jr., 1 April 1822, from Tralee

Gives Primrose authority to collect his rents.

SOURCE : O'Connell MSS, UCD

946

To his daughter Kate, Merrion Square

Tralee, 1 [and 3] April 1822

My own own Kate,

What a cruel thing it is to your father's heart to part with his sweet Kate. . . . I part with you, my Kate, but for a short period. I part with you for your advantage and that of *all of us.* We must in these dreadful times practise economy and then, my child, the journey will be such an advantage to you and my heart's darling Nell and to my sweet Betty. You will be such accomplished young ladies when you come back and in the meantime there is so much of novelty to be seen by you—such a difference in the habits, manners, appearance, buildings, in short, in everything that you will doubly relish the changes. First, the change from this country to that and next the return to Ireland. You must all write to me long letters and give me with freshness the impressions made upon you by all the objects which will surround you. I expect to join you in the vintage which is the gayest time of the year, and I flatter myself that the time will not be the less gay for the arrival of your father. Oh how I shall long for the summer assizes! The King made the last late,[1] but all the kings in Europe would not keep me from you all next summer. If God spares me life and health, I will be off from Cork the hour the assizes are over and my delay in Bordeaux will be short indeed. . . .

Cork, 3 April

. . . I enclose in this letter four half notes for £10 each which you will give the sweetest, best and dearest darling woman that ever lived. Can you find you *such* a woman? You will easily know her by her *cock-nose*. . . .

SOURCE : Fitz-Simon Papers
1   George IV's visit to Ireland in 1821 had the effect of delaying the holding of the summer assizes.

947

To his wife, Merrion Square

Cork, 3 April 1822

My darling love,

. . . My brother James is greatly pleased at my family going to France. All he fears as usual is that they will not practise economy there for want of *skill* in that art. I believe he thinks that if they had a lesson or two from ' the Madame '[1] they would learn it better. But, darling, he little knows what a powerful impulse the desire of returning to your husband and your house is to you and he still less knows what a clear and distinct mind my Mary has although, indeed, James is not at all disposed to undervalue you. . . .

SOURCE : NLI, MSS 5759
1   James's tight-fisted mother-in-law, Madame O'Donoghue.

948

To his wife, Merrion Square

Cork, 4 April 1822

My own darling love,

. . . The *first* thing you will do, darling, is to make James Sugrue bring you my note for £138.10.0 from Dr. Wilson and let me know that you have got it. The *second* is to give your mother £15, the *third* to take £25 for your own use. These three sums being added together make £178.10.0. Then keep £21.10.0 more for yourself, that is, I mean for the house, etc., etc. and you will thus have applied £200 out of the £300 above mentioned. That is, you will have in your own hands £46.10.0 for house expenses etc. over your mother's £15 and the amount of Dr. Wilson's bill. And you will have £100 in hands for *bill money* besides Cooper's £50. Send over to Mr. Cooper's to know if Mr. Cooper[1] of Cashel has left a note of mine there payable the 28th of March because if he has, you are ready to take it up. Let me know the result.

Call also at Cooper's,[2] the coach-maker, and inquire whether he could get you anything *decent* for your carriage and harness complete[3] as you are going to France for a couple of years. There is no harm in just making this inquiry. Let me also know whether you have any prospect of either setting the house or selling the horses. You see, heart, I am not alarmed at the prospect of French disturbances. It is not at all improbable but that the Bourbon Government may crumble but it is quite plain that there will not be a civil war or any strife that would render life insecure even in the capital, and in all the changes since 1794 strangers have been perfectly safe in the provinces. It is my opinion that commotion is not now to be dreaded in the slightest degree. You may imagine that I am powerfully persuaded of this when I allow you and the sacred pledges of our single-hearted love to leave me. I am to be sure deeply anxious to have *you* and them completely independent but *you know* I would not willingly expose you to any risk. . . .

SOURCE : Fitz-Simon Papers

1 Samuel Cooper, Killenure, Cashel, Co. Tipperary.
2 Henry Cooper, coach-builder, 25 Mary Street, Dublin. High sheriff of Dublin city, 1823.
3 That is, for their sale.

949

To William Conyngham Plunket, House of Commons, London

Cork, 4 April 1822

(Private)

My dear Sir,

I saw with extreme regret the uncertainty in which your mind is respecting the discussion of our question this sessions. As one of the sufferers I hope you will not think me obtrusive in writing to you on this subject. I do so because I perceive you think that there is a difference of opinion amongst the Catholics themselves on this point. If there be *any*—which give me leave to say I much doubt—at all events you may credit me when I solemnly assure you that out of every 100 Catholics of the upper classes 99 are for a speedy discussion. The Catholic clergy of the second order are unanimous in wishing for it because they are convinced that at this moment every man in the House must admit the zeal and energy the Catholic clergy have evinced during the present disturbances.[1] This testimony you will cheerfully bear. This testimony Mr. Goulburn,[2] our mortal enemy, and even Mr. Peel *must* now admit to be true. You cannot conceive what a mitigation to the misery of a defeat the unanimous voice of Parliament in favour of our clergy would be. Besides, discussion always did us good and we ought to *dare* our enemies at this moment to attribute to bigotry or zeal for the Catholic religion any part of the present tumults. These will at all events be precious advantages—to have admitted in Parliament *the innocence* of the Catholic religion as any part of *the immediate* cause of the troubles now raging and also to have praised and *admired* by all parties the exertions and loyalty of the Catholic clergy.

All these you forego if you postpone the discussion until the next sessions, and we of course remain as rigidly unemancipated as if we were defeated upon a discussion for which it is *the least* possible consolation that we had a majority in the Commons last time. If we had, there was then a majority the other way in the Lords which fairly neutralized any good effects to be derived from the liberality of the House of Commons.

To remain in our present degraded state is to be sure a severe injury but men bear *injuries*. To refuse us the poor and paltry consolation of a discussion will, I think, be looked on by very many as an insult and few indeed have the Christian fortitude to bear insults without a wish for vengeance. God help us. How little is it necessary to blow up another flame in poor Ireland. We are tolerably accustomed also to a defeat but we are little used to have our hopes and wishes adjourned as a matter that may wait for leisure hours and sunny seasons. Let me then most earnestly implore of you *to discuss* our question whatever be the result.

But after all can the result be doubtful? Catholic Portugal and Catholic Spain are really consolidating their liberties. Are we for ever to despair? Alexander[3] is either curbed or goes to war. If the latter—which I believe—what scenes will follow he is wise who can tell. If *he* be curbed, is he likely to forgive England for her interference? Then look at home. Was there ever misery equal to that of the Irish?[4] And I ask with confidence was there ever more exemplary conduct than that of the educated portion of the Catholics and of the entire Catholic clergy? What would the state of this country be if our clergy were neutral? What if they fanned the flame? Who then could reckon on extinguishing the conflagration other-wise than with blood, and blood is just the very worst cement of civil society? For my part in the present state of England, Ireland and Europe I cannot bring myself to believe that the Parliament would be mad enough to reject our just claims. Do not mistake me. I do not say a word of this in the way of menace. We have been as humble and courteous in our petitions as we are really submissive in our inclinations. We are sincerely attached to constitutional connection with England. When I say we I mean the Catholic clergy and Catholic gentry including the upper class of farmers, but the people, the physical force is ready to turn out. Let them have but an occasion or give them officers and they will soon find an occasion.

I fear I tire you in thus candidly disclosing my hopes, wishes and fears. I hope you will excuse me for troubling you with these unconnected notions. I write out of the fullness of my mind and only fling out my thoughts in disjointed portions. I wish not to weary you or I could write a dissertation on the state of Ireland. I feel that you are quite at liberty to make any use you please of this hurried letter if it be possible that it could be useful. But I know that I have no right either to continue it or to recollect that I wrote it.

You will be glad to hear that all Kerry with the exception of the Limerick border is returning to *perfect* tranquillity. This you may rely on although the tithes are now again *being* exacted with iron rigour, but then Dr. Elrington,[5] the Bishop of Limerick, has written a pamphlet to prove that tithes are not a grievance in Ireland! ! !

The western and southern parts of the county of Cork are also becoming tranquil. The horrid spirit of retaliation which the frequent use of the Insurrection Act and the Saurin system generally has excited or generated in Limerick is not likely to be raised here. Serjeant Lloyd[6] has conducted himself in an exemplary manner. He is a sweet-tempered, amiable gentleman. Serjeant Torrens[7] is a little too much on the *fortiter* but, above all, there is Serjeant Lefroy who goes this circuit as judge, preaching bad sermons and displaying as little law as possible. I believe his is the most complete *failure* which any times can have produced. For my part I was so little in Chancery[8] that I believed he deserved his high reputation there but no, he wants an authority for every legal principle and supercedes the jury with as little ceremony and as much decision as if his own share of the trial was not quite enough for him.

I am quite inexcusable in trespassing so long upon you.

SOURCE : Papers of Mrs. Nicholas Shorter

1 The winter of 1821/22 witnessed a great increase in agrarian crimes and disturbances. In order to deal with this situation the government passed the Insurrection Act for Ireland (3 Geo. IV c.1) which received the royal assent on 11 February 1822.

2 Henry Goulburn (1784-1856), chief secretary for Ireland, 1821-27; chancellor of the exchequer, 1828-30, 1841-46; home secretary, 1834-35. Took a prominent part in resisting Plunket's Catholic Emancipation bill, 1821. See *DNB*.

3 Alexander I (1777-1825), czar of Russia, 1801-25. About this time he was suspected by many of having warlike designs on the Ottoman Empire.

4 Ireland was now beginning to suffer from a famine produced by a partial failure of the potato crop of the previous year.

5 Thomas Elrington (1760-1835), a native of Dublin; educated Trinity College, Dublin. Provost, 1811-20; bishop of Limerick, 1820-22; bishop of Ferns, 1822-35. Author of *Inquiry whether the Disturbances in Ireland have Originated in Tythes*, 1822.

6 John Lloyd (1761-1835), son of Richard Lloyd and a native of Limerick. Resided at 2 Merrion Square, West. Second serjeant, 13 May 1822.

7 Robert Torrens (1775-1856), a native of Co. Londonderry; justice of
   the common pleas, 1823-56.
8 In a letter to W. C. Plunket in 1827 (see letter 1431) O'Connell said:
   'The supposed hostility to me of Lord Manners has prevented my
   having the same business in chancery which I have in all the other
   courts. Let me do Lord Manners the justice to say that he never
   treated me badly in his court but the clients were afraid to employ
   me there.'

950

To his wife, Merrion Square

Cork, 5 April 1822

My *own* darling Love,

Will you, can you forgive me for the cruel and ferocious
letter I wrote you, my darling Heart, last night? Oh yes, you
can for you are all mildness; you will because you are all
sweetness and goodness. You will, my *own, own* darling
Mary, because you will attribute it to trial and haste and you
will receive my earnest entreaty for forgiveness as the request
of the man whose whole life is devoted to make you and your
children happy. Oh darling, how cruel was it of me to send
away that letter on a Thursday night so that by the present
arrangement of the coaches you cannot get this letter till
Monday morning. I would not, however, let this day pass
without soliciting your pardon.

The fact is just this, my own love, that I am greatly
pressed for money this month. I never in my life was so much
so. You see that by the list of bills which I have to pay. I
had determined that the bill you make James Sugrue take up
should be protested in case John Hickson pressed it on me.
I wrote to him to say that I could not take it up and I would
actually have felt a pleasure in its being protested if *he* had
not withdrawn it, then, darling, I had with difficulty made
some arrangements which would have brought me near the
other outstanding bills all of which I am extremely desirous to
take up. I had just got myself into a comfortable state of hope
of being able to accomplish all this when you have disarranged
me completely by taking up this bill. Indeed after my letter to
Hickson, I did not think it would be called for at all and still
less could I have imagined that you, my darling Mary, would
have committed so large a share of my resources to take up

a bill I did not mention especially as I had in the spirit, but without the intention of a precaution, sent you a list of the frightful number of bills *still* remaining. . . .

I know, my dearest treasure, you would not for the world's wealth do anything but what you thought would please me. I know *that,* my own Mary, perfectly well. It *will please me* excessively if you pardon me cheerfully and affectionately. My letter was to be sure a barbarous one, unbecoming a gentleman or a Christian, but it gives you an opportunity of behaving generously to me in return and I know my love too well not to be sure you will do what is generous. We are nearly twenty years married, darling, and this is my *first offence.* It shall, I hope, sweetest, be my last. I wish I were near you to pat your cheek and press your sweet lips as a seal to my forgiveness. . . .

SOURCE : Fitz-Simon Papers

951

To his wife, Merrion Square

Cork, 6 April 1822

My darling Love,

I wrote you a long letter of apology yesterday and I have but one moment to write to you at present. We may still get through this month unless James Sugrue has *also* taken up Dr. Wilson's bill. . . .

Do not call or send to Mr. Cooper's in the Square about the £50 bill and, if it is called for, say you will immediately write to me about it and have an answer by return of post. . . . How I regret that I wrote to you so harshly on the subject. Nothing shall ever again induce me to do so. But, darling, I shall say no more on the subject save that I fondly believe you will forgive me.

Will you be able to make all your arrangements so as to sail from Dublin on the 29th of this month, next Monday three weeks it will be? . . .

Let me know with precision *how* much money you have after reimbursing Sugrue the sum he paid towards John Hickson's bill. The list of bills this month is certainly tremendous but still I hope to get over it. I hope not to have such a month for a good while to come.

SOURCE : Fitz-Simon Papers

952

To his wife, Merrion Square

Cork, 7 April 1822

My darling Love,

I am quite nervous about the letter I shall get from you this evening in answer to my most improper epistle of Thursday. Darling, allow me again to beg your pardon. Indeed, my true Love, I do most bitterly regret having written one single line that could give you displeasure or uneasiness. I never will again do so and I believe I never did so before. No, darling, I will not, but on the contrary I will endeavour by a tenfold increase of tender affection to compensate you for the uneasiness I have thus given you. Do, my sweetest, forgive your fond husband. But why do I ask when I know you have already forgiven me, for you are the best as well as the sweetest of women. My *own own* Mary, my heart doats of you.

. . . I have as much as will take up Eyre's[1] bill of £40 to be due on Wednesday and I will send it to you in case James Sugrue has taken up Dr. Wilson's note as well as Hickson's bill. If he have not, then you have already money enough 'for the bills which will be due on Wednesday and Thursday, and for Friday I will, please God, send you abundant provision though there will that day be about £200 due. These were what terrified me darling.

. . . How I long to have you settled in France. I should indeed before now have heard from the General[2] but I suppose he will not give any unnecessary delay. I am quite sure of the kindness of his intentions and, in truth, whether he approves of it or not, I will not give up my plan because I am convinced it is that which will give *us,* darling, independence and happiness at the price of a sacrifice which we are both ready to make for the good of our children. . . .

SOURCE : Fitz-Simon Papers

1 Unidentified.
2 Count O'Connell.

953

To his wife, Merrion Square

Cork, 8 April 1822

[No salutation]

If you had a mind, my darling heart's love, to wring your husband's very soul you could not have done it more effectually than by writing the sweet, gentle, uncomplaining letter I got from you last night. Oh, how could I be so base as to write such a letter as I did to such a woman. May the great God of heaven bless you, is my fervent prayer. I expected that you would have at least reproached me in some degree and vindicated yourself with at any rate some firmness. But I did not know what the complying gentleness of your tender nature is capable of and now to my exquisite satisfaction I find that my own darling thinks she was wrong merely because her husband unjustly accused her. It was this disposition of yours, Mary, that fascinated me in early life and that made me continue your lover for twenty years after I became your husband, and indeed, I love you now more than ever I did and I respect you still more than I love you. I do not ask you any more for forgiveness because it would be doing you an injustice to think that a sentiment of anger could be harboured towards me in such an affectionate mind as yours. I was literally insane when I wrote my letter to you and, darling, I now believe that it is on the whole much for the best that you paid that bill of Hickson's. I perceive by a letter I got last night from James Sugrue that Dr. Wilson's bill lies over unpaid. Let it be so, darling, for a few days longer. You have therefore got from me in half notes between you and James Sugrue £200 and he has got £100 from Roger[1] so that, as you gave him the other £50, you will have only to add £12.10.0 to it. Then, giving your mother £15 . . . you will still have £172.10.0 in hands. Take out of that £42.10.0 for house expenses, it will leave you £130 out of which you will, before this reaches you, pay tomorrow £40— Eyre's bill—and the day you get this, £50 Higgins' bill and you will have £40 towards meeting the bills due on Thursday. I believe my letter of yesterday was erroneous in supposing that Eyre's £40 would not be due until Wednesday. I hope this error will not occasion a protest as in the list I sent I marked down a £40 bill as due the 9th. I will, please God,

send you a banker's bill for at least £200. The bills which are
to be paid are 9th £40 to Eyre, 10th £50 to Higgins, 11th
£58 *with interest* to Mr. Mahon[2]—same day, 11th, £138.10.0
to Dr. Wilson, a *fresh* bill not the one already due, 15th
£69.19.0 to Roose, 25th £75 Clongowes Wood payable, I
think, to Elliot,[3] 28th £50 to Cooper. All these we must take
up. They may not be accurate as to the precise day but they
are nearly so. I do not believe any other bill can possibly *call*
and there certainly is not one which I should wish to have protested. Believe me, sweetest, to be your more than ever
devotedly attached,

Daniel O'Connell

[P.S.] Tell *each* of them how I love them. Tell Dan so twice.

SOURCE : Fitz-Simon Papers
1   Roger O'Sullivan.
2   Nicholas Mahon.
3   J. Elliott, merchant, proprietor of London and Dublin Parcel Office,
    33 Lower Sackville Street, Dublin.

954

To his wife, Merrion Square

Cork, 9 April 1822

My darling Heart,

After paying Eyre's bill £40 and Higgins' for £50 you will,
I perceive, I mean after your mother's £15, the £12.10.0 to
J[ames] Sugrue and £20 for the house, have £62.10.0.

There will be two bills due on the 11th, one to Mr. Mahon
for £58 *and interest,* another to Dr. Wilson for £138.10.0.
Darling, I have been kept so late in court that I cannot send
you a large bill this day but it shall go to you or to James
Sugrue tomorrow without fail. I have written to Mr. Mahon
to request that he would advance the difference for me to James
Sugrue for 24 hours. I am sure he will not refuse me. James
Sugrue will on Friday give you the surplus of the bill I shall
send him.

Sweetest love, I thank you from the bottom of my heart for
your most kind and affectionate letter. It is so like you, my own
heart's dearest treasure.

How I long to hear that Mr. Coppinger has bought the
horses. It is *too good,* I fear, to be true.

Darling love, put off your journey from the 29th of this month to the first Monday in May, Monday the 6th. Write to Finn on the subject so soon as you have determined.

Darling, I got through the Lent admirably. In fact, except the last week in part, it was no Lent at all.

SOURCE : Fitz-Simon Papers

954a

From William Conyngham Plunket

43 Conduit St. [London], 10 April 1822

Draft
(Private)

My dear Sir,

I have been out of town for some days which has prevented my answering your letter of the 4th inst. I shall proceed with the most entire frankness to state my opinions on the very important subject to which you advert.

I have always looked to the question as one equally involving the best interests both of Protestants and Catholics and on which it was the duty of an honest member of the Legislature or of the community to act on his own unbiased judgement without being bound by the prevailing wishes or opinions of either ; at the same time with an anxious desire to attend to such wishes and to conciliate, and as far as might be done consistently with the essential interests of the cause, to accommodate to the opinions of those who were most interested in the event.

Acting under these impressions it has frequently been my lot to differ from large portions of the Roman Catholic Body, not only as to the measures to be pursued but as to the time and mode of bringing them forward, and I have much satisfaction in thinking (and I believe I do not deceive myself in so thinking) that in abiding by my own views I have served the best interests of the cause and have rather gained the confidence even of those who had originally differed from me. On such principles I must always act, not meaning however to say that I should take on myself the very serious responsibility of declining to bring forward the measure at a time which I might think inexpedient if I found that the general sentiment

of the Roman Catholics themselves and the general opinion
of their Protestant Friends decidedly differed from my own.
Such a course would, I admit, be arrogant and might besides,
connected as I now am with the present government, give rise
to jealousies which I should deeply regret. Subject to these
observations I do not hesitate to say that my opinion is strongly
against bringing forward the question during the present
session and that it is equally strong for introducing it early in
the next.

I agree with you that the conduct of the Roman Catholic
gentry and clergy has been such during the late disturbances
as to give them strong additional claims on the justice and
good feeling of Parliament. I agree that the attention of the
House should be called to the subject and the fullest testimony
borne to the excellence of a conduct which goes beyond all
praise and defies all contradiction; but all this can be done and
will be done again and again on the various occasions which
must arise during the session on the discussions on Irish affairs;
and there is no necessity with a reference to this object to have
a separate discussion on the Roman Catholic question. I cannot
agree with you that the question rests where it was before the
last session and that the rejection of the proposed measure in
the Lords has neutralized its adoption by the Commons. In
my opinion the cause has made an advance the value of which
is almost incalculable and that the having the deliberate sense
of the Commons of the United Empire in favour of the admission to parliament [? ensures] the ultimate success of the
measure at no distant period unless by some unwise and intemperate course on the part of the R[oman] Catholics this
natural and steady progress should be interrupted. You will
probably give me credit for being able to form some rational
conjecture as to the probability of carrying the measure at
present; my opinion is that it certainly will not pass the Lords;
and my strong apprehension is that it will not reach that
House. It appears to me that you state the matter much too
strongly, and excuse me for saying, without any ground to rest
on, when you say that not having the discussion during the
present session can be considered as an insult to the Body. The
question never has been considered as an annual one. Mr.
Grattan[1] has declined bringing it forward as such; I myself
declined it the year before last, and I am convinced that the
very most unfortunate shape it could assume would be that of
being necessarily and of course brought before Parliament

every year. It would not only lose its interest but its friends
who, though willing to expose themselves to some unpleasant
differences with their constituents (I mean the English Members for counties and open places) in order to carry, or
essentially to advance the measure, will not submit to be
annually dragged forward merely for discussion. In addition
to this there are many persons on the ministerial side of the
House who have been amongst the steadiest and most efficient
friends of the Roman Catholics who may feel themselves
placed in a situation of some awkwardness if in consequence
of a determination to bring it on every session, the question
should become liable to be considered as one of attack and
embarrassment. With reference to the prospect of success it
seems most material to look to the opinion of those persons.
You can estimate as well as I can do, the prejudice it must
sustain if brought forward against their judgement even
although they should give it their entire support. As to the
reasons which make the present moment appear inexpedient,
they are many but they all resolve themselves into one question
—is it likely that the measure, if now brought forward, will be
carried or advanced? My own judgement, on a not inattentive
consideration and with reasonable means of judging, is that it
is likely, by so doing, to be thrown back for many years. In
all this I may be mistaken. To go into the particulars on
which I form this conclusion would be endless and useless:
most of them are such as will naturally present themselves to
your own understanding. I hope in a few days to have better
means than I have at present of being fully informed of the
opinions of the friends of the measure as well on the opposition
as on the ministerial side of the House. What effect Mr.
Canning's intended motion[2] may have on their minds I cannot
exactly anticipate. It strikes me that if I were now to give
notice of the general measure such a step would infallibly
defeat his, which I should deprecate, not only because I should
consider the success of his measure an important step gained but
because its being so defeated would give rise to great dissatisfac-
tion on the part of the English noblemen who have always
so fairly and gallantly made common cause with the entire
Body. I need not add that let the measure be brought forward
when it may, it must have not only my concurrence but my
most cordial and zealous support. With respect to the measure
itself, if it be brought forward, it cannot be offered to the
House by me, or with the most distant hope of success by any-

body, in a shape substantially different from that in which it was last year offered to the House of Lords. I persuade myself that in that shape it will be considered by the great body of the Roman Catholics, clergy and laity, as a measure of contentment and satisfaction. This observation applies to the question at all times, but I mention it more particularly in reference to the point now under consideration, because I should hope that in the interval between this and the next session the opinion of the See of Rome might be notified in such a way as to secure an acquiescence in the proposed regulations. As to the opinion of the great body of the Rom. Caths. on the expediency of the immediate discussion, by proposing the question directly to Parliament, you have so much better means of forming a judgement, as well from being on the spot as from your extensive acquaintance with almost all its members, that it would be absurd in me to make any assertion. I own however I cannot but think you miscalculate when you say that 99 in 100 of the better ranks are decidedly for it; but still further I must entertain a strong hope that even of those who are friends to an immediate measure a great proportion would be disposed finally to acquiesce in the well considered opinions of those whom they know to be their sincere friends, even if that opinion were to lead to a postponement to the next session. Above all I cannot believe they would urge on the measure, with a strong expectation of defeat, merely for the sake of an immediate discussion in addition to that which in all its parts it received last session. I have written a very long and rambling dissertation, but I am a good deal pressed by business and I think it more important to answer without delay than to wait to methodize what perhaps is not very well worth arrangement.

[P.S.]   I have no objection to the substance of this being communicated to individuals but would not wish the letter itself to be handed over or any copy taken.

SOURCE : Papers of Mrs. Nicholas Shorter

1   The celebrated Henry Grattan who had died in June 1820.
2   See letter 958, note 3.

955

To his wife, Merrion Square

Cork, 11 April 1822

My darling Heart,

I enclose you a bill on the Pims for £350. . . . There were due this day two bills, one to Mr. Mahon, £58 with interest— call it £60—and the other, £138.10.0, to the College. As you had £62.10.0 in hands you will be able to repay Mr. Mahon the amount of his advance for this day and have £211 or there-abouts to spare out of the £350 bill. Now the other bills this month are 15th £69.19.0, 25th £75, and 28th £50, total £194.15.0. This will allow you to put up cash for all the bills due this month and leave you at least £16.5.0 for house expenses. I hope to hear that you have got from Coppinger his bill at 91 days for the horses but it is *too good* to be real-ized. I wish also we had £150 for the carriage and harness but that is quite too good to be realized. It would be quite *a make*. Speak again to O'Mara about my own horse. You are now as great a woman of business as ever Mrs. Delany[1] was. Are you getting rid of servants? If the coach-horses are sold you can dismiss the helper, I presume, but I know you will do everything for the best. . . .

Is Maurice[2] studying? I suppose not or you would gladly have told me of his diligence. Just say to him from me that he made me a solemn promise to go to his Easter duty[3] and that I am most sincerely sorry to see that his promise in that respect also is not of the slightest avail. It is bitterly painful to me to say so. . . .

SOURCE : Fitz-Simon Papers

1 Presumably Mary Delany (1700-88), wife of the Rev. Patrick Delany, an Englishwoman who lived for some years at Delville, Glasnevin, Co. Dublin. See *DNB*.

2 His eldest son.

3 The obligation then on Catholics to receive Holy Communion between Ash Wednesday and Ascension Thursday.

956

To his wife, Merrion Square

Cork, Saturday, 13 April 1822

My own love,

Another *blank* for the horses. Could you not get £60 or £70 or £80 for them at the farming repository? I am impatient to have them disposed of but let that not worry you. . . . Oh God, how it wrings my heart to part with you and with what a tremulous anxiety I will watch over every sixpence until I am fully able to have you back again! I will hug every tenpenny as a link in the chain that is to draw back my Mary to me. . . .

Hickson's letter is *so far* satisfactory but upon the whole I am *now* better pleased that we paid the bill, much better so that, Darling, I was not a little wrong in my passion at that which I now admit was all for the better. . . .[1]

You may, darling, put up a bill until my arrival. I cannot exactly say when that will be but the assizes here finish on Tuesday, the 16th of this month, and I can leave this the next day for Dublin unless I am obliged to go back to Limerick. I will not do the latter unless I get a *special fee*. I could not refuse a cool hundred. But unless I get *that* I will not go. . . .

Are my children talking about their journey? I hope they are in spirits about it. My darlings, what scenes of novelty are open for them! Have you communicated to Finn the time of your departure? Mention in your answer to this where in Kilkenny I could see Finn as I pass through. . . .

SOURCE : Fitz-Simon Papers
1   See letter 950 et seq.

957

To his wife, Merrion Square

Cork, 15 April 1822

My darling love,

I am sincerely sorry that I did make the £350 bill payable to Mr. Mahon. I had no notion that James Sugrue could have taken up the bills without Mahon's assistance and it gives me much satisfaction to find that he could. Darling, I hope the inconvenience was but short from my blunder.

. . . I have to pick up two sons of Morgan's friend Mr. Burke in Clonmel to take them to Clongowes. He was so attentive to my poor fellow when in a foreign land that we must retaliate although the taking them to Maynooth will *cost* me a day which at present I can very badly afford. I must also take the Connors from Clongowes. They cannot afford to remain there. Ask James Sugrue whether we can place Dan Connor[1] in any mercantile house where he could for the present earn a livelihood, I mean subsistence as a clerk. Maurice Connor must go back to Tralee. The affairs of that family are in a sad way from the dreadful fall in the times. I am afflicted to think of the dismal prospect they have before them.

I have had a violent cold and cough in the latter end of the week and yesterday I got a warm plaster to my chest and have, thank God, got complete relief. . . .

. . . I really regret having to take up the Burkes just at this moment when I am doubly impatient to be with you all. I am impatient too to see Blake[2] before his departure for England.

I will talk to you, darling, about Morgan and Baron O'Brady[3] when we meet. I do not like the military life for him if I could help it. But I see he will do nothing else and we must submit. I however think that when the General[4] sees him he will be desirous to have him in the French service if my poor fellow will but give up his absurd attachment to the English. I decidedly will not consent to his going into the British service. . . .

SOURCE : Fitz-Simon Papers

1 Daniel Connor (1807—19 May 1879), fourth son of James Connor and nephew of O'Connell's wife. Assumed surname of O'Connor Kerry; colonel in 43rd Austrian Infantry. Created a baron of the Austrian Empire.
2 Anthony Richard Blake.
3 Thomas Freiherr von Brady (O'Brady) (1752-1827), retired from the Austrian army with the rank of master of ordnance, 1809.
4 Count O'Connell.

958

To his wife, ' Dame Irlandaise', Poste Restante, à Bordeaux,
Department de la Gironde

Merrion Square, 3 [and 4] May 1822

My darling heart's own Love,

I begin this letter the day after you left me. It is a kind of
consolation to me to talk thus to you and my heart wants
some comfort for I am a lonely and miserable wretch with all
that I love torn from me and those sweet and endearing ties
which made existence a pleasure rent asunder. How my heart
travels with you and my children in your packet-boat—sea-
sick and crowded in that small sloop a speck on the ocean. I
fancy myself present and blame myself for all you suffer.
My sweet boy, my darling little prater complaining to his *Mud*
who can give him no relief. My girls, my own sweet girls,
suffering themselves and double sufferers by seeing their
mother in torture. I do not forget my John and Morgan but
they are able to bear it. Oh my Mary, that I was with you
or that you were with me. I found last night when I went to
my solitary room my little boy's lance and a judgement of
his. Oh, how they wrung my heart. It is my own cruel fault
that occasions the necessity of separating from you who are
always good and from my girls who have never been anything
but sweetness to their father's heart. I watched the wind all day
yesterday. With us it was mild and fair. At night it blew
fresh and I could not sleep because it blew on *our* windows.
I called them *our* but they are *my* melancholy windows. It
moaned too as it does at the south before a storm and it made
me miserable. . . . I made a great argument in the Chancery for
young Leslie[1] of Tarbert in a cause in which he is *robbed* by
the inattention of those who were formerly concerned for him.
The Chancellor[2] heard me right well. If you had been at home
I would have returned in great glee. You would have known
by me that I had succeeded. Canning's motion in favour of
the Catholic peers has been carried by a majority of five.[3]
I have not as yet had any offer for the horses. . . . I believe
I have secured Mr. Forde's[4] place for John the coachman.[5]
All the servants left us this day. Oh you cannot possibly think
how lonely the house is. It is the most cruel and cold feeling
which makes it chill to my very heart. . . . When any of

you write to me say as much about yourselves as possible. Give me every particular no matter how light or trivial. Tell me all you say, do and think. Tell me the entire story of your voyage, how each of you bore it, who was least sick and when you all recovered. Tell me the impression the strange country and people make on you all. In short, what I want is to hear as much as possible about every one of you. Let me have three letters a week while you are in Bordeaux and two a week afterwards. Get such paper as this and write small. There is nothing that I could tell you of us all. Maurice dined yesterday at the King's Inns and left me with those two little Burkes.[6] I was unable to say a word to them. Maurice, they, and I eat our fish with great solemnity together this day. I do not think I can get them off for Clongowes before Monday. That day Maurice and I will dine at the King's Inn. On Tuesday we dine at our club.[7] I have stopped both the *Observers* and care as little about the theatre as if it were in New York. . . . No Kerry news. All are actually starving in the County of Clare and nearly so in the County of Kerry. It is horrible to think of the state of the poor people. We went up in great state yesterday after court to Alderman McKenny with his plate.[8] The Duke of Leinster, Lord Meath,[9] Lord Cloncurry, Lord Killeen,[10] Sir Thos. Esmonde and a host of first-rate citizens. He had a splendid collation for us and I took the opportunity of speaking to Lord Meath about Mrs. Shiel.[11] He promises to do everything necessary. . . .

4 May 1822

. . . My love, do you not now reproach that loose and profligate waste of money to many and many an ungrateful and undeserving object which makes it necessary for us to separate? No, my love, you do not reproach it but my own heart does, and the misery I now endure is nothing but the punishment I deserve for not being more attentive.

I am *now* just returned from court, from one of the busiest days I ever knew, from speaking in every court and being wanted everywhere I had not time to mourn and I came back to my solitude and my sorrows with spirits neither exhausted or [sic] wearied but astonished at their own calm. I heard too from Kerry this day, that is, I saw *those* who came from it, *all* our friends are well. The distress extreme and the want spreading. . . .

Alderman McKenny has been just here with a brief in a

cause of his own and five guineas. You may be assured I
will take care of him. . . .

[P.S.] Remember me also to poor Hannah and Julia.[12]

SOURCE : Fitz-Simon Papers

1   Probably Robert Leslie (1792-1827), Tarbert House, Co. Kerry,
    eldest son of Robert Leslie, J.P., Tarbert House.
2   The lord chancellor, Lord Manners.
3   On 30 April 1822 George Canning proposed a motion in the
    Commons for leave to introduce a bill to repeal ' the Act of the 30th
    of Charles II ' under which Catholic peers were excluded from the
    House of Lords. It was carried by 249 votes to 244. The bill passed
    the Commons but on 22 June it was defeated in the Lords by 129
    votes to 171.
4   Probably William Ford (1791-1860), attorney, 26 Arran Quay,
    Dublin, and Kilcairn, Navan, Co. Meath.
5   O'Connell was dismissing the coachman for economy sake.
6   Alexander and John Burke.
7   The Irish Club (see letter 907).
8   On 2 May 1822 Alderman Thomas McKenny was presented with
    a ' service of plate ' in recognition of his services to the nation
    (FJ, 3 May 1822).
9   John Chambre (Brabazon), tenth earl of Meath (1772-1851), lord
    lieutenant of Co. Dublin 1831-51; created Baron Chaworth (U.K.)
    1831.
10 Arthur James (Plunkett) (1791-1869), styled Lord Killeen, 1793-
    1836; M.P. for Co. Meath, 1830-32. Succeeded as ninth earl of
    Fingall, 1836.
11 To obtain a position for her now that she was leaving O'Connell's
    employment as housekeeper.
12 Maidservants whom Mary O'Connell had brought with her to
    France.

959

To his wife at Bordeaux

[Dublin], Sunday 5 [6, 8 and 9] May 1822

My darling own love,

I have resolved to write to you by way of Journal, that is,
to write something every day. I beg of some one of you to do
the same. I will write different letters in one, and your one
letter may contain different days' accounts written by different
persons. My mind is more at ease this day; the weather has

become moderate and the fears which my long letter of yesterday and the day before contained are now like the wind quite tranquillized. I now flatter myself that you are getting fast to the end of your voyage and perhaps tomorrow will take you up the Garonne. . . . Maurice and the young Burkes are gone to Mass. Tell Morgan he forgot to give me Mr. Burke's address. Let me have it in the first letter that arrives from you. . . .

Monday, May the 6th.

. . . They now say Canning's bill[1] will pass. The Bar are about to address the late Chief Justice.[2] I mean to oppose it as strongly as I can. He was a plausible tool of bigotry. We are going to have better times for the farmers and to get some rents as it seems determined to get rid of the idea of returning to cash payments and they will let out the bank-notes again.[3] I am delighted at it as you may be certain I will avail myself of the opportunity to pay off every shilling I owe out of my lands, I may say, out of them alone. I hope the ministers will persevere in getting out the bank-notes. It would certainly make a difference of from £1,500 to £2,000 a year to me at the very least and now, darling, I have become really *avaricious* as far as a strong affection for money can make me but I hope my motives are pure. They refer, darling, to my debts and to you and my children. I have the young Burkes here still. I expect Finn here by the Carlow coach. If so, this letter will probably go with him. Tell my Nell that her father expects she will learn Spanish and German as well as French and especially Italian. I hope the summer after next to take *them* and you into Italy. If the rents come in you may depend on it. Tell my Kate I will be satisfied with her being a French and Italian scholar. As to my Betty I will not yet decide. . . . I wish you would retard his [Danny's] speaking French in order not to interfere with his English.

Wednesday, 8th May.

I wrote nothing yesterday I was so busy, first, in court, next, at *our* Education Society[4] and next, at our club[5] where I dined. There was a requisition to the father of the Bar to call a meeting to address Chief Justice Downes on his retiring from office. The meeting was called for half after three this day but I went round the hall with great *ferocity,* collected some myrmidons and, lo and behold! the worthies who signed for

the meeting gave the matter up and thus without any further
trouble I have defeated the intolerants for so much. A barrister
who loves a peer says the meeting was given up for fear I
should sing the song, ' All in the Downs '. The education
meeting was held yesterday at the Rotunda. Dr. Troy was in
the chair. Lord Cloncurry spoke well, so did Hamilton Rowan
and the meeting greeted the latter with great cordiality. There
was a more heartfelt cheer of applause for him than I have
often witnessed. The fact is the poor fellows shouted for him
as they would *for the Pikes*. I wept at feeding my own Nell's
pigeons and yet when I came to speak and got a glimpse at the
ridiculous nature of the Kildare Street pretenders[6] I almost
convulsed the meeting with laughter. Maurice went down to
Clongowes yesterday with the young Burkes.[7] I am very happy
to be rid of them. I dined quite alone this day and felt as
melancholy sitting by myself as you may imagine. Maurice is
however now—9 o'clock—returned after safely delivering his
charge. Poor Keller[8] died three days ago of a bilious fever. . . .
He has left his family in dire distress. . . . I hope and trust
the Bar will do something for them. I stirred the matter as
much as I could this day in the Hall. His children are real
objects of compassion. William Finn came to Carlow on
Monday but, I understand, was to go back again to Kilkenny
to attend a public meeting either this day or tomorrow to
prevent, if he could, the proclaiming the barony in which his
own property is situated. . . .

Thursday, 9th May.

. . . The Government is sending down potatoes in great
abundance to the South. They will scarcely be in time, the
distress is so very very great. I will send this letter off tomorrow, please God, without waiting any longer for Finn.
You will, I see, be detained a good while at Bordeaux for
him. . . . I do not like letters written across. I would rather
pay three times the postage than get such letters and, besides,
I am told that they stop such letters in Paris and read them.
Do not write to me in that way but write to me very long
letters. I got a letter this morning from Edward Connor. Dr.
Purdon has offered for their house but as the window tax is
certainly to be taken off they will be likely to get a higher rent.
Master Ellis told me yesterday that the window tax[9] would
certainly be taken off and they have orders at the Custom
House to give up collecting it. . . .

source : Fitz-Simon Papers

1   See letter 958, note 3.
2   William Downes.
3   See letter 1546, note 8.
4   Irish National Society for the Education of the Poor of Ireland.
    See letter 841, note 1.
5   The Irish Club formed in 1821 by Cloncurry, Alderman McKenny
    and others. See letter 907.
6   *Recte* Kildare Place Society.
7   Alexander and John Burke.
8   Jeremiah Keller, called to the bar, 1779; second son of Philip Keller,
    Deliger, Co. Cork.
9   The Irish window and hearth taxes were abolished by an act
    (3 Geo. IV c. 54) in July 1822. The decision to abolish them was
    announced in the Commons by the chancellor of the exchequer,
    Nicholas Vansittart, on 24 May (*DEP, 28 May 1822*).

960

From John Bric

Morning Chronicle Office, 7 May 1822

My Dear Sir,

. . . The honour of corresponding with you, the pleasure
of express[ing] my sincere and warm feelings towards you, I
ever felt greater than delicacy will allow me to describe. Those
feelings are too strong and too old to be abated by temporary
absence. Believe me, I never think on you without praying for
an increase to your prosperity and an exaltation of your fame.

The state of the political world you know as well, better
than I do—everything uncertain, the signs of the times
promising little of repose.

The affairs of England precarious—the Minister,[1] deserted
by his old partisans, has been defeated night after night—confused and uncertain in his measures, he one night abandons a
project which a few nights before he held out for the relief of
the landed interest of the nation. Those are strange things and
surely they afford evidence that the system so long pursued is
tottering at last. The force of events are yet to be exemplified.
Oh good debt,[2] thou art reserved to bring about strange and
mighty alterations. Canning's motion,[3] you see, has been
successful. It is doubted whether the Bill will pass the
Commons, if sent to the Lords it would put them in an

awkward situation. Whether it go there or not it will never go to the foot of the throne. Mr. Plunket has put off the general discussion.[4] Well, we must wait. After that discussion, whenever it shall come on, and the defeat which I anticipate will follow, Irishmen had better look down at their shoe-strings and trust to time, to chance, to revenge, and not to men, for their freedom.

We are to have a meeting for the relief of your starving population this day. Why is there no general meeting for the same purpose in Dublin?[5] Try to make up a meeting and distinguish yourself there. The public mind of this country is turned with anxiety to the state of Ireland at this moment, and surely it will be the eternal shame of Ireland if one man be allowed to starve there whilst another has a shilling to spare. Your benevolence I am sure must anticipate any suggestion of mine. For humanity sake and the honour of our land, let some public effort be made in the metropolis. . . .

SOURCE : Fitz-Simon Papers

1 A reference to the difficulties of Lord Londonderry (formerly Castlereagh) in introducing to the Commons measures designed to relieve the agricultural interest in the current depression by a loan and by inserting a sliding scale in the Corn Laws. The difficulties are discussed in the *Annual Register* for 1822, pp. 98 et seq.

2 The national debt, the payment of the interest on which was widely felt to be a very heavy burden.

3 See letter 958, note 3.

4 In the Commons debate of 30 April on Canning's motion (see letter 958, note 3) Plunket had intimated he was not for the present bringing forward a motion on the Catholic claims (*FJ*, 4 May 1822).

5 See letter 963, note 1.

961

To John Primrose, Jr., Hillgrove

Merrion Square, 9 May 1822

My dear John,

In future you will oblige me by writing to me once a month—the post after the first of each month—and send me an abstract of your cash account. I take for granted that you have not been able to get any money worth speaking of or I should have heard from you. I want very much £200 by the 19th of this month or the twentieth. You spoke of your

father's getting to that amount from my uncle[1] but I suppose
you were not able to accomplish it. Try and if possible send
me to that amount. It is the College[2] rent and fines which
make me want it. Let me hear from you without delay.

My family have sailed from Bordeaux the 2nd of this
month. I have not of course heard as yet of their arrival nor
can I for near a week. I feel most lonely and miserable in
their absence. Maurice is the only one of my children with
me.

SOURCE : O'Connell MSS, UCD
1 Hunting-Cap.
2 Trinity College, Dublin.

962

To his wife at Bordeaux

Merrion Square, 14 May 1822

My darling Mary,

. . . Oh, darling, I am tempted to great sin on the subject of my poor Uncle Maurice. He is showing several symptoms of decay. The principal one is a swelling in his legs.
. . . May the great God forbid that I should ever form the
least wish for property that would make me for one moment
look to his death as a desirable event. It would indeed be
wrong, and his illness *may* prevent me from being with you
as early as I otherwise should. . . . I think you had better
take your *lodgings* at Pau only by the month. I am uneasy
about the heat of the weather for you in summer. I believe you
may go nearer the mountains than Pau. . . .

There is no kind of Kerry news. . . . The famine is nearly
complete in that county and as yet but little has been done to
alleviate it. They however talk of doing great things. In the
meantime the people are starving.

My trade goes on flourishingly. All the rest of the Bar
are complaining but I never was doing so much. In your
absence I have nothing to take up a moment of my time but
law. I rise at half after four, breakfast at ¼ after eight, dine at
a quarter after five and go to bed between nine and ten. I
am, thank God, in perfect health and will be in good spirits
as soon as I hear of your safe arrival at Bordeaux. . . .

SOURCE : Fitz-Simon Papers

963

To his wife at Bordeaux, redirected to Pau

[Dublin] Wednesday, 15 [16, 18, 20, 21, 22
and 23] May 1822

My own darling, darling Mary,

This is my fourth letter and I have not yet had one line *in
reply*. Oh, how I long for one line from you! . . .

William Finn is gone. He has sailed in the *St. Patrick*
steam vessel for Bristol. . . . I do not get any letters myself.
All my Kerry news comes from others. But as I wrote near a
week ago to Primrose on business I trust I shall get direct and
positive intelligence in a few days. Darling, my professional
business continues in full blow and I am busy wiping off old
scores. There are many and many of them before me but let us
trust in God and hope for the best. I have, after all, a light
heart when my family misfortune does not oppress it and I
have future hopes which console me.

Thursday, 16th May 1822

. . . I am just going to the Lord Mayor's to a meeting
about the Southern distress.

Saturday, 18th May

The meeting at the Mansion House went off poorly, bad
speaking and not much money subscribed.[1] I wanted them to
adjourn to the Exchange to render the subscription universal
but I was strongly opposed, especially by Eneas MacDonnell.

The English post has just called. I rushed to the door but
no letter, no letter from you, Mary. Oh my Mary! Is it possible you and my children could have been out in the gale of
the 10th? How miserable I am! What a vile wretch! It was
for my own follies and idle gratifications that I made it necessary to separate from you and my children. I deserve the
punishment. . . . I rave, darling, when I think of being now
sixteen days separated from you without hearing of your safety.
. . . Maurice is perfectly well, not studying much but improved and improving in appearance, as fidgety however as
ever. I have not yet sold the carriage but expect to get from
£100 to £120 clear for it. . . . I wish I was rid of it. It has
been at Cooper's for near a week. I dine tomorrow at Richard

O'Gorman's, the next day at a charity dinner and thus my housekeeping is light. The money I paid Mrs. Shiel for this week is only £3.10.6 for everything, postage and all. I have borrowed an excellent horse . . . while my own is sick, quite a treasure of a horse for a fat man.

Monday, 20th May 1822

I was *unable* to continue my journal. Indeed I *was* very miserable. Your eldest son and I wept at our breakfast this morning plentifully. The storm of the 9th ran in my head and I spent last night in a very feverish state. . . . On my way home I called at Elliott's and waited in his office till he got his letters. I had there the delight to read a letter from the captain of the *Dorset* dated from Bordeaux on the 9th, boasting of his passage and saying *all* his passengers were well. I will love that fellow for ever. And now, you saucy cocknosed vixen, why did not some one of you write to me by the same packet? . . . Have I not a right to be angry but the fact is nothing could make me angry this evening. I have had a bitter load taken off my heart. . . .

Tuesday, 21 May

I am waiting with impatience to hear *of you*. Tomorrow's post—how I long for it. . . . Term is over love, that is, the law term is over and we will have something of a short vacation. I have made a party for Howth on Sunday *afternoon* as you are arrived safe, that is, I go as one of the party for I am as stingy as possible.

Wednesday, 22 May

What shall I say? What shall I do? Oh Mary, what is the meaning of all this? . . . How could you all use me so ill, how could you all be so cruel to me? Sure you must have known that Elliott would inform me of your arrival and yet you all pass two days on land without writing to me. . . . I cannot forgive my sister Ally or Morgan. He, however, cares nothing for me. What I say or do is quite a matter of indifference to him. It is plain some of you must be ill. I stamp and rave and know not what to do. It is so cruel, so malignant not to write. Oh, it would be troublesome to Mr. Morgan, would it? Mr. Knox wrote and his letter is in town these two days. The Captain's letter is in town these two days. . . . Oh, perhaps to save some lousy[2] postage you wrote across the letter. They stop all such letters in France.

Thursday, 23 May

Darling, I had this moment the happiness of getting your first letter. It is dated the 11th. My mind is at ease and I smile when I look back at the virulence with which I wrote yesterday. I will not blot any part of it out that you may see how bitter my anguish was when I found that I was left without a letter for *three* days after everybody else had heard. Darling, my next shall be to Kate. I will begin it tomorrow. The account from my Uncle is favourable today. The swellings have got down. He is a surprising old man. My business is greater than ever. I have been all day haranguing in the courts. . . . I live with the most scrupulous regularity. Never a soul near us at meals. Maurice dined this day at Howth with Father Keogh. I sat as usual solitary.

SOURCE : Fitz-Simon Papers

1 O'Connell subscribed £25 and became a member of the committee set up at this meeting to supervise the raising of funds for the relief of the distress in the south and west of Ireland (*FJ*, *DEP*, 18 May 1822).
2 An old slang term denoting a thick skin on a pot of stale paint. Its modern use dates from World War I.

964

To his daughter Kate, Pau

Merrion Square, 24 [27, 28 and 30] May 1822

My own sweetest darling Kate,

What a pet of mine you are, Kate. I doat of all my children but you, my sweetest child, have put tendrils round my heart and it clings to you with the fondest affection. I will tell you a secret. I used to weep more when I named you and Danny than when I named any other of my children. You, too, frightened me, sweet Kate, for about ten days before you went you said to me one morning at breakfast, ' I am sure we shall all be drowned going to Bordeaux.' I used to think of that, Kate, and if anything had happened to you that phrase would have been written with letters of fire on my soul. . . . This is my fifth letter. I wrote two to your darling mother, then one to Ellen, then one to be put this day into the office for your sweet mother. Darling, tell your beloved mother that it is not possible to describe the joy and satisfaction her letter gave me. . . . She bids me burn it. What a chance she has of my burning a letter of hers! I now want, my sweetest Kate, details of your travelling, not stiff letters telling me you are well and send me your love and have no more to say. You have all plenty to say. Give me journals, say to me everything that happened in the packet-boat, everything you see and hear, how you like the people. . . . In short, darling Kate, it will be quite a treat to me to chat as it were with you all by letter and hear you talk amongst yourselves. . . . I myself have an alarm clock fixed between four and half after four. Maurice sleeps in the room with me and *growls* at the clock awaking him. It rings some minutes and I defy the seven sleepers not to wake at it. I breakfast at *eight by the hall clock*. We dine at the usual hour. I work incessantly but I am, thank God, in perfect health and my mind is quiet since I heard from the sweetest, dearest and best of living women.

. . . *I got* another verdict in the Common Pleas. I do not think I ever did more or perhaps so much business in any one day. I heard nothing from Kerry today. The benefits are going on at the theatre. . . . I made Maurice a present of a ticket in honour of you. . . .

Monday, 27 May

I was not able to write anything to my sweet Kate on Saturday. I was in court very early and very late. . . . Yesterday afternoon we made a party to dine at Howth—James Sugrue, Roger,[1] Mr. Hart, Costello[2] and James Sugrue's partner, Mr. Jones,[3] Maurice and I. We set off after three and saw the steam packet arrive against wind and tide. It is, to be sure, a most wonderful invention. She came across in the teeth of wind and tide in nine hours. We dined at the inn and were very pleasant and merry. Maurice and I rode and came home in the cool of the evening but too late to write anything to my Kate. This day we go out to dine at O'Mara's at Glencullen to meet Lord Rossmore[4] who, I believe, wants your father's assistance to canvass the Catholic peers should the bill[5] for their emancipation which is now before the Lords pass into a law. Between you and me, sweet Kate, I think the bigotry of the Protestant peers will throw it out. It is to be discussed on the

31st [30th?] of this month.[6] You see what a politician I am
making of my own fair Kate, her father's dearest darling.

Tuesday, 28 May

Maurice and I went yesterday to Glencullen. I went in a
chaise, Maurice rode. The day was charming. . . . I left
Maurice at O'Mara's and he will stay there till tomorrow. I
came home and had the delight to find a letter from my Nell
with a *cover* from my ever loved Mary before me. It is dated
the 16th. . . . I pay double postage for a letter and *a cover*
. . . so that I ought to get two full sheets in every letter just as
I write to you all. Let me have two sheets in every letter in
future. . . . Tell me something too of Hannah and Julia.[7]
How do they get on with the French servants? I think poor
Hannah must often be at a loss how to get on at all. I should
be glad to see her attempting to make herself understood by a
person who knew nothing of English. Darling Kate, I got this
day *The Fortunes of Nigel*[8] and read already [a] great part of
a volume. I like it very much. The scene is in England at the
court of King James the first but the characters are chiefly
Scotch. . . .

Thursday, 30 May

I finished *Nigel* and I like it very much. It is a beautiful
and interesting story, more natural than most of Scott's late
novels. I promise you a great treat in it. As usual I sat up the
first night I got it until twelve midnight and *neglected* my
business to finish it. I was very busy all day yesterday for,
although this is vacation with everybody else, it is none with
me and I have this day a *great speech* to make in a cause in
court which will make a good deal of noise. I intend to be
very *pathetic*. . . . I expect this day or tomorrow to hear
from you all but as yet your letters do not enter into sufficient
details. For my part I tell you everything that passes, even to
your pigeons which I take great care of. I love your pigeons,
sweet Kate, because they belong to my children. . . . There
is nothing but grief and woe in Kerry. The people starving
and the gentry in bitter want. No rents, no money, the fever
and famine raging. May the great God be merciful to them all.
Talk to all my children about me. Tell my Morgan I long to
hear *of him* and from him. Is he learning *anything*? . . .
You must all *chat* with me in your letters. I hate *stiff*
letters. . . .

SOURCE : Fitz-Simon Papers

1   Roger O'Sullivan.

2   Patrick Costello, solicitor and wit; engaged in Catholic agitation and anti-tithe campaign. In 1832 he unsuccessfully contested Waterford city. He died 13 July 1858 at 57 Lower Mount Street, Dublin.

3   A member of the firm of Arnold Jones & Co., 3 Cooke's Lane, Watling Street, Dublin, manufacturers of oil, vitriol and bleaching salts.

4   Warner William (Westenra), second Baron Rossmore (I) (1765-1842), M.P. for Co. Monaghan, 1800-1801; created Baron Rossmore of Monaghan (U.K.), 1838.

5   See letter 958, note 3.

6   It was discussed, in fact, on 21 June 1822.

7   Maidservant with O'Connell's family from 1817.

8   By Sir Walter Scott (3 vols., Edinburgh 1822).

965

From his wife

[Incomplete copy of letter]

26 May 1822

My dearest love,

With what delight did I press to my heart your sweet, your long wished for letter. My own, own Dan, do not fret. I wish you could see me and your children so happy and contented. . . . You are, heart, much more religious than your Mary and from the moment it was deemed necessary for me to come with my family to France, I put on the resolution to bear it like a Christian. Do not, my own love, make me unhappy by those reproaches you cast on yourself. . . . You never deserved any from me. You have been the best and most beloved of husbands and you will continue such to the last hour of my life. I think, heart, instead of upbraiding yourself for sending your children from you, you will rejoice when you meet them next August.

SOURCE : O'Connell Papers, NLI 13651

966

From Philip Harding[1] to Merrion Square

27 May 1822 [postmarked Macroom]

Dear Sir,

As I perceive your name on the Dublin Committee[2] I beg leave to call your attention to the state of Macroom and its neighbourhood. From its having been the principal seat of disturbance the distress is perhaps greater than in many other places and requires, I assure you, immediate relief. Employment seems to be, as it ought, the wish of all the benevolent subscribers at both sides of the water. Now there is here a new chapel about half finished and, for want of [about two words missing] there it must remain. I therefore [? ask] your humane and friendly assistance, solicit some portion of the Dublin fund towards relieving the poor of Macroom which can now be effected in a most excellent and praiseworthy manner by finishing the Chapel.

SOURCE : O'Connell Papers, NLI 13647
1 Philip Harding, Firville (Bealick), Macroom, Co. Cork. Died 3 July 1841. Landowner.
2 Established at the Mansion House meeting on 16 May to raise funds for relieving distress. See letter 963.

967

From his brother James to Merrion Square

Killarney, 31 May 1822

My Dear Dan,

You will receive a letter from Kean Mahony by the same post with this, enclosing resolutions entered into by a meeting held in Iveragh for the relief of the poor. You have also an account of the subscriptions entered into, in addition to that small sum I received of the first £500 remitted from London for the relief of the poor of this County—£44—which as yet was all the aid the inhabitants of Iveragh, consisting of a wretched population of eighteen thousand, received out of *all the money* subscribed for the South of Ireland. It is true I got a letter on Sunday last written from the Mansion House, Dublin, and signed P. Singer[1] and Hugh O'Connor[2] enclosing me £50 for the relief of the poor in my vicinity but *as that letter* was directed to Killarney, I apprehended the Committee[3] in Dublin may intend this sum for the poor of this town and neighbourhood. I, however, in my reply to P. Singer and Mr. O'Connor *take it for granted* this money was to be laid out for the poor of Iveragh and sign my letter as Treasurer to the local committee of that district but, of course, until I hear more on the subject, I will feel myself bound to hold the £50 at the disposal of the Secretaries of the Dublin Committee. . . .

SOURCE : O'Connell MSS, UCD

1   Paul Singer, called to the bar in 1796, I Upper Temple Street, Dublin.
2   Hugh O'Connor, merchant, Mountjoy Square, Dublin.
3   See letter 966, note 2.

968

To his wife, Pau

Merrion Square, 31 May [and 1, 2, 5 and
6 June] 1822

My own darling Mary,

. . . Be, darling, like me in love with every farthing because the pence saved will hurry the reunion of our family. I wish to be quite a miser. How I *long* to be out of debt. How I regret owing a shilling. I suppose, darling, you keep an accurate account of every *cent* you pay though the French money will bother you at first. If you have not already begun to keep such an account I entreat of you to do so from the moment you receive this letter. Take first an account of how much money you have still in hands, and then at the other side begin to put down your expenses and, darling, every Monday morning deduct the expenditure from the sum in hands and ascertain how *the cash* stands, and once a month at least let me know how the balance is . . . and let me know what you have that I may be prepared to send you more money quite in time before any want could possibly reach you. . . .

The jury trials are continuing and I have decidedly the lead of all other counsel in point of quantity of business. I am kept late each day but am not obliged to be in court as early as usual because it is Baron Smith who sits.

Saturday, 1 June

The *Dorset* is arrived. I will go on board her this day or tomorrow to thank the captain and crew for their attention to you all. . . . Yesterday was a day of great professional triumph. There were two special jury cases in both of which I succeeded. One was against Ball's Bank,[1] the other against the 'Kildare Street Bible Education Society'.[2] I was greatly delighted in beating those scoundrels. They failed by reason of the inaccuracy with which they keep their accounts, and it appeared that for three years they never accounted with the public for their stock of books, paper, slates, quills, etc., etc. of the value of from £6,000 to £10,000, so that they are covered with disgrace and ridicule. You know how I dislike the canting hypocrites that belong to that association, and you will easily form an idea of how cheerful you would have found me at dinner if I had had my family about me but, alas, I came home to a miserable solitary table, for even Maurice dined out, and had to spend my wretched evening as well as I possibly could. The letters from my children were to be sure a great comfort to me although the darlings do not write with that *flow* which I could wish for. . . . This, darling, ought to be vacation but you know there is no vacation for your husband. Blessed be the will of God.

Sunday, 2 June

. . . This day I was obliged to go to the Clondalkin Charity Sermon[3] four miles out of town. Mr. L'Estrange is about this time on his way home. Do you recollect *my quarrel* with you about him? But, darling, for once I was right. I would not give a meal's meat to a human being for any consideration other than charity if I could afford and practise that. There is no kind of Kerry news. The distress and starvation great, no rents, no money, *all* gone to complete ruin. I do not know what the gentry will do if there be another year of this description and that there will is, I think, quite clear unless we have some great change in the political affairs of England, but while the present ministers remain in office there is no hope for this wretched country. The Catholic Peers bill[4] will certainly be thrown out in the Lords by a frightful majority. It is now postponed . . . because Lord Grey's *only* mother died! An admirable reason truly. The King takes no part and that is very nearly as bad as if he were decided in his opposition. The old fellow, they say, is looking out for another wife, I believe it. . . . It [*Nigel*] is indeed a sweet novel, and Scott has adver-tised a ' dramatic poem '.[5] I hope he will not fail in the drama as miserably as Lord Byron has. It is near nine o'clock so, darling, I must go to bed to be up soon after four, I hope. . . .

Wednesday, 5th June

. . . Maurice is at O'Mara's, John Howley,[6] Curran and a large party of young people are there and here I am by myself, solitary and sufficiently miserable, working away like a windrawer. No matter. Darling, be as penurious as you pos-sibly can, that is, if you wish that I should soon have my family about me. If you *do not,* why you may be extravagant. That's all because as long as I have a guinea, you shall com-mand it. . . . There is not a word of news from Kerry, every-thing going on there as badly as possible but the season is remarkably early. We never had so warm a month of May and beginning of June. You who dislike heat so much must, I fear, feel very much oppressed. I tremble to think how this terrible hot weather must affect you. Tell me the truth, darling, as to how you bear it. . . .

There came in to me yesterday a Mr. Reilly[7] who has just finished *his education* as an engraver in London. He was very anxious to get a portrait of me to engrave and was quite delighted at my allowing him to engrave Gubbins' picture of me. He does it purely as a speculation of his own and he promises to have the engraving in about six weeks. I hope to carry you over a proof impression in August. I will have noth-ing under it but my simple name and surname and beneath the two lines, ' Hereditary bondsmen etc.' He seems to me to be a young man of talent and he showed me some good speci-mens of his engravings. I think *this time* we shall not be dis-appointed. He was greatly pleased at *his success.* . . .

Thursday, 6th June

I had the great pleasure last night of get[ting] your letter of 26th May, that is, written up to the 26th on which day you were to have left Bordeaux. I therefore direct this to Pau. . . . Maurice is come in from O'Mara's. He desires his love to all, to you especially. He promises to write by the *Dorset* but you know he deals much in the future tense or rather what the Greeks call a tense, of a little more than future. He is really a fine youth. May God bless and direct him ! . . . Darling, your letter pleased me extremely. It contains many details, and I like details about you all. Do you write to me once a week and get the boys and girls also to write, each of them once a week in addition, that is, alternately. . . .

SOURCE : Fitz-Simon Papers

1   Ball's Bank, Henry Street, one of Dublin's most famous private banks. Founded about 1810, it was taken over by the Northern Banking Company Ltd. in 1888. Its directors in 1822 were Benjamin Ball, Matthew James Plunkett, Philip Doyne, Jr., and Henry Samuel Close.
2   That is, the Kildare Place Society. The case is not mentioned in the newspapers.
3   The annual sermon in aid of the free school of the Carmelite Brothers at Clondalkin, Co. Dublin, founded in 1813 and of which O'Connell was president.
4   See letter 958, note 3.
5   Very probably *Halidon Hill : A Dramatic Sketch from Scottish History,* published in Edinburgh on 24 June 1822 (William Ruff, ' A Bibliography of the Poetical Works of Sir Walter Scott, 1796-1832 ', in *Edinburgh Bibliographical Society Transactions,* I, part 2 [1936-37], 213).
6   John Howley (1789-1866), son of John Howley, Rich Hill, Co. Limerick; K.C., 1835; knighted, 1865.
7   B. O'Reilly, 176 North King Street, Dublin. The engraving is dated 1 February 1823.

969

To Nicholas P. O'Gorman

Merrion Square, 22 June 1822

My dear O'Gorman,

I beg leave to deposit the enclosed letter[1] with you as a document[2] of great importance to the Catholics of Ireland. I deposit it with you in your capacity of Secretary to the Catholics and for public purposes, and I request you as such secretary to call a meeting of such noblemen and gentlemen as take a part in managing our affairs, to consider the propriety of either petitioning Parliament or instituting a prosecution on the subject of this letter and of the conspiracy which it proves to convert the judicial office into an engine of calumny and bigotry.

Very faithfully yours,
Daniel O'Connell

P.S. Acknowledge the receipt of this. I think the meeting should be private.

SOURCE : FitzPatrick, *Corr.*, I, 81

1 There is a copy of this letter in the Earl Grey Papers, University of Durham, as follows:

Dublin, 9 August

Dear Lord Norbury,

I transcribe for you a very sensible part of Lord Rosse's letter to me.

'As Lord Norbury goes our circuit and as he is personally acquainted with the gentlemen of our County, a hint to him may be of use. He is in the habit of talking individually to them in his chamber at Phillipstown and, if he were to impress upon them the consequence of the measure, viz., that however they may think otherwise, the Catholics would in spite of them, elect Catholic members (if such were eligible), that the Catholic members would then have the nomination of the sheriffs, and in many instances, perhaps of the judges; and that the Protestants would be put in the background as the Catholics were formerly, I think he would bring the effect of the measure home to themselves, and satisfy them that they could scarcely submit to live in the country if it were passed.'

So far Lord Rosse. But what he suggests in another part of his letter.

'That if Protestant gentlemen who have votes and influence and interest, would give those venal members to understand that if they will purchase Catholic votes, that by betraying their country and its constitution, they shall infallibly lose theirs, it would alter their conduct though it could neither make them honest or respectable.'

If you will judiciously administer a little of this medicine to the King's County or any other members of parliament that may fall in your way, you will deserve well.

. . . Many thanks for your letter and its good intelligence from Maryborough. Jebb is a valuable fellow and of the sort that is much wanted.

Affectionately and truly yours,
William Saurin

2 A full account by O'Connell of how he came by the letter appears in letter 1024. O'Connell enclosed the above copy with his letter to Earl Grey of 24 June 1822.

970

To Francis Hely-Hutchinson[1]

Merrion Square, 22 June 1822

My dear Sir,

I write lest you should be detained at home on my account in the morning. I felt the justice of your sentiments to a certain extent as hastily expressed in our short conversation this day but it was too short to enable me to explain to you the precise situation in which I stood as a trustee for a numerous but unfortunate class of subjects. I will not give you the trouble to listen to any details on that subject as the custody of Mr. Saurin's letter[2] is no longer with me and that the subject is about to be taken up by the Catholics at large. This supercedes the occasion of paying you my respects in the morning if I am right in supposing that it was with reference to that letter that you wished to speak with me. If it related to any other subject I will cheerfully wait on you at any time which may best suit your convenience.

SOURCE : Donoughmore Papers

1 Francis Hely-Hutchinson (1759-1827), brother of the first and second earls of Donoughmore; M.P. for Dublin University 1790-97; Naas, 1798-1800.
2 See letter 969, note 1.

971

From his daughter Ellen

Pau [France], Saturday morning, 22 June 1822

My dear Father,

. . . Kate was very proud that you wrote her a long letter without a word of scolding while you gave me *two*. I hope, however, that I shall not incur them again as I have begun my letter pretty high and intend, as you do not like it, never to be either *dutiful* or *affectionate* again at least to the former extent. I was delighted to find you were in better spirits than when you wrote me such a sad letter that made us all cry. . . . Pau seems to be a very pleasant town. . . .

[P.S.] . . . I had another letter written to you but by mistake crossed a few lines of it so was obliged to tear it as Mama says (making a pun at your expense) ' that it would make you very *cross* to have anybody *cross* a letter to you '. . . .

SOURCE : Kenneigh Papers

972

To Earl Grey

Merrion Square, Dublin, 24 June 1822

My Lord,

The interest your Lordship has always evinced in the affairs of this wretched because ill-governed country induces me to take the liberty of transmitting to you a copy of a document which will, I think, give you an idea of the nature of the springs by which our political system is put in motion. It is a copy of a letter[1] from the late Attorney-General of Ireland, Mr. Saurin, to the Chief Justice of the Common Pleas, Lord Norbury,[2] containing, as I think, clear evidence of a conspiracy to pervert the judicial character into an engine of calumny and bigotry. This letter was found in the streets about a week ago by a respectable person and is now deposited with Mr. O'Gorman as the Secretary of the Catholics of Ireland. There is no doubt of its being genuine and, should a prosecution be instituted upon it in consequence of an address of either House of Parliament, its authenticity can be established beyond controversy.

This letter cannot as I humbly conceive be considered as private property. It is evidence of crime and therefore belongs to the public. It is evidence of a crime of a very atrocious description and of one which necessarily would be committed in secret and of which no evidence could be obtained, save either by accident, as in this instance, or by the wilful treachery of an informer whose testimony should on public grounds be used however his conduct may be impeached.

Mr. Saurin, the writer of the letter in question, has been for sixteen years *the* efficient organ of the Irish Government. He is still, though out of office, the chief adviser of Lord Manners who is himself a *principal* in the management of this wretched country. I entreat of your Lordship to excuse me for taking this liberty with you. I assure you no man living estimates more highly than I do your Lordship's public character and services to our unhappy people.

SOURCE : Earl Grey Papers

1 See letter 969, note 1.
2 John (Toler) (1745-1831); created Baron Norbury, 1800, Viscount Glandine and earl of Norbury, 1827. See *DNB*.

973

To Thomas Spring Rice

Merrion Square, 24 June 1822

My dear Sir,

I feel it right to enclose you a copy of a curious document which is now in the hands of Mr. O'Gorman as Secretary to the Catholics of Ireland. It is a letter[1] of the late Attorney-General for Ireland to Chief Justice Lord Norbury and contains a pretty specimen of the vile purposes to which the Bench in Ireland may be prostituted. It seems to be a roving commission to a judge to create every kind of ill blood by every species of calumny. I beg of you as a friend to the purity of the judicial character to take this document into your most serious consideration. It would in my humble judgment afford strong evidence of a conspiracy between Lord Rosse,[2] Mr. Saurin and Lord Norbury to pervert the judicial office into a political engine of calumny and bigotry. It opens views upon us of the secret management of the anti-liberal part of the Irish administration which will be quite frightful when you recollect that the writer of it has been the efficient organ of the Irish government for about sixteen years and is still the confidential adviser of our Chancellor[3] as well as his bosom friend. There is *no doubt* of this letter being genuine.

The history of it is this. It was found on the quay near the Four Courts on last Wednesday week, the 12th of June, by a young attorney who is a Catholic. It had no cover nor any address. It must have been formerly in an envelope. The gentleman who found it in some days after communicated its contents in conversation with a Catholic clergyman who obtained and transmitted the document to me to be made use of for public purposes. I have accordingly deposited it with Mr. O'Gorman, our Secretary, and it is probable that a public meeting will be held relative to it. In the meantime you are at liberty to make any use you please of it. There is no Irish Member who possesses near so much of the public confidence as you already do and I am quite candid when I express my decided opinion that you deserve the confidence and gratitude of your country in the highest degree.

SOURCE : Monteagle Papers, NLI 13367 (2)

1   See letter 969, note 1.
2   Lawrence (Parsons), second earl of Rosse (1758-1841), a lord of the treasury, 1805-09; joint postmaster-general, 1809-31. A leading opponent of the Union. See *DNB*.
3   Lord Manners.

974

To William Conyngham Plunket

Merrion Square, 1 July 1822

My dear Sir,

I had the honour to receive your letter of the 25th of June, and am sincerely sorry to see that you think the plain evidence of a foul and most dangerous crime—the perversion of the administration of Justice to political purposes[1]—should be sacrificed to some notion of etiquette. I am indeed very sorry for it.

I hope and trust that, if any Catholic had been guilty of an attempt to corrupt a judge and to pervert the administration of so sacred a thing as public justice to any purpose injurious to the State, or even to the meanest Protestant in that state, such Catholics would be prosecuted with the utmost rigour of the law. In the case of a Catholic so offending I should be desirous that the usual modes of obtaining evidence of secret conspiracies, namely, the giving rewards to any associate who would betray and prove guilt, would be resorted to. Such crimes require and justify the hiring, at wages, of that kind of treachery which all honest men abhor, but must make use of, otherwise secret conspiracies would go unpunished. In the case of an offending Catholic I should hope that his crime would be thus sifted, detected, and punished. I am not so foolish or so uncandid as to assert that the case of a Protestant who conspires to injure the Catholics' case can in the present temper of Society in these countries, and under the present system, with at least one half the administration in both decided enemies of Catholic rights and liberties—I am not, I say, so foolish and uncandid as to assert that under such a system the crimes of Catholics and Protestants against each other should be weighed in the same scales of gold; neither theory nor practice warrant me to say so. But yet *this* is so plain, so distinct, so enormous an offence; the evidence of it has been procured in so guiltless a way—no reward, no price has or can by any the remotest possibility be now or hereafter paid for it; it is handed to us by that kind of chance which is sometimes absurdly, and at other times perhaps piously, called ' providential ', it furnishes so strong, so striking a feature in the causes of Irish misery that I cannot bring myself to believe but that on reflection you will see the necessity, or at least the propriety, of not allowing these offenders to escape.

Under these circumstances I feel it to be my duty again, and in the most respectful manner possible, to tender you the copy of this letter and to offer you the proof of the original, and also of the manner in which it has been procured.

I am happy that, as this letter is addressed to you merely as a public man on a public subject, it does not require from you any reply. Its contents are dictated by perhaps a mistaken, but certainly a strong as well as painful sense of public duty. . . .

SOURCE : FitzPatrick, *Corr.,* I, 81-3
1   See letter 969, note 1.

975

To Lord Cloncurry

Merrion Square, 6 July 1822

My dear Lord,

I thought I could have the pleasure of spending tomorrow with you, but I now find I cannot. I must, very reluctantly, deprive myself of that honour. I do, indeed, want very much to converse with you and, if the following Sunday be dry, I will try and find you at home sometime in the forenoon of it. I begin to think that it would be possible to *take a position* favourable to reform before the next sessions commence, especially if the Duke of Leinster could be brought into action. The country gentlemen are *now* smarting and between loss of rents and the pressure of tithes and the horrors of the ' Constabulary Bill ',[1] there are many who would now come forward that have been hitherto neutral or adverse. It would, at all events, be right to try.

SOURCE : Cloncurry, *Personal Recollections,* p. 214

1 This bill was introduced to the Commons by Goulburn on 24 May 1822 and in due course became law (3 Geo. IV c. 103). Its purpose was to increase the number of police and stipendiary magistrates and to bring them more directly under the control of the central government thus reducing the power and influence of landlords (Hereward Senior, *Orangeism in Ireland and Britain,* 1795-1836 [London and Toronto 1966], p. 200; Oliver MacDonagh, *Ireland* [Englewood Cliffs, N.J., 1968], pp. 24-5). No doubt one of the ' horrors ' was the increase in local taxation (rates) which this reorganization would involve.

976

From John Devereux to Merrion Square

Palace of Bogota, 16 July 1822

Private

My ever dear friend,

I have barely time, the courier being on the point of starting, to enclose you a letter for my dearest Morgan. I return immediately[1] to Europe under the most flattering auspices charged with a high diplomatic mission[2] from this government to the states of Europe. This honour I did not covet or seek but as I was for returning, the Government intimated to me in the most flattering terms that it was their wish to confer on me some mark of their distinguished favour and confidence, such in fine as the government of the United States conferred on the illustrious Lafayette when he returned at the conclusion of the Revolutionary struggle of that country, only that his was confined solely to his own country.

I have written to the president requesting it as a favour that his Excellency would grant a leave of absence to your cousin Maurice who is now a full captain in the Rifles commanding the finest company in that Regt. to which he is also acting Adjutant-Major. As I have now realized, my dearest friend, a splendid sufficiency, I shall charge myself specially with the care of poor Maurice.[3] Independent of the pleasure it affords myself I am aware it will afford you and your dear Lady still greater pleasure, that I should have him with me as my private secretary. I only fear that the fine youth will not reach this city before my departure. If not, I shall make such arrangements for him in pecuniary matters so that he can follow me with all speed. . . .

Recall me dearly to Counsellor Finlay, Counsellor O'Gorman and his worthy brother. Also to Mr. William Murphy. You must excuse this hasty scrawl, but I treat you now with all the familiarity of a brother!—and such you are to me by adoption, having no brother or sister now alive.

Let me know by a few lines if you would have any objection to act as one of my trustees to a fortune I wish to settle on my betrothed bride previous to marriage. This I wish to do not only from the devoted affection I bear my fond idol, but also that it shall be a proof I did not seek her fortune when I aspired to the honour of her hand. Out of what is already realized to me, I can conveniently settle on her one hundred thousand pounds. A shilling of her fortune I am resolved never under any circumstances to accept of. . . .

SOURCE : O'Connell MSS, UCD

1 Devereux did not in fact leave until the middle of 1823.
2 Devereux was appointed to a diplomatic mission to Russia and Scandinavia by the vice-president of Colombia in Bolívar's absence, but the congress refused to approve it. The vice-president, Santander, said that Devereux himself made the offer to go without any remuneration.
3 Maurice O'Connell was already dead when this letter was written (see letter 980). He died on 2 April, a few days before the battle of Bombona at which his regiment distinguished itself.

977

This letter, from Sir Francis Burdett, 22 July 1824, was taken from the Irish Monthly, *XI (1883), 342-3, which gives the date erroneously as 1822 and the addressee as O'Connell. In fact, the letter was addressed to Stephen Coppinger (FJ, 26 July 1824.)*

978

From Count O'Connell to Merrion Square, redirected to Cork

[5 August 1822]

[Salutation and most of one line illegible]

   . . . from Limerick has reached me yesterday evening, transmitted from Paris. A few days before I received one from Morgan of the 23d. Your family were all quite well and in great glee from the prospect of seeing you soon. I was aware of the want of good professors (masters) at Pau. The province you contemplated, *Perigord*, is, I believe, still worse in that respect. The chief town, *Périgueux,* is a poor place. The gentry, once very opulent, are now in low circumstances and the new breed of those who now rule the land pay but little attention to a refined education. If I were to offer my opinion I conceive that *Toulouse* would be an eligible place of residence. The city is large, inhabited by a great number of very respectable families, therefore I presume that good masters of every description may be had there. The country is beautiful, the climate healthy and living as cheap, I believe, as at Pau, the distance between both inconsiderable. . . . I rejoice to see your professional reputation and your receipts daily increasing. As to your lands, surely they must, though bad the times, produce something. Otherwise the soil will be abandoned and the land become a wilderness.

   I shall be truly happy, my dear Dan, the day all your debts are paid. Then and not till then will you enjoy peace of mind and real independence. Then and not sooner will it be in your power to make some provision for your family. I wish with all my heart that Baron O'Brady's answer to your letter may meet your views for Morgan. As he has fixed his heart on entering the service, that of Austria is preferable to any other. . . .

[P.S.] . . . We are here on our way to Paris, and we hope you will give us a few days *en passant*. Let me earnestly request of you neither to see nor communicate whilst in France with any individual of the *Libéraux faction*. I trust you will comply with my request.

SOURCE : Fitz-Simon Papers

979

To John Primrose, Jr., Hillgrove

Merrion Square, 31 August 1822

My dear John,

I left Cork yesterday morning at six and arrived here at the same hour today. I intend going by the steamboat of Monday evening to Liverpool and thence as fast as I can to Pau.

I wrote you a hasty letter from Cork. I now return to its contents. What I wish is: 1st that you should get up from Myles McSwiney all my account books, receipts, etc. 2dly that you should take special care of the plantations. This I entrust to you as my most anxious desire, and allow me to say I know *nothing* which I would take as an excuse for your neglecting it. I supercede everybody else but you in that case and therefore in truth you cannot have any excuse. Pardon me for writing so peremptorily to you on the subject. 3dly As butter *must* fall, urge my tenants out. I will allow 5$^{s.}$ over every quality for butter, given either to Tom Fitzgerald[1] or Charles Sugrue, for butter delivered in all September, and should butter rise higher than the present quality—that is more than two shillings per hundredweight—before the 1st of December, I will allow the difference and do you allow the tenants accordingly. 4^{thly} Get John Connell to go to every farm and sell off all extra and unproductive dry stock, otherwise the tenants will accumulate too much of that kind of stock and all will be likely to perish in the spring. Allow the tenants 2$^{s.}$ for every pound sterling they pay you out of the price of stock sold this or the next month. 5^{thly} Exert yourself as much as possible to send money here for James Sugrue for me. . . .

. . . James Sugrue will settle the College[2] gale here but of that you need say nothing. All you need do is to send him the money as fast as you can. . . .

SOURCE : O'Connell MSS, UCD

1   Thomas Fitzgerald, Mallow Lane, Cork, butter merchant. Married Kitty McCarthy.
2   Trinity College, Dublin.

980

From Arthur Sandes[1] to Merrion Square

Quito, 10 September 1822

Sir,

Although I have not the honour of a personal acquaintance, I feel it my painful duty to announce to you the death of your relative, Mr. Maurice O'Connell, Lieutenant in the Regiment under my command, who fell a victim to a malignant fever on the 2d of April last. Brave, generous, sincere and possessing qualities which raise the esteem and talents which arrest the attention of mankind, Mr. O'Connell's character was truly Irish, uniting in it all those virtues for which the sons of our country are so justly celebrated, being always worthy of his ancient and honourable name and of that love of liberty which had engaged him in the defence of an oppressed people. . . .

[Additional tributes to his ability, popularity, etc.]

As a friend to liberty you will be pleased to hear of the success of the last campaign . . . the Spaniards having solely possession of Puerto Carello. All other parts of the country enjoy a state of the most profound tranquillity and the inhabitants are beginning to reap the fruit of the numerous sacrifices which they have made to emancipate themselves from the tyranny of Spain. . . .

P.S. I request you will do me the favour to let my friends in Kerry know that I am well.

SOURCE : O'Connell MSS, UCD

1 Arthur Sandes (1793-1832), Greenville, Co. Kerry; veteran of the Napoleonic Wars; commander of the 1st Venezuelan Rifles, a unit of the first expedition to South America; colonel in Venezuelan army, 1822, and brigadier-general, 1825; later a general in Ecuador, where he married and died. An Irish speaker. A street was named after him in Quito.

981

To James Sugrue, 3 Cooke's Lane, Watling Street, Dublin

Bordeaux, 7 October 1822

My dear James,

Charles McCarthy[1] carries with him two parcels of law papers. Get my clerk Connor to deliver them. He lives at No. 12 Trinity St. . . .

I have drawn upon you for £30. Accept the bill. I will be myself in Dublin before it can become due.

Pau did not agree with my family. We are on our way to Tours. We have taken a furnished house there for six months for £72. My stay there will be very short. I will see you, please God, early in November, certainly before the first business day of term.

My opinion of France and Frenchmen is not raised by a near inspection. Their climate is to me detestable. Nor can I endure the parched and sunburned appearance of the country. After all, poor Ireland is the spot if she had but justice. The French seem very discontented. In truth they are full of all manner of uncharitableness. The Bourbons are indeed far from being popular. I should not be surprised to hear one day of their starting a new race of revolution.

[P.S.] What a treat an Irish newspaper would be to me.

SOURCE : NLI, MSS 5759

1 Captain of the vessel *Erin*.

982

To his wife, 'Dame Irlandaise', No. 6 Rue de la Guerche, à Tours, Dept. de L'Indre & Loire

Merrion Square, Thursday, 19 [20, 21 and 23] December 1822

[No salutation]

. . . We have had great *work* since I wrote on Tuesday. The City is *wild* about addresses[1] to Lord Wellesley. The Lord Mayor has called an aggregate for tomorrow at the Exchange, and *I* thought the best course was to sink the Catholic meeting into the general body of the citizens. According I called this day a meeting for that purpose. Lord Killeen was in the chair.

I was, as usual, opposed by Nic Mahon and by Eneas Mac-Donnell. We had great debating and a division on which *we* had a great majority. The result is that we all go to the Exchange tomorrow, and I hope we will have a *great day* for Ireland. Marquis Wellesley is most highly indignant. His physician has been examined before the Privy Council and I am told swears that the piece of timber which was flung at him would have been as mortal as a pistol bullet had it been thrown half a foot lower. It broke, it seems, part of the panel. I do not think there ever was the least opportunity of putting down the Orange faction till now, but now, unless we throw away the game we have in our hands, it will reduce the matter to this. Either the government must put down the Orangemen or be put down by them. There is no other alternative. The Lord Mayor, Fleming,[2] is high in the patriotic interest. It is hoped he will soon be placed at the head of the police in the room of Alderman Darley.

Friday, 20 December

I had written the first page last night and was going to bed when Hugh O'Connor of Mountjoy Square came for me to join a committee at Milliken's to assist in preparing an address, etc. I was obliged to go and listen to several speeches from Sir A. Bradley King and was kept up until after midnight. We were at it in [the] morning again and at length *agreed to disagree,* and so away we went to the meeting—the Lord Mayor took the chair at twelve. The speakers were the Duke of Leinster, Lord Cloncurry, Sir Frederick Flood,[3] Sir Charles Morgan,[4] Luke White,[5] Mr. Guinness,[6] Governor of the Bank [of Ireland], O'Conor Don, Hugh O'Connor, one Daniel O'Connell, the two Grattans,[7] Counsellors Leader, Sheil and MacDonnell. There never was such a meeting in Ireland. The Exchange was crowded to the greatest excess. I was the only person who made himself heard throughout. There was the greatest unanimity and good feeling, and the Orange faction were branded with deserved reprobation. Not a human being to defend the miscreants or to say one word in their favour. They had not the courage to utter even a single hiss or a solitary no. In short, darling, it was a great day for Ireland. I never saw any public day like it. I think it is the commencement of better days and more cheering scenes. But after all, Darling, what can or ought to cheer me as I have passed another post without hearing. Oh Mary, it makes me sad indeed. Indeed, love, you punish me too much. However *tomorrow*. This is the 11th day since I heard from you, own dearest Mary.

Saturday, 21 December

. . . The turn politics are taking in this town is really surprising. It is not, I hope, superstitious to call it providential. I never thought the Orangemen would have committed themselves as they have done. Only think that the ruffians who are taken up[8] for attacking the Lord-Lieutenant, at least the leaders of them who are in Newgate, are first cousins of one of the Sheriffs. His name is Thorpe, and he is the scoundrel who at his dinner turned away the Secretary to the Lord-Lieutenant sooner than give up his toast of ' the Glorious Memory '. You may imagine what a curious revolution it is in Dublin when the Catholics are admitted to be the only genuine loyalists. For the first time has this truth reached the Castle. Every one of the Orange rascals is now disavowing his tenets and, if things continue in the present temper, there will be no finding out or discovering an Orangeman for love or money. The Corporation presented their address this day. Ours is to be presented on Tuesday. I believe we shall have an immense procession. We go from the Mansion House to the Castle. I suppose I shall get another shake hands from His Excellency. If we had hired at large wages the Orangemen, they would not have done our business half so well. . . . Pray for me, darling, at your devotions and Communion. Why, my dearest love, should you not become a weekly communicant? It is but a little trouble, love, and it is a great happiness. Own darling, good night. God bless you.

Monday, 23 December

. . . We are to go up tomorrow to the Castle in great state. The Committee are to be in court dress so that I shall have this second turn out of my court dress [about one word missing] but I will not wear a powdered wig. I will take Maurice with me in plain clothes. The only persons in full costume being the Committee of 21. . . . I am anxious to know how the Lord-Lieutenant will receive me *after* my letter.[9] But I hope my late *loyalty* will compensate for the letter. If it does not, why then, darling, I do not care a two penny ticket for all the Lord-Lieutenants and viceroys and kings to boot in Europe. You ask me if there is to be war between France and Spain. I think, darling, that there will. I do not see how the Legitimates[10] can possibly allow Spain to be free unless she is so in full despite of her miscreants. To be sure it is a perilous thing to attack Spain, that it is, and therefore I have my doubts, and sometimes strong doubts. But upon the whole I think there *must* be war.[11] It would be an excuse for letting out the paper money again. We shall, I believe, darling, have war. And even as it may seem to bring you the more speedily home I shall not be sorry for it. I mean as far as I am individually inclined to yield to my private feelings. . . .

[P.S.] You will be surprised to hear that I am great favourite with the *Dublin Evening Post*.[12] Indeed I believe the mode in which I have taken up this business has pleased everybody. There is novelty in being puffed off in the [*Dublin Evening*] *Post*. As to the Orangemen, it is actually ludicrous to see the way in which they are backing out of this affair. They are a paltry set and I hope will soon cease to have any political influence or existence. At all events the present occurrence can do nothing but good. . . .

SOURCE : Fitz-Simon Papers

1 The presence of Wellesley at a performance of Oliver Goldsmith's *She Stoops to Conquer* at the New Theatre Royal, Dublin, on 14 December 1822, produced a riot by Orangemen in which a bottle was thrown at the lord-lieutenant during the playing of ' God Save the King '. The lord mayor was petitioned to call a meeting of citizens for the purpose of adopting an address of support to the lord-lieutenant. The Catholics met at D'Arcy's Tavern on 19 December and resolved to join the rest of the citizens at the ' Grand Public Meeting ' which by now the lord mayor had arranged at the Royal Exchange for the following day (*FJ*, 14-21 Dec. 1822).

2 John Smyth Fleming, Smock Alley, Dublin; alderman, 1816-41; lord mayor of Dublin, 1823. He had forbidden the traditional 12 July decoration of King William's statue in College Green (*DEP*, 2 Nov. 1822).

3 Sir Frederick Flood (1741-1824), Banna Lodge, Camolin, Co. Wexford; M.P. for Co. Wexford, 1812-18; created baronet, 1780.

4 Sir Charles Morgan, second baronet (1760-1846), M.P. for Brecon, 1787-96; Monmouth Co., 1796-1831. See *DNB*.

5 Luke White (c. 1740-1824), 6 Gardiner's Row, Dublin, and Woodlands, Co. Dublin. Wealthy bookseller and publisher. M.P. for Co. Leitrim, 1812-24. Father of first Baron Annaly.

6   Arthur Guinness, J.P. (1768-1855), Beaumont House, Co. Dublin,
    and 33 Granby Row, Dublin; second son of the founder of
    Guinness's brewery whom he succeeded as head of the firm in
    1803. Director of the Bank of Ireland, 1808-39; governor, 1820-22;
    supporter of Catholic Emancipation and one of the five treasurers
    of the O'Connell testimonial fund, 1829.
7   James and Henry Grattan.
8   A number of alleged culprits were lodged in Newgate Jail, Dublin,
    on 15 December (*FJ*, 16, 17 Dec. 1822). The charges preferred
    against them for conspiracy to riot and simple riot were eventually,
    in effect, dismissed by the city grand jury (*FJ*, 3 Jan. 1823).
9   Probably his public letter to Wellesley of 11 July 1822; *DEP*,
    13 July 1822.
10 That is, those in France like Chateaubriand who disliked the principles of the French Revolution and supported French intervention
    in Spain in order to restore the full authority of the Spanish
    monarchy.
11 This prediction proved to be correct. On 7 April 1823 a French army
    invaded Spain to restore the authority of her Bourbon king,
    Ferdinand VII.
12 The editorial in the issue of 21 December, which was devoted
    mainly to a lengthy report of the previous day's meeting, eulogized
    O'Connell, adding that ' as no man possesses more influence when
    he exerts himself in the right way, we are convinced that no man
    can speak to the public with greater effect '.

983

To his wife at Tours

Merrion Square, 26 [27 and 31]
December 1822

My own darling Love,

. . . On Tuesday the 24th my last letter went off to you.
On that day we assembled at the Mayor's and went up in great
procession at about two o'clock to the Castle. I was in Court
dress but with an unpowdered wig. There were at least from
twenty to thirty in Court dresses, the rest in plain clothes. The
Duke of Leinster and Lord Meath were of the party. Dr. Troy
and Dr. Murray were in the dresses in which the King received
them. The scene at the Castle began with a great scramble for
refreshments. It was quite a bear garden. Of course I kept free
of that scene. There was a quantity of wine and cakes
demolished in high style and a college lad, tall and strong in

his cap and gown, got his share of the wine and distinguished himself afterwards by translating his Connaught dialect of broken English into worse Latin to everybody he could get to listen to him. The Lord-Lieutenant arrived about three o'clock. We were then ushered into a large room called St. Patrick's Hall. It has rising seats at the sides, three rows one above the other, a canopy and throne at the end. The seats were crowded. The committee[1] filled the centre of the room. The Lord-Lieutenant ordered a chair for Dr. Troy. My worthy collegian fell in with the Committee and got talking his bad Latin. I never saw a more vulgar hound. The Lord-Lieutenant was surrounded by a suite in superb uniforms. The address was badly read by the Mayor, the answer admirably delivered by the Marquis and there were bursts of applause which I believe to be very much out of rule. Then there was a levée at which all those in Court dress were admitted. My friend the collegian got in by means of his cap and gown and notwithstanding his thick shoes, and I believe, worsted stockings. As the Lord-Lieutenant went round the circle bowing to each of us, the collegian followed with his nose occasionally almost in the Marquis' face. It was provoking and ludicrous. At last he fastened on Dr. Troy who could not get rid of him until I interfered and took him off. Then an aide-de-camp came and got a beefeater or battle-axe guard man to take my worthy collegian into custody and turn him out. If I had my children at home I would make them laugh for an hour at the grotesque and impudent conduct of the fellow. It has not been noticed in any newspapers but it was not the less laughable and provoking. I do not think I shall soon forget the figure of *the animal*. The Lord-Lieutenant received us most kindly. His answer was admirable. In short, every thing in this respect is going on as well as possible. Maurice made his first appearance at the Castle and drank a couple of glasses of *royal* wine. Yesterday in the evening Maurice and I rode out to Glencullen where we dined and slept. Oh, darling, it is beautifully cold. There never was such weather in Ireland. The wind is south-east, cold, clear, sharp and delightful. I walked in this morning from Glencullen and let O'Mara's messenger ride the horse. I take it to be full nine miles for it cost me two hours and a half to walk it and I ran a great deal of the first two miles. I afterwards refreshed myself with a warm bath, the first bath by the by which I have taken since I returned to Ireland. My legs are battered, I mean my feet, from the walk. I dined on a brace of wild ducks that I got from Kerry. . . . I fear I will not be able to go to Kerry for a full week yet, and I am beginning to be impatient for another letter from you. Darling heart, good night.

Friday, 27 December.

I spent my day at home working for you and my children. Mrs. Blaquiere[2] called here this day but I did not see her. Her husband who used to ride about on a white horse (you remember he and his former wife were visitors of ours in Westland Row) is confined in a madhouse. . . . We have a strong report that the King is married or going to marry a daughter of Marquis Conyngham and for my part I believe that there is some truth in the report. It would be a delightful thing to keep the Duke of York from all chance of the throne. . . . This evening there came a letter for him [Maurice] from Morgan which I opened and read. I could not for the life of me avoid reading a letter from Tours, from Tours in which my heart is wrapt. Tell my own own Danny that I will write to him the moment I hear that he can read. . . . I do not think I shall be able to leave this for Kerry before the 6th of January and I must be back again in one fortnight. I wish I could avoid going down at all. . . . Tell Ellen that Moore's *Loves of the Angels*[3] is come out. I got it a while ago and read it in half an hour. It is only an account of three angels that fell in love with three ladies and although the subject is not very promising it is really an exquisitely beautiful little poem. A separated husband and wife are described and the evils of separation,

> All this they bear but not the less
> Have moments rich in happiness
> Blest meetings after many a day
> Of widowhood past far away
> When the loved fair again is seen.

This is what your husband looks to as the recompense of this his solitary widowhood. Oh, how I long to see again the loved face of my Mary and those of my loved girls and boys. How I wish I was reading this poem for them. It is short, a mere trifle for such a poet, but exquisitely sweet and not stained with a single indelicate thought. The poetry is full of Moore's magic. In spite of the *Edinburgh Review* Moore is the very prince of poets. There is more melody and harmony in his versification than in any other poet I ever read.

All our accounts are warlike. You will certainly have war. Stock-jobbing is endeavouring to keep the fact out of sight but depend upon it you will have war. . . .

31 December

. . . Maurice and I have a round of invitations. We dine this day at Alderman McKenny's, tomorrow with Mr. Milliken,[4] the day after at Mr. Somers', the day after at Mr. Roose's, the lottery office keeper. I am also tomorrow to go up to the Park[5] on the occasion of presenting a Catholic address from Derry.[6] . . . Tell my own Dan that I cannot write to him until I get a certificate in due form from Ellen that he can read, for it would be very idle to write directly to a boy who could not read. I submit that to his own good sense and delicacy. I got also this day a letter from poor Devereux[7] from Santa Fé de Bogota dated in July last. He is coming home to ' his idol '. He writes in his usual strain. He is to bring home £100,000, no less I assure you. They say in Kerry that ' half would not be bad '. There is also a letter for Morgan in which Devereux promises to bring Morgan home his pay and prize money. I believe Morgan will not buy many cakes with the remittance. What you will be glad of is to hear that little Maurice[8] is well and has a company in Sandes' Regiment. Colonel Hall[9] however is no more. Poor fellow! He was not, however, so attentive to Morgan as I think he might have been. There is also some Featherstone dead.[10] I do not know who he was. I believe I will not be able to go at all to Kerry. . . .

SOURCE : Fitz-Simon Papers

1 The presentation of the loyal address to the lord-lieutenant was in the hands of an *ad hoc* committee of twenty-one, set up at the Royal Exchange meeting of 20 December (see letter 982, note 1).

2 Eliza, second daughter of William Roper, Rathfarnham Castle, Co. Dublin. Married 1818 Peter Boyle de Blaquiere, son of first Baron de Blaquiere.

3 Published on 23 December and attacked in the leading journals on religious grounds. See Wilfred S. Dowden, ed., *The Letters of Thomas Moore*, 2 vols. (Oxford 1964), II, 512 n.

4 Richard Milliken, 104 Grafton Street, Dublin; bookseller to the king and to Dublin University.

5 Phoenix Park, where the vice-regal residence was situated.

6 Unidentified, but possibly in support of the lord-lieutenant as was the Kerry address. See letter 987, note 6.

7 Devereux was at this time endeavouring to collect the cost of his expedition from the government of Gran Colombia.

8 Maurice O'Connell of the Irish Legion (see letter 828, note 3).

9 See note 10.

10 This information seems to be inaccurate. Col. Francis Hall was assassinated in Quito, Ecuador, in 1833. There is no Featherstone listed among the legion. There is, however, a George Featherston-haugh who was killed at the battle of Bompona on 7 April 1822. O'Connell seems to have confused Hall with Featherstonhaugh, who sailed with Wilson's Hussars to Venezuela in 1818 as an artillery officer and later joined the Rifles. The mistake about his death arises from Devereux's letter of 16 July 1822 to Morgan O'Connell which was included in a letter of the same date to O'Connell. The letter reads: ' Poor Featherstone Hall is gone. Col. Hall still remains at Caraccas at the head of the Topographical Department of the Republic ' (Fitz-Simon Papers).

984

To John Kent Johnston,[1] 1 Eden Quay

Merrion Square, 28 December 1822

My dear Sir,

. . . I will give you . . . a copy of the memorial of the conveyance[2] under which my father took the fee simple lands. They were sequestered during the usurpation of Cromwell and granted to Sir William Petty, an ancestor to the present Marquis of Lansdowne. They were let for three lives dependent on 99 years renewable for ever at small rents and fines about the year 1694, and the interest in these leases vested in my father who obtained the last renewal in 1795.[3] In the year 1807 the present Marquis of Lansdowne, then Lord Henry Petty, advertised the sale of the fee, and my father became the purchaser of his own lands at 25 years purchase. The convey-ance of the fee was accordingly executed to him and it recites the title fully. As soon as the registry office opens in the ensuing week you shall have this statement in *professional* form with the documents necessary to sustain it. . . . The lands are: Carhen house and demesne containing 600 acres at the least; Upper Liss, Lower Liss with the mill and forge holdings. . . .

SOURCE : O'Connell MSS, UCD

1 Agent to the European Life Insurance and Annuity Co. of London.

2 O'Connell was trying to raise a loan from the European Life

Insurance and Annuity Co. of London on a mortgage of part of
his landed estate.
3 The 'Act to prevent the further Growth of Popery' of 1703
(2 Anne c. 6), which, among other things, prohibited Catholics
from taking leases for more than thirty-one years, was not retro-
spective. Thus a lease held by a Catholic, such as the one described
by O'Connell in the above letter, was free from interference throughout the eighteenth century.

985

To John Primrose, Jr., Hillgrove

Merrion Square, 31 December 1822

My dear John,

I got your letter and am very much obliged to you for your
exertions. I got credit in account from James Sugrue for £400
remitted by you to him. It was an immense deal under the
circumstances. What have you done since?

I expected to be able to go down this vacation and as yet
do not despair. . . . Let me know at the same time if you
have any money to send me. I am not pressing although I
would not refuse money nor would I at all distress the people
beyond that pressure which they require to make them pay
anything. Give a receipt in full to any man who you think acts
honestly and pays you what he can and give the people such
abatements as you deem necessary. I desire, in truth, nothing
but what they can fairly give me. . . .

SOURCE : O'Connell MSS, UCD

986

To Myles McSwiney[1]

Merrion Square, 31 December 1822

My dear Myles,

Give John Primrose every deed and lease of mine in your
possession. I implore of you to give them without delay.

Yours ever affectionately,

Daniel O'Connell

SOURCE : O'Connell MSS, UCD
1 This letter was appended to letter 985.

987

To his wife at Tours

Merrion Square, 8 [and 9] January 1823

My own darli ıg Mary,

. . . I could not beforehand believe it possible that I should
pass an entire week in health and spirits without writing a
word to my Mary. The fact is, heart, that I was a bit of an old
rake. I dined out almost every day [one or two words illegible]
I then went to bed late. I had neither evening nor morning
to write to you in. On Tuesday the 31st of December, *we* dined
with Alderman McKenny. He had a large party. Champagne
and very fine burgundy. Maurice stayed there dancing until
five in the morning. New Year's Day we dined with Mr.
Milliken in Grafton St. When his little children began to come
in I thought they would never stop. It really had a comical
effect to see them enter one by one. The last was a sweet little
duck one year and a half old, a fine fat, merry little girl walking in as stout as the rest. On Thursday I dined at Mr. Somers'
who has taken the corner house of Upper Mount St. here near
us. Its drawing-room is in this square. Dan Mahony of Dunloe
Castle dined there . . . on Friday I dined with Roose[1] . . .
Sunday we dined [about three words illegible] at Rice Hussey's
and met Mr. Spring Rice [about two words illegible] patriot.
Only think that the Corporation of Dublin have voted him his
freedom and presented it to him in great state.[2] We had this
day a very respectable meeting[3] of the County of Dublin. I
never in my life was so pleased with any meeting. It went off
in the very best style. We carried everything. There was a
swaddling looking young parson[4] who spoke a speech in
defence of the Orangemen. He would not have been heard but
for me, I believe. However I was even with him by treating
him to a sermon by way of reply to the great amusement and
delight of the meeting. I ended by giving him a text to preach
on next Sunday. We carried our resolutions and a beautiful
address drawn up by young Curran. I threw in a few slight
points into it in order to make it bear the more strongly on
the Orangemen [several lines illegible] Plunket was in a
beautiful rage and Lord [? Wellesley] continues so. They are
to proceed now by a criminal information and we shall have
some pleasant work next term [about two words illegible]
Orangemen. I thought it better not to give any [? annoyance]

as our enemies are doing our business. Is it not a delight [one or two words illegible] to have the Orangemen[5] and the Government at daggers [? drawn]? I believe I am to dine at the Park with the Lord-Lieutenant [one or two words illegible] as he recovers from a slight indisposition under which [about two words illegible] and he sent me a particular apology for not having [about one word illegible] me at his last levée. . . .

Thursday, 9 January

Darling, I had a short time ago to open the door for my brother John who came up in the night coach. He came with the Kerry address[6] and is now asleep in my bed. . . . Dublin is as dull as anything can be. . . .

SOURCE : Fitz-Simon Papers

1 David C. Roose (died 1836), stockbroker and state lottery office keeper, 7 Upper Fitzwilliam Street, Dublin; knighted, 1830. Roose is credited with having suggested to P. V. FitzPatrick on 22 June 1828 that O'Connell should stand in the forthcoming by-election for Co. Clare. FitzPatrick immediately conveyed the suggestion to O'Connell whose first reaction was not enthusiastic. The idea that a Catholic should confront the Penal Laws by standing for parliament had been asserted by John Keogh (FitzPatrick, Corr., I, 159-61).

2 Not reported in the newspapers.

3 A meeting of the freeholders of Co. Dublin in Kilmainham courthouse on 8 January 1823, held to deplore the recent outrage on Wellesley (see letter 982) and to express support for his administration (FJ and DEP, 9 Jan. 1823).

4 Edward Tighe Gregory, Rutland Street, Dublin (born c. 1793), formerly curate of St. Dolough's, Co. Dublin; author of pamphlets on religious and political topics.

5 Upon the city grand jury's dismissing the bills of indictment against the Orangemen allegedly responsible for the outrage on Wellesley (see letter 982), Plunket as attorney-general filed new charges against six of them. Their trial, which began in the court of king's bench on 3 February 1823 and lasted five days, ended in the acquittal of one and the disagreement of the jury in the cases of the other five. See Richard Wilson Greene, A Report of the Trial of James Forbes, etc. for a Conspiracy to Create a Riot (Dublin 1823).

6 'The gentry, clergy and freeholders of the County of Kerry' were presenting to the lord-lieutenant an address expressing indignation 'at the late base and traitorous attack on your Excellency's person' and offering congratulations 'upon the fortunate miscarriage of the vile attempt' (FJ, 28 Jan. 1823). Other counties presented similar addresses.

988

To his wife at Tours

Merrion Square, 11 [and 15] January 1823

My own darling love,

I begin my *next* letter to you being at present determined
not to allow any Tuesday to pass over without sending off a
letter. I am, darling to dine this day with the Lord-Lieutenant,
of course by invitation. I go in Arthur Blennerhassett's[1] carriage
or, rather, I believe, Harry Grady's. Blake is in town and lives
at the Park. I will before I close this letter give you an account
of the ' Castle '. Everything is going on as well as possible. The
Orangemen are doing their own business more effectually than
we could. I really expect to be emancipated this sessions.
Canning is become a great favourite with the King and is now
seriously determined on bringing forward the Catholic question. It will come on in an early part of the sessions, and who
knows but I would be able to ' frank ' my letters before that
sessions are over. At all events, darling, I look forward with
hope to the ensuing sessions. The ministry cannot afford to
leave Ireland as she is. The radicals in England are pressing
on them *hard*. The taxes are becoming very unproductive. The
interest of the debt cannot be paid, and we certainly are on the
eve of great events whilst I have taken my station in the midst
of moderation, good temper and conciliation. It really succeeds
admirably. Infinitely better than violence, and you may rely
on it, love, that I do not sacrifice one atom of principle. . . .
On Thursday we had a great dinner at Morrison's given by
the Chamber of Commerce. Spring Rice was there and he and
your humble servant made *sundry* speeches. It was a mixture
of all parties and went off admirably. If I can add a line when I
come in this night I will.

Wednesday, 15 January

. . . The fact is, darling, I never was anything like so much
employed. I refuse as much business as would be sufficient for
another lawyer. . . . Well, darling, I dined at the Park on
Saturday. You may believe I kept the abstinence. I went in
Arthur Blennerhassett's carriage. The state certainly is dignified. We were received by three livery servants at the outwards
door who demanded our names and announced us, as it seemed

to me, to persons at both sides of an elegant hall. We then [? were shown] into a handsome antechamber where one of the ushers attended. He again got our names and showed us into a spacious and very elegant drawing-room where we were introduced to the Aide-de-Camp in waiting. In this room we remained until dinner. The company consisted of about twenty persons exclusive of the Lord-Lieutenant's staff and officers or household. Judge Day, the Knight of Kerry, etc., were of the party. The Lord-Lieutenant continued too ill to dine with us. About seven we were shown across another room, in which there was an excellent band of music, to the dinner room. The service of gilt plate is really [one word missing]. Of course the whole dinner service was plate. The [? gilt] service, except plates, which were china, was in gold. The knives were gold with agate handles. I dined principally of a fine turbot. The dessert itself was excellent and abundance of ices. The champagne was good as any I ever drank and in great quantities. One of the footmen, perceiving I was observing the fast, took special care to let me know everything of that description at the table. It was, on the whole, a new scene to me and one a good deal gratifying. The Lord-Lieutenant is, thank God, convalescent. Are you not surprised at my writing so much about a dinner? I had a great deal of conversation with his private Secretary, Capt. Johnson.[2] I never abused the Orangemen in my days of what they called intemperance with half the violence with which they are now abused at the Castle. It is delightful to see these changes. Plunket brings on our question early in the Sessions. Now or never. My brother John has no Kerry news save that the eldest son of Frederick Mullins[3] is going to marry one of black Arthur's daughters. He is a fine young fellow of nineteen and his mother is said to be wild at this sacrifice. The old gentleman at Derrynane has had a slight attack about the heart, but it is over without danger or much pain. Edward Fitzgerald, who lives at Kenneigh where John Hayes resided, was robbed last week by seven armed men, undisguised. It it said they intended to rob Derrynane, but luckily they have been detected and four of them lodged in gaol. They were strangers and were harboured by a tenant of John Segerson's of Cove. . . . How are poor Hannah and Julia? How does the cold weather agree with Julia? Hannah bustles about so as to be able to bear it better. John's[4] wife is breeding, but James' wife is not although he told me last summer he thought she was. I suppose he will have but a very small family.

That is what as a prudent fellow he would much like. I suppose he is gone off for Derrynane. It was a most audacious robbery at Fitzgerald's.[5] The robbers came in at about nine o'clock while the family were at cards in the parlour. They got but £15.

SOURCE : Fitz-Simon Papers

1 Probably Arthur Blennerhassett, Jr., of Elmgrove and later of Ballyseedy, Tralee; high sheriff of Kerry, 1821; M.P. for Co. Kerry, 1837-41. Married Frances Deane, daughter of Henry Deane Grady.

2 Capt. Edward I. Johnston, private secretary to the lord-lieutenant Marquis Wellesley, 1822-23.

3 Probably Rev. Frederick Ferriter Mullins (born 1778) whose eldest son, Frederick W. Mullins, was nineteen. This marriage apparently did not take place.

4 His brother.

5 Of Kenneigh, Waterville, Co. Kerry.

989

From his brother James to Merrion Square

Killarney, 12 January 1823

My Dear Dan,

. . . I was delighted to hear from Roger O'Sullivan that your professional *income* was greater for the year 1822 than ever it was, so that with such resources, if you only *have fortitude* enough to persevere in living as you do at present for three or four years, you will not only be able to avoid *those damned kites and bills* but actually pay a large part of your bond debts. . . .

Roger O'Sullivan showed your letter to Kit Gallwey[1] which annoyed Gallwey very much as you say you suppose he *can now get the money* for Lord Kenmare elsewhere and does not wish to take my uncle's. Indeed, I think Roger ought not to have shown your letter. As a fox hunter or *half-pay officer he may do* so but by indiscretion of this kind he is not likely to add much to his business *as an attorney*. The fact is poor Gallwey has a most difficult card to play with *these damned* trustees of Lord Kenmare's who, I fear, are anxious to deprive him of the agency and he only waits their sanction to take the money.

SOURCE : O'Connell MSS, UCD
1   Christopher Gallwey, J.P. (1781-1861), eldest son of Thomas Gallwey
    and Maria Mahony (Dunloe); land agent to earl of Kenmare, 1817-61.
    Married Lucy Grehan.

990

To his wife at Tours

Merrion Square, Friday, 17 [and 22]
January 1823

My own darling Mary,

. . . My brother John continues here still but I believe he
will soon be relieved as the Lord-Lieutenant is much better.[1]
John is very impatient to be back again to his family. No blame
to him. Where can anybody be well except with his
family. . . .

There is nothing stirring here. The Orangemen are circulating *squibs* of all kinds, play-bills, ' racing calendars ', etc.
It is however pleasant to see them at daggers drawn with Government. Plunket has promised me to bring on the Catholic
question the very first week of the ensuing sessions. I have read
Peveril of the Peak[2] and will send it to you by Mr. Sweetman.
I think you will like it extremely. It will be one of his most
popular novels and yet it does not please me as much even as
the last, although this certainly is a highly amusing book. It
does not resemble any one of his former productions. It has no
' Meg Merrilies '[3] of any kind. Its date is from shortly before
the Restoration until the close of Titus Oates' plot. You may
imagine how hurried I must have been when I allowed Maurice
and John to read it before me, but I got hold of it last and
finished it, to do which I was obliged to sit up until a quarter
before five this morning.

Wednesday, 22nd January.

. . . At length my brother John has got leave to go home.
The Lord-Lieutenant received the Kerry and Tralee addresses
yesterday. John and I took a coach, *not* a hackney, and gave a
seat to Arthur Blennerhassett. Judge Day, the Knight [of
Kerry], Maurice King[4] and Maurice Leyne[5] formed with us the
deputation. Lord Wellesley was very civil to me. He shook
hands with me twice and said civil things. He is a very nice old
gentleman, full of fire and spirit and with all the appearance of

a decided character. We were kept in an antechamber some
time where we got refreshments. He read his answers distinctly
and was plainly affected by our County address. . . . [? They]
have not as yet dismissed a single Orangeman from office and,
until they do, I will not give them credit for their good wishes.
I have reason to think that the Orangemen are quite determined
to give the government a bit of a fright. They are, it is said,
making their musters. I have just sent an offer to government
to raise a regiment of 1,000 men for them in Dublin so that, if
accepted, when I go to you next I will sport for my children
my major's uniform. Seriously, darling, I have made the offer
and perhaps it would be accepted. If it be, we will take the
uniform of the Guards. The fact is the Orangemen are growing
daily more audacious and it would be quite a triumph to put
them down. How *my* poor troops would be delighted to be
hunting Orangemen. I confess it would amuse me to have one
good day's running after the rascals. I have written a letter to
Blake which I believe and hope he will show to some of the
ministry on the subject of the state of the Orange party. Master
Ellis is very busy, they say, organizing his gang. The fact is,
love, that if they do not receive a check from Government they
will put down the Government itself. My brother John went
off this morning. Maurice got through his examination tolerably well but, of course, did not go near the premium. He has
now no further chance because the next, which will be the
final examination for his degree, is one in which no premium
is or can be given to any part of the class. He will then go to
London and keep his Easter term and, as Trinity term commences in a fortnight after the Easter, he had better, I think,
keep both before he joins you. This, however, shall be as you
please. I do not either like to leave my girls without a male
protector when my darling Morgan shall have left you. One
cannot possibly be too strict and exact amongst those rascally
French. I know my darling girls are delicacy personified, but
it is not possible to be half guarded enough at their time of life.
I will therefore let you have Maurice as soon after Morgan
leaves you as possible. It will be another pang to my heart to
part with Maurice but that cannot be helped. It is for his good
and it would be much for his good if he would avail himself of
the leisure Tours would afford him to study Law, History,
Mathematics and Chemistry. . . . When you come down in
Boulanger Cartion's[6] books to 1,000 francs, let me know. I
will instantly tell you how you are to be replenished. I really

am surprised at your having held out so long on the money I
left you. Darling, I know how anxious you are to be an
economist and I thank you for it. . . .

SOURCE : Fitz-Simon Papers
1 See letter 987, note 6.
2 By Sir Walter Scott (Edinburgh 1822).
3 A character in Walter Scott's *Guy Mannering; or, The Astrologer,*
   first published in 1815.
4 Probably Maurice King, attorney, The Mall, Tralee.
5 Maurice Leyne (1791-1865), second son of Maurice Leyne, M.D.,
   Tralee.
6 Boulanger Cartion, a banker in Tours.

991

To his wife at Tours

[Merrion Square], Wednesday, 22 [24, 25,
26 and 27] January 1823

My own darling Mary,

Your letter of the 13th I got this evening. . . . You used
to get letters at that vile Pau in 12 days, but I suppose the
French detain the letters in their offices and probably read some
of them. It is likely enough. They are capable of anything. . . .
As to the servant maid, she is getting on very well. I like her
although James[1] does not. He has made two or three attempts
to get me to part with her and even got Maurice to apply or,
rather, suggest that she was not fit, but the woman is orderly
and quiet and unobtrusive, dresses my dinner sufficiently.
Besides she is steady, advanced in life and, I am told, religious,
and here she shall, please God, remain until *my commander*
is reinstated in authority here. Do you know the cocknosed
personage I allude to?

Friday, 24 January

Two days of term are over, two busy but bitterly cold days.
We have the severest frost I can remember. There was more
snow in the year 1813, but there was not such a strong easterly
wind with constant freezing at night. The weather, however, is
to me very pleasing as far as I am myself concerned. I wear
my large cloak cut sufficient short for walking. It is very warm
and I carry an oak stick to prevent a fall on the ice and so walk

off or, rather, trot to court. The Attorney-General had made all his arrangements to try the Orangemen this term.[2] I thought they would not be tried until Easter term but I find that there was this day an order made which ensures that the scoundrels will be tried within this term. If the Attorney-General does not take care he will have an Orange jury packed upon him as sure as he lives, but I am tired of giving cautions. You ask me, darling, about my debts. I am paying them off by degrees. They were greater than you had any idea of. They were of two kinds, bills and bonds. The bond debts require little beside the payment of interest and insurance, but in that way they run away with a load of money without getting lighter in themselves. The bills must be paid to the hour. I have made but little way hitherto with the bonds but I have worked myself a great deal through the bills. Tradesmen were constantly drawing on me and I had an immense number of that kind to pay while fresh ones were daily accumulating. At present there is no accumulation and I promise you I am paying off the old. During Novr. and Decr. I paid £611 some shillings without getting a penny save out of my profession—a great deal for two months and I began then with a solitary pound and some silver which was all I had about me when Maurice and I arrived here. By May-day I expect to be pretty well over matters of this description, I mean bills, and then, darling I will *attack* the bonds. Every hundred pounds I receive shall instantly go to lighten the interest. Alas, I fear it will take another year to complete my *freedom* but, darling, another year will do it. And I never again will conceal a thought of mine from you. It was to save you from mental suffering that I was guilty of concealment. The fact is that I always looked to the resources to come from my Uncle Maurice's succession as the means of paying off, and I went in debt on that speculation. God forgive me if even I was ever so criminal as to wish for his death. I hope I have been in some measure punished for it, and I trust none of my family will ever entertain such a wish. I am sure, darling, you will not although, if he lives—and his health is good—my family must remain in France until next summer twelve month. Beyond that it cannot be necessary and at that time I will, please God, have my affairs in such order that I will show you my income and debts, if any, and we will live and manage accordingly. Darling, we will pay ready money for everything and upon no account will we run up bills of any kind. So much for a long history in reply to your questions. I have, sweetest, many and many a forgiveness to ask of you on this subject, but I appeal to your affections for my pardon.

Saturday, 25 January

Darling, there never was in my memory such weather as this known in Ireland. It is much colder than the Russian year —beginning of 1813. . . . You would laugh to see me go to court this day in my gallowses [sic] over my boots, my great cloak on, a white cravat over my neck handkerchief and a great cudgel in my hand. It is quite laborious to walk the streets. . . . I only go to Court and I really enjoy the cold. In fact I perceive it but little. . . . This is a bitter winter all over the Continent. Here the mails can with difficulty travel, and I think we are fairly in for another fortnight of this kind. . . . There is at present no political news. The English are busy and bustling and certainly there never was so much discontent afloat amongst them. I think they will press hard upon the Ministry this next sessions. I wish they would issue the bank-notes again until at least I had got rid of my debts. That is a selfish wish, darling, but it is not for myself alone that I feel. What a comfort to me if I had my wife and children about me. That is my first and last thought. Darling, keep up your spirits —all will, please God, be yet well. Let me know when you approach the last 1,000 francs. It is not possible to be a greater economist than you are. Maurice and I have got great presents of wild fowl. We make our dinner tomorrow of woodcock, teal and snipe from Kerry. We have a brace of County Clare woodcock for Monday.

Sunday, 26 January

. . . Can you conjecture why the Waters were removed from Tours? I am sincerely sorry for it both on their account and yours. I never saw any French lady I liked so well as Madame de Waters.[3] I suppose they were thought not to be ultra enough for the vile blockheads that are urging on the worthy but helpless old King to resign his throne and the re-establishment of religion for objects which would be pernicious if attained, and yet they seemed to me, and I saw and talked to them in confidence, to be as staunch Bourbonists as it was possible. You now see I was right when I told you there would be war. To be sure the state of England is an obstacle. You have no idea how they are boiling over in England. Cobbett and Hunt are carrying petitions and resolutions which five years ago would be called treason, and they are carrying these petitions at meetings of the *first* gentry in the land. In fact, darling, the ministers know not what to do nor the people either. I expect that the result must be favourable to the Catholics.

Monday, 27 January

. . . This is really a dismal day but *our* excellent fires and close rooms are so different from the French *gazebos* that we do not mind the cold. . . .

SOURCE : Fitz-Simon Papers
1 O'Connell's man-servant.
2 For the outrage upon Lord Wellesley (see letter 982).
3 Probably married to one of the Waters family whose ancestors came from Ballymacdoyle, Co. Kerry.

992

To William Conyngham Plunket

Merrion Square, 22 January 1823

Private

My dear Sir,

You will perhaps smile at the gravity with which I profess to have become an alarmist; but I cannot avoid having a strong belief that the Orangemen intend to make some exhibition of their force to overawe Lord Wellesley's Government. You well know that if such a thing be attempted, it is not in human nature that it should end in mere show. I have nothing of legal evidence, or even of a *tendency* to legal evidence, to offer to you on this subject. But I do myself believe it, more especially as Master Ellis and Mr. Saurin are so very active amongst their partisans. But these are matters on which, if there be any just reason for my *fears,* you must have better information than you could get from me, who, after all, *know* nothing, save from the sensation made amongst the Catholic population by the species of armed preparation of their Orange neighbours.

But my object is just to tell you that, should you deem it a wise or proper measure, it would be very easy to increase the yeomanry force of Dublin by a thousand or twelve hundred men, to be officered and armed by Government but without any kind of pay. I believe the Opposition noblemen resident near Dublin would take the command; and I am certain that it would be easy to get unexceptionable gentlemen, half of them Protestants, the other half Catholics, to become officers; and I will answer for the privates in forty-eight hours.

As they would take no pay, they would require to be called volunteers, not yeomanry. If you should deem this suggestion of any practical utility, you will make use of it; if not, forget it was made, and forgive me for taking up so much of your valuable time at this moment; and do not take the trouble of sending me any answer in the latter case.

SOURCE : Papers of Mrs. Nicholas Shorter

993

From his brother James to Merrion Square

Killarney, 23 January 1823

My Dear Dan,

. . . He [Hunting-Cap] had a most fortunate escape of not being robbed by the party that broke into Edward Fitzgerald's.[1] They came within a hundred yards of Derrynane House the same night Fitzgerald was robbed, but they then thought it too near day to break into the house and took up their lodgings near Cove, determined to rob John Segerson and my uncle next night. They were, as I presume you heard, attacked by Richard Murphy, the High Constable for Iveragh (in their retreat) and five out of the nine of the Banditti were lodged in Tralee Jail. Four of them were originally natives of Iveragh and Dunkerron and brought the five more from Limerick and Waterford.

. . . [Hunting-Cap] is greatly pleased at the way you conducted yourself at the late meetings in Dublin.[2] Tell John[3] he was very glad he went with the address.

Kit Gallwey got no answer yet from Lord Kenmare's trustees. I will not of course give the £4,200 unless the *exact security* you point out is given, but I rather think his Lordship's trustees or their attorney, Mr. B[   ],[4] will be glad to give the money as 6% on such an estate is a great thing *and they will* take care to get ample security. . . .[5]

SOURCE : O'Connell MSS, UCD

1 See letter 988.
2 See letters 982 and 987.
3 O'Connell's brother.
4 Name illegible.
5 This sentence is difficult to understand. There may be mistakes in transcription since James O'Connell's handwriting is almost illegible.

994

To Bishop Doyle[1]

Merrion Square, 26 January 1823

My Lord,

I cannot refuse the President and members of one of the very meritorious orphan charities of this city to obtrude a request upon your Lordship. The charity I allude to is the Summerhill Female Orphanage. A few, indeed very few, individuals have by personal exertions sustained this ' amiable and useful charity ' for many years. I need not tell you that amongst the miseries of the present period, one of the bitterest to some minds is that the very sources of charity are dried up and that those hands which *would* distribute cheerfully are empty. The result of such a state of public and private affairs does—without any of the exaggeration *supposed* to be usual on such occasions—leave this charity almost entirely dependent on the produce of the next annual sermon which is fixed for Sunday, the 13th of April, being the Sunday after Low Sunday, I fear an unpropitious time for my request to which I now return. It is an earnest but most respectful entreaty that you, my Lord, would be pleased to preach that sermon, unless it should interfere with some of those sacred duties which belong to your venerable office. With these I do not and I could not interfere but if with perfect *safety* to them, your Lordship could allow us to announce your name as the preacher,[2] you would not only do an essential and vital service to an interesting charity but, what is of infinitely less value, leave another and a deep impression of gratitude on the mind of one who has the honour to be, with sentiments of profound respect and esteem, My Lord,

> Your Lordship's most obedient, faithful and devoted
> servant,
>
> Daniel O'Connell

SOURCE : Kildare and Leighlin Diocesan Archives

1 James Warren Doyle, O.S.A. (1786-1834), Carlow; bishop of Kildare and Leighlin, 1819-34. Author of numerous works under his episcopal initials J.K.L. See *DNB*.
2 The preacher eventually announced was the Rev. A. O'Connell (*FJ*, 10 April 1823).

995

From Edward I. Johnston to Merrion Square

Phoenix Park [Dublin], 31 January 1823

My dear Sir,

I have the honour to acknowledge the receipt of your letter of the 28th instant and to acquaint you that his Excellency will have great pleasure in receiving the address[1] from the Roman Catholic Clergy, Gentry and Inhabitants of the City and Liberties of Londonderry at the Phoenix Park tomorrow at a half past four o'clock.

SOURCE : O'Connell Papers, NLI 13647

1 See letter 987, note 6, for a description of an address of probably the same tenor as the above.

996

To his wife at Tours

[Merrion Square] Wednesday, 5 [9, 10 and
11] February 1823

My darling Mary,

. . . Darling, I was with the Lord-Lieutenant on Saturday for an hour and was exceedingly well received. We were tête-à-tête. You may imagine what a change it is when I have become a great Castle man, but I am not changed, darling. I am as true to Ireland and to reform and to Liberty as ever I was. Be assured, sweetest, I never will give up my principles. On Sunday it was arranged that I should go on *a mission* to the country preparatory to the election. Sir Hans Hamilton[1] having died, the County is sharply contested between Sir Compton Domville[2] and Col. White,[3] the third son of Luke White, not the son who opposed Talbot[4] but a younger son. Domville set up in the Orange interest and avows the most direct no-popery principles. White is a liberal and his father is a decided reformer. The son will also support reform. There was a chaise and four ready for me *after Mass,* and off we drove to the towns of Rush and Skerries, two towns on the coast beyond Howth.

Sunday, 9 February

The reason, or at least one reason, for not writing for the last four days was *the election*. It is still going on and is now very doubtful although at one time the popular candidate was 222 ahead. He boasts still of 162 but I am beginning to be alarmed. But to return—this day week I went down to the towns of Rush and Skerries and harangued in the streets of each. It was amusing; a kind of wild day, very cold, half snowy. I was then quite fresh for the ensuing day on which the election began. I spoke for an hour and a quarter, I believe, at the least. I never was in my life so well satisfied with myself. Perhaps that is a bad criterion to judge by. I was the only person who made anything like a *speech*. On Monday also the state trials commenced. Your friend Cooper, the coach-maker, was the Sheriff and a most abominable panel of jurors he returned. Everybody apprehended they would acquit the Orangemen and certainly the great majority of them were strongly inclined to do so. The trials lasted from Monday until late on Friday. The Jury were then enclosed for the night and next day were discharged by consent, it being found that they would not agree.[5] We consider it as a good feature in the times that the Government thus perceive that, as long as the Orange faction subsists, it will be impossible to administer justice in Ireland against any of that vile party, a truth that the Catholics have been long in the habit of declaring, but we were not believed or regarded. Now the Government itself experiences the mischief of such an association. You will be glad to hear that there is leave for meat during Lent every day but Wednesday. I will consult with a physician and only fast as he directs me. That I promise you. The Munster circuit commences the third of March. I hope I

will be able to avoid going to Ennis. If I can I think it likely
that I will. I enclose you, my own darling, a bill for £100
British. This, I calculate, will produce you 2,450 francs at the
least. I am glad to anticipate your wishes in sending it to you.
Plunket, I believe, sailed this morning for Holyhead. The
Catholic question comes on the 20th. There is really reason
now to expect success but we shall see.

Monday, 10 February
    Darling, we are getting on famously for White. I will not
close this till tomorrow so as to tell you the final result.

Tuesday, 11 February
    The election will be over this day. We deem it impossible
for White not to succeed so you may reckon upon it that he is
returned. This is really a great triumph and shows what the
Catholics can do. . . . I do not hear when Mr. Sweetman is
to start. His father[6] is a decided patriot. It was he seconded
Mr. White. . . .

SOURCE : Fitz-Simon Papers
1   Sir Hans Hamilton (c. 1752-1822), Sheephill, Co. Dublin; M.P. for
    Co. Dublin, 1798-1800, 1801-22.
2   Sir John Compton Pocklington Domvile (c. 1776-1857), created
    baronet, 1815; Templeogue and Santry, both Co. Dublin; M.P. for
    Bossiney, 1818-26; Oakhampton, 1826-30; Plympton, 1830-32.
3   Henry White (1789-1873), *recte* fourth son of Luke White, M.P.;
    M.P. for Co. Dublin, 1823-32; Co. Longford, 1837-47, 1857-63;
    served in 14th Light Dragoons. Created Baron Annaly, 1863.
4   Richard Wogan Talbot. At the general election of 1820 he was
    opposed by Col. Thomas White.
5   See letter 987, note 5.
6   William Sweetman, brewer, Aston's Quay, Dublin, and Raheny,
    Co. Dublin.

996a

To William Conyngham Plunket, House of Commons, London

Merrion Square, 10 February 1823

Dear Sir,
    Will your leisure allow you to recollect the conversations
I have troubled you with on the subject of ' Judgements ' in our

courts. You know it is now nearly impossible to make out a *clear* title to a purchaser of lands in Ireland. Nine-tenths of the money lent for a century last past [*sic*] in Ireland were lent on judgements, and our habits have been too *inaccurate* to allow *us* to think of going to the trouble of satisfying those judgements which were not required to be satisfied for some particular purpose. The consequence is that no search can be made for any name without finding a multitude of judgements against *that name*. It is no answer to the objection arising from such judgements that the name being the same the person was different. How is that to be proved and how is any purchaser to *preserve* the proof of such difference. The antiquity of a judgement also is no reason why it should be considered as no encumbrance because however old, it may under O'Neil's act[1] be revived against any one tene-tenant and that would keep it alive against everybody else. In short, it is a crying grievance. Landed property sells for thirty-five years purchase in France *because* it is so easy to ascertain encumbrances. The 'inscription' list shows at once and conclusively how the property is affected. In Ireland at present sixteen or eighteen years purchase is all that can be got, and it is impossible to compel a reluctant purchaser to complete his purchase. But I fear I weary you by repeating things which are familiar to you.

I will, if you permit, send you the draft of a remedial bill. It will include with judgements all bonds to the crown, a different provision however for the latter. As to judgements, what I propose is that no judgement shall affect lands in the hands of a purchaser for value unless a memorial similar—*mutatis mutandis*—to the memorials of assignments of judgements shall be enrolled and renewed once in every twenty years, setting forth by name, like an inquisition upon an elegit[2] the lands which the pltff [plaintiff] in the judgement seeks to affect by that judgement. The pltffs [plaintiffs] should be at liberty to put in a new memorial as often as they please so as to include all new acquisitions of the defts [defendants]. It seems to me that I would thus simplify searches and increase the facility of transfers of property and the security of the purchaser.

As to crown bonds, I would require that all crown bonds should be enrolled within six months from the execution in the exchequer. In this I include all bonds which are passed by sureties for public officers of every kind—collectors of county and barony cess, grand jury officers, makers of post roads, builders of gaols, etc. At present the practice is most slovenly. The public suffers more than individuals but purchasers are always at a loss how to discover the existence of such bonds, and in one instance from Waterford a purchaser suffered a very great loss by reason of a dormant bond of this nature. There is an Irish statute which gives to *all* debts to the crown, even including simple contract debts, the force of a statute staple. If you allow it, I will send you my draft including both these points.

I have the pleasure to tell you that Mr. R. N. Bennett, who was counsel for the Ribbonmen at some of the late trials, has got a communication from the leaders by which they offer on the terms of an amnesty to give up their arms, to take the oath of allegiance and another oath never again to belong to any secret or illegal association. They have named the Rev. Mr. Lube[3] and the Rev. Mr. Yore,[4] two Catholic clergymen of the parish of St. James in this city, into whose hands they are ready to give up their arms and to take these oaths provided those gentlemen get authority to administer them. They—the clergymen—are willing to make a return to government *upon oath* of the number of persons who will come in and take the above oaths. It seems to me that it would be desirable to give these people an amnesty on these terms, and I submit it to your judgement. There is not in the world a people more inclined to an affectionate loyalty than the Irish if the government will give up affording countenance to the Orangemen. I am quite sure you have too much good feeling and, I may say, good taste to countenance that faction. Indeed, they are your enemies to the full as much as ours.

Pray excuse this long and hasty letter. I sincerely hope your journey has not injured your health. *Ireland wants you much.*

SOURCE : Papers of Mrs. Nicholas Shorter

1 Unidentified.

2 A writ of execution which entitled a creditor to take possession of either a debtor's land or, if he (the creditor) chose, the debtor's chattels.

3 Rev. Andrew Lube (died 1831), parish priest of St. James's, 1810-31.

4 Rev. William Yore (1781-1864), Catholic curate of St. James's and chaplain to Kilmainham jail, 1810-25; curate, St. Michael and St. John's, Exchange Street, Dublin, 1825-28; parish priest and vicar-general, St. Paul's, Dublin, 1828-64. A native of Dublin, educated and ordained at Carlow college.

997

*From John Barclay Sheil, M.D., 16 Westmoreland St., Dublin,
14 February 1823*

Has arranged for a dinner with O'Connell and Sir Henry
Conyngham Montgomery.[1]

SOURCE : O'Connell MSS, UCD

1 Sir Henry Cunningham Montgomery (c. 1769-1830), The Hall,
Co. Donegal. M.P. for St. Michael, Cornwall, 15 January–12 May
1807. Created baronet, 1808.

998

From his son Daniel[1] to Merrion Square

Tours, 17 [and 19] February 1823

My Darling Fado,

I received your letter on Shrove Tuesday night, everybody
but Mrs. Sweetman[2] was gone. Mod[3] gave a party that night
and asked young Russell[4] and young Sweetman to come to *us*
with their Mamas. . . . I speak French better than *Old
Woman Mod Mary.* Sometimes she tells me to speak to the
maids for her so as to bring wood and things of that kind,
though she speaks it very well and is picking up like me
myself. It's Mod that I say my lessons to and she takes a great
deal of pains with me. . . .

I hope we won't have war, I mean I hope we *will* for I
changed my mind since Ellen wrote the beginning. The town
is full of soldiers. Some of the Duc d'Angoulème's horses and
a regt. of foot came in and we saw them going about with
billets but none of them came to us yet. . . . I hope. we won't
have either officers or soldiers. We wouldn't care if they were
Irish officers and soldiers but the nasty French! . . .

Wednesday, 19th February

I was at *two* balls, one pleasanter than the other. I danced
a little at Mrs. Frizell's but I did not dance at all at Mrs. Hay's.
I am learning to dance. . . . Johnny and I gave a party about
a fortnight ago. We had young Frizell, the three Butlers, the
two Russells and Henry Sweetman.[5] . . .

SOURCE : O'Connell Papers, NLI 13645
1 This letter is in the handwriting of his sister Ellen.
2 Wife of William Sweetman, Jr.
3 His mother.
4 Obviously a son of Mr. Russell who lived at Tours (see letter 1011).
5 Son of William Sweetman, Jr.

999

To his wife at Tours

Merrion Square, 19 February 1823

My darling Love,

. . . I suppose you heard of our victory for Mr. White. He was returned the day my last letter was sent by a majority of 145.[1] It was and is a matter of great importance to put down so distinctly the Orange principle. It shows the English government that the Orangemen are weak in physical as well as moral strength. Darling, we had an immense chairing. I never saw such a crowd. I was in the first carriage next to White's chair or rather on the box where Billy Murphy and I took our stand. We passed through the Liberty[2] etc., stopped to give four cheers for the King at the Castle gate and so went on to College Green. The College lads attacked the people with stones etc. but they were soon put to the rout. I had a great view of part of the battle. In short no popular triumph was ever half so great. . . .

It is scarcely worth my while to go circuit at all and if we are emancipated as I think we will, I shall be in silk[3] next term with probably a right to frank my letters—but all in good time. Darling, do not be uneasy about the Lent. I give you my sacred word of honour I am perfectly well able to bear without inconvenience the present Lent. I never was, I repeat it, better or stouter. You know, heart, I told you from the beginning that there would be war. I am now all anxiety to see what I must do about my family. If I could afford it at this moment I would have you all home instantly. That, however, we must not think of unless in a case of necessity. I will write to the General[4] on the subject in a few days when the policy of England becomes more declared. . . . I did not fix on Versailles, love, because I heard that the class of British subjects there are of a very despicable description although perhaps it is not a true account. . . .

Tell my children, darling, that I doat of them, especially my own Danny. I entirely agree with him that the French are very inferior to the Irish. Maurice got Kate's letter. If you should have soldiers or officers quartered on you, take care to divide the house with them so as that you or my girls should not be at all in their presence or company. Make Morgan sleep either in the *salle-a-manger* or in the closet back of your bedroom and get a *palate* for Julia and Hannah[5] in your bedroom. In short, they are a kind of people not to be associated with. Perhaps Boulanger could get you an exemption or perhaps the General could if you were to apply to him.

SOURCE : Fitz-Simon Papers

1 The result of the poll, declared on 11 February, was 994 votes for Lt. Col. Henry White and 849 for Sir Compton Domvile (*Saunders News-Letter,* 12 Feb. 1823). On 13 February, White was chaired by a victory procession from Kilmainham into the centre of the city (*FJ*, 14 Feb. 1823).

2 The Liberty or Liberties consisted of the area of Dublin around Meath Street and St. Patrick's Cathedral which, being outside the city limits, was part of Dublin County. According to the *Freeman's Journal* of 14 February 1823 the Liberties contained many county electors who had voted for White. When the procession reached College Green a fight took place with the students of Trinity College (the college authorities maintained that the students merely defended themselves against attack). 'A hostile mob [allegedly Domvile's supporters] assembled opposite the house of Mr. O'Connell but a remonstrance from that gentleman induced them to disperse without doing any damage' (*FJ*, 15 Feb. 1823). O'Connell's account contradicts this (see letter 1006).

3 That is, a K.C.

4 His uncle, Count O'Connell.

5 Maidservants.

1000

From John Bric to Merrion Square

London, 22 February 1823

My Dear Sir,

. . . I would have written to you without hesitation if I had anything valuable to communicate on the great and unexpected events that have occurred since last I had the pleasure of seeing you. At home and abroad they are equally delightful to contemplate. The contest abroad[1] *must* serve the cause of freedom even though for a moment its banners should be trodden down by armed mercenaries, and at home—Oh God, how gratifying! Let me thank you from the bottom of my heart for the part, the wise and able part you have taken in this business.[2] You have hit the thing between wind and water and whilst you have justly elevated your own name you have done much for your country. The result of the trial[3] will, I dare say, be gratifying to the turbulent and foolish Orange. To you, to us all, the conduct of a Corporation jury can give neither surprise nor pain. It is rather pleasant to see this expressive reaction on a government who have so long fostered this furious and bloody banditti. The proceedings will tell on the people of this country, and the Administration is placed in that situation that to remain stationary is impossible, it must do something. It is reported and believed that Peel and the Churchmen made an effort to have the Marquis recalled. It failed. Well informed persons say that Mr. Peel is himself more likely to walk away. It is a poor devil and is breaking down fast. Every human being here condemns his ridiculous speech[4] in reply to Brougham. The French papers have very properly taken a hold of it. You can have no idea how impatiently public men here look for the arrival[5] of Plunket. He has acted like a true-hearted Irishman and has my respect and heartfelt prayers. . . .

Feby. 19th [*recte* 29th]
   Seven or eight days have passed since I wrote the preceding. Nothing has since occurred. The question of peace or war remains undetermined. The general opinion here is that the Cabinet are likely to come to an open rupture on the Irish question—Peel, the Hertfords and the Duke of York on one side—Canning and everyone else on the other. Lord Liverpool, it is supposed, will not exert his power against the country. The *Courier* speaks the sentiments of the former party, it made a most coarse and hostile attack on Lord Wellesley and Plunket a few evenings since.[6] The Catholic question has been postponed to the 17th of April. I sincerely congratulate you on the success of your appeal[7] to the College rioters. . . .
   May I expect a line from you, would you give me any encouragement to the Bar? *I can command a £100 a year certain*. I hope Mrs. O'Connell and the young ladies are well.

SOURCE : Fitz-Simon Papers

1   Presumably a reference to the proposed intervention in Spain by the
    French government for the purpose of restoring Ferdinand VII's
    authority.
2   A reference to O'Connell's reaction to the outrage upon Lord
    Wellesley (see letter 982 et seq.).
3   See letter 987, note 5.
4   Probably a reference to the Commons debate of 4 February on the
    king's speech when Peel rejected Brougham's plea for intervention
    on the side of Spain (*Hansard*, N.S., VIII, 65-70).
5   Plunket was on his way to Westminster to propose a new motion
    on Emancipation.
6   Issue of 17 February 1823, because of the dismissal of an Orange
    official, Sir Charles Vernon, from Irish government service (*FJ*,
    20 Feb. 1823).
7   Apparently a reference to O'Connell's appeal to the alleged sup-
    porters of Domvile to disperse (see letter 999, note 2).

1001

To his wife at Tours

Merrion Square, 5 [and 6] March 1823

My own and only Love,

Thank our sweet boy for me for the pleasure his darling
letter[1] gave me, and give his sweet lips three kisses for his
doating father. . . . Since I wrote last I had a busy week of
it. I gave up miserable Ennis and am now preparing to start
for Limerick. I spent this day at home clearing off my table
and have made great progress. I will resume my journal to you
on circuit. I dined yesterday with Maurice at Scully's.[2] He is
grown, you will perceive, very hospitable of late, but I would
as lief he did not ask me because I would rather stay at home
and work for the return of my wife and children. Last Thursday was a levée day at the Castle. I went there, of course in
Court dress, and was received by the Lord-Lieutenant with
marked kindness. It was a most crowded levée although it was
said all the Orangemen would stay away, but they had not the
courage to do so. They were afraid of the loss of their places
and so cringed with as much sycophancy as if the Lord-
Lieutenant was of their ' own kidney '. It was to me an amusing sight enough. Darling heart, I felt very cold in my white
silk stockings although I had warm ones underneath. I was

lucky in being able to get from court there. The crowd was nearly as great as at the King's Levée, and Dr. Troy and Dr. Murray were there in full canonicals.

Thursday, 6 March

First as to politics. Darling, there is no doubt of war, not the least. The only doubt is whether England will engage in it. The people are very anxious for war. All their sentiments of public liberty, all their prejudices against the French and all hopes of raising prices depend on war or are turned towards it. But the ministry are unwilling to increase the debt and are afraid of a bankruptcy. So that England will keep at peace as long as she possibly can, and she will not go to war at all if the Spaniards submit like the scoundrel Neapolitans. There is indeed great danger of treachery in Spain, the greatest danger —but if they be only tolerably unanimous, we are at the beginning of a contest which will one way or the other give a new face to Europe. In the meantime I think of my own family. How happy should I be to be able to bring them home or to have any possibility of doing so. The only thing I can do is to lay my plan for getting them one stage nearer me. Your idea of Devonshire has quite delighted me and for the present I have resolved to put it into practice. I will be with you before the close of August and immediately bring you to Paris where we will spend a fortnight or three weeks to show my girls everything worth seeing, and then we will go down by Rouen to Havre and cross from that to Southampton. I will in the meantime make inquiries for a proper place in Devonshire. I am convinced you can live there as cheap as you could in rascally France. Oh how I hate France. I hate it in all moods and tenses, past, present and to come. My entire attention will be taken up with maturing this plan. Maurice can live with you and go up to keep his terms. I also can spend three weeks with you at Christmas, almost as much time as I had with you last year. I arrived the 18th of September and left you I think the 22nd October. Now I could reach you by the 20th December and stay with you till the 18th of January. In short, darling, I am all alive to having you so much nearer me. I was even thinking of getting a furnished house in Kerry, but certainly Devonshire is much better. It is warm and genial too in winter and it would be a seasoning of you on your way home. You are wedded to the house you are in while at Tours, and we must pay for it until August next. But that can be at the worst but a sacrifice of ten or fifteen pounds even should you leave it sooner. I have arranged everything for my departure tomorrow morning before four o'clock. I spent yesterday and this day at home and I finished my toil before I sat down to this pleasure. . . . In point of money, darling, the times are really dreadful. My profession however is holding out well, hitherto it has been on the increase. It is more than it was up to this time last year. . . .

Darling, I think of Exeter for you for the next winter. At all events we will stop at Exeter in the first instance, if you please, and you can thence look about you. There is an elegant chapel and many Catholics. But before I decide, I will have your opinion. I dare say that we shall get lodgings for my entire family for £10 a month or £120 a year. I am indeed quite sure that we shall. How much a month did we pay in Bath? Winter, however, is *the season* there and we were in it at a comparatively cheap time. But since, prices have greatly fallen. Darling, I am now going to shave and then to bed. I will be off, please God, *long* before 4 in the morning. I think it better go all the way in one day than sleep out of my warm bed. I have a very warm one in Limerick.

SOURCE : Fitz-Simon Papers
1   Letter 998.
2   Denys Scully, who lived at 13 (now 75) Merrion Square South.

1002
To his wife at Tours

Limerick, Monday, 10 [and 12] March 1823

My darling love,
    . . . I left Dublin on Friday the 7th at half after 4 in the morning and easily reached this town by 8 in the afternoon. I was not one bit fatigued although, darling, it was a *fast* day and I of course kept the fast. There is nothing so idle as to think that there is the least difficulty for a man with my health and strength of frame to keep the fast. I assure you, my love, I am quite convinced that it is actually of use to my health. Almost all the diseases of persons in the upper classes do at middle life arise from repletion or overmuch food in the stomach, and there can be no cure for that so complete as a Lent regularly kept. Be assured that if I felt the slightest attack on

my health I would immediately give up the fasting. Depend on that, darling. I cling to life with too much tenacity to follow any practice which could injure my health. It would do your heart good to see me dine, even yesterday, although I eat three eggs for breakfast I was able to call for beef three times and mutton twice and to eat apple pie besides.

Tuesday, 12 March
. . . Depend on it that as long as you remain in France you will be exposed to great delays occasioned in getting my letters as it is, I believe, a well known fact that the French Government is not at all scrupulous in opening private correspondence and detaining letters to ascertain whether they shall be opened or not. . . . With respect to Ireland, darling, believe me there is not the least danger to me. I never knew a period in which there was so little of personal hostility towards me. I assure you I have experienced ten times as much enmity from Catholics as I now do from the Orangemen. On the contrary, it has become a kind of fashion amongst them to praise my candour and moderation. The truth is that they have quite enough to do to fight the Government and have not leisure to attack others. I assure you that in all their political squibs and party publications—and they are very numerous—I am spared to such a degree that I have jocosely said more than once that I was quite jealous that they should bestow so little thought upon me, and that at a time when there was not half as much calumny going I had full nine-tenths of it to my own share, whereas at present I do not get above a tithe of the whole. Besides, I do assure you, darling, that I never knew a period of less personal danger from political causes in Ireland than the present. There is in truth a *great cry* but as the proverb says— *little wool*. The Orangemen are clamorous and contemptible since government ceased to take part with them and every day shows their weakness. I do not, my Mary, my own Mary, deceive you. Indeed I do not. The next thing on which you may set your mind at rest is the recall of Marquis Wellesley. Take my word for it, sweetest. *He will not be recalled.* He is firm in the government of Ireland. The next thing you are anxious about is the war. Darling, the war between France and Spain is certain. It is inevitable. The Bourbons and their Ultra party have committed themselves. They *must* now go to war. Nothing short of another revolution in France could prevent the war. And whatever the English newspapers may

say I see no symptom whatsoever of any danger of a new revolution in France. The French people are probably the only people in the world utterly unfit for liberty or for any rational system of government. They want moral temperament, if I may use the expression. They are indeed an odious people, no disinterested devotedness to country, no noble emulation of virtue, no generous sacrifice of self for the good of others, no decency to conceal the broadest features of political depravity. With such a people nothing will do but the strong government of the Bourbons, and while the Bourbon government is repressing their political tendency to crime they are also fortunately and, I hope providentially, engaged in the restoration of that pure Catholic worship which alone contains genuine Christianity. The churches will soon be all filled with zealous and active clergy, with a clergy ill-provided for with the goods of this world and *therefore* (amongst other reasons) the more fit to attend to the concerns of eternity. I have, love, run on I know not how with this dissertation. I will conclude it by remarking that I am convinced nothing so useful to the Catholic religion as the fall of Napoleon could have been devised by human ingenuity. His colossal power was wielded to enslave the Church, to promote practical atheists to the first stations, to discountenance the mild and modest virtues of the Christian and to expose to ridicule, reproach and persecution every being animated with zeal to promote Christian truth and practice Christian charities. Darling, you will think that I preach on these subjects, but they really are topics which I have turned much and long in my mind and I write thus only the overflowings of deep reflection and I indulge in them because I believe you have no objection *to see* your husband's thoughts. With respect, darling, to the reports of peace, you are not to give them the least credit. There is in France as well as in England a class of individuals of very great wealth who are deeply interested in keeping up to the last possible moment the reports of peace. Those are the stock-jobbers. They are ruined by thousands by the fall in the funds which has been occasioned by the prospect of war. The British funds have already fallen at a rate which exceeds eleven per cent and, darling, the present fundholders who wish to sell out circulate and pay the newspapers for publishing reports of peace that they may be able to sell out before a further fall takes place and which will assuredly take place so soon as war is admitted to be quite certain. So that my opinion, you see, is decidedly warlike. As to England joining in the war, *that* will depend on the length during which war shall continue between France and Spain. If the Spaniards, like the very base Neapolitans, *give in* without a long and ardent struggle, then indeed England will continue at peace. But if the spirit of national independence and the love of liberty enable the Spaniards to hold out for six months, England *must* take part in the contest and be involved in the fight whether she will or no. War would be *useful*, very useful to Ireland. The English cannot go to war without emancipating *us*. They cannot go to war without a general reform of abuses, without a revision of contracts and, in short, without doing justice to all parties. Darling, the times are big with events of the deepest magnitude. May God direct them for the best for poor Ireland, but *that* he will at all events. His will is *the best* and indeed the only good. Darling, to descend to our private concerns, I repeat my determination to bring you and my children this next autumn to the south of England. This is a determination from which nothing, I think, can shake me. You would live quite as cheap at Exeter. . . .

. . . Did I tell you that I continue under *the direction* of Mr. Coleman? It is not right to change these matters, and without the slightest disparagement to anybody else, there cannot well be anybody more calculated for all his duties than Mr. Coleman.[1] Do you, darling, and my girls go to Communion at least once a month. Take care, sweetest, to get my John to do so. *This* is the age to make an impression on his mind, otherwise it will be too late. Say to me, my love, if you and the girls go monthly. It will be a great comfort to me to hear that you do and my girls will be glad that, besides higher motives, their poor father is pleased with them. Oh tell them, sweetest, how I long to press them to my heart of hearts, give them and my boys my *tenderest, tenderest* love. I believe they will all be glad to get out of France. At least it is a great pleasure to me to think I shall please them by bringing them one stage nearer home. We will, please God, spend a full fortnight in Paris so as to see everything worth seeing and, before you return from Exeter, I promise my girls a sight of London. I could rave of the happiness of having you all so much nearer me.

SOURCE : Fitz-Simon Papers

1   Rev. Patrick Coleman (died 1838), educated Paris and Maynooth, curate at Townsend Street chapel for many years; P.P. of St. Paul's, Dublin, 1825-28; St. Michan's, Dublin, 1828-38. Sometime vicar general.

1003

From John Bric

London, *Morning Chronicle* Office,
12 March 1823

My dear Sir,

. . . You have read the debates.[1] I don't blame the ministers for the part they have taken. They are evidently afraid of the high Orange party in Ireland. They are opposed here by a strong faction (the Duke of York's). They have a difficult part to play. If all that ought to be done shall not be done, if a direct, enlarged and manly policy shall not be pursued, still we must not complain, we have gained all through. We must not blame Mr. Plunket in particular, who has personally suffered, who is hated by our enemies. The Irish here look up to him with strong feeling. I understand he was walking in the Park on Sunday last and greeted by a number of young Irishmen in a way that astonished the cold and sober temper of the English. Don't be enthusiastic with respect to the issue of the Catholic question. It will be carried in the Commons but the noble lords will reconsider the bill. You may expect to hear from me in a day or two.

SOURCE : Fitz-Simon Papers

1 Most likely the Commons debate of 3 and 5 March on James Abercromby's motion of stricture on Orange societies in Ireland. In the same week the Commons also debated the Irish church establishment, the Jesuits in Ireland and Irish tithes.

1004

To his wife at Tours

Limerick, 14 [and 17] March 1823

My darling Love,

. . . We had a great day of it yesterday. There was a most important trial[1] against ' the Corporation ', that is, against one of the sheriffs. Lord Gort was in court and I indulged myself in painting the profligacy of the Corporation in its truest colours. It would please you, darling, if you were to know the quantity of applause I received. I had an opportunity too of condemning in strong and sarcastic terms the vice of duelling.

In short, they all say I never made half so good a speech in my life.[2] I dined with a large party at a very rich papist's, a Mr. Kelly,[3] who bought great estates during the war. I intend to start for Tralee in the morning and I will send this letter thence. Charles O'Connell[4] of the County of Clare goes with me to assist Roger O'Sullivan in the management of the assizes. As you know, they cannot expect much aid from Sir Robert Blennerhassett.[5] I hope my brother John will be foreman of the Grand Jury. It will be idle affectation in Roger not to make him foreman.

Tralee, 17 March

I came here from Limerick on Saturday the 15th. The new road is not as yet *finished* and so I had to come by that scoundrel ferry at the Cashin.[6] It is quite a dreary journey though it might easily be made a pleasant one . . . .

I dined this day with Rick.[7] He had excellent fish for Maurice and me especially delicious scallops; only think, large scallops costing only 1s. 8d., or two tenpennies the dozen. This is the first week of Lent I have to pass without any meat as there has been no leave in Kerry but Lent is now, one may say, over as the next week would be a black fast at any rate. I assure you solemnly, darling, I never in my life had so little reason to complain of my diet. It is no inconvenience whatsoever to me to fast, not the least, you may make your mind perfectly easy on that subject. . . . You will smile when I tell you as a secret that I have already commenced my canvass to represent this county in the next parliament. I can have no secret from you but I have really begun to canvass and will ascertain before the week is over what my prospect of success is likely to be. In fact, if the Catholics are emancipated there can be little doubt of my getting into parliament if I choose and, darling, there is no other person to represent this county. Colonel Crosbie has not the least chance of sitting again; his health is much impaired and his fortune gone. Charles Herbert[8] is dead, Sir John Godfrey[9] involved in a sea of debt. Blennerhassett[10] of Elmgrove must retire to live on half-pay. There is nobody but one of the Kenmare family who could be thought of, and I believe I will be able to ascertain that the Kenmare family will not think of seeking the County. I write all this to you because when I write to you I am only thinking aloud. Say nothing of it, darling. I would not wish that it should reach the ears of any Kerryman in Tours for the present. I allude in

particular to Richard Mahony.[11] The old gentleman at Derrynane is amazingly well and has stamina in him to live many a
long year. . . . Parson Dowling of Iveragh is also dead. Poor
wretched man he left, I believe, a large family. He was an
unamiable creature at least in politics. . . . You can form
no idea of the distress of the country gentlemen, not a shilling
to be had for rents of any lands. . . . Did I tell you I made
the best speech I ever uttered at Limerick? At least *so* they
all say. . . .

SOURCE : Fitz-Simon Papers

1   *John Norris Russell* v. *William Taylor.* Taylor was found guilty of
    publishing a libel on Russell (*DEP,* 18 Mar. 1823).
2   'Mr. O'Connell closed the plaintiff's case in one of the most
    splendid philippics ever heard in the court; it was attended with
    a burst of applause, and had a powerful effect upon the court and
    jury ' (*DEP,* 18 Mar. 1823).
3   Probably John Peter Kelly, D.L. (1775-1871), Ballintlea and Firgrove,
    both Co. Clare, who purchased in 1811 the estates of the Ingoldsby
    Massy family in Co. Limerick.
4   Charles O'Connell (1792-1874), Liscannor and Ennis, both Co. Clare;
    attorney; died unmarried. Second son of Maurice O'Connell of
    Moyresk and Braintree, Co. Clare.
5   Sir Robert Blennerhassett, second baronet (1769-1831), high sheriff
    of Kerry, 1823.
6   The Cashin is the estuary of the river Feale and enters the Atlantic
    about twelve miles north of Tralee.
7   His brother-in-law Rickard O'Connell.
8   Probably Charles Herbert, Torc, Killarney.
9   Sir John Godfrey, second baronet (1763-1824), Bushfield, Co. Kerry,
    landowner.
10 Probably Arthur Blennerhassett, Jr.
11 Probably one of the Mahonys of Dromore, Kenmare, Co. Kerry.

1005

To his wife at Tours

Tralee, 19 [20, 21, and 22] March 1823

My own Mary,

     . . . On this subject [the state of Ireland] you may indeed
believe me when I tell you that your fears are most perfectly
groundless. The little idle Orange *talk*, with which the party
papers were filled, was all the mischief which existed and that is

now completely over. I never knew so little of real danger in
political party in this country. Lord Wellesley is certainly
secure.

Tralee, 20 March

I continue. Lord Wellesley has been publicly *avowed* by all
the members of the Administration. There is now no longer
any apprehension of his removal and the Orangemen have
ceased to hope it. For my own part too I never was so well
treated in political life. Darling, I most solemnly assure you
(and did I *ever* deceive you) that your fears are quite idle and
vain and that there never was a safer time for me than the
present. . . .

The only Kerry news is that Kean Mahony is going to be
married to Miss Cronin[1] of the Park and she is ready to go
with him to reside in Iveragh, not being as saucy as some other
cocknosed people. I wish I had, however, a house fit for anybody with or without a cocknose amongst my native mountains
or anywhere else out of both Dublin and France. How sore my
heart is at times, and I hate France with a mortal hatred.

Friday, 21 March

. . . Your son is going to a ball this night. As I keep him
from following the practice of others in respect to eating meat,
I do not like to prevent his going to the ball. He and I dined
with Rick.[2] He, I mean your son, looked very handsome and
neatly dressed. I could not help kissing him and I exclaimed,
' Oh, how like your darling mother you look! ' He does, love,
he does look very like you. It is a pity he is not more steady
but I ought to love him for your sake. . . .

The County of Cork has again got into a frightful state of
disturbance. Did I tell you that a party of robbers had got into
Iveragh and robbed Fitzgerald's house at Kenneigh? Yes, I
recollect I did.[3] Well, two of the wretches have been capitally
convicted and will be executed. My old uncle had a great escape
from them. They were to have robbed him the same night if
they had not been a little too late, and so they put it off till
the ensuing night but were taken up in the interval. . . .

Tralee, 22 March

Darling, as soon as you receive this, call with Ellen as an
interpreter to the house of the banker Boulanger Cartion. Let

her tell him from me that I am extremely grateful to him for his great kindness in preventing soldiers or officers from being billeted on my family. . . .

SOURCE : Fitz-Simon Papers

1 Mary Anne Cronin, only daughter of Daniel Duggan Cronin, The Park, Killarney; married 1823 Kean Mahony, Castlequin, Cahirciveen, Co. Kerry.
2 His brother-in-law Rickard O'Connell.
3 See letters 988 and 993.

1006

To his wife at Tours

Cork, 25 [and 26] March 1823

My darling Love,

. . . The fact is that the first Lent I attempted to fast I used to drink too much wine which I foolishly conceived would serve me as additional nourishment, and it was, I am sure, the excess of wine which made me ill. This Lent I *manage* the matter much better as I content myself with a tumbler of *sweet* punch made of ' the native ' which is, I believe, the liquor in the world least injurious to the health. . . . It is quite idle for healthy people to say that they cannot fast or live upon a single meal. How many thousands, I may say millions, have not one good meal to live on and yet do all manner of work on one *bad* meal in the 24 hours. . . . The stay of Lord Wellesley in Ireland is fixed. He remains with the approbation of the entire cabinet, and the rage of the Orangemen, which was *mighty* like a puddle in a storm, is abating very fast. They begin to see that all chance of plunder is gone except through the old and legitimate channel of the Government and they are acting accordingly. The discussion in the House of Commons on Mr. Abercromby's[1] motion[2] was eminently useful. The Orangemen got no kind of support from anybody but Mr. Dawson.[3] The Knight of Kerry replied to him in an admirable speech. What miserable reports you must see of the proceedings in Parliament when you say that you are dissatisfied with the Knight this session. You must know that in his life he never yet *shone* until this session. His answer to Dawson, his speech on the tithe question and another speech of his on Irish politics were amongst the best pronounced in parliament.[4] The London papers for the first time praised him highly and all the liberal press in Ireland vied with each other in commending him. How strange that he should be so reported as to dissatisfy you! In fact he has raised himself very high this session, and take my word for it that he has deserved it. I say this, I assure you, love, without the least partiality. To return to the debate on the Orange question. The bill[5] which Mr. Goulburn[6] undertook to bring in will be quite fatal to them. It is one which is already in operation in England to prevent combination amongst mechanics. It makes it an indictable offence to belong to any society bound together by any oath. This coming from a no popery man as Mr. Goulburn is, strikes deeply into the Orange. Mr. Peel's speech was perhaps the worst symptom for the Orangemen of the entire.[7] It was an attempt to prove that even while he was in Ireland he did not encourage the Orange system! ! ! An attempt which proves at least this—that he does not now think that to encourage Orangeism would be laudable, for otherwise he would not endeavour to show that he *had* discouraged the system. No matter how unfounded that attempt, it proves to the Orangemen that they cannot reckon on him. So much for the accuracy of the information derived from Mr. Bolton! ! ![8] I now proceed to answer your question about the bill for a commutation of tithes.[9] I like the *principle* of that bill well, that is, I like any change in the tithes because, in the first place, I am decidedly of opinion that tithes should be abolished *in toto* and this meddling with them by parliament admits *a right* in the parliament to do with them as they deem most expedient. That is *one step* gained towards the abolition. In the next place I would, if tithes are to last, infinitely prefer that they should be paid by an amiable tax in money fixed in some way than that they should continue in their present state. So far this bill will go at all events. I have not as yet read the bill itself, and it is impossible to collect its details from the newspapers. It has, however, been ordered to be printed and I will probably tell you what I think of it in another letter. Darling, I perceive also by your letter that you think our house was nearly attacked by the mob. I am astonished I did not mention *the fact* to you as it really occurred. But I believe I did. It was a perfectly friendly group that came to our house, upwards of one hundred who were collected because they heard that the [Trinity] College lads intended to attack me. I had considerable difficulty in persuading them that their apprehensions were vain and that I was perfectly prepared to meet any assault. This was the circumstance which the newspapers, with their usual inattention to facts, misrepresented into a hostile mob *persuaded* by me to go away without doing any injury, a story as destitute of probability as it was of truth.

Cork, 26 March

. . . I saw my poor Kitty's[10] family. They are all well and lively but their property is suffering dreadfully from the times. There never were such times. Young Primrose is managing my affairs and I am greatly satisfied with him. If I had him in the place of Myles McSwiney for some years past it would make a difference of *many, many* thousands to me. I can, however, acquit Myles of all but neglect. I never saw anything more strict and accurate than Primrose's accounts. The poor bishop[11] is suffering much from the gout. His temper is of infinite service to him under that affliction. I came from Killarney on Monday in the coach with a sister of Parson Hyde[12] and two nice girls, her daughters. She told me as we left the coach that I had quite won her daughters' hearts! ! ! Only think of that, my old woman, as a puff to my vanity. There is enough to fret you besides my fasting about which you are so saucy. . . . I already enjoy in idea the beef-steak Aunt Nagle threatens me with on next Sunday morning. It is I that will eat it with a relish. . . .

Roger[13] took no oaths when sworn in sub-sheriff but to perform the duty, etc., none of the vile oaths. I found out more than a year ago that it was a mistake to suppose Catholics could not be sub-sheriffs and published my opinion on the subject.[14] The consequence is that there are very many Catholics in that office this year and there will be more in future, but *I* expect emancipation this session. . . . I am impatient to know whether you approve of my Devonshire plan.[15] . . .

SOURCE : Fitz-Simon Papers

1 James Abercromby (1776-1858); judge advocate general, 1827-28; chief baron of the exchequer (Scotland), 1830-32; speaker of the House of Commons, 1835-39; created 1839 Baron Dunfermline. See *DNB*.

2 A motion of stricture on Orange societies in Ireland. See letter 1003, note 1.

3 George Robert Dawson (1790-1856), Castledawson, Co. Londonderry; M.P. for Co. Londonderry, 1815-30; Harwich, 1830-32. Under-

secretary of state for home department, 1822-27; married 1816 Mary, sister of Robert Peel, M.P., the future prime minister. See *DNB*.

4 The last speech referred to was probably the Knight's contribution to the debate on the Irish church establishment on 4 March. He also spoke on the debate on the Jesuits in Ireland on the following day.

5 In the debate on Orange societies in Ireland on 5 March Goulburn had suggested the possibility of a government measure to curb the activities of the Orangemen (*Hansard*, N.S., VIII, 465). No such bill was presented.

6 Henry Goulburn.

7 On Abercromby's motion on Orange societies on 5 March.

8 Unidentified.

9 The Irish Tithes Composition Bill, introduced by Goulburn to the Commons on 6 March 1823, which in due course became law (4 Geo. IV c. 99). Under this tithe payers could negotiate with tithe owners for the fixing of the tithe as a lump sum instead of as a proportion of produce payable in kind. See Angus Macintyre, *The Liberator : Daniel O'Connell and the Irish Party*, 1830-1847 (London 1965), pp. 170-1.

10 His sister Kitty Moynihan.

11 Dr. Charles Sugrue, bishop of Kerry.

12 Rev. Arthur Hyde (1763-1834), vicar of Killarney, 1809-33. He had six sisters, three of whom married.

13 Roger O'Sullivan.

14 This opinion was published in the *Freeman's Journal* of 24 February 1820.

15 See letter 1001.

1007

To his wife at Tours

Cork, 26 [27 and 28] March 1823

My own Mary,

If I cannot please you about fasting I will endeavour to do it by writing, that is, if you will allow quantity to make up for the deficiency of quality. Indeed you say I gratify you in everything else, and are you not therefore bound in common *honesty* to admit that I would have great pleasure to gratify in that particular also if I had not that which you will pardon me for calling a higher duty, namely, my obedience to the Church? I would indeed do anything in my power to please you. Indeed I would, Mary. It is and has been the happiness of my life to endeavour to please you, my own sweetest Mary, my comfort, my love, my dearest darling Mary; but surely, dearest,

I have *a command* to fast if I am able to do it, and if I was not, I assure you I would at once give it up. The Lent is now over and here I am as hale and as hearty as man can be, somewhat thinner, I admit, but not one bit the worse for that. You would have smiled if you saw me eat my breakfast last Sunday, a goose egg, then a turkey egg and then a hen egg. I shall grow too fat when Lent is over. . . . Both John and James were on the Grand Jury and Richard Mahony of Portmagee got on as a talisman, that is, upon the default of Rowland Eager who could not attend, being laid up in the gout.

27 March
        . . . I will, however, contrive to get Miss Edgeworth's early lessons for children[1] sent . . . to darling Danny. . . . My sister Ellen is here looking very well and has become extremely attentive to her religious duties. She spends her time at Chapel or in attending the sick. In short, she is quite well in every respect and resigned to her situation. Poor thing, one's heart ought to bleed for her. She has survived her partner and almost all her earthly comforts. . . . Let me know whether I write sufficiently distinctly for you as your writing sometimes puzzles me which I attribute in a great degree to the rascally quality of the French paper.

Good Friday, 28th March
        I have now a heavy and a doleful task to perform—tidings of death and woe. My Honora,[2] my poor Honora, my ever loved darling sister is gone, is no more. She was my earliest favourite, the first being I ever loved. She is gone. We were nine. The hand of death has been amongst us and there remain but eight. Who will be next? She died of a terrific typhus fever. She died on Sunday last, the twelfth day. She has left a mournful husband and a long family of daughters just at the age when they most want a mother's tender advice and a mother's watchful eye. . . . How my mind runs back to our early days when we were gay and lively, and she was the mistress of all our sports and comfortess in all our little afflictions. We all loved her and she used to manage us all. . . . Oh, how I want my Mary's bosom to lay my afflicted head on. How one embrace from my sweet Mary would soften that cold, rigid feeling which the view of a sister's grave excites. Oh, that I had my sweet children now near me but, again I say, may the will of God be done and that alone. . . .

SOURCE : Fitz-Simon Papers

1   Maria Edgeworth's *Early Lessons*, of which the seventh edition was published in London in 1820.
2   His sister Honoria O'Sullivan.

1008

To his wife at Tours

Cork, 2 [3 and 4] April 1823

My darling Heart,

The reason why I did not write for some days past was not the affliction occasioned by my own poor sister's death but more principally from the pressure of business. That pressure, however, was of eminent use in taking off my mind from unpleasant and bitter recollections, and the very nature of those trials, in what so large a portion falls on me, has served to dissipate altogether that gloom which would otherwise settle upon me. . . . These assizes are passing over with rapidity. They have been heavy. I have already received in this town alone £220 or thereabouts, and I am likely to receive more. I wish I had always been as careful of my money and I would not now be separated from my sweet Danny and his mother. I wish I could even see the brat shouting amongst his little French playfellows. The plan of coming to Exeter delights me. There will be no difficulty in becoming acquainted with any Catholics of that vicinity we please or of being accommodated in that town. There are many Catholics there as I understand. . . .

Thursday, 3 April 1823

Maurice is still in Kerry. . . . I will get rid of his mare by turning her out as a breeding mare at Derrynane and I will have my own horse *taken up* to Dublin. I want him to ride between this and the long vacation to the shower bath which has done so much to banish my rheumatism. . . .

We have here many reports of disaffection in the French army but in general they can easily be traced to stock-jobbing. Not that I should be surprised if there were an unwillingness to march to Spain. Oh, how I wish you were out of that cursed France! The Bourbons were as secure as any family ever was upon a throne if they had not been so silly as to engage in this preposterous war with Spain, and now they have put their dynasty on the hazard of a dice. They have, however, done a good deal already for the Catholic religion and perhaps it would be better now that the bishops' sees are filled if the close connection between Church and State were not drawn still more tight. I do not like to have our priests preaching despotism and I hate the idea of coupling the awful name of God with that of any earthly power. I saw a cross near Paris erected ' A Dieu et au Roi ', ' To God and the King '. I could not help feeling a sensation of blasphemy. . . . The war fit has gone by in England. They will not go to war with France unless they are forced by future events. As to Ireland, the Orange cry is certainly abating. Even Baron McClelland of hanging notoriety is discountenancing the Orange in the North.[1] In the south and especially in this county the disturbances are quite unabated. The new plan of the Whiteboys is to burn everything. Houses, barns, corn, hay, turf stacks, everything. We hear, even during the assizes, of burnings every night. And this rage is spreading fast. The unfortunate wretches find out that they can burn with the least possible chance of being detected. In short, this system is now assuming the most appalling attitude. The misery of the country gentlemen is at its height without the least appearance of any mitigation. . . .

Friday, 4 April.
      . . . I will not have a happy day till you are out of France. . . . The poor Irish have miseries and consequent vices but they have not the native depravity of the French. The faults of the Irish are the produce of foreign oppression. They owe their causes to the evils entailed on them by foreign subjugation and by the tyranny exercised over them by strangers. Alas, however, the picture they now present is most doleful. I did not think I should live to see such a total annihilation of property. Farms which have been let thirty years ago and which were considered as valuable as estates are now surrendered. It is well to have a trade. . . .

SOURCE : Fitz-Simon Papers
1   In giving judgement in a riot case at Downpatrick on 25 March, Judge McClelland condemned ' the disgraceful fact, which was admitted on all hands that a large band of Orangemen should be suffered to parade at a funeral and with guns and headed with fifes and drums and all the material of civil war ' (*Patriot,* 1 April 1823).

1009

To his wife at Tours

Cork, Tuesday, 8 [and 10] April 1823

My darling Love,

I had the pleasure of receiving yesterday your letter *up* to Good Friday. Your mind is *now* quite at ease about my fasting. I assure you that I have not suffered in the slightest possible degree from it, and that I am now again beginning to grow too fat. . . . Maurice,[1] however, occupied the middle place on the roof [of the coach to Dublin] yet I feel very unpleasant at his travelling in that way. My regret, however, is nothing on that score compared with that excited by his terrible increase of 'fidgets'. It is, my love, vain to conceal it from ourselves. It must be an organic defect or, if it be habit, it is increasing on him to a cruel degree. My heart is quite sore about him. I wish you would at once sit down and write to him on the subject. I am wearied and heartsore. He actually has got a trick of lolling out his tongue round his lips which is childish and absurd in its appearance. I would not write to you on this subject if it did not affect me deeply, deeply. Now, darling, that I am writing on this subject I recur to my poor Morgan.[2] I cannot bear the idea of his going into that rascally Austrian service. I would infinitely prefer his staying at home altogether and becoming an attorney. I will, however, say no more of this until I have your opinion on it. If it concurs with mine, consult him and, if he will accede to our wishes, then consider it as determined. I will, however, be guided by your advice. I never, my sweetest Mary, did wrong when I took your advice. Write to me as speedily as possible on the subject. I will not write to the General[3] about him till I hear from you.

Thursday, April 10

. . . I dined yesterday at Dr. Bullen's.[4] He has another little duck of a daughter, the sweetest baby I ever saw. . . . I hugged the darling and sounded my watch for it and it chatted with me at a great rate. I bothered the baby however when she told me that she was a great prate roast. 'Pray Miss,' said I, 'how do you roast your prate?' It amused her greatly and made her very entertaining. I write this nonsense, darling, because children are the first want of my heart. . . . The O'Mullanes are always in *hot* water. The extravagance of James[5] in his lifetime and the fall in the times have *very*, very much embarrassed them. In fact, everybody who depended on interests in land is nearly ruined and totally so if they owed any debts. The worst is that the prices must fall still lower before they can possibly mend. You may now judge how true my account of the Orangemen was. The country is as quiet as far as relates to them as if we never had a riot at the theatre[6] or any difference between them and the Government. In fact, nothing can equal the oblivion in which the *great events* of the present Administration are now thrown into. Not a word going, the same idle and cheerless routine that you have so long seen while Saurin was Attorney-General. I am told Peel and Plunket have come to a compromise by which Peel agrees to give up the Orangemen provided Plunket will give up the Catholics. I believe that this compromise has been *in substance* arranged. The Catholic bill will be brought in and probably carried through the house of Commons to be rejected in the Lords. The King is very ill. The Duke of York somewhat recovered but greatly broken. To mortal eye things look badly but who knows what Providence intends for this wretched country. The Patriots have been defeated in Portugal and what is worse, the people seem disposed to resist the forces of the Cortes. I suppose some harsh invasion has been made upon their religious rights or feelings. It is, however, a most fortunate thing for the Bourbon French that such a rebellion should just now subsist in Portugal. . . .

SOURCE : Fitz-Simon Papers

1 His son.
2 His son.
3 His uncle Count O'Connell.
4 Either Denis B. or William Bullen, both physicians of 82 South Mall, Cork.
5 James O'Mullane, Merchants Quay, Cork (died before 1815), first cousin of O'Connell. Residuary legatee and sole executor of his father, John O'Mullane (died 1806).
6 See letter 982, note 1.

1010

To his wife at Tours

Merrion Square, Friday, 18 April 1823

My own sweetest Love,

. . . Maurice is in excellent health and somewhat more attentive to himself. I watch him now as a cat would watch cream. There is not much business in the Hall, but although I have been but five days at home I have already got 110 guineas. Now, darling, I come to the subject which interests you most, namely getting out of that rascally France. I wish it *may* be in my power to get you out of it during the month of May. I enclose you £100 British. . . . If I can possibly do it I will proceed thus. First, I will arrange lodgings for you at or very near Exeter. Secondly, I will if possible send you another £100, and that I hope will be sufficient to bring you to Paris by the 10th of May. I would then join you there by the close of the ensuing week and, giving my girls in all a stay of ten or twelve days at Paris, I would be able to accompany you to Rouen and Havre and thence across to Southampton and so fix you at Exeter and be back for the sitting day of the ensuing term, the 30th of May. Such is the outline of my present plan, but it will require £300 to carry it into effect and fix you at Exeter. . . . At Exeter I could spend my Christmas with you besides, of course, six weeks of the long vacation and I should almost, alas that almost, feel you at home if you were there. . . . Three days will easily bring you to Paris. I will postpone until my next the subject of your taking lodgings there but you know we must not *sponge* on the General's family.[1] . . .

[P.S.] Speak to each of my children about me. Tell my Nell of my tender love. Do not quiz her about anybody but especially about Richard Mahony[2] for, besides its being of course idle, I could not consent that my grandchildren should be *doomed* not to be Catholics. . . . Politics are grown quieter here much but we are all alive with Mr. Owen's plan.[3] There is to be a great meeting[4] tomorrow. I will go there if I can and make *a speech*. Darling, how I wish my girls were there to listen to me. Lord Wellesley is, I think, yielding to the Orange scoundrels. He cannot help it. He is not supported by anybody but he *will* remain. That is the *only* comfort.

SOURCE : Fitz-Simon Papers

1 That is, the married stepdaughters of Count O'Connell.
2 See letter 1004, note 11.
3 Robert Owen (1771-1858), the Welsh utopian socialist, made a very
  extensive tour of Ireland between the autumn of 1822 and the early
  summer of 1823 in order to study Irish social conditions and to
  publicize his ' New System of Society '—model villages organized
  on socialistic lines whose inhabitants would want for none of the
  necessities of life (Podmore, *Robert Owen*, I, 277-82).
4 Owen addressed large meetings at the Rotunda on 12, 19 and 24
  April. At the second meeting, alluded to in this letter, O'Connell
  attempted to speak in support of Owen but was obliged by a noisy
  minority to sit down (*FJ*, 14, 22, 23, 25 April 1823; *Patriot*, 17, 24,
  26 April 1823).

1011

From his wife to Merrion Square

Tours, 20 April 1823

My dearest love,

I received your letter last night which certainly did not help
to add to my repose. The description you give of my poor
Maurice makes me truly unhappy, but if his restlessness is a
disease, he is to be pitied and not condemned. When last I had
the happiness of seeing him there was a great change for the
better. Perhaps his constitution is more weakened by his
growth. I will hope anything to be the cause of all this misery
to you but an incurable disorder. My next letter shall be to him,
and my earnest advice shall be that he should at once use the
shower-bath. When he is with me I shall take great pains with
him, and if this fidgeting be merely a habit, I do not despair
of his getting quite free from it. Now, love, to answer you on
the subject of Morgan's becoming an attorney. I totally and
entirely disapprove of it. It is a profession I never wished for
any son of mine, but at present thinking of fixing Morgan to
any *trade* but [two or three words missing] is quite idle. You
don't know Morgan as [? I do]. Believe me, he is too fond
of liberty ever to submit to the control of any person for a
period of five years, much less consent to be bound to a *desk*.
The time for giving Morgan a profession is gone by, and you
are now too much committed with your uncle[1] to change your
mind. It would not be treating him well after all the trouble

he has taken and the obligations he is under to the Austrian Ambassador. The enclosed letter will show you what he still will do for Morgan. Can you, Dan, in justice to your other sons, refuse this commission for Morgan? Why should not Morgan get on as well as other young men in the Austrian service? Mr. Russell,[2] who resides here, has his second son in that service. He is only three years in it and he is already a lieutenant. Surely Morgan has better interest than he had. *He* has also health and a disposition to be happy in whatever situation he is in, but, believe me, it would be lost money to give him any other profession but the army. I repeat, I know Morgan better than you. . . . I have not spoken to Morgan on the subject of your letter nor shall I.

SOURCE : O'Connell Papers, NLI 13651

1   Count O'Connell.
2   Unidentified.

1012

From Thomas Spring Rice

Duchess St. [London], 26 April [1823]

My dear Sir,

Late courts here pressed so hard upon me that I have been unable to write.

We are for the present checked in our onward course but I do not in any respect feel discouraged.[1] Disapproving as I much do the secession of Burdett, etc., it worked well for us, for we should not have had as good a division as we might have expected; and as it is that calamity was averted. *All I am confident* will yet be well with prudence. The quieter we are the better. A false move would now play the Orangemen's game. If the inquiry into the conduct of the Sheriff[2] turns out as I expect we shall stand higher and stronger than ever. Indeed I think our case would then be irresistable.

Pray send me the Catholic Charity bill.[3] Relying on you I have not put this matter into other hands.

SOURCE : Fitz-Simon Papers

1   On 17 April the Commons debated the ' Catholic Claims '. Burdett and Hume expressed chagrin that the cabinet was not sponsoring an Emancipation measure and, with other members of the opposi-

tion, left the House in protest. Consequently they were not present
to vote on a motion that the debate be adjourned indefinitely which
passed by 313 to 111.

2   The Commons inquiry into the conduct of Sheriff Charles Thorpe
of Dublin city (see letter 1020, note 1).

3   On 3 July 1823 leave was given to Sir Henry Parnell and Sir John
Newport to introduce a bill to enable Roman Catholics to make and
execute gifts and grants for pious and charitable purposes. The bill
was not introduced.

1013

To his wife at Tours

Merrion Square, 28 April 1823

My darling love,

The delay in writing to you for much more than a week
has been occasioned principally by my anxiety that this letter
should contain something conclusive about your departure
from Tours. I regret excessively that it cannot simply because
I have not as yet *mastered* the funds sufficient for that purpose.
. . . I have heard from Bric who has been lately down at
Exeter. The place is cheap, commodious, pleasant and the
climate mild, the packets between Havre and Southampton
excellent, the passage from 14 to 20 hours and a good deal of
it smooth water. . . .

I have not time to write politics. The priest who was
sentenced to a year's imprisonment was guilty of no other
offence than attending a sick woman who sent for him in spite
of an Orange husband. The conviction[1] was atrocious but I
believe I shall easily get rid of it. I have this day caused a writ
of error to issue. With respect to the Catholic cause you must
have been astounded at the result. We are, however, beginning
a general rally in Dublin. We are to get up the Catholic Board
again[2] and to take the strongest measures the law will allow
to enforce our cause on the attention of parliament. I believe
what has happened is all for the best. . . .

SOURCE : Fitz-Simon Papers

1   Unidentified.

2   A reference to the Catholic Association, the founding of which had
been planned at a dinner party in the Fitz-Simon home at Glencullen
in the Dublin mountains on 8 February. The attendance consisted of
Mr. and Mrs. Thomas O'Mara (host and hostess), Christopher

Fitz-Simon, Lord Killeen, Richard Lalor Sheil and O'Connell (information supplied by Lt. Col. M. O'Connell Fitz-Simon, M.C.).

On 25 April a preliminary meeting of Catholics took place in Dublin, Lord Killeen in the chair. The attendance included Sir Thomas Esmonde, Sir John Burke, Hon. Thomas Barnewall, Nicholas Mahon, William Murphy, Hugh O'Connor and John Howley, Jr. It was decided to form a Catholic organization because of (as Hugh O'Connor put it) ' the present deplorable state of Catholic Affairs ', and to hold an aggregate meeting on 10 May. The meeting appointed Nicholas Purcell O'Gorman as ' Secretary to the Roman Catholics of Ireland ' (*DEP*, 26 April and 1 May 1823). The aggregate meeting took place in Townsend Street chapel on 10 May, Lord Killeen in the chair. It passed several resolutions among which was one to form an association in Dublin to assist the Emancipation cause and to hold a meeting on the following Monday, 12 May, for that purpose (*DEP*, 13 May 1823). This meeting was held accordingly in Dempsey's City of Dublin Tavern, Sackville Street, Lord Killeen in the chair. It resolved ' That an Association of Catholic Gentlemen should be formed and that an Annual Subscription of One Guinea should constitute a Member ' and ' That the name of our Association be " The Catholic Association " ' (*DEP*, 13 May 1823).

1014

To his wife at Tours

Merrion Square, 1 May 1823

My darling love,

. . . I have settled everything for your accommodation at Exeter, that is, I have ascertained the facility of our wishes being carried into effect there. All that remains is your approval of the plan. If you approve of it you may reckon on my cooperation. If your letter in answer to mine of the 18th of April approves of my going for you to Paris I *shall meet you there about* the 20th of this month. . . . Get Morgan to write to John Egan[1] to take handsome lodgings for you not far from the General's.[2] Let him also write to the General. I will write to him by the next post to that which takes this letter. If Morgan kept up his intimacy with Nancy McCarthy's[3] family she would take lodgings for you. I beg of you, love, *for my sake,* that is, if *you love me*, to forget what passed and forgive her and see her and her daughters. Let the lodgings be handsome, eight or ten Napoleons can make no great difference if paid more than you otherwise would. But, darling, you *must* not trust my girls to Madame d'Etchegoyen[4] without your own attention, that is, do not let them go to any party without your being with them. Observe this, darling, strictly while in Paris. It is your fond husband's only *command*. . . . Morgan knows the Rue Richelieu. It was in it we lodged at a *shabby* hotel called Hotel d'Irlande. I would not wish you to go there. Get to the Hotel des Colonies and you can remain there till you get lodgings. Hire a job carriage, you can get a handsome one for five or six or, at the worst, ten francs by the day. Show my girls every-thing. Do not lose time because I will be obliged to hurry you off when I arrive. . . . Your advice with respect to Morgan is decisive, and it will be a melancholy pleasure to me to embrace my own darling boy before we part for years. . . . Perhaps by starting very early you could go from Tours to Orleans in a day. As far as Blois the road is good. It is deep with loose clay-like sand between that and Orleans. . . .

SOURCE : Fitz-Simon Papers
1 Unidentified.
2 Count O'Connell.
3 Nancy McCarthy, daughter of Timothy McCarthy and Elizabeth O'Connell (O'Connell's aunt). She married (1) Darby Mahony (died 1796 in Kingston, Jamaica) and (2) her cousin Charles McCarthy.
4 Count O'Connell's stepdaughter.

1015

From Thomas Spring Rice

Duchess St. [London], Saturday
[c. early May 1823]

My dear O'Connell,

Have you forgotten my bill for Catholic charities?[1] I hope not. Pray let me have the draft as soon as you can.

I hope all looks well here with calmness and good sense. . . .

SOURCE : O'Connell Papers, NLI 13648
1 See letter 1012.

1016

From John Devereux

Bogotá, 6 May 1823

My dearest friend,

It is now some months since I apprised you and my dear Morgan of the premature and most melancholy event[1] which must have penetrated your hearts with the deepest sorrow and which, my dear friend, I have never ceased to contemplate with mingled emotions of exquisite sympathy and grief. I appreciated so highly the excellence and merits of our dear departed Maurice that I had him named and appointed by the Government, Secretary to the Legation to Russia, and had delighted myself with the prospect of soon presenting him to you and his family in that capacity as my cherished and most confidential friend! The solemn decree, alas, is gone forth, which has ordained it otherwise; and while I most sincerely condole with you, my dear Sir, and his family on this truly afflictive bereavement, I doubt not that you have enjoyed that support which arises from an acquiescence in the dispensations of the Almighty, in the consciousness that whatever mystery involve them, they are the appointment of infinite wisdom.

I would have set out on my mission[2] four months since but for a piece of information which I communicated to you and Morgan at the time and which has since been confirmed to me beyond the possibility of a doubt, namely, the marriage of the girl I so much adored to another. It has, my dear friend, as you may suppose, given me great pain; yet on consideration I begin to consider it a misfortune of that class which a reflecting mind will most easily overcome, for it is accompanied by no self-reproach, and regret must be mingled by a certain degree of contempt at the instability of human affections. We cannot justly quarrel with anyone for not loving us, or for ceasing to love us because the will is free, but we can console ourselves for the loss of affections which have proved too weak to endure the great tests of time and absence. I shall soon set out on my mission and, as I propose taking France in my way to Russia, I hope to have the happiness of hailing once more your dear and most estimable Lady and family. Enclosed is a letter for my dearest Morgan which you'll have the goodness to forward to him.

Recall me dearly to Counsellor Finlay and his Lady and also to the excellent Mr. Burrowes and Mr. Martin³ the solicitor— Ely Place. . . .

SOURCE : Fitz-Simon Papers
1 See letter 980.
2 See letter 976.
3 James Charles Martin, 2 Ely Place, Dublin.

1017

From his wife to Merrion Square

Tours, 7 [8, 9, 10 and 11] May 1823

My dearest love,

I cannot express my astonishment not having as yet heard your final determination respecting Morgan. . . . You complain, love, of the times and the want of money and yet you hesitate to accept a situation for your son so advantageous in every respect. You must be aware of the great expense this young man is at present to you and that the longer he is *thus* provided *for* the more unwilling he will be to do anything for himself. . . .

Thursday, 8 May

We met . . . another acquaintance of mine, a Mrs. Hirton [?],¹ wife also to a naval captain who resides here. *She* is making a great noise amongst the Protestants in consequence of her constant attendance during Lent to the sermons preached in the Cathedral. Her husband has forbidden her to go there any more. . . . I am *one* of her confidantes, the other two are a very pious old French lady and a most exemplary clergyman. You must therefore, love, be very discreet on *this* subject until I give you permission to speak *freely*. She told me before she left England she was most prejudiced against the Catholic religion but since she came to this country she had made it her *study*. She had read a great deal and the more she read the more convinced she was that she was in error. She believes firmly in every article of our faith. She does not *now* want *book*s of controversy but books of instruction. I have promised to lend her some and at the same time to introduce her to my director. *He* is of all others the best qualified for the instruction of a convert. I give you *this* intelligence, darling, knowing how you will rejoice at the return of even *one strayed sheep to the fold*. Mrs. Hirton [?] is quite an educated, well informed woman and of high family. You can't think how indignant she is at the treatment of the Irish Catholics. She wishes much to know you not more for your patriotism than for your piety. Would to God it were possible for you to converse with her. . . .

Friday, 9 May

. . . As for the Catholic cause, *it* is in my opinion *now* past redemption.

Saturday, 10 May

. . . I am now going with Ellen and John to the cathedral to pay a *visit* to Mr. Dubois. He attends *there* every Saturday from twelve until nearly four o'clock and, with the exception of one, all his penitents are Irish. Our family is so large we go on separate Saturdays generally three each Saturday.

Sunday, 11 May

. . . until I hear from you again I will not leave this. Indeed it would be quite impossible for us to make the rapid journey you point out to Exeter without a very great loss and a loss of your time which in such bad times as the present I think you cannot afford. . . .

SOURCE : O'Connell Papers, NLI 13651

1   Unidentified. The name is illegible and could be Hirton, Kinton or Kirton.

1018

From John Bric, London, 9 May 1823

In reply to O'Connell's queries Bric sends information about sailings from France to England and about living accommodation at Exeter.

SOURCE : Fitz-Simon Papers

1019

To John Kent Johnston, Eden Quay

Merrion Square, 10 May 1823

My dear Sir,

I believe the delay in concluding with the European Company[1] has a good deal arisen through my fault. I really have
too much to do for others to be able to attend to minute details
of my own, but I fancy much of this delay was caused by my
stating to Mr. Mannin[2] that some persons to whom I am indebted were unwilling to accept payment, being desirous I
should continue to pay them interest. . . .

[P.S.] I shall become a subscriber to Owen's Society.[3] He *may*
do some good and cannot do any harm.

SOURCE : O'Connell MSS, UCD
1 See letter 984.
2 Unidentified.
3 Hibernian Philanthropic Society, founded by Robert Owen, which
held its first meeting at Morrison's Great Rooms, Dublin, on 3 May
1823 (*Patriot,* 6 May 1823). Despite initial enthusiasm, the society
folded up before the end of one year (Podmore, *Robert Owen,*
I, 281-2).

1020

From Richard Milliken to Merrion Square

39 Paternoster Row, London, 14 May 1823

Private

My dear Sir,

I read with heartfelt pleasure óf your exertions in the cause
of justice and was happy at hearing of the fruits of some [of]
them. You are aware of the small interest that Irish affairs
excite in this country. Even this inquiry,[1] it is thought, will all
end in smoke and that our worthy Sheriff will walk away in
triumph, so do not let our friend exult too much. It is reported
that one of our ex-sub-sheriffs asked the other night where
Perceval *was shot* and said [that] perhaps our friend, Mr.

Plunket, might 'meet the same fate'. I believe this[2] will be mentioned in the House tonight. You heard of Mr. Graham[3] and
his sword-cane. In the streets you meet with Mr. Graham,
Handwich,[4] Leader,[5] Sibthorpe[6] walking together. The fellow
who serves the summonses, Golding,[7] watches closely Mr.
Blake's[8] Chambers to report which of our friends go there, and
to show you the treachery of their own party, men who are
afraid to speak to me on the lobby, if we meet on the stairs or
when they are not seen, they give me a squeeze or a hearty
shake of the hand, but I dislike such dubious characters and
think you will agree with me that *Poole*[9] was one of our best
witnesses. I ask your attention to a pamphlet[10] which I presume
he [*recte* you] will have read by this time in which your name
is mentioned *not ill-naturedly*. I wish I could name the author
but this I will say to *you* that I would prefer his pen to any that
I know at our side of the water. Ask Stewart[11] for the sheets
should it not be quite ready for publication, and favour me
with your opinion respecting it. I think it will make some
noise. That high-spirited gentleman and member of the Corporation, *Mr. Archer,*[12] whose transgressions I had forgiven
last year at the request of Mr. Rees[13] and Mr. Martin Kane,[14]
has, in my absence (the time he always attempts his injuries),
written to Lord Wellesley requesting ' his business, stating his
loyalty, his having served the office of sheriff and his father[15]
having been *twice sheriff* of the Co. Wicklow, a matter unpre-
cedented, and that he hears that prejudicial reports have been
circulated about him which *he believes* to be without foundation' and, strange to say, that although I have the most un-
bounded confidence of Lord Wellesley's most particular friends
who have honoured him with the most confidential matters, I
would not be surprised at this gentleman obtaining what he
seeks but, please God, I will exhibit him truly before that.

[P.S.] I ask you for one chance word to my poor wife as you
pass by.

SOURCE : O'Connell Papers, NLI 13647

1 A Commons committee of the whole House was inquiring into the
   conduct of Sheriff Charles Thorpe, the official who had empanelled
   an Orange jury in order that those Orangemen accused of the
   ' Bottle Riot ' (see letter 982, note 1) might be acquitted. Some fifty
   witnesses had come from Dublin, several of whom are named in
   this letter. The examination is recorded in *Minutes of Evidence
   taken before the Committee of the Whole House Appointed to*

Inquire into the Conduct of the Sheriff of the City of Dublin,
pp. 545-790, H.C. 1823 (308) VI.

2   There is no evidence of this being mentioned.

3   William Graham, printer, Orangeman, twice charged with riot,
    examined on 9 May 1823, carried a sword-stick.

4   Either of the brothers Henry and Mathew Handwich, carpenters,
    both of whom had been on charges dismissed by the grand jury
    and had subsequently been prosecuted by Plunket.

5   William Leader (Leadour), tallow-chandler, Orangeman, examined
    9 May.

6   Thomas Sibthorpe, born in Dublin c. 1798; son of Luke Sibthorpe,
    who represented the smiths on the common council; medical
    student at Trinity College, Dublin, since 1815; M.B., 1826; examined
    by Commons 9 May 1823.

7   P. Golding, bailiff, otherwise unidentified.

8   Probably Anthony Richard Blake.

9   William Poole, Co. Dublin landowner, member of the corporation
    since 1802, representing corporation of brewers, examined 6 May
    and described Thorpe as a ' Protestant ascendancy man ' who ' had
    the panel in his pocket '.

10 *Recent Scenes and Occurrences in Ireland or Animadversions on a
    Pamphlet entitled ' One Year of the Administration of the Marquess
    Wellesley ' in a letter to a friend in England,* published on 16 May
    1823 by Richard Milliken himself (*FJ*, 16 May 1823).

11 Presumably an employee at Milliken's printing works in Dublin.

12 Probably Charles P. Archer, 34 Dame Street, Dublin, H.M. Book-
    seller in Ireland, sheriff's peer. He was high sheriff of Dublin city
    in 1816.

13 Unidentified.

14 Unidentified.

15 Thomas Archer, Mount John, Newtownmountkennedy, Co. Wicklow;
    high sheriff, 1799 and 1800.

1021

To his wife at Tours

Dublin, 19 May 1823

My darling Love,

I have got your letter up to the 11th since I sent off mine
dated yesterday. I write this to say that I will not go for you till
after circuit. I had actually paid for my passage to Liverpool
in the steam packet of Wednesday and made all my arrangements. Well, darling, they are all over. Send Morgan at once

to Paris. He will find his old valet Thadee Peter there. I will write again to the General tomorrow and a long letter to you the day after. . . .

SOURCE : Fitz-Simon Papers

1022

To his wife at Tours

Merrion Square, Thursday, 22 [and 23] May 1823

My darling love,

I now recommence my journal to you which I have discontinued since the Cork assizes. . . . I got while I was in Cork a letter from you complaining of your own health and of that of my Nell and Kate and . . . I took for granted that it was a kind of petition to me to remove you if I could, and I immediately turned all my thoughts towards effecting that object. . . . Behold what must have been my astonishment when I got your first letter refusing to come off. . . . I got your letter refusing to stir even after getting my remittances. . . . I am, however, sure you have done quite right. . . . You are certainly right. . . . You have already approved of Exeter for the winter and we will get a good house *furnished* there at the rate of 100 guineas a year, that is, well and comfortably furnished, and I trust in God that before another winter I will have you all again merry in Merrion Square. I hope you have sent Morgan to Paris to the General. I will write to the latter tomorrow. Surely I told you, darling, that I approved of what you decided about him. I am sorry enough to have to tell you that Maurice will, I fear, never be cured of his shocking and foolish gesticulations. I do all I can but all, I fear, in vain. He has now got a trick of gapping and, as it were, slapping with his mouth that has a very silly effect. Poor fellow. What a cruelty it is of him to abandon himself to these miserable sillinesses. He has the present term to keep before he can go to London, but indeed I doubt whether you will not think it useless to go to the expense of giving him any profession. You shall, however, be the sole judge of that when he spends a month or two with you at Exeter. For my part I am nearly hopeless. . . . John[1] has left his eldest son at a school within a mile of Carlow. . . . I have got and read Scott's new novel, *Quentin Durward*.[2] I like it much.

Friday, 23 May [dated 24 in error]

Darling, you may rely on it that the name of the English lady[3] shall never escape my lips without your express permission founded on hers. God is very good to her and she ought to love him with intense gratitude. The more she considers, the more convinced will she be of the truth and purity of the Catholic faith, this faith which has had perpetual continuance from the days of the apostles to ours. We can tell the precise year when every sect began. When they endeavour to retort this upon us, no two of them agree in fixing the period when our religion began, and the date given by each of them is shown at once to be false by the clear proofs of the Catholic faith having existed before that date. In truth, Protestantism is unfortunately but the first step to infidelity. But, sweetest love, you will, I am sure, tell the excellent lady in question that the best way to be a Catholic is to excel in the performance of every duty. Mildness and attention towards everybody. Her husband should perceive by a thousand little attentions and those manners which sweeten life that his wife was rendered the better woman by embracing a better religion. There are a thousand cares in a family which may be performed in the spirit of the most perfect Christian charity and would go farther to soften down all opposition to the public profession of the Catholic faith than anything else. My Mr. Coleman's maxim too is ' beaucoup de piété, beaucoup de gaieté '. There is a ready cheerfulness which belongs to a conscience free from guilt which is superior to all the joys this world can give. These hints, darling, you will use discreetly or not at all as you think fit. As you are in her confidence you will do right to suggest this as the most easy mode to overcome opposition and perhaps to have the still greater happiness of getting her husband to think more seriously of the Catholic religion when he sees its mild and gentle precept making the performance of every duty more light and cheerful. Tell my children, darling, of their father's fondest love. I hope they have an opportunity of studying general and local history. They ought to know everything relative to France and especially to the Béarn where they were and Tours where they are. I wish my girls to read more books than you do, sweetest. Pray yield to me in this particular. Exeter is the place where they will have, if you please, books in plenty. . . .

SOURCE : Fitz-Simon Papers
1 His brother.
2 By Sir Walter Scott (Edinburgh 1823).
3 See letter 1017.

1023

To his wife at Tours

Merrion Square, 23 [24, 25, 26 and 28] May 1823

[No salutation]

. . . Darling, I passed the greater part of this day in court. I arose before six, worked till breakfast hour, but not breakfast, for this you know is a fast. Went to court, was concerned in jury cases until I spoke to evidence to a special jury between three and four and then came home with a right good appetite for a fine trout James got me, the first I have seen this long time. . . . I give you these details that we may again fall in the habit of this kind of communication because everything you and my children do is to me matter of great interest. Begin again with telling me what you all do every day. I have read *Quentin Durward*. I told you before I like it much. The scene is in France and Flanders up to Liege. The period the reign of Louis the 11th. The book opens on the banks of the Cher about a couple of leagues below Tours at a place called Plessis-les-Tours. I think I know it. The first scene finds the hero wading across the river Cher. This local interest made it not the less dear to me as you may well imagine. I think my girls will be delighted with it, and I will take care to send it to them and to you by the first possible opportunity. . . .

Saturday, 24 May

I remained in bed this morning until seven because it was the second fast day in succession and I did not like to exhaust myself by early rising. I was in court from about half after eleven till past three. I made three speeches to juries, in two of which I was very successful and in the third I had no reason to complain. I then went to the Catholic Association where we had great debating. The principal question was whether we would allow Protestants to be members of the Association by paying a subscription just as Catholics might. You will easily imagine that I was of *this* way of thinking and carried it by a triumphant majority. I wish we may find Protestants liberal enough to join us, that is all; we have done our part. The next motion was that we should allow no visitors but Protestants, that is, that no Catholic should come into the Board without paying one guinea a year. This we also carried, so that you see we have in our little parliament set the Protestants a good example. . . .

Sunday, 25 May

. . . You have I suppose seen by the newspapers that Dr. Troy is dead.[1] He arrived at a fine old age and died in sentiments of the purest religion. May the great and good God be merciful to his soul. Dr. Murray succeeds as a matter of course but cannot take the archiepiscopal *throne* until a notification is made to Rome. However, his right of succession is long since decided. Dr. Troy died without a guinea. He was a most charitable man and never was known to refuse giving what he could to a person in distress. He governed the Catholic Church in Ireland in a stormy period and was very much beloved by his own clergy. Darling, I mean to take a bath on my way to O'Mara's.[2] I prayed for you this morning and for the English lady.[3]

Monday, 26 May

I slept at O'Mara's last night and rode in this morning. . . . I remained at home working the far greater part of the day. . . . You have but two months more to stay at Tours for you will have to be at Madon,[4] I presume, early in August. I wrote to the General on the subject. If Boulanger Cartion has continued as civil as he was at first, get the General when he comes to Tours to pay him a visit and to thank him. I would be very glad to have *that* done unless the General expresses some unwillingness. Of course you will not in that case urge him. Darling, before you receive *Quentin Durward* go with your girls to see the castle built or at least inhabited by Louis the 11th at Plessis-les-Tours. It cannot be more than two miles and a half from Tours. It will give an additional interest to the story to have seen it before you read the book. Let me know whether you are not *now* full of money. When you got the £100 you had about £8 in bank, that is 200 francs, and everything paid including three months of the house rent. . . . Now, darling, remember to give me this information with precision and exactness. . . . I suppose you hear regularly of the examination[5] which is going on in the House of Commons. As far as it goes it does some service and no injury at all. But the vile English ministry are not disposed to do any kind of justice to Ireland nor will they until in some hour of distress and national degradation they want us excessively. I trust they will not wait until it is too late. Kerry is now quiet except some of the northern parts of it. Raymond's[6] house and offices at Riversdale were burned down by some of the unfortunate miscreants. He will suffer little as a presentment will certainly be granted and the county must pay.[7] The counties of Cork and Limerick continue very much disturbed as does part of Clare. Ribbonism is probably extending itself. So much the worse.

Wednesday, 28 May

I wrote *nothing* yesterday but did a great deal of work. I laboured at home until past eleven. I then went to the Custom House on a revenue trial until three, then to the Exchange upon a bankrupt question, then to the Catholic Association where we passed a great many resolutions,[8] and then home where I did a horse load of business before I went to bed having eaten my solitary dinner at home. . . . Edward Connor is come up this day from Tralee. He stops here. He brings no news but that all our friends there are well and that everybody in the country is as poor as a church-mouse. I bought some books for my Danny and some for John. They consist of a tolerably complete collection of school books called *Pinnock Cathechisms*.[9] They are upon almost every literary subject, and I promise you he can scarcely ask a rational question for which an answer can be wanting if you have the aid of these little books. I also will send by the *Dorset* the book Mrs. Donaldson wished for and seven volumes of Miss Edgeworth's.[10] They are of a small size and contain the continuation and sequel to *Early Lessons*. I hope I have hit on the right ones. . . . Write to Mrs. Harrison.[11] . . . You ought, love, to pay the postage of all letters you write to her. The poor woman cannot afford to be put to the expense of postage and ought not to afford it for strangers. But you are yourself so considerate that, surely, I need not say anything to remind you of these matters. . . .

SOURCE : Fitz-Simon Papers

1 Archbishop Troy died on 11 May at his house in Rutland Square, Dublin.

2 Glencullen, Co. Dublin (the Fitz-Simon house).
3 See letter 1017.
4 Chateau de Madon, near Blois.
5 See letter 1020.
6 George Raymond, Riversdale, Listowel, Co. Kerry.
7 In Ireland malicious damage was (and still is) chargeable on the county ratepayers.
8 This meeting (Joseph McDonnell in the chair) passed resolutions on rules of procedure (*DEP*, 29 May 1823).
9 'A series of short manuals of popular instruction, by means of question and answer, on almost every conceivable subject' (see *DNB*, s.v. 'Pinnock, William').
10 See letter 1007, note 1.
11 Unidentified.

1024

To Henry Brougham

Merrion Square, 26 May 1823

Dear Sir,

I did not send you last summer a copy of Mr. Saurin's letter.[1] I ought to have done so but the truth is that I felt you had treated me *slightly* in ' the affair of the Queen '[2] and without reflecting on how very little claim I had on your attention, I sacrificed a chance of doing some good to an idle, private or personal pique.

I now avail myself of your *first* letter to give you the following detail. Mr. Saurin's letter was found without any cover or direction on Ormond Quay in this city [Dublin] early in June 1822 by a young gentleman whose name is Monaghan.[3] He had been apprentice to an attorney, a Mr. Gibbs,[4] who is Deputy Clerk of the Crown of the Connaught Circuit. He was then put out of his apprenticeship. I am ignorant whether or not he has been since admitted an attorney, but at all events he can be easily found to prove the finding. He gave the letter to the Rev. Mr. Burke,[5] the parish priest of Summerhill in the County of Meath. That gentleman it was who communicated the contents to me, and I got the original from him and deposited it with Mr. O'Gorman, Secretary to the Catholics of Ireland, with whom it remains for any public purpose.

Such is the history of the finding of that letter. I am decidedly of opinion that evidence of crime is in its nature public property, and if you think fit to make any use of that document as any such evidence, you will at your discretion bring forward or suppress the names of the individuals I have thus mentioned. My name is also entirely at your service in that respect. I would not take the part I did with regard to Saurin's letter unless I had been convinced that I was right and, being of that opinion, I care very little for any obloquy which may follow my empowering you to make a full statement of the manner in which Mr. Saurin's letter was procured.

I write a second letter[6] on the subject of the administration of justice in Ireland. You must blame yourself if you find this correspondence troublesome. I write by your invitation.

SOURCE : Brougham MSS, University College London

1 See letter 969, note 1.
2 The appointment of an attorney-general for Ireland for Queen Caroline.
3 Unidentified.
4 George Gibbs, attorney, 35 York Street, Dublin, deputy clerk of the crown, Co. Longford. Longford was in the north-west, not the Connaught, circuit.
5 Rev. John Burke (died 1845), P.P. of Summerhill, 1824-26; Athboy, 1826-30; Castlepollard, 1830-45. A vigorous supporter of the Emancipation and anti-tithe movements, attracting the admiration of William Cobbett in his *Political Register* of 24 September 1831.
6 Unidentified.

1025
To his wife at Tours

Merrion Square, Friday,
30 [and 31 May, 2 and 3 June] 1823

My darling love,

. . . Yesterday I breakfasted out as usual on a holiday and after spending some time at home and the library I dined at the friary of Adam and Eve Chapel where we had Dr. Murray and a great quantity of the *Clergy*. I am sorry to tell you that Scully[1] was like to meet a very serious accident. He was out riding and came down on the crown of his head—whether by the fault of his horse or of something of a fit is not known. I went to see him and was convinced he was gone. I found him vomiting, which in such a case is considered a sign of fracture, and he seemed to me to be a little deranged. But I learn that his life is not at present despaired of. Tomorrow, I suppose, will nearly decide his fate. He had grown perfectly square being full as broad as he was long. His manners certainly were not or, I should say, are not in his favour, but he does not want good qualities. He is enormously rich but his family are young and involved in litigation. He would be a great loss to them indeed.

Saturday, 31st May

I have the pleasure to tell you that Scully's fall which I thought so dangerous turns out to be a mere nothing. I am, however, convinced it was near apoplexy and, as his skull was not fractured, the quantity of blood he lost from his head only served to do him good. . . .

Monday, 2 June

I dined yesterday in the country at Mr. Corballis'.[2] Edward Connor went with me. We had Doctor Murray there and altogether a very pleasant party. Their place is very much to my taste. I took my first cold shower-bath yesterday and was not a little pleased with myself for taking it. . . . I have had this a very busy day in court and I am going to dine at a Charity dinner. . . . I expect, sweetest, a couple of special retainers for circuit. That makes circuit pass in the manner most pleasant, especially the summer circuit. One of the special retainers is for Wexford, the other for Galway. . . .

Tuesday 3 June

. . . I spent yesterday evening at a charity dinner where I made a great variety of speeches, this day in court *arguing* cases. . . .

SOURCE : Fitz-Simon Papers
1 Denys Scully.
2 Richard Corballis, merchant, Upper Mount Street, Dublin, and Roebuck, Co. Dublin.

1026

From Henry Brougham

London, Monday [2 June 1823]

Dear Sir,

I have to thank you for much very valuable information in your two letters[1] received today. It is precisely of the kind I wished and you may depend on your name not being used.

Pray favour me with your opinion upon the probable effect in Ireland of our late strange proceedings as to Sir A. B. King.[2]

Allow me to set you right touching my apparent neglect of your most just claims in the matter of the Queen's[3] law appointments. I assure you it was partly through necessity, from the strong opinions entertained by lawyers here, and partly through the melancholy accident[4] that soon followed and cut short all further proceedings. But for that I believe it would have been tried and of course in your person.

SOURCE : Fitz-Simon Papers

1 See letter 1024.
2 The Commons committee, which was inquiring into the conduct of Sheriff Thorpe, repeatedly examined Sir Abraham Bradley King on 23 and 26 May. Twice lord mayor of Dublin and a former deputy grand master of the Orangemen of Ireland, King refused throughout (claiming privilege because of his Orange oath) to answer whether Orangemen were bound as such to regard Catholics like the Amalekites whom Joshua had urged the Israelites to vanquish (*Hansard*, N.S., IX, 490-535).
3 Queen Caroline.
4 The death of Queen Caroline on 7 August 1821.

1027

To his wife at Tours

Saturday, 7 [and 9, 10 and 13] June 1823

[No salutation]

. . . It will, in truth, be enough for you to be at Exeter before the winter sets in. I think you will have beyond any comparison a more pleasant winter there than at Tours. . . .

Monday, 9 June

. . . I went out yesterday after Mass to Blanchardstown. There was a great meeting of the school society there and a large public dinner.[1] I presided and we had great speeching. I rode home in the evening. There was a good deal of rain but I came in dry by means of an umbrella. I rode a very safe horse but cruelly slow. I however liked the evening. It was something in the wild style of Iveragh to travel in as I did, borrowing a horse from I knew not who. We had on Saturday a great meeting of the Association,[2] great debating, attacking the Orangemen as violently as we possibly can. There is no use in any other line of conduct. We shall next week have a petition[3] before parliament on the administration of justice in Ireland. We give it to Mr. Brougham. It is to be sure nearly useless but it is some comfort to keep the scoundrels in a state of uneasiness and disquiet if they will not grant us our rights. Judge Fletcher, my neighbour, is dead. He has left a large fortune to his only child, his son, the barrister who is an odd looking but a worthy creature. He will be succeeded it is said by Sergeant Torrens. Who is to succeed the Sergeant is not known. I wish it were Tom Goold with all his oddities.

Tuesday, 10 June

. . . I now think that my wife and children have grown careless of me and that those who once loved me have ceased to do so. Oh, my dearest Mary, I am indeed far from being happy. I do not think your letters are as affectionate as they used to be. None of my children write to me. . . . May God help us, love. I blame myself and have only myself to blame for our separation. . . .

Friday, June 13

. . . Your brother Rick is here and my brother James. The former came here to purchase new gums to his teeth, the latter to purchase an estate. . . . Darling, my heart is *heavy, heavy* at the length of your absence from me. My children have, I think, almost ceased to love their father. Even my Kate I am sometimes jealous of. My Betsey never loved her father much and I scolded my Nell so much about growing fat that I suppose she resents it. Give them all my *tenderest tenderest* love. . . .

SOURCE : Fitz-Simon Papers
1 Not reported in the press.
2 Catholic Association.
3 The petition sought a remedy for the alleged corruption of justice
   by the Orange party. Bearing 2,000 signatures it was presented to
   the Commons by Brougham on 25 June 1823 (*Hansard*, N.S., IX,
   1203).

1928

To Lord Donoughmore,[1] Bulstrode St., London

10 June 1823

My Lord,

I feel so much respect and gratitude towards your Lordship for your personal kindness to myself, and the unwearied zeal with which you have always advocated the cause of the Catholics of Ireland upon its true principles, that (however unnecessary in itself) I cannot avoid making a short comment to your Lordship on a recent occurrence amongst us. I mean the giving a partial Catholic petition to Earl Grey instead of respectfully entreating of your Lordship to present it for us.[2] The persons who act with me amongst the Catholics are, believe me, deeply penetrated with the same sentiments towards your Lordship that I am. And however a few individuals may think that, in transferring the petition from Mr. Plunket to Mr. Brougham in the Commons I intended any disrespect to the former, they are greatly mistaken, although upon that mistake may be founded the selection of Earl Grey in the House of Lords. I have only to add that the Catholics of Ireland, for whom your Lordship has been pleased to accept the management of their general petition,[3] are filled with sentiments of the most perfect conviction of the debt of gratitude they owe you and of the inestimable value of your services in our cause. For my humble self, I have so many additional motives to be devoted to your most estimable family that I should blush to belong to any body which could forget for one moment how deeply indebted we are to your Lordship. There is no danger of any such forgetfulness. And I now write only to show how jealous we should be of anything which could bear the appearance of such danger.

SOURCE : Donoughmore Papers

1 This letter bears the note: 'The kindest possible letter and the
   most gratifying to my feelings upon what had passed in the recent
   meeting of the R.C. Committee when the petition to Parliament
   respecting the administration of justice which he had moved should
   be presented to the House of Lords by me, was entrusted to Lord
   Grey.'
2 See letter 1031, notes 1 and 2.
3 A petition seeking Emancipation, resolved on at the Catholic
   aggregate meeting of 10 May (*DEP*, 13 May 1823).

1029

From Henry Brougham

London, 12 June 1823

Dear Sir,

I have to express to you my high sense of the honour conferred on me, through your means, in being entrusted with the
Petition[1] to the Commons.

The friends of the Roman Catholic body here all agree in
regarding this application as highly precious, the subject-matter
being at all times important and especially at the present
moment, and there being no doubt that, if a case can be made
out of a general unfairness in administering justice between
Catholic and Protestant, a most triumphant answer will be
given to all who say that the Penal Laws and their consequences
are no practical grievance to the body of the Roman Catholic
people.

Viewing it entirely in this light, as I have abandoned my
own motion[2] which stood for next Wednesday, I have resolved,
beside presenting the Petition, to move on Wednesday next,
18th, that it be referred to the Grand Committee on Courts of
Justice. This proceeding will afford full scope for discussion
and whether we prevail or not, will do much practical good.

In addition to the facts I already possess, I am desirous of
receiving any other information which you may collect, illustra-
tive of Lord Redesdale's position, that there are two kinds of
Law and Justice in Ireland.

SOURCE : O'Connell Papers, NLI 13647. Also *Irish Monthly*, XII
        (1884), 104.

1 See letter 1027, note 3.
2 On 11 June Brougham informed the Commons that he would

withdraw his notice as to the state of Ireland (when this notice had been given has not been identified). He added that he would present a Catholic petition the next day and, at a later date, would move that it be referred to a committee of the whole House (*DEP*, 14 June 1823).

1030

To his wife at Tours

Merrion Square, 14 [and 16 and 17] June 1823

My darling Love,

I had the happiness of receiving your letter dated up to the 6th this day. . . . Darling, your letter is not calculated to raise my spirits. There is an air of coldness and, I think, of vexation in it which is far from being cheering to me. I never again shall, I perceive, have anybody really to love me, and after all why should I? You are as angry with me about what I said of my girls' reading as if I had meant to offend.[1] *Indeed,* indeed I did not. Forgive me, darling, I will avoid such topics in future. How bitterly do I regret that I placed myself in a situation to be compelled to separate from my family. . . . Did I say anything which called for the reproach that I wished your girls to read books which clergymen could condemn as inconsistent with religion? If I did I entirely retract it and beg of you, my dearest Mary, to be convinced that I did not intend to say any such thing. . . . John, I perceive by your letter, is turning out badly. He was a *great great* favourite of mine but idleness is so miserable and mean a quality that I would entertain no great hope of him if he were idle, and I am sure he must be very idle when you tell me of it. It is a sad thing for me to have my boys disappoint me thus. I did indeed entertain considerable expectations of my poor John, but idleness at his age, believe me, is almost incurable. . . . I wish Kate would write to me but no, love, leave them all in that respect to themselves. . . . Politics look as badly as possible. The dastard Spaniards did not strike one blow for Liberty.[2]

Monday, 16 June

. . . Darling love, let me implore of you not to write to me upon any topic which has in it the slightest tincture of vexation towards your poor husband. I desire your pity, darling, so long separated from all my heart holds dear, and I feel that weariness of the heart which the Swiss experience when they think of their fond home. . . .

Tuesday, 17 June

Speak very seriously to my John for me. Tell him I am literally shocked at his being idle. Idleness shows a want of energy and an absence of that thirst for knowledge without which no person can be fit for anything save base and mechanical pursuits. He shall not have my fondness if he does not give up idleness at once and for ever. I work fifteen or sixteen hours out of the 24. I will only ask him to work 5 or 6. . . .

SOURCE : Fitz-Simon Papers
1 See letter 1022.
2 A reference to the ease with which the French forces which crossed into Spain on 7 April 1823 were able to occupy the country.

1031

From Lord Donoughmore

Bulstrode St., Manchester Square [London],
18 June 1823

Copy

My dear Sir,

I have been far from well for these few days past but am now much better or I should have thought myself unpardonable in letting a moment pass without expressing to you my best thanks for your friendly communication and for the honour which you did me by your kind support upon a late occasion.[1] Indeed with your valuable testimony that I have been at all times ready to do my best for my Catholic countrymen, I was enabled to look with much comparative indifference as to what the sentiments might be of several other individuals of that meeting upon the subject of so unimportant a person as myself. At all events whatever my political transgressions may have been I have no sins of neglect to lay to my charge as relating to the interests of the Roman Catholic body; and your earnest and manly and talented mind was prepared to render more than justice where you felt that the intentions and the heart were sound.

I have no right to complain that I did not appear upon a late occasion to find equal favour in every man's sight, and undoubtedly I could have no title to a monopoly in the presentation of the petitions of my Catholic countrymen upon all subjects whatever. But one thing I feel that I have a right to claim from them and from all those who put themselves forward in their cause and that is to be free from misrepresentation; and I therefore consider that I have just ground to complain of the statement of a learned gentleman[2] when he urged as a reason for not giving the late petition to me that it ought to be given to a person of the same cast of political opinion with Mr. Brougham. If the learned gentleman intended thereby to declare that such was not the case so far as regarded Mr. Brougham's opinion and mine, the learned gentleman would not make a declaration consistent with the fact. My political feelings are those of opposition to his Majesty's present ministers with whom I scarcely know any public measure which has been questioned, in which I have ever agreed. I should therefore wish that the learned gentleman would henceforward be good enough to spare his comments upon my parliamentary conduct.

SOURCE : Donoughmore Papers

1 The occasion was a meeting of the Catholic Association on 7 June when O'Connell proposed that Donoughmore, as a proved friend of the Catholics, should be asked to present the current petition (complaining of the administration of justice in Ireland) to the Lords (*DEP*, 10 June 1823).
2 Richard Lalor Sheil, who at the above meeting insisted that the petition be confided to Lord Grey since he was of the same politics as Brougham who would be presenting it to the Commons (*DEP*, 10 June 1823).

1032

To his wife at Tours

Merrion Square, Wednesday, 18 [and 19, 20 and 21] June 1823

My darling Mary,

I sent off a letter yesterday for you and wrote it in a good deal of mental suffering. My mind is now more at ease. Perhaps it is that term being now over I feel more distinctly the period approach when I shall have the happiness to see you and my darling children. . . . The fury of the Orange party is high though I hope it will meet with more distinct opposition from Lord Wellesley than it has hitherto done. Yet there are but little grounds for such hope. . . .

Kean Mahony was married last week to Miss Cronin and Shea Lawlor[1] to the second daughter of Dan Mahony of Dunloe Castle. He of course gets no fortune by her. His own affairs are, I believe, a good deal embarrassed, but so are those of almost every country gentleman with very few exceptions.

Thursday, the 19th June.

Darling, sweetest darling, I have just got your letter to the 12th, that is to this day week. I believe you are quite right, sweetest Mary, and that what I want is *petting*. Indeed I want those that I love, and in the meantime it is not possible to be more pleased than I am at the account you give me of my children. . . . I believe, love, I will send you your son Maurice. Poor fellow, my heart bleeds when I think how foolishly he is throwing himself away. You will soon perceive that it is not possible to overcome by mild means his propensities to silly and idle gesticulation. You will then, darling, *acquit* me. I believe, love, that I am to get a patent of precedence.[2] It will, if I get it, entitle me to a silk gown and a place amongst the King's Counsel. I would not, you know, take it if it were either ' Place, pension or office ', but I believe I may take it as it is a mere right of preaudience. However, it is probable that Lord Manners will use every effort in his power to prevent my getting it. The idea is due to the Chief Justice, who, you know, is Charles Bushe. He spoke of me in the most flattering terms to the Lord-Lieutenant, and Blake, the English barrister, gave me to understand that the matter was settled. Darling, I mention Blake's name only in confidence. He has taken the office of *Remembrancer*, for that is the name of his office, with a salary of £3,000 and the office is for life. It is very fortunate for the Catholics that he should be here. It would make a difference of at least a thousand pounds a year to me to have the silk gown and of course I would not sacrifice one particle of my independence to get it.

Friday, the 20th June.

. . . You will find him [Maurice] much changed for the worse. Alas, alas. I must however submit. It is better I should send him to you than keep him here. I know not what to do

with him. Your brother and mine are still here. So is Edward
Connor and O'Donoghue.³ It is ludicrous to see the difference
between our dinner and that which they would have if you
were here. . . . There was a dreadful battle the other day
between the Orangemen and the Catholics at a place called
Maghera.⁴ The Catholics were armed with common hand
sticks, the Orangemen with muskets loaded with ball cartridges.
Of the Catholics there were something about 12 killed and from
50 to 60 wounded. The accounts I have from the Castle this day
are that I am certainly to get the silk gown by a patent of
precedence. I can scarcely believe it myself although I am
assured it is the fact. It would help to bring home my wife and
children.

Saturday, 21 June
    . . . Why, sweetest, are you so angry about my sending
to pay any trifle which might be due to Mrs. Harrison?
Darling, I *could not* entertain an idea derogatory to you.
Believe that, my Mary. I wrote to the General not to take the
trouble of a journey to Tours as you were all to see him at
Madon. That was all, sweetest. . . .

SOURCE : Fitz-Simon Papers
1 John Shea Lawlor (born 1798), son of John Lawlor, corn merchant.
   Called to the bar, 1830. Married 1823 Margaret, daughter of Daniel
   Mahony, Dunloe Castle, Killarney, Co. Kerry.
2 A patent of precedence (precedency) was granted by the crown
   and enabled a barrister to practise as a K.C. (see letter 930, note 6).
   It was an honour very rarely granted.
3 Probably Charles James, O'Donoghue of the Glens (1807-33).
4 A riot took place on 12 June at a fair at Maghera, Co. Londonderry,
   resulting in the deaths of several people (*DEP,* 17, 19 June 1823).

1033

To his wife at Tours

Merrion Square,
Wednesday, 25 [and 26 and 27] June 1823

My darling Love,
    . . . On Sunday I went to Mr. Corballis. My brother James
and Maurice dined with me there. Rick¹ and Edward Connor
dined here. . . . There is nothing at all *new* in Kerry nor

here save the *old* story, party spirit oppression and no hopes
of any amendment. I never knew appearances so unfavourable for the country and its friends as they are at the present
moment or so much cause to be dispirited on every account.
Despotism is succeeding in Spain[2] and Portugal[3] and the
Orange system in England and Ireland. It is generally thought
here that the only chance the Catholics of Ireland have is
from the Bourbons who will become so powerful after their
conquest of Spain that they may terrify the English into better
treatment of the Catholics of Ireland, but these are speculations
to be laughed at. Darling, I must send you money as soon
as I possibly can so as to have your arrangements made to get
you to Madon as early in August *as you are asked* and wish
to go. How mistaken you are when you say I am ashamed of
my family. I am proud, darling, of my family and I would
be truly sorry to contrast any of them with any French lady
I ever saw.

Thursday, 26 June

. . . I sent . . . quite a library for my Danny, and a
Latin and Greek grammar for my poor John. It delights me
to hear that he is growing more diligent. Tell him he must
work hard if he wishes to please his father. All I ask of him
is work. . . . The business, darling, is very considerable and
I am at the top of the wheel. I receive no less than £600 this
month and there are *five* days of the month yet to come for
I am writing to you now at an early hour. My brother James
talks of coming with me to Madon to see the General. It
would delight you all to see him. . . .

Friday, 27 June

The town is ringing with a miracle of Prince Hohenlohe's[4]
affected on a Miss Lalor[5] at Maryboro. It was published last
night in the [*Dublin*] *Evening Post* under the sanction of Dr.
Doyle, the Catholic Bishop of Carlow.[6] There is no doubt at
all of the fact. Miss Lalor was deprived of her speech more
than six years ago. She had two or three medical men in
attendance and no less than eight Dublin physicians consulted.
Prince Hohenlohe was requested by the Bishop to intercede
for her, and his answer fixed the 10th of June as the day on
which he was to say Mass for her. Accordingly on that day she
was instantaneously cured and is as well as ever she was in

her life. Protestants and Catholics were equally witnesses of
this miracle, and the bishop, who is a man of the highest character for talents as well as integrity, has affixed his name to
the public account of it. It will create a sensation all over
Europe because Dr. Doyle is admitted by the very worst of
the Orange faction to be a man of the utmost ability and
probity. The former, at least, is beyond controversy, and he
would be a fool man indeed if he were to expose himself to
be detected in a false statement which he would certainly be
if his account of this miracle were not certainly true.[7] Darling,
the circuits are fixed. I do not think I will go any part of my
own. I have already special retainers for Wexford and Galway
and for Trim in the County of Meath. . . .

SOURCE : Fitz-Simon Papers
1 Mary O'Connell's brother Rickard O'Connell.
2 As a result of the French invasion of Spain, the *Liberales* were being
   overthrown and the harsh reactionary rule of Ferdinand VII was
   being restored.
3 John VI's younger son, Miguel, was at this time leading an absolutist
   movement against the weak constitutional regime of the Cortes.
4 Prince Alexander Leopold Franz Emerich von Hohenlohe Walden-
   burg Schillingfürst (1794-1850). Ordained a Catholic priest in 1815,
   he soon became renowned for the miraculous cures attributed to
   him.
5 Miss Maria Lalor, born c. 1805, daughter of James Lalor, Rosskelton,
   near Maryborough, Queen's County (*DEP,* 26 June 1823).
6 *Recte* bishop of Kildare and Leighlin and residing at Carlow town.
7 A quite different view of this and another cure was expressed by
   ' A Rational Christian ' in a pamphlet, *An Exposure of the Late
   Irish Miracles* . . . (Dublin 1823).

1034

From his son Morgan to Merrion Square

Paris, Wednesday, 25 June 1823

My Dear Father,

Tomorrow being the day appointed for my departure for
Italy I write this to inform you of it and also that my uncle[1]
is much better. He desires me give you his affectionate love
and that as soon as he is able he will write to you. I write to
my mother today also and will write to her again from Lyons,
Turin, and Milan but don't intend to write again to you till

I reach Vicenza and am settled with the regiment.[2] Of course you have all the news from Spain to a greater extent than we have except through the English papers by which I see a great account of the meetings of the Catholic Association and of Sir Harcourt Lees'[3] proclamation.[4] I suppose you heard that Lady Holland,[5] Lady Oxford[6] and Mrs. Hutchinson[7] were ordered by the police to quit Paris. They were accused of seeing people at their houses who were inimical to the Bourbons and to the Government. I saw old Louis drive out the other day. The carriage was open and the poor old man looked very ill indeed, thin and yellow. I also saw the Duchess of Berri,[8] an ugly squint-eyed little woman. I wrote to Tours today and my uncle[9] desired me state to my Mamma that, as he was afraid his illness would hinder them from going to Madon so soon as he could wish, still that as soon as she had got rid of her house, she could come up and take possession of Madon till you go for them. They'd be supplied with everything by the housekeeper that they could want. The General has also put me in funds for the campaign. He has given 600 francs in money for my travelling expenses of which 150 are paid for my place to Milan. He has also given me a bill for 1,200 francs on Vienna, 600 of which he thinks will be about the amount of the money necessary to be lodged with the paymaster of the regiment for my equipment, and the other 600 is to be my allowance till the 1st of January next, and he says that I'll always get the bill cashed by the paymaster of the regiment. . . . Richard Mahony intends starting almost immediately for Ireland. He says that in a letter from his brother Denis he was told the prices are rising in Kerry. . . . The General has bought a new watch for Ellen, much handsomer than her last and engaged to go well. . . . You can't think how it annoys me every day at D'Etchegoyen's to be obliged to sit still and listen to such opinions as they and their friends give about the war and the whole batch of the Bourbons and Ultras. I am sometimes almost tempted to attack one of them. . . .

[P.S.] On second thoughts I believe I had better write to you from Milan. Baron O'Brady is at Vienna. Wouldn't it be as well if you were to write to him and enclose the letter to me to Vicenza and I'll take care to get it delivered. His regiment is the 1st Infantry of the line and I'm sure he'll be most happy to give Charles Connor[10] an appointment to a battalion of his. My address in Italy is à Mons. M. O'Connell, Cadet dans le 4me régiment de chevaux légers à Vicenza.

SOURCE : O'Connell Papers, NLI 13645

1 Count O'Connell.
2 The 4th Leger Cavalry in the Austrian army.
3 Rev. Sir Harcourt Lees, second baronet (1776-1852), Seapoint, Blackrock, Co. Dublin. Pamphleteer in opposition to Catholic Emancipation. See *DNB*.
4 'The Address of Sir Harcourt Lees, Bart. to the Orangemen of Ireland', 3 June 1823, urging them not to be provoked into disorder while warning them against the consequences of recent Catholic activity which he termed 'the Popish Plot' (*DEP,* 12 June 1823).
5 Elizabeth (1770-1845), the divorced wife of Sir Godfrey Webster, fourth baronet; daughter of Richard Vassall, Jamaica; married 1797 Henry Richard (Fox-Vassall), third Baron Holland.
6 Jane Elizabeth (1773-1824), wife of the fifth earl of Oxford.
7 Probably Mrs. Woodcock (usually known as Mrs. Hutchinson) who lived with Christopher Hely-Hutchinson for some years and whose salon in Paris was a meeting-place for people of radical political outlook (see Harold Kurtz, *The Trial of Marshal Ney: His Last Years and Death* [London 1957], pp. 267-8).
8 Caroline Ferdinande Louise (de Bourbon), duchesse de Berry (1798-1833), wife of Charles Ferdinand (D'Artois), duc de Berry (who was assassinated in Paris, 13 February 1820).
9 His grand-uncle Count O'Connell.
10 Charles J. Connor (O'Connor) (1801-61), C.C. of Sandyford and Glencullen, Co. Dublin; son of James Connor and nephew of O'Connell's wife.

1035

From Henry Brougham

London, Friday [27 June 1823]

My dear Sir,

The petition[1] was fully debated last night on my motion[2] and I was ably supported by Hutchinson, Parnell, Abercromby. Never did I see debate so wholly on one side. Our facts were admitted and even confirmed, so was the state of Ireland. The bulk of their argument was an attack on the Catholic Association and on the *violence* and *style* of the petition which I defended and also showed them they had no right to be nice after all their crimes against Ireland, either as to men's words or actions.

The means of obtaining Saurin's letter[3] were again attacked and I believe those who in a luckless hour chose that topic have little reason to rejoice for it opened up the Queen's case[4] on them. One great point they made was that leading Catholics did not concur in the petition, but I denied this and predicted that this treatment of it would rally every R.C. in Ireland round you. I am going to give other proofs today.

SOURCE : Fitz-Simon Papers

1   See letter 1027, note 3.
2   The motion was 'That the said petition be referred to the Grand Committee for Courts of Justice'. It was defeated by 139 votes to 59.
3   See letters 969 and 1024.
4   That of Queen Caroline.

1036

To his wife at Tours

Merrion Square, Sunday, 29 [and 30 June,
1 and 2 July] 1823

My darling Love,

. . . Maurice has not *as yet* gone to his duty.[1] He says he *will* but that, alas, is likely to continue in the future tense, it *will* be. He has, however, improved in regard to his fidgety tricks, and I now plainly perceive that he can get rid of them if he chooses. . . . We had yesterday a chancery suit between Davy Fitzgerald,[2] the attorney, and Arthur Blennerhassett[3] of Ballyseedy for £300 in which honest Davy was defeated. Blennerhassett is living with his wife in Kerry but I do not imagine that they will long continue to reside there. His affairs are considerably deranged and he must I think shortly retire from out of the way of the Sheriff. In fact nine-tenths of the country gentlemen in Kerry are ruined. The total want of rents has swept them clean. It is, however, said—and I incline to believe it—that there is a prospect of an improvement in prices which will, if it continues, give us something out of our lands. I am more anxious on your account than on my own *much, much, much*. I implore of you to send me an immediate account of the General.[4] . . . I feel very, very anxious about his health. He really would be a cruel loss to me as if God spares his life, he will certainly push forward our darling Morgan to such a rank as would give him independence.

Besides we have every reason to love him as the best and most generous of men. . . .

Monday, 30th June

    . . . I had a great day of this. There was an action[5] tried in the King's Bench brought by a gentleman against a lady for not marrying him. I was counsel for the lady and we beat the swain out of court. . . . I was also busy in *twenty* other causes. Mr. Brougham has written to me about my silk gown.[6] He will speak of it in Parliament. So far so good. I believe still that I am to get it and the best is, darling, that I can do without it. I am beginning to think that there is a chance of amendment for *us* farmers. Better prices are springing up for agricultural produce. . . .

1 July

    Darling, there is not the least symptom of Orange display this day, neither is there any likelihood of there being any in this town on the 12th. But with respect to the Catholic address[7] to the King, you are right when you say that it is useless. . . .

2 July

    . . . Darling, I am very, very busy. It would please you to see how my business increases and yet I do not get out of my difficulties. The truth is the load was too heavy for me and I am only just beginning to see a possibility of getting rid of it. Do you, however, sweetest, keep up your spirits. Another year in England will bring *all* round again so that *if ever* I live to succeed to my Uncle's[8] property I will have the pleasure of being out of debt. I never could get on but for the immense income of my profession. In June alone I received £700 and paid it all away, but it extinguishes so much. . . .

SOURCE : Fitz-Simon Papers

1   Easter Duty—the obligation for Catholics to receive the Sacraments during the period from Ash Wednesday to Trinity Sunday, or as soon as possible thereafter.
2   David Fitzgerald, attorney, 14 North Earl Street, Dublin, second son of David Fitzgerald, Ardrivale, Co. Kerry, and Catherine Twiss.
3   Arthur Blennerhassett, Sr., Ballyseedy, Tralee, Co. Kerry; married Dorcas, daughter of George Twiss.
4   Count O'Connell.
5   *Edward Fairfield* v. *Eliza Walker* (DEP, 3 July 1823).
6   That is, a patent of precedency.

7   This address was passed by an aggregate meeting of the Catholics
    of Ireland in Dublin on 10 May. It described what it considered
    the desperate state of the Catholics because of the Penal Laws and
    the unjust administration of law. It asked the king to take their
    grievances into his consideration and to recommend to parliament
    the redress of those grievances (*DEP*, 13 May 1823).
8   Hunting-Cap.

1037

To Lord Donoughmore

Merrion Square, 2 July 1823

My Lord,

I beg leave respectfully to solicit your Lordship's attention
to the bill[1] before the House of Lords relative to the profession
of attorneys in Ireland. The reason why I make this request is
because I am convinced *by experience* that bill is calculated to
do much mischief to the public. Having no other motives I
venture to hope that my testimony will add to the impression
which I perceive by the public papers[2] has already been made
on your Lordship's mind on this subject.

Your Lordship has been always so kind and condescending
to any request of mine that I am thus tempted to trespass on
you. . . .

SOURCE : Donoughmore Papers

1   The Court of Chancery Bill introduced to the Lords on 25 June
    (enacted as 4 Geo. IV c. 61). Section XII of this act debarred
    officers and clerks of that court from practising as solicitors or
    attorneys.
2   Donoughmore formally dissented on 23 June from the third reading
    of the Grand Jury Presentment Bill, objecting to any increase in the
    salaries of clerks of the crown while clerks of the peace were
    shown no favour (*Lords Journal*, LV, 807; *FJ*, 27 June 1823).

1038

To his wife at Tours

Merrion Square, 4 [and 6 and 8] July 1823

My darling heart's love,

I bitterly regret that I wrote those letters which have
afflicted you,[1] my sweetest Mary. I am the cause of your banish-

ment from house and home, and then I have the cruelty to inflict upon you additional misery by letting the overflowings of my bitterness fall on you but, dearest love, the truth is that my sorrow arises from our separation. . . . I place all my bliss in this world in making you all happy. I never will *scold* any one of my girls again. Oh, Mary, how I shall doat of them. I also got a letter[2] from my Morgan to say that the General[3] was much better. You do not know all the reasons you have to love him. . . . The D'Etchegoyens will not be able to leave Paris by the first of August. The General proposes that you and my family should take possession of the Chateau at Madon before they get there. But that, I suppose, you will not relish. Neither indeed does it strike me as a good plan. . . . Rick[4] and I dined with O'Mara[5] who was surgeon to Napoleon. We dined with him at Lyons[6] the Atty's. He is a plain, unaffected young man, greatly attached to the memory of the unfortunate great man. He had a beautiful snuff-box given to him by Napoleon, gold with the N and Crown and many bees and stars. It was a beautiful article and the association of ideas made it really interesting. . . .

Darling, the cause of Liberty is put down everywhere. The dastard Spaniards are crouching[7] and the Portuguese are again become ' Base Lusian Slaves—the lowest of the low '.[8] In short, the rascally Ultras in all countries in Europe triumph, and the only consolation to be found in this world is in family affection. I bear public misfortunes with quite a philosophical tranquillity. . . . I have three cases making together two hundred guineas for Wexford. . . .

Sunday, 6th July
    . . .

Tuesday, 8th July
    . . . You will not be sorry to hear that the *New Monthly Magazine*[9] just published, one of the best in London, has given a brilliant character of me. It was plainly written by some very sincere friend.[10] I will take it with me to you. It has, however, the extreme folly to describe me as a handsome man. Darling, you may be satisfied with *that* but others will laugh at it. . . .

SOURCE : Fitz-Simon Papers
1   Letters 1027 and 1030 meet this description.
2   Letter 1034.
3   Count O'Connell.

4 His brother-in-law Rickard O'Connell.
5 Edward Barry O'Meara (1786-1836), surgeon on board the *Belle-rophon* when it received Napoleon, 1815; surgeon to Napoleon at St. Helena, 1815-18. See *DNB*.
6 Either Joseph, 6 Arran Quay, or John C. Lyons, 93 St. Stephen's Green, Dublin.
7 A reference to the success of the French invading forces in Spain.
8 See letter 1033, note 3.
9 'Sketches of the Irish Bar, No. VI', in *New Monthly Magazine*, VIII (1823) 1-10.
10 The writer was William Henry Curran.

1039

To John Kent Johnston

Merrion Square, 5 July 1823

Copy

My dear Sir,

I wish to complain to you of the conduct of your Company to me. After having finally arranged everything and complied with every condition, I have had my trouble for nothing and they have broken off.[1] I do not wish you should enter into any expostulations on the subject with them, I merely wish you to know the fact. It is not worth-while to be angry, but for your sake I am sorry for it as they plainly are persons not to be dealt with.

SOURCE : O'Connell MSS, UCD
1 See letter 984.

1040

From Lord Donoughmore

Bulstrode St., Manchester Square [London], 5 July 1823

Copy

My dear Sir,

You will not, as I trust, doubt the ready attention which your letter which I have this moment found upon my table upon the subject of the bills[1] now in their progress relating to the profession of attorneys, would command at my hands. But from what I heard at the House of Lords yesterday respecting these bills, I rather expect that they will pass with little or no amendment.

For myself I have taken my leave of the House for the present session as my brother, Lord Hutchinson, and I propose leaving town for Knocklofty in the course of Monday week.

SOURCE : Donoughmore Papers

1 For one of these two bills see letter 1037, note 1. The second was the bill for the better administration of justice in the equity side of the Court of Exchequer introduced to the Lords on 7 July and enacted as 4 Geo. IV c. 70. Section XI of this act debarred officers of the Court of Exchequer from practising as solicitors or attorneys.

1041

From the Knight of Kerry to Merrion Square

Bath, 9 July 1823

My dear O'Connell,

I have this moment received your letter of the 5th.[1] I wish much that it caught me in London. I could in that case have easily found out and made approaches to individuals having influence with ' Atlas '.[2] It is difficult, as you will understand, to make adequate inquiry by letter but as soon as I learn the names I shall do my best. . . .

I dare say you will agree with me that, in my peculiar situation, *neutrality* was the proper course in the war against my colleague,[3] rather more justifiable than that of England in the affairs of Spain. All matters now coming before the House are influenced by the physical *exhaustion* of members, and this state favours the conservative principle of Ministers, viz., ' to do nothing '. Such a system may in their foreign relations only produce contempt and degradation but applied to Ireland is calculated to engender civil war. I will not ask whether any wise, but can any honest man wish to leave Ireland to itself under the present paroxisms?

SOURCE : O'Connell MSS, UCD

1 Not extant.
2 Robert Peel. A hostile English newspaper applied this epithet to Peel in 1815 (Fagan, *O'Connell*, I, 205).
3 James Crosbie, M.P. for Co. Kerry. On 26 June Brougham had

presented a petition from George Rowan charging Crosbie with
accepting bribes for procuring official appointments (*Hansard,* N.S.,
IX, 1253-5). On the following day Brougham read part of a letter
from an unnamed M.P. in support of Rowan's character (ibid.,
pp. 1318-19). On 1 July the Knight of Kerry stated that he had
written the above letter but had done so only in response to
Brougham's query. He had had nothing to do with the petition
and did not wish to give any corroboration to it (ibid., pp. 1363-5).

1042

To his wife at Tours

Merrion Square, 13 July 1823

[No salutation]

. . . I now have the happiness to tell you that our dear
Maurice has been at Communion and I hope will be *there*
again before he leaves town. It is an ease to my mind and
ought to be so to my conscience. . . . You ask whether I
approve of your plan of going to Paris so soon as your term
of the house is out. Why, love, I believe I would approve of
anything you may propose. My judgement is really so warped
when I come to consider anything *you* propose that I am incapable of making a sound decision. But in this instance there
can be no doubt that you are right. It would be a *wild* plan
to have you go occupy a chateau in *the plains* without any
owner to take the management. Write to the General fully on
the subject. I will also write to him from Wexford. . . .

I am excessively anxious that my own girls should see
Paris thoroughly. I will, please God, spend three weeks there
with you, myself. We will visit Versailles, St. Cloud, etc. In
short I will endeavour to make you all as happy as I possibly
can. I anticipate with pleasure the joy of being with you to
see that proud but filthy capital. The contrast between it and
London is excessive. . . . He [Maurice] will take with him
' My Character ',[1] *Quentin Durward* and Debrett's *Peerage*
in two vols. for that learned lady, Miss Betsey O'Connell,
whom you call an authoress to quiz your old husband but
which husband cherishes in his heart his darling Betsey,
authoress or not. . . .

There is no political news. The country quieter. The
friends of freedom almost broken-hearted by the bare pol-
troonery of the miserable Spaniards[2] and the villainy of the

lousy Portuguese.[3] Darling, that is an ugly word but there is no other to describe the wretches. The 12th yesterday went off without the slightest noise, not in confusion. The statue was not dressed, not an Orange visible. I never saw a more tranquil day. I met a fellow in the streets who told me it was I did it all! ! ! . . .

SOURCE : Fitz-Simon Papers
1   No doubt in the *New Monthly Magazine* (see letter 1038, note 9).
2   See letter 1030, note 2.
3   See letter 1033, note 3.

1043
From Henry Brougham

Lambton, 30 July 1823

My dear Sir,

I ought long ago to have acknowledged the great obligations under which you have laid me by the kind and far too partial manner in which you were pleased to mention me at the late meeting.[1] I received the accounts while extremely busy on this circuit at York, and I deferred writing until I should find a little time to express how sincerely I felt my debt of gratitude to you. One who has lived long in public life becomes very indifferent to ordinary praise and blame but he learns the better how to prize the ' *laudari a laudato* '. I never shall be able to repay the obligation but I may endeavour to lighten it by tendering the currency you chiefly value, I mean my anxious efforts for your oppressed country and the interests of civil and religious liberty.

Allow me now to explain why I postponed mentioning in the late discussion on the Chancellor,[2] the important subject of your rank. I have met with no dissenting voice among either lawyers or political men upon the propriety of Lord W[ellesley's] making a point of this, but those to whom I stated my opinion, while they concurred clearly and strongly, thought the mooting such a point *now* in Parliament might be made the pretext, if not be the cause, of the present *half-measure-men* in Dublin objecting to it. At all events they deemed it fit to wait till next session before we broached the matter (which is one of some delicacy) publicly. To their arguments I yielded, knowing from experience the obstinate and powerful hostility of the Chancellor (Ld. Eldon), a man who never hesitates or scruples when a real or supposed interest of his own is in question, whatever he may do when the interests of others require him to be decisive. One who to pursue his bigoted prejudices or to gratify a personal pique or to exercise his revenge in safety for wrongs, which he may not have had the manliness to resist or to resent openly at the time (as in my case, at the Queen's trial), will have recourse to every kind of secret persecution. You would hardly believe the kind of *false pretences* to which he has been driven in vindicating himself from the charges of our Bar here as to the withholding of my rank and the total indifference he shows to the inconveniences he occasions both to the suitors and to the profession, including his own Tory partisans, whom he has thrown out of business for the sake of a last attempt (which has signally failed) to injure me. His bigotry on the Catholic question may produce the same effects in your case, resembling mine as it does in some respects, it will for that reason be the more odious in his eyes and, were I now to mention it, he would be fixed in personal opposition to it. Therefore, my wish is that you should have the matter brought before Lord Wellesley by the suggestion of some common friend and that he should urge it before anything is said in Parliament. If this fails, then next session it must be brought forward as part of the case which we all look forward to with much expectation and unabated zeal.

SOURCE : O'Connell Papers, NLI 13647

1 The meeting of the Catholic Association on 12 July when O'Connell paid a tribute to Brougham for his speech in the Commons on 25 June when presenting the petition from Irish Catholics complaining of the inequality of the administration of the law (*DEP*, 15 July 1823).

2 Probably Lord Manners, the lord chancellor of Ireland, whom Brougham attacked in his second speech in the Commons on 26 June on the administration of justice in Ireland (*Hansard*, N.S., IX, 1311-17).

1044

From Walter White, Lieut. 11th Regt. and Acting Town Major, Royal Barracks, Dublin, 31 July 1823

Seeks O'Connell's help in his aim to become assistant town major.

SOURCE : O'Connell Papers, NLI 13647

1045

To Bishop Doyle, Carlow

Limerick, 1 August 1823

Confidential

My Lord,

I beg your kind attention to a circumstance which may in the hand of God be of use to his Church in Ireland.

There is in this town a Miss Mary Fitzgibbon, a near relation of the late and present Earl of Clare. She is a Catholic, a convert I believe, and as a lady of rare and most exemplary piety, she has resisted many temptations and some minor persecutions to desert ' the ancient faith '. Her Protestant relations are of two classes, the one liberal and so inclined to Catholicity as to be won over by any striking event, that is, as far as human means could assist their conversion. The other class of relatives are very inimical to the Catholic faith and have shown, as I am informed, much animosity to this lady for her fidelity and zeal in the cause of truth. This lady has been affected for some time past with a cancerous tumour and has been pronounced by her physicians to be incurable.

Her spiritual director, the Rev. Mr. Coll,[1] a man of the most exemplary piety and of apostolic zeal accompanied with that simplicity which belongs to a heart full of divine love, has *made* me promise to write to your Lordship on this subject, principally to put him in the way of having a discreet and proper application made to Prince Hohenlohe for his intercession on her behalf.

Should it please God to restore this lady through the intercession of that holy clergyman and by the efficacy of the pure sacrifice, it would probably be a mercy to many and many who are now in error. It is not for such as me to estimate the divine bounty, but as far as human reason can see darkly into the ways of Providence, it would appear that this is an occasion in which much edification and consolation may be given to Catholics and an evidence afforded to Protestants which it would be difficult to resist.

Any reply you may think fit to give me on the subject had better be addressed to the Rev. Mr. Coll, Limerick, or to the Rev. Dr. Hogan,[2] Limerick. The latter is the parish priest of this parish and is a clergyman of the very first respectability. Either of these gentlemen would be happy to communicate with your Lordship on this interesting subject.

SOURCE : Kildare and Leighlin Diocesan Archives

1 Rev. Thomas Coll, C.C. (c. 1791-1857), St. Michael's parish; P.P. Newcastlewest, Co. Limerick, 1826-57, where O'Connell was frequently his guest.
2 Rev. Patrick Hogan (c. 1776-1839), P.P. St. Michael's, 1813-39.

1046

From his brother James to Killarney

Derrynane, Nine o'clock, Thursday night,
4 September 1823

My Dear Dan,

I this moment received both your letters and was shocked to perceive the state of embarrassment you are in with respect to pecuniary matters. When we parted last Friday I told you I was satisfied to join you in a bond for any sum not exceeding fifteen hundred pounds and am, of course, still ready to do so. . . . Until I received your letter (notwithstanding what you told me in Cork), I did hope the demands on you were not of so pressing a nature and that your creditors would give you some time to look out for means to pay them. I again repeat, my dearest fellow, I do not know what is to be done. . . .

SOURCE : O'Connell MSS, UCD

1047

To John Primrose, Jr.

Killarney, 6 September 1823

My dear John,

I am just off for Cork. . . . You have not a moment to lose in forwarding the £140 to Jerry McCarthy. In truth it ought to be off by this. A day's delay when a bill is out is often ruinous.

SOURCE : O'Connell MSS, UCD

1048

From his brother James to care of Charles Sugrue, Cork

Hillgrove, 8 September 1823

My Dear Dan,

[James refers to a letter he had written but which O'Connell apparently did not get owing to his leaving Tralee] . . . but that is not of the slightest consequence as it merely contained a decided refusal on my part to part with the money I have in the Funds and now for *the last time I declare I will not do so.* I have no other means to meet the *to me* very heavy engagements I entered into and my credit and character are at stake, neither of which will I, if I can, forfeit. Surely no year has passed these 15 years that bills of yours were not protested for non-payment, and yet one would suppose by your letters to me, that if you got this small sum I *happen* to have in the Funds, you would be rid of all future embarrassment. Under no circumstances would I wish, my dear Brother, to hurt your feelings . . . but, if your affairs are in the desperate situation you represent them, why did you not make some arrangements to meet these demands now pressing on you, either by a sale of the very *small property you have* out of settlement . . . or by the sale of a life annuity? You must be aware that within a short period I have paid for your account £500 and I joined you in a note to Paul Jones for £100. You cannot forget that my brother John and I seven years ago gave you £1,700 of our share of the General's money, not one penny of either principal or interest did we since receive. That was applied to take up bills of yours and, when you talk of the security afforded by the conveying your property to me for any money I may advance, do you forget that your present debts amount *at least* to double the value of your life use of it and, as to the plan of economy adopted by you with respect to your family, it is indeed a very novel one. In the course of a few months they move from Dublin to Pau, from that to Tours, now they are in the most expensive part of Paris and will wind up by fixing their residence in England, the dearest country in Europe to live in. In fact, I must think of my wife and family and, though you may think it extraordinary that I do not comply with your request, no impartial man living will agree with you in that opinion. The resources of your profession are enormous, if not squandered or dissipated. I never ceased warning you against the course you were running, and when I executed the annuity deed to Mr. Hickson in which *I covenanted* to pay him, I did so then, *though an unmarried man,* with considerable reluctance. The General's bounty enabled you to redeem it and now, if you are again compelled to raise money in that way, you must wait for means to redeem it until the death of that dear and venerated uncle at Derrynane, a period not very remote I fear, from the advanced time of life he has come to.

SOURCE : O'Connell MSS, UCD

1049

From his brother James to Cork, care of Charles Sugrue

Derrynane, Thursday Night, 11 September 1823

My Dear Dan,

I this evening received your voluminous letter of the 9th inst. and now, for *the third and last time, most solemnly declare* I will not give you the small sum I have in the Funds. . . . Nothing, I am convinced, but the greatest distress would induce you to persevere in endeavouring to get this money from me. My credit and character are at stake. . . . You talk of being able to repay me in the month of November. In the name of common sense, how? . . .

You, my dear Dan, describe in the most glowing terms the ruin to you and your family unless you can procure money. I cannot give it to you except at the utmost risk of the ruin of my wife and family. Have they not the same claims on me that yours have on you? Are they less dear to me though I have not your powers of eloquence in giving utterance to my feelings?

In a letter I wrote to Charles Sugrue the 9th inst. I desired him tell you to call on John[1] to come forward and join me in endeavouring to procure money *for your present urgent purposes.* His property is worth twice what mine is, even including Ballybegin, and on the death of our dear and venerated uncle, his fortune will be without exaggeration four times more valuable than mine. You are equally dear to us both, you have ever been a most affectionate brother and indeed we had a right to be proud of you. We both cheerfully gave you £1,700 of our share of the General's money seven years ago. . . .

You no doubt gave us the best security you had to offer *but since that period to this hour we did not receive one shilling principal or interest.* I do not wish to again repeat that within the last 16 months I am involved over £600 for you. . . . I do not wish to hurt your feelings but I must say there is no instance of a man who ruined and dissipated his own and his children's property, having too scrupulous a regard for the interests of those who have not such strong claims on him. I will not attempt to conceal from you the danger to you and your family should my poor uncle hear of your embarrassments, yet I am willing to hope, even in that event, he would not vent the sins of the father on his innocent children but, of course, every nerve should be strained to prevent its coming to his knowledge, and I need not say I have ever been as anxious to promote your interest and that of your family with him as I have my own. . . . You will be most fortunate if means are had to enable you to resume your professional avocations in Dublin next month. . . .

SOURCE : O'Connell MSS, UCD
1 His brother.

1050

From his brother James

Carhen, Tuesday morning, 15 [*recte* 16]
September 1823

My dear Dan,

Your letter of the 15th inst. *covering another Bond for my signature I have* this moment received and I return you that bond *executed by me.* You have long since received from Charles Sugrue Mr. Fagan's[1] bond *with my signature to it,* I having *once* promised you I would go as far as £1,500 and will join you *in another bond* for the remaining £500 but I have *on my knees bound myself by an oath, during the rest of my life never again to join you in bill, bond or note or in any other security, either verbal or otherwise, for one guinea and, further, I have solemnly sworn on my knees never to give you in any one year during my life any sum of money exceeding twenty pounds. This oath I have taken without any evasion, equivocation or mental reservation.* Now where you are to get *my remaining* £500 I really do not know. [James then states that his mother-in-law, Madame O'Donoghue, is extremely tightfisted about money and could not be prevailed upon to assist O'Connell financially.] . . . I have lived for near 6 years in the same house with her in the utmost harmony. It has in a pecuniary way been of equal advantage to her family and to mine. I would be the basest of human beings were I capable of saying an unkind thing of her but you are greatly mistaken in thinking *I can exercise such an influence over her private concerns as would enable* me to prevail on her to pay monies. . . .

I also received with your letter your bond to me for £1,500 and Drew Atkins'[2] letter informing me you executed a mortgage to *me for that* sum. This, I am aware, is the only security you could give with an insurance on your life, and it surprises me not a little that you should *talk of my perfect safety in securing* you in procuring this money. Surely you do not mean to say you do not owe at least three times as much as your life interest in your paternal property is worth, and the only valuable part of it being freehold, the numerous previous judgement creditors of yours take precedence of my mortgage. Then as to your chattel property, it is only a College[3] interest which in a few years will leave no profits and even on that you executed a mortgage to John and me and there is now due to us over £1,000 principal and interest. Then as to your profession, surely *ill-health* or *arrest for debt* would completely knock you up. I have said in a former letter and I now repeat it that it is an insult on common sense to have you talk of *the security* you can offer for money . . . [remainder of letter missing]

SOURCE : O'Connell MSS, UCD
1 Probably William Trant Fagan, J.P., D.L. (1801-59), Feltrim, Co. Cork, son of James Fagan. M.P. for Cork city, 1847-65.
2 John Drew Atkins, attorney.
3 That is, under lease from Trinity College, Dublin.

1051

To his wife, Hotel Durand, No. 4 Place Vendôme, Paris

Cork, 17 September 1823

My darling love,

You will be pleased to get a short letter. I have the happiness to tell you that I have made satisfactory arrangements which will permit me to leave this either this evening or tomorrow morning at farthest before day.[1] My heart is light and my spirits revived at being at length able to accomplish my objects. Darling, all is well.

I sent you by the post of the 15th half an English bank post bill for £50. . . .

SOURCE : Fitz-Simon Papers
1 O'Connell left Dublin for France on 23 September (*CMC*, 26 Sept. 1823).

1052

From John England, Bishop of Charleston[1]

Charleston, S.C. [U.S.A.], 4 October 1823

My dear Friend,

My conscience has often smote me for having left unfulfilled a promise which you extorted from me four or five years ago to give you in writing my notions of what is true *liberty* in a Roman Catholic. I have now snatched a few moments to redeem my word. I have thrown hastily together what has frequently been the reflections of my leisure—such as it is it belongs to you—if worth using to be used as you think proper.[2] I would have extended it much more had I leisure, for I confess I should like to have more minutely and better described that disgusting mixture of foppery, folly, infidelity and ignorance which at both sides of the Atlantic usurps the name of liberality. If I know my own heart I hold bigotry in as great abhorrence as I do infidelity or heresy, and I place the persecutor (I care not for his creed) at least upon the same line on the scale of immorality with the heresiarch. Yet, I acknowledge the singleness of truth and I yield to the force of evidence.

I have been sick of the sweet, soft-tongued, lisping, ranting declamation of half-educated, unthinking Index and Review reading, perfumed young drawing-room decorations. I have in vain endeavoured to find some meaning in the specious assertions of pompous and respectable-looking gentlemen who saw much and grew old to no purpose. I have been shocked at the gross fabrications and palpable falsehoods which Hume and most other English writers of what is called history have put forward. I have been obliged to wade through and decompose much of that area of misrepresentation of Catholicity which deluges every land into which a vent could be found for the effusion of the British press. I have then looked back and seen that fashion compels an association with the first class; custom and the decencies of life require that the second should be respected. Education makes the third class; authority, pride, sloth and self-interest preserve the fourth; then the world is chiefly governed by fashion, custom, the decencies of life, education, pride, sloth and self-interest—how difficult a task is it to draw the world from under their influence. And as that interest is principally directed against true liberality and in favour of its deceitful competitor, we must not be astonished at finding so much spoken in favour of what is so little reduced to practice. I am overwhelmed with occupations and yet I made time to write you a letter and a dissertation. You are not more occupied than I am. I do not require an essay but I look for a letter. You may without impiety snatch a moment from those morning devotions at which you are detected through the half-closed parlour shutter, and even in the presence of a crucifix, scribble a few lines to an expatriated Bishop who was once your fellow-agitator and your ghostly father.

I have to thank my Dublin friends for enabling the Rev. Mr. Swiney[3] to come hither. We needed his assistance greatly, and a few more of the same description would have the effect of at once enabling me to afford an opportunity of practising their religious duties to thousands of Catholics who have not seen a priest during many years. My own exertions to try and afford an opportunity to some of them who live several hundred miles apart and several hundred miles from this have more than once nearly cost me my life. With *five good priests* more than I now have, moderately speaking, I could do with some safety ten times as much good as I now do with great risk to my life; but they should be trustworthy, unambitious religious men who would cheerfully undergo privations. Will you inform my friend, the Bishop of Kerry,[4] that the Rev. Mr. O'Donoghue,[5] whom he sent to me (such as he knows him to be), has rendered me the most essential services and done more for the advantages of religion in two years in this diocese than he could have done in any part of Ireland during his life.

I had serious thoughts of visiting Ireland, for poor and wretched and oppressed as she is, I think in a short time I could procure eight or ten good priests to aid me and as much as would pay the expense of their passages and such an additional sum as would launch them fairly upon the missions, but

I cannot just now. Yet were I to have one or two clergymen whom I could depend upon, in addition to those now with me, I hope I should be able next summer to effect my object.

I am led to hope that the Christian benevolence of Dublin will not be confined to Mr. Swiney's case. May God pour his blessings upon the contributors. They will of course have all the merit of the good which he has begun and will continue to do here. Perhaps your Archbishop would have the kindness to permit an occasional sermon to be preached, and you could easily find a preacher who would advocate our cause. This would aid your friend.

By a late regulation no Irish bishop can give to a clergyman an *exeat* for this mission until the American bishop consents to receive the person who desires to come. The regulation was very necessary. But to facilitate the proper selection of clergymen for my dioceses I request and hereby authorize his Grace, Dr. Murray, the Archbishop of Dublin, Rev. Dr. Crotty[6] of Maynooth, Rev. Andrew Fitzgerald of Carlow,[7] the Rev. Thos. O'Keeffe of Cork[8] and my brother, Rev. Thos. R. England, or any of them to consent in my name and on my behalf to receive unto the Diocese of Charleston any clergyman of whose zeal, prudence, disinterestedness, piety and literary attainments they or either of them shall be satisfied. And I shall feel myself obliged to any bishop who will, upon the certificate of either of the gentlemen above named, grant to a good clergyman desirous of aiding me an *exeat*; and I shall consider any pecuniary aid, given to a person so received, as a favour conferred upon myself and as a donation to this diocese.

Books for students in Theology and pious books for distribution would be very useful and acceptable, and many such could be spared. We are about forming a library for the clergy and for our seminary to which many clergymen in Ireland could make (to us) very valuable presents without inconvenience to themselves. Should you get such, send them to my friend Edward Hore[9] of Liverpool to whom for many favours I am greatly obliged. If books be directed to me with the addition of ' President of the Charleston Catholic Book Society ', for the use of the Society, they will be imported duty free as the Legislature of this State has incorporated that Society, and the United States remits all such duties to literary or pious corporations. I have much more to write if I had leisure but I am now going to a fort at which the colonel of artillery tells me there are some Irish Catholics who wish to receive the

Sacraments and many of whom have not had an opportunity for many years. I daresay they do their duty as well as the British Artillery who would not, when I was amongst you, enlist a Catholic. I have met many highly respectable Catholic officers in the War Department at Washington, and when I had the honour of an introduction to the President, the first clerk in the Secretary of State's office who conducted me was a Catholic. I was accompanied by a Jesuit and a Roman Catholic gentleman. The President was the only Protestant present, and yet you may inform Sir Harcourt Lees that we did not kill him. [P.S.] Did Lord Fingall and the aristocrats ever inform the public what was got by their breaking up the Catholic body at the moment when victory hovered over its ranks? You may be certain if you admit them to leadership they will play you the same trick again. Such folk have been doing the same thing during the last 250 years.

What in the name of wonder did Lord Killeen or Lord Kenmare do for Catholicity? If I know them, these men would say that God Almighty ought not to have cured Mrs. Stuart[10] as the miracle would *agitate* the bigoted Orangemen and annoy *our friends* of the opposition. Tell my old friend Dr. Sheridan that I was delighted to see his manly and sensible letter.

SOURCE : *Dublin Evening Post*, 5 Feb. 1824

1 The first paragraph of this letter is published in Sebastian Messmer, *Works of the Right Reverend John England, First Bishop of Charleston,* 7 vols. (Cleveland, Ohio, 1908),V, 506-7.

2 This essay on liberty is published in ibid, pp. 507-14.

3 Rev. Edward Swiney.

4 Dr. Charles Sugrue.

5 Rev. Francis O'Donoghue.

6 Rev. Bartholomew Crotty (1769-1846), rector of Irish College in Lisbon, 1801-11; president of St. Patrick's College, Maynooth, 1813-33; bishop of Cloyne and Ross, 1833-46.

7 Rev. Andrew Fitzgerald, O.P. (1763-1843), educated at the University of Louvain; president of St. Patrick's College, Carlow, 1814-43.

8 Rev. Thomas O'Keeffe, dean of Cork (died 8 April 1847).

9 Unidentified.

10 Mary Stuart, a Carmelite nun in Ranelagh, Dublin, who it was alleged was cured by Prince Alexander von Hohenlohe and recovered the use of her limbs.

1053

From his brother James to Merrion Square

Killarney, 3 November 1823

My Dear Dan,

I received your letter of the 30th ult. and was glad to hear you arrived in Dublin in good health and that you fixed your family in Southampton where I trust they will live with all the economy the present state of your affairs require. I have no doubt they will, if you made them acquainted with the magnitude of your debts. You should fix an annual sum for Maurice's support in London where I presume he must often be to attend terms. He could and ought to live very well on 200 guineas a year, including clothes, etc. His bare clothes in Dublin cost him that sum, I know I am under the mark when I say so. He is blessed with a good constitution and with talents that ensure success at the Bar if he applies but, my dear fellow, I have reason to know he thinks he will have a large landed property. It is cruel not to undeceive him.

With respect to your plan of bringing your family to live at Derrynane for next summer, I do not think it practicable. My dear uncle is in his 95th year. He now wishes to have no person at Derrynane *for more than two days* (except John, you or myself). *This I know.* . . . This plan [bringing the family to Derrynane for the summer] must be abandoned. In fact I see nothing for you to do but to leave your family in some cheap part of England or Wales until you can afford to bring them to Dublin to your own house but, in the name of God, make them *fix their residence* somewhere, I mean not for a few months but for years. *Their tour* to the Continent, which was intended to be of use to your finances, has beyond all doubt contributed to add largely to your debts. This however is a subject I will never again renew. If what you have suffered heretofore by your waste of money has not cured you, anything I could say would of course make no impression. . . .

SOURCE : O'Connell MSS, UCD

1054

From Rev. Peter Kenney to Merrion Square

Clongowes Wood [College], Clane,
6 November 1823

My Dear Sir,

I hope that you will excuse this second trouble on the subject of the Masters Alexander and John Burke.[1] On the 9th June last I furnished to you their account then amounting to £150.14.8. This account was all payable on the 7th May last and the greater part of it due long before that time. Another half year will be payable on the 7th of December next which (with extras) will probably add £60 more to above stated sum. I enter into this detail through an apprehension that the account sent in June may not have reached you, as you probably were then from home. I may be allowed to add that it is a greater inconvenience than is generally imagined to allow these accounts to remain so long unsettled. The difficulty of getting in debts long due to this house makes the charge of providing for this large establishment a very arduous undertaking. I should feel particularly obliged by a line from you on the subject.

The Master Burkes are both very well: they are quiet, well conducted boys but they do not show much talent and will not make any great progress in a classical course of studies. They came here so very backward for their age that they have yet much to learn in the more necessary departments of English education, Arithmetic, writing, etc. I should mention that the elder boy, Alexander, applied in his mother's name for leave to go home last August. This I refused without your permission as the visit would be attended with considerable expense, whilst his stay here during the vacation was not attended with any extra charge. If you could give me any late news of my worthy friend Counsellor Scully's health, I should feel really obliged. I am unwilling to trouble good Mrs. Scully on so distressing a subject and yet I know no other member of the family to whom I could address my inquiries. . . .

SOURCE : O'Connell Papers, NLI 13647
1   Sons of Sgt. Maj. William Burke of Devereux's Irish Legion.

1055

To his wife, 129 High St., Southampton

Merrion Square, 10 November 1823

My own darling Mary,

I have no excuse for not having written *again* to my sweetest love but that John wrote long letters and I have been very very busy. . . . Did you see the speech[1] I made about you, flowing from my heart. I ought to have said more but I was overpowered, at least, darling, I ought to be so. . . . I have not as yet sent John to school[2] but will without further delay. I heard from Morgan and will certainly write to him and send him money before the week is over. . . . I need not give you any Irish news because I send you regularly the Irish papers of which, as you may perceive, I engross no small share. . . .

SOURCE : Fitz-Simon Papers

1 Unidentified. It is probable that he made this speech at the annual dinner of the Trinitarian Orphan Society at Spaddichini's Royal Hotel, College Green, Dublin, on 3 November (*FJ*, 4 Nov. 1823).
2 Clongowes Wood College.

1056

From William Somerville[1]

Baltimore, United States, 10 November 1823

Dear Sir,

I have taken the liberty to enclose you by the ship *Franklin* to Liverpool a volume of letters on France which you will oblige me by accepting as a testimonial of the recollection I entertain of the civilities I received from you when in Dublin with General Devereux. The interference of the Holy Alliance in the affairs of the South of Europe[2] has interrupted the natural course of events in that part of the world since my return home and has damped the ardour of the hopes with which its prospects inspired me in 1820; yet I trust the volume will not be found entirely void of interest to one who is animated, like yourself, by a fervent zeal for the happiness of mankind. . . .

source : O'Connell MSS, UCD

1 Major William Clark Somerville (1790-1826), born Bloomsbury, Maryland. Joined Venezuelan army before 1817. Author of several works, including *Letters from Paris on the Causes and Consequences of the French Revolution*. Died in Auxerre, France. Owing to paper damage the surname, Somerville, in the above letter is missing. It has been identified by the substance of the letter.

2 The Congress of Verona had assembled on 20 October 1822 to decide what the great powers should do about the insurrectionary situations in Greece, Italy and Spain.

1057

From his brother James to care of Charles Sugrue, Cork

Killarney, 19 November 1823

My Dear Dan,

When I received your last letter I had only time to execute the bond for £500 and enclose it to you which I trust arrived in Dublin this morning.

With respect to what you mention about fixing your family in Killarney, I really do not know what opinion to offer. You could, I think, get a small furnished house here for about 100 guineas a year. That is the sum a Mrs. Jackson pays for the house next to Mrs. O'Donoghue's which was lately occupied by the Blands. It is just such *a one as ours* and in Killarney there is no better to be let. . . . Once they were fixed here they, I think, could live respectably on seven hundred pounds a year and, of course, keep a carriage and two men-servants, but perhaps including clothes, etc., it would be better fix the annual expenditure at £800. . . . In order to enable you to make any way in the discharge of your debts it will be absolutely necessary that your family should *fix themselves in some place for three years at least*. There is no use in regretting what is past but, surely, surely, the expense of travelling and changing from place as they have done from the time they left Dublin until now must be ruinous. It would be an insult to common sense to attempt to deny this. I will now with the greatest candour tell you the view I take of your affairs provided you have *nerve enough* to pursue a plan of prudence and economy which can alone save you and your children from ruin.

I take for granted your debts amount to *at least* twenty

thousand pounds. I know *where you owe* £15,000 of this (the interest of £20,000 together with the premiums on insurance cannot come to less than [one word missing] hundred pounds a year, the expense of your family including Maurice, now at the Temple, *at least* £1,000 and your own in Dublin, of course, including the rent of your house, your living in Dublin, circuit expenses, public and private charities and other heavy expenses that must attend your *former indiscretions* (which I thank God do not now exist) cannot be calculated at less than £600 a year, so that *the aggregate* cannot be rated at less than £3,200 per annum.

To meet this large sum your landed property I rate at a clear £1,000 a year, and the receipts by your profession £5,000 a year. This would leave £2,800 to apply to the discharge of your debts, and need I here observe that everything depends on the fixed and persevering prudence of every member of your family. The paying debts in theory appears very easy but in practice it is very slow and difficult. You, my dear Dan, have ever been of a most sanguine disposition, but unless your family and you reflect on the magnitude of your debts and limit their expenses, you will be unable to give them the means of existence, should Providence call you out of the world. The permanent landed property you will be in possession of on my dear Uncle's death, including what you got by your father, will not amount to over twelve hundred pounds a year. The value of that rascally College property is not worth mentioning and the Derrynane property ceases with your own life. . . .

SOURCE : O'Connell MSS, UCD

1058

From Denys Scully to Merrion Square

Merrion Square, 23 November 1823

Dear O'Connell,

I am sorry to be troublesome to you but I am extremely in want of the thousand pounds which you promised to pay me in December last, and I shall be exceedingly obliged to you if you will endeavour to collect this money for me and pay it to me in the course of a week. I don't know what I shall do if you disappoint me now, for I have contracted very heavy engagements which I am wholly unable to discharge without the help of this money. The two notes of a thousand pounds are dated upwards of eight years ago, and you promised faithfully to have them paid in the summer following their date, yet they are still unpaid though I confidently expected the contrary. Try and stir yourself and endeavour to get rid of this engagement without delay. I expect your speedy compliance with this my desire, and I am, yours very faithfully,

D. Scully.

SOURCE : O'Connell Papers, NLI 13647

1059

To Denys Scully

Merrion Square, 26 November 1823

My dear Scully,

I am excessively pressed this being the last week of the Law term, but I will certainly see you on the subject of your letter on Monday at ten o'clock in the morning. I trust I shall be able to satisfy you. . . .

SOURCE : Scully Papers

1060

To Daniel O'Connell, Kilgorey, Tulla, Co. Clare[1]

Merrion Square, 28 November 1823

My dear Dan,

I send you the Act of Parliament[2] under another cover. It will cost you more postage than it is worth unless I can get a frank and it will afford you very little information. It is a gross and rank job throughout, calculated to turn the tithes into fifths. There is no parleying with it. You must resist it *in limine* or you are in the parson's power.

The vestry at which you are to attend on Tuesday is, I take for granted, the first in your parish, that is, I presume that there has been no prior vestry under this tithe act. If there have, you are late for any serious opposition after once consenting to proceed under the act. You must oppose it at the first meeting and get that meeting if possible adjourned *sine die*.

The vestry should be composed of persons who have paid upwards of 20 shillings in the whole for county cess charges or jury rates within the last year preceding the vestry. Nobody else is entitled to attend. If seven such persons do not attend, the vestry is to be adjourned *sine die* and the business is at an end. That you will perceive by the 11th section. If seven vestrymen do attend, then the chair is to be taken and I would advise you to endeavour to have the chair filled with some person favourable to the measure if the votes are likely to be nearly equal, because the chairman has no vote except in the case of an equality of suffrages.

When the chair is taken there comes the tug of war. You must if possible procure a majority to refuse going into the act. Move an adjournment *sine die*. Do not let them entertain the subject at all because, if they do, the appointment of Commissioners can be forced and the certificate of the Commissioners will be conclusive. There is no mode of stopping the thing if a majority of the Vestry sanction the measure. You must put forth all your strength to procure a majority of the Vestry against it, and at all events, should there be a majority against you for entertaining the subject, procure if possible a limited adjournment for further consideration and for appointment of a Commissioner. But indeed your best exertions would be useless if they had once gone so far as to have agreed to entertain the measure. There is no longer any control, all is in the power of the bishop and the Commissioners, and the Commissioners, while they are valuing every acre in the parish, are entitled to 30 shillings a day each to be paid out of the treasury in the first instance and afterwards to be levied off the parish and which alone would be no small burden to a parish. The Commissioners when appointed cannot give the Clergyman less than the average of the seven years preceding 1821 and that average is not to be calculated upon what was actually paid to the parson but upon what was agreed to be paid to him, so that I repeat if you do not throw it out at the first vestry there is very little use in attempting any battle afterwards. You see therefore that you must rally your forces and meet the mischief in the first instance.

I am promised a frank for tomorrow.

SOURCE : NLI, MSS 5759
1 This letter was written by another hand and signed by O'Connell.
2 The Irish Tithes Compositions Act (4 Geo. IV c. 99) which received
   the royal assent on 19 July 1823.

1061

To his wife, High Street, Southampton

Merrion Square, 30 November
[and 2, 3 December] 1823

[No salutation]

I heartily thank you, darling, for your *second* letter.
Indeed, it will cheer me to hear twice a week from you. But let
me confess my painful disappointment at finding my hopes
now gone, and that we are not to have another doat. I did
imagine you would not have mentioned the subject to me at
all unless you were quite certain. I love you, sweetest, still,
but ought I not to love you more if my wishes were realized.
May the great God bless and preserve you to me at any rate.

Darling, I have had a very busy time of it and received
more money, thank God, than I ever did. It was indeed wanting, but if I could reckon on a few months of equal success
I would begin to conquer my difficulties. However, we can
reckon on such abundant means only during term and for
some days after. They then cease, comparatively speaking.
. . . I received from the 3rd of November to the 30th, that is
in 28 days, £760 and something over. But for rascally outstanding bills I would therefore have begun upon the principal of my debts. However, I trust in God I will soon be able
to begin upon them. If God in his infinite mercy grants me to
continue in health and strength I will look forward with cheerfulness to restoring my Mary and her girls to their warm home
and to all the happiness a fond husband and doating father
can bestow.

2 December

I have written to my Morgan and sent him through a
London banker something more than he has asked for mess
and ale. Poor fellow, I have been at least three weeks later
than I ought to have been with him. I have not sent John
off and I doubt whether I shall be able to write to Mr. Kenny,
the Clongowes Superior, tomorrow. If I can, I will. We had

a great discussion this day at the Dublin Library[1] on the subject of the *Mail*—we kicked out the wretch by a majority of 227 to 147. The Catholics for the first time stood together. Your son John was the first vote in the majority. It was truly one of the most extraordinary political days I have seen in my time. I am quite pleased with the victory.

December 3rd

I have settled to have John go to Clongowes next week. Everything is arranged. I got a letter from you last night with much less pleasure than your letters usually give, and I own with some surprise that you should, after my former letter, continue another reproach on the subject of my visits to Miss Gaghran.[2] I own I think I, least of all, deserved this repetition. Surely I said enough on that subject—at least I think I did—to set your mind at ease. But why it should be otherwise, I confess I am at a loss to understand. I never in my life showed the slightest tinge of preference to any being above[3] you, and why *now*, when I would not look at any other woman for a moment, you should thus persevere in an angry correspondence on a subject so trivial—at least in my estimation— is to me quite unintelligible. I have only to repeat my solemn promise of never again seeing her without your express permission. I therefore implore of you to discharge from your mind any uneasy sensations I might have caused you on this subject.

Can you for one moment doubt that, if I thought it would have given you the slightest pain, I ever would have paid her a visit? If you think I would, you do indeed wrong me. I have no shred of gratification in her visit, and if I had, you little know, it seems, how cheerfully, how [indecipherable; page torn] I would sacrifice it to you whom both duty and tender affection bid me cherish, and I do cherish in the inmost recesses of my heart and with the tenderest love. Spare me then, I conjure you, or rather spare yourself any painful expressions on this subject. I repeat that you shall never again have the slightest cause to reproach me, and indeed, if you did not think otherwise, I would assert that you have not at present any such cause. Moreover, darling, forgive me, I conjure you, this time, and it shall be the last. Depend on it, you shall have no ' Lord or Master '—I know of course who you allude to—she [he?] always treated you I think with respect and affection—but at all events she [he?] certainly shall have nothing of interference with you of any kind save the mere exchange of friendly civilities. To that I readily pledge myself. I could as little endure as you could any dominion over you, so that on that subject you may rest satisfied.

You see, darling, how long I have been writing this letter. The fact is that the *nisi prius* has begun and I am kept in court very late every day. I take great care of myself, however, sweetest. I have my cloak taken to court at four o'clock and come home very warm. Indeed I never, thank God, was in better health and, if you and my girls were here, I should be in excellent spirits. Give my children my tenderest, tenderest love and believe me, own darling Mary, with the greatest truth and [indecipherable] tenderness.

Your fondest,
Daniel O'Connell[4]

SOURCE : *Irish Times*, 15 May 1947

1 A general meeting of the Dublin Library Society at their new building in D'Olier Street, called ' to take into consideration the propriety of discontinuing the *Dublin Evening Mail* in consequence of its having become the vehicle of individual and malicious slander '. An attempt by Rev. Edward Tighe Gregory to have the meeting drop the issue was defeated by 227 to 147, and then the motion to discontinue taking the *Mail* was passed by a large majority without a division (*FJ*, 3 Dec. 1823).

2 O'Connell's daughters' governess, identified by a comparison of the above letter with letter 1063. The lady's name was scratched out on the original so that there was a hole in the page at this point.

3 ' Above ' frequently had the colloquial meaning of ' other than '.

4 This letter, obviously once part of the Fitz-Simon Papers, was presented to Mr. Sean O'Faoláin about 1946 and he published it, as above, in the *Irish Times*. Whether it is still extant is not known.

1062

To Denys Scully

Merrion Square, 1 December 1823

My dear Scully,

I find that I cannot make a definitive arrangement with you before Friday next. I will call on you that morning, please God, at half after ten and, believe me, it will give me the greatest pleasure if I can that morning hand you at least £1,000. . . .

SOURCE : Scully Papers

1063

To his wife at Southampton

Merrion Square, 7 [and 9] December 1823

My darling love,

. . . And as to her [Kate], darling, I need not I am sure tell you to be cautious and not allow it to be *said* that she could form any attachment for Mr. Jackson. There are three things to be observed. First, darling, I would insist that *all* her children should be brought up Catholics. I would not consent to any exception. Secondly, we know nothing of the family or means of the young gentleman. Thirdly, he was said to have been of a sarcastic and indeed of something of a slanderous temper. He may to be sure be falsely accused, and for my own part I cannot recollect I ever saw the slightest reason to think that he was guilty of any such disposition. I only repeat the rumour to put you on your guard. I have settled everything for John's going to Clongowes and he will be there certainly during the ensuing week. . . .

We had yesterday a great cause[1] between Lord Bandon[2] and Sir Augustus Warren[3] about the affairs of the ancient Bank of Warren and Co. which closed in the year 1784. I was counsel for Sir Augustus and I may tell you that I made an impression which has been already much spoken of. It would amuse you, could you have seen how attentive Lord Manners was to me. I got the [? commission] for the tabinet and I will send to Miss Gaghran to [? have it] executed. Darling, be assured I will not go myself [two or three words illegible] have been too much fretted at your repeating the same *scolding* on this subject twice. Pardon me, my dearest love, and attribute my angry emotions to that irritability which is overscored by the misery I endure at being so long separated from you and my darling children. It is difficult for me not to be fretful in absence from such sweet darling treasures whom my follies, not to call them by the more proper name of vices, have banished from their *sweet home*. Pity me, love, and do not be angry with me. I have not the heart to talk to James[4] about the subjects you write. I will however give poor John[5] warning tomorrow to look out for some other place and, unless he can get one, that he must shift for himself. He is a worthy attached old man and I do not love to change those who are about me but every shilling saved brings you nearer home and that will console me for everything. . . . Did I tell you I sent Morgan his half yearly allowance, £32.10.0 British? It will be about £70 a year Irish money. I have received with Ellen's [letter] a very kind letter from Vienna from Baron O'Connell. He promises attention to Morgan and says he was a schoolfellow of your father's as well as of mine.

9th December
. . . Edward Connor was here last week. We made a clumsy effort to have him sworn an attorney a year too soon but failed. . . . They [Irish affairs] are dull and dismal but there is one good feature. Prices are rising fast. If the current runs that way for some time longer we shall have rents again.

SOURCE : Fitz-Simon Papers

1   *Earl of Bandon and Others* v. *Sir Augustus Warren*. The case was instituted to regulate the proportions which the partners in the late Bank of Warren and Co. had to pay of the losses (£100,000) incurred. On 9 December the lord chancellor gave judgement in favour of the defendant (*CMC,* 12 Dec. 1823). The affairs of the bank were wound up by 1825, (Eoin O'Kelly, *Old Private Banks and Bankers of Munster* [Cork 1959], p. 51).

2   Francis (Bernard) (1755-1830); created 1793 Baron Bandon, 1795 Viscount Bandon, both in the Irish peerage; 1800 Viscount Bernard and earl of Bandon.

3   Sir Augustus Warren, third baronet (1791-1863), Warren's Court, Macroom, Co. Cork. Succeeded his father, 1821.

4   His man-servant.

5   Coachman.

1064

From Richard Granaghan,[1] Mullingar Gaol, 7 December 1823, to Merrion Square

The writer seeks O'Connell's assistance in obtaining redress. He was appointed agent by Lady Westmeath[2] to collect an annuity of £1,300 and arrears from Lord Westmeath.[3] He is innocent of the charge of assault sworn against him by ' a creature of Lord Westmeath '.

SOURCE : O'Connell Papers, NLI 13647

1   Unidentified.

2   Emily Anne Bennet Elizabeth (Cecil) (1789-1858), daughter of first

marquis of Salisbury. She obtained a divorce from Lord Westmeath
in 1827.
3 George Thomas John (Nugent), eighth earl of Westmeath (1785-
   1871), created 1822 marquis of Westmeath.

1065

To his wife at Southampton

Merrion Square, 11 December 1823

My own love,
  . . . We will, please God, go to Communion together on
the morning of New Year's Day and, darling, I beg of you
and my children to go to Communion also on Christmas Day.
Promise me, darling, to do so. I came in this day from a busy
and bustling day's work. Richard Mahony of Portmagee dined
with me, the first and only dinner I gave since I left you. He
came up to get some money due to him for the hire of a boat
employed about the building [three or four words illegible]
great Skelligs Rock.[1] . . .
  The late fairs have been very good. In short, the farming
times are improved though as yet we have not begun to taste
sweets of the changes. If they would bring me back another
£1,000 a year, darling, they would indeed be welcome, but
blessed be the will of God in all things and at all times. . . .
How I wish there was a good steam packet between this and
Bristol. . . . I am truly happy to hear your account of Maurice.
Oh darling, it would cheer my heart to find him diligent,
economical and religious. I perceive your *friend* Jackson has
gone off. I am not sorry for it, darling. I did not relish the
idea of his *thinking* of my sweet, sweet Kate. She is indeed
the greatest possible doat of mine. . . . Good night. God
bless you, darling.

12 December, Friday
  . . . I hope to carry you Scott's *last* novel.[2] That is an Irish
phrase because I mean his next. My John will certainly go to
Clongowes early next week. What a shame for me to have
kept him for near two months idle. He is a sweet, good boy
and a very great favourite of mine. . . .

SOURCE : Fitz-Simon Papers
1 The two lighthouses on the Skellig Rock about twelve miles off the
   Kerry coast were being built at this time and were completed in 1826.
2 Sir Walter Scott's *St. Ronan's Well,* published in December 1823.

1066

To his wife, 129 High St., Southampton

Merrion Square, 14 [and 19] December 1823

My own and only Love,

. . . We will, darling, if you please begin the new year by
going *all* together to Communion. Do not however, sweetest,
omit Christmas Day. I wish Maurice would join us. Speak
to him, dearest. . . . My sweet John goes tomorrow to Clongowes and leaves me quite alone. . . .

Friday, 18th [*recte* 19] December

. . . I had another triumph on Monday, darling, in a
great cause[1] against the Corporation of Cork. We beat the
rascals heartily but, what is more strange still, one of the
special jury who had the case had a miracle performed in his
house that morning. He is a Mr. Andrew Rorke,[2] a very
respectable man of landed fortune. His daughter had been
taken ill with the measles at the Ursuline Convent in Cork
and was obliged to come home in wretched health. She was
daily growing worse, an incessant cough, pain in her side and
confirmed consumption. Her father consulted two English
physicians. Surgeon Crampton[3] was her attending physician.
She could not stand or lie down but was for many months
supported in bed by what is called a bed chair. Her lungs
were declared by Crampton to be impostumated and last week
he told [one or two words illegible] that her recovery was
impossible. Well, darling [about two words illegible] the
15th being one of Prince Hohenlohe's [about three words
illegible] she received the holy sacrament [nearly two lines
illegible] made her in one moment well. She arose, dressed
herself, prostrated herself in adoration, breakfasted, dined,
slept and is as well as any human being. In one moment,
darling. Blessed and glorified be the God of the Christians.
Now and for ever. This has made, and is making, a sensation.
I believe it will be hard now to find a subterfuge. Darling,
all the evidence will be collected, I expect, and I also expect
to be one of the persons employed for that purpose. It was the
Rev. Mr. Aylmer[4] of Clongowes who said the mass for her.
In short, sweetest, it is another proof, I trust, of the bounty
of God to his faithful people and a mercy to all who hear of

it with humility and faith. My girls will rejoice to hear it. Give them my tenderest love. Darling, my sweet little John is at length settled at Clongowes. My darling shed a tear as he left me and he has left his father lonely. My sweet child, he is a great, great doat of my fond heart. . . . I have done with court, I finished yesterday. This is my first day at home and I have done an immense deal towards clearing my table. I promise you that by the time I start for ' the Association ' tomorrow I will be far advanced towards getting rid of my present arrear. It is true more will probably come and then I have my pecuniary arrangements to make. . . .

SOURCE : Fitz-Simon Papers

1 *Cork Corporation* v. *Thomas Shinkwin.* The corporation claimed the exclusive ownership of all markets in Cork and were now taking action against the defendant for maintaining a meat market erected in 1809. The jury decided in favour of Shinkwin (*CMC,* 17, 19 Dec. 1823).
2 Of 5 Mountjoy Place, Dublin.
3 Philip Crampton, M.D. (1777-1858), a celebrated Dublin surgeon; created baronet, 1839. See *DNB.*
4 Charles Aylmer, S.J. (1786-1847), born at Painstown, Co. Kildare; rector of Clongowes Wood College, 1817-20. See *DNB.*

1067

From Rev. Peter Kenney, S.J.

Clongowes Wood [College], Clane,
16 December 1823

Dear Sir,

I was from home when your son arrived yesterday and I now hasten to express the pleasure which I feel in adding your third son[1] to the number of our pupils. . . . I am much gratified by your promise of spending a day here before the expiration of the Christmas holidays. As the days are short I hope that you will make up your mind to sleep here that night that we may have more leisure to enjoy your company and conversation.

It were well that some decision were made relative to the future education of the Burkes.[2] They are both very deficient in talent, at least in that talent which is required for literary pursuits. Alexander is now growing very big and it would be much more useful to him to attend solely to an English education than to spend his time in the elements of languages of which he never will know much. . . .

SOURCE : O'Connell Papers, NLI 13647
1 John.
2 Alexander and John Burke (see letter 1054).

1068

To Denys Scully

Merrion Square, 20 December 1823

My dear Scully,

However reluctant to trespass upon you—which indeed I am—I must throw myself on your indulgence for another week. I got rid of my court business only on Thursday and yesterday began to be able to attend to my own affairs. I will be *definitive* with you by giving me another week, that is, by this day week you shall have money or leave to put me to the sword. . . .

SOURCE : Scully Papers

1069

To his wife, 129 High St., Southampton, 23 and 24 December 1823, from Merrion Square

' The fairs continue to improve.'

SOURCE : Fitz-Simon Papers

1070

From his wife to Merrion Square

Southampton, 23 December [1823]

My dearest love,

. . . *We* can think and speak of nothing but your coming. Until this day we had our hopes and fears but the *certainty* you give *us* this day has put *them* all to flight. . . . Maurice

got a very kind letter from your uncle¹ this morning, written
by himself. He tells him he has written to his Uncle Maurice
on the subject of allowing Maurice two hundred a year while
he is at the Temple. . . . May the great God preserve and
bless him [Count O'Connell]. I cannot tell you how much I
esteem and love this best of men. . . .

   This is a most horrid, stupid place for young people. The
stiff, starched, proud English will not visit without letters of
introduction. We shall not regret much our departure from
England, but when we meet, love, we must talk and consider
well upon our future place of residence. . . . What prevented
you, love, from attending the *last* Catholic meeting?² Only I
read of you at the dinner at Morrison's³ I should have been
quite unhappy as I would have supposed some accident
occurred to keep you from *agitating*. I was amused, love, at
your undeserved encomium on our *good* thing.⁴ Surely, heart,
if he was well inclined towards the Irish what was to prevent
him from showing it by more than words? His ingratitude to
the Irish has only confirmed the *good* opinion I always had
of him. . . .

   SOURCE : O'Connell Papers, NLI 13651
1   Count O'Connell.
2   The meeting of the Catholic Association on 13 December.
3   At the annual dinner in aid of the Orphan's Friend Society in
    Morrison's Hotel, Dawson Street, Dubin, at which O'Connell
    presided (*FJ*, 16 Dec. 1823).
4   A reference to Wellesley, the lord-lieutenant. At the above dinner
    O'Connell 'bore testimony to his Excellency's excellent intentions
    with regard to Ireland but they were rendered of no avail by the
    circumstances in which he was placed' (*FJ*, 16 Dec. 1823).

1071

From his wife to Merrion Square

Southampton, 28 December 1823

My dearest love,

   . . . Charles Connor is with us since Christmas Eve. As
the poor fellow had no situation as yet in London, I asked him
to spend the Christmas holidays with us. He is an excellent
creature and most religious. *He* went with the girls and I to
Communion on Christmas Day. I am sorry to say Maurice

did not accompany us. That unfortunate manner of putting off he has got was alone the cause, but he will certainly go before the holidays are over. He is a very good boy and, in my opinion, as innocent as he was five years ago. . . . I am quite shocked at the sum of money you have paid for our tabinet. Such a price! I had no notion but that you would get *ours* at the *Liberty* for at least four shillings a yard. Why, darling, did you give such a price? . . . I wish, my heart, I could execute your commission but it is impossible. At this time the people of any trade will not work and could a carpenter be got to make the footboard,[1] I fear Mr. Arnold[2] would refuse to go to any more expense for our accommodation, particularly as we did not ask to have it done when first we came to the house. *You must* not have any *cramps* while you are with us. *It* is the constant sitting at home that [? gives] you cramps, love. You will be constantly on foot with your daughters. The Oxford coach arrives every day, Sunday excepted, at Bath. From there there is a coach to this place from Shrewsbury. You cannot miss getting coaches to Bath and Bristol. The Christmas holidays don't interfere with the coaches. They come and go as usual. Don't let James forget to give you the articles I have so often asked you to bring. If *they* are forgotten *now* it will be *his* fault. Reeve's[3] *History of the Bible* is in the house. The other articles James has. . . .[4]

SOURCE : O'Connell Papers, NLI 13651

1 An upright board set across the foot of a bed.
2 The owner of the house being rented by O'Connell's wife.
3 Joseph Reeve (1733-1820), English Jesuit and biblical scholar. Educated St. Omer. Appointed chaplain to the fourth Baron Clifford of Chudleigh, 1767, at Ugbrooke Park, Devon, where he remained until his death. In 1780 he published *History of the Holy Bible,* a free translation of Nicolas Fontaine's work. See *DNB*.
4 On the outside of the letter is written: ' Should Mr O'Connell leave Ireland before *this* letter reaches Dublin, *it* is to be kept until his return.'

Index of Persons

In this index no distinction is made between persons mentioned in letters and those mentioned in notes, or between a name mentioned once or more than once in a letter and its notes. Numbers in italics indicate that the person is either the writer or the recipient of the letter; a form of relationship after a name indicates relationship to Daniel O'Connell. All numerical references are to letter numbers.